The Grand American
AVENUE

1850 · 1920

The Grand American

AVENUE

1850 - 1920

Jan Cigliano
Sarah Bradford Landau

Editors

The Octagon
The Museum of The American Architectural Foundation

POMEGRANATE ARTBOOKS • SAN FRANCISCO

THE OCTAGON MUSEUM
Washington, D.C.
April 15–July 10, 1994

THE HISTORIC NEW ORLEANS COLLECTION
New Orleans, Louisiana
September 13–December 10, 1994

THE CHICAGO ARCHITECTURE FOUNDATION AT
THE HAROLD WASHINGTON LIBRARY CENTER
Chicago, Illinois
January 21–March 18, 1995

THE NEW-YORK HISTORICAL SOCIETY
New York, New York
April 16–July 16, 1995

Published by
POMEGRANATE ARTBOOKS
Box 6099
Rohnert Park, California 94927

In association with
THE OCTAGON
The Museum of The American Architectural Foundation
1799 New York Avenue, N.W.
Washington, D.C. 20006

Library of Congress Catalog Card Number 94-66197

ISBN 1-56640-679-X (paperback)
ISBN 1-56640-680-3 (hardcover)

Designed by Bonnie Smetts Design

FIRST EDITION

Printed in Korea

CONTENTS

The exhibition
"The Grand American Avenue: 1850–1920"
is organized by
The Octagon Museum of The American Architectural Foundation
and sponsored by
Lila Wallace-Reader's Digest Fund.

Additional support has been provided by
The National Endowment for the Arts,
The Graham Foundation for Advanced Studies in the Fine Arts,
The College of Fellows of the American Institute of Architects, and
The Construction Information Group of McGraw-Hill, Inc.

FOREWORD

THE LATE NINETEENTH AND EARLY TWENTIETH CENTURIES witnessed sweeping industrial, economic, and social changes in the development of this country's cities. This book and the exhibition of the same title, *The Grand American Avenue: 1850–1920*, examine how these forces, evidenced along the major thoroughfares of our nation's cities, affected American architecture, urban design and development, city planning, and, in later years, social, preservation, and environmental issues.

We at the American Architectural Foundation are grateful for the major support and commitment of the Lila Wallace-Reader's Digest Fund in support of this project. Initial research was undertaken with grants from the National Endowment for the Arts, the Graham Foundation for Advanced Studies in the Fine Arts, the College of Fellows of the American Institute of Architects, and the Construction Information Group of McGraw-Hill, Inc.

Sherry C. Birk, curator of the Prints and Drawings Collection of The Octagon, The Museum of the American Architectural Foundation, recognized the resources within that repository to support the idea for this project. As project director, she has devoted herself to the exhibition, this publication, and the accompanying *Educational Resource Guide* and video production with great energy, enthusiasm, and professionalism. Under Birk's leadership, the Grand American Avenue project has been brought to fruition through the dedicated collective efforts of every member of the staff of the American Architectural Foundation and the Octagon Museum. Members of the American Institute of Architects staff have also lent their assistance and expertise to the project in a most cooperative manner.

No project of this magnitude would be possible without the participation of the many individuals, private collectors, museums, public institutions, and private organizations whose objects form the content of the exhibition. We extend our deep appreciation to them.

NORMAN L. KOONCE, FAIA
President
The American Architectural Foundation

PREFACE

BETWEEN 1850 AND 1920 dynamic forces dramatically changed the shape of America's cities. Wars occurred, transportation developed, industry changed, invention and creativity prevailed, and fortunes were amassed and lost. This publication and exhibition of the same title, *The Grand American Avenue:1850–1920*, explore the architectural, urban, cultural, and social themes of avenues in twelve American cities affected by these forces. The project represents the first effort to examine a group of "grand avenues" collectively and to evaluate their impact on the development of American cities throughout the country during this time. While particular streets in specific cities have been studied, an overview examining the underlying social and economic circumstances, urban design issues, and architectural and landscape influences has not been previously undertaken. Distinct differences and common patterns that caused the rise, dramatic change, or eventual decline of each avenue and its place in the urban development of America's cities as they exist today are presented in the exhibition and discussed extensively in the publication.

Selecting the twelve avenues for the project was indeed challenging, as virtually every city and town has its "grand avenue." The goal was to examine a variety of styles, themes, and social issues that were simultaneously occurring throughout America. Six of these avenues were selected to be presented in the exhibition to illustrate the unique qualities contributing to the rise, development, and change of each avenue, while demonstrating themes common to them all. A national geographical focus presenting a wide variety of avenues throughout the United States was paramount. Knowledge of scholarly research in progress on specific avenues across the country was extremely helpful. The availability and accessibility of objects such as architectural drawings, historic photographs, paintings, decorative art objects, architectural fragments, and furniture were explored to ensure that the avenues could be visually presented in an exciting and cohesive way.

It was recognized at the beginning that the museum exhibition would not travel extensively due to the large number of objects included and the need to protect them for future generations. Therefore, a panel reproduction version of the original museum exhibition has been produced to travel to a wide variety of sites over an extended period of time.

An *Educational Resource Guide* will travel with both versions of the exhibition. It is a basic user's guide providing information about how to utilize local and national resources to maximize the grand avenue project in any area of the country. Further, two video productions (a twenty-six-minute version for extended programming and a nine-minute version for use with the exhibition) are available.

During the six-year production of this project, wars have occurred, transportation has made the world a smaller place, creativity and ingenuity have brought us into the computer age, and extraordinary telecommunications systems have been developed that allow immediate global access to data. This progress, like the seven decades under review in this study, has affected the growth, development, and social and environmental condition of our cities.

Finally, it is not the purpose of this project to be the definitive study of grand avenues across the United States, as it is clear that each avenue deserves its own exhibition. It is hoped that this general overview will serve as a catalyst for further research. Perhaps as a result we can learn from the past, evaluate the present, and improve the future of our cities for succeeding generations.

SHERRY C. BIRK, *Curator*
Prints and Drawings Collection
The Octagon, The Museum of the American Architectural Foundation

INTRODUCTION

"DELAWARE AVENUE IS TO BUFFALO what Euclid Avenue is to Cleveland, Summit Avenue to St. Paul, Commonwealth Avenue to Boston...," the *House Beautiful* critic exclaimed in 1904, herself preferring the beauty of Delaware Avenue.[1] The list might have gone on and on. In scores of cities and towns across America during the second half of the nineteenth century, local luminaries of business and culture built linear promenades of elegant residences. In each place their cumulative actions over decades created private community enclaves and spaces of authority, architecture for display, and broad streets intended to impress. For both nouveau riche and established gentry, the cost of entry to America's grand avenues was wealth, first and foremost, followed by cultural and civic leadership, and, quite importantly, a bent for architectural display. The grand avenues of America arose as advertisements of achievement.

As industrial enterprise enriched communities along the Atlantic coast, into upstate New York, and further across the continent, artistic progress claimed one local avenue after another. This enthusiasm signified more than an interest in architectural aesthetics. The ostensibly infinite expanse of urban space prompted leading entrepreneurs to pursue high-stakes land development: real estate speculation played an important role in the building of these residential promenades. While it is true that businessmen sponsored many of the Western world's most beautiful streets, squares, and crescents, nowhere was the drive for material progress so vigorous as in post–Civil War America. The marketplace determined the shape of the nineteenth-century city, and the convenience of commerce and the community—expressed in its most fashionable form—fostered the development of the grand avenue. These would be the roots of its nineteenth-century inception, as well as it twentieth-century fate.

As a community, and an expression of cultural and entrepreneurial achievement, the grand avenue visions that emerged across the nation represented a distinctly American urban ideology. They had their theoretical origins in Renaissance city planning ideals and reflected fragments of images that could be found in numerous European cities and towns built in the shadow of Imperial Rome.[2] Combining the idea of the city garden with a faith in economic power, the grand avenue evolved to become a highly valued space imbued with civic function. The notion that the broad, tree-lined urban boulevard marked the landscape as a special place was just the context for planting Berlin's Unter den Linden with two thousand nut and lime trees in 1647 (Figures 1 and 2).

For New World travelers, the most memorable sight among Europe's *grands travaux* was the 275-foot-wide Avenue des Champs-Élysées, expanded by Napoleon III and his planner Georges-Eugène Haussmann from

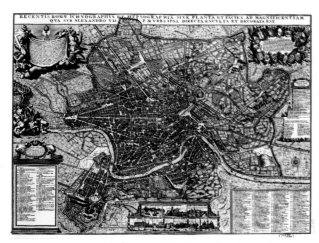

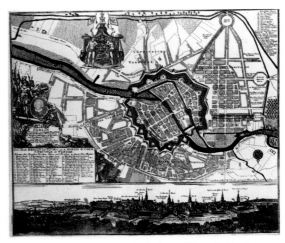

Figure 1. Iconographic plan of Rome, c. 1667. Portrays Renaissance city planning ideals.

Figure 2. Berlin, c. 1750. Shows the landscaped Unter den Linden, lower right quadrant.

1853 to 1870 to accommodate commercial traffic and promote royal power (Figure 3). Perhaps the monumental arches and gated entrances on the grand avenues of American cities—on Fifth and St. Charles Avenues, Vandeventer Place and Ward Parkway—were intended to recall the Arc de Triomphe at the entrance to the Champs-Élysées, or the Brandenburg Gate at the Unter den Linden, or even the triumphal arches erected at each end of St. Petersburg's Nevsky Prospekt. It is no wonder that the Campus Martius, the monumental core of sixteenth-century Rome, was replicated two centuries later on Detroit's Woodward Avenue.

The patrons and designers of the twelve grand avenues in this book drew inspiration from several sources: Charles Pierre L'Enfant looked to his native France, especially Versailles, in his 1791 plan of Washington's principal avenues, including Massachusetts Avenue[3]; Joseph Ellicott, who laid out Buffalo's meridian street plan in 1804, referred to French models; Colonel Collinson Pierrepoint Edwards Burgwyn of Richmond looked to Paris's boulevards and Commonwealth Avenue in Boston for the initial 1887 layout of Monument Avenue; and Los Angeleans incrementally adopted the "linear city" concept along Wilshire Boulevard, which had its origins in ancient Egypt. One can see from just these few examples that there was neither a continuity of theory from the Renaissance to the twentieth century, nor from Europe to America. We also know from the European travel journals of landscape architect Frederick Law Olmsted and architect Richard Morris Hunt—each of whom beautified a half-dozen or more grand avenues—that many of the designers who helped shape the urban and architectural face of America's grand avenues looked to several, not just one or two, European references.[4]

American patrons also fueled the international traffic of ideas, ongoing since the seventeenth century. The squares of Charleston (1680), Philadelphia (1682), and Annapolis (1694) followed the dream of Sir Christopher Wren's 1666 Baroque plan for London, to create green pleasure grounds for people. By the mid-nineteenth century, fashion-conscious society had become absorbed with the France of Louis Napoleon III in all manners of life, as Mosette Broderick observes in her discussion about Fifth Avenue patrons. The American passion for Grand Tour travels and European styles and customs encompassed every corner of the Continent. Having said this, however, the influence of European references should be qualified by the understanding that not each and every patron or designer traveled abroad; one of the greatest proponents of classical principles, Daniel H. Burnham, had not even toured Europe until 1896, three years after the World's Columbian Exposition in Chicago.

The cultural impulse for America's grand avenues was distinct to this country's prospering society. Unlike the tree-lined promenades that graced the Continental landscape, which state authorities laid out to herald the patronage of the bourgeoisie, the premier residential boulevards in American cities were created by private citizens and arose out of democratic ideals about commerce, culture, and community building. This is why many grand avenues became "the best address" of the city's leading churches, synagogues, museums, libraries, shops, and businesses. It is also why such men as Harrison Gray Otis and Samuel Clemens moved from one grand avenue to another as they made their homes in new cities. Perhaps this is also why the legacy has lived on for decades beyond the physical artifact in many cities and towns. These avenues were "the open-air salons of the city," claimed Charles Mulford Robinson in 1904, "adorned to stamp it with majesty."[5]

Acknowledgment by outsiders of the grand avenue's superiority solidified the neighborhood and further perpetuated its development. Yet when such regard diminished and the avenue's civic function clashed with competing community forces, the grand avenue lost its social and economic sovereignty. As Stephen Fox writes about Galveston's Broadway in the mid-1920s, the esplanade's strong appeal to commerce and the

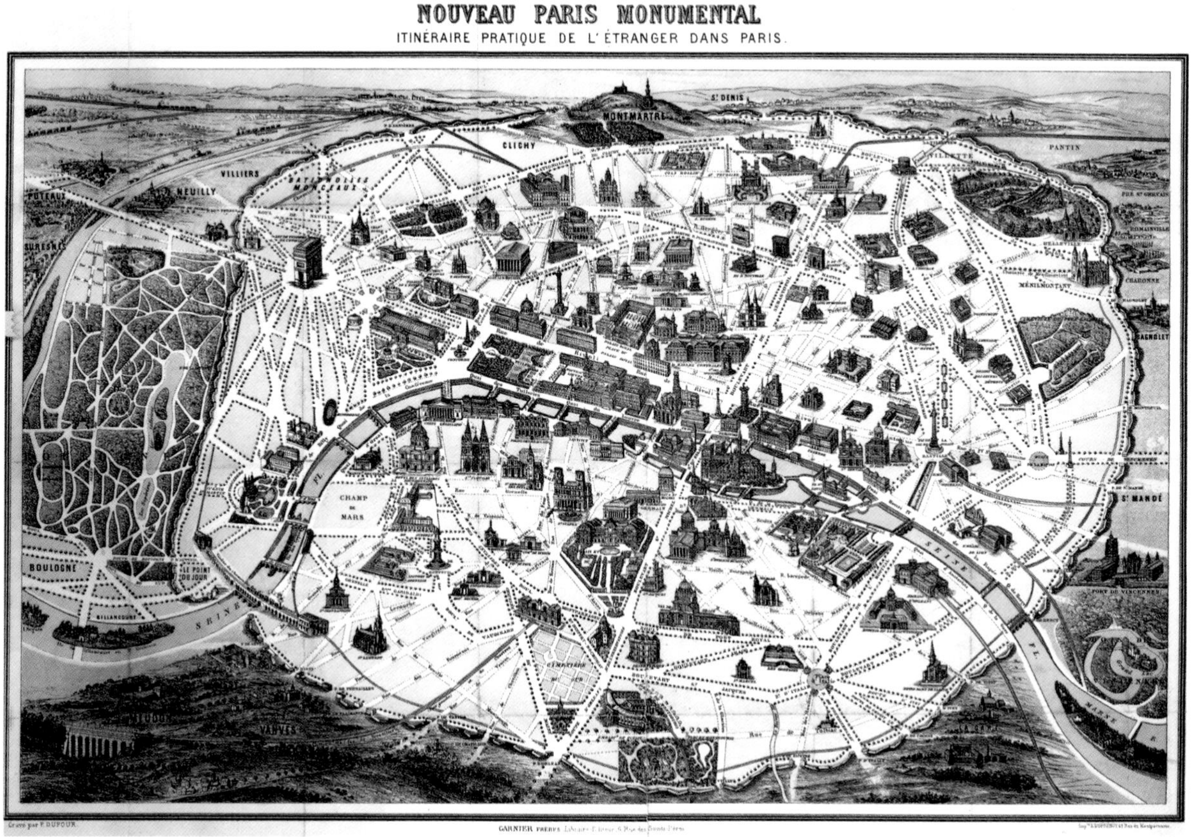

Figure 3. "Nouveau Paris Monumental," c. 1865. Displays the broad vistas and hierarchical urban order created by Napoleon III and Georges-Eugène Haussmann, 1853–70.

automobile overwhelmed protests by the Galveston Civic League and halted the advancement of the tree-lined grand avenue.

In this last decade of the twentieth century, one might ask why we should be concerned with how the higher ranks of society chose to live in the late nineteenth century, especially in light of wide-ranging criticisms of elitist social and architectural history. The answer is that the grand avenue figured prominently in the development of urban communities across the nation, and became a conspicuous microcosm of each city's health—for better or ill—in the twentieth century. While historians have tended to approach American city development from the perspective of one place, one period, or one subject, most, admittedly, have failed to examine this particular phenomenon. Among the multitude of urban studies, only one seminal publication, Robinson's *Modern Civic Art* (1904), devoted an entire chapter to "great avenues" in the United States. Even fifty years later, urbanist Christopher Tunnard underscored the need for additional scholarship, emphasizing that "the residential avenue has received no attention as a city planning phenomenon."[6]

ACHIEVEMENT AS ADVERTISEMENT

Most eighteenth-century cities and towns were laid out to support a fledgling mercantile society, centering around coastal ports and commercial exchanges. Upper-strata families preferred attached or row houses within walking distance of ports and markets, clustering near in-town greenswards around Rittenhouse Square in Philadelphia, Bull Street in Savannah, Meeting Street in Charleston, and St. John's Square in New York City. Many cities, in fact, had more than one fashionable enclave, each supported by their patrons' ethnic and entrepreneurial proclivities. Any thought of living beyond the congested urban center not only meant long and uncomfortable commutes until the 1840s, but unlighted and ungraded roads, and no municipal health or fire systems.[7] The country was stark wilderness, home to the lower classes in many places and certainly not desirable for elegant living.

Technological advances changed all this. Beginning in the 1840s, booming canal and railroad industries shifted city life away from port-oriented markets. Privately financed horse-drawn railways and sewer-and-water lines paved the way for expanded urban districts and promoted real estate speculation on the outer fringes. Quite conveniently horsecar and utility lines tended to radiate out from the city's center in a linear fashion, to follow the main traveled roads and emerging affluent neighborhoods on the city's periphery.[8] And even though wealthy residents shunned the rail lines for their personal use, they built on the street with the finest improvements and highest value. Indeed, on most grand avenues building activity escalated just after the completion of major "public" projects, many actually funded by residents and builders. In this way, the private realm created the infrastructure of the public realm: it provided the vision and funded the improvements.

Drawn by premier locations, commerce often followed the carriage trade. After midcentury, shops and business blocks tended to crowd in on the fashionable residential district nearest the downtown core, and affluent families turned their sights beyond the city center to greener pastures in less congested quarters.

Within a decade or two, America's entrepreneurial class had transformed the midtown-to-uptown section of the most attractive street leading out to the country into a linear parade ground of stylish mansions. Many of Chicago's "first" families in the early 1870s moved westward from the teaming commercial district on Michigan Avenue, to the exclusively residential enclave along Prairie Avenue, a crowd-free sanctuary with breathtaking views across Lake Michigan, writes Mary Alice Molloy.

As the nation's urban centers grew to house one-third of the population during the second half of the nineteenth century, the grand avenue became a dominant urban form—romantic sensibilities mixed with classical ideals. During this period Americans generally acquired a newfound love for the panorama of the breathlessly growing city, a fondness which supported a new national iconography of sweeping bird's-eye views, captured in thousands of artistic engravings and lithographs. While the urban demography of the early nineteenth century had provided few settings for such Renaissance luxuries as spacious plazas and landscaped promenades—in 1800 less than five percent of the population lived in urban areas of 10,000 or more—commercial prosperity heightened cosmopolitan instincts to spawn inspirational cityscapes.

By conscious intent or osmosis, new ideas about elegant and unified streetscapes seemed to enter Americans' consciousness through cumulative tradition. The ideal of a semiurban, landscaped parade ground of free-standing residences emerged in no one decade across America, nor in any one trendsetting city. To be sure, the fashion of Romantic gardening espoused by Andrew Jackson Downing in *Landscape Gardening* (1841) and *The Horticulturalist* (1846)—"architectural beauty must be considered conjointly with the beauty of the landscape"—claimed avid devotees among upper- and middle-class patrons alike.[9] Moreover, the great landscape architect Olmsted created widespread enthusiasm for naturally sculpted parks and gardens and the visual advantages of long avenues through his widely lauded landscape designs.

The vision that emerged after mid-century portrayed the residential street as a continuous parklike environment of houses, not separated by fences, but knit together in a picturesque sequence of lawns and trees and sidewalks and paving. In the oldest urban centers along the Atlantic seaboard, the grand avenue grew out of seventeenth- and eighteenth-century settlement patterns, seamlessly connected to the town's grid network. In the young industrializing urban areas of upstate New York and the Midwest, many city plats of the 1790s and early 1800s exhibited classical influences, featuring broad radial streets and long boulevards. In the southern and western regions of the United States, most grand avenues emerged later in the nation's economic rise, from 1870 to 1890. Conceived as exclusive—some even speculative—land developments on the fringe of the urban area, many captured the essence of Romantic influences by breaking away from rectilinear and radial patterns to follow the land's natural contours, as in New Orleans, Richmond, and Kansas City.

Often among the broadest streets in the city, spanning up to 200 feet in width, and often enjoying lofty elevations and picturesque views, grand avenues took on an aura of grandeur simply by their natural sitings. The streets' residents and land developers, and even some progressive municipalities, crowned these promenades with arcades of shade trees, the most popular technique for harmonizing street vistas in the last quarter of the nineteenth century. James Hillhouse of New Haven was among the first American land developers to decorate his private street, his namesake, when he lined it with elms in 1792. Charles Dickens was so impressed with Hillhouse Avenue during an 1868 visit that he declared the shaded promenade "the most beautiful street in America."[10] Yet the idea of landscaping urban streets was slow to take hold in this country, in contrast to the European fancy for dressing principal byways with shade trees. By the 1870s, however, rows and double rows of American elms framed the channels along Eastern and Midwestern avenues, while live oaks, palms, and sugar maples thrived in temperate Southern climates.

Landscaped squares and circles also guided the advance of urban processionals. In Washington, D.C., and Richmond, for example, eminent personalities in these Southern capitals staged their homes along the broad, tree-lined streets—Massachusetts and Monument Avenues—majestically punctuated by statues of Civil War heroes. Parkland also spread a velveteen blanket across bucolic cityscapes, though city plans prior to the 1850s omitted such public pleasure grounds. Philadelphia created the first, Fairmount Park, beginning in 1855, followed by New York City with Central Park between Fifth and Eighth Avenues in 1858. Acknowledgment of the economic value and aesthetic beauty of "natural" urban oases prompted grand avenue residents in Detroit, Cleveland, and Buffalo to assemble vast expanses out in the borderland of their residence-streets, donating the pristine acreage to the city for public parks. By extension, several patrons after 1870 sponsored massive park-and-boulevard projects, conceived with their avenue at the heart of the system: they hoped to ward off the spillage of unruly urban growth and enhance the elegance of the city's streets.

This goal was shared by a growing number of wealthy Americans and community builders who discovered the merits of restrictive covenants to control the use of land and the design of structures and streets. As the noise and smells of center-city industry thickened and the prevalence of disease and immigrant labor spread, as commercial building continued at an unrelenting pace, more and more affluent families chose to make their homes in privately developed subdivisions. While the patrons of such unrestricted streets as Fifth and Prairie Avenues could rely only on the private marketplace (and neighborly pressure) to determine who bought and built what where, exclusionary private streets represented an entrepreneurial form of controlled development, an American variant of authoritarian European planning. Boston's Back Bay, started in 1858, was among the first speculative developments in the country to center around a residential boulevard, the 200-foot-wide Commonwealth Avenue. It was built by a public-private partnership that transformed landfill over former mudflats into a luxurious neighborhood regulated by strict height and setback covenants, a testament to the art of unified street planning.[11] Yet nowhere in the nation did the culture of the private street flourish as it did in St. Louis, where Vandeventer Place in 1870 was the third of nineteen such streets to be developed. It was the most elegant of the city's private streets in the post–Civil War decades, the grand avenue of St. Louis, observes Charles Savage, thanks to legally binding covenants that governed the lovely parklike atmosphere.

Ward Parkway's developer, the J. C. Nichols Company, also established rigorous regulations to dictate design, development, and maintenance to assure it would remain Kansas City's most prestigious residential address, according to William Worley. In Los Angeles, Henry Gaylord Wilshire had envisioned a similar degree of control over his affluent residential subdivision when he first succeeded in banning transit lines and trucks on Wilshire Boulevard. But within three decades, after commercial builders had won piecemeal rezonings along the street, writes Thomas S. Hines, the boulevard had become "the great white way" linking the downtown commercial core with prosperous neighborhoods around Hollywood, Beverly Hills, West Adams Heights, and Wilshire, ending almost sixteen miles beyond at the Pacific cliffs in Santa Monica. The emergence of Wilshire Boulevard as the grand avenue of Los Angeles came late in the nineteenth century and evolved faster, in a compressed series of episodes in the city's horizontal sprawl. Its evolution marked time to the speed of the automobile, rather than the strolling pedestrian. As a street destined to accommodate the motorized vehicle, its rolling hills and residential neighborhoods were soon replaced in the early decades of the twentieth century by a commercial, auto-oriented culture. It signified the finale of elegant residential enclaves and the new civic dominance of commercial promenades.

COMMUNITY NEIGHBORHOODS

That the grand avenue emerged in an age of extraordinary growth nationwide owed much to the commercial and social eminence of the patrons who created these streets. Through their coherence and genuine grandeur, grand avenues acquired a certain notoriety as self-contained communities even as they asserted a dignified vision of urban life, an integrating element that went straight to the heart of the town's identity. In fact, many patrons looked to the street and the neighborhood life it supported as a means to deepen their roots in the prosperous communities they were creating through their enterprise. Such showcases of wealth inevitably attracted quite controversial figures—oil magnate John D. Rockefeller (Figure 4), industrialist Andrew Mellon, real estate capitalist "Big Jim" Fisk, meatpacker P. D. Armour, coffee importer Lafayette Folger, and liquor wholesaler Tom Pendergast. The women, too, may have lacked opportunities to occupy key business and political positions, yet they contributed thousands of hours and dollars to social welfare organizations and arts and educational institutions. Perhaps not so prevalent, but very prominent for their works and wisdom, were the few artistic personalities who redefined the edges of staid society—Samuel Clemens, Judah Touro, John Hay, Alice Pike Barney, and Mary Pickford.

The camaraderie shared with neighbors—whether they liked one another or not—reinforced the prestige of the linear neighborhood, nurturing a

Figure 4. John D. Rockefeller, 1910.

collective pride that loomed larger than its sheer physical presence. Over time, grand avenues across America gained local recognition as the ceremonial parade ground. Here is where the corteges of assassinated presidents Abraham Lincoln and William McKinley traveled in Cleveland and Buffalo; where Memorial Day veterans marched in Richmond; and where New York's famed St. Patrick's Day parade captured the attention of millions nationwide. Indeed this civic presence was just what patrons intended, for themselves and their streets, as they endowed their grand avenues with truly great museums, libraries, symphony halls, and colleges and universities (Figure 5). In Detroit, for example, after Woodward Avenue's Thomas W. Palmer, a U.S. senator and ambassador to Spain, donated 140 acres of pristine farmland along his residence-street for public parkland, his neighbors framed the open green with the Detroit Institute of Arts by Paul Cret (1927) and the Detroit Public Library by Cass Gilbert (1921).[12]

Such an active appetite for culture gave rise to one common trait among most grand avenue patrons: a genuine appreciation for the design arts. As an essential part of their everyday lives, these people embraced the inherent value of fine art and architecture by investing huge fortunes in their houses, furniture, paintings, art objects, gardens, the commercial buildings they built, and the streets themselves. A diversity of styles gathered

Figure 5. Touro Synagogue, St. Charles Avenue, New Orleans, c. 1925.

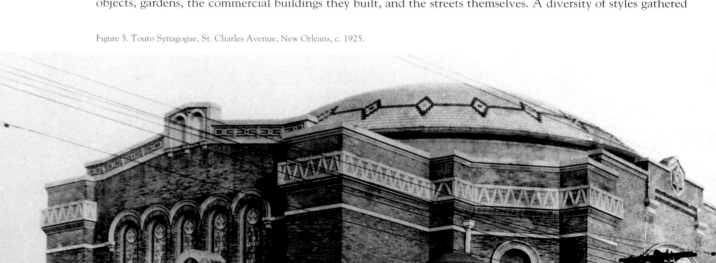

along most grand avenues, together adding up to a larger architectural idea that brought all the variations into harmony. The street was the place for builders and architects to show off, and their clients happily obliged.

Not all patrons placed a premium on ostentatious scale and stylistic panache. A minority preferred modest personal comfort. But the majority indulged lively enthusiasms for high decor and retained local and national architects known to be masters of many aesthetics. Thanks to high-speed rail travel and regular steamship schedules abroad, as well as the inflow of talented German and Scottish artisans and the widespread distribution of architectural publications, wealthy patrons in the postbellum decades enjoyed countless opportunities for architectural self-improvement. Some acquired sophisticated tastes and some clearly did not. Regardless, a keen competitive spirit—who could build the better house—raised the temperature on more than one street in this book.

The local architectural scene was perhaps the most impressionable. Grand avenue patronage shaped careers—star-makers for one local luminary whose signature stamped the streetscape. Architect-of-the-avenue stature elevated James L. Silsbee on Delaware Avenue, Charles F. Schweinfurth on Euclid, Thomas Sully on St. Charles, Jules Henri de Sibour along Massachusetts Avenue, Eames & Young on Vandeventer Place, and Nicholas Joseph Clayton along Broadway.[13] On the national level, an elite coterie of the country's most prominent architects claimed credit for residential designs on several grand avenues, notably Richard Upjohn, Richard Morris Hunt, Henry Hobson Richardson, Burnham & Root, McKim, Mead & White (apparently the most popular), Peabody & Stearns, William Lawrence Bottomley, and John Russell Pope. Such eminent designers as William LeBaron Jenney, Louis Sullivan, and Greene & Greene authored at least one commission. And for the interiors, whether patrons lived in Detroit or Galveston or New Orleans, most took the New York–bound train to have rooms and furnishings by Herter Brothers, John La Farge, Marquand & Co., William Morris, and Louis Comfort Tiffany, the most prolific.[14]

As showy and clever as these houses appeared inside and out, patrons most poignantly exhibited their entrepreneurial bent in an insatiable enthusiasm for advanced technology, or better yet, personalized mechanical trinkets. To be sure, income-tax-free wealth before 1913 bought domestic luxuries that predated mass markets by a decade or more—central heating in the mid-1850s, electric lighting and elevators in the 1880s, intercoms in the 1890s, and interior garages in the earliest years of the new century. But it was patrons' love for inventive gadgets that pushed the architects and builders—albeit, infrequently and sporadically—to incorporate such innovative devices as rudimentary air conditioners and humidifiers into several early twentieth-century houses.

AN ALTERED IMAGE

For all this magnificence, the speculative marketplace played the greatest role in shaping the twentieth-century image of the grand avenue. Ironically, it was the patrons themselves who transformed initially remote areas into highly valued districts. Where these elegant streets ran through the heart of prospering downtowns, the grand avenue became enormously vulnerable to surging land prices and an expanding populace. An assortment of higher densities and income-producing uses—apartment buildings, hotels, department stores, and office buildings—gathered along the premier street. The residents were also changing. Second- and third-generation homeowners, who were less wedded to the grand avenue vision than their ancestors, increasingly outnumbered the original creators that remained. All felt burdened by the extraordinary expense of voluminous houses, what with escalating property taxes and maintenance costs. Grand dame Mrs. Richard Townsend of Washington, D.C., recalls Sue Kohler, spent a small fortune after 1910 just to maintain the thirty-four servants who were the linchpins in the daily operation of her Massachusetts Avenue mansion. This is when the architectural moderation of St. Charles Avenue patrons, writes S. Frederick Starr, paid off handsomely by enabling homeowners to preserve the stately residential image.

Beyond the sheer expense of monumentalism, many affluent urbanites became disheartened by the harsh realities crowding in around their elegant environments. Year by year, mounting ethnic and cultural diversity altered the urban street's public image and weakened the personal influence of grand avenue patrons. Noisy streets, choked with autos and streetcars and pedestrian crowds, denied the exclusiveness these people sought. Even so, believing that beautiful cityscapes could influence human behavior, just as Olmsted had argued, civic-minded advocates chaired municipal art societies and park-and-boulevard commissions in the 1880s and 1890s. Many resided on the grand avenues of their cities. Yet as they waved their banners of public welfare and social reform, their deepest desire was to preserve their cherished streetscapes by reining in pluralistic forces.

This is why the awesome sight of the White City at the 1893 Columbian Exposition inspired municipal art societies nationwide to organize the maiden City Beautiful conference in 1899. These City Beautiful proponents spoke of creating harmonious urban landscapes across their towns and cities, often invoking visions that had actually developed on hundreds of grand avenues over the past five decades. They advocated "scientific" methods to cope with "modern" problems and brought nationally prominent designers into scores of cities to restore the landscape's economic value and civic dignity, particularly their own coveted properties.[15]

Grand avenues that emerged late in the century and reached their peak growth during the period 1900 to 1910 benefited greatly from City Beautiful proposals. In Richmond, for example, Monument Avenue patrons drew inspiration from plans for Washington, D.C. (1901), Cleveland (1903), and Chicago (1909), according to Richard Guy Wilson. In Los Angeles, as well, Charles Mulford Robinson centered the 1908 plan for "Los Angeles, the City Beautiful" around Wilshire Boulevard, coming at a crucial moment in the evolution of this grand avenue, argues Hines. Aggrandizing the city's principal street was difficult enough, but creating a grand avenue out of whole cloth, dressed in the guise of a City Beautiful plan, was virtually impossible in America's free market. That it partially succeeded in Philadelphia, where civic leaders and the Art Federation undertook a Haussmann-like effort to superimpose Fairmount Parkway on William Penn's seventeenth-century grid, was testimony to the plan's public merits and the sponsors' will.[16] Even in such places as Detroit and Cleveland, patrons and major business interests attempted but failed to formalize the street's dignity as its supremacy ebbed. The plans neither carried the force of law nor aligned with the will of commerce.

One is at a loss to understand why such entrepreneurial minds as those who sponsored the beautification of Detroit and Cleveland and Chicago, among other cities, failed to incorporate a legal mechanism to enforce these monumental blueprints. Maybe they were not yet reconciled to the realities of their diminishing civic influence; it was not as if land-use covenants were unknown or untested. Restricted urban districts had gained widespread credibility over the last five decades. The problem, Herbert Croly argued around 1910, was that the grandiose qualities of these plans were removed from the realities of the marketplace.[17] The lobbying power of mercantile interests, which paid bounteous tax revenues to city coffers, was so forceful, and ethnic diversity and congestion so pervasive, most grand avenue patrons in fact lacked both the will and the ability to create protected residential zones in the heart of fast-growing cities.[18]

Just as nineteenth-century grand avenue patrons had sponsored or built the street infrastructure to support their residential environments, twentieth-century commercial and transit interests now persuaded city officials to increase the capacity of roads and sewers to meet their economic needs. Street widenings after the mid-1920s transformed green promenades into concrete arteries. And where they rose, tall buildings on center-city grand avenues totally disrupted the harmony of the streetscape. Convenience overwhelmed the grandeur of Broadway and Delaware and Euclid Avenues, while commerce reigned on Fifth Avenue and Wilshire Boulevard. Yet in such places as Washington, D.C., New Orleans, and Kansas City, where the grand avenue emerged late in the century and extended well beyond the commercial core—cities in which economic pressures were weak anyway—these residential promenades largely avoided conflict with high-density commercial uses.

Affluent Americans a century before may have felt secure amid congestion, but now they felt only hostility. Mixed confusions about crowds, nearby factories, and incoherent images on their streets gave rise to various responses in different cities and different circumstances. Early on, residents who were stubbornly committed to living in town regardless, built such fortress-like domiciles as the 1886 Glessner house on Prairie Avenue, which by then was engulfed on all sides by factory smoke and the din of passing trains. Many residents led tax revolts against city officials down through the 1930s. And in places such as St. Louis, where expanding suburban areas afforded the choice between inner-city noise and working-class neighbors or a quiet semirural and homogeneous enclave, wealthy residents chose the latter. Perhaps it was their speculative mindsets that enabled them to leave their magnificent (and expensive) urban mansions behind for spacious grounds in the suburbs. Perhaps it was their estrangement from a formerly elegant environment they no longer could control.

Those grand avenues endowed with noble civic functions, such as Massachusetts Avenue, tended to be most resilient to twentieth-century urban pressures because of their larger public purpose. Yet streets laid out as exclusive residential neighborhoods, such as Vandeventer Place and Prairie Avenue, became most vulnerable to urban expansion and heightened densification around the turn of the century. Grand avenues that gained a strong commercial presence thrived or died over the years in concert with the general enterprise of the city or town.

LOOKING FORWARD

Today, the grand avenue's legacy lives on in many forms: in novels and songs and movies, in collector post-cards, in institutional landmarks and parks along the street, and, in all too few cases, as elegant residential promenades. Historic districts along Delaware, Prairie, Monument, and Broadway Avenues have helped to preserve a portion of the legacy—"a symbol of attainment" in Buffalo, "that remarkable street" in Chicago, "the site of memorials to the Confederacy" in Richmond, and the "Queen of the Mexican Gulf" in Galveston. But the greatest legacy the grand avenue bequeathed to subsequent generations was an indigenous cultural identity, a collective vision of economic and civic achievement in a democratic society.

In this book, America's grand avenues have been defined according to four elements: original function (residential); socioeconomic class (upper strata); architectural design (elegant, sometimes ostentatious, and technologically innovative); and urban design (straight, landscaped streets punctuated by monumental features). The exploration is presented in twelve essays, each portraying the forces that shaped the grand avenue in one city. Through a collective profile, the reader may see differences in urban form, street patterns, economic circumstances, geographical conditions, social customs, political environments, and architectural vocabularies.

JAN CIGLIANO
Washington, D.C.

The Grand American
AVENUE
1850-1920

Chapter One

FIFTH

Avenue

New York, New York

For 150 years people the world over have equated success in the United States with an address on Fifth Avenue. This banal sounding, numerically named boulevard housed America's wealthiest citizens, and its shops provided them with the most elegant and desirable commodities. Fifth Avenue has seemed to us a promenade of silk-hatted gentlemen with elaborately attired ladies rather as we see in the Fred Astaire film in which the famous entertainer sings "Easter Parade." The refrain from the song is, "On the avenue, Fifth Avenue," which Mr. Astaire sings as he glides past enlarged photographs of the former mansions on the street.

Fifth Avenue was a creation of the fluid social climate of nineteenth-century New York, and its diversified architectural story may have been the most significant residential boulevard in America for a full century (Figure 1).

At the beginning of the nineteenth century, the upper three-quarters of the island of Manhattan was given over to a series of farms located on a set of hills and valleys punctuated by brooks, rivers, and streams with occasional marshes. Despite these natural obstacles, New York City was on the way to becoming the premier city of the nation.

The leaders of eighteenth-century New York, the Dutch and English settlers called the Knickerbockers, were feeling the pinch of the increasing growth of trade in the tight confines of the southern tip of New York City. These local merchants were able to afford a comfortable home living in brick Federal row houses located at St. John's Square and Greenwich Street on the western side of the island. A group of these merchants moved uptown to Second Avenue where the city was more peaceful. This move was the beginning of a northward movement in the city.

ESSAY BY MOSETTE BRODERICK

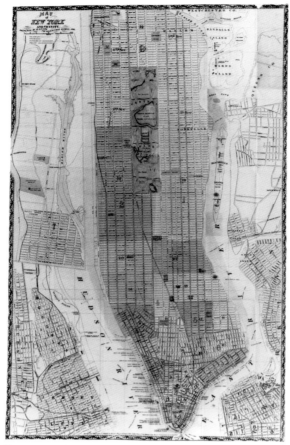

Figure 1. Map of New York and vicinity, 1865. Fifth Avenue runs north-south adjacent to the east edge of Central Park.

New York City's future growth was laid out in the city's first planning document, "The Randel Plan," or "Commissioners' Map," completed in 1811. This gridiron method of arrangement of the city for future development ignored the topography of the existing land. The empty land at the edge of the then-built city was organized into cross streets and avenues arranged by number, not by name.

Fifth Avenue first appears on this 1811 Commissioners' map, but the city would not get the title for the land along it until 1824 when the section of Fifth Avenue from Art Street (long demapped) to Thirteenth Street was opened. Six years later the city could sell plots from Thirteenth to Twenty-fourth Street, and the avenue was opened up to Forty-second Street in 1837.

The Commissioners' new plan began at the former burial ground of recent use, today's Washington Square Park. Even the city's most avaricious developer could not figure a way to build over the Potter's Field of just a few years earlier, so the plot had to be left as open ground. The City declared this the parade ground when it was opened to the public in 1828. The neatly fenced-in green rectangle proved a boon to row-house builders who would rapidly surround it with houses before moving northward (Figure 2).

A few Scottish merchants who felt affluent enough to build larger houses than those available for rent in the increasingly crowded Greenwich Street area, leased plots at the north of Washington Square on land held by the charity called "Sailor's Snug Harbor." The builders of numbers 1 through 13 Washington Square North provided New York City with the highest-quality Greek Revival row houses yet built. The red brick row acted as a bridge for these well-off merchants to attract others of their class, making a horizontal corridor from Knickerbocker Second Avenue over to the land-locked road at the middle of the island, Fifth Avenue. Washington Square North's first residents could look out their rear windows at their own gardens, then northward at the empty land beyond inhabited only by grazing red cows. Henry J. Brevoort, Jr., was probably the first city house builder to round the bend on to Fifth Avenue in 1834. Brevoort was a member of the old landholding family whose farm lay just to the east. Brevoort continued the established tradition of the red brick house in New York City, but added fancy stucco panels and a distinctive central door portico. This fine, freestanding house has long been believed to be the work of Town & Davis, but this matter is open to dispute (Figure 3).[1]

Above Washington Square a few houses were built near the upper reaches of the dirt lane that would eventually be the avenue. New York State's future governor, Edwin D. Morgan, built a house on the east side at Thirty-seventh Street set back from the proposed avenue.[2] In the spacious front yard Morgan staged seasonal displays. In summer he had a garden; in winter, a skating pond. Just above Morgan's house was the large hilltop country residence of John Taylor, a wooden Greek Revival summer house in the vicinity of what would be Fortieth Street today.

Hills did indeed characterize the future avenue. Steep peaks interrupted the country lanes of the upper island requiring sturdy horses to be stationed at the bases of these rocky sections. Those riding in carriages used the "hill" horses to pull the vehicles up the steeper grades. The horses wore metal bells that made a gay noise as they plodded upward, a sound children always enjoyed hearing.

Surely these hills would inhibit the development of Fifth Avenue. On that assumption, New York City's water commissioners took city land on the western side of Fifth Avenue from Fortieth to Forty-second Street and would create there the first large, safe water source for the cholera-plagued island. The Croton Reservoir was built between 1837 and 1842, and when it opened, the Egyptian-styled, battered-wall holding tank was a wonder of modern technology. Those who journeyed to view the new Croton Reservoir and enjoy the latest fad of walking atop its thick walls, could take refreshment on the return trip southward at Colonel Thompson's Madison Square roadhouse, which sat back from the traffic at Twenty-third Street.[3] The roadhouse flourished with the horse-loving youth of the city from 1829 to 1850 and was a well-known watering spot until the city pushed northward.

As horses sped up the dirt lane in 1843–44, their riders would have looked with mild surprise at two twin houses being built on the west side of Fifth Avenue at Eighteenth Street on what was then almost suburban land. Henry H. Elliott, an iron merchant at 27 Wall Street, and Robert C. Townsend, a dry goods merchant at

Figure 2. View of Washington Square parade ground from the southwest side, c. 1850.

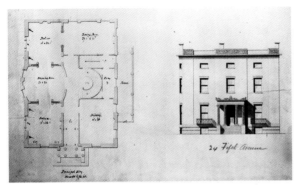

Figure 3. Brevoort residence, 24 Fifth Avenue, 1834, architect unknown. Plan and elevation, watercolor. Demolished.

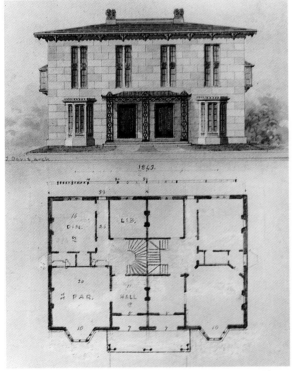

Figure 4. Elliott and Townsend residences, Eighteenth Street and Fifth Avenue, 1843–44, Town & Davis, architects. Plan and elevation, watercolor. Demolished.

33 Nassau Street, commissioned the firm of Town & Davis to build "two low, pretty dwellings of white marble with bits of lawn in front of them."[4] The Town & Davis houses had an almost rural appearance, but urban materials were used, including fine ornamental railings. These Town & Davis houses may have had the first bay windows in New York City (Figure 4).[5]

Though Town & Davis seem to be the first architects building houses on Fifth Avenue, the church builders were already on the avenue. The newly celebrated English-born architect, Richard Upjohn, began an Episcopal Church for Fifth Avenue at the northwest corner of Tenth Street in 1840. This Church of the Ascension, as did his then-being-built Trinity Church at Wall Street, helped to make the old utilitarian material of the city, brownstone, into a fashionable covering for new structures. Trinity and the Church of the Ascension, both still standing, made brownstone a material of choice for New Yorkers. Just four years later at Eleventh Street on an open lot, another English-born architect, Joseph C. Wells, built the First Presbyterian Church for the Scottish population. Also built of brownstone, this church still stands. Brownstone now seemed to be *the* material for Fifth Avenue (Figure 5).

As Fifth Avenue slowly awakened from its country character, the city's builders abandoned the red brick of the Federal and Greek Revival row houses for the new Renaissance *palazzo*-inspired house fronted with New Jersey's Belleville brownstone (Figure 6). In England, Charles Barry had made the Italian Renaissance *palazzo* the inspiration for his famous clubhouses on Pall Mall. The Barryesque *palazzo* came across the Atlantic and became the inspiration for the ubiquitous brownstone house popular in the 1850s and 1860s, built on Fifth Avenue from its start to Central Park and on the side streets as well. This house so became the norm that all row houses are commonly called "brownstones."

Although the brownstone was the forte of the speculative builder, its greatest designer of the 1850s was inspired by the real thing, not an illustration in a book. Frederick Diaper came to New York and practiced in

Figure 5. View looking south at Fifth Avenue and Fourteenth Street, 1865. Row houses with First Presbyterian Church, 1844 (Joseph C. Wells, architect) and the Church of the Ascension, 1840 (Richard Upjohn, architect) in the distance.

Figure 6. Unusually wide brownstone residence, New York City, c. 1850, Calvin Pollard, architect. Elevation, watercolor.

the Greek Revival mode before becoming the master of the Renaissance Revival brownstone. Diaper, who had studied in England with Robert Smirke, had more specific architectural ability and training than the average English builder/opportunist who came to the United States in search of economic gain and improved professional status. Diaper had a sure eye and a good sense of proportion which made his fine Renaissance Revival houses of the later 1840s and early 1850s the talk of the town.

The Diaper houses were known for a more sophisticated internal plan as well as for grand exterior appearance, making his houses much sought after by wealthy city men such as the two New York City brothers, Henry and David Parish, and a new settler in the city from Germany, the young August Belmont. For bachelor Belmont, whose European sophistication acquired at the circle of the Rothschild bankers put staid mercantile New Yorkers in awe, Diaper built a house at 82 Fifth Avenue at the southwestern corner of Fourteenth Street in 1847. Belmont would soon marry and require a larger house for his growing family. Instead of building a large house on a side street, Belmont's wife, the daughter of Commodore Perry, insisted on remaining on Fifth Avenue. Belmont resolved his need for space, a proper wine cellar, and a house that continued to support his image of a continental gentleman, plus his wife's insistence on Fifth Avenue, by purchasing a seven-year-old house at 109 Fifth Avenue (at Eighteenth Street) from the merchant who built it, John Gihon. Gihon had built the broad-fronted, double house for his family but decided to move them to true suburbia—Yonkers—in 1859. The Gihon house was perhaps Diaper's biggest and would become home to the family until the death of August Belmont in the 1880s (Figure 7).

Figure 7. Gihon-Belmont residence, 109 Fifth Avenue, 1852, Frederick Diaper, architect. Demolished.

If Diaper was the grand man's architect of the 1850s, then yet another British-born New Yorker, Griffith Thomas, was the proper businessman's builder. Griffith Thomas, who came to America with a wave of English builders determined to improve their lot, had a father here. Thomas Thomas, father of Griffith, had settled in America in the late 1820s. The Welsh father and son would build many important city buildings, from St. Peter's Catholic Church in the financial district (extant) to the Grand Opera House. Griffith Thomas was the master of the speculatively built Renaissance Revival brownstone house. Thomas had a flourishing commercial business while being an immensely successful house builder. Thomas was "Mr." Worth Street, building the textile capital of mid-nineteenth-century America there as well as designing numerous bank buildings and insurance offices. Thomas carried on an enormous practice because he was a practical man. Unlike Diaper, who built for image-conscious wealthy men, Thomas built for the more modest, cost-conscious American merchant. Thomas finished his buildings at the cost he had promised and completed them on time. As a result he received continuous employment and boasted that he had built at least three buildings on each block of Fifth Avenue from Washington Square to Central Park.[6] Sadly for Thomas, his numerous commissions were inadequate for his high standard of living. He died in 1879 soon after the death of both his sons and well behind in the rent for his office.

In fact, Griffith Thomas did not build as many houses as he claimed, but in the Union Square to Forty-second Street area, he did build many houses for the speculative builder's world. Griffith Thomas's precise, cost-effective work caused him to be one of the primary architects for the great landowning family of mid-nineteenth-century New York, John Jacob and William Backhouse Astor. For the Astor estate, Thomas built

Figure 8. Fifth Avenue, west side, looking north from Thirty-third Street, c. 1877. J. J. Astor residence, (left), 1859, architect unknown. W. B. Astor residence (right), 1856, Griffith Thomas, architect. Demolished.

the better houses. The Astors owned great swathes of land in the blocks of the Thirties, on and near Fifth Avenue. For the Astor estate's second-grade houses, a local builder and distant relative of Mrs. William Henry Vanderbilt, Peter Kissam was asked to produce respective units of exactly the same house. The Astor estate used Kissam for routine residences and Thomas for better houses.[7]

W. B. Astor's two sons were given wonderful house sites for their own families in the mid-1850s. The Lafayette Row Astors saw the march of the city, which Fifth Avenue was then leading, as inevitable and for the two young couples when his sons married, W. B. Astor gave each a corner property on Fifth Avenue— John Jacob Astor II at the northwest corner of Thirty-third Street and W. B. Astor II at the southwest corner of Thirty-fourth Street. The marriage residences of the third-generation Astors would act as a magnet. W. B. Astor hoped to lead renters to his tracts of houses planned for the blocks just to the sides of Fifth Avenue (Figure 8). Although we cannot be sure who built either of the mid-1850s houses for the Astor heirs, the John Jacob Astor house of 1859 was brick, while the W. B. Astor house was Griffith Thomas's signature brownstone.

W. B. Astor II had married a formidable woman. Caroline Schermerhorn Astor was a child of the venerable and well-connected Old New York Schermerhorns. With the infusion of major Astor money, Mrs. Astor set out on a successful journey to make herself the apogee of New York City's emerging and conspicuous upper social class. She would, in fact, become the famous Mrs. Astor.

Thus Caroline Schermerhorn Astor wished a house to go with her ambitions. We must assume that the better of the family architects, Griffith Thomas, did her house in 1856. The house was built before New York City kept records and the house was not specifically singled-out in Thomas's obituaries, but the W. B. Astor house closely resembles the well-known Marshall O. Roberts house on lower Fifth Avenue,[8] which was repeatedly listed as a major work of Thomas's. Thomas listed himself as architect for the Astors, and combining the fact that the Astor house resembles the Roberts house and that Griffith Thomas was hired to do the extension on the house on September 11, 1875, it seems reasonable to assume that he was the builder of Mrs. Astor's mansion. The extension of 1875 was a perfect cube thirty-five feet by thirty-five feet, one story high and cost the large, for the period, sum of $16,000. The extension was, of course, the famous ballroom where Mrs. Astor and Ward McAllister would find New York's top "400" could fit.

Griffith Thomas was the architect for the first purpose-built clubhouse in New York City—the Union Club on the northwest corner of Fifth Avenue and Twenty-first Street in 1854–55. This Renaissance Revival *palazzo* in brownstone sat among the brick and brownstone houses of these blocks and provided gentlemen with a convenient place to congregate when they needed to extricate themselves from domestic life (Figure 9).

On the site of Colonel Thompson's roadhouse, Griffith Thomas built (1857 to 1859) the first major commercial building on the thus far sanctified-for-domestic-purposes-only land, Fifth Avenue. For Amos Eno, Griffith Thomas (with assistance from a William Washburn) married houses with commerce and helped to create the famous Fifth Avenue Hotel. The Eno venture was a risky one. The developer chose to build the most lavish hotel New York had seen and to place it well *above* the city's commercial district. Given its location amongst houses and its construction by a specialist in both residential and commercial properties, Eno hoped that the hotel would be regarded as part of the house-bound neighborhood. Each guest was expected to treat the amenities of the hotel as his own—to consider the hotel an extension of one's own house. To be sure, the Renaissance Revival light stone building was larger than private houses, but it blended in amongst them as being only slightly taller than a residence. The hotel provided a "vertical incline railroad," that is, passenger elevator, for guests unwilling to walk up the stairs to the upper chambers. But the walk was well worth the trek—each guest room had a fireplace for cozy warmth in the rooms in winter and year-round guests could congregate in the magnificent public

Figure 9. Fifth Avenue at Twenty-first Street, looking south, c. 1865. The Union Clubhouse (right), 1855, Griffith Thomas, architect. Demolished.

Figure 10. View from the southeast of Fifth Avenue and Twenty-third Street. The Fifth Avenue Hotel, 1857–59, Griffith Thomas and William Washburn, architects. Demolished. Photograph not dated.

rooms on the first floor. The red and black marble floor of the dining room was dramatic and guests were welcomed to four meals a day covered by the hotel charge rate of $2.50 a day. People ate at long family-style tables so conversation could readily be found and, should a hotel guest have a friend visit, the guest could be brought to a meal gratis. Mr. Eno's policy was to include a paying customer's social obligations in as gracious a manner as one might do at home. The reputation of the Fifth Avenue Hotel was so high that when Charles Dickens made his second visit to the U.S., he stayed at the hotel. Even more proof of Mr. Eno's brilliant success in placing the hotel among private houses high above the hotel district came in 1860 when the Prince of Wales, on a visit to New York, chose the Fifth Avenue Hotel as his place of residence (Figures 10 and 11).

Figure 11. View of a dining room, c. 1880. The Fifth Avenue Hotel, Fifth Avenue at Twenty-third Street, 1857–59, Griffith Thomas and William Washburn, architects. Demolished.

11

MATTERS FRENCH

During this early period of Fifth Avenue's development, the English influence was quite clear—several of the avenue's architects were either British-born or relied on illustrations from English publications as sources for the details on the Greek Revival and Renaissance Revival houses. Indeed, New York looked almost exclusively to England for architectural information until the middle of the nineteenth century. But when it came to fashion or the decoration of the entertaining rooms in the new brownstones, things English were considered quite passé. "Everything English is decidedly *mauvais ton*; English materials, English fashions, English accent, English manner are all terms of reproach."[10]

The English novelist Anthony Trollope toured North America in 1861–62 and wrote, "The taste of America is becoming French in its conversations, French in its comforts and French in its discomforts, French in its eating, and French in its dress, French in its manners, and will become French in its art."[11]

Figure 12. Hart M. Shiff residence, 32 Fifth Avenue, 1850, Detlef Lienau, architect. Demolished.

In New York City, French influence in the world of buildings began with the arrival of the French merchant and banker, Hart M. Shiff, from his New World home in New Orleans. Mr. Shiff bought a Fifth Avenue lot for his family's new home on the southwest corner of Tenth Street at 32 Fifth Avenue. Mr. Shiff hired the Danish/German-born architect, Detlef Lienau, to build his new abode and the contract drawings were signed on May 4, 1850. The resulting red brick and brownstone house was a novelty in America as it had a steep slate roof—the first mansard roof in New York City. The house was noted as being exceptional in its day[12] and Lienau had to work carefully with the carpenter who built the roof as the builders did not know how to construct this new style—a popular feature of residential French architecture in the second quarter of the nineteenth century.[13]

The choice of a French-influenced builder for a French-born client is logical indeed, even though the design coincided with an increasing francophilic tendency in the fashion-conscious world of the U.S. One can only wonder if Shiff and Lienau discussed the design of the row house later in 1850 as a small pencil doodle on the elevation contract drawing shows a Francois Ier chateau with corner turrets.[14] The Shiff lot was a large, double-sized plot fifty feet wide, thus suitable for a freestanding "chateau," but this novel idea did not go further and a somewhat conventional house with some French features was built over the next two years (Figure 12). Sadly for Shiff, he died halfway through construction of the house and never resided in his style-setting home. Shortly after the house was completed, the Shiff family sold the property to the son of the owner of the

Fifth Avenue Hotel, the famous collector of New York prints, Amos F. Eno. Eno lived in the house until his death. The house was then torn down and replaced by an apartment building in 1923.

Although Shiff never called his house home, the roofline his carpenters suffered so to construct became the symbol of fashion-conscious New Yorkers for the next twenty years. The mansard roof became an outward symbol of sophistication and many new buildings were later completed with this visual allusion to the Second Empire of Louis Napoleon. In New York City, many row houses were to be built with the addition on an extra story in the French manner. In vintage photographs showing conventional row houses with low, token mansards, one can be sure that the roof was a jazzy new alteration of the 1860s and 1870s.

In row-house building, the mansard became identified with families who might have chosen to travel abroad and emulate a continental life. Although well-off Americans had made the Grand Tour to Europe from the 1830s on, these folks returned to the U.S. content to display objects purchased on their tour, but also to return to conventional New York manners. The success of August Belmont in smart society combined with regular steamship schedules caused Americans to consider more travel abroad and to sojourn there longer. The Americans of the 1850s and 1860s who frequented the resorts and watering holes of Europe as well as the cultural capitals, looked for acceptance of Americans as social equals to wealthy Europeans. In many places these American social climbers failed, but in the France of Louis Napoleon, they found a kindred, well-off smart set who dominated Second Empire society. Americans gained access to these circles and returned home determined to exhibit French social values at home. The effects of the court of Louis Napoleon on the dress, architecture, manners, and cuisine of East Coast Americans became dramatic in the years just after the Civil War and began the Europhilia phase of American society which flourished from the 1860s to the great depression of the 1930s.

The old mode of living of New York City's early Knickerbocker gentry died—a victim of economic growth and the replacement of the old order by a new wealthy crowd determined to break down the walls of society via a display of money. A sobering rhyme, "Nothing to Wear," was written in 1857 about a New York City belle of the era:

> Miss Flora McFlimsey of Madison Square, had made three separate journeys to Paris, and her father assures me, each time she was there,…she spent six continuous weeks without stopping, in one continuous round of shopping. And yet, though scarce three months have passed since the day, this merchandise went, on twelve carts up Broadway, this same Miss McFlimsey, of Madison Square, at last time we met her was in utter dispair because she had nothing whatever to wear![15]

The sheer exhibition of money became the ticket to success in New York City society from the Civil War to the present day.

The two Astor houses on Thirty-third and Thirty-fourth Streets reflected this social change. The earlier house, that of W. B. Astor II, built of correct New York City brownstone, reflected the staid nature of the Astor who married a Knickerbocker. John Jacob Astor II, in his pressed Philadelphia brick house built just three years later, made a nod to the newer French-inspired style. His Thirty-third Street house had pronounced corner quoins, an elaborate entry portico, and a stubby mansard roof.

Though the younger Astors' houses were the talk of the town in the 1850s, just a few years later on the northern corner of Thirty-fourth Street at Fifth Avenue, A. T. Stewart's purchase of the ungainly brownstone house of Samuel P. "Sarsaparilla" Townsend was the center of attention.[16] Stewart, the Irish-born dry goods merchant who built America's first department store, had traveled to Europe himself several times in the 1850s and early 1860s with his wife and her young nieces. The Stewart entourage stayed in Paris and in French resorts while Stewart attended business meetings. Back in New York, Stewart's business flourished

Figure 13. A. T. Stewart residence, northwest corner of Thirty-fourth Street and Fifth Avenue, 1864–69, John Kellum, architect. Demolished. Photograph c. 1883.

with his great new uptown store on Broadway at Ninth Street which had opened during the early days of the Civil War. Stewart had, wisely, and in the manner of the Astor family, invested in a large group of real estate properties in his adopted city. Flush with success in 1864, the aging Stewart and his wife purchased the Townsend property.

Stewart himself inspired little confidence in his level of taste. The Knickerbocker diarist, George Templeton Strong, noted with dissatisfaction that he was "up Fifth Avenue this morning to call on Mrs. William Astor…the great, hideous one hundred-thousand dollar Townsend-Sarsaparilla-Springer house on the other side of Thirty-fourth Street has just been bought by A. T. Stewart, who has razed it to the ground and tells William Astor he is going to lay out one million on a new white marble *palazzo*. I suppose it will be just ten times as ugly and barbaric as its predecessor, if that be conceivable."[17] Stewart hired the carpenter/architect of his iron store to build him a new house and seems to have had to cajole John Kellum into designing a house grand enough to stop Stewart's neighbors in their tracks.[18] Stewart's house, completed in 1869, was the showiest house in

Figure 14. Nos. 4, 5, and 6 Fifth Avenue. John Taylor Johnston residence, 6 Fifth Avenue, 1856, Alfred J. Bloor, architect. Demolished. Photograph not dated.

New York City to the day and may have been the costliest private house in the nation.

A. T. Stewart's big corner house was separated from the Avenue by a deep moat, and its entrance was on Thirty-fourth Street. The house was cut white stone[19] which made it stand out dramatically from its neighbors (Figure 13). Although Stewart liked to claim he built the first white marble palace, he was here copying a significant earlier house. John Taylor Johnston, the well-liked descendant of two notable Scottish families, had built a stunning new house on Fifth Avenue at Eighth Street. In 1856, John Taylor Johnston, who had grown up on Washington Square, turned the corner and built on Fifth Avenue. Johnston, who was a figure in the railroad world, hired a student of Diaper, Alfred J. Bloor, to build him a fine Renaissance *palazzo*. Bloor provided just such a house, but used a different facing material. Bloor used Lee Quarry Stone (from Massachusetts), which was the color of slate for the Johnston house. When the house was finished it was subtly different from its neighbors, but not shockingly so. However, Lee Quarry Stone whitens, and in the next decade and a half the house became quite white.[20] So, when Stewart contemplated building his house, he had the inspiration of Johnston's newly whitening house twenty-six blocks to the south (Figure 14).

Surely A. T. Stewart could hardly ignore his social betters across Thirty-fourth Street. Stewart was not part of New York society, a fact that did not distress him terribly as acquisition of capital was his delight. But a man as wealthy as Stewart, whose fortune rivaled that of the Astors, had to have his house make a statement about its relation to its neighbors. Although the white stone came on inspiration, the form of the house was based on that used for the John Jacob Astor II house. Like the Astor house, the Stewart residence had a short mansard roof pierced by dormer windows. Stewart had determined to outbuild the Knickerbockers and the new Astors. He forced New York City to notice his house which, in the end, with the furnishings and the pictures he bought, may have cost him over two million 1870 dollars. Stewart opened the door for "house as statement" and instructed the city and the world that the lavish expenditure of dollars made a person impossible to ignore. Following Stewart's example, newly rich Americans came to Fifth Avenue to lay coffers of gold before the gods of society. Inevitably, it worked. Sheer money bought presence in what was called the "shoddy" aristocracy. Shortly, we shall see how the Vanderbilts took on Stewart and transformed the west side of Fifth Avenue from Fifty-first to Fifty-seventh Streets into Vanderbilt Street. The Vanderbilts, unlike Stewart, did wish to join society and they succeeded—their homes bought entry into New York's elite.

If Stewart made New Yorkers notice the corner of Thirty-fourth Street[21] and Fifth Avenue in 1869, just twenty blocks to the north was the howling wilderness—an area whose primary residents were goats (Figure 15).[22] It was here on the frontier of the new Central Park that two sisters made a very astute business move.

Figure 15. View in Central Park, looking south from Sixty-fourth Street. Lithograph, 1859.

Figure 16. Madison Avenue looking northwest from Fifty-fifth Street, c. 1870. Mary Mason Jones residence (far left of row at what was Fifth Avenue), 1868, Robert Mook, architect.

The Mason girls, Rebecca and Mary, had both married Jones boys. They were both widowed early and shared portions of a farm their father had purchased. Old John Mason, a city merchant, had bought a farm which stretched from Fifty-fourth to Fifty-sixth Streets and from Fifty-seventh to Sixty-third Streets between Fifth Avenue and Fourth Avenue. The parcels John Mason acquired were reasonable in price as urbanization of the area seemed a century away. In fact urban growth at Fifth Avenue from Fifty-seventh to Fifty-eighth Streets in 1868 looked still to be decades off when the widowed Mary Mason Jones returned from a visit to Paris. Mary Mason Jones, who belonged to old, Knickerbocker, mercantile New York, felt commerce was about to invade lower Fifth Avenue. With incredible daring she hired Robert Mook to build a whole block of houses—an entire terrace scheme in the northern wilds. How did Mrs. Jones envision filling her new houses in an area of chaos? She had a two-fold scheme—to make a startling, glamorous row with unified appearance in emulation of contemporary Second Empire Paris—and to move right in herself (Figure 16).

Robert Mook was a mid-century architect who received some important commissions, yet we know little about him. We do know his father, Thomas Mook, owned the Bull's Head cattle yard on Fifth Avenue between Forty-fourth and Forty-sixth Streets. Ironically, it was the Bull's Head cattle yards that had inhibited the growth of Fifth Avenue in many people's minds, as its presence kept the speculative builder at bay until the yards moved west to Eleventh Avenue in the early 1850s. Thus Fifth Avenue was saved from the mess and smell of slaughtered animals.

Robert Mook and Mrs. Jones began their project for a terrace of white houses. At about the time that they began the southern corner house that would be Mrs. Jones's own residence, her sister, Rebecca Colford Jones with her architect, Detlef Lienau, began contemplating a second Jones row. It would seem logical that all four discussed the design of these two terraces, as they would have to be very special to lure wealthy New Yorkers to the goat fields (Figure 17).

Figure 17. Rebecca Colford Jones row, 1869–70, Detlef Lienau, architect. Elevation, watercolor. Demolished.

Robert Mook's terrace was the more striking of the rows. The tall houses were crowned with a newer, high-pitched mansard more authentically Second Empire than the earlier squat roofs. The tall corner pavilion-roof houses were modeled on the new work at the Louvre in Paris which Mrs. Jones had surely seen on her recent visit.[23]

The line of French inspiration for the owner-commissioned houses took a new turn in the 1870s when the formula of Second Empire style pervaded the commercial world of iron-fronted banks and warehouses and made the new style routine. Further, the Franco-Prussian War and the fall of Louis Napoleon ended the direct inspiration of the French court for upwardly mobile Americans.

The fashion-conscious still turned to France for inspiration—now to the country chateau. In the middle of the nineteenth century, new owners of wine-growing estates in France that were bereft of a genuine chateau commissioned an appropriate replica. These nouveau riche families were the same folk that American railroad barons studied on visits abroad. It is not surprising that the new American rich turned to the chateau for architectural inspiration. Further reinforcement could be found in the homes of established families. In London, the architect William Burn had built a chateau in Whitehall for the Duke of Buccleuch in the mid-1850s called Montagu House. The prominence of Burn's urban chateau would have made an impression on American visitors in the nineteenth century who may well have been inspired by the British version of the chateau for the streets of New York City. Unlike the nineteenth-century French wine-country chateaux, Montagu house has been demolished.

The chateau first appears in the United States as the unbuilt variant on Lienau's design for Hart Shiff. It may well be that R. M. Hunt proposed a chateau for the showman/speculator "Big Jim" Fisk. Fisk, like Hunt, was a native of Brattleboro, Vermont, where he came from humble stock. Fisk's father was a peddler who sold tin at the home of Hunt's senator-father. When Fisk made his entry into New York in the late 1860s, he purchased the Pike's (Grand) Opera House and gave Hunt and his family run of the place, an honor the Hunts

Figure 18. Jim Fisk residence, Fifth Avenue at Seventieth Street, 1870, Richard Morris Hunt, architect. Elevation, watercolor. Unbuilt.

Figure 19. The "Vanderbilt" portion of Fifth Avenue, Fiftieth to Fifty-Seventh Streets, west side. W. K. Vanderbilt residence (top left), 1878, Richard Morris Hunt, architect. Cornelius Vanderbilt residence (top right), 1879, George B. Post, architect. W. H. Vanderbilt double residence (bottom), 1879–82, John B. Snook and Herter Brothers, architects. All residences demolished. Wood engraving, 1882.

did not use.[24] In 1870 Fisk contemplated building a house at Seventieth Street and Fifth Avenue and asked the amused patrician, Hunt, to design a house for the womanizing, flamboyant Fisk. Fisk, who owned the largest boat on the Hudson and whom Hunt called a rough-cut diamond with enormous appetites, might have seemed the proper baronial type to have a François I chateau (Figure 18). Sadly, the Fisk episode never reached fruition as Fisk's adulterous daliance with Josie Mansfield ended in a shootout at the Broadway Central Hotel in 1871. Ironically, Josiah M. Fiske, a man who had absolutely no family relation to Fisk, would build a chateau on the site years later.

Hunt would find a client for the chateau a few years later when the Alabama-born parvenu, Alva Forbes Smith, married the second grandson of Commodore Vanderbilt. Alva Vanderbilt may have spent some time during the Civil War years in Paris—certainly the children of cotton factors did escape the destruction of the South in the world of Louis Napoleon. Alva Vanderbilt would be a francophile for life, residing in France when she was widowed by her second husband, O. H. P. Belmont. It would be Alva and her first husband, William Kissam Vanderbilt, who would build the first true chateau on Fifth Avenue. Following the settlement of the court case against the sisters and brothers of William Henry Vanderbilt, the three primary beneficiaries, William Henry and his two sons, Cornelius and William Kissam Vanderbilt, commenced private houses on Fifth Avenue on a scale that comes close to that of A. T. Stewart. As had Stewart, Alva Vanderbilt chose light-colored stone for her house. Stewart's house had a mansard roof as a gesture to fashionable France. Alva Vanderbilt's house was now an accurate archeological study closely based on late medieval chateaux (Figure 19).

Between the era of the first houses on the Avenue and the period of the grand statement houses of the last quarter of the nineteenth century, the architectural world had changed. American architects of the mid-century often had no familiarity with European buildings as they had often not traveled abroad. By the second half of the century, Americans were following the footsteps of R. M. Hunt, many spending time at the École des Beaux-Arts in Paris. The knowledge gained in Europe allowed these designers to work in sophisticated historical vocabularies. Hunt created an assembly of correct features to create the Fifth Avenue chateau. Within its Bloomington, Indiana, limestone walls, Alva Vanderbilt accomplished her goal. She forced New York society to take up the Vanderbilt clan. Sheer exposure of money in a fancy house made the grandchildren of the coarse Commodore acceptable to the city's elite (and changing) 400.

THE VANDERBILT BALL

The inaugural event for the Vanderbilt houses was the party put on by William Kissam Vanderbilt and his wife, Alva. The party was part of a military-like assault on New York society put together by Mrs. Vanderbilt who, along with her husband's entire family, had been excluded from the annual January event given by *the* Mrs. Astor. Determined that the family fortune gave her the right to be a principal in the *bon ton* world, Mrs. Vanderbilt built her stage with her baronial house, filled the press with information about its wonders (often we read that the house was built of imported French Caen stone; it was actually among the first buildings in the county built of gray Indiana limestone), and created great curiosity among the elite, who were eager to see the interior. Alva Vanderbilt then tantalized the city by sending out a massive mailing of invitations for a costume ball to be held on the Monday after Easter, March 24, 1883. The brilliant Mrs. Vanderbilt sent out so many invitations that anyone who owned fancy dress clothes was on her list. The few who noticed themselves among the uninvited evidently sent out warnings within Easter eggs, predicting trouble at the party. The attempt to frighten people away from the party was a failure.

One significant person did not receive an invitation—Mrs. W. B. Astor, who had snubbed the Vanderbilts. Cunningly, Alva allowed Mrs. Astor's daughter Carrie to practice the formal quadrille dances then favored at parties, only to inform the girl just before the party that though she had gone to great trouble to prepare for the entertainment, her family had not been invited. The sobbing teenager ran home to press her mother into amending her snobbery. Carrie Astor won and Mrs. W. B. Astor grimly took her carriage up the avenue to the Vanderbilt door and accepted social defeat from Mrs. Vanderbilt. An invitation to the party was promptly issued.

The Vanderbilt ball was an extravaganza with over 800 guests appearing in costume. Costume parties had a history in New York earlier in the century, but they were forbidden after an unfortunate elopement, said to be the result of such parties. The Vanderbilt ball re-set the fashion for the other costume fetes of the century.

The guests arrived on the red carpet late in the evening on Monday. Tired city businessmen, forced by their wives into costume, unhappily walked up the steps of the house, but were willing to wear tight costume leggings for a glimpse of the Vanderbilt chambers. Women were ushered to Mrs. Vanderbilt's room with its then-novel

Figure 20. The Fletcher residence, Seventy-ninth Street at Fifth Avenue, 1899, C. P. H. Gilbert, architect. Oil on canvas, date unknown.

gold bathroom fixtures. At 1:00 A.M. the assembled guests feasted in the rose-bedecked top-floor gymnasium. Under the strong white calcium light of the new electrical bulbs, people gawked at the immense rooms and lavish floral decor. A series of nine quadrilles was then performed by groups imitating horses and tea cups and dressed to enhance the theme of the set dance.[25]

All the newspapers were filled with accounts of the party and, as Mrs. Vanderbilt could contemplate contentedly, no one would be able to ignore the Vanderbilts any longer.

The success of the Vanderbilt chateau led to a veritable plague of such houses along Fifth Avenue. Alva Vanderbilt's own brother-in-law, Cornelius Vanderbilt, built his own chateau at Fifty-seventh Street. For Mr. Fletcher of *Castoria* fame, a chateau still stands at Seventy-ninth Street (Figure 20). Its neighbor across the street for Isaac Brokaw came down in the mid-1960s, but the Fletcher house inspired Frieda Schiff to ask for a similar house also by the architect C. P. H. Gilbert as her wedding gift when she married Felix Warburg. The Warburg mansion stands today as the home of the Jewish Museum.

As Beaux-Arts-influenced artists conjured up palatial residences for affluent families settling on Fifth Avenue, historical styles were put forth with clear erudition. For those able to afford the incredibly high cost of a plot of land on the avenue, their architect turned the undeveloped land into a perfect specimen of a

Figure 21. View of east side of Fifth Avenue at Sixty-third Street, 1869. Runyon W. Martin residence, 1865–69, Jacob Wrey Mould, architect. One of earliest houses built opposite Central Park.

Figure 22. Funeral procession of General Grant, Fifth Avenue at Fortieth Street, 1885. William Henry Vanderbilt residence (left of the parade, mansard roof), John B. Snook, architect. Union League Club (the tall building to the south) with flag at half-mast. All buildings demolished. Photograph from Croton Reservoir.

Figure 23. Washington Inaugural Centennial parade, view from Fifth Avenue at Thirty-ninth Street, looking north, 1889. Croton Reservoir and Bristol Hotel (far left), Griffith Thomas, architect. All buildings demolished.

favored period in European architecture. The owners of the house could proudly equate themselves by the appearance of their house with Italian bankers, French aristocrats, and British lords—each house spoke for the desired identity of its owner. Elizabeth Drexel Lehr wrote of her childhood on Fifth Avenue, "When I grew up I watched it [Fifth Avenue] pass from the era of modest, discrete-looking brick and brownstone houses, each with its high stoop striving to look as much like its neighbor as possible, to the splendors of the great, gaudy palaces which proudly reared their Italian, Gothic, or Oriental structures to house the new millionaires" (Figure 21).[26]

Figure 24. Senator William A. Clark residence, Seventy-seventh Street at Fifth Avenue, 1904, Lord, Hewlett & Hull with K. M. Murchison, architects. Demolition photograph, 1927.

In the last quarter of the nineteenth century, Fifth Avenue was indeed the nation's showcase of town houses. As New York's wealthy formed the fashion parade, those who had made a fortune elsewhere flocked to America's most prestigious street. The new millionaires took on the East Coast's most fluid society—the one to which only money mattered—and set up housekeeping next to Astors and Vanderbilts (Figures 22 and 23). From California returned D. O. Mills. From Cleveland came the Rockefellers. From the caldron of steel in Pittsburgh came Frick and Carnegie. Even a "copper-king" senator, William A. Clark of Montana, made a 130-room palace on Fifth Avenue his home (Figure 24). The apogee of success for the social climbing American millionaire became Fifth Avenue. Promenading in one's best on Sunday was the custom on the avenue, a walk restricted, in the main, to those resident on the street.

Refronting the Avenue / Putting on a New Face

We have concentrated thus far on the origins of Fifth Avenue's residential development in terms of individual commissions. Fifth Avenue's house-building phase began as individual commissions just off Washington Square Park and continued as individual houses from Fifty-seventh Street northward. In between Fourteenth and Fifty-seventh Streets, speculative builders made the avenue. The runs of rather similar brownstone fronts pushed relentlessly northward, although high land prices kept many lots barren of building for long stretches of time. Tall wooden walls hid the gaps in the run of row houses and advertising whizzes plastered the walls with bevies of lurid bills. The bright posters on the wooden walls were quite a contrast to the completed houses.

The Barry-inspired brownstone was home to the more conservative of the city's wealthy. Behind the substantial mahogany doors with their silvered handles and hinges, Edith Wharton placed many of her characters. Author Wharton had returned to New York after travel abroad and lamented the monotony of the chocolate-colored houses and the absence of grand building.[27]

By the 1860s, many were echoing the sentiment of Edith Wharton about the monotony of the formerly dignified brownstone. Now brownstone fronts were going out of style and architect/builders were beginning to rail against the speculatively built, conservative house. "What artist…used any sketchbook in transversing our much vaunted Fifth Avenue? When he has seen one house he has seen them all. The same everlasting high stoops and gloomy brownstone fronts; …the same huge cornices bristling with overpowering consoles and projections, and often looking in their proportions, like whole regiments of petrified buffaloes leaping headlong over the roof...."[28]

Naturally, the new profession of architect wished to wrestle the private house market out of the hands of the builder/speculator, and the hue and cry against the brownstone had a strong tone of self service. But many New Yorkers liked the practical, if repetitive, houses of a professional speculative builder, especially in the middle years of the century.[29] A host of speculators bought two or three plots at a time and employed an "in-house" architect/builder to produce a brownstone. The top of the line firms of architect/builders on Fifth Avenue at midcentury were the English-born Duggin & Crossman (later Charles Buek & Co.) and John H. Sherwood. In the middle range was Robert Lynd and closer to the bottom was Edward Kirkpatrick. Two architectural partnerships also developed their own properties while acting as architects for other commissions. In the middle of the avenue, especially the streets of the Fifties, was the territory of D. & J. Jardine, while Sixty-seventh to Sixty-ninth Streets from Fifth Avenue over to Madison was the land of Lamb & Wheeler (later Lamb & Rich).

As Americans reacted against the conformity of the brownstone front, blocks when finally fully built upon often had a very mixed appearance. Part of the eight houses on a 200-foot-block frontage might be brownstones; but other plots, particularly the highly valued corner sites, might appear to be engaged in martial combat, with houses fighting for architectural presence against their very neighbors.

In fact, the problem of architectural rivalry on Fifth Avenue blocks only became worse as the century progressed. By the 1880s and 1890s, the owners of the brownstones were feeling the need to update their "respectable" houses. The chateaux of the *arrivistes* became the norm just a few years after the Vanderbilts completed their houses. Even staid old Mrs. W. B. Astor finally deserted her brownstone house on Thirty-fourth Street in 1896 for a Loire chateau by the same architect, R. M. Hunt, who had built for the upstart Alva Vanderbilt on Fifty-first Street. New York City Buildings Department records from the 1880s to World War I are filled with alterations made to the classic brownstone houses. Refrontings were done up and down the avenue as everyone joined the vogue of the individual-appearing house. Left far behind was Mrs. Wharton's hated stone. All the new fronts were white stone and brick. The Vanderbilts had arrived and conquered and the European-trained architects now killed off the brownstone front.

Fifth Avenue was New York City's showcase of building. Tourists visited the avenue to stare in wonderment at the wealth there displayed. Charles Follen McKim, it was noted, used to walk past the Vanderbilt houses when he was unable to sleep at night. Assured by the calming effect of millions of dollars safely ensconced behind the stone walls, he seems to have been able to return home and rest.[30] Fifth Avenue was canonized—the home of wealth for ages to come. Everyone who lived on Fifth Avenue was wealthy and all, it seemed, was right with the world.

But was this really true? Actually, well-mixed with the homes of people of good and great fortune were houses of people without excess cash. Widows in reduced circumstance turned their Fifth Avenue homes into boardinghouses.[31] Respectable people who could not afford to buy or rent a house on the avenue came to board. Behind the doors of the older brick and brownstone houses could be a diversified group of tenants.

The boardinghouse was tolerable for single people and perhaps young couples, but for mature people it was not a proper house.[32] By the 1870s, a new dwelling type came to Fifth Avenue—the apartment hotel. The apartment hotel provided young couples starting out with a fashionable address. Older couples could also stay in the hotel as could people who traveled much of the year. In the apartment hotel, management existed to provide household services such as laundry, kitchen, and a trusted battery of servants, sparing tenants from searching for their own staff. The first family apartment hotel on Fifth Avenue, Haight House, was created out of the former home of R. K. Haight, designed by John B. Snook. Haight had died and his heirs converted the Fifteenth Street house into an apartment hotel for twenty families and fifteen bachelors. The architect of the conversion, Stephen D. Hatch, added two more stories to the house and a mansard roof to increase the volume of the building.[33]

In 1871–72, François Cottenet built an apartment hotel on the site of his family residence at 35–37 Fifth Avenue on the northeast corner of Tenth Street. The layout of the Grosvenor (a name closely based on the development of London's Grosvenor estate in the 1860s) Apartment Hotel was clever. All apartments had sunny rooms and were served by the new elevator. Suites cost $650 to $2,200 a year to rent, but the tenants were provided with servants and did not have to fit out a house. This home-like hotel was a discreet neighbor on the avenue. It did not appear to be a multiple dwelling and its architect, Detlef Lienau, made it conform to the appearance of the houses next door.

In 1872, on the west side of Fifth Avenue just north of Twenty-sixth Street, the top three floors in a five-story commercial building built by Alfred H. Thorp were set aside for apartments. Apartments, like the apartment hotel, were new methods of dealing with the incredibly high cost of city land[34] as well as the cost of keeping a city household. The apartment house story begins in an earlier decade in New York, but this building with stores on the ground floor and apartments above seems to be the first official apartments built on the avenue. The Thorp apartment house was built across the street from the first apartment house built for Fifth Avenue, but not used as such at the south side of Twenty-seventh Street. R. M. Hunt had been commissioned to build the Stevens House apartment block in 1870 and the building was completed in 1872 when Thorp's block was ready. But while Hunt was constructing Stevens House, Paran Stevens, its owner, had died and litigation ensued between the architect and the widow Stevens. The ambitious Mrs. Stevens hired Arthur Gilman on July 3, 1873, to alter Stevens House and add to the property thirty-four more feet on the Fifth Avenue side of the building. The finished building was then turned into an apartment hotel.[35]

In 1873, at the end of July, August Belmont's old house, then owned by Henry van Shaik, was turned into a French flat apartment house by D. & J. Jardine at a cost of $48,000.

In 1875, two older houses on Fifth Avenue near Thirteenth Street and Thirty-seventh Street were altered to become boardinghouses by their owners.[36] The following year, Griffith Thomas made his own new house at 504 Fifth Avenue just across Forty-second Street from the Croton Reservoir into a flats building. Thomas used a new lighter sandstone for this house, but financial reversals kept him from being able to occupy the place. He sold the house to William H. Webb, who had Thomas add two floors to his house and

Figure 25. Fifth Avenue, looking north from Fortieth Street. The Bristol Hotel (the former Griffith Thomas residence) just north of the reservoir, 500 Fifth Avenue, Griffith Thomas, architect. All buildings demolished.

extend it deeply westward to create a large apartment house—the Bristol—which remained on Fifth Avenue until the 1920s.

In the same year that the Bristol became an apartment house (Figure 25), two more older houses were converted[37] and Lienau altered the Grosvenor flats building for a new owner, J. H. Gautier.

In 1877, house developer John H. Sherwood turned the northeast corner of Fifth Avenue at Forty-fourth Street into French flats, creating a zone of apartment hotels and flats in the streets between the Bristol at Forty-second Street to the later apartment hotels, the Windsor at Forty-seventh Street and the Buckingham on the site of present-day Saks Fifth Avenue.[38] The conversion of houses to French flats even extended to Fifty-second Street in 1881 when the showy new house of Anna Lohman (Mrs. Charles Lohman) built by Duggin & Crossman was renovated (Figure 26). Mrs. Lohman was the famous Mme. Restell, the best-known of New York City's

Figure 26. View of Fifth Avenue, 1882, four years after the death of Mme. Restell. The fancy house, left, may be a version of Mme. Restell's residence.

upper-class abortionists. Mme. Restell had taunted polite society for whom she worked by building her own house on Fifth Avenue. The dwelling of the well-known society problem solver caused neighboring property values to decline as no one wished Mme. Restell next door. The New York City arbiters of justice finally went after Mme. Restell, and in the face of certain legal action against her, the abortionist committed suicide in her bathtub in 1878. The estate of Mme. Restell then wanted no part of the house and Robert Mook was called upon to turn the house at 657 Fifth Avenue into French flats at a cost of $60,000.

In the 1870s, most apartment hotels and French flats were renovations of existing buildings. The first purpose-built upper-class apartment house of Fifth Avenue intended to look like a multiple dwelling, not a house, was the Knickerbocker at 245 Fifth Avenue[39] of 1882–83. The Knickerbocker was developed by Hubert, Pirrson & Co. with some help by the young and as yet architecturally untrained Ernest Flagg.

Figure 27. Plaza Apartment House (later the first Plaza Hotel), c. 1886, Phyfe & Campbell, architects. Shown here before alteration by McKim, Mead & White, architects, for New York Life Insurance Company.

Ernest Flagg had another experience with a Fifth Avenue apartment house venture, one that proved a disaster for his father, who had tried to develop a co-operative apartment house on the site of one of the avenue's old winter skating ponds. By the 1880s, the properties proved too valuable for leisure pastimes and a large parcel of twelve lots passed through a complex series of mortgages from Laura L. Appleton to Jared Bradley Flagg and his associates for $850,000. The Flagg group issued a prospectus[40] for a joint stock company, the Fifth Avenue Plaza House Club, which called for the building of a co-operative apartment house to be designed by William A. Potter with interiors to be provided by the young Ernest Flagg. The stock venture failed to attract buyers since, as the Record & Guide explained, "the promoters were anxious for too large a profit."[41]

The property then passed to John C. Anderson for the sum the Flagg group had paid for it and Anderson took back a second mortgage from two men who proposed to build an apartment house on the site. These two new players were John C. Phyfe and James Campbell, who sought financial backing from New York Life Insurance for the building. Carl Pfeiffer was hired to design the structure. Pfeiffer proposed a building that was a cross between the design of the Dakota by H. J. Hardenbergh and the new flats building of London built in the Queen Anne style. There were to be thirty-six apartments with a restaurant in the building. The individual apartments would be two stories with the bedrooms on the upper floor. The apartment house which would have been built around an open court was to be pressed brick with stone and terra cotta trim.[42] Shortly after Pfeiffer's plans were completed, Phyfe and Campbell became involved in costly litigation with several of the heirs of earlier owners of the property. At this point the rather mysterious Phyfe and Campbell abandoned Pfeiffer's design and built the apartment house illustrated here (Figure 27). The completed design forced Pfeiffer to print a notice divorcing the architect from the building, stating that he was "in no way responsible

Figure 28. The first Plaza Hotel (formerly the Plaza Apartment House), 1890, after alteration by McKim, Mead & White, architects. Demolished. Photograph, 1897.

for the architectural merits or demerits of the building as erected."[43]

Phyfe and Campbell appear to have completed the apartment house but not, perhaps, the interiors, when New York Life pulled the plug by foreclosing on their building mortgage. The insurance company had the unhappy job of completing the building, fitting it out as a hotel. The creation of the hotel was done by McKim, Mead & White, who removed the mansard roof, added classical detail to the facade, and provided suitably elaborate interiors (Figure 28). The hotel was leased to David and Frederick A. Hammond, proprietors of the Murray Hill Hotel, for a set period of time. The hotel opened on October 1, 1890. At the end of the lease, the hotel site was sold to the Geo. A. Fuller Company and demolished for the present hotel building completed by H. J. Hardenbergh in 1907.

COMMERCE INVADES THE AVENUE

At the beginning of the age of splendor, Mary Mason Jones predicted a commercial invasion of lower Fifth Avenue effectively killing domestic life. Mrs. Jones and other sages of the era were correct. Shops rooted into the brick and brownstone houses directly after the Civil War in 1867 when the firm of Gambrill and Post produced a two-story building for Brewster & Co. at the northwest corner of Fifth Avenue and Fourteenth Street.[44] The following year at 170 Fifth Avenue on the southwest corner of Twenty-second Street, Russell Sturgis, the architect and also the editor of *The Crayon*, built a store for John Hoey that had lodging above the shop. Two months after Sturgis applied for a building permit, Louis Burger, a prolific commercial architect of the period, requested permission for a piano factory and showroom for Albert Weber at the southwest corner of Sixteenth Street and Fifth Avenue. In 1869 Knoedler Gallery displayed its collection of recent French Barbizon-school paintings in a former house at Fifth Avenue and Twenty-second Street, seemingly in the Russell Sturgis-designed shop. From 1870 on, stores were cut into old houses each year and a few new buildings were built with shops below and flats above.[45] Stores and shops were not welcomed at the beginning of Fifth Avenue, where, by now, old avenue families had successfully resisted the tide of change. But from Fourteenth Street to Twenty-third Street, a new first-class shopping district of small stores was created. The shops were mainly piano salesrooms (Figure 29), galleries, and fine clothiers at first, but the decorative suppliers for the city called the section around Twentieth Street home in the later 1880s, uprooting themselves from their old district at Broadway and Broome Street.

Figure 29. Chickering Concert Hall, Fifth Avenue at Eighteenth Street (on the site of the Elliott and Townsend houses), c. 1875, George B. Post, architect. Demolished. Photograph, c. 1900.

The invasion of business was complete when August Belmont's double house at Eighteenth Street was sold by his heirs for $650,000 so that a tall building could be constructed on the site. The current Belmonts were then living further up on Fifth Avenue at Eighty-first Street. The fashionable Belmonts did not want the family home as Eighteenth Street was now undergoing rapid transformation. Shops for the gentry were shoehorned into the avenue between Fourteenth Street and Twenty-third Street, and became a magnet for the garment business. In the 1890s and 1900s, the nine-block stretch became an extension of the East Side of Washington Square—the city's wholesale textile and clothing manufacturing district. Fifth Avenue had a new tone, a new sound, and a new appearance as Robert Maynicke built tall buildings for the clothiers' offices and manufacturing spaces.

Naturally house owners were upset by the invasion of commerce, although the record sums paid for the houses by developers were the talk of the town. A group of people interested in saving Fifth Avenue from factories, the noisiest of the tenants in the new buildings, was formed in 1907. This new self-interest group, the Fifth Avenue Association, admitted that the land on the avenue was too expensive for single-family use and promoted the concept of offices on Fifth Avenue in the lower stretches and apartment buildings on the upper street. The Fifth Avenue Association was formed as a subtle method of controlling the future on the avenue. Manufacturing clearly brought negative status to the avenue and brought in factory workers. Association members did not like the social tone of the garment workers and their bosses, who dressed differently from the norm and who spoke foreign tongues amongst themselves. Offices were certainly preferable as business workers spoke English and dressed more acceptably. Following the disastrous Asch Building Triangle Shirtwaist fire of 1911, when many of the garment workers just east of Washington Square tragically perished in the city's worst fire, the Fifth Avenue Association made the most of the disaster to keep their mandate of office use for the buildings. The Association also used the fire as a pretext for keeping out new, even taller buildings, specifying the height limit of 125 feet on its avenue buildings and those east and west of Fifth. Thus the Fifth Avenue Association created the present appearance of lower Fifth Avenue with its even cornice line that properly respects the width of the street. Unlike some civic groups, the Association acknowledged the reality of the situation and set about making the best they could of the commercial invasion. It was the example of height control fixed by the Fifth Avenue Association that led in part to the creation of New York City's 1916 Zoning Resolution—the nation's first effective urban planning document.

The Fifth Avenue Association would hold its sway over the lower avenue until the Depression, but at midtown in the office building boom of the later 1920s, several taller structures were built.[46] At Rockefeller Center, the investing family prudently held the tall buildings back from the avenue with 30 Rockefeller Center rising a third of the block westward towards Sixth Avenue.

In these same boom years, the upper avenue appeared to be engaged in a game of demolition dominos. Almost in unison, the wreckers destroyed the opulent homes of the 1880s and 1890s in one great sweep of 1926–27. The older mansions sold by widows of the houses' builders were replaced with luxurious apartment houses. Often the property held deed restrictions that required first-class residences on the site, thus forestalling a continuation of the office and department store boom taking place in the blocks of the Forties and Fifties. Upper Fifth Avenue across from the park would continue to be strictly residential, but now for multiple-dwelling units.

Fifth Avenue continued in a (sort of) image limbo after the Second World War. Apartment houses filled in on the upper avenue and a few remaining houses, such as Henry Clay Frick's briefly used mansion, became cultural institutions. But below the park, confusion reigned.

The commercial invasion of Fifth Avenue had been limited to the first-class shop and luxury services. Parallel to Fifth Avenue on Broadway and Sixth Avenues from Fourteenth to Twenty-third Streets stretched the City's new behemoths, the department stores of Ladies' Mile. The grand stores of the last quarter of the nineteenth century sold a tremendous range of goods from the moderately priced to the very pricey. The march of the dry goods emporia had begun on Broadway. Once New York City's first elevated line was undertaken on Sixth Avenue, the shopping street moved westward under the trestles of the new elevated roadbed.

Benjamin Altman, the son of a Bavarian Jewish family that had settled in New York in 1835, took a small dry goods shop on Sixth Avenue in 1870. Watching the creation of the world's first above-ground means of transportation inspired the youthful merchant to take a lease on property at the southwest corner of Nineteenth Street. Altman hired the well-known residential and commercial architects, D. & J. Jardine, to build him a cast-iron fronted store that in the next twenty years was enlarged to cover the entire block from Eighteenth to Nineteenth Streets. As Altman finished his building, Ladies' Mile seemed at its height. Across the street from him, the successful Chicago merchant, Henry Siegel, built his new store seemingly assuring the area continued commercial pre-eminence. But Altman sought a higher level of merchandising. Altman specialized in first-rate fabrics that he brought together from all over the world. Once purchased, the goods would be sent to the homes of his customers in fastidiously maintained maroon vehicles. In his leisure time Altman began to collect Chinese porcelains in his home at 626 Fifth Avenue on Fifty-first Street. Altman gradually turned his attention to works of art and an increasingly sophisticated manner of living. Despite his new life as an art collector, Altman did not forget his business. At virtually the same moment that Siegel opened the Siegel-Cooper store, Altman began quietly buying lots on Fifth Avenue near Thirty-fourth Street. Encouraged by the Astor family's creation of a glorious new hostelry, the Waldorf, then Waldorf-Astoria, on the western side of Fifth Avenue between Thirty-third and Thirty-fourth Streets (on the site of the old Astor houses), Altman saw a place on Fifth Avenue for his elegant emporium. As the century changed, Altman kept quietly buying lots. He must have been overjoyed when the Pennsylvania Railroad announced the coming of its new station nearby at Thirty-third Street and Seventh Avenue. On Fourth Avenue, the Grand Central Station was undergoing electrification and would shortly be replaced with the present building.

In 1905 Altman hired Trowbridge & Livingston to build the store on Fifth Avenue that would reflect Altman's image and make it blend with the neighboring houses. Altman's designers faced a problem rather like that Siegel had encountered with the north corner of his site on Sixth Avenue—a holdout. Altman was unable to obtain 1 East Thirty-fourth Street. The former brownstone-fronted house had been in commercial use for several decades and had been remodeled by McKim, Mead & White for use by the gallery Knoedler & Co. (Figure 30). Altman would not acquire the Knoedler site until 1911, when the Fifth Avenue frontage of Altman's was completed (Figure 31). Two years later, but before the final Madison Avenue portion of the store would be built, Altman died at home attended by his faithful companion, Michael Friedsam.[47] Altman was generous to his employees and his city in his will.

Figure 30. Knoedler & Company, 1 East Thirty-fourth Street, prior to 1911. Remodeled for the gallery by McKim, Mead & White, architects.

Gradually the other department stores abandoned Ladies' Mile and joined Altman on Fifth Avenue to the north of Thirty-fourth Street. The row houses and mansions were nibbled away by department stores. From World War I to the 1970s, Fifth Avenue became the nation's elite shopping

Figure 31. B. Altman & Company, Fifth Avenue at Thirty-fourth Street, after 1911, Trowbridge & Livingston, architects.

street. Gorham's and Tiffany's (Figure 32) moved to the avenue in 1906. Both jewelry and silver stores were designed by McKim, Mead & White just above Altman's store. Lord & Taylor arrived eight years later followed by W. & J. Sloane's furnishings and Saks Fifth Avenue; Bergdorf Goodman's replaced the Cornelius Vanderbilt house in 1928. Between Saks and Bergdorf's, De Pinna's, Best & Co.'s store for children, Bonwit Teller's, and the Tailored Woman were major stops on the new Ladies' Mile. To the world, the avenue now conjured up fashionable shopping, not living. For fifty years people came to New York to shop on Fifth Avenue, and it may well have been the most significant street in twentieth-century retailing history. Shopping as an elegant experience for the upper and middle classes was seemingly firmly established on Fifth Avenue.

Figure 32. Fifth Avenue looking south to Thirty-seventh Street. Tiffany store, 1904–1906, McKim, Mead & White, architects; Birch Burdett Long, renderer. Residences are demolished; store is extant.

Figure 33. Empire State Building under construction, Fifth Avenue looking south from Fortieth Street, c. 1930.

But in the 1950s and 1960s, among the fancy stores appeared the nefarious and long-living "Going Out of Business" store intent on milking tourists shopping on an unfamiliar avenue. Then, the airline ticket office appeared. In the 1960s, New Yorkers began to wonder what Fifth Avenue was. The New York zoning code was amended to try to keep residential property on the avenue; Olympic Tower on Fifty-first Street benefited from the encouragement of apartment houses under the new zoning measure. But the pendulum had swung too far. The appearance of a fast-food shop, Roy Rogers, seemed to mark the end of the battle. Fifth Avenue was on the way to becoming an ordinary street in the city. No longer did one have to dress up especially well to appear on the boulevard—it had become part of midtown (Figure 33).

Today, as the lives of the century-old department stores are snuffed out on the avenue due to the bad debt of the take-over kings of the 1980s, Fifth Avenue at midtown seems doomed to follow other grand boulevards to oblivion. In 1990, Paul Goldberger, the *New York Times'* architectural critic, wondered if "Fifth Avenue (had) become beside the point."[48] As we reflect on the tall buildings recently completed in midtown and on the empty department stores, we can only decide that Fifth Avenue has lost its special shopping status to the chic shops of Madison Avenue, SoHo, and Columbus Avenue. Today, manufacturers of candy bars and the makers of elegant automobiles would not choose to conjure up Fifth Avenue to sell their product.

Perhaps the restoration of that beacon of learning in its midst, the research center of the New York Public Library, at Forty-second Street and

Bryant Park, may bring back spirit to the commercial section of the avenue. A new life for the empty Altman's store would certainly rejuvenate this once grand avenue.

The upper third of Fifth Avenue across the street from the park still retains most of its old glory. Cultural institutions sit beside embassies among fine apartment houses. The current ultimate apartment may be located on Park Avenue or on Fifth Avenue. The remarketing of Park Avenue after World War I made it into a luxurious boulevard for apartment houses. But Park Avenue cannot offer the spectacular sunsets visible in an upper floor on Fifth Avenue. While one can debate the elite quality of Park versus Fifth Avenues, one can only wonder where Flora McFlimsey now lives. Perhaps she has gone to Katonah, Great Neck, or even Beverly Hills.

ACKNOWLEDGMENTS

I would like to thank the Graham Foundation and especially Carter H. Manny, Jr., for making it possible to do the research on Fifth Avenue. Eventually this will result in a comprehensive book on the avenue.

I would like to thank Robin Sand and Lydia Latchinova for helping me do research on the Fifth Avenue project. My thanks also to Sarah Bradford Landau, who encouraged this work. I am also grateful to Andrew Saint for his comments and to Kayla Baker Stotzky for her endless wisdom.

Several books are of continued assistance in this work. Invaluable is Henry Collins Brown's *Fifth Avenue Old and New*, New York, 1924. Also helpful is my section on the history of some late nineteenth-century row houses in the book on the *Villard Houses: Life Story of a Landmark*, New York, 1980. Of special interest is the section on the earlier row houses by Sarah Bradford Landau.

MOSETTE BRODERICK

CHAPTER TWO

DELAWARE

Avenue

BUFFALO, NEW YORK

DELAWARE AVENUE BEGINS AT THE TERRACE, high ground above the shore of Lake Erie, and runs northward several blocks to Niagara Square, the focus of Joseph Ellicott's 1804 plan for Buffalo. Leaving the north side of the square, which began its existence as a residential quarter but today is surrounded by civic buildings, the broad, straight thoroughfare extends far out to the city limits and beyond. In the late nineteenth century, the three-mile stretch of street from the square to Delaware Park, an idyllic pastoral landscape laid out by Frederick Law Olmsted and Calvert Vaux, became one of the nation's celebrated places of residence.

1804-43: THE STREET IN THE WILDERNESS

The conclusion of the French and Indian War in 1763 ended French domination of the Niagara Frontier and marked the advent of permanent settlement of the area. This trend increased after the Revolution, and in 1804 Joseph Ellicott (1760–1826) mapped a town on the banks of Lake Erie at the mouth of the Buffalo Creek. The site of the city was part of the vast land holdings of the Holland Land Company, a Dutch firm that had purchased most of western New York.[1] Ellicott, who was the local Holland Land Company agent, had earlier in his career helped his brother Andrew survey Pierre L'Enfant's plan for the new capital at Washington.

The influence of L'Enfant's Washington is readily apparent in Ellicott's design for Buffalo (first named New Amsterdam). Niagara Square, located near the lakefront, became the center from which eight streets radiated in several directions. Among the streets passing through Niagara Square was Delaware

ESSAY BY FRANCIS R. KOWSKY

Street (after 1879 called Delaware Avenue), which Ellicott is said to have named for one of the Indian groups that frequented the portage road around nearby Niagara Falls. Apparently in Ellicott's mind the street was destined to become a magnificent residential district.

Despite Ellicott's lofty vision for the new city—he said that the site was "developed by nature for the grand emporium of the Western world"—Buffalo remained for the first quarter of the nineteenth century an inconsequential village. During that time, the poet Timothy Dwight visited the settlement and reported that "the inhabitants are a usual collection of adventurers, and have the usual character of such adventurers thus collected when remote from regular society retaining but little sense of government or religion."[2] A few years later, British troops invading from Canada during the War of 1812 burned most of the buildings that were standing at the time. The destruction, however, was a blow from which the populace, which had fled in advance of the attack, quickly recovered.

In 1832, when the town incorporated as a city, Niagara Square was its chief residential quarter. Comfortable, free-standing residences must have given it more the air of a New England town commons than the look of urban residential squares in eastern cities. One of the early residents of the square was Samuel Wilkeson, the man largely responsible for the creation of Buffalo's harbor and one of the promoters of the Erie Canal. His handsome dwelling (Figure 1), erected in the 1820s, was one of the best examples of the late Federal style of domestic architecture that New England settlers had brought with them to western New York.

Another early dwelling upon the square was owned by Henry H. Sizer, whose wealth came from produce and shipping interests (Figure 2). The red brick house was erected in 1836 by Benjamin Rathbun, Buffalo's

Figure 1. Samuel Wilkeson house, 1820s. Demolished. Photograph, c. 1912.

first speculative builder and was a far more urban-looking structure than the Wilkeson house. Its severe Greek Revival lines produced an impression of conservative dignity that it shared with other buildings of the time, particularly the costly Philander Hodge house that went up at the corner of Delaware and Chippewa in 1835–36 and which architectural historian Henry-Russell Hitchcock called "solid, solemn and heavy detailed."[3] The Sizer house, which was the first building in Buffalo to be illuminated by gas lights, survived

Figure 2. Henry H. Sizer house, c. 1836. Demolished. Photograph, c. 1912.

well into the twentieth century when, in an expanded form, it served as the offices of the Spencer Kellogg Oil Company.[4]

"By the 1830s and for the rest of the century," wrote historians Richard Brown and Bob Watson, "the lawyers came as close as any group in Buffalo to constituting an aristocracy." Indeed, men of the legal profession erected many of the city's finest early dwellings. In 1836, Heman B. Potter, the region's first district attorney, moved into a splendid house on Niagara Square for which the prominent New York City firm of Ithiel Town and Alexander J. Davis furnished designs (Figure 3). The late Federal-style dwelling (so like others of the time in Buffalo in its cubic mass, end chimneys, and roofline balustrade) faced the south side of the square from where it was entered through a Greek Revival columned porch raised several feet above street level. (The east elevation looked onto Delaware Avenue.)

"I intend to have no carved or filigree work about my house, outside or inside; plain but *very* neat," Potter admonished his architects, whom he also asked to model his entrance on doorways he had seen on Waverly Place in New York City.[5] Why Potter engaged Town and Davis is not known, but his choice illuminated the strong economic and cul-

Figure 3. Heman B. Potter house, 1835–36, Ithiel Town and Alexander J. Davis, architects. Photograph, c. 1912.

tural ties that bound Buffalo to New York with the development of the Erie Canal (of which Potter was a prime supporter). "The Buffalonians," stated a local newspaper the year Potter moved to Niagara Square, "are determined not to be behind New York in any particulars."[6] Heman Potter's fine house, which later descended to his son-in-law, attorney George Babcock, was the first building in Buffalo known to have been designed by

Figure 4. Dr. Ebenezer Johnson house, 1833.

a nationally prominent architectural firm. In future years, out-of-town firms would furnish plans for many of the houses along Delaware Avenue.

The initial portion of the street north of the square opened to traffic in 1826. The first important dwelling to be erected here was the stone house built by Buffalo's first mayor, Dr. Ebenezer Johnson (Figure 4). Assisted by a loan from Ellicott, Johnson, who like many of those who settled western New York came from New England, set up medical practice in the village around 1810. Following the War of 1812, he gave up medicine to pursue various real estate and business ventures that, for a time, proved highly successful. In 1833, he erected his large stone house on a 25-acre piece of land that fronted on the avenue in the area that today is bounded by Chippewa and Tupper Streets. Unfortunately, as is the case with most of the early dwellings on Delaware Avenue, the name of the architect is unknown. The Johnson Cottage, as it came to be called, was a Palladian-style villa set amid park-like grounds. Emulating the Villa Rotunda, the house proclaimed its importance by means of a central dome (later replaced by a glass lantern) and large recessed porch that formed a gracious and protected entrance.

In 1835, a young Massachusetts woman named Ellen Bigelow visited the Johnsons with her family on their way to a new home in the West. She left a vivid account of the Johnson's new dwelling in which she found "everything conducive to comfort."[7] Surrounding the house were the first extensive landscaped grounds in western New York. Ellen Bigelow remembered them as "consisting of a fine flower garden, a kitchen garden well supplied with hot beds, and in the rear an extensive park in which deer were wandering about, apparently as much at home as in their native woods." Entering the property through a gateway on Delaware Avenue, along which Johnson had planted a row of elm trees, one approached the house by a carriage road that, Ellen Bigelow recalled, "separated and wound around a large and closely shaven grass plat in the form of a heart.

From each of these walks a flight of stone steps led to a broad piazza, where young ladies were playing battle-door." The Bigelows were clearly pleased to find Johnson installed as a country gentleman on the edge of the wilderness—not far away, remembered Samuel Welch, an early Buffalo resident, the street in front of Dr. Johnson's house became a "straggling country road, but little used"[8]—and they probably hoped to repeat his success in their new home in Illinois. But the visitor lamented the crass tenor of life beyond the bounds of the Johnson's civilized domicile. Perhaps unaware that she was faulting the source of her host's fortune, she complained that land speculation, "'the root of all evil' seems to me the main, if not the only, spring of action to be found in the city." Demolished in 1917 after having been used as a school, Johnson Cottage presaged in its scale, suburban character, and social aspirations many succeeding residences on the avenue.

Another significant addition to Delaware Avenue in the 1830s was the construction between Allen and North Streets of the U.S. Army's Poinsett Barracks. President Martin Van Buren authorized the post in 1838 after the British burning of the American vessel *Caroline* on the Niagara River. Increased American military presence at Buffalo was undertaken to stabilize the volatile border region and to prevent another war with England. Poinsett Barracks was dismantled later in the nineteenth century, with the exception of the large house that had been built for the chief surgeon. After 1845, when the garrison withdrew to fight in the Mexican War, the house became the private residence of Joseph G. Masten, a judge and early mayor of the city. Masten

Figure 5. Poinsett Barracks House (commonly known as the Wilcox House; presently Theodore Roosevelt National Historic Site), 1838.

added a grand Tuscan Doric portico (Figure 5) to what had originally been the rear of the building, for the house had been constructed to face the parade ground on the east. From a subsequent owner, Ansley Wilcox, the building is today popularly known as the Wilcox house.[9]

A few years before the creation of Poinsett Barracks, the land on which it was to stand had been included in the site of the University of Western New York, an ambitious undertaking supported by many leading citizens.[10] Foremost among the group was the Reverend Asa T. Hopkins, minister of the First Presbyterian Church. His friend, Judge Ebenezer Walden, donated nine acres of land at what was to be the intersection of Delaware Avenue and North Street, an elevated site that enjoyed a beautiful prospect of the lake. (The site forms the foreground of the view in Figure 6.) On this high ground, noted Hopkins, Timothy Dwight had stood in 1804 "to sketch the description of our circumambient scenery which he incorporated in his travels."[11] From here, Dwight had written, "The lake opens in boundless view, and presents in a perfect manner the blending of unlimited waters with the sky."[12] Once the state legislature had passed the act incorporating the university, Hopkins, a Yale graduate, wrote to the president of his alma mater, Jeremiah Day, for advice on administration and—perhaps at the suggestion of Heman Potter—contacted A. J. Davis for architectural plans. In September 1836, Davis, who had projected Greek and Gothic revival buildings for New York University (1831–32), Girard College (1832–33), and Bristol College (1835–36), gave Hopkins sketches for the new institution.[13] Unfortunately, none of the sketches has survived. Despite Hopkins's valiant efforts, nothing came of the university project, which fell victim to the 1837 economic depression.

Mayor Johnson's commodious dwelling, the University of Western New York, and the Poinsett Barracks were early signs of the growing prosperity and strategic importance that the Niagara region had assumed following the opening of the Erie Canal in 1825. The canal, which had Buffalo as its western terminus, had been promoted by Joseph Ellicott and his political ally, Governor DeWitt Clinton, to link western New York directly to New York City and the markets of the seaboard. With the inauguration of the canal, the great age of commerce and industry began in New York State, and the wilderness character of the western region steadily disappeared. As the western focus of this development, Buffalo, by the end of the nineteenth century, evolved into the metropolis for which it had been prepared by Ellicott's ambitious city plan.

1843-65: THE STREET OF INTIMATIONS

In 1843 the first railroad came to Buffalo, an event that further strengthened commercial ties with New York City and the East. Soon other lines joined the city to the coal fields of Pennsylvania, thus making available the cheap fuel used in the manufacture of iron and steel. The Civil War also enhanced the city's position as a transportation center, and by the close of the conflict Buffalo was a major transfer point for east-west rail traffic.

The prosperity of the 1850s and 1860s stimulated much construction on Delaware Avenue. An early view of the street (Figure 6), shows a long tree-lined vista toward the lake from near North Street. Beyond this point, the street remained rural; a small tree-shaded cemetery marked the junction with North Street, and the nearby Jubilee Springs Water Company, established in 1837 on a site along the avenue near the present Gates Circle, continued to serve as the main municipal water supply. Westminster Presbyterian Church, designed by Harlow

Figure 6. "Bird's-Eye View of the City of Buffalo from Westminster Church on Delaware Avenue," 1875. The Aaron Rumsey house is visible at the lower right.

M. Wilcox of Buffalo and erected in 1852 above North Street, enjoyed a pleasant pastoral setting for its graceful spire and simple round-arched windows. Further out, Charles E. Clark developed the new Forest Lawn Cemetery in 1850 on 80 acres he purchased from Erastus Granger, who had taken title to it in the early nineteenth century from the Six Indian Nations. Located three miles north of Niagara Square, Forest Lawn, which grew to 230 acres in 1865, assumed the character of a Romantic rural cemetery. This style of gardening had been popularized by Andrew Jackson Downing, whose books and essays in *The Horticulturist* enjoyed a wide readership in western New York. In Buffalo, Lewis F. Allen, who operated a successful farm implement business, was a correspondent of Downing's and a trustee of the cemetery. Forest Lawn's winding roads and wooded hillsides—the planner is unknown, but we know that the trustees sought advice from Adolph Strauch of Cincinnati's Spring Grove Cemetery—anticipated the design of the great park that after the Civil War Frederick Law Olmsted laid out adjacent to it.

Figure 7. George B. Webster house, c. 1853, Richard Upjohn, architect. Demolished. Photograph, c. 1912.

The Romantic tradition that brought into being evocative landscapes such as that of Forest Lawn was also responsible for the Gothic Revival, an architectural movement that was well-represented on Delaware Avenue. In 1848 Richard Upjohn was invited to Buffalo to design St. Paul's Episcopal Church, a building he is said to have regarded as his best church.[14] As a result of his work at St. Paul's, the famous New York architect was asked by George B. Webster, a local insurance agent and one of the members of the vestry, to design a house for him on Delaware Avenue (Figure 7). The brick villa (located on the southwest corner of Delaware and Utica) was a fine example of Gothic Revival domestic architecture that included decorative verge boards and tall gables. Not far away, Charles Taintor in 1857 built another Gothic villa (later known as the Jewett Homestead and since demolished) that attracted attention for its extensively landscaped grounds. Described as "one of the finest mansions in this section of the country,"[15] the Taintor house gave eloquent testimony to the popularity of Downing's ideas in western New York. Another beautiful Gothic dwelling was that built at 262 Delaware by attorney John H. Ganson in 1866 as a double residence. Entrances to each house (the other half was owned by another lawyer, John C. Sibley) were on the sides; the street facade was given over to a series of tall windows fronted by lacey iron balconies. The delicate and strict lines of the house, the proportions of which paid a lingering debt to the Federal style, made it one of the most distinguished designs of the period (Figure 8).

The towered and vine-draped Walter Cary house, built in 1852 at 184 Delaware, was also a conservative version of the Gothic style (Figure 9). Cary, a physician whose father had been an agent of the Holland Land Company, was a man of culture and refinement, and for many decades his house was one of the brightest spots in the social and cultural life of the city. It was also the home of Cary's vibrant sister-in-law, Maria Love. "The dinners and receptions in that mansion have been proverbial," wrote the *Buffalo Courier*, which called Miss Love the "outstanding figure" of Delaware Avenue's cultural aspirations.[16] Maria, who together with Walter Cary commissioned portraits from Augustus Saint-Gaudens, devoted her considerable energy and talents to a number of high-minded causes, including shepherding escaped slaves across the border to Canada. After the Civil War, as prime mover of the Ladies Monument Association, she sought in vain to erect in Niagara

Figure 8. John H. Ganson double house, 1850s. Demolished.

Figure 9. Walter Cary house, 1852.

Square an arch designed by H. H. Richardson to commemorate the city's war dead.

On the east side of Delaware Avenue where it leaves the north side of Niagara Square stood the grandest of Buffalo's Gothic homes, the James Hollister house (Figure 10). Hollister was one of several enterprising brothers who owned, among other types of businesses, a chain of checkerboard-painted stores extending from central New York into Ohio.[17] He erected his house, which resembled the Gothic designs of the eminent A. J. Davis, in 1852 and resided there until 1858. In that year the dwelling was bought by Millard Fillmore, who came to live there several years after his presidency. It had been Fillmore who as president had asked Downing to prepare a plan for a public pleasure ground stretching from the White House to the Capitol, and as a private citizen he played a role in Buffalo's park movement. And certainly Downing would have approved of the splendid Gothic villa in which Fillmore lived until his death in 1874, for it resembled the landscape architect's own home.

But without doubt, the finest Gothic Revival dwelling in the city was the board and batten cottage of the Reverend John C. Lord (Figure 11). Lord was a Presbyterian minister and a great promoter of culture in the city. His house, which was erected in 1852 and located near the present Potomac Avenue, stood within grounds landscaped in the new informal style popularized by Downing. A lawyer before becoming a minister, Lord, who occupied the house until his death in 1877, was a persuasive preacher and writer. His sermon "On the Higher Law as Applicable to the Fugitive Slave Bill," delivered on Thanksgiving Day 1850, attracted national attention for the principle of "higher morality" it expounded. Seward and Webster, and many others, subscribed to his notion that upright men must be prepared to disobey unjust laws.[18] From all we know of Lord, he embodied the refinement, erudition, and Christian virtue that Downing felt were best expressed by the Gothic style.

The Gothic Revival shared the national limelight with the contemporary Italianate style, and Delaware Avenue possessed a number of these types of dwellings. The house erected around 1845

Figure 10. James Hollister house, 1852. Demolished.

Figure 11. The Rev. John C. Lord house, 1852. Demolished. Photograph, c. 1912.

at 340 Delaware and owned later in the nineteenth century by Dr. Charles Cary (the son of Walter Cary and for many years the dean of the School of Medicine at the University of Buffalo) actually combined Greek and Italian elements. (It has since been demolished.) Generally, however, the form, which was also popular with the readers of Downing, fused the serenity of the classical style with the more asymmetric and informal notions of planning associated with Gothic Revival design.

Among the most impressive houses in the Italianate style were those of Edmund J. Newman, owner of flour and cement manufactures; Wilson Shannon Bissell, postmaster general in Grover Cleveland's first cabinet;

and Benjamin Rogers, a local physician. All of these dwellings (since demolished) conformed to the cubic type with central cupola. The William H. Peabody residence, at the northeast corner of Delaware and Allen, was a fine example of the asymmetrically planned Tuscan villa. It had a handsome tower and graceful arcaded porch. (It, too, has been demolished.) The Rufus L. Howard house at 251 Delaware, however, displayed the most flamboyant ornament of any of its Italianate neighbors, indicating a date in the later 1850s (Figure 12). The exterior was festooned with ornate labels over the windows, long pendants beneath the eaves, and flagrant finials on the roof. Howard, who had made his fortune by perfecting and marketing the first mechanical lawn mowers, owned his own iron works. The exuberant ornament on his house, however, appears to have come from Buffalo's Eagle Iron Works; the vase-crowned labels above the round-headed windows on the second floor as well as the bracketed pediment over the large central window repeat patterns illustrated in the firm's catalogue of cast-iron architectural elements.[19]

Figure 12. Rufus L. Howard house, c. 1858. Demolished.

The largest of the Italianate-style houses on the avenue belonged to Aaron Rumsey, the owner of a successful leather tanning business. At the northwest corner of North Street and Delaware, the Rumsey house, which was constructed of brick painted a light grayish tan and capped by a large cupola, profited from its elevated site. (The house appears at the lower right of Figure 6.) The pretty grounds included a conservatory.[20] After the war, the Italianate style lost ground to the growing American interest in French architecture.

The so-called Second Empire–style became synonymous with the urbanity of Paris. Already before the war, Delaware Avenue possessed notable examples of the new style. The mansard-roofed Myron P. Bush house, at the northwest corner of Delaware and Summer Street, was built in 1859 by an architect from Boston named J. D. Towle.[21] Surrounded by five acres of landscaped grounds, the Bush residence (since demolished) was an impressive mansion in which lived a family that owed its fortune to leather manufacturing. Even more grand than the Bush property were the house and grounds of Bronson C. Rumsey, successor to Aaron in running the family tanning business and one of the founders of the Manufacturers and Traders Bank. In 1862, he erected a handsome mansard-roofed dwelling at Delaware and Tracy Street (since demolished). The designers were Henry and Edward Rose, brothers from England about whom very little is known.[22] The Rumsey house, which Henry-Russell Hitchcock called "solid, pretentious but dignified,"[23] had sumptuously decorated interiors, but the property behind the dwelling was its most notable feature. Here the Rose brothers laid out extensive grounds. In addition to terraces, lawns, walks, and fountains, the grounds contained a Grecian temple summer house and a dreamy lake with a chalet boat house. "Rumsey Park" hosted many gay parties and social events. Moreover, in the era before public parks, the Rumseys generously invited neighborhood children to use the grounds. One of those who came to skate there in winter was young F. Scott Fitzgerald, who as a boy of eight lived near Delaware Avenue.

Two other significant Second Empire dwellings erected on the avenue were built according to the plans of a local architect named George Allison. Although Allison may not have traveled abroad, his Charles F. Sternberg house (1869) at 414 Delaware was described by the *Buffalo Morning Express* as "of the latest style of French architecture."[24] Sternberg, who had amassed his fortune in the shipping and storage business, dwelt in comfortable interiors graced by many floor-to-ceiling windows and decorated on the inside with heavy carved black walnut woodwork, much of which remains intact. The house that Allison designed, also in 1869, for Third National Bank president Abraham Altman at the southeast corner of Delaware Avenue and Summer Street (and since demolished) was even more grandiose than the Sternberg residence. "As the city of Brooklyn from its many church edifices takes the name of 'City of Churches,' so Delaware street, from the number of costly residences, may be styled the 'Street of Palaces,'" stated the *Buffalo Morning Express* in an article devoted to a description of Altman's new $100,000 domicile.[25]

1865-1901: The Street of Attainment

The close of the Civil War marked the beginning of the golden age of Buffalo as an industrial and transportation center and the glory period of Delaware Avenue as the city's premier residential street. Its residents remained prosperous and optimistic about the future, despite setbacks during periods of national recession, until after World War II. In the 1890s, when engineers harnessed Niagara Falls to produce electrical energy, the city assumed new importance. During the 1901 Pan American Exposition, the "City of Lights" drew the world's attention to Buffalo's pre-eminent position in the new age of electrification.

The festivities were marred, however, by the shocking murder of President William McKinley, who on September 6, 1901, was shot while visiting the exposition. A few days later, McKinley died in the Delaware Avenue home of John G. Milburn, a distinguished lawyer who acted as exposition president. "Within the hour, that particular…block in the avenue assumed national as well as international importance," wrote a reporter who described the time of McKinley's death as the "avenue's day of gloom." With the homes of William H. Glenny, the proprietor of one of the country's largest crockery businesses, and E. Carlton Sprague, a foremost Buffalo attorney, nearby on West Ferry Street serving as emergency meeting places of McKinley's cabinet, "the attention of the world was centered on this particular four corners of Delaware Avenue."[26] Vice President Theodore Roosevelt hurried to Buffalo from a hunting trip in the Adirondacks and on the afternoon of September 14 took the oath of office as president in the Delaware Avenue home of his friend Ansley Wilcox. Wilcox, a respected lawyer and crusader for civil service reform, had remodeled the former Poinsett Barracks house from Judge Masten's days, asking Buffalo architect George Cary in the mid-1880s to make changes and additions. In the front parlor on the south side of the house, Roosevelt was sworn in as the president of the United States. Immediately after the brief and simple ceremony, Roosevelt, with characteristic sangfroid, "dashed up [Delaware Avenue] in a carriage and refusing all protection from secret service men arrived to pay his tribute to the late president and also to confer with the members of the cabinet."[27]

The solemn drama of the "avenue's day of gloom" ended when McKinley's body was carried from the Milburn house to lie in state at City Hall. Wrote one eyewitness, "All the pomp and circumstance of military escort, bands of music playing Chopin's funeral music and carriages containing diplomats, members of the cabinet and other distinguished guests, wended a sorrowful way through weeping throngs."[28]

The Delaware Avenue that McKinley's cortege followed in 1901 was at the peak of its beauty and splendor. By that time, it had become a major artery in the new park and parkway system that Frederick Law Olmsted and Calvert Vaux designed for the city in 1870. Taking his inspiration from Baron Haussmann's Paris, Olmsted, who thought Buffalo possessed the nation's best urban plan, created a network of existing streets and new parkways that connected all parts of the city with the three parks he designed for the northern section of town.[29] The major pleasure ground was The Park (present-day Delaware Park), a 230-acre masterpiece of pastoral landscape (Figure 13). In Olmsted's system, Delaware Avenue was the main link between the downtown area and Delaware Park, some three miles away. From Niagara Square, the street passed beneath double rows of elms, a favorite tree of Olmsted's because of its graceful wineglass form and its associations with New England town life. Where the avenue left the north side of Niagara Square, Olmsted had hoped the city would erect the Soldiers and Sailors Arch that in 1874 he asked his friend H. H. Richardson to design (Figure 14). In this regard, Olmsted was reviving an idea of Ellicott who, citing the example of Paris, had proposed a

Figure 13. The Park (present-day Delaware Park), 1870–76, Frederick Law Olmsted and Calvert Vaux, architects. Photograph, c. 1912.

triumphal arch be erected in Niagara Square.[30] Unfortunately, despite Olmsted's urging and the fund-raising efforts of Maria Love, Richardson's arch never was constructed.[31]

Not far from the site of the proposed arch, Richardson designed a new house for William Dorsheimer (Figure 15).[32] Perhaps at the suggestion of Olmsted, who was a friend of Richardson, Dorsheimer asked the young architect in October of 1868 to plan a house for him at 434 Delaware. The scheme that Richardson drew up was a pure example of the type of house being built in the suburbs of Paris during the years that Richardson studied at the École des Beaux-Arts. Lacking the heavy ornamentation and inflated proportions of other Second Empire houses such as the Altman and Sternberg residences, the Dorsheimer house conveyed restraint and Neo-Grec rationalism, while at the same time recalling, especially in its materials, the seventeenth-century architecture of Louis XIII. The elegant dwelling, in appearance so unlike Richardson's later work, must have pleased its owner, who could point out to his neighbors—including the nativist Fillmore, who had built a political career on anti-German sentiment— that it represented the latest in contemporary design.

Figure 14. Soldiers and Sailors Arch, 1874, H. H. Richardson, architect.

Figure 15. William Dorsheimer house, 1868, H. H. Richardson, architect.

Dorsheimer, who had gone to Harvard and later become a successful lawyer, was one of the most prominent Buffalonians of German descent and one of the minority of avenue residents who were not of British background. Since the late 1840s, Buffalo's German community, centered on the east side of town, had grown steadily. By the 1870s, Germans comprised nearly half of the city's population. "Two distinct human elements furnished the rock from which Buffalo was being built," wrote historian Allan Nevins, "the granite of New England, and the softer, mellower marble of Germany."[33] The Germans exerted a profound influence on the economic, political, and cultural life of the city—Nevins attributed to them "an appreciation of the uses of leisure which many New Englanders lacked." The German community, and especially Dorsheimer, fostered the creation of Olmsted's park system and promoted the candidacy of reform-minded Grover Cleveland, who became mayor in 1882. Dorsheimer himself had state and national political ambitions and in 1874 he became Samuel Tilden's lieutenant-governor. In this position he controlled the building of the new capitol in Albany, a project he succeeded in wresting from the original architect and giving to Richardson, Olmsted, and Leopold Eidlitz.

A few doors away from Dorsheimer lived Samuel Clemens, later to become famous as Mark Twain. Clemens arrived in Buffalo in 1872 with expectations of making a success of the *Buffalo Courier*, a newspaper of which he was part owner. The Second Empire–style house where he and his wife lived at 472 Delaware was a gift from his father-in-law who presented it to him as a surprise the night Clemens arrived in town with his bride.[34] Unfortunately, Clemens's stay in Buffalo was marred by the tragedy of his father-in-law's death, the premature birth and extended illness of the couple's first child, and indifferent financial success. After two years, the Clemenses abandoned Buffalo for Elmira.

The decades of the 1870s and 1880s were nationally the time of eclecticism and experimentation in

Figure 16. See House, Alexander Oakey and Alfred J. Bloor, architects. Photograph, 1877.

American domestic architecture, forces that were most strongly concentrated in the High Victorian Gothic and Queen Anne movements. The former movement was scantily represented on the avenue and elsewhere in Buffalo, while the Queen Anne style took the city by storm, especially in the more solid middle-class neighborhoods. The house at 440 Delaware, possibly designed by Cyrus K. Porter, was a mild-mannered version of High Victorian Gothic, with a pointed arch window and corner colonnette distinguishing its facade. Milton E. Beebe (born 1840) designed a more pronounced example of the style for lumberman Nelson Holland, whose banded brick and stone house stood at 916 Delaware (since demolished). Probably because of Olmsted's connection with the city, several of his High Victorian architect associates in New York obtained work in Buffalo.[35] Alexander Oakey, an Olmsted friend, actually opened an office in the city for a brief time, in partnership with Alfred J. Bloor, who had worked with Olmsted on the United States Sanitary Commission during the Civil War. Oakey and Bloor prepared a design for the Episcopal See House to stand at Delaware and Tupper Street (Figure 16). Their scheme conformed to the foundation walls of an unfinished church that had been begun in 1869 according to plans by Arthur Gilman of Boston. The limestone and red brick design[36] generally resembled the work of William Burges in England and contained many picturesque details, including a large perpendicular window lighting the staircase and a flying buttress above the entrance. If it had been built, the See House would have been among the most imaginative dwellings in Buffalo.

The foundations of Gilman's church were used in the 1880s to erect Trinity Episcopal Church, which went up according to plans by the local architect Cyrus K. Porter. The broad, aisleless nave and massive beamed ceiling create one of the loftiest church spaces in the city. The interior is made even more beautiful by the superb stained-glass windows by John La Farge and the Tiffany studios. On a bright day, the procession of colored windows that ring the dark and spacious interior glow like gems.[37] Few places in America can rival the quality of this pyrotechnic display of Victorian colorism.

If architects and clients in Buffalo tended to shy away from the high seriousness of Victorian Gothic, both welcomed the warm and relaxed atmosphere for living that the Queen Anne style evoked. Buffalo, with its nearby sources of timber, is a city that in its older quarters possesses many fine examples of this "free classic" style that was popular through the 1890s. No architecture more perfectly expressed the nineteenth-century notion of domesticity than these warmly textured, broad-roofed, generously proportioned dwellings. Many of these structures were erected by speculative builders, men who most often got their designs from pattern books and trade magazines. On Delaware Avenue, however, there were constructed a

Figure 17. Mrs. Bainbridge Folwell house, c. 1885, James Lyman Silsbee, architect. Demolished. Photograph, c. 1886.

number of architect-designed Queen Anne houses. James Lyman Silsbee, who for a time had an office in Buffalo before moving to Chicago, designed at least three strikingly picturesque Queen Anne houses here. The large stone and shingle dwelling he built around 1884 for Mrs. Bainbridge Folwell at 713 Delaware attracted international attention when two photographs of it appeared in *L'Architecture Americaine*, a portfolio of architectural views by the New York City photographer Albert Levy that was published in Paris in 1886 (Figure 17).[38] The steep roofs, slender chimneys, banks of windows, and delicate low-relief decoration in gables showed Silsbee's consummate mastery of this free-ranging style. H. H. Little, a local architect, erected in the early 1880s a more restrained version of Queen Anne at 869 Delaware for William W. Sloan.[39] Sloan had come to Buffalo from Northern Ireland in 1848 with 13 cents to his name. By dint of hard work and a sharp eye for business, he achieved success, first in the malt business and later in banking. When his new home was ready, he and his wife undertook a trip abroad to purchase luxurious furniture and bric-a-brac. This was an oft-told story of new wealth and its haste to acquire the trappings of culture. Sloan lived out his life in his commodious house, never suffering that reversal of fortune that seems all too often to have defeated many self-made men.[40]

As well as being the time of the Queen Anne movement, the decade of the 1880s saw Richardson's star rise to its apogee. Buffalo had given him his first truly important commission, the Buffalo State Hospital of 1870, and the city also became the location of his last work, the Delaware Avenue mansion of William Gratwick (Figure 18).[41] Commissioned only two months before Richardson's death, the building was completed by Shepley, Rutan and Coolidge. Photographs taken when the house was new reveal that the exterior

Figure 18. William Gratwick house, 1886, H. H. Richardson, architect. The photograph shows the north elevation; the east elevation faced Delaware Avenue. Demolished.

Figure 19. Harry Hamlin house, 1889, Marling and Burdette, architects. Demolished.

rather faithfully followed Richardson's intentions. The interiors, however, may have been more heavily deco-rated than Richardson would have liked—if the Glessner house is any guide. The acres of luxurious furnish-ings must have reflected Gratwick's notion of how a wealthy individual should live. Self-made, Gratwick had gained his fortune in lake shipping and in lumbering. His house, which he himself had few years to enjoy, was undoubtedly intended to crown his success, and it is not known if he chose Richardson as his architect for any other reason than his golden reputation. Tragically for American architecture, the massive dwelling came down within thirty years of its construction.

The Gratwick house inspired several imitations along Delaware Avenue. Foremost among this group was the house at 1014 Delaware designed in 1889 by the Buffalo firm of Marling and Burdette for Harry Hamlin, vice president of the American Glucose Company (Figure 19). Henry Burdette had actually worked for a time in Richardson's office, and one assumes that he had the upper hand in what was a thoughtful interpretation of Richardson's principles. The carefully detailed Hamlin house, which was built of brick, echoed the refinement of surfaces of Richardson's Sever Hall at Harvard and the powerful masses of his Gratwick house. The granite Edward Michaels house (1893) at 741 Delaware by Boston architect A. Phillips Rhinn also paid homage to the Gratwick house. Rhinn, however, streamlined Richardson's masses and details and showed signs of European modernism. The Charles W. Pardee house at 938 Delaware emulated Richardson's Romanesque heaviness and rough-hewn surfaces. But its clumsy composition only served to point up by contrast with the Gratwick house the difference between the genius of the master and failings of less-talented imitators. Finally,

Figure 20. Mrs. Erzalia Metcalfe house, 1882, McKim, Mead & White, architects. Demolished.

Figure 21. George L. Williams house, 1895, McKim, Mead & White, architects.

Figure 22. Robert Keating Root house, 1896, McKim, Mead & White, architects. Demolished. Photograph shows garden elevation.

the Albert J. Wright house at 512 Delaware paid homage to the Gratwick house in a more under-stated manner. The corner tower and recessed porch at the side of the facade emulated major elements of Richardson's design. Furthermore, a thick drapery of vines grew across the surface of the Wright house. This form of natural decoration Richardson—proba-bly due to the influence of his friend Olmsted—liked to see envelop his stone dwellings.

But despite the power of Richardson's example, his architecture, as well as the picturesque styles of the 1870s and 1880s, gave way to the rising tide of neoclassicism that nearly overwhelmed national taste during the last decade of the nineteenth cen-tury. Chief among the practitioners of this imperious display was the New York City firm of McKim, Mead & White. In 1882, the young office received its first commission in Buffalo, the Erzalia Metcalfe house, located just west of Delaware Avenue on North Street (Figure 20). It may have been socialite Frances Wolcott (nee Metcalfe) who asked the firm to design the dwelling for her mother, for Frances associated with the writers and artists—including John La Farge, Augustus Saint-Gaudens, Stanford White, and Charles McKim—who clustered around Mariana Griswold Van Rensselaer in New York. The brick, stone, and shingle Colonial Revival house was a masterpiece of the partners' early period and sur-passed in originality their more well-known neoclas-sical works.[42] Its demolition in 1982 for a parking lot was a grievous loss to the city.

McKim, Mead & White eventually were to erect three more dwellings at the corner of Delaware Avenue and North Street. In February 1895, real estate broker Charles H. Williams hired the firm to design a house at 690 Delaware, a commission entrusted primarily to Stanford White, assisted by Edward York. The red brick and limestone dwelling is distinguished on the exterior by a two-story semi-circular stone portico and on the inside by an expansive stairhall that fills the entire center of the plan. Next door, at the corner of North Street, Charles's brother George, a wealthy banker, demolished the Italianate Aaron Rumsey residence and erected the largest dwelling by the firm in Buffalo. The George L. Williams house, which in general resembles McKim, Mead & White's Vanderbilt house at Hyde Park, New York, of approximately the same date, later became the residence of newspaper publisher Edward Butler (Figure 21). Prominent in Republican politics, Butler had expected McKinley for dinner the evening the president was shot. The fourth residence by the firm at this location belonged to industrialist Robert Keating Root, whose 1896 house at 650 Delaware was an accomplished essay in Georgian Revival (Figure 22).[43]

These three later McKim, Mead & White houses were the subject of an article by Virginia Robie in the July 1904 issue of *House Beautiful.* In addition to her glowing description of the dwellings and their "rare and beautiful" furnishings from the "remote corners of Europe," Robie provided her readers with a vivid description of the avenue, which by the early twentieth century had assumed a park-like character that would have pleased Olmsted. "Delaware Avenue is to Buffalo," she wrote,

> what Euclid Avenue is to Cleveland, Summit Avenue to St. Paul, Commonwealth Avenue to Boston, and the Lake Shore Drive to Chicago,—with this difference, that Delaware Avenue is more beautiful. Many of the dwellings on this famous street have the character of country houses. They are surrounded by broad lawns, shaded by fine trees, and inclosed by hedges and high fences of ornamental iron…. Nature and the landscape-gardeners have done much for Delaware Avenue and provided each dwelling with a setting.[44]

Figure 23. The Midway, 1889–95.

Locally, architects Edward B. Green (1855–1950) and William C. Wicks (1854–1919), who formed a partnership in the 1880s, specialized in the dignified neoclassicism that McKim, Mead & White had succeeded in placing in the forefront of American architecture. The house they designed for George Forman at 884 Delaware is an especially fine example of this style. Green and Wicks were also chosen by Henry M. Birge, the owner of a well-known wallpaper company, to be the architects of his residence at 477 Delaware. The Birge house, erected between 1889 and 1895, is part of a distinguished row of dwellings known as the Midway, so called because of its location halfway between Niagara Square and Delaware Park. In a city that overwhelmingly preferred detached dwellings, the Midway evolved house-by-house according to strict covenants that governed height and design. All the houses are in some version of neoclassical design; in their totality they create the most urbane streetscape in the city (Figure 23).[45]

In addition to the construction of houses, the 1890s saw the beginnings of club life on the avenue. In 1896, Green and Wicks transformed a former church building into the Twentieth Century Club, the city's oldest women's club (Figure 24).[46] The elegant Renaissance facade of the clubhouse is distinguished by an arcade of Ionic columns on the *piano nobile*, directly above the street-level entrance. In 1901, a newly formed civic organization met at the club to map plans for the aesthetic improvement of Buffalo. In April, artists John La Farge and J. Q. A. Ward addressed the Committee on Municipal Art that had been set up by the local chapter of the American Institute of Architects. John DeWitt, president of the Municipal Art Society in New York, and the art patron Charles DeKay offered advice on fashioning a permanent body to promote the cause of civic art. Out of this meeting came the Society for Beautifying Buffalo, an organization that until 1906 fostered City Beautiful ideals.[47]

Figure 24. Twentieth Century Club, 1896, Edward B. Green and William C. Wicks, architects.

During the 1880s and 1890s, Delaware Avenue had achieved its exalted status as one of the eminent addresses in America. Here in a sort of linear paradise of many mansions set amidst tree-shaded lawns and elegant gardens most of the city's sixty millionaires lived in a manner that would have astonished antebellum residents. The avenue epitomized Samuel Gomper's observation that "modern society is based on one simple fact, the practical separation of the capitalist class from the great mass of workers. It is not so much a difference in industrial rank as social status...a distinction scarcely noticeable in the United States before the previous generation."[48]

But in her autobiography, Mabel Dodge Luhan confirmed what many outsiders suspected—behind the avenue's glittering, clannish socializing stretched a bleak intellectual landscape. "On Delaware Avenue," she wrote, "you knew everyone you met on the street, but the people never talked to each other except of outward things. There was hardly any real intimacy between friends and people had no confidence in each other.... In those days only the outermost rim of life was given any conscious attention."[49] The child of Charles and Sara Ganson, Mabel endured an unhappy childhood on the avenue until she, like her contemporary Frances Metcalfe, escaped to Europe and New York. Mabel eventually settled in Taos, where after a series of marriages and love affairs, she befriended D. H. Lawrence, who shared with her a deep respect for Pueblo culture. The Ganson's house, a large Italianate villa near the northeast corner of Delaware and North Street that had been built for lumberman Jerome Pierce (and since demolished), was during Mabel's girlhood the scene of many fashionable parties. But normal domestic life, regulated by convention and overseen by servants, was barren of affection—Mabel's father, a taciturn businessman, was known to fly a flag at half-mast whenever his wife returned from a trip. Mabel's sharp-focused portrait of the way of life of her parents and their friends shocked many locals, as surely the author intended. The society editor of the *Courier Express* cautioned her readers to draw a "heavy veil of discretion...over certain pages devoted to personal experiences, which are purely salacious and calculated to disgust the most advanced modernist."[50] Turning over the rock of America's new wealth, Mabel Luhan provided social historians with a rare close-up look at ethical deterioration—anomie, one writer called it—among the upper classes.[51] In Luhan's opinion, the life of ease exacted a toll on the spirit that people in lesser circumstances were not asked to pay.

1901-30: THE STREET IN TRANSITION

For the first three decades of the twentieth century, Delaware Avenue—especially the section beyond North Street—remained the most desirable residential address in the city. In fact, many older mansions of the 1860s and 1870s gave way to new, more palatial constructions. But also during this time, local and national economic and social forces began a process that would reshape the city and diminish the luster of its most resplendent thoroughfare.

At the beginning of the century, the Colonial Revival style enjoyed considerable popularity in Buffalo. The example of McKim, Mead & White's Root house may have locally stimulated this taste, which by 1900 had become an American preoccupation. Charles Platt, who built a national reputation for his informed recreations of Federal architecture, was commissioned by two clients in 1911 to design houses next to each other on Delaware Avenue. For H. Tracy Balcom, a dealer in musical instruments, Platt designed a brick and sandstone Neo-Georgian house at 1193 Delaware. In the drawing room, which measured forty by twenty-four feet, Balcom installed an organ, which he was fond of playing for guests, and on the ceiling of the third-floor billiard room he himself painted nostalgic scenes of Italy. A lovely enclosed garden, another specialty of Platt, a devoted student of Italian Renaissance horticulture, once grew behind the house.

Also in 1911, Willis O. Chapin, a local attorney and the first president of the Society for Beautifying Buffalo, asked Platt to design a house for him next to the Balcom property. This gray stone dwelling at 1205 Delaware has large mullioned and transomed bay windows that offer ample insurance for bright, cheerful interiors during Buffalo's gray winter days.

In 1915, the widow of Seymour H. Knox announced that she would build a residence costing one million dollars on property she had purchased on Delaware Avenue north of Summer Street.[52] The new house in the French Baroque style was designed by New York City architect Charles Pierpont H. Gilbert and replaced an older Italianate house that stood on the property. Farther up the avenue, near Utica Street, Seymour H. Knox, Sr., her husband, had erected a few years before a formidable marble and Roman brick mansion. Knox had begun his career in Reading, Pennsylvania, in the 1860s when he and his cousin and partner F. W. Woolworth had introduced the five-and-dime store to American retailing. In the 1880s, Knox moved to Buffalo where he opened a comparable store on Lafayette Square. The success of this and like ventures led Knox in 1912 to consolidate his holdings with those of several other firms under the name of F. W. Woolworth. Knox, who became the new corporation's first vice president and oversaw some 800 stores nationwide, also became involved in banking in Buffalo where he, and later his son, Seymour H. Knox, Jr., were generous patrons of art and music. They gave many works to the nascent Albright Art Gallery, which because of their continued support is now named the Albright-Knox Art Gallery.

Mrs. Knox had decided to build her new home next to the rambling stone mansion at 786 Delaware that Edward B. Green had designed in 1913 for Stephen M. Clement, the president of the Marine National Bank. Always a competent academic designer, Green produced for Clement a handsome Tudor-style dwelling, in the design of which Henry-Russell Hitchcock saw "some of the virtues of the earlier Richardsonian precedent despite [its] lack of originality."[53] Together with the Saturn Club (1922) by Buffalonian Duane Lyman (1887–1966) at 977 Delaware, Green's Clement house is the best example of Tudor Revival architecture in the city.

Most of the residential building activity that took place on the avenue in the early twentieth century occurred north of North Street.[54] Reflecting the new importance that mansions erected here gave to the upper avenue, embellishments were made to the street itself. Gates Circle, the point at which the avenue meets Olmsted's parkway system, received in 1904 a large granite fountain originally installed at the Pan American Exposition. Designed by E. B. Green and donated to the city by Mrs. Charles W. Pardee, the fountain was the first piece of City Beautiful ornament to grace the Buffalo cityscape. Apparently, the spirit that animated such groups as the Society for Beautifying Buffalo was making itself felt in town.

But while the construction of mansions went forward unabated along the upper reaches of the avenue, in the downtown section the pressures of commerce and government began to transform the street. The portion of Delaware Avenue below Niagara Square had by the third quarter of the nineteenth century already lost its residential character. In 1869, the Roman Catholic diocese constructed a large Victorian Gothic school building at the corner of Church Street, behind Patrick Keeley's St. Joseph Cathedral (1850). Farther up the street stood the municipal jail, across from which the city erected in 1874 a new city hall, for which Rochester architect A. J. Warner drew the plans. Warner's Quincy granite Victorian Gothic structure—which was to influence the design of Richardson's Allegheny County Courthouse in Pittsburgh—occupied former Franklin Square. The space around the building was land-scaped by Olmsted, who was soon to undertake a similar job designing the U.S. Capitol grounds.

Around Niagara Square, a number of imposing buildings went up in the early twentieth century replacing earlier houses and giving the area a monumental character. In 1907, the city erected in the center of the square Carrère and Hastings's memorial to McKinley. An obelisk surrounded by four brooding lions (carved by A. Phimister Proctor), it resembled fountain obelisks the firm had designed for the grounds of the 1893 World's Columbian Exposition in Chicago. (Carrère and Hastings had also been the chief architects of the Pan American Exposition.) The McKinley Monument still pro-

Figure 25. City Hall, 1929, John Wade, architect.

vides an effective point of focus for the several streets that converge on the square.

Wishing to capitalize on the monument's prominence, Green and Wicks drew up, in 1925, an elaborate proposal to make the obelisk the centerpiece of a commanding City Beautiful place bordered by neoclassical public buildings in the manner of the Place de la Concord in Paris.[55] But while nothing resulted from this scheme, Niagara Square did become the center of municipal government when in 1929 the new city hall went up there (Figure 25). Designed by John Wade, a native of New York who had set up practice in Buffalo in 1921, City Hall, which includes the site of the Wilkeson house, is a Hugh Ferriss dream come true, an impressively scaled and richly detailed Art Deco skyscraper that towers above the historic square. Unfortunately, it began the pernicious practice, followed by far less redeeming projects, of building over Ellicott's radiating streets.

Other buildings erected around Niagara Square between the wars include Green and Wick's Buffalo Athletic Club (1924), Bley and Lyman's Federal Courthouse (1936), and George B. Post and Sons's Statler

Hotel (1923), the first of many hotels erected nationally by Ellsworth M. Statler. The presence of the Colonial Revival Statler at Niagara Square (where it replaced the Hollister-Fillmore house) accelerated the commercial development that gradually overtook the two-mile stretch of Delaware Avenue between downtown and North Street. Already in 1888 Margaret Armstrong had moved her millinery store from Main Street to the corner of Delaware and Mohawk, an event that marked the beginning of business life on the street. In 1901, the nine-story Tourraine Hotel opened, hoping to draw trade from visitors attending the Pan American Exposition, and a few years later the Spencer Kellogg linseed oil corporation converted the Sizer house to its use. By 1919, when Statler decided to erect his nineteen-story hotel—said to have been the largest building in the state outside of New York City—there were twenty-four businesses along lower Delaware Avenue. "The transformation of Delaware avenue was inevitable," wrote realtor Richard W.

Figure 26. Walter Cary house during demolition.

Goode in 1925. "Its history," he said, "is that of similarly located streets in other cities—East avenue in Rochester, Euclid avenue in Cleveland, Woodward avenue in Detroit, and many others—fine residences growing old, giving way to boarding houses, and they in turn to business."[56] The economic cycle was clearly evident to Louis Graham Smith, another local realtor, who commented on the dramatic rise of avenue property values as a result of the change from houses to shops.[57] The poignant sight of a mansion being demolished, like Walter Cary's fine old Gothic house (Figure 26), became a common one along the avenue. Reflecting on the demise in 1934 of McKim, Mead & White's Root house, which went down to make way for business, the society editor of the *Buffalo Express* penned a fitting epitaph for many other residences that would suffer a similar fate: "It is with regret," she wrote, "that we have to chronicle that so artistic a dwelling place…should stand empty of all human habitation. If as though it said, 'The Play is Ended.'"[58]

The rise of commerce on Delaware Avenue can be attributed to several factors. One was the post–World War I rise in rentals on nearby Main Street, the traditional commercial street of the city. Another was the advent of public transportation along the avenue north of Chippewa that made it accessible to many more people than before. (Motorized bus service began on the avenue in November 1924.) And, of course, the coming of the automobile increased traffic on the street. The Packard car company opened its showroom in 1915 at 284 Delaware, and service stations appeared on Niagara Square in 1927 and at Delaware and Virginia and Delaware and Tracy in 1936. In 1923, the five-story Statler Garage (recently demolished) went up at the corner of Mohawk Street to accommodate shoppers and hotel guests, but unlike later "ramps" it showed respect for the street with shops at ground level.

From the beginning of the age of commercialization on the avenue, merchants sought to retain the tone of quality that people had long associated with a Delaware Avenue address. To obtain advice on how best to manage the transition, the merchants who constituted the Delaware Avenue Association (organized in 1923) invited the president of the Fifth Avenue Association to Buffalo to explain how the process had been carried out in New York City. Eventually certain rules and regulations agreed to by Fifth Avenue businessmen were adopted by their Delaware Avenue counterparts. "Delaware Avenue always has been a source of pride to Buffalonians," stated Goode, "and the object of the Delaware Avenue Association is to make its business portion as attractive a commercial thoroughfare as it formerly was a residence street."[59] The Association succeeded in 1924 in having the city widen the avenue from Niagara Square almost up to North Street. The widening of the roadway from forty feet to sixty feet was accompanied by the laying of new sewer lines, the placement of traffic signals, and the installation at one-hundred-foot intervals of 1500-candle-power electric light standards.[60] The modernization of the avenue, however, occasioned the destruction of most of the splendid elm trees that had lined the thoroughfare, two rows on each side, since even before Olmsted's day. The effort by many citizens both on and off the avenue—including artist Charles Burchfield, who had come to town in 1923 to work in the Birge wallpaper factory—to stay the massacre of the trees was to no avail. "A platoon of the city's oldest residents went under the executioner's ax yesterday," wrote the *Buffalo Courier*. "They were in the way."[61] It was the first of many preservation battles that were doomed to fail in a city that, like many others, came to pride itself on the destruction of its distinctive charms in the name of jobs and progress. The City Beautiful Movement and all the optimistic idealism for which the Society for Beautifying Buffalo stood died with the widening of the avenue. But what the realtors and city fathers could not recognize at the time was that Delaware Avenue was only a stopping place for business on its migration to the suburbs.

Figure 27. Bley-Lyman Building, 1920s, Lawrence Bley and Duane Lyman, architects.

The widening of the avenue was followed by the demolition of many houses and their replacement by businesses. A number of these were designed in Classical style in keeping with the desire to maintain the image of a "high-grade" street. The architectural partners Lawrence Bley and Duane Lyman took a special interest in the affairs of the avenue. Their own building near the corner of Allen Street had a ground-level arcade of shop fronts above which broad expanses of plate glass lighted their offices (Figure 27). Bley and Lyman also designed the elegant Art Deco Vars Building at 344–352 Delaware and may have planned the handsome *palazzo* of shops and offices on the northwest corner of Delaware and Tupper. Dr. Johnson's house and property were replaced by Delaware Court, a long two-story building of shops and offices.

In many cases, the old mansions were retained and converted for business use by the addition of single- or double-story shop fronts in their former front lawns. The 1920s shop erected in front of the Queen Anne

Figure 28. Shops in front of older houses, 300 block of Delaware Avenue, 1920s.

Figure 29. View of Delaware Avenue above North Street, c. 1920.

house at 360 Delaware (Figure 28) is representative of this class of conversion. A number of early dwellings were saved by this process and yet stand along lower Delaware Avenue.

Above North Street, the residential character of the avenue survived (Figure 29). The sylvan streetscape that Virginia Robie talked about endured for many years, until disease effectively put an end to the graceful native elm. But while business was held at bay at North Street, apartment houses began to make their appearance in the residential section of the street. By the 1920s, several large apartment blocks, gracefully detailed with ashlar ground floors and tasteful Classical ornament, were erected there. Notable is the Westbrook (No. 675, including the site of the Charles Ganson house) by Robert North and Olaf Shelgren, architects of many of Buffalo's well-designed traditionally styled modern buildings (Figure 30). Another grand apartment house was the Campanile, designed by Frank B. Kelly, who moved to Buffalo from Canada in 1921. Its Spanish style attested to the Pan American Exposition's lingering influence on local architecture.

Constructed as the Great Depression was about to begin, the Campanile, like its contemporary, City Hall, marked the beginning of Buffalo's economic decline. No large single or multiple dwelling rose on the avenue until the 1960s when the skyline was disfigured by two out-of-scale turquoise brick apartments, one on either side of the street between Lexington and Cleveland. These buildings testified that, whatever its limitations might have been, the age when architects and clients believed that a Delaware Avenue address demanded certain standards of taste had passed.

EPILOGUE: THE STREET OF MEMORY

After World War II, more and more families moved away from the avenue. The mansions they left behind were either demolished, turned into multiple dwellings, or taken over by institutions. Landscaped grounds suf-

Figure 30. Westbrook Apartments, 1920s, Robert North and Olaf Shelgren, architects.

fered from the lack of professional care and the street, gradually denuded of its trees, acquired, for those aware of its former glory, a forlorn aspect. The devotion to art and culture and civic pride that had animated so many of the avenue's wealthy home-owners lacked staying power. As Downing had warned his readers in the 1840s, a grandiose residence erected by a flush generation would likely become an unbearable burden to another. The culture that so many of the residences of Delaware Avenue had purchased abroad and proudly enshrined in expensive domiciles proved to be an ephemeral affair, and nearly all signs of it on the avenue, other than many of the buildings themselves, were gone by the 1960s.

Religious properties, however, were less affected by the ravages of change. Today they are often the brightest reminders of the street's former gentility and urbanity. A notable exception to this general truth, however, is the demise of the "new" St. Joseph Cathedral, which the Catholic diocese erected at the northeast corner of Delaware and Utica in 1912.

A sign to the predominantly Protestant residents of the avenue that Catholicism, the religion of the immigrant classes, was a powerful force in the life of the city, the white marble cathedral was declared in the mid-1970s in need of repair. After selling the windows, the bishop demolished the church. In its place rose a high-rise residence for the elderly, a blessing for many, no doubt, but architecturally the gray concrete structure offers nothing to the spirit.

Despite many losses, much of the physical evidence of old Delaware Avenue endures. Increasingly it is cared for by corporations, who like the former families find in the mansion a discreet but effective symbol of attainment. But before this trend set in, it fell to the preservation community to come to the aid of the mansions. In the early 1970s, the Delaware Avenue Association and the Landmark Society of the Niagara Frontier successfully opposed the leveling of a group of them for an office building. This victory halted the depletion of the avenue's historic resources. Local historic district and National Register status now offer some protection for many of the houses on the street, and public sentiment, more easily roused when wealth and fame are associated with architecture, would undoubtedly prevent any major structure from being lost. (Little attention, however, is paid to the shop-fronted houses of the 1870s and 1880s on lower Delaware.) With the course to demolition restricted, the momentum of decline appears to have been stemmed. And perhaps someday the owners of Delaware Avenue property will share the urbane vision of city life that Buffalonian Samuel Welch, a man who took pride in the appearance of his city, articulated in 1891. "What is the good life for," he asked, "unless you can enjoy it? What contributes more to its enjoyment than to have your lot cast where surroundings are pleasant; made more beautiful by cultivation, education, and refinement?"[62]

ACKNOWLEDGMENTS

The author is indebted to Austin Fox, Olaf William Shelgren, Jr., and William Loos, Rare Book Librarian, Buffalo and Erie County Public Library, for generously sharing with him their wide knowledge of Buffalo and its architecture and for offering many observations and suggestions that greatly improved the content and form of this chapter.

FRANCIS R. KOWSKY

Chapter Three

WOODWARD
Avenue
Detroit, Michigan

A tattered Woodward Avenue stands today as Detroit's ceremonial main street. Long ago, Civil War soldiers marched off to war and returned home to a hero's parade along this once proud route. Political rallies, visiting dignitaries, and society weddings and funerals have showcased their rites of passage here, too. Extending northwest toward Pontiac, the two-and-a-half miles of Woodward Avenue from the Detroit River at the downtown center to the Michigan Central Railroad viaduct emerged as Detroit's premier residential address in the second half of the nineteenth century (Figure 1). After midcentury, the avenue was developed rapidly northward from the river's edge thanks to the heady wealth generated from maritime and rail trade as well as the city's flat terrain. Ironically, this open landscape that lent itself so well to long, expansive residential vistas also fostered the rapid spread of commercial and retail establishments along the thoroughfare after 1890 (Figure 2).

By 1920, the urban commercial pursuits and the suburban residential preferences of those leading families who had formerly transformed Woodward Avenue into Detroit's grandest promenade contributed to this exposé of urban blight.

Detroit's Beginnings

Said to be "the oldest continuously inhabited community between the Appalachians and the Rocky Mountains,"[1] Detroit was founded in 1701 as a strategic military outpost by Antoine de la Mothe Cadillac. The straits between Lake Erie and Lake St. Clair gave the original settlement the name "Détroit." Six decades

ESSAY BY Thomas W. Brunk

Figure 1. Bird's-eye view of Detroit, looking northwest from intersection of Jefferson and Woodward Avenues, 1887.

Figure 2. Aerial view of Detroit, looking north from Detroit River, 1935.

later in 1763, this French settlement came under British control at the end of the French and Indian War. Almost a century after its founding, Detroit became an American village in 1796. It was incorporated as a town in 1802 and was named the Michigan Territory capital three years later by President Thomas Jefferson.[2]

Fire swept through the town on June 11, 1805, moving rapidly from one frame structure to the next, leaving only one building standing. The territory's leading magistrate, Augustus B. Woodward, envisioned a grandiose rebuilding plan modeled after Pierre L'Enfant's 1796 plan for Washington, D.C. Woodward's scheme prescribed equilateral triangles radiating from a central park called Grand Circus, and geometric districts formed by circles, squares, and triangles. The 1807 plan designated the location of important civic buildings and public spaces and parks, which Woodward, as L'Enfant in Washington, dispersed throughout the city.[3]

Woodward's baroque vision clashed with the pragmatic interests of Detroit's landholders, business leaders, and politicians, who abandoned many of the monumental elements in favor of more profitable land development schemes. The Grand Circus planned for the intersection of Woodward and Adams Avenues was reduced to a half-circle park, broad avenues were narrowed, and a strict rectilinear street plan was imposed on Woodward's axial plan, compromising its civic grandeur. Judge Woodward's plan was further confounded by the city's laissez-faire land development policy which until 1873 allowed private property owners to subdivide and lay out streets as their individual interests dictated.[4] Even with all these variances, pivotal features of Woodward's plan did survive. Campus Martius, the square at the heart of the plan and the city, provided a unified civic core anchored by the City Halls of 1835 and 1868, the Detroit Opera House (1869), the Soldiers & Sailors Monument (1872), and the Merrill Fountain (1901) (Figure 3).[5] Woodward Avenue, the city's north-south axis, became Detroit's civic processional (Figure 4).

In the early decades of the nineteenth century, Detroit was a small village—only 1,422 residents in 1820—with a declining fur trade being the chief industry. As private capital shifted focus in the antebellum years to the region's rich natural resources of timber, copper, iron ore, and the Great Lakes themselves, the

Figure 3. Campus Martius, looking west down Michigan Avenue, c. 1890. Soldiers & Sailors Monument (foreground), 1872, R. Rogers, architect. Detroit City Hall (left), 1871, J. Anderson, architect.

economy and the village flourished. The population nearly doubled each decade between 1840 and 1870, and brisk trade on the Detroit River and expanding railroad lines opened Detroit to international markets. Fresh wealth flowed into the young city, attracting industrious entrepreneurs of the 1850s and 1860s to Detroit where the manufactured goods such as railroad cars, ships, stoves, steam engines, iron, steel, and pharmaceuticals represented the core of commerce. Prosperity prevailed through the 1920s, when the city's population exceeded one million residents.[6]

Fostering the growth of this young region were the roadways that spanned Detroit's flat topography to outlying settlements. Territorial surveyors in the 1820s shaped this geography by platting what were to become the main-traveled routes through the woodlands. Among these routes, Woodward

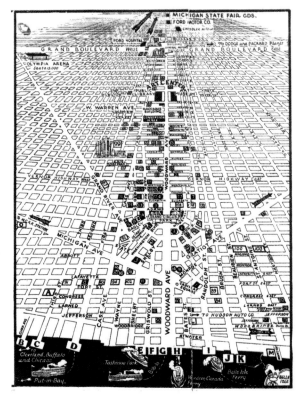

Figure 4. Map of Detroit, 1931.

Figure 5. Woodward Avenue and State Street, c. 1890.

Avenue, also known as the Pontiac Road or the Saginaw Turnpike, fulfilled Chief Justice Woodward's plan by becoming the principal northward road through the center of the developing urban village.[7] In November 1849, a private toll-road enterprise, chartered by the General Plank-Road Act of the previous year, seized upon Woodward Avenue's emerging function by opening the eighteen-mile-long Detroit-Pontiac Toll Road to incoming and local travelers. The completion of the Erie Canal in 1825 brought a full tide of immigration to the region. Detroit prospered and, as the frontier receded, an increasingly stronger business climate provided the private capital to stimulate cultural and architectural interests.

Beginning in the 1830s, the town's most affluent residents created fashionable residential districts within walking distance of their downtown business establishments (Figure 5). An increasing working-class population congested these close-in districts with boardinghouses, saloons, and brothels, pushing wealthy families accustomed to more elegant surroundings outward along the city's major avenues—west on Fort Street, east on Jefferson Avenue, and north on Woodward Avenue. During the 1860s and 1870s, ever-more industrious commercial and manufacturing enterprises overwhelmed the bustling Detroit River bank area near Jefferson Avenue and West Fort Street.[8] Almost by default, born out of the capitalistic endeavors of Detroit's business and civic leaders, Woodward Avenue became the city's linear neighborhood of affluence and grandeur.

EARLY DEVELOPMENT ALONG THE AVENUE

The downtown retail district was concentrated on Jefferson Avenue until the 1850s, when merchants began moving to Woodward Avenue as it was fast becoming the city's most prestigious residential and business address.[9] In an effort to preempt this commercial development, residents living near Campus Martius petitioned the city in 1850 to have it made into an urban park and pleasure ground.[10] Campus Martius was fenced and landscaped with green lawns and shade trees. The transformation was startling. The *Free Press* lauded the new look of Campus Martius, "with its young trees and its oat crop springing up fresh and green among the bricks and mortar surroundings." Impressed by the effect on the emerging grand avenue that such landscaping could impart, the reporter argued for beautification of the area between the square and City Hall because, "It would make Woodward Avenue one of the pleasantest [*sic*], as it is now one of the busiest and most important thoroughfares of the city."[11] The suggested improvements did not occur, nor did city officials maintain Campus Martius. Freely roaming cattle and other animals destroyed the lawn and ornamental plants, and within two years the square looked more like a forlorn pasture than an elegant park. "The supposed shade trees are only poles," the *Detroit Daily Advertiser* reported, "and the only green thing on the square is a big Dock Weed."[12]

A turning point in the residential development of the avenue came in 1852, when the portion north of Grand Circus to the plank road was widened and paved.[13] Previously known as Witherell's Lane because of its narrow, rustic character and Judge Witherell's nearby home, this section of Woodward was officially dignified as an avenue in 1867.[14] The Detroit-Pontiac Toll Road was only a memory, yet Woodward Avenue continued to be among the city's most heavily traveled routes.[15] Four privately operated street railway lines using horse-drawn cars began operation in 1863 along Jefferson, Woodward, Gratiot, and Michigan Avenues, capitalizing on the growing residential and commercial appeal of these streets.[16] Campus Martius posed no barrier to aspiring retailers, who leaped beyond this intersection by 1870 and steadily pushed northward toward Grand Circus Park and the emerging first-class residential district beyond.[17]

Lower Woodward Avenue was lined with dry goods stores, grocers, and other merchants. The tremendous growth of retail trade in the downtown area increased congestion and drove up the property values, again pushing residents out.

By 1886, thirteen transportation lines had established a foothold—each competing for the patronage of the growing, outward-moving population. The outlying area began to rapidly build up as the sylvan property on the outskirts of Detroit became more attractive to the wealthy for residential expansion (Figure 6).[18]

Figure 6. Woodward Avenue, looking north from Rowena (now Mack) Avenue, 1896. Westminster Presbyterian Church spire is at left.

RESIDENTIAL DEVELOPMENT

Upper Woodward Avenue of the antebellum years was a woodland region, the choice of wealthy residents looking to escape the congestion of the city center. The procession of stately residences along Detroit's semi-urban thoroughfare beyond the Campus Martius in the 1840s was led by prominent citizens who, in their quest for quieter surroundings, found proximity to their downtown businesses. The early development of the avenue was governed in part by the idiosyncratic residential and commercial subdivision of the extensive landholdings of its owners, some of whom were avenue residents. Often these individuals shared business partnerships, or civic, religious, and social affiliations, and in many instances were related by blood or marriage. The residential growth of the avenue reflected increased personal wealth, expanded mobility, and a desire to

Figure 7. Central business district on lower Woodward Avenue, c. 1900.

remove one's family from the growing downtown congestion (Figure 7).

Colonel John Elishu Winder, clerk of the United States District Court, was among the first to establish a substantial residential estate on Woodward Avenue, just north of Grand Circus Park. He purchased ten acres of land for $1,500 in 1842 and the following year built a wooden Greek Revival mansion with a stately two-story front portico.[19] Winder set his home back some three hundred feet from the roadway, enhancing its grandeur.

Within two years, Reverend George Duffield, pastor of the First Presbyterian Church, affirmed his prominence in the community by building a substantial masonry residence with a Doric-columned porch opposite the intersection of Winder Street.[20] Duffield's architectural taste was influenced by his pastoral tenure in Philadelphia and New York City. While the design of Duffield's home was sophisticated by Detroit standards, not all citizens viewed his architectural statement as a savvy investment of his resources. Not only was it the largest home in the city, but it was located just outside the northern city limit. Residents ridiculed Duffield in the countryside and referred to his residence as "Parson's Folly."[21] Nonetheless, Reverend Duffield combined the best qualities of a growing city with those afforded by communion with nature and indulged his earthbound enthusiasm for creating romantic landscapes through an elaborate garden of specimen plants and flowers acquired during his travels. Even the wild ivy that covered the north side of his home had been shipped to Detroit from England's Melrose Abbey.[22] Duffield lived in the home for almost a quarter-century until his death in 1868; after that it was remodeled into a two-family dwelling. In 1883 the elegant Duffield residence was demolished to accommodate outward-sprawling commercial and retail development.

Figure 8. Woodward Avenue and Sproat Street, northwest corner, c. 1916. David Whitney, Jr., residence (far left corner), 1872, Mortimer L. Smith, architect. Jacob S. Farrand residence (right), 1854. Westminster Presbyterian Church spire (background).

Jacob Shaw Farrand, a druggist, city official, and banker, built a brick mansion on Woodward in 1854, one mile north of his downtown Woodward Avenue store (Figure 8). Farrand may have represented the city's affluent vanguard in his choice of a borderland residence but, as other Midwestern patrons, he certainly demonstrated latent tendencies in his architectural taste by choosing the Greek Revival style for his house at a time when the Eastern establishment had moved well beyond classical forms to embrace romantic Gothic and Italianate styles. Farrand, proud of his civic achievements, reinforced his social standing by building his substantial Woodward Avenue mansion. Like many of his peers, Farrand, who arrived in Detroit from New York State almost two decades before, invested as much of his business acumen over the next sixty years in public service as he did in the creation of his personal wealth. He served as deputy revenue collector for the port and district of Detroit, military secretary to the governor, city alderman, county supervisor, president and member of Detroit's Common Council, president of the police commission, commissioner of the water board, a member of the board of education, and was active in the Presbyterian Church.[23] Following her husband's death in 1891, Mrs. Farrand continued to live in the home until her death in 1910. About 1920, the house was demolished to make way for encroaching retail concerns.

Woodward Avenue differed from other grand avenues in the East and Midwest in that the city's growing Jewish community developed a substantial residential core on Woodward Avenue prior to the Civil War. Simon Mandlebaum, an influential businessman, erected a grand "Romanesque" mansion on the northeast corner of Woodward and Adelaide Street in 1858 designed by architect Sheldon Smith. The Mandlebaum residence cost $14,000 to build and featured all "modern improvements," including water and gas. It was reported that the house could "hardly be surpassed in point of convenience, or external beauty, by any dwelling in the city."[24] Mandlebaum lived in the home with his wife and daughter until 1862, when he sold it for $20,000 to Emil S. Heineman. Heineman had settled in Detroit in 1851, after leaving Bavaria because of religious intolerance, and established a wholesale clothing business in 1853. Following the outbreak of the Civil War, Heineman became a major supplier of military clothing to federal and local troops.[25] Heineman was president of the Hebrew Relief Society of the Beth El Jewish Society. His wife, Fanny (Butzel) Heineman, was president and secretary of the Detroit Ladies' Society for Support of Hebrew Widows and Orphans in the State of Michigan for many years.[26]

Perhaps the most romantic of the early Woodward Avenue mansions was that of Thomas Witherell Palmer (Figure 9).[27] Known for his resourcefulness, straightforward methods, and large, well-executed business schemes, Palmer was an influential real estate and lumber merchant in 1864 when he purchased a parcel of land on Woodward Avenue one-half mile north of the city limit. There was a small one-and-a-half story wooden farmhouse on the property to which Palmer made additions as his needs or fancies dictated. Palmer's investment coupled with his recognized real estate sagacity did much to stimulate residential development

Figure 9. Thomas W. Palmer residence, east side of Woodward Avenue, between Farnsworth and Kirby Streets, 1864–71. Currently the site of the Detroit Institute of Arts.

outward on the avenue. Ten years and $70,000 later, Palmer had transformed the modest frame dwelling into a grand Italianate villa complete with an abundantly landscaped lawn punctuated with statuary, a greenhouse, and ancillary outbuildings.[28]

The Palmer residence uniquely incorporated two square towers—a short central tower and a taller tower on the south side crowned with a belvedere and flagpole. In the early 1870s, Palmer undertook his last major alterations. The Buffalo firm of Hersey and Company was hired to remodel the interior using "handsomely veneered" French burl walnut at a cost of $25,000.[29]

In 1873 Palmer was appointed to the first Detroit Board of Estimates and in 1878 was elected to the Michigan Senate. He pushed for legislation

Figure 10. Wallace-Stephens-Pingree residence, 1020 Woodward Avenue, 1864/1883. Currently the site of Horace H. Rackham Educational Memorial Building.

that allowed Detroit to acquire Belle Isle as a city park and to establish a system of boulevards and parks within the city. He was elected a U.S. senator in 1883, supporting the right of women to vote and the creation of the Department of Agriculture, while opposing the continuation of unrestricted immigration.[30] In March 1889, he became U.S. ambassador to Spain. Palmer remained in Madrid for thirteen months, then resigned his post to return to Detroit.

Palmer, a noted art collector, was among the founders of the Detroit Museum of Art and served as the museum's first president from 1885 to 1892. President Harrison appointed Palmer to the World's Columbian Exposition Committee in June 1890, and he served as its president. In 1893, Palmer and his wife donated their 140-acre summer estate on the west side of Woodward Avenue, about seven miles from the river's edge, to Detroit for a recreational facility. Palmer Park remains one of Detroit's major urban parks.

The wooden construction of Palmer's villa contributed to its demise. A fire in the south tower above the library on March 29, 1895, resulted in substantial damage. Repairs were made, but eight months later a second and more serious fire in the butler's pantry proved too disastrous to repair and the well-known landmark was taken down.[31] This prime location remained vacant until 1922, when ground was broken for the new Detroit Institute of Arts building.[32]

Stone merchant James P. Wallace built an elegant Second Empire residence in 1864 using sandstone quarried along Lake Huron (Figure 10).[33] As with many of the early avenue mansions, the architect of Wallace's residence in not known. Wallace died in 1879, but his family lived in the mansion until 1882, when it was sold to lumber merchant Henry Stephens. Stephens hired architect William Scott to design a $6,000 stone rear addition, including a ballroom and additional staff quarters. Four years later the house became the property of wealthy shoe manufacturer Hazen S. Pingree. The exterior of the house was altered at various times, each alteration adding more ornate French flourishes.[34]

Pingree arrived in Detroit just following the Civil War, a distinguished Union veteran and survivor of the notorious Andersonville Prison. He engaged in the shoe business with Henry P. Baldwin & Company for a short time before establishing his own shoe manufacturing firm, Pingree & Smith.[35]

In 1889, Pingree was elected mayor of Detroit on the Republican ticket and "set about righting wrongs and reforming many of the antiquated ways of doing the city's business."[36] Pingree took on the street railway companies and the gas company, securing valuable concessions. He promoted beautification of the city and paving of its major streets with asphalt. Pingree was reelected mayor an unprecedented three times and under his administration Detroit gained the title of "The City Beautiful." His success as mayor is attributed to his unwavering opposition to "monopolistic corporations." For many Detroit residents, Pingree was nothing short of a hero because of his efforts to help the unemployed following the money panic of 1893. He introduced a program of public works as a means of reducing a staggering ten percent unemployment. In 1894, Pingree rallied private support to turn vacant private land into public "potato patches," thereby reducing food shortages. His plan was widely acclaimed and embraced by other cities. Cultivation of these garden plots continued through 1896. Indeed, "Potato Patch Pingree" became nationally known as the champion of the needy. Pingree was elected governor of Michigan in 1896. He is credited with remodeling the state's assessment and taxation systems.

Pingree's taste for things French was fully indulged in his residence. The central hall exhibited a tapestry that had reportedly belonged to Napoleon Bonaparte. The sitting room had French medallion-back chairs covered with expensive satin damask, heavy draperies, and marquetry furniture with marble tops. The drawing room was the most spectacular, with gilt Louis XV furniture covered with exquisite Gobelin tapestry, a large Aubusson carpet, crystal chandeliers, wall sconces, and an ornate marble mantel. The decorative effect was enhanced with Pingree's extensive art collection.

Known as the "Grindstone House" because of its stone construction, the mansion was converted into a garage in 1919. Lamenting the fate of the elegant Pingree mansion, the *Detroit Saturday Night* sarcastically noted, "The Pingree homestead at 1020 Woodward Avenue has been sold and will be converted into a garage—news item. To what base uses may we return—Shakespeare."[37]

The architectural statements of these early Woodward Avenue residents induced other prominent citizens to build along Woodward Avenue during the 1870s and 1880s.

THE GROWTH DECADES, 1871-90

Cyrenius A. Newcomb established a dry goods business in downtown Detroit in 1868.[38] From 1869 to 1874 Newcomb lived on Woodward between Sibley and Sproat, and in 1874 erected a brick Italianate residence with a low-pitched roof and square cupola several blocks north near Kirby Street. Newcomb, Endicott & Company led the commercial movement up Woodward in anticipation of the avenue's growth. Initially, the shop was located in the Merrill Block on the northeast corner of Woodward and Jefferson. In 1869, the firm moved into the newly completed Opera House Block on Campus Martius, which was then considered outside the business center, but trade followed. Dexter M. Ferry built a building on the east side of Woodward just north of State Street in 1881 to accommodate Newcomb's growing firm.

Newcomb was a devoted member of the Universalist Church, a founding member of the Detroit Museum of Art, and served for many years as a museum trustee. At his death in 1915 he was president of the Anderson Electric Car Company.[39]

A superb example of Second Empire design carried to its logical extreme was the Wilhelm Boeing residence built on Woodward Avenue in 1875 (Figure 11). Boeing garnered his fortune in pine lands, lumbering, and the manufacturing of woodworking tools. His mansion imitated the latest French building fashion and commanded a striking presence on the avenue. Unfortunately the architect's identity is not known. The impressive central tower, crowned with a curved pyramidal roof, took on pavilion proportions in this design. By 1910, this grand mansion had been subdivided into the six-unit Davis Apartment Building.

Architect Mortimer L. Smith restated the traditional Victorian house using pseudo-Swiss details in his 1876 late Picturesque-style residence for shoe manufacturer Richard H. Fyfe (Figure 12). The rustic charm of the Swiss chalet idiom with its gabled roof, decorative trusses, stickwork, broad verandas, and jutting balconies was a delightful bit of whimsy that added to the avenue's diversity.

Figure 11. Wilhelm Boeing residence, 1875, architect unknown. Subdivided into six apartments in 1910.

Figure 12. Richard H. Fyfe residence, southwest corner of Woodward Avenue and Hancock Street, 1876, Mortimer L. Smith, architect.

The Woodward Avenue mansions of Wellington R. Burt and Simon J. Murphy were published in *L'Architecture Américaine* in 1886.[40] Mason & Rice's 1881 mansion for Burt was a fine example of the Queen Anne style. The architects cleverly incorporated a full double-deck porch wrapped around the corner tower, creating recessed areas on both the side and the avenue facades. The conical tower roof, diverse window sur-

Figure 13. Woodward Avenue and Putnam Street, west side, c. 1896. Edward Smith residence (left), 1887. Simon J. Murphy residence (right), 1883, William and John Scott, architects.

rounds, and distinctive front gable set this house apart from its neighbors.[41] The interior differed from the usual Victorian arrangement in that the kitchen and service rooms were isolated from the main portion of the house through the use of ingenuously contrived passageways. The parlor, sitting room, library, dining room, and hall were designed with large sliding doors that could be opened to create a grand space for large parties.[42]

Simon J. Murphy's 1883 Victorian brick residence replaced the more modest clapboard home of lumberman Charles D. Farlin on the northwest corner of Putnam (Figure 13).[43] Murphy made his fortune as a pioneer lumberman in Michigan and later in real estate investments, which included erecting the thirteen-story Penobscot Building in 1905.[44]

SOCIAL, RELIGIOUS, AND RECREATIONAL ACTIVITIES

The outward residential growth of the avenue attracted recreational and religious organizations. The first Michigan State Fair was held on Woodward Avenue just south of Duffield Street in September 1849. By the late 1850s, a Ladies' Driving Park was established on the west side of Woodward Avenue north of Davenport Street. This park was the site of the Michigan State Fairs from 1858 through 1862. During the winter months of the 1860s, part of this site was flooded to create a skating rink, which was so popular with residents that a second rink was created at Woodward and Edmund Place.

The Peninsular Cricket Club was established on April 5, 1858, with grounds on the west side of Woodward between Canfield and Forest.[45] A "great base ball tournament" was held on the grounds in August of 1867, but the highlight came in September 1879 when the All-England Eleven cricket team matched skills with the Detroit club. The English cricketers emerged the victors to the chagrin of Detroit fans.

The Amateur Athletic Association purchased the five-acre cricket club site in 1887 and leased it to the newly incorporated Detroit Athletic Club. The club erected a handsome brick clubhouse "old Colonial in feeling with slight Romanesque treatment" designed by Joseph V. Gearing (Figure 14).[46] The clubhouse was a horizontal brick mass with two projecting bays covered with a hipped roof. Along the rear of the building was a large balcony overlooking the extensive athletic field. The building featured a bowling alley in one of its bays and an exterior toboggan slide that was open to the public for an admission fee. With its fine facilities for outdoor sports, the DAC was the center for baseball, football, track, tennis, cycling, and cricket. A national track meet at the DAC in 1888 drew some 4,000 spectators to watch 120 athletes from all parts of the country. However, by 1902 the DAC was in financial trouble due to rising property values, and ever-increasing taxes and maintenance costs. There was much discussion of closing, but the club remained in operation with deficits subsidized by members' personal generosity until January 1913, when the organization was dissolved. A new Detroit Athletic Club was formed and erected its fine clubhouse designed by Albert Kahn on Madison Street in 1915. The Woodward Avenue property was eventually sold and used for various sports and commercial interests.[47]

An eighteen-acre public Recreation Park was built two blocks east of Woodward Avenue at the northeast corner of Brady Street in 1878–79, just behind Harper Hospital, which accommodated nearly all athletic interests. This facility remained in operation until 1894, when the land was subdivided into residential lots around a boulevard called Brush Boulevard Park.

Just as the wealthy citizens moved outward from the city center to more tranquil locations, they moved their religious institutions outward as well. Many churches were located on or near lower Woodward Avenue

Figure 14. Detroit Athletic Club, west side of Woodward Avenue between Canfield and Forest Streets, 1887, J.V. Gearing, architect.

Figure 15. St. John's Protestant Episcopal Church, 1860, Jordan & Anderson, architects. Relocated when Woodward Avenue was widened in 1935.

Figure 16. Woodward Avenue, looking north from Grand Circus Park, c. 1900. The spires of Central Methodist Church (1866, G.W. Lloyd, architect) and St. John's Protestant Episcopal Church (1860, Jordan & Anderson, architects) rise above the growing commercial district.

in the 1840s, including Mariners Protestant Episcopal, the First Methodist Episcopal, St. Paul's Episcopal, and the First Presbyterian.

St. John's Protestant Episcopal Church, organized in 1858, was the first religious institution to build on Woodward Avenue above Grand Circus Park (Figure 15). Henry P. Baldwin, a prosperous shoe manufacturer and later governor of Michigan, was building his home on the northwest corner of Woodward and High Street in 1858 when he conceived the idea of establishing Detroit's sixth Episcopal parish in this outlying area.[48] He purchased and donated a lot on the southeast corner of Woodward and High Street and underwrote the building of a chapel designed by Jordan & Anderson in 1859. Two weeks after the chapel was opened, Baldwin offered to donate $17,000 toward building a church.[49] As the church's principal lay leader and benefactor, Baldwin served on the building committee that handpicked architects Jordan & Anderson for the church commission.

The Victorian Gothic St. John's Church recalls Jordan's earlier designs for the Fort Street Presbyterian Church (1855), Jefferson Avenue Presbyterian Church (1855), and the chapel at Elmwood Cemetery (1856). The exterior is rubble limestone that was quarried downriver from Detroit. The Kellys Island sandstone tracery adds novelty to the facade.[50]

The Central Methodist Episcopal chapel and church were built just following the end of the Civil War on the northeast corner of Woodward and East Adams Avenue (Figure 16). Designed by Gordon W. Lloyd, the Central Methodist Episcopal Church was a landmark signaling the elegant residential district just beyond and the beginning of a vista punctuated by a variety of church spires, hence the title "Piety Hill."

The Westminster Presbyterian Church at the northwest corner of Parsons was the result of a design evolution of more than a dozen years (Figure 17). The original chapel was built in 1873–74, but subsequent additions of 1879, 1880, and 1887 created one of the avenue's most unusual ecclesiastic buildings. Although High Victorian Gothic, many of its decorative features included Byzantine and Eastern elements arranged in a purely arbitrary design. The plan was a cruciform type covered by a huge glass dome at the crossing. Interior decorative mosaics and surface treatments were executed by Louis Tiffany.[51] Gordon W. Lloyd's design was nothing short of exotic, with its banded Saracenic arches, chimneys concealed in minarets, and an awkwardly conceived corner belfry tower.[52] This landmark stood until 1918, when it was demolished for the construction of Orchestra Hall.

The 1887 Gothic Revival Woodward Avenue Baptist Church was located at the southeast corner of Winder Street (Figure 18). Architect Mortimer L. Smith dramatically replaced the traditional large stone interior piers with thin iron columns, thus greatly opening the worship area. Unfortunately, the church was almost completely redesigned because of the widening of Woodward Avenue in 1935, and was subsequently destroyed by fire in 1989.

Other significant nineteenth-century churches on Woodward Avenue were Second Congregational Church (Mortimer L. Smith, 1872), First Presbyterian Church (Mason & Rice, 1889), First Unitarian Church (Donaldson & Meier, 1890), First Congregational Church (John Lyman Faxon, 1890), and Church of the Holy Rosary (Malcomson & Higginbotham, 1896).[53]

St. Paul's Episcopal Cathedral on Woodward and Hancock was the last major church built in this residential district. In July 1892, St. Paul's Episcopal Church and St. Joseph's Protestant Episcopal Church[54] merged and purchased the B. F. Farrington residence on the northeast corner of Hancock Avenue with the ultimate plan of erecting a cathedral church on the site. Four years later, a stone chapel and parish house were erected at the rear of the Farrington residence to serve the needs of the congregation. Distinguished ecclesiastical architect and exponent of the Gothic Revival style, Ralph

Figure 17. Westminster Presbyterian Church, northwest corner of Woodward Avenue and Parsons Street, 1874–80. G. W. Lloyd, architect. Demolished, 1918. Currently the site of Orchestra Hall.

Figure 18. Woodward Avenue, looking south from Sibley Street. Left to right, Woodward Avenue Baptist Church, 1887, M.L. Smith, architect; St. John's Protestant Episcopal Church, 1860, Jordon & Anderson, architects; Central Methodist Episcopal Church, 1866, G. W. Lloyd, architect.

Adams Cram of the Boston firm of Cram, Goodhue & Ferguson, was selected as architect for the proposed cathedral church.[55] Architect George D. Mason, a member of the parish, was selected as the associate architect to supervise the construction. Ground was broken in 1908 and the building was dedicated in 1911. St. Paul's was consecrated as the cathedral church on October 12, 1919.

In St. Paul's design, Cram adapted early Gothic architecture to fit modern ideals, conditions, and construction. Reinforced concrete was used in the construction of walls, arches, columns, and the floor. The exterior and interior rely on proportion and harmony, rather than on applied ornamentation, for their success. The building incorporates work by some of the best artists working at the time. The large east window was executed by the London firm of Heaton, Butler & Bayne. John Kirchmayer carved the elaborate reredos, which were first exhibited at the Boston Museum of Art before being installed in the church. Perhaps the most unusual feature of the church is the handcrafted tile paving designed and executed by Mary Chase Perry and Horace J. Caulkins, founders of Detroit's Pewabic Pottery. Although departing from long-established paving conventions, Pewabic Pottery maintained the Gothic spirit of the church and significantly added to the artistic effect through the tile designs and specially made glazes. Cram, a deeply religious man, referred to St. Paul's Cathedral as "a sermon in stone."

THE ARCHITECTS

The earliest Woodward Avenue residences were designed and constructed by an active cadre of "architect and master builders," such as James Shearer. Active in Detroit from about 1853 to 1865, Shearer formed a partnership with journeyman carpenter James Dewey in 1853 and operated his own millwork on Woodbridge and Beaubien. He designed and built his home in 1856–57 on the southeast corner of Woodward and Canfield, near the toll gate, then the city's northern limit. Shearer promoted his professional reputation by advertising his Woodward Avenue residence as an example of his fine credentials as an architect and builder. This, in turn, added credence to upper Woodward Avenue as an emerging first-class residential district. Shearer undoubtedly designed and built several of the early Woodward residences. Politically active, Shearer served as a ward alderman representing eastern Woodward Avenue in 1861–62 and was appointed a member of the Committee on Plans for the new city hall in 1859. He eventually subdivided his property at Woodward and Canfield into twenty-five residential lots.

Architects as a professional group began emerging in Detroit during the late 1850s, primarily in the area of church design. Albert H. Jordan arrived in Detroit from Hartford, Connecticut, and established a solid reputation as a church architect with his commissions for the First Congregational Church (1854), First Presbyterian Church (1855), Jefferson Avenue Presbyterian Church (1855), Fort Street Presbyterian Church (1855), and the chapel at Elmwood Cemetery (1856). James Anderson, a young Scottish draftsman in the office, became Jordan's partner about 1857, and their work branched into commercial, civic, and residential areas.[56] Their Woodward Avenue commissions included the Henry P. Baldwin residence (1858) and St. John's

Episcopal Chapel, church, and rectory (1858–61). While Jordan seems to have been active in Detroit until 1860, Anderson was responsible for the design of City Hall (1870–71).[57]

The role of Jordan and Anderson was challenged by the arrival of Gordon W. Lloyd (1833–1904) in Detroit in 1858. Lloyd was born in Cambridge, England, and came with his family to Quebec at age six. Following the death of his father, Lloyd returned in 1847 to England, where he entered the architectural office of his uncle Ewan Christian.[58] Lloyd attended night classes at the Royal Academy and, like many aspiring architects, finished his formal education with a sketching tour of the Continent. Lloyd sailed for America in 1858 and settled in Detroit, where he soon received several important commissions. Among the first was Christ Episcopal Church in 1861 on Jefferson Avenue, a Gothic design with a more medieval flavor than the Jordan churches. Lloyd was given more design freedom in his 1866 Central Methodist Episcopal Church on the northeast corner of Woodward Avenue and East Adams. The corner tower with its broach spire gave a strong vertical accent to the rugged masonry facade notable for its restrained ornamentation. Lloyd designed two Woodward Avenue residences—for George F. Moore (1880) and David Whitney, Jr. (1890)—and the Westminster Presbyterian Church (1874–80).

Sheldon Smith (1818–68) began his Detroit practice in 1855. Smith was a farmer and a teacher before turning to architecture about 1852 in Sandusky, Ohio.[59] His first Detroit commission seems to have been an addition to the Garrison House Hotel on Jefferson at Cass Avenue in 1854.[60] Sheldon Smith's plans for the $66,000 Detroit House of Correction in 1859 established his reputation as an architect who could successfully undertake major projects. The Simon Mandlebaum residence (1858) is his only known residential work on Woodward Avenue. The largest project of his career, the Detroit Opera House, was on the drawing board at the time of his death in 1868. The design is credited to his son Mortimer L. Smith (1840–96), who began working with him as a draftsman in 1857 and was made a principal in the firm Sheldon Smith and Son in 1861. Young Smith demonstrated his architectural ability in this artistic 1868 Second Empire design. Prominently located on the Campus Martius, the Opera House featured elegant shops on the first floor and an auditorium that seated 2,800 (Figure 19).[61]

Mortimer L. Smith was a colorful figure in Detroit. Handsome and athletic, he was an accomplished artist who regularly exhibited his paintings and for a time vacillated between painting and architecture as his profession of choice. Smith designed several Woodward Avenue residences, commercial buildings, and churches. Notable among the residences were those for David Whitney, Jr. (1871), Richard H. Fyfe (1876), Joseph Black (1877), Joseph B. H. Bratshaw (1880), William H. Stevens (1883), and Maxwell Fisher (1890). Commercial and ecclesiastic work on the avenue included the Godfrey Block (1871), Woodward Avenue (Second) Congregational Church (1872), Newcomb-Endicott Building (1879), Beal Block (1885), and Woodward Avenue Baptist Church (1887).

One of the most prolific architects working along Woodward Avenue was William Scott, a native of England who settled in Canada with his family in 1853. Scott is first listed in the *Detroit City Directory* in 1872 as the chief engineer for the Detroit, Lansing & Lake Michigan Railroad and the Detroit & Bay City

Figure 19. Woodward Avenue and Campus Martius, northeast corner, c. 1895. Detroit Opera House, 1869, Sheldon and Mortimer L. Smith, architects.

Railroad.[62] Scott's son John (1850–1928) followed his father in the study of civil engineering and in 1874 joined his father to form the architectural office of William Scott & Son. The following year the firm became William Scott & Company, Architects and Civil Engineers. The firm included William, his sons John and Arthur H. Scott, and Alfred Wood. William Scott retired in 1887 and his sons reorganized as John Scott and Company, which by 1890 was one of the leading architectural offices in Detroit.

The firm's earliest known Woodward Avenue residence was for Wells W. Leggett, agent for the Brush Electric Light Company, in 1882. Several important Woodward Avenue residential commissions followed: Simon J. Murphy (1883), Charles H. Smith (1884), William C. Colburn (1884), Charles H. Hodges (1884), Frank J. Hecker (1889), and George L. Beecher (1893). John Scott and Company was well represented on adjacent residential streets, and by numerous commercial buildings and factories.

The firm of Mason and Rice was responsible for several fine Woodward Avenue residences and a major church during the thirty-year period between 1881 and 1911. George D. Mason (1856–1948) came with his parents to Detroit in 1870 and began his study of architecture with Mortimer L. Smith in 1873 at age sixteen. The next five years he worked in the office of Henry T. Brush and Hugh Smith. Mason visited the

Philadelphia Centennial Exposition in 1876. In 1878, he formed a partnership with Zachariah Rice.[63] Mason and Rice became a large and aggressive firm undertaking varied design work, including churches, hotels, major public buildings, and commercial structures, as well as fine residential work.

Mason was keenly interested in the advancement of architecture as a profession and was instrumental in establishing the Michigan Chapter of the American Institute of Architects in 1887. In 1911 Mason was elected the United States delegate to the International Congress of Architects held in Rome, Italy. He spearheaded the effort to establish the Michigan State Board for Registration of Architects and served as its first president from 1915 to 1919. After three-quarters of a century of active architectural practice, Mason was affectionately known as the Dean of Michigan Architects when he died one month short of age ninety-two. His Woodward Avenue commissions included residences for John Burt and Wellington Burt (1881), David Carter (1883), Edward H. Butler (1885), William V. Moore (1889), the First Presbyterian Church (1889), Albert L. Stephens residence (1890), the Woodward Apartments (1902), Temple Beth El (1902), and the last major residence to be erected on Woodward, that for Lemuel W. Bowen (1911).

Detroit's architects matured as a professional community during the 1880s. The Detroit Association of Architects was formed on April 3, 1884, with twenty charter members. The group hoped to set standards for architectural work and to obtain a consensus on a scale of prices for work to combat the intrusion of builders and carpenters, but this early association was short lived. In October 1887 six members of the earlier group and other peers organized the Michigan State Association of Architects.[64] This group associated themselves with the Western Association of Architects the following month. In January 1890 the Michigan association reorganized to conform with the requirements of the American Institute of Architects and officially became the Michigan Chapter of the American Institute of Architects in March 1890.[65]

THE GOLDEN DECADE, 1891-1900

Colonel Frank J. Hecker's French Renaissance mansion (Figure 20) brought a grandeur to Woodward Avenue that was more commonly associated with the mansions of New York's Fifth Avenue or Chicago's Prairie Avenue or Drexel Boulevard.[66] Frank J. Hecker and his business partner, Charles Lang Freer, amassed their fortunes from the building of railroad freight cars and associated enterprises. They each purchased two adjoining lots on the northeast corner of Woodward and East Ferry Avenue in 1886.[67] Hecker desired something different from the prevailing Queen Anne or Romanesque residential designs. Consequently, his architect John Scott recruited Louis Kamper from the New York firm of

Figure 20. Frank J. Hecker residence, northeast corner of Woodward and East Ferry Avenues, 1889, Louis Kamper (for John Scott & Company), architect. Elevation and first-floor plan.

McKim, Mead & White to design a French Chateau–style mansion for Hecker in 1888.[68] The Hecker plan is based on the square with corner towers. The light buff Bedford, Indiana, limestone with a green tile roof was a relief from the commonly used dark Lake Superior sandstone and red tile roofs. The first-floor plan was unencumbered in that the sliding double doors between the rooms and the large stairhall allowed the space to be opened up for grand parties (Figure 21). A large stained-glass window dominated the south-side landing, bringing colorful light into the heart of the house.

The oval dining room featured specially made built-in mahogany cabinets and a domed ceiling. Its walls were treated with a copper metallic finish and the ceiling with silver gilt. The small octagonal room off the dining room had an ornately painted ceiling. Carefully selected woods were combined for maximum effect throughout. White quarter-sawn oak was used in the hall; English oak with exquisite burl panels was used in the library. The parlor and music rooms were executed in a French manner with silk fabric panels, carved moldings, and gilded wood details. Intricate geometric patterns were created in the parquet floors of each room. Elmer Ellsworth Garnsey was brought from New York to superintend the general decorative scheme and to create ornate painted ceiling designs.[69]

Upon completion, the Hecker residence was acclaimed for the successful collaboration of archi-

Figure 21. Interior view of Frank J. Hecker residence, c. 1893. First floor hall.

Figure 22. Woodward Avenue, looking down East Ferry Avenue, c. 1892. Frank J. Hecker residence (corner), 1889, Louis Kamper (for John Scott & Company), architect. Charles L. Freer residence (adjacent), 1890–91, Wilson Eyre, Jr., architect.

tects, artists, designers, and decorators. The *Detroit Free Press* wrote that the house was "…designed and executed along the true lines of legitimate art."[70] *The Critic* called Hecker's residence "The Finest House in Michigan," adding that, "While there are other residences here in Detroit on which more lavish outlay has been made, Col. Hecker obtained a better result by not knowing more than his architects. He told them how much he wished to expend and left them alone" (Figure 22).[71]

The most famous residence in the neighborhood was that of internationally known art collector and founder of the Freer Gallery of Art in Washington, D.C., Charles Lang Freer (Figures 23 to 25). Although not directly on Woodward Avenue, Freer's remarkable Shingle-style residence stood out between Hecker's turreted chateau and the exuberant neighboring Queen Anne residences. Freer began collecting art in the mid-1880s and, through diligent study and association with artists, he developed a keen aesthetic sense. He selected Philadelphia architect Wilson Eyre, Jr., to design his residence in 1890.

Freer's home is one of the finest monuments of the period in Detroit. There is a distinctive transition from the Queen Anne toward a modern, organic architecture that expresses new fluid patterns of living. Corner fireplaces, built-in cabinets and furniture, and the skillfully designed two-story central hall with a double freestanding fireplace defies fixed architectural traditions. The house is a testament to Freer's discerning aesthetic. The unusual stippled metallic wall finishes provided a

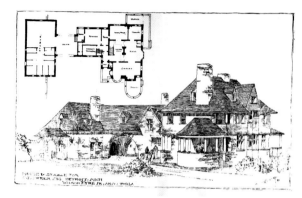

Figure 23. Charles L. Freer residence, Woodward and East Ferry Avenues, 1890–91, Wilson Eyre, Jr., architect. Residence and stable, renderings.

Figure 24. Charles L. Freer residence. Art gallery, with exhibition of paintings by James McNeill Whistler, c. 1907.

Figure 25. Louise Hecker Fletcher (playing with a dog in the Freer garden), c. 1903. Freer residence appears in the background.

unique background for Freer's priceless collection of ancient Eastern and contemporary American art works. As Freer's collection grew, Eyre was called upon to expand the residence.[72] The first major addition was necessitated in 1904 when Freer purchased James McNeill Whistler's celebrated Peacock Room and brought it to

Detroit from London (Figure 24). Originally created for English shipping magnate Frederick Leyland in 1876, the Peacock Room is now in the Freer Gallery of Art in Washington.

Freer first offered his important collection and the funds necessary to build a museum to the Smithsonian Institution in 1902, but it was not until 1906 that this unique gift was accepted. Conditions of the gift provided that the collection remain in Freer's possession during his lifetime. News of the gift put Freer's Detroit residence in the international spotlight as the Freer Gallery. Baedeker's 1909 guide to the United States described the collection and provided tourists with instructions for admittance.[73] Freer died in 1919 and the collection was moved to Washington. His residence was sold the following year to the Merrill-Palmer School, which occupies the building today.

Lumber baron David Whitney, Jr., commissioned architect Gordon W. Lloyd to design Woodward Avenue's most lavish mansion in 1889–90 (Figure 26).[74] Whitney came to Detroit from Massachusetts in 1857 and made millions from investment in pine lands and the buying and shipping of lumber. He was well connected in lake-marine transportation and owned an extensive fleet of steam barges.

Figure 26. David Whitney, Jr., residence, 4421 Woodward Avenue, 1889–90, Gordon W. Lloyd, architect. Currently the Whitney Restaurant.

The *Detroit News* referred to the "Whitney Palace" as "the finest ever erected in Detroit."[75] The exterior is of rough pink Jasper stone from South Dakota mixed with polished gray granite columns and tooled moldings and cornices. Whitney moved into his new home in December 1893. The *Detroit Free Press* called the residence "An American Palace" and praised it as "the most substantial residence in this part of the country, one which will fairly vie with the Potter Palmer Palace in Chicago."[76] The style was called "Romanesque." The grand hall was the largest room, with a floor of English tile mosaic in a Flemish design with tones of sage, olive, red, and buff. There was a mahogany elevator adjacent to the grand staircase that took guests to either the third-floor picture gallery or the basement billiard room. Mrs. Whitney's suite was appointed with Louis XV furniture.[77] Lloyd's design for the Whitney residence was not his most successful due to the confusion from too many unrelated elements. The enlivened facade lacks the harmony and serenity achieved by Hecker at a lesser expense through careful planning.

Whitney invested in residential property along lower Woodward Avenue in anticipation of the northward commercial trend and commissioned Lloyd to design the Grand Circus Building at Park Street and Woodward in 1885.[78]

The Avenue's Demise

Woodward Avenue developed along individual tastes without the benefit of an agreed-upon master plan. Trees along the avenue were untrimmed and branched out too low, vacant lots were neglected, and unsightly fences of every type added to the eyesores. There was a great variance between the magnificence of the buildings and the haphazard maintenance of the yards and plantings. By 1890 residents interested in preserving and enhancing the residential character of the avenue organized the Woodward Avenue Improvement Association to beautify and give the avenue a "park-like" appearance in the portion from Adelaide north to the Michigan Central Railroad crossing. The Association's membership included long-time residents such as Heineman, Fyfe, and Pingree and others such as Hecker who were just erecting their homes.

The Association retained respected Belgian-born "landscape artist" Eutrope Ferrand to study the question and develop a plan. Ferrand candidly outlined his findings to the Association in a letter: "In order to get the best results, we have to take the avenue as a whole and in some measure deprive each separate piece of property of its individuality, so as to imagine a thoroughfare across a large park."[79]

He recommended that all front and side fences or hedges be removed and that any rear fences be covered with plantings. The only variety of shade trees for Woodward Avenue, according to Ferrand, was the American weeping elm because of its large size and uniform shape. The trees were to be regularly spaced in a straight line along the avenue with the lawn between the street and homes kept free of large trees to preserve the view.

A lengthy meeting was held in Mayor Pingree's office on July 2, 1890, to discuss Ferrand's proposal. Ferrand was hired as consultant by the Association with the proviso that property owners were individually responsible to pay Ferrand for their lot improvements. Pingree engaged Ferrand to begin on his block that same week.[80] Ferrand was hired by Frank J. Hecker and Charles L. Freer to landscape their residences.

In spite of these efforts, the Association could do little to stop the encroaching noise and air pollution from rapidly growing industrial corridors flanking the avenue and the use of soft coal and wood fuels. Ironically, many of the offending industries were owned and operated by avenue residents.

The economic panic of 1893 idled many of Detroit's largest industries and left ten percent of the city's population out of work. With increasing demands for social change, life on the avenue changed. After 1893, only one major residence was erected on Woodward Avenue, that of Lemuel W. Bowen in 1911–14. Designed by George D. Mason, it was erected on the site of the Cyrenius A. Newcomb mansion, on the west side of Woodward between Kirby and West Ferry. It seems curious in light of the commercial direction the avenue was taking that Bowen, an organizer of the Cadillac Automobile Company, invested so much in his elegant English Renaissance Revival residence and extensive gardens. Indeed, six years after moving in, he was surrounded by boardinghouses, auto garages, and other such enterprises.

Property values soared as various commercial and retail interests vied for choice avenue locations. This rapidly changing character deterred any further residential development and drove many longtime residents to relocate.[81]

In 1910, the Detroit Museum of Art trustees purchased the vacant eight-and-a-half-acre Palmer-Merrill-Ferry tract for $216,400 as the site for a new art museum. In an effort to establish a cultural center, the

Figure 27. Lower Woodward Avenue, looking toward Windsor, Ontario, Canada, 1893. Elk's ceremonial arch spans the avenue.

Figure 28. Ford Motor Company's 25,000 employees, Highland Park Plant, Woodward Avenue and Manchester Street, c. 1913.

museum trustees with the support of the mayor and the City Planning Department lobbied the Library Commission to purchase the residential block across Woodward as the site for the new public library. Several mansions still remained on this site, and the Library Commission knew that the cost would be higher than was paid for the museum site. Not all property owners complied with the Commission's plea to sell at the lowest cash price per parcel. Some refused to sell for the appraised value, and condemnation proceedings followed. The Commission had to pay a whopping $1,194,349.72 for the site, nearly double their original estimate.[82]

Indicative of the crass commercialism on Woodward Avenue, the proposed art center had not even gotten off the drawing board when a cartoon of the proposed new museum appeared in *The Little Stick* captioned "Garages to the right of it, garages to the left of it, garages in front of it, our new art center." Lightly written over the face of the cartoon was "honk!"[83]

With the rapid growth of industry and commerce (Figure 27), Detroit of the twentieth century moved from the "City Beautiful" to "Detroit the Dynamic." In spite of the dramatic transformation, residents such as Hecker and Freer had no intention of abandoning their homes. In a candid letter to former Detroiter Thomas S. Jerome, Freer summarized conditions in 1911:

> …if you were to suddenly find yourself back here, you would be greatly astonished at the marvelous growth of the city. Business is scattered throughout Woodward Avenue from the Boulevard to the River, and the suburbs are extending wonderfully. Nearly all of your old friends are removing their homes to Grosse Pointe and business, generally, seems to be very prosperous here. I am afraid that the old-time charm of Detroit as a resident city has almost completely fled. Smoke, dirt, noise and all the unfavorable features of a large manufacturing center are, by degrees, spreading over the entire old residential portion of our city. I, for one, however, do not feel like tearing up my present home in search of quieter surroundings at Grosse Pointe or any other place near our city.[84]

Henry Ford's 1909 Highland Park plant, located on Woodward at Manchester, increased congestion along the avenue and encouraged the emergence of automobile garages and showrooms all along Woodward (Figure 28). Ford's announcement of the five-dollar-a-day wage in January 1914 set in motion an enormous

Figure 29. Woodward Avenue, looking west down West Grand Boulevard intersection, c. 1924.

influx of people from rural areas looking for jobs, and Woodward Avenue led them to the Promised Land. The rapid expansion of the automobile industry, related manufacturing, and a flood of workers demanding housing, concentrated on and near Woodward Avenue, sealed the avenue's demise as a fine residential district (Figure 29).

Woodward Avenue was widened in 1935 and many of its grand churches were moved backward or so altered as to confound the architects' original conceptions. One by one the grand mansions either met the wrecking ball immediately or experienced years of ignominious re-use, usually not even remotely related to their original function. Today, only five mansions remain on Woodward Avenue.[85] The Whitney and Hecker mansions have been sympathetically refurbished, one for use as an elegant restaurant and the other for a law firm's office. Efforts are being made to refurbish the Beecher mansion, now used as offices for

Figure 30. Woodward Avenue, looking south from Warren Avenue, 1989. St. Paul's Episcopal Cathedral (left), 1908–11, Ralph Adams Cram, architect.

Wayne State University. The Bowen house serves as the Michigan Health Care Corporation's Adult Mental Health Hospital, and the Smith house provides office space for the Detroit Public Schools.

A drive up Woodward Avenue from the Detroit River is a sad experience—a tale of two cities (Figure 30). Many of the blocks above Grand Circus Park are as vacant now as they were in the 1860s, ripe for development, but waiting for a growing population and a healthy, expanding city core to embrace them.

CHAPTER FOUR

EUCLID
Avenue
CLEVELAND, OHIO

THE 1893 BAEDEKER'S GUIDEBOOK to the continental United States recommended Euclid Avenue as "one of the most beautiful residence-streets in America."[1] Only one other street, Fifth Avenue in New York, had such an honor bestowed on it by this travelers' bible. Another encomium, from internationally acclaimed scholar John Fiske, lauded the avenue for its magnificent vistas, which reminded him of "the nave and aisles of a huge cathedral." In his 1879 lecture on "American Political Ideas" to the Royal Institution of Great Britain, Fiske poignantly captured the avenue's special qualities: "In Cleveland...there is a street some five or six miles in length and five hundred feet in width, bordered on each side with a double row of arching trees, and with handsome stone houses, of sufficient variety and freedom in architectural design, standing at intervals of from one to two hundred feet" along the entire length of the street.[2] Fiske's measurements were actually grander than the avenue—eighty feet wide and four miles long—but his conclusions were quite valid. Euclid Avenue exemplified, for Fiske, the New England village ideal, wherein abundant land and private ownership created a more fluid political and social structure than the authoritarian feudal system in England. Samuel Clemens, among other critics, had no difficulty arguing that Euclid Avenue was not the country's best example of an open social system—a neighborhood unpenetrable by "poor white trash," he claimed—but Fiske, undaunted by contrary evidence, serenely viewed it as a vision of the system's success in America.[3]

Also known as Prosperity Street and Millionaires' Row, Euclid Avenue was distinguished during the second half of the nineteenth century for its architec-

ESSAY BY JAN CIGLIANO

Figure 1. View of Euclid Avenue, looking east from Twenty-sixth Street on north side, c. 1920.

ture and the eminence of those who resided there. Extending from downtown Public Square eastward to Ninetieth Street, Euclid Avenue was a kind of linear roll call of the residences of Cleveland's business and cultural leaders. The avenue's patrons commissioned the finest architects of the prosperous post–Civil War years, 1865–1910, to design elegant mansions that would reflect and enhance their own economic and social positions. For these patrons, the design arts were much more than a frill; they were an essential part of their everyday lives. In their houses, furniture, paintings, art objects, gardens, the commercial buildings they built, and the street itself, the avenue's residents embraced the inherent value of great art and architecture (Figure 1).

Most of the houses that gave notice to this architectural showcase were built during the great age when Cleveland was being transformed by tremendous industrial growth. The progressive fortunes of capital and culture that built the residences and created the vision for Euclid Avenue were the same fortunes that drove the iron-and-oil port city. The commitment of money, energy, and creative vision by residents sprang from the same values that they invested in the city's development. The avenue was as much a monument to the strong and dynamic Midwestern industrial center they had created as it was to their personal fortunes and accomplishments. Euclid Avenue was probably the most important integrating element in the city during the formative years of Cleveland's development. Undoubtedly, however, more than a few of the mansions were pretentious, a reflection of the patrons' aspirations. But if the architecture was bold and flamboyant, it was no more so than the patrons' business style. If rooms were big and ceilings high, they were no less so than the occupants' realized aspirations.

The most interesting questions to pose about Cleveland's grand avenue are how it came to be and why it survived for such a brief period in Cleveland's history. In the 1850s, Euclid Avenue still competed with Franklin Boulevard in Ohio City, west of the Cuyahoga River, as the premier address of Cleveland capitalists. Bankers, lawyers, and commercial entrepreneurs gravitated east of the river, while many leaders of Cleveland industry and shipbuilding settled on the west side.[4] Euclid Avenue triumphed in this competition chiefly because of its proximity to the downtown business district and Public Square offices, and because it was the city's center spine. But commerce expanded over the decades at the sacrifice of the residential neighborhood of its principal promoters. By the turn of the century, no other could rival the avenue as the city's main commercial street. Even though Euclid Avenue entrepreneurs were sanguine about their triumphs, they did not envision further financial gains adversely affecting their private environment. But without municipal control of planning and development, the architectural glory of Euclid Avenue gradually faded and disappeared. The neighborhood that brought fame to Euclid Avenue, and to Cleveland, thrived for only sixty years, between about 1850 and 1910.

Euclid Avenue's place in the history of Cleveland's physical and cultural development is not diminished by its short life. It is really that much greater, because of its remarkable presence, and now its absence. The avenue's origins, its very reasons for being at all, were not remarkable. It was an urban neighborhood—the gathering of families who lived in one place for the purpose of reinforcing their collective activities. What is remarkable is who these people were, the size and style of the houses they built, and the central position their avenue had in the city's urban development. Ironically, it was the tremendous success of Cleveland's industry and commerce that nurtured the rise and fostered the fall of this grand avenue.

A Grand Avenue Takes Shape, 1816-55

The Connecticut Land Company, which settled Cleveland and the surrounding Western Reserve's three million acres in 1796, chose to make Cleveland the city center of "New Connecticut," as the reserve was then called. Over the century after its founding, Cleveland grew from a rural village of seven residents to a driven industrial metropolis of 381,000 people. Even so, an instinctual rural pattern of life characterized this urban place, as it remained a western New England outpost for decades into the nineteenth century. Indeed, many

Easterners who visited Cleveland in the 1850s and 1860s were struck by the strong resemblance to the Connecticut motherland—rural streetscapes, red barns, white houses, and village greens.[5]

By 1870, however, two out of five of Cleveland's 92,829 residents were foreign-born, distancing New England's cultural hold toward the cosmopolitan urbanism of Europe. Many who hailed from northeastern towns and villages, though, did not easily lose their New Connecticut bent. Their allegiances were undeniably rooted in the traditions of their eastern counterparts, influ-

Figure 2. Map of city of Cleveland, 1892. Twenty-eight-square-mile radius.

encing Euclid Avenue residents' choice of architectural styles, interior furnishings, designer fashions, attitudes, and customs.

By 1910, Cleveland was the nation's sixth largest city, with over 560,000 residents. Its location at the center of multiple trade routes from the East, the South, and the West, not to mention the northern terminus of the 309-mile Ohio Canal, enabled local entrepreneurs to exploit lake, canal, and rail trade and build the city's import-export industries from a deficit of over $80,000 in 1825 to a profitable $300 million business by 1896 (Figure 2). At century's end, iron producers and oil refiners held the reins of Cleveland's industrial wealth, both boasting $10 million industries and running second only to their counterparts in New York.[6]

Euclid Avenue emerged only gradually as the residential promenade of Cleveland through the early nineteenth century. The neighborhood first began around Public Square and moved eastward toward University Circle as the century matured. In the early 1800s, Euclid was known as the "girdled road" for the encircling markers around the bark of its trees, and as the Buffalo Stage Road since it carried four-horse passenger coaches to and from Buffalo, New York. In its earliest days, it was an unpaved, unlighted path through the woods. It was scarred and rutted by the wheels of stagecoaches and frequented by wolves and other wild animals. Four blocks beyond Public Square, only a few acres of the primeval forest had been cleared and fenced.[7]

An important turning point in Euclid's history came in the early 1830s when a dozen or so leading citizens built their homes along it, most of whom were canal merchants and attorneys who had their offices on Public Square and nearby Superior Avenue. They apparently chose Euclid as their residence to live within walking distance of their businesses yet distant enough from the mercantile activity around Superior Avenue and the river. All had recently arrived in Cleveland from New England or upstate New York. Most were from small farming and mercantile towns, though a few hailed from such urban centers as Boston, New Haven, Hartford, or Buffalo. They worked closely with one another during the day and chose to live among one another, true to the tradition of their native towns (Figure 3).

East of this small neighborhood, further out beyond the developed edge of the village, a few venturesome settlers built vast homesteads. These rural gentry laid the path for future eastward development by laying out extensive 100- and 200-acre farms, which were later subdivided during the postwar years into valuable Euclid Avenue frontage. By the mid-1840s, the two miles along the north side between Thirteenth and Fortieth Streets were controlled by four men. The country estates of physician John M. Sterling and merchants Nathan

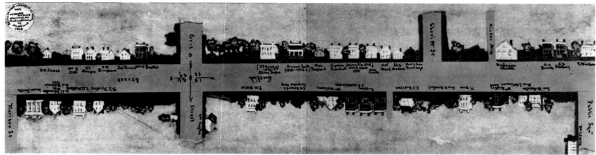

Figure 3. The unpaved road, 1846–47. Facsimile, 1908.

Perry, Peter Weddell, and Samuel Dodge were really quite in keeping with the street's pastoral landscape. Indeed, little could these men realize that by preserving the natural, open vistas of their property they were creating the hallmark of Euclid Avenue.[8]

The topography of the land surrounding the street also played a role in the avenue's streetscape design. An east-west ridge rose gradually from Lake Erie and reached its peak elevation of about 100 feet above sea level on the north side, where these early houses were sited. The top of the ridge—overlooking the lake to the north and the avenue to the south—provided a splendid site for the palatial residences. Once established, by the early 1850s, the principle of building on the ridge and away from the avenue became an honored convention. A few observers even wondered if Euclid Avenue residents aspired to a European tradition. Humorist Artemus Ward suspected that the depth of the avenue set-backs—a generous 100 to 300 feet of rolling lawns—was artfully measured to pronounce "the length of the owner's pedigree." A case in point, Ward mockingly observed, was "one resident who discovered the other day that his maternal grandfather, six times removed, was associate master-of-the-mews in the household of the third Duke of Gillyflower" and was preparing to move his house back fifty feet. The design of Euclid Avenue grounds and houses, in Ward's view, were "calculated to strike awe to the plebian heart."[9] Cast-iron fences, uniformly installed by all avenue residents, further reinforced the exclusiveness of the neighborhood, screening the spacious, manicured lawns from the many passers-by who strolled along the avenue. This barrier was heightened by residents' propensity to erect these formidable fences along the public sidewalk, but not between their private homes. For four miles, one yard flowed into another, interrupted only by side streets, and the railroad crossing and commercial blocks at Fifty-fifth Street. The result was a continuous parklike vista of landscaped lawns, finely pruned shrubbery, and shaded walkways.

The Finest Avenue in the West

Euclid Avenue's position as the city's premier residential address had been established by the early 1850s. And Cleveland's good standing among Eastern and Western critics ultimately focused on the "noted street."[10] One visitor in 1857 posed the rhetorical question, "Where is there a street west of a New York avenue, that can vie with Euclid?" Where, indeed? A *New York World* reporter suggested in 1863 that it was "the finest avenue in the west," distinguished by "a double row of charming villas and gardens where one might sigh to dwell." In 1866 another *New York World* reporter pronounced Euclid "the Fifth Avenue of the city"—a stunning compliment from a Manhattanite.[11] Even British novelist Anthony Trollope favorably compared the double row of "the beautiful American elm" that arched over the street to the "little paltry trees" that decorated Paris' boulevards. And Samuel Clemens, the typically caustic chronicler, singled out the avenue as "one of the finest streets in America."[12]

The vision that took shape on Euclid Avenue, first voiced by residents as early as 1855, was "a continuous avenue of shade running like the Boulevards of Brussels…a drive and a promenade of about 5 miles." This explicit form and function, a broad tree-lined processional, was quite sophisticated for its day: it predated by more than a decade the completion of the great scheme fabricated for Paris by Napoleon III and Baron Haussmann, undertaken from 1853 to 1870. Armed with an irrepressible vision and enthusiasm from their European Grand Tour travels, avenue residents sustained their dream of a boulevard through the early 1870s, to "make Euclid Avenue the finest thoroughfare in the world."[13] The strongest push by private citizens to make the avenue the spine of a city-sponsored boulevard scheme occurred in the mid-1890s, but it too ultimately failed. At no time was the idea of a European boulevard adopted as formal policy by Cleveland's public officials.

Rather, the parklike setting was created by the coordinated actions of residents. Such men as Union Telegraph founder Jeptha Wade, Standard Oil founder John D. Rockefeller, and General Electric founder Charles F. Brush built their modern fortunes and Euclid Avenue estates with the belief that they would be passed on to their heirs to preserve. These people, unlike the established gentry in New York or Philadelphia, were not aggrandizing deep-rooted family wealth with their new avenue residences. They were nouveaux riches, and they needed roots. Their desire to stage themselves along the city's principal parade ground reflected the prestige of an avenue address and indicated a commitment by the family to its residence and its street.[14]

The families who built Euclid Avenue were builders of property. It is an understatement to say that these entrepreneurial individuals were materialists; they thought and acted mostly on the basis of concrete interests rather than philosophical ideas. Few of the men were artists, writers, or scholars; most were capitalists engaged in such pursuits as canal routes, railroad tracks, ore and copper products, nuts and bolts, electric dynamos, and oil. In architecture, as in business, they recognized the value of physical property and of their own leadership in advancing striking architectural form. Many patrons worked with their architects and builders in the design and construction of their houses, from overseeing the rendering of the original plans to the management of contractors and the selection of Tiffany skylights and Herter Brothers furniture. The results were often as much a product of the owner's tastes as those of the builder or architect. Patrons showed themselves to be pliant stylists; they accepted the new and did not cling to the old. But they did not set trends either. They influenced local design to the extent that their architects and builders wrapped currently popular styles around expensive, magnificent forms.

Their conventional aesthetic leanings were entirely consistent with their traditional values and formal lifestyles. Novelties and innovations in structural and mechanical systems distinguished these houses from others in the city. In fact, patrons' progressive, even inventive, attitudes about the vast possibilities available in material resources inspired them to encourage their builders and architects to incorporate the most modern techniques available. Euclid Avenue houses led the way in introducing the first running water, central ventilation, electric lighting and wiring, and the first elevator and steel-frame construction in a Cleveland residence. The patrons and their residences helped advance the art and science of local house construction, ultimately raising the quality of life for others, as such innovations subsequently became standardized and affordable to the larger population.

Figure 4. Nathan Perry residence, 2157 Euclid Avenue, c. 1830. Jonathan Goldsmith, masterbuilder. Alterations by Peabody & Stearns, architects. Photograph, 1930s.

COUNTRY VILLAS, 1840-75

The first houses built on the street were modest frame dwellings. They were rooted stylistically in the plain vernacular of the villages from which their owners had come. The architecture, like the road, was rustic and utilitarian. The residence built for Nathan Perry around 1830 was typical: a gabled roof, clapboard siding, and little detailing to differentiate this house from any other. The Perry house, home to four generations of the Perry-Payne-Bingham-Blossom family, was also typical among avenue residences, especially those built after 1850, as the inherited domicile of children and grandchildren. In the 1890s, when Charles Bingham came into possession of his wife's family home, he retained Boston architects Peabody & Stearns to expand and "neoclassicize" the old Nathan Perry house, adding a tower, porch columns, wings, and rear addition (Figure 4).

The severe classicism that had shaped the street's original appearance began to give way by the mid-1840s to an enthusiasm for more picturesque forms. Patrons chose one of the two European transplants then in fashion among American homebuilders: the Italianate villa and the Gothic country house, both more romantic in their inspiration than the austere earlier residences. The Italianate villa was exceptionally popular among Euclid Avenue patrons from the 1840s through the 1860s—most appropriate for an urbane city street. Gothic styling, however, was much less popular and was usually adopted by residents whose farmhouses dotted the street's woodland region beyond the village's eastern boundaries.

The residences of railroad magnates Joseph and Jacob Perkins were among the finest Italianate villas. Unlike their neighbors before them, the Perkins brothers went beyond Cleveland for their architect to the eminent professional of the day, Richard Upjohn of New York City. Upjohn's design for Joseph Perkins's residence (Figure 5), built in 1851–53, was similar to other Italianate villas the architect was then working on, notably the J. H. Birch house in Chicago.[15]

Once Upjohn had completed the drawings and sent them off to Perkins in Ohio, the client managed the

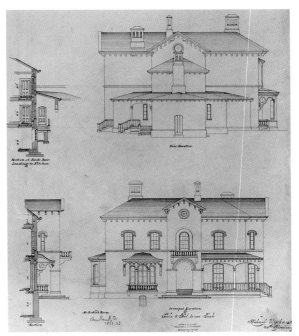

Figure 5. Joseph Perkins residence, 2719 Euclid Avenue, 1851–53, Richard Upjohn, architect. Original rendering by Richard Upjohn.

execution and retained as construction managers the city's leading building and architectural firm of Heard & Porter—who designed many of the avenue's residences in the 1850s and 1860s. Joseph Perkins personally purchased the stone, brick, lumber, nails, and glass, and negotiated the contracts for the stone mason and day laborers. The house cost Perkins $47,580, more than he had wished to spend, but, as he told Upjohn, he was "entirely satisfied with the design" and this was "strong consolation."[16] So much so that Perkins also called upon Upjohn to advise him on the design for the grounds and summer house, one of the few noted occasions a patron afforded Upjohn the chance to apply his talent as a landscape architect.[17] Upon its completion, one local observer commented that the Perkins residence resembled "the comfortable country home of a family of wealth and taste in England"—just as Andrew Jackson Downing had envisioned and Upjohn had made possible through his exceptional talent.[18]

To be sure, the residence fit well with the sophisticated pursuits of its occupants. Joseph and Martha Steele Perkins had purchased the Euclid Avenue lot and commissioned Upjohn prior to moving to Cleveland from Warren, Ohio, in 1852. Once here, they and their children and grandchildren made Euclid Avenue their home for over seventy years. Joseph, a son of the wealthy General Simon Perkins family of Warren, had worked in his father's railroad businesses before arriving in the city. He came to preside over the Bank of Commerce, a position he held for two decades (1852–72), and, with his brother Jacob, built the Cleveland & Mahoning Railroad, which opened the plentiful Mahoning Valley coal fields to the city's industrialists beginning in 1852. For her part, Martha Perkins led hundreds of women in the organization of the local Women's Christian Temperance Union in 1874. In her mission to abolish alcohol abuse, she went frequently to slum flats in the crowded River Street district to counsel those in impoverished homes and sailors' saloons—places quite apart from her pleasant Euclid Avenue surroundings.[19]

House and grounds were just one part of the enthusiasm for the design arts that residents of the street indulged in at this time. They took as much pride and pleasure in the manner of life they led within their homes as they did in their public architecture. The interior domain became as much a focus of the owners' and designers' attentions as the exterior. A variety of motifs played behind the reserved uniformity of exterior facades. In the 1850s a liberated enthusiasm for things sculptural in rooms and furnishings anticipated lavish post–Civil War taste. Freed from the constraints of classical orders, marble fireplaces displayed bold, arched openings and stairways spiraled up from one floor to the next—all characteristic of Italianate interior designs.

Builders decorated rooms with deeply molded cornices and carved woodwork, while many avenue families cluttered the modest spaces with furniture and artifacts.

Exteriors, too, adopted the Italianate's high-relief interior look. The Euclid Avenue residence was treated as one big sculptural piece, cast out of textured building materials, and surmounted by magnificent rooftop embellishments of iron balustrades, cupolas, and prominent gables. The orchestrated use of different masonries was quite popular on Euclid during this period of romantic design, thanks in part to bounteous regional reserves of clay and sandstone readily available to Cleveland builders.[20] In 1865–66, entrepreneur Jeptha H. Wade, and his banker son, Randall, created adjoining estates in the refined Italianate villa style (Figure 6). While many of their neighbors were building on Euclid's central parade ground between Twelfth and Thirtieth Streets, the Wades, one of the richest and most influential families in the city in the second half of the nineteenth century, chose instead to build on its rural borderland at Fortieth Street. Wade had been familiar with Cleveland since 1850, when he brought the telegraph to the city. In 1866 he moved his family to town from Columbus, choosing Euclid Avenue as the locale from which they would "not wish to move."[21] And here the family and subsequent generations stayed for nearly seven decades.

Father and son, both artists, jointly planned their residences, each at a cost of $200,000—an extraordinarily high sum in that postwar day—and surrounded them by vast landscaped gardens in keeping with the Downing ethos. The lavish interiors of parlors, drawing and reception rooms, and hallways were as much a product of the Wades' artistic visions as they were of architect and craftsmen. The rooms and halls were customized with gilt moldings and elaborate frescoes, becoming showcases for the Wade family's exquisite art collection acquired in world travels. Jeptha's third-floor ballroom doubled as his private picture gallery, and masterpieces by Reynolds, Turner, Renoir, and Monet lined the walls of the great hall and music room in

Figure 6. Randall and Jeptha H. Wade estates, 3903 and 3917 Euclid Avenue, 1865–66. Rendering in *Lake Atlas*, 1874.

Randall's house. His dining room was custom-designed around the gilded chairs and gold mirrors, and, so pleased was he with the effect, he exclaimed to his father that it "goes off in good style, *very nice*."[22] The Wades personally selected all furniture and carpets from the finest New York houses and designers, and ensured that each residence was mechanically *au courant* with such conveniences as central steam heating, running water, and gas fixtures. Each bedroom even adjoined a private bathroom, and a temperature-controlled wine cellar housed Jeptha's vintage collection.[23]

The street on which Wade chose tó build his estate was the home of many of the city's most prominent leaders and most opulent residences. Even so, had the Euclid Avenue story ended in the mid-1860s, it would not have been worthy of grand avenue fame. That coveted status was still being shaped, rising to its heyday in the post–Civil War decades. On Euclid Avenue, and throughout the country, the postwar period was exceptional for its buoyant prosperity and intense building activity. In just fifteen years, between 1865 and 1880, 130 new houses appeared on the avenue, more than doubling the size of the neighborhood.

Figure 7. John D. Rockefeller residence, 3920 Euclid Avenue, 1866–68, Simeon C. Porter, architect.

The mansard roof was the chief hallmark of the houses in the 1860s; it crowned country villas out on the eastern borderland around Seventieth Street as well as the urban townhouses built closer in. Among the most stately, if stylistically unremarkable, was the residence of John D. Rockefeller, who purchased a brick mansion designed by Cleveland architect Simeon C. Porter in 1868, two years before the twenty-nine-year-old founded the Standard Oil Company (Figure 7). Eleven years after settling into his residence, in 1879, Rockefeller bought the adjacent house and lot to create a two-acre estate with 230 feet of avenue frontage.[24] Rockefeller's mansion struck a high profile, for this southside residence commanded a prominent intersection and was sited uncharacteristically high on its deep, rolling grounds. It was also long identified with the ambitious endeavors of its nationally acclaimed owner.

Rockefeller was closer to being a native Clevelander than most of his neighbors—he had lived and worked in the city since age fifteen, and many of his family's deepest roots were planted in the community. Here he met and married Laura Spelman, a schoolteacher, in 1864, and started the oil refining business of Rockefeller & Andrews with Samuel Andrews in 1865 and then Standard Oil in 1870. Once he had embarked on his drive to consolidate and control the region's oil refineries, Rockefeller fast became known as a tough and often ruthless entrepreneur. At the same time, he did more than any other parishioner to support the Euclid Avenue Baptist Church, and did so out of a piety that appears genuine.[25]

Aside from their church activities, the Rockefellers socialized little with others on the avenue. They had a fondness for simple living, in contrast to many of their neighbors, and brought in private tutors for their four children. Rockefeller had only a few close friends, notably business partner Henry Flagler, who lived across the avenue and walked or rode with him to and from the office each day.[26] After a decade on the avenue, the family vacated the Euclid Avenue house for their 79-acre Forest Hill estate, four miles out in the country. Then in 1884, Rockefeller bought the family's New York City townhouse on Fifty-fourth Street at Fifth Avenue, and divided time between it and the Cleveland country house. Meanwhile the avenue residence stood as a grand mansion occupied only by a maid. Decades later, around the turn of the century, Rockefeller leased it as a sanitarium for alcoholics, which neighbors Edward A. Merritt disparaged as the "drunk cure establishment" and Homer Wade II, son of Randall Wade, dubbed the "liquor effect eliminator establishment."[27]

The oil mogul engendered little affection from most of his neighbors, or from other Clevelanders; instead he was regarded mostly with ire mixed with envy. Over the years, troubled by a tax dispute with the state and by bad press, Rockefeller forever lost his love for his adopted city. Paradoxically he maintained the avenue residence until his death in 1937, when it was promptly razed in accordance with his will.[28] The property was sold and redeveloped as a parking lot and gas station.

In the years before the residence was razed, many were struck by the disparity between its relatively unpretentious design and its owner's extraordinary affluence. The disparity was magnified when the house of the richest man in America was compared to others being built along the avenue in the postwar years, more lavish in their picturesque effect. The architects responsible for creating these

Figure 8. John and Clara Stone Hay residence (left), 1235 Euclid Avenue, 1875–76, Joseph Ireland, architect. Residences (right) of Amasa Stone, 1255 Euclid, and William Boardman, 1303 Euclid. Photograph, 1920s.

more dramatic mansions were Heard and Porter, who had dissolved their ten-year partnership in 1860, and New York emigre Joseph Ireland, who in 1865 opened an office in the industrial city. Their patrons, all prosperous businessmen, many of them active connoisseurs, shared credit for advancing the scale and style of architectural design along Euclid Avenue.

This sculptural elegance culminated in the 1870s and early 1880s in the form of a High Victorian Gothic indulgence. The most popular decorative features echoed the furniture of British designer Sir Charles Eastlake: spindled porch columns resembling legs of chairs, and geometrical cornice motifs reminiscent of ornamental borders on beds and mirrors. Patrons and architects also filled up interior spaces with "sincere" so-called Eastlake furniture, bookcases, and doors. "Sincerity" was the utmost design virtue. Eclecticism was so rampant that specific styles were sometimes impossible to identify. Patrons also devoted abundant resources to their grounds, which became outdoor museums for fanciful whims, taking on a furnished look with larger-than-life iron statuary of cherubs, goddesses, deer, and classical serpents.

Among the finest residences built in this spirit was the home of writer and diplomat John Hay, which distinguished itself by its luxurious gabled and traceried front (Figure 8). Designed by architect Ireland, it was built as a wedding present to John and Clara Stone Hay from Clara's father, railroad magnate Amasa Stone, and stood next door to the Stone home. Building of the connubial manse began within "an hour or so" of the couple's arrival from Manhattan in 1875, Hay reported to his friend Whitelaw Reid, and "ever since my ears have been full of the muffled click of the chisels of some half hundred workmen on the soft yellow stone."[29] Surely he exaggerated the size of the crew, industrious as the masons might have appeared. But then Hay enjoyed good drama and clearly the construction of his sandstone house captured his imagination. Father-in-law Stone, creator of decorative woodwork that he was, lavished upon his daughter and son-in-law's house the finest woodcarving and cabinetwork money could buy. He hired the talented German artisan John Herkomer, who was admired locally for his workmanship. In the 1870s and 1880s, the inflow of immigrant German and Scottish carpenters and masons, such as Herkomer, contributed to the skilled finery of the Hay house and others along the avenue and in Cleveland, as in other cities.[30]

John Hay was among the truly great figures who lived on Euclid. His blue-ribbon resume portrayed a man of venerable intellect and energy—the private secretary to President Abraham Lincoln, an editor of the *New York Tribune*, coauthor with John Nicolay of Lincoln's masterful biography, ambassador to Great Britain, and secretary of state under Presidents William McKinley and Theodore Roosevelt. By temperament he was very much the scholar; by profession he was the perfect diplomat—handsome, disarming, witty, brilliant, a charming cosmopolitan. Once married, he gave up his job at the *Tribune* and came to Cleveland to appease Clara's father and to write Lincoln's biography. As a man of relative leisure who was mildly amused by his newfound affluence, he became a wonderfully astute observer of Cleveland's glamorous society. This all began with the design and building of his own residence.

Hay carried on a long and lively correspondence with his sister-in-law Flora Stone, whom he adored from a safe distance and who was traveling abroad at this time, providing her with a closeup narrative of the house's construction. He happily described the west parlor to Flora as a "perfectly lovely" room, the best he had ever seen, and privately donned it "the Pavilion de Flore," meant as a not-so-subtle endearment to his sister-in-law. Meanwhile Hay seemed to value his alliance with architect Ireland. So enthusiastic was his involvement that he was cheered when he could present the architect with the drawing room mantelpiece two months ahead of schedule, enabling Ireland to design the room's wainscoting with this centerpiece in place. Moreover, John and Clara worked with their prominent New York interior designer, Herter Brothers, to select all fireplace mantels, carpets, and furniture to achieve the "sincere" but comfortable Eastlake ambience.[31]

SANDSTONE PILES, 1880-95

The picturesque front of the Hay residence was among a few that engaged such carpenter-like detail, adding a playful touch to the avenue's bold streetscape. Most of the residences of this period, rather, held to the more *serious* High Victorian manner. By the 1880s the sculptural touches that had first appeared in the late 1840s were now in full play, patterned after the buildings of eminent Eastern architects widely published and admired in the trade press. The light and angular demeanor of young Ireland's Gothic villa designs had evolved into the bolder, more masculine forms of a mature romantic architect. Over one hundred houses were built on Euclid Avenue in the fifteen years between 1881 and 1896; most were constructed of sandstone and most were designed in variations of the High Victorian Gothic or the Romanesque Revival style.

Ireland had favored the use of wood and stone to enhance the Hay house composition. But most other avenue architects and patrons at the time preferred a uniform family of masonry materials for both walls and ornament. The English-derived High Victorian manner changed all this. The use of the so-called "honest" building materials of stone and wood now prevailed, accented by a touch of carved wooden tracery. To turn out their designs, Cleveland architects—Levi T. Scofield, Joseph Ireland, the young partnership of Forest Coburn and Frank Barnum, and recently arrived Pennsylvania native George H. Smith—called on a large and growing field of local builders, painters, and craftsmen, most of whom had, within the decade, emigrated to the city from Ireland, Scotland, and England.

The houses built on Euclid Avenue in the 1880s were spectacular when compared to others going up in downtown Cleveland's finer neighborhoods, but modest when they stood beside the effusive statement of their neighbor Samuel Andrews. He retained the lesser-known local architect Walter Blythe, a former partner and son-in-law of Charles Heard, and began design of his mansion in 1882. Andrews, who was a former member of Rockefeller's close-knit Standard Oil clan, stood out against the avenue's self-consciously genteel landscape. His residence had the same impact. Like most of his peers, Andrews rose to affluence from near poverty; unlike them, he enjoyed a brash and pretentious way of life. He had developed the lucrative process to extract kerosene from crude oil, but in 1874 Rockefeller and Andrews parted over irreconcilable differences. He then went to work for neighbor Charles Otis, Sr., at the American Wire Company.[32]

Andrews was a thoroughly enigmatic character, and his life, like his personality, was filled with more questions than answers. An Englishman who had arrived in Manhattan in 1857, he clearly looked back across the Atlantic to his native land for inspiration in the style of his residence (Figure 9). One account claims that an English mansion Andrews knew from his boyhood was the model for Blythe's preliminary design. Plans were reportedly drawn up in London and sent to Cleveland, along with two dozen joiners, wood carvers, and other craftsmen. The thirty-room residence housed 18,000 square feet on three floors. Just to magnify the spectacle, it was dramatically set back 280 feet from the street and approached by a serpentine carriage drive (Figure 10). The mansion was also the first Cleveland residence with a basement-to-attic elevator, a convenience of only the wealthy in 1885. After three years of building and decorating, the Andrews family moved into their new home. For unknown rea-

Figure 9. Samuel Andrews residence, 3033 Euclid Avenue; preliminary design, Walter Blythe, architect. Rendering by Otto Kuetenik, c. 1882.

sons, they moved to New York City three years later, leaving the Euclid Avenue house vacant.[33] For all its haunting opulence, the Andrews residence was a catastrophe for its owners in its extravagant operations and costly maintenance. But also for its meaning: it was only a monument, not a home. The sandstone pile stood furnished but unoccupied for thirty years. No explanation at the time or since could account for Andrews's ambition to build such a fabulous palace and then leave it to ruin. In its most useful role, the house was immortalized as a dramatic stage set for three Hollywood-produced movies.[34]

The Andrews house symbolized a lost innocence that now characterized the residential neighborhood. Euclid Avenue had long since grown beyond its bucolic ambience. It was very much an urban city street, itself a linear stage set for large, expensive city houses. By the mid-1880s, the elaborate Romanesque Revival manner had captured the attention of most patrons, becoming the preeminent style on the avenue during the

Figure 10. Samuel Andrews residence, 3033 Euclid Avenue, 1882–85, Walter Blythe, architect. Photograph, 1889.

active building period of the 1880s and 1890s. Sandstone, the principal ingredient in the Romanesque recipe, was very fitting for the high style favored by Euclid Avenue patrons, for it was the source of one of Ohio's major industries; Cuyahoga County was the home to the largest stonecutting plant in the country, the Independence Stone Company, and the quarries near Independence were the main reserves for the sandstone shipped by the B&O Railroad to the East and around the Midwest.[35]

The fully mature neo-Romanesque style arrived on Euclid Avenue with the arrival in Cleveland in 1882 and 1883 of Boston architects Peabody & Stearns and Charles F. Schweinfurth, respectively. Such local architects as Scofield, Blythe, and the firm of Coburn & Barnum had already worked in the style, and may even have influenced these Eastern designers to some extent, but their arrival navigated a grander phase in which the best ideas nationally inspired the city's best architects.

Standard Tool Company president Charles W. Bingham tapped the East Coast architectural establishment when he hired Peabody & Stearns to design his avenue residence (Figures 11 and 12). Over the years, Bingham maintained a close association with this prominent firm, which designed his avenue house in 1882–83 and his Glenville country cottage in 1887–88. The talent apparent in the firm's work, as well as a mutual rapport, prompted Bingham to retain the architects again in the late 1890s to design extensive interior alterations and a wing and stable at the rear of the old Nathan Perry house, originally built in 1830 by Bingham's wife's great-grandfather. While the Bingham houses were the only residential commissions of

Peabody & Stearns in Cleveland, the firm's esteemed portfolio was distinguished by the many palatial residences on other grand avenues, the majority of the architects' private clients similar in stature to the Binghams of Cleveland.[36]

Quite possibly, Bingham introduced his neighbor, Sylvester T. Everett, to Peabody & Stearns' chief designer, Julius A. Schweinfurth, and his brother, Charles.[37] The senior Boston architects freely permitted their designer to take on outside jobs, thus enabling the Schweinfurth brothers to move their ad hoc practice to Cleveland in the spring of 1883 at the behest of one of the city's foremost bankers and railroad entrepreneurs. This was the beginning of a long and fruitful career on Euclid Avenue for Charles Schweinfurth (Figure 13). Everett had purchased the northeast corner of Fortieth Street across from the family homestead of his wife, Alice Wade, granddaughter of Jeptha Wade. Then he engaged Cleveland architect and sculptor Levi Scofield to draw up preliminary plans. But it soon became clear to Everett that Scofield could not meet his expectations. Having toured the European continent, and enjoying close ties with a distinguished array of the nation's business and political leaders, Everett was acquainted with many of the great works of contemporary art and architecture and was a demanding and well-versed patron. He called on the Schweinfurth brothers to see if they could produce a superior design. Their first rough sketches indicated to Everett that they could indeed "make a much more substantial looking house" than Scofield could turn out. Everett dropped the Cleveland architect, hired the Boston designers, and instructed the Schweinfurths to "go ahead as fast as possible with the work."[38]

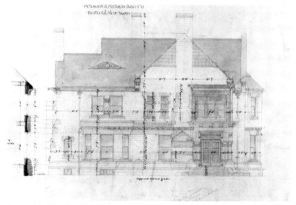

Figure 11. Charles W. Bingham residence, 2445 Euclid Avenue, Peabody & Stearns, architects. Original rendering of front elevation, 1883.

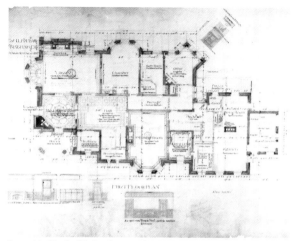

Figure 12. Charles W. Bingham residence, 2445 Euclid Avenue, Peabody & Stearns, architects. Original rendering of first-floor plan, 1883.

Figure 13. Charles F. Schweinfurth, architect. Photograph, not dated.

Figure 14. Sylvester T. Everett residence, 4111 Euclid Avenue, 1883–87, Charles F. and Julius Schweinfurth, architects. Photograph, 1917.

Figure 15. Sylvester T. Everett residence, 4111 Euclid Avenue, 1883–87. Moorish wishing-well room with inlaid tile mosaic, sandalwood paneling, and star-shaped fountain. Photograph, 1937.

Everett's Hummelstone mansion took over four years (1883–87) to design, construct, and furnish (Figures 14 and 15). The influence of Boston architect H. H. Richardson was to be seen in the strong, controlled emphasis on contrasting vertical and horizontal elements, the richly carved rounded windows and arches, and the polychromatic stonework. When his former Boston associates completed the Everett house, Richardson gave their design his "high commendation."[39] It was as grandiose as it was handsome. The mansion had over 20,000 square feet on three floors, with thirty-five principal rooms and forty fireplaces. Immense stained-glass windows inlaid with images of Richard the Lion-hearted and the Everett coat of arms dominated the great hall and broad stairway. The most unique room was surely that built for Everett's young wife Alice, who had a deathly fear of thunderstorms. Always protective of his wife's comfort, Everett ordered the architects to add a windowless and soundproofed sitting room to which she could flee during rough weather. For himself, Everett had the architects face the den fireplace with hand-painted tiles depicting twenty of his favorite Shakespearean plays—he was said to have memorized all of Shakespeare's major plays. So for a man who had grown up on a modest Trumbull County farm in a family of eleven children, he had achieved a distinction far exceeding even his own expectations. Alice Wade, however, twenty years her husband's junior, was quite accustomed to such elegance. She "expected everything but the moon" from Everett, according to their daughter, "and he nearly always could supply it."[40] Certainly he did so with their new home, which rivaled the splendid Wade residence in which she had been raised.

The Everetts' baronial pile, which some found forbidding and all viewed as awesome, was a legend in its time and widely believed to be among the most expensive homes in Cleveland. The Everett and Bingham families, who lived in their Euclid Avenue homes for over 35 years, together expanded the vision of grand

house design beyond the city's venue and, in so doing, introduced the stylistic bent of Richardsonian Romanesque to Cleveland. But not everyone who built a Romanesque mansion on Euclid Avenue sought to imitate the robust Richardsonian mold or retained Charles Schweinfurth to design it. Other patrons preferred the sculptural definition of a more subdued neo-Romanesque form. The enormous residence of Charles F. Brush, inventor of electric arc lighting, was one of the finest in this vein.

In 1887 Brush bought and demolished the former residence of Henry M. Flagler and retained architect George H. Smith to design a neo-Romanesque villa to take its place.[41] To no one's surprise, the inventor's home was the first in the city to be wired for electricity (Figure 16). And with a demeanor like the broad-shouldered, deep-chested Brush himself, who stood over six feet tall, the imposing house encompassed almost 40,000 square feet on three floors and towered over the avenue from its 160-foot landscaped vista. To the rear stood the largest windmill in the world, which generated the power to fuel the house's ten tons of storage batteries. It must have appeared in this late-nineteenth-century setting as the satellite dish does in late-twentieth-century backyards (Figure 17).

Figure 16. Charles F. and Mary Brush residence, 3725 Euclid Avenue, 1887–88, George H. Smith, architect.

Figure 17. Largest windmill in the world, built by Charles F. Brush in his Euclid Avenue backyard. Photograph, 1889.

Sharing the domestic enthusiasm of many of their neighbors, Charles and Mary Brush collaborated with Smith in the house's planning, especially for the interior. The main attraction stood in the main hall at the foot of the circular mahogany staircase: Brush's enormous pipe organ, which reached up three floors to the ballroom.[42] Brush closely supervised the work of the prolific Herter Brothers and the brilliant decorative artist Louis Tiffany, who designed all the lighting fixtures, stained-glass windows, transoms, and skylights.[43] Undoubtedly at Brush's request, Smith's design was a kind of revival showcase for a blend of the Romanesque and Renaissance styles. It is appropriate that this Renaissance man had such a house. He was a genius, with more than fifty inventions to his name. At age twenty-seven, he invented the first electric open-coiled dynamo. Within three years, in 1879, he threw a switch that dramatically illuminated Cleveland's Public Square with arc lamps and inaugurated electric streetlighting throughout the world. His was an invention that profoundly transformed the quality of urban life, chiefly because of his own facility in its use and promotion. He founded the Brush Electric Light and Power Company in 1881 to build central power stations and arc lamps for Cleveland and other major cities such as New York, Boston, Philadelphia, Baltimore, and San Francisco. The firm consolidated with Edison Electric in 1892 to form the General Electric conglomerate.[44]

Brush's ceaseless laboratory work was centered in the basement of his residence. Following his retirement in 1891, his home became his scientific headquarters; after the death of his wife, Mary, his research became his companion and his laboratory his retreat.[45] Few of Brush's neighbors could claim his affinity for the world of electrons and neutrons; just as few shared his preference in house style during the age of Richardson. Yet whatever the strain, the Romanesque in all its various forms remained the fashion of the day among Euclid Avenue patrons. In the 1890s the preeminent avenue architects Schweinfurth and Coburn & Barnum introduced yet another variation on the basic theme by emphasizing Tudor references—prominent gables, crenelated roofs, and slender, capped chimney stacks. Indeed, it was Schweinfurth, an avid collector of European patternbooks and medieval motifs, who brought the Tudor tendency to its highest level on the avenue. This was the style chosen by one of Schweinfurth's many demanding clients, banker and iron merchant David Z. Norton.

For Norton's avenue residence, Schweinfurth in 1897 drew up two design schemes, conceived to match the new wealth the patron had achieved as co-owner of Oglebay, Norton & Company. The architect's first plans presented an elegant rendition of the academic Adamesque, or neo-Federal manner, a style revived by leading architects in the late 1890s. Schweinfurth's genteel, high-style design showed lavish carved swags and classical ornament draping the principal facades. Nothing of its kind, so delicate and refined, had yet been built on Euclid Avenue, and Norton rejected the scheme.[46] Instead, this native Clevelander, attuned to the prevailing taste among his grand avenue neighbors, chose a more conventional sandstone house with Romanesque and Tudor motifs (Figure 18).

The corner residence proclaimed itself to the avenue by the imported Venetian lion statues that stood on either side of the arched doorway. This masculine theme was carried into the interior in the heavy use of dark wooden wall panels, thick ceiling beams, and raised doorway moldings (Figure 19). The "Napoleon Room,"

Figure 18. David Z. and Mary Norton residence, 7301 Euclid Avenue, 1897–98, Charles F. Schweinfurth, architect. Photograph, 1939.

Figure 19. David Z. and Mary Norton residence, 7301 Euclid Avenue, 1897–98. Main Hall. Photograph, 1939.

the finest chamber on the main floor, showcased David Norton's exquisite Napoleona collection and revealed his and his wife's fondness for the romance of chivalry. Medieval armored statues standing guard in the great hall reflected the same enthusiasm.[47] Upstairs, as was the custom in many Euclid Avenue houses, the master bedroom and private bath were at the front of the house overlooking the avenue and taking in the southern sun. The three children enjoyed the luxury of their own private rooms, and shared a bath among them.

The Nortons, cosmopolitan in their interests, thrived in their avenue residence. Having lived in only this city and on Euclid Avenue for decades, both David Norton and his wife, Mary—who was the daughter of Cleveland's first mayor, William B. Castle—were established figures in the city's downtown cultural and social life. Among the many fraternal and sports clubs

111

of which David was a fixture, he spent most of his leisure hours with his avenue cronies at the Union and University clubs and the Country and Castalia sporting clubs. Mary Norton, who was unique among her female peers for her schooling in Switzerland and at Vassar College, was founder of the Musical Arts Association and an officer of the Cleveland Institute of Music. Their sons, Robert and Laurence, exploited the leisurely pleasures of their parents' wealth and became the wardens of the family home after their parents' deaths in 1928. In 1937, forty years after the Nortons first moved in, the residence was one of only eight private homes remaining on the avenue.[48]

In their day, the neo-Romanesque houses defined the architectural theme of this grand avenue. But after the turn of the century, patrons showed diminished enthusiasm for the romance of Romanesque forms and, instead, a heightened interest in the more recently revived Renaissance and classical styles. This ushered in a new era in residential design on Euclid Avenue. The street itself entered a new era. It was during this period that the long and delicate balance between the grand residential avenue and the commercial main street tipped to favor commerce.

IMPERIAL ELEGANCE, 1895-1910

Downtown Cleveland had become a major city by 1895—active, dense, and populous. Euclid Avenue was the very heart of this pulse as the city's premier residential street and also, by this date, its best business address. Commercial blocks, four and five stories tall, had first gone up on the avenue in the 1850s around Public Square. Over the years, offices, stores, and the streetcar line inched up the avenue, reducing the early neighborhood to just a pleasant memory. As the new century dawned, retailers, showrooms, and small industries moved in to capitalize on the crowds of people, carriages, and trolley cars. Downtown businesses maneuvered for a visible foothold on the city's grandest promenade (Figure 20).

These commercial pressures prompted Euclid Avenue residents to think about the civic function of their street as both a place of private homes and a parklike boulevard developed according to a unified vision. They manifested their interests in several ways, most obviously in their protests against commerce, transit, and high property assessments. Yet a more conservative, even subtle, response appeared in the shifting architectural preference of those who built on the avenue around the turn of the century. If

Figure 20. Euclid Avenue looking east from Ninth Street, 1898.

Figure 21. Ambrose Swasey residence (left), 7808 Euclid Avenue, and Worcester R. Warner residence (right), 7808 Euclid Avenue, 1891–92, Richard Morris Hunt, architect.

the Romanesque spirit portrayed the avenue in its finest hour, the imperial classicism of the following decade, 1900 to 1910, would come to symbolize the neighborhood's peak of elegance and the beginning of its fall.

For Euclid Avenue patrons, who advanced more cautiously beyond their Romanesque allegiance, this revision in architectural taste occurred at a time when house building was ebbing and stylistic changes were magnified. In the fifteen years between 1895 and 1910, only sixty residences were built on Euclid Avenue, far fewer than in earlier decades. The architects were also largely a new group, a younger generation well-equipped to respond to the avenue's clientele, thanks to their professional training in the classics, most at the Massachusetts Institute of Technology.[49] Meanwhile, Schweinfurth, the neo-Romanesque master, remained in the forefront by shifting his design style to respond to the changing fashion and the tastes of his Euclid Avenue clients. Some patrons bypassed local talent altogether to call on the services of prestigious out-of-town architects—now a customary practice on this grand avenue as on others—Richard Morris Hunt and McKim, Mead & White of New York, and Peabody & Stearns of Boston. This "gradual invasion" by designers "whose standing and training are the best," according to architect J. Milton Dyer, who became well-established among Euclid Avenue patrons during this period, was the most uplifting influence for local architects.[50]

Indeed, in 1891, six years before Norton had rejected Schweinfurth's proposed neoclassical design, Ambrose Swasey and Worcester R. Warner advanced the avenue's artistic standards when they retained Hunt to design their adjacent houses (Figure 21). Warner & Swasey, both engineers and friends and business associates since age nineteen, were fairly modest, genial characters and prudent in their personal expenditures. Hunt, by contrast, born into the monied elite of old New York, was admired as a prolific and talented designer of the Eastern establishment. The choice of Hunt by the more frugal partners, then, might have appeared a surprising one except for the fact that Hunt and Warner had previously worked together on major building projects in Cleveland and Washington, D.C.[51] Similar to much of his residential work at this time, the details of Hunt's modest city houses for Warner and Swasey were inspired by the English Tudor and early French Renaissance periods. In contrast to the architect's Vanderbilt and Astor Fifth Avenue mansions, however, these Euclid Avenue townhouses lacked grandiose pretensions, as did their patrons. Hunt created the two residences to be viewed as one composition, symmetrical about a central driveway and Warner's observatory to the rear.

Independent and yet related, the two houses reflected their owners' attitudes toward one another. Warner and Swasey's fifty-year partnership, which began back in Exeter, New Hampshire, grew into an "intimate business association," in Warner's words. A decade before they built their avenue residences, they had come to Cleveland together from Chicago to establish their engineering firm of Warner & Swasey, an international leader in the design and manufacture of telescopes and astronomical instruments. The partners' scientific and business successes were no accident: each man was a talented mechanical engineer with an eye for invention and profit. Their best-known commissions were the huge telescopes for the Lick and Yerkes Observatories.[52]

Warner, like so many of his contemporaries after the turn of the century, left his city residence for the leisurely life in the country, moving after two decades in 1911 to Tarrytown-on-the-Hudson nearby the estate of his old friend, John D. Rockefeller. But Swasey stayed on long after Warner's departure and the death of his wife, Lavinia, in 1913.[53] As an old man, in 1937, he observed how his own avenue had been changed by the progressive age in which he lived. It was cause for pride as well as chagrin. At age ninety-one, he returned to his parents' farm in Exeter to die amidst the peaceful countryside of his childhood. Two years later his Euclid Avenue house was razed, the symbolic close of his and Warner's remarkable partnership.

The Samuel Mather family was another among the venerable institutions of the avenue—Samuel, a prolific philanthropist and chairman of Pickands, Mather & Company, and Flora, his wife, a leading benefactress of numerable social welfare institutions. Samuel, who was the son of one of the Connecticut Land Company's largest shareholders, had moved to Euclid Avenue with his parents in 1865 at age fifteen. Flora, daughter of Amasa and Julia Stone, was born and raised there. After 1891, once their Schweinfurth-designed summer house in Bratenahl was completed, they spent only about half the year in their avenue residence, the old Amasa Stone homestead. Even so, Flora and Samuel Mather's ties with the avenue remained as strong as ever. Such commitment was cause for them to decide in 1907 to build a house of their own making; Samuel also still enjoyed his daily half-mile walk to his downtown office. They commissioned Charles Schweinfurth to plan their American classic residence, an impressive Tudor Gothic design for house and grounds that signified their view of the grand avenue and the family's place on it. By this time, iron ore merchant Mather was recognized as the architect's chief promoter, having worked with one another on several projects.[54] His choice of architect was therefore not at all surprising; the fact that he decided to build a $3 million residence on Euclid Avenue as late as 1907 was much more so.[55] But Mather was not one to accept passively the momentum of commercial change that was bearing down on the residential neighborhood. Rather, he sought to educate others by the force of his own actions. He thus bought the old Jacob Perkins house (1853), demolished it, and retained Schweinfurth to design a new mansion in its place (Figures 22 and 23).

This turned out to be Schweinfurth's largest residential commission and the largest house ever built on Euclid Avenue. The architect's composition covered two-and-a-half acres of formal gardens, squash courts, an eight-car garage, and the forty-three-room residence. The house, set back against an expansive 600-foot lawn, was the centerpiece of this highly structured scheme, deliberately measured in the best Renaissance fashion. It was a triumphant display of architecture, landscape, and civic art. For Schweinfurth, the Mather commission represented the climax of his artistic development: it combined his natural talent in the anticlassical dialect with his developed skill in academic forms.

At the same time Schweinfurth was at work on the Mather residence, the architect was also in the midst of designing the magnificent Trinity Cathedral, four blocks west on Euclid Avenue. The two buildings shared common traits in the leaded windows, stone battlements, and Tudoresque archways—delicacies that he perfected over the years through his many trips to Spain and England. Even in the early 1890s, when Schweinfurth was still preoccupied with the Romanesque, Cleveland *Plain Dealer* reporter S. J. Kelly, who visited the architect at his studio, marveled at how thoroughly the designer's mind dwelt on days of chivalry, cloistered monks, and high arched churches of medieval times."[56] His architectural signature, if nothing else, was drawn from the days of chivalry.

Schweinfurth had another celebrated trait that endeared him to clients and gave pause to his contractors: he was a stubborn perfectionist in the execution of his plans and the choice of materials. Within the trade, Schweinfurth was revered and feared as "a terror to contractors who varied a

Figure 22. Samuel and Flora Mather residence, 2605 Euclid Avenue, 1907–12, Charles F. Schweinfurth, architect. Formerly a portion of the site of Jacob Perkins residence. Photograph, 1932.

Figure 23. Samuel and Flora Mather residence, 2605 Euclid Avenue, 1907–12. Backyard showing squash courts at left rear.

hairs [*sic*] breadth from his designs." In one of his more dramatic outbursts, in 1915, he axed to destruction a gold leaf ceiling in the making in the Cuyahoga County Courthouse. The workman on the job, surprised and fiercely angered, struck Schweinfurth across his face with a monkey wrench and blinded him in one eye. Years later, young Philip Mather asked his father which of the architect's eyes was the glass one, and his father replied, "Look for the gleam of human kindness; that is his glass eye."[57] The architect's volatile temperament, however, always protected his clients' best interests and was little hindrance in his fine camaraderie with the Mathers.

Samuel and Flora personally shaped the original house plans with Schweinfurth. Flora's study was located beyond the first-floor public rooms, adjacent to an elevator for her use. Then there was Samuel's billiard room and den. On the second floor, the patrons' spacious bedrooms, joined by marble baths, looked out to the avenue, while the children's rooms and guest bedrooms faced the rear gardens. Seven servants' rooms were on the third floor, as was a ballroom that seated three hundred. Construction began in 1909. Three years later, in the autumn of 1912, the house was finally ready for the Mather family.[58] Yet the family had changed in important ways since its new home was first conceived as a public reception hall and private sanctuary. Flora Stone Mather, gracious matron and mother of four, never saw her contribution to the avenue rise above ground level. She died of breast cancer at the age of fifty-seven.[59] Her daughter Constance became the lady of the house, taking over her mother's responsibilities as hostess for her father's social gatherings. Samuel Mather, sixty-two years old in 1912, was recognized as one of Cleveland's most expansive corporate capitalists: the officer of at least nine companies and a director of more than two dozen iron, banking, and transportation concerns.

Thanks to his wealth, and his respect for the building arts, he made an indelible mark on the city through the building programs he spearheaded. The value of his work endures almost a century later, as most of the projects he sponsored are still standing. His own avenue residence is one. It passed to the Cleveland Institute of Music when he died in 1931, then to the Cleveland Automobile Club in 1940. The state acquired the property for Cleveland State University in 1969 and restored the residence in 1978.[60]

With their celebration of European roots, the Mathers and other avenue residents also rediscovered the classic symbols of their own New World culture. Ironically, the neo-Federal and Academic Classical residences built

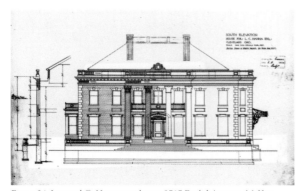

Figure 24. Leonard C. Hanna residence, 2717 Euclid Avenue, McKim, Mead & White, architects. Formerly a portion of the site of Jacob Perkins residence. Original rendering of south front elevation, 1902.

during the grand avenue's final decades were designed in a genre similar to those of the avenue's first decades, though they were clearly built on a much grander scale. Leonard C. Hanna, brother of political mastermind Marcus A. Hanna, even went so far as to commission the famed New York firm of McKim, Mead & White in 1901 to design his new residence (Figure 24). The mansion was a stunning example of the sumptuous high-style neo-Federal manner, with its two-story portico graced with fluted columns and rooftop balustrade. The patron exercised no apparent reserve, which, in retrospect, is astonishing in view of the late period in which he built and the house's proximity to the avenue's expanding commercial district.

Hanna, who took over leadership of the M. A. Hanna Company after his brother's death in 1904, knew McKim, Mead & White's work in Washington and New York, just as his urban establishment friends and colleagues were among their clientele. He undoubtedly brought the firm to his hometown of Cleveland to bestow upon its grand avenue, through his own residence, some of the same artistic splendor the firm had created in New York, Washington, and Boston. The Hanna·residence, its grounds landscaped by Julius A. Schweinfurth, who was then a chief designer in McKim, Mead & White's Manhattan office, was completed in 1904. Within fifteen years the Hanna family left Euclid Avenue for the serenity and beauty of the lakefront, and turned the house over to the Cleveland Museum of Natural History.[61]

A Grand Tradition

Entrepreneur Anthony Carlin commissioned the last house on Euclid Avenue, constructed in 1910–12, marking the end of the age of elegant building. The real legacy of Carlin's house, though, was that it was also the last residence to be occupied in the avenue's grand tradition. The patron's son John and his wife, who lived there after the senior Carlin had died, remained on the avenue as long as possible—until the noise, traffic, and soot became unbearable. The last residents memorialized their departure in 1950 by throwing the notorious "last dinner dance," a formal farewell party for Euclid Avenue. The Carlins and their guests were commemorating the most genial ritual that had occurred hundreds of times in hundreds of Euclid drawing rooms over more than a hundred years.[62]

The same fresh wealth that financed the building of the homes defined the social life of its residents. This new money created a fluid society that welcomed newcomers and was less tied to the rigid observances that molded the established domains of "proper" Boston and "old" New York. Since Cleveland had only really begun to prosper in the 1840s and 1850s, it was without an entrenched elite tradition in the post–Civil War decades. The families of Euclid Avenue created this tradition. And while Fifth Avenue's grand dame Mrs. Astor led New York society and Prairie Avenue's McCormicks and Fields presided over Chicago, a fraternity of people, most of whom lived on Euclid Avenue, embodied Cleveland high society. The visual continuity of the long street no doubt concealed differences among the various households, yet there was much that bound these personalities together in a common life. Indeed, camaraderie seeded this linear neighborhood and perpetuated it over time (Figure 25).

Over the decades, intermarriages, family friendships, social affairs and clubs, and front-porch meanderings knit this society together, as they did the smaller, divergent groups within it. Most everyone knew everyone else, at least casually, and each family belonged informally to at least one of the many coteries that distinguished one block from the next. And it is not surprising that if a Mather, Wade, Bingham, or Norton lived on one street—even in one house—for decades and through multiple generations, he or she would be bonded,

Figure 25. *The Perils of Society*, movie playbill, 1916.

for better or worse, with his or her neighbors and rooted in the pace and patterns of the place. Because the grand avenue itself loomed so large among these people, their lives were oriented outward to the street and their visibility on it. It was a picture window on their world.

Most Euclid Avenue households were large, active places, as were most of the homes on the nation's grand avenues. They doubled as hostelries for visiting relatives and friends, social centers for intimate and gala dinners and dances and concerts, and domiciles of the families—often extending to include married children, grandchildren, in-laws, and other distant relatives.[63] A total of eight people lived in a "typical" avenue residence in the postwar decades, including live-in servants. In a time when all meals were eaten at home and hand-drawn hot tubs supplemented central plumbing, and kerosene room heaters were indispensable for such voluminous rooms, servants were the linchpins in the smooth operation of both mansions and families.

After midcentury, few Euclid Avenue households were without a cast of servants. Over the decades, the number and native origins of the servants changed along with the wealth of the families and the complexion of the city's foreign-born population, most of them Irish or German immigrants.[64] Most households had at least one man, who was the family's coachman, gardener, and chief butler. Two or three female domestics, properly clad in starched uniforms, tended the family's cooking, housekeeping, errands, and children, really running these houses. The butler or cook was chief of the internal hierarchy and responsible for managing the staff and arranging menus and schedules with the lady of the house.

The relations between family members and their servants encompassed the full spectrum of emotions, from affection to indifference to insolence. Housekeepers who virtually became members of the family were far fewer than those who were employed only one or two years and became a source of discord. At one end of the spectrum, Martha (Mrs. Joseph) Perkins enjoyed the "warmest affection" from her housekeepers because she took care of their comfort and happiness. Flora Stone Mather, however, felt beset by an incompetent maid and a troublemaking nursemaid; Mrs. Mather concluded that it would be less work to take care of the children herself than to referee quarrels among her housekeepers.[65] In spite of these internal dramas, Euclid Avenue servants enjoyed a good deal of freedom to come and go as they pleased. In most of the houses built before 1880, the servants' bedrooms were located on the same floor as the family's in the rear section; in later residences they were up on the third floor, along with the ballroom. Only a few housekeepers enjoyed the privacy of a small house at the back of the property.[66]

A group portrait of each Euclid Avenue home does not add up to a uniform set of values or just one vision of domestic life on the avenue. The diversity among generations and families made life interesting and kept the avenue a lively place. It was still a neighborhood, though, connected by four miles of a continuous processional of grandeur, one that families recognized they were a part of, whether they lived down around Twenty-first Street or up at Eighty-ninth Street. Just as the protocol of society respected certain conventions, so too did daily life. Glimpses into avenue homes portray a picture of both the banal and glamorous, taking in a full array of rituals from daily trips to the market to evening soirees and dinner dances. Food, drink, and good cheer were emblazoned across the culture of this grand avenue, as in other wealthy households around the country. To consume it, digest it, and savor it suggested that the rituals of hospitality were carefully minded to keep an evening an orderly event.

Afternoon teas were a favorite ritual, some being informal at-homes, where anyone could stop by, while others were by invitation only. Out-of-towner John Hay, the great diplomat and consummate writer, was accorded a royal welcome when he brought his new wife, Clara Stone, back to her native avenue in 1875. Hay, not one to buck the pageantry of tradition nor miss the opportunity to observe social nuances in action,

Figure 26. Coaching day. Four-in-Hand Club preparing to depart for a ride in the country. Charles A. Otis, Jr., residence (left), 3436 Euclid Avenue. Edward A. Merritt residence (right), 3424 Euclid Avenue.

soon became acclimated to his neighbors' love of socializing over tea and pastries.[67] But he could not understand how the neighborhood could eat so much and yet stay so healthy.

The fit constitutions of many avenue residents may partially be attributed to their extensive outdoor activities—gardening, walking, gaming, or driving about (Figure 26). Carriage drives and sleigh rides along the avenue, through the parks and further out into the countryside, were a universal favorite. During the second half of the nineteenth century, families, friends, and lovers spent many a balmy evening or weekend afternoon in refreshing outings. Driving was a source of calm for some and hearty sport for others. But the families' love for the horse and carriage quickly gave way to the motorized vehicle when it appeared on the scene in the 1890s. These affluent families avidly acquired the latest models for their use and play, as fast as the dealers could roll them out on the showroom floors.

The exhibitionist traits apparent in the equestrian and architectural enthusiasms of Euclid Avenue families also revealed themselves in their savoir-faire in formal affairs. The extravagance that others noted, and some criticized, simply reflected a joy for formal celebrations. These families took the greatest pleasure—and invested

Figure 27. Dickens party, *Bleak House* dress-up, 1889.

the most social energy—in dinner parties and receptions. Dance lists for 700 guests in the 1890s were not unheard of. These sumptuous evenings took full advantage of the opulent residences—from the spacious entrance hall, up the sweeping staircase, to the grand ballroom on the third floor. With so many social events to attend, hosts and hostesses staged many a theme party, fantastic affairs in which all guests dressed up in costume. It is no coincidence that these were also all the rage back East. In this Western city of restrained personalities, such frivolity was repeated time and again—a Southern cake walk, a Dickensonian dress-up, a baby party with waiters serving champagne in nursing bottles (Figure 27).[68]

Just as animated group rituals bonded this neighborhood, so did the exclusive city and sports clubs and fraternal orders, many headquartered right on Euclid Avenue. To these Clevelanders, and their social counterparts in New York or Chicago or wherever, the "Club" was part of the lifeblood of their street. For these liberal-minded Clevelanders, who took pleasure in diversity, there was a place for every passion, and every group had its place. Each club—the Union, the University, the Four-in-Hand, the Tavern, the Rowfant—deepened the ties and extended the geographic boundaries of Euclid Avenue society. For this life of grandeur, the avenue was as much an institution of social people as it was a panorama of residences. And yet personal pleasures, as great as they might have been, would not deplete the families' civic-minded pursuit to bring pleasure and improvement to others in the city.

The energy that residents of Euclid Avenue invested in the larger Cleveland community in fact exceeded that reserved for their own recreation. They had not only the wealth and community pride—and the women

Figure 28. University Circle, c. 1940.

the luxury of leisure time—necessary to direct major philanthropic and cultural endeavors, but collectively they possessed a deep evangelical spirit that appeared genuine by its products. Born out of pious New England roots, these Clevelanders were as generous on behalf of others' well-being as they were selfish about their own. They appreciated the fact that they had the means to give something back to the community from which they had prospered so handsomely. Early in his career, Rockefeller stated, "I believe it every man's duty to get all he honestly can, and to give all he can."[69] This solid civic pride was one of the few beliefs the oil magnate shared with his fellow neighbors. Euclid Avenue men and women led the way in consistently contributing their time, energy, and money to the development of the city's civic, religious, educational, and charitable institutions.

They built their greatest legacy at the eastern end of the grand avenue, the magnificent cultural park around University Circle (Figure 28). The ambitions and tastes that shaped this cultural park's growth during the late nineteenth and early twentieth centuries were chiefly those of particular Euclid Avenue patrons and benefactors who gave their collections, money, and management to the Cleveland Museum of Art, the Cleveland Orchestra, the Cleveland Institute of Music, Western Reserve Historical Society, and Case Western Reserve University. Jeptha Wade was among the chief benefactors, amassing and landscaping the nucleus of this area, 82-acre Wade Park, then giving it to the city in 1892. Wade and other patrons saw University Circle as not just a socially desirable playground, a pleasant educational amenity in the park, but also as good business for the city. The creation of this campus-in-the-park was a natural extension of Euclid patrons' vision of their avenue as a civic processional. Euclid Avenue alone, a shaded linear landscape connecting the Public Square with University Circle, and the open country beyond, had become the megastructure of the city's urban landscape.[70]

THE FALL OF CLEVELAND'S RESIDENTIAL PROMENADE, 1910-50

By the mid-1890s, this grand avenue reached its zenith: more than 260 residences lined the linear landscape between Ninth and Ninetieth Streets, six times the forty-five that stood there a half-century before. But over the next fifteen years, progressive forces weakened the bonds that shaped the social and architectural neighborhood. Cleveland "had but one Euclid Avenue," architectural critic I. T. Frary eulogized in 1918, "no other street could take its place." But by then, he realized, it was too late to redeem the glory of the past; the progressive forces were too great and well advanced to resurrect the pride that had been at the heart of residents' vision through the decades.[71] By 1921, only 130 houses were still standing, and in 1950 the last family left Euclid to make its home in the Shaker Heights suburbs. The Carlin's last dinner dance drew down the curtain once and for all.

The collective impact of traffic and transit lines on the avenue, commercial development pressures, extraordinarily high property values, and the spread of nearby low-income neighborhoods led to the decline of the residential neighborhood between 1910 and 1950. Through these years, avenue residents became less and less devoted to their once unassailable allegiance to the monumental grand avenue vision. This changing attitude, consciously or unconsciously, recognized that progress—represented by industry and commerce, ironically, from their own business enterprise—would and probably should shape the future development of the downtown area. These affluent residents were now quite frankly willing to move beyond the city's center to their new residential havens in the Heights and along the lake shore.

The downtown business district that emerged around Public Square in the 1860s and 1870s had continued to prosper and expand toward the growing eastern residential areas. By the mid-1890s, the length between the Square and Ninth Street was solidly built up with retail arcades and large stone and brick office buildings. Whether a Clevelander's interest was in business, banking, shopping, the theater, or a hotel, this urban district had it all. Mass transit officials did their part too, relentlessly lobbying to run the street railway between Ninth and Fortieth Streets—the forbidden length known as Millionaires' Row. Thanks to the impetus of populist mayor Tom Johnson, who lived on the avenue and had made his fortune in street railway consolidations, they had installed electric street cars along the Euclid line by 1889.[72] Not to be outdone, however, avenue residents petitioned the city in 1896 to designate Euclid a boulevard, to integrate the avenue into Cleveland's park system and control its use by a city park-and-boulevard commission. Their intent was to halt advancing commercialization in the residential neighborhood, to preserve the principle of the country in the city.[73]

After a good deal of debate, the city council adopted the boulevard plan in 1897. But it was a close vote, twelve in favor and ten opposed.[74] The council's endorsement turned out to be a hollow victory for Euclid Avenue residents and the park commission. The city failed to take even the first step to commence work on the public project. In the meantime, a majority of Clevelanders and some council members continued to demand streetcar access along the most direct route between the city's center and the eastern suburbs, to wit, Euclid Avenue. The boulevard plan had become a political football. All efforts to move forward were blocked. After three years, in 1900, the council responded to the voice of its constituency and unanimously rescinded the park commission's control of the avenue.[75] The boulevard plan was filed away deep in the city's archives.

Within two years of the repeal, however, Mayor Johnson appointed the now well-known Group Plan Commission to create a grand mall surrounded by major public buildings (Figure 29). Even if it was more grandiose than the park-and-boulevard plan, the mayor, a vigorous advocate of municipal facilities for the masses, promoted the idea for its public merits. The Chamber of Commerce and local AIA chapter, who financed and had promoted the project since the mid-1890s, endorsed it on its ceremonial merits. In point of fact, many of the Chamber members who now backed the Group Plan were among the very avenue residents who had led the park-and-boulevard campaign five years before. For all constituencies, it was viewed as an orderly response to apparent chaotic urban expansion.

The esteemed designers brought in by the city— Daniel Burnham of Chicago and Arnold Brunner and John Carrère of New York—expanded their Cleveland clients' vision of monumental civic design to encompass the entire city. Burnham recommended that the outlying parks be incorporated into the scheme, specifically via the main processional connecting these parks: Euclid Avenue. Under a new guise, the failed boulevard plan was revived.[76] The 1903 Cleveland Group Plan was the first so-called City Beautiful plan in the country to be enacted after the 1901 McMillan Plan in Washington, D.C. While the unsuccessful Euclid boulevard plan had attempted to realize just this, the Cleveland Group Plan's successful implementation stemmed from its stated public purpose. Its success was also due to the caliber of its designers and the political power of its exponents, notably the mayor's office and the Chamber of Commerce.

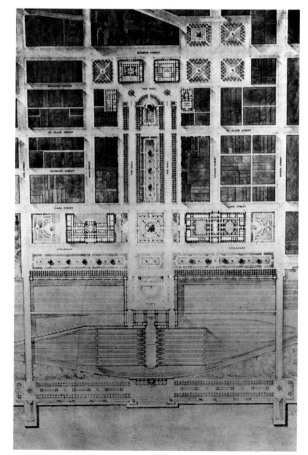

Figure 29. Cleveland Group Plan, 1903. Euclid Avenue and Public Square (top); the Mall and proposed Union Station along lakefront (bottom).

In spite of these efforts, Euclid Avenue remained without peer in its appeal to commercial interests. Such posh retailers as Halle Brothers had located on the avenue as early as the 1880s with an eye for capitalizing on the prestigious address and its affluent clientele. The soaring value of avenue property confirmed this appeal and dimmed the prospects of future residential growth.[77] The streetcar magnates, always at the ready, played directly into the hands of business and the city tax collector. In 1890 the East Cleveland Street Railroad petitioned the city council to lay tracks along the entire street. The proposal was supported by a majority of the affected property owners, mostly businesses, but was adamantly opposed by the Committee of Euclid Avenue Property Owners, mostly residents—Charles Bingham, Charles Brush, Leonard Hanna, and Samuel Mather, among others.[78] At issue was the redefinition of Euclid Avenue, to recognize its crucial role in the city's expansion. Businesses and elected city officials urged change. Residents, steeped in long-term commitment to their exclusive homes and grand avenue, defended the status quo. Within seven years, however, compelling pressures by commerce and transit interests overwhelmed the resistance of a diminishing and weakened residential community. In 1915 an electric street railway ran along the full length of the avenue.[79] This was a critical moment in the life of Euclid Avenue.

In truth, other factors besides the street railway were disrupting the residential neighborhood. New commercial and institutional buildings were dramatically reshaping the scale of the street as the avenue came to be recognized as the premier center of commerce, culture, and institutional life. Now, as commercial demand for prime property increased in downtown Cleveland, as the technology of mass transit and the private automobile made travel to prosperous residential areas outside the city easier, and as industrial pollution and an emerging poor neighborhood two blocks away made for a less attractive living environment in the central city, Euclid's stature as Cleveland's grand avenue fell.[80] It was no longer the pleasant place to live that it once was, especially for families accustomed to privacy amidst elegant, countrified surroundings.

By the mid-1920s, a number of the magnificent houses on the avenue had been sold and subdivided into rental apartments. For those residents who remained, they disliked the downgraded property as much as their new neighbors. This presumably entered into the thinking of Charles Brush and John Rockefeller, who stipulated that their houses were to be razed immediately after they died; they shuddered at the thought of multiple families occupying their personal havens. For these men and their former neighbors, their commitment to living on the avenue, previously unshakable, now faltered. Those families that remained met with another adverse force after the turn of the century, this one a real drain on their wealth. City officials uniformly ratcheted up real estate taxes 200 percent between 1900 and 1910, and 300 to 500 percent over the next decade.[81] These were affluent people, to be sure, some even millionaires, but such a tax burden became too onerous and simply unacceptable. Assessments depreciated some during the economic depression in the 1930s—most of the value was in the land—but not enough.[82] Residents had a final response: move off the avenue, raze their houses, and sell the land. A number of residents donated or sold their homes to tax-exempt, philanthropic institutions. By 1938 only four families remained.

The community of shared interests that was centered around the avenue waned as the street's elegance gradually disappeared. Yet these families did not leave with the melancholy that subsequent generations felt in looking back. The patrons of Euclid Avenue, from the early decades to the last, were on the leading edge in all they did. They were as progressive in business as they were in the architectural drama of their residences and where they chose to live. In establishing the new enclaves in Bratenahl, the Heights, Wickliffe, and Willoughby, they deliberately and increasingly chose to disperse their energies and capital in other places rather than maintaining a singular presence on the avenue. For most, the automobile bridged the miles between Public Square and their enclaves out east. And while they abhorred congestion on their own street, they enthusiastically embraced the auto for their personal use: it enabled them happily to choose the comforts of nonurban living and commute to their downtown offices, clubs, churches, and shops.[83]

EPILOGUE: THE RISE OF CLEVELAND'S MAIN STREET, 1910-60

The physical transformation of Euclid Avenue in the twentieth century occurred gradually over five decades, just as the creation of the grand avenue had taken shape in the nineteenth century. The difference now, though, was an absence of a common vision. The new high-rise bank and office buildings appeared to be designed in isolation from the world around them. The modern builders gave little apparent thought to repairing the world around them or building a new one.[84] Euclid Avenue "is the visual testament to the unwillingness of people to work together for mutual advantages," exclaimed the *Architectural Forum* staff writer in 1959.[85] What an interesting counterpoint to testimonials by residents a century before. But after decades of seeking to create a linear showcase, avenue patrons had succeeded *too* well by the early 1900s in creating a pleasure ground open to all. It had become the downtown main street, the geographic center of the city, and the hub of Clevelanders' daily lives (Figure 30).

By the end of World War II in 1945, a number of tax-exempt institutions, which did not have to pay property taxes and, anyway, were at the mercy of such beneficence as former Euclid Avenue families could provide, moved into the mansions that remained. The avenue by now had gained an institutional signature. And of

Figure 30. Euclid Avenue looking east from Fourteenth Street, 1940s.

Figure 31. Demolition of Leonard C. Hanna residence, 2717 Euclid Avenue, 1958.

course there were the Union Club, the University Club, and the eleven Christian churches standing along the Avenue. Had the city's institutional life played a primary role in the politics and commerce of Cleveland, as it did in such capital cities as Washington, D.C., and Richmond, Virginia, these remaining residences might have been protected by a renewed monumental stature. But the nonprofit institutions of Cleveland's Euclid Avenue, while honored for their social value, took a backseat to private capital and industry. Thus when city officials in 1949 were laying out a massive new highway system to absorb the wartime employment boom and traffic gridlock, they red-lined Euclid Avenue around Twenty-second Street—the once glorious central parade ground—as one of seven radials feeding into the new innerbelt.[86] Between 1950 and 1959, the city seized and demolished thirty mansions, for all practical purposes, disposable assets in the way of civic progress. The mass leveling gutted what little remained of the former neighborhood (Figure 31). It was the grand avenue's final fall.

The innerbelt, opened in 1960, gave rise to a spurt of new hotel and office development, an uneven collection of glass-walled structures. Yet beyond the interchange there were mostly rooming houses, filling stations, lunch counters, parking lots, and deteriorating houses and grounds. No architectural landscape here, certainly no grand avenue. The street that had been "the pride and very backbone" of the city, journalist James Lister of *The Clevelander* reported, had become a "honky-tonk." Another reproach in 1965, by architect Edward Durrell Stone, called the former grand avenue "a disgrace."[87] Thanks only to the strength of family ties, the legacy of Euclid Avenue has survived in its downtown clubs, churches, and cultural and philanthropic institutions. Withal, the seven houses that stand at this writing are glorious postscripts of Euclid Avenue's historic grandeur.

Chapter Five

PRAIRIE
Avenue
Chicago, Illinois

Late-twentieth-century eyes might well perceive the entire Prairie Avenue episode as a massive case of Second City Syndrome. Under the influence of this malady, Chicagoans praise themselves with faint damns, as when a turn-of-the-century booster bragged that his city had "more miles of railroad, more vessel tonnage, more freight, larger parks, dirtier streets, a sootier atmosphere, a more malodorous river, more gamblers, more good things, more bad things, than any other city."[1] The statements are true, more or less, and just to make sure, many of them include words like "perhaps" and "probably." A hearer is usually brought up short, however, and suspects too much protesting: why make a superlative of a shortcoming? The speaker may merely be compensating for not being first or best or New York, but the suspicion is aroused that the greater the superlative, the more real, or at least the more deeply felt, the shortcoming.

The street called Prairie Avenue and the people who lived there in the last quarter of the nineteenth century garnered an inordinate share of these jingoistic self-deprecations. "Perhaps," said an 1898 guidebook, "no where else on earth can so many wealthy households be found grouped together." Prairie Avenue was "justly famous as the most expensive street in America west of Fifth Avenue." The John Wesley Doane house, at 1827 Prairie Avenue, was "probably the finest house west of New York"; the avenue's parties were catered by Kinsley's, "the Delmonico's of the West"; the legendary merchant prince Marshall Field, who lived at 1905 Prairie Avenue, owned a painting by Jean François Millet which, though small, was "far superior to the *Angelus*." "That remarkable street" was home to "merchants whose business affects every mart on earth" and who pos-

---

essay by Mary Alice Molloy

129

sessed "wealth that at last aroused the jealousy of New York."[2] Praise of "the most looked-up-to street in the city" stressed the wealth of the residents. The "sunny street that held the sifted few" was "illustrative of all that is rich and splendid in city life." "The habitat of notably solvent citizens" was "the center of Chicago's wealth and the citadel of her social aristocracy." "This golden spot," this "Nest of Millionaires" was the "hub of Chicago aristocracy and Americanism."[3]

THAT REMARKABLE STREET

Chicago flairs out from the western shore of Lake Michigan into three sections, two of which are separated from its business core, the Loop, by branches of the Chicago River. In the earliest years of the city's history, the West Side appeared likely to become the most prestigious section,[4] although eventually the Near North Side and its Gold Coast captured that honor, and retained it. But in the years immediately after the Civil War, the South Side offered the lure of open spaces without the major handicap of the other two areas, the need to cross a branch of a very busy river to reach the Loop (Figure 1).

The gradual eastward curve of Lake Michigan creates much of the South Side. A new street is inserted along the shore every two to four blocks, so that Michigan Avenue, which faces the lake at Congress Street, is ten blocks west of it at Thirty-first Street, just two and a half miles south. By all odds Michigan Avenue

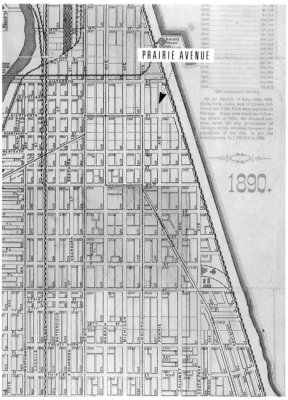

Figure 1. Blanchard's map of Chicago, 1890. Prairie Avenue runs north-south beginning near the lakefront below the rail yard, upper right.

should have become the premier South Side street. Its downtown lakefront site gave it special cachet; it was a direct line into and out of the heart of the city; and it was slated to become a macadamized carriage way along the boulevard system, a strong lure for those with a taste for fine horses.[5] But somehow events in 1870 shifted focus two blocks east of there, to Prairie Avenue. That year the South Side's first $100,000 home, built for Daniel M. Thompson, a grain elevator owner, was under construction on several 200-foot-deep lots on the corner of Prairie Avenue and Twentieth Street. Also that year, ground was broken for Marshall Field's elegant residence, and George M. Pullman, the railway palace car builder, negotiated the purchase of the northeast corner of Prairie Avenue and Eighteenth Street. Pullman paid the highest price to date per frontage foot for a Chicago residential site. Prairie Avenue for a distance of six blocks was about to become, and would remain for more than three decades, Chicago's "residence street par excellence."[6]

To reach this "neighborhood of Million-aires…celebrated in local annals," guidebooks of the 1880s and 1890s directed visitors south on Michigan Avenue past Twelfth Street, where the lakefront park ends. For the next four blocks most of that shore land was railroad yards, which are only now being redeveloped. Tourists were directed to turn left at Sixteenth Street, where two blocks of small houses buffered the residential quarter to the south from the rail yards. A right turn at a point near the lake's edge

Figure 2. Upper Prairie Avenue, looking south on west side from Eighteenth Street, c. 1890.

placed one at the start of upper Prairie Avenue (Figure 2). (Today, 1920s landfill makes this spot considerably inland.) Between Sixteenth and Eighteenth Streets only a rail line, which the guides never mentioned, separated the homes on the east side from the water. South of there Calumet Avenue became the first of many streets to take over the lakefront spot. Each travel guide found special delights to dwell on, but all directed attention to the homes of "Chicago's chief trinity of millionaires," Pullman, Field, and meat packer Philip D. Armour. Tourists were specifically asked to take note of the ornate bronze doors of the Pullman mansion.[7]

At Twenty-second Street, now Cermak Road, tourists passed out of this "aristocratic quarter" and into a zone of "struggle between business and comfort." The carefully maintained pavement degenerated into a worn stone roadway as Cottage Grove Avenue, following an old stagecoach route, cut a diagonal swath across Prairie Avenue and adjacent streets.[8] Along the jumble of streets thus created were apartments and shops, private schools, and a dancing academy. There were also churches and synagogues and a medical school and a hospital, but no deep lots suitable for elegant homes. At the water's edge were the McAvoy and Seipp breweries and a series of railroad switching yards. The paved and graded roadbed returned at Twenty-sixth Street, and the scene again became "Parisian in cleanliness" as one entered lower Prairie Avenue (Figure 3). Along

Figure 3. Lower Prairie Avenue, east side of 2700 block, 1903. Charles L. Hutchinson residence (center), 2709 Prairie Avenue.

this fresh rank of stately homes of wholesalers, financiers, and railroad presidents, special attention was drawn to "a house made beautiful with treasures of art,"[9] the residence of Charles L. Hutchinson, banker, trader, and president of the Art Institute of Chicago. At Thirtieth Street, apartment buildings began to intrude, and at Thirty-first, Prairie Avenue was declared at an end and tourists were directed back to Michigan Avenue. In fact, the street continues southward for another eleven miles, virtually to the city's southern limits, but beginning at Thirty-first there are four north-south streets instead of three between Indiana Avenue and South Park Boulevard (now Dr. Martin Luther King, Jr. Drive) (Figure 4). Prairie Avenue never again has lots deep enough to encourage mansion building. Nevertheless everyone, except perhaps the residents of lower Prairie Avenue, acknowledged that the street as Chicago's holy of holies had ended at Twenty-second.

Guidebooks warned visitors not to be disappointed when they did not find palaces on vast estates.

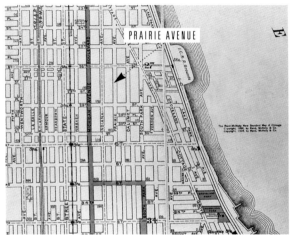

Figure 4. Map of Chicago, Rand-McNally & Co., 1904. Prairie Avenue, center, runs north-south. Blocks become narrower south of Thirty-first Street (lower right).

Ostentation, they claimed, played no part in the lives of the "solidly wealthy," who were "not of the Veneering variety." Critics Montgomery Schuyler and C. H. Blackall concurred. They stressed the livability and comfort manifested in Chicago's wealthy neighborhoods in general and especially along Prairie Avenue. Schuyler, however, noted the unnaturalness of a fashionable quarter developing on the edge of a lake but cut off from the water by railroad lines. He saw Prairie Avenue as striving for a "character of suburbanity" while leaving the best views to the horses in the stables in the rear. Aware that Chicago was freer of sham palaces than else-where, he wondered why the anarchism that permeated news from Chicago throughout the 1880s had "sprung up" in what appeared to be the "most democratic" of American cities.[10]

Schuyler captured what all the superlatives tried to disguise, that apart from the convenience of having a commuter railroad at one's doorstep, Prairie Avenue's setting had little to recommend it. The Lake Michigan shore land on which Prairie Avenue was built was an ill-favored marsh capable of sustaining only a few cottonwood trees from the mouth of the Chicago River for four miles south to present-day Thirty-first Street. The native Potawatomis had had the wisdom to avoid the area. The soldiers at Fort Dearborn, which was built at the mouth of the river in 1803, had learned that the shallow soil, excessive humidity, persistent cold, damp winds, short growing season, and swarms of insects and birds thwarted all agricultural or horticultural pursuits.[11] Prairie Avenue at Eighteenth Street is the accepted site where Indians slaughtered evacuees from the fort during the War of 1812. This fact may at first have repelled development of what was in effect a cemetery, but the 1812 massacre eventually became an attraction, as if Prairie Avenue should be occupied only by those whose success most vindicated the pioneers' sacrifice. The residents nurtured a cottonwood in the middle of

Eighteenth Street that they had determined was the actual massacre site. When it died, they sent its wood to the Chicago Historical Society and erected a sculpture romanticizing the slaughter.[12] They also had to sacrifice peace and quiet and had to live not only with the noises, dirt, and smells of adjacent railroads and breweries but also with the uncomfortable knowledge that the city's licensed vice district began at State Street, four blocks west of Prairie Avenue. Initially contained in the vicinity of the Loop train stations, the district grew inexorably southward.

Retreat of Merchants and Citizens of Means

The notion of ever being fashionable could not possibly have occurred to Prairie Avenue's initial residents and developers. The street's first home was that of brick manufacturer John N. Staples (Figure 5). This gentleman's rural villa was a two-story-plus-cupola structure of Italianate persuasion. Chicagoans would have described it as Southern and regarded it as a contribution of the sizable Virginia contingent among the city's early settlers.[13] It was built facing the lake midway along the first block sometime prior to June 1852, when the Illinois Central railroad obtained the right to build a trestle in Lake Michigan in exchange for a stone breakwater that would halt erosion of the shoreline. Service on the lakefront tracks began in 1856 with three daily round trips to south suburban Hyde Park, and, the shore having been stabilized, development began. Initially it was concentrated around an outpost at Twenty-sixth Street and the lakefront known as Carville. The short-lived American Car Company attempted to launch a railroad car industry there. Workers' cottages were erected on adjacent streets. In 1856 John B. Sherman, a future Prairie Avenue resident, organized a stockyard out of the few cattle holding pens around Myrick's Tavern at Cottage Grove Avenue and Twenty-ninth Street. In 1858 St. James Catholic Church was established in a frame building at 2709 Prairie Avenue to serve the largely Irish population.

Significant residential development on or near upper Prairie Avenue came slowly and halted altogether during the Civil War. Nonetheless, by 1861, when Chicago had become the world's largest railway center, travelers passing on the sixteen daily trains noticed "houses which must be the retreat of merchants and citizens of means."[14] Among these was the home built for lawyer Wirt Dexter at 1721 Prairie Avenue in about 1863. Dexter, whose Boston antecedents included a member of John Adams' cabinet, chose a rambling clapboarded New England farmhouse updated with an Italianate cupola.

The building pace increased markedly immedi-

Figure 5. John N. Staples residence, 1702 Prairie Avenue, 1852–53, architect unknown. Demolished.

ately after the war as developers set up townhouses in clusters throughout the length of upper Prairie Avenue. New residents included railroad conductors Herbert Whiting and Charles W. Wheeler; furrier James A. Smith; distiller John Pahlman; hardware man Joseph Liebenstein; clothier Morris Einstein; grocers Granville S. Ingraham, Henry C. Durand, and Samuel A. Tolman; lawyers John Forsythe, George Sloan, and Edward Roby; and real estate men F. R. Otis and H. O. Stone. Only Einstein, Tolman, Otis, and Stone would become well known in Chicago business and remain on Prairie Avenue throughout its heyday.

Tolman, Otis, and Stone occupied a set of townhouses built at 2031–2035 Prairie Avenue in 1869. These were slim three-story, stone-faced, flat-roofed residences with trapezoidal bays. John Wellborn Root, an architect with strong Prairie Avenue associations, observed that such houses as these shared most features, inside and out, with the New York brownstone of this period. But Chicago streets looked "gayer and less solid" than East Coast ones, mostly because the facing stone was not brownstone but the local buff-colored Lemont lime-stone.[15] Somehow this stone become known as Athens marble, and houses that employed it were commonly called marble fronts. The marble fronts, or their alternatives, brick houses with Athens marble trim, were typically narrow homes set on twenty-five-foot lots, the city standard.

Marble fronts and rambling frame houses in ranks of forty or more would never make an avenue remarkable, but the announcement of the Thompson house improved the chances (Figure 6). This dark brick building with its extremely pronounced brownstone window caps was designed by Chicagoan Lavall B. Dixon. The tower that topped its entrance pavilion stood heads over everything else on upper Prairie Avenue. The house may have been what inspired one guidebook to assert that Prairie Avenue residents favored "the new style of rococo and belittled church architecture."[16] The grounds of the massive structure were rivaled in expanse ultimately only by the Pullman property. After a decade, Thompson's son-in-law, meat packer Samuel Allerton, took over the house and made the stable the envy of the horse-mad set.

Whether spurred by Thompson's example or by some other impulse, upper Prairie Avenue became impressive enough that the May 1874 issue of *The Land Owner* presented it as "one of the most fashionable

Figure 6. Thompson/Allerton residence, 1936 Prairie Avenue, c. 1869–70, Lavall B. Dixon, architect. Demolished.

and handsomely-built of all our South-Side thoroughfares" (Figure 7). Boosterism of every sort was rampant that year as an antidote to the grim realities of recovery from the Great Chicago Fire of 1871 and the Panic of 1873. The publication included an engraved collage portraying the homes of Thompson, Pullman, and Field along with those of Louis Wahl, who owned a glue works, millinery wholesaler Edson Keith, insurance man A. A. Dewey, shoe and boot maker Charles M. Henderson, and coal and pig iron dealer Robert Law. All of the houses were portrayed in equally

Figure 7. "Residences of Prominent Citizens on Prairie Avenue," 1874. George Pullman residence, lower left, under construction and illustrated without front veranda.

spacious surroundings, liberally spattered with fledgling elm trees, and the writer proclaimed that "no city in the world can rival Chicago in its residences." Another publication of that year also singled out the Keith and Wahl houses for illustration.[17] Given an additional fifteen new or remodeled houses completed with stone fronts and mansard roofs in the next few years, the overriding impression of Prairie Avenue became fixed in the Second Empire, or General Grant, mode (Figure 8). By the mid-1880s this streetscape would be regarded as "modern and United States and almost monotonously stiff in architecture and style."[18] What is most remarkable is that at this time

Figure 8. Prairie Avenue, west side of 1800–1900 block, c. 1906. Left to right, Edson Keith residence, 1870, J. W. Roberts, architect. Elbridge Keith residence, 1870, J. W. Roberts, architect. Fernando Jones residence, 1866, J. M. VanOsdel, architect. Daniel B. Shipman residence, c. 1873, architect unknown.

Marshall Field, who would later be lionized and whose home would be the essence of all that Prairie Avenue stood for, was accorded only the briefest mention.[19]

HABITATS OF NOTABLY SOLVENT CITIZENS

Of the large homes built on upper Prairie Avenue in the 1870s, four merit consideration. Three of them, those built for William Gold Hibbard, partner in a wholesale hardware business, Marshall Field, and George Pullman, were early works of architects who had been exposed directly or indirectly to the Neo-Grec buildings of contemporary Paris.[20] The fourth, the John B. Sherman house, constituted a shift away from French influences.

William LeBaron Jenney, who had received technical training in France and would make major contributions to skyscraper architecture, was the first to employ consciously what he called Modern French architecture when he designed the Hibbard house at 1701 Prairie Avenue in 1868 (Figure 9). He restricted the ornamentation of the brick walls to accents of construction features. Pilasters, for example, articulated advancing and receding planes across the front elevation. The Hibbard plans showed particular sensitivity both to the site on the east side of the first block of Prairie Avenue, with Lake Michigan at its back, and to the size of the Hibbard family (Figure 10).

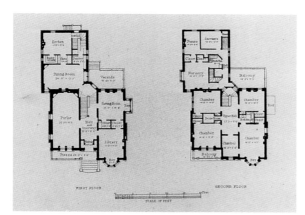

Figure 9. William G. Hibbard residence, 1701 Prairie Avenue, 1868, William LeBaron Jenney, architect. Elevation, 1869.

Figure 10. William G. Hibbard residence, 1701 Prairie Avenue, 1868, William LeBaron Jenney, architect. First- and second-floor plans, 1869. Demolished.

A large veranda with a balcony above it at the southeast corner offered a sheltered and unobstructed view of the lake as "a pleasant resort during warm summer afternoons and evenings."[21] A bay window off the second-floor nursery offered small children a similar option. The height of the ceilings in the dining and kitchen wing was reduced to allow access to the nursery from the turn of the stairs. This device, which Hibbard maintained was common to his roots in upstate New York, established the nursery and the six children who occupied it as the focus of the household.[22] The Hibbard house as executed exhibited Frederick Law Olmsted's criticism of Jenney, with whom he dealt while planning the town of Riverside, Illinois. To the great landscape designer, the young architect had "not been a sufficient student" while in Paris and was not yet "working with a sure hand and fixed principles."[23]

In contrast, the Marshall Field house (Figure 11) was the work of a very sure hand, that of Richard Morris Hunt, and it deserved praise as the "first really artistic dwelling-house" in Chicago.[24]

Figure 11. Marshall Field residence, 1905 Prairie Avenue, 1871, Richard Morris Hunt, architect. Demolished. Photograph, c. 1889.

Distinguished by Victor Hugo's *style tricolor*—blue-gray slate mansard roof, red brick walls, light stone trim—the Field house followed the strict formulae expected of a French middle-class detached suburban house during the years Hunt had lived and studied in Paris. In particular, it maintained the value of the garden elevation as the foremost one by making the southern facade more symmetrical and imposing than the entrance facade.[25] Hunt's success at this is confirmed by the fact that published views of the house all show this facade.

The Field plan was skillfully adapted from the characteristic French one of four rooms around a central stairwell and demonstrated why Montgomery Schuyler found Hunt's buildings of this period to be "incidentally and intrinsically extremely "interesting" (Figure 12).[26] A central hall ran the full length of the house to terminate at a swirling staircase (Figure 13). Three of the four rooms were octagonal; for the one on the north side, corners were simply sliced off a rectangle, but the two rooms to the south were the result of a hexagonal swelling midway down the long hall and the insertion of a small cross-axial passage there that led

137

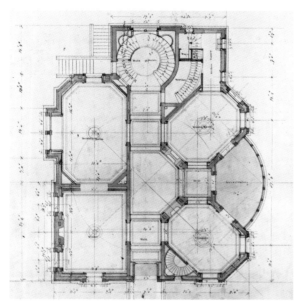

Figure 12. Marshall Field residence, 1905 Prairie Avenue, 1871, Richard Morris Hunt, architect. First-floor plan, watercolor.

Figure 13. Marshall Field residence, 1905 Prairie Avenue, 1871. First-floor hall.

to a conservatory bowing out of the southern facade. The angled sides of the hexagon were the fireplace ends of the two southern rooms, which both had window or door openings on all of their four short sides and on the wall shared with the conservatory, leaving only one solid wall in one room and two in the other. The effect was to have southern light flooding half of the house and penetrating deeply into the long hallway.[27] This emphasis on a southern orientation probably appealed strongly to Field, who, as the head of a rapidly growing dry goods business, would have been more aware than most of French strides in department store design that used wells to light huge spaces.[28]

The Pullman house at 1729 Prairie Avenue, begun in 1871, was a melding of French architecture with what appears to have been a good deal of second-guessing by the client (Figure 14). The architect, Henry S. Jaffray, had spent four years in Hunt's New York office in the late 1850s.[29] The Pullman house, with a number of additions designed by S. S. Beman, was Prairie Avenue's showiest place and meant for a flamboyant lifestyle. It incorporated a 200-seat theater, an organ, a bowling alley, and a billiard room in addition to at least three parlors and an extensive conservatory. It was also the first Prairie Avenue house to take its corner site seriously and to be clad on all sides in stone, a brownstone and not Athens marble. Strong articulation of the horizontals and variations in fenestration from floor to floor recalled Hunt's work while Jaffray was with him.[30] The Eighteenth Street facade, with a porte-cochère more prominent than the Prairie Avenue porch, may have been intended as an urban variant of the monumental French garden elevation.

The Pullman house took a good deal longer to build than the usual two years of the other houses. The family did not move in until early in 1876, and they could not entertain until the following January. It was

September 1878 before the hallway of rich woods was completed to the satisfaction of a client who had been trained as a cabinetmaker. Most of the delay appears to have been caused by the changes in design, such as the inclusion or exclusion of a bay window, and by dickering for the lowest contract prices.[31] Descriptions of George Pullman's character indicate that he may have been attempting to outdo the Field house by choosing a more expensive-looking, all-stone building. Or perhaps, since the Pullmans were the one family to respect Prairie Avenue's lake setting and to attempt ambitious groundskeeping, they may simply have perceived a uniform presentation as the appropriate backdrop for their plans.[32]

Figure 14. George M. Pullman residence, 1729 Prairie Avenue, 1871–76, Henry S. Jaffray, architect. Demolished. Photograph, c. 1910.

The lessening of the thrall of things French after the fall of the Second Empire in 1870 made its first Prairie Avenue appearance on the Sherman house, built in 1874 on the southwest corner of Twenty-first Street (Figure 15). John Wellborn

Figure 15. John B. Sherman residence, 2100 Prairie Avenue, 1874, Burnham & Root, architects. Demolished. Rendering by John Wellborn Root.

Root, who would be the most distinguished of the wave of new talent that rebuilt Chicago after the Great Fire, introduced the change in this, the first major design of his partnership with Daniel Hudson Burnham. By calling upon elements of Ruskinian Gothic architecture, Root produced a design he came to regard as revolutionary, especially the roof.[33] This was high-pitched and multiplaned and dotted with finials; the mansard's curve had been banished. In addition, the corner was marked in a dramatic way. The rectangular oriel on the upper floor supported by a single dark blue granite column gave the house "a certain allure or style indicating personality,"[34] a claim new to Chicago architecture. The plan was also at odds with the compact French one; a long hall took a dead bead on the dining room at the end and left rooms of contrived shapes and a tucked-away staircase strewn to either side.[35]

THE MAYFAIR DISTRICT OF CHICAGO

Lower Prairie Avenue's story took a different twist. In 1865 Sherman spearheaded the consolidation of Chicago's stock handling and slaughtering operations into a single Union Stock Yards placed a good two miles inland. The removal of Sherman's lakefront yards and the failure of the railroad car company left Carville considerably depressed. In 1880 St. James parish followed its parishioners and moved to new build-

Figure 16. Lower Prairie Avenue, west side of 2700 block, 1903. Left to right: A. C. Bartlett residence, 1886, Cobb and Frost, architects. Hiram Kelly residence, 1887, Cobb and Frost, architects. A. A. Sprague residence, 1883, Burnham & Root, architects. O. S. A. Sprague residence, 1888, Burling and Whitehouse, architects. William J. Watson residence, 1884, Treat and Foltz, architects.

Figure 17. Edwin Pardridge residence, 2808 Prairie Avenue, 1886, Wheelock and Clay, architects. Demolished. Photograph, c. 1890.

ings four blocks further west. Charles Hutchinson bought the church's Prairie Avenue land and built homes on it for his sister and himself.[36] By 1885 he had singlehandedly created a second exclusive Prairie Avenue enclave by acquiring several other large parcels and reselling them to his family, friends, and business associates. These included Hutchinson's father-in-law, restaurateur H. M. Kinsley; A. C. Bartlett, Hibbard's partner; wholesale grocers A. A. and Otho Sprague; and Marvin Hughitt, president of the North Western railroad (Figure 16).[37] Hutchinson was also instrumental in locating St. Paul's Universalist Church on Prairie Avenue at Thirtieth Street. The rugged stone edifice designed by Burling and Whitehouse in 1887 featured a colored-glass lantern that may have come from the La Farge studios.

Lower Prairie Avenue achieved a certain secluded ambience because it was not interrupted by cross streets from Twenty-sixth to Twenty-ninth Streets. The nascent architectural journals, especially *Inland Architect*, recorded virtually all of the district's houses as they came from the drawing boards of the city's most popular architects. Initially these exhibited the twin vogues of the Queen Anne and Richardsonian Romanesque, but all subsequent fashions were represented as construction continued until after 1905. Architects visiting Chicago were instructed to make sure they saw the home of Edwin Pardridge, a dry goods merchant turned grain trader, at 2808 Prairie Avenue (Figure 17). An 1886 design by the firm of Wheelock and Clay, this vaguely chateauesque mansion was distinguished by an "eccentricity of color." Details in the bright tones of blue enamel, buff brick, and copper stood out sharply against the more somber brown and terra cotta walls and purple slate roof.[38]

ALL THAT IS RICH AND SPLENDID IN CITY LIFE

While lower Prairie Avenue was flowering in the early 1880s, the few remaining lots on upper Prairie Avenue were being filled in, primarily by large and lavish residences north of the Marshall Field house. These included the chocolaty cube of O. R. Keith, one of the millinery family (Figure 18); the "palace" of importer John Wesley Doane; and two Burnham & Root designs, the sedate Thomas Dent house and the distinctive yellow residence of Joseph Sears, developer of cottonseed oil.[39]

Field's 1883 buyout of his partner, Levi Leiter, for a reputed $3 million in cash confirmed him as Chicago's richest citizen by far. He and his home were thereafter the principal attractions of Prairie Avenue, and the street's new architecture respected that to a rare degree. On the Field house, an especially prominent windowless angled wall at the southwestern corner was actually a side of one of the bays that gave balance and monumentality to the garden elevation. Each of the new homes was designed with a prominent element of some description at the same location. Although the architects Field's neighbors employed missed, or ignored, the subtleties of Hunt's design, their use of this device created a streetscape of impressive vistas, especially when approached from the south (Figure 19). The press extolled the new "unrivaled character of the neighborhood," which should be obvious even to someone "born on Fifth avenue, New York, [or] reared at Clifton, Cincinnati; or Euclid avenue, Cleveland; or Grand avenue, Milwaukee."[40]

The Doane house attracted considerable attention during construction (Figure 20). The high, tapering, crested roof of its angled bay achieved a preeminence on the east side of the street that the tower of the Thompson/Allerton house had on the west side. Because of its interiors, not its stark exterior, it was "entitled to rank with the semi-palatial residences of older cities." Its architect,

Figure 18. O. R. Keith residence, 1901 Prairie Avenue, c. 1882, Lavall B. Dixon, architect. Roofline and interiors modified for Norman B. Ream in 1887, Burnham & Root, architects. Demolished.

Figure 19. Prairie Avenue, looking north of Nineteenth Street on east side, before 1890. Left to right: George M. Pullman residence, 1871, Henry S. Jaffray, architect. Coleman-Ames residence, 1886, Cobb and Frost, architects. Joseph Sears residence, c. 1882, Burnham & Root, architects. Thomas I. Dent residence, 1881, Burnham & Root, architects. John Wesley Doane residence, 1882, T. V. Wadskier, architect. O. R. Keith residence, Lavall B. Dixon, architect.

Figure 20. John Wesley Doane residence, 1827 Prairie Avenue, 1882, T. V. Wadskier, architect. Demolished.

T. V. Wadskier, was noted for the personal attention he devoted to his clients' needs.[41] Doane's included exceptionally rich appointments and the first domestic use of electric lighting in Chicago, befitting a founder of the Western Edison Light Company. The house featured a stair hall that was thirty feet square and fifteen feet high, large by even the most generous American standards (Figure 21). Its spacious effect was expanded by a galleried central opening topped with a stained-glass dome illuminated electrically at night. Bronze medallions and metallic wall and ceiling coverings throughout rooms of oak, cherry, mahogany, or bird's-eye maple were chosen to respond to 250 incandescent lights.[42]

Figure 21. John Wesley Doane residence, 1827 Prairie Avenue, 1882. First-floor main hall. Demolished.

The completion of houses clearly meant for entertaining, such as the Pullman and Doane mansions, indicated that lifestyles on Prairie Avenue had changed considerably from the days when each family had a cow that was led off to pasture every morning. Then dinner invitations were issued for 6:30 on the dot, and Sunday afternoons were reserved for informal visiting along the street. In the 1870s, New Year's Day headed the social calendar; the hostess garnering the largest number of calling cards was unquestionably the social leader, until the next New Year.[43] In that decade the Hibbards purportedly entertained several evenings a week throughout the winter months with dinner parties for about twenty adults who later adjourned to the basement bowling alley.[44] Children recalled playing games on the open lands south of Twenty-second Street, fishing on the lakefront in summers, and skating in the winters on a rink Marshall Field maintained. Field, although reserved, even cold, with adults, was always a favorite with children.[45]

In contrast, the reception that the Doanes hosted on November 10, 1882, to celebrate their silver wedding anniversary and inaugurate their new home, had a guest list comprised of four hundred of Chicago's citizens of "wealth, youth, and beauty." The exterior of the house was flooded in calcium light, and flowers and plants of all colors and types almost but not quite hid the "fountain of fragrant perfumes," and the elaborate mantels, pillars, balustrades, and railings.[46] The best-remembered event of this era was the Mikado Ball, given by the Fields for their children in 1885. For the occasion the ground floor of the house was converted into a stage setting from the Gilbert and Sullivan operetta, two boxcars brought in food from Sherry's of New York, and favors were designed by the painter James Abbott McNeill Whistler. Field is alleged to have spent $75,000 on the event.[47] It was not unusual for the Pullmans to celebrate a wedding anniversary with dinner and a play in their theater followed by dancing, nor for them to invite 500 to an afternoon reception to meet an opera star.[48] Mrs. Pullman instituted an exclusive dancing class at which men who had dedicated their lives to rising above their circumstances could devote the same intensity to learning to enjoy their success.[49]

Chicago society women as a group were regarded as intelligent, thoughtful, individual, and not flirtatious.[50] Two Prairie Avenue women, both of them beautiful and witty, were undisputed social leaders, Josephine Moore (Mrs. Wirt) Dexter and Elizabeth Yager (Mrs. H. O.) Stone.[51] Mrs. Dexter, who carried her tall height "like a goddess," shared her husband's passion for music and his reputation as a "wonderfully entertaining" conversationalist. The Dexters focused their parties around their fireside and restricted their guest lists to persons with whom they had things in common. For twenty years they were hosts to such visiting New England notables as orator Wendell Phillips, poet James Russell Lowell, essayist Ralph Waldo Emerson, and clergyman Theodore Parker.[52] Mrs. Stone, "a believer in total harmony," was noted for the obviously sincere pleasure she took in fostering artists. The "thoroughly individual" salon-parlor in her marble front townhome featured a chapel organ and a plethora of small tables littered with busts, books, loose photographs, exotic porcelains, souvenirs, and lamps.[53] Mrs. Stone's most renowned entertainment was an afternoon reception for Oscar Wilde during his celebrated 1882 American lecture tour.

For the men, social as well as business contacts were fostered during noontime dining at their downtown clubs. The Chicago Club maintained a "millionaires' table" frequented by Field and Pullman. Closer to home, the Calumet Club, opened at Michigan Avenue and Twentieth Street in 1883, was a favored site for poker evenings. It also hosted the city's first important annual art show and events for the children of the membership. The Standard Club, at Michigan Avenue and Twenty-fourth, offered similar facilities for Jewish families. The residents appear to have been most proud of Washington Park racetrack, which opened in 1884 (Figure 22). The annual meetings there were occasions for parades of the avenue's finest horses and vehicles along the four miles of smooth boulevards leading to the Sixty-first Street track.[54] Most important, however, was the club without a clubhouse, the Commercial, which was founded in 1877 on a Boston model to allow sixty public-spirited, generally self-made men to foster the growth and prosperity of Chicago. In the late 1880s, when Doane was the club president, the overwhelming majority of the membership lived on the fashionable South Side streets, sixteen on Prairie Avenue alone.[55] At monthly meetings club members raised and debated issues affecting the city and determined whether to act on them. Major civic endeavors they initiated ranged from reversing the flow of the Chicago River to sponsoring the World's Columbian Exposition of 1893 to assigning Daniel Burnham, a member, to devise a comprehensive plan for Chicago.

Commercial Club membership also provided a man with the best solicitation list in town, and Charles L. Hutchinson made excellent use of it. In 1880 the club discussed whether it was time to foster the growth of the arts in Chicago. The Art Institute of Chicago had begun with a meeting in May 1879 that is believed to have been held in the George Armour home at 1945 Prairie Avenue.[56] Three and a half years later, the twenty-eight-year-old Hutchinson took on the presidency, which he kept for forty-three years. By 1907 he had transformed the vestiges of an art school into an organization he announced he was no longer ashamed of.[57] In the process he approached his Commercial Club associates and Prairie Avenue neighbors whenever he needed funds to purchase single objects or entire collections. For classical antiquities, for example, he turned to P. D. Armour, who proved to have been less than honest when he insisted in an interview that his culture was all in his wife's name. In 1890 Hutchinson established himself and the Art Institute as collectors to watch by fine tuning "Chicago hustle" on his first major foray. Learning that fifteen paintings of Dutch masters from the Demidoff collection could be bought outright ahead of their scheduled auction, Hutchinson cabled to Field, Armour, and

Figure 22. Washington Park Racetrack clubhouse, 1883, Solon S. Beman, architect. Demolished.

a few others in Chicago, who promptly agreed to buy the paintings until the Art Institute could find donors for them. A list of seven of the eventual donors includes four Prairie Avenue names.[58]

Prairie Avenue residents, including Hutchinson himself, were not adventurous art collectors. They filled their walls with works of acknowledged masters and successful French Salon painters. In Arthur Meeker's novel *Prairie Avenue*, set in 1885, the daughter of the millionaire modeled after Marshall Field was probably least fictionalized when she guided a visitor through her father's collection. She recited "without looking at their labels, the names and prices of all of the pictures in the picture gallery—from 'Sheridan's Ride' to 'A Sunset in Holland'—and could tell which ones Papa had picked up at a Calumet Club show for a song, which imported at vast expense from New York or Europe."[59] The Pullmans so prized *Happy Moments*, a painting by Adolphe-William Bouguereau (Figure 23), that they gave it pride of place when they stripped everything else from their parlor for their daughter Florence's wedding in 1896.[60]

Figure 23. George M. Pullman residence, 1729 Prairie Avenue. Main Salon. Bouguereau's *Happy Moments* is behind the piano (center). Demolished.

In contrast, musical talent and the appreciation and support of it were very strong on Prairie Avenue. Unquestionably the hundreds of musicales, recitals, and concerts held over the years in virtually every home on the street prepared the milieu for the success of the Chicago Symphony Orchestra, founded in 1891. High points among these events were the champagne supper musicales at which Louise Stager (Mrs. Frank) Gorton was the first to bring together artists and socialites. She enhanced the ambience of these evenings by adding a delicate Federal-style music room to the rear of her 1870s brownstone at 2120 Prairie Avenue (Figure 24).[61] The most frequently told and never contradicted piece of Prairie Avenue lore concerns Ignace Paderewski, who received a healthy stipend for a concert in the home of grain trader Charles

Figure 24. Frank S. Gorton residence, 2120 Prairie Avenue. Music room addition, 1891, architect unknown. Demolished. Photograph, c. 1896.

Schwartz. After the performance the renowned pianist was invited to join the men at the poker table. He left having restored the fee and a good deal more to his host's pocket.[62]

THE HUB OF CHICAGO ARISTOCRACY AND AMERICANISM

The years that surrounded the Chicago Haymarket "riot" of May 1886 were known as "the comfortable 80s" on Prairie Avenue. Residents and visitors alike insisted that the street was "serene," "unbelievably pastoral," and "as quiet as a country lane" with an "air of genteel refinement and elegant luxury."[63] Reality was, of course, different. Trains skirting Prairie Avenue now numbered sixty a day.[64] The noise rattled windowpanes, coal smoke blackened buildings, and molten cinders were littered everywhere. Residents placed cheesecloth over their heat registers to keep some of the soot off of their furnishings; a window left ajar at night meant cinders in slippers by morning. The original cottonwoods had succumbed quickly to the railroad's pollution, and elms introduced into the unfriendly soil had to be constantly replaced to keep their ranks unbroken. In a hundred years of photographs, no view of Prairie Avenue has ever included a mature tree. And the red light district was becoming firmly entrenched at Twenty-second and State Streets.[65]

Figure 25. John J. Glessner residence, 1800 Prairie Avenue, 1885–87, Henry Hobson Richardson, architect. Photograph of house under construction, c. June 1887.

Figure 26. John J. Glessner residence, 1800 Prairie Avenue, 1885–87. Library. Photograph, 1923.

Furthermore, elements regarded as even less savory occasionally intruded, as they did on Thanksgiving Day 1884. That afternoon socialists marched through the city's aristocratic neighborhoods flaunting their "black emblems of want and despair in the faces of rich robbers."[66] Shortly after this, the Commercial Club established a subscription fund to purchase six hundred acres north of Chicago. With remarkable high-handedness they gave the land to the federal government and pushed legislation through Congress to create a military base so that troops would be near Chicago if needed. The city police and the state militia having been perceived as inadequate to suppress this and subsequent anarchist activities, it was "therefore, the duty of the club members, as citizens, to take the lead in the important matter of the protection and promotion of the city's commercial interests."[67]

This was the Prairie Avenue that John J. Glessner, a partner in a farm implements business, presented to Henry Hobson Richardson in May 1885 when he showed him the southwest corner of Eighteenth Street. After only a few moments, the Boston architect asked, "Have you the courage to build the house without windows on the street front?"[68] Richardson had a clear idea of how to keep out the realities of Prairie Avenue while getting light into a building at the northern end of a block. He designed a U with massive stone walls hugging the property lines on three sides and sheltering a courtyard to the south (Figure 25). As Hunt had done fifteen years earlier, Richardson may have called on the French suburban model, shifting it this time to suit the urban setting that Prairie Avenue had become. But he did so over the neighborhood's strong objections. A delegation visited Glessner at his office to point out that Prairie Avenue houses were set back from their lot lines. George Pullman waxed incensed at the millionaires' table for several days over reports, erroneous ones, that the house would have no windows facing the streets. Mrs. Dexter sent a letter recommending a bay window. Feathers were smoothed at last when Marshall Field announced, "That house is coming out all right."[69] The Glessners made careful note of all such remarks, which fill five and a half typescript pages. Charming though they may appear today, they record the very strong emotions of people who really felt they had the right to dictate another's dream house.

As the Glessners took their places in Prairie Avenue social life, it was obvious that they and their house represented a second shift in the street's ambience. They did not have fabled wealth, nor was their home furnished with an ivory and gold salon indebted to the tastes of a French court. The sunny yellow combination parlor and music room espoused Arts and Crafts principles; prized Modern Gothic pieces were retained throughout the house and augmented generously with William Morris's designs. Editor, essayist, and novelist Charles Dudley Warner captured the tenor of what was new when he brought a companion along to see that the Glessner library displayed "little of the Pullman Palace Car" (Figure 26).[70]

The change pervaded all future construction on upper Prairie Avenue. In the street's last mansion-sized house, designed by S. S. Beman in 1890–92 for piano and organ maker William W. Kimball, a living hall with an organ in its second-floor gallery replaced the assorted reception and

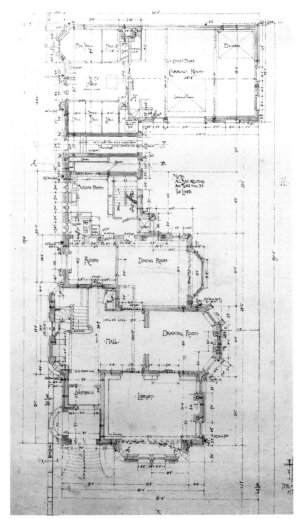

Figure 27. William W. Kimball residence, 1801 Prairie Avenue, 1890–92, Solon S. Beman, architect. First-floor plan, working drawing, 1890.

Figure 28. William W. Kimball residence, 1801 Prairie Avenue, 1890–92.

147

Figure 29. Max A. Meyer residence, 2009 Prairie Avenue, 1888, Burnham & Root, architects. Demolished. Perspective, watercolor.

Figure 30. Hugh McBirney residence, 1625 Prairie Avenue, 1890, Francis M. Whitehouse, architect. Demolished.

public rooms of the past (Figure 27). The front room in this house, which is standing at 1801 Prairie Avenue, is a very large library; a token parlor is slipped in behind it. The exterior is chateauesque, modeled on sixteenth-century features of Brittany's Chateau de Josselin (Figure 28).[71]

More typical, however, were the townhouses being squeezed into the few spaces left between existing homes. These proved to be excellent tests of their architects' mettle. The William H. Reid house, an 1894 Renaissance Revival design by Beers, Clay, and Dutton standing at 2013 Prairie Avenue, features a central music room cum stairhall under a domed skylight. This affectation required the first use of a steel frame in a Chicago residence. Burnham & Root gave the George H. Wheeler house, erected at 1812 Prairie Avenue in 1884, a Dutch vernacular flavor, and enlivened the "most humane and lovely" Max A. Meyer house of 1888, built at 2009 Prairie Avenue, with copings and moldings of a French Gothic persuasion (Figure 29). Both houses had the strongly frontal gable ends that characterized Root's late work. Cobb and Frost adapted the device effectively in 1888 on the Richardsonian Harriet P. Rees house, still standing at 2110 Prairie Avenue, and in 1889 Francis M. Whitehouse honed it down finely on the Hugh McBirney, Jr., house at 1625 Prairie Avenue (Figure 30).[72]

Remodelings were as numerous as new construction throughout the 1880s. The most active practitioners were the various relatives of novelist Arthur Meeker, who added stables, squash courts, and even rooftop children's playrooms to a number of houses. Most affected was the house at 1919 Prairie Avenue. In 1883, Meeker's grandparents, the William H. Murrays, had S. S. Beman wrap a brick and terra cotta envelope around an 1867 frame house there. Mrs. Murray's brother, Charles Schwartz, added to it in 1887, and Marshall Field, Jr., made major alterations in 1902, so that it became hard to know "what it thought it was originally trying to be."[73] Architecturally the most significant change was undertaken by the Dexters in 1889, when they, like the Glessners before them, drew the wrath of the community by erecting out to the sidewalk an addition of "no particular style" (Figure 31). Their architect was Arthur Little of Boston, and in recent years this "noble and elegiac" house has been described as a worthy culmination to the opening phase of this unique architect's career. It was a significant building in the introduction of the Federal Revival not merely in Chicago but nationally.[74]

Wirt Dexter died of a heart attack in May 1890, within months of the completion of the addition. By 1898 over thirty of the upper Prairie Avenue residences housed widows and widowers. Among the dead were George M. Pullman, Mrs. Marshall Field, Charles Schwartz, Mrs. John Sherman, Max Meyer, Mrs. George Wheeler, and Edson Keith. Doane and P. D. Armour would die in 1901, Sherman in 1902, Hibbard in 1903, and Field in 1906. Guidebooks had been noting since the early 1890s that many houses on the "avenue of avenues" were "comparatively old" and some were even "weatherworn." The pastor of Second Presbyterian Church, at Michigan Avenue and Twentieth Street, acknowledged the situation in 1892, when he proposed preparing to move on with the congregation. Others were not so insightful. New homes were constructed on both

Figure 31. Wirt Dexter residence, 1721 Prairie Avenue, 1889 addition and alterations, Arthur Little, architect. Original frame structure visible at the left. Demolished. Photograph, c. 1891.

parts of Prairie Avenue until 1905, and patriarchs such as Field, Glessner, and especially Hibbard, attempted to keep their children in houses nearby. They succeeded only for a while. By 1900 the automobile permitted the new generation to live far from the railroad's soot without making too many of the concessions their parents had faced. They chose Hyde Park to the south, the Gold Coast on the near North Side, or even the northern and western suburbs. The new mobility came at the same time that Chicago society stabilized into a tightly organized, exclusive circle. An address on the right street was no longer all that was sufficient for entree. The first house to be demolished was Robert Law's. The showplace published in 1874 had become a drab olive-green white elephant. The year was 1910.[75]

THE WORLD'S ONLY LANDMARK DEMOLITION SITE

On lower Prairie Avenue, decline came swiftly and followed a classic model. A 1912 police raid found "sporting houses" as far east of the licensed district as Indiana Avenue, at the back doors of Prairie Avenue homes.

The 1914 *Blue Book* recorded a sharp drop in the number of lower Prairie Avenue addresses. In 1917 a renowned madam, Vic Shaw, openly moved her operations into the house at 2904 Prairie Avenue. The following year St. Paul's Universalist gave up its facility to another congregation. By 1927 the lower Prairie Avenue area had become the South Side badlands; by 1940 it was the worst slum in Chicago. Its buildings were bulldozed in the early 1950s to make room for public housing.[76]

Upper Prairie Avenue's decline followed a pattern all its own. The introduction of trucks required larger loading docks on warehouses that could now be sited away from the central business district. Indiana Avenue was particularly vulnerable to such buildings because it carried a trolley line. In 1905 two factories were built there, at Eighteenth Street and at Twentieth Street. On Michigan Avenue between 1908 and 1910, owners unloaded their houses on auto manufacturers, who demolished them wholesale and built showrooms. The transformation to Automobile Row was complete in less than two years. Other construction in the area was associated with the printing industry, attracted to the adjacent rail lines. The new character of the area was fixed by 1917, when R. R. Donnelley, the nation's largest printer, began its huge Lakeside Press building on Calumet Avenue.[77]

Curiously, the first factory on Prairie Avenue itself was not associated with printing. It was the Hump Hairpin building, erected in 1915 on the site of the Thompson/Allerton house (Figure 32). Its one-story layout and raked brick elevations were not concessions to the residential locale but dictates of an efficient, economical stamping operation.[78] Publishers and businesses associated with printing took over several of the mansions. Plans for neo-Colonial cottages were marketed out of the Doane house. The P. D. Armour, H. O. Stone, and Edson Keith houses were subdivided for roomers.[79] The Murray/Field, Jr., house was a "center for inebriety." The Architects Club was headquartered in the Kimball house. A terra cotta firm took over the Hibbard house. The Sherman house was a medical school with dubious credentials. A dressmaker operated out of the Gorton home.

Real estate experts claimed that the land was worth more without the houses. In 1922 Pullman's daughters accepted this and ordered the vast mansion and greenhouses demolished. At the start of the 1930s, the street

Figure 32. Hump Hairpin Manufacturing Company, 1918 Prairie Avenue, 1915, Alfred S. Alschuler, architect. Photograph, c. 1920.

seemed at a glance to retain most of its old appearance, but the Doane mansion stood abandoned, its exotic woods exposed to the weather, and ducks and chickens ran wild in the Sherman house. By the end of the decade, twenty-six wrecking permits had been executed. Vacant lands were used for concession stands during the 1933–34 Century of Progress Exposition, which occupied the adjacent lakefront landfill. For a while the Field house had a reprieve of sorts; in 1936 it was ruthlessly altered to house Laszlo Moholy-Nagy's New Bauhaus. At least fifty houses were gone by 1946, when the photographer Walker Evens captured the F. R. Otis townhouse alone against a backdrop of printing plants (Figure 33).[80]

The Field house was lost in 1955. It took another decade before the burgeoning preservation movement found the street and launched an effort to save the Glessner house and protect it within the cocoon of a landmark district. By the time success was assured in 1978, there were a mere eight houses left standing among printing plants, parking lots, and derelict spaces. Today a "restored" streetscape uses plaques in niches formed of old iron fencing to stand in for lost mansions. The lure of the suburbs and the effects of the technological revolution on the printing industry are making the factories the new derelict spots in this museum of urban change. Second City Syndrome, however, had never abandoned the street. The Prairie Avenue Historic District, officially opened in 1978, has been called "the world's only Landmark Demolition Site."[81]

Figure 33. F. R. Otis residence, 2033 Prairie Avenue, 1869, architect unknown. Set against a backdrop of printing plants, 1946. Demolished.

ACKNOWLEDGMENTS

When asked, I envisioned writing an article that would meld the work of others and be full of gratitude to them. I didn't do that, and now I am indebted in addition to virtually every reference librarian and architectural and photographic collection curator in Chicago, every landmarks office staff member in Illinois, and architectural historians across the continent. Given that immense obligation, I hope I have been able to repay the most pressing debts by conveying here some of the all-compelling fascination that Prairie Avenue has for Victor Dyer, Jethro M. Hurt III, Dale Cowell, Elaine Harrington, and especially for Allan Vagner and Jack Simmerling.

MARY ALICE MOLLOY

CHAPTER SIX

ST. CHARLES

Avenue

NEW ORLEANS, LOUISIANA

IN A LYRICAL ASIDE IN HIS SARDONIC NOVEL *A Confederacy of Dunces*, John Kennedy
Toole wrote:

> The ancient oaks of St. Charles Avenue arched over the avenue like a canopy....St.
> Charles Avenue must be the loveliest place in the world. From time to time...passed
> the slowly rocking street cars that seemed to be leisurely moving toward no special des-
> tination, following their route through the old mansions on either side...everything
> looked so calm, so prosperous.

Toole nicely captured the subtropical mood of the United States' southernmost
grand avenue. Winding in generous curves corresponding roughly to the crescent
bend in the Mississippi's course west of downtown and the Vieux Carre, St.
Charles Avenue continues for four miles from Lee Circle near the city's center to
the once politically autonomous Carrollton neighborhood (Figure 1). Now
invaded by fast-food restaurants, budget hotels, and gas stations in its lower
reaches, most of the upper half of St. Charles Avenue's course still exudes the
combination of stateliness and dignified ease noted by Toole.

St. Charles Avenue's most rapid development began in the same years
Haussmann was cutting grand avenues through Paris. But it owes none of its character to French antecedents, which were the prototype for grand avenues in most
parts of the westernized world. Indeed, in many respects this grand avenue in what
was once La Nouvelle Orleans owes less to France than do most other great
American avenues of the period. It is also set off from most American avenues in
other respects as well. Thanks to the live oaks (*Quercus viriginiana*), St. Charles is

ESSAY BY S. FREDERICK STARR

Figure 1. Map showing the course of the New Orleans and Carrollton Rail Road and hence of St. Charles Avenue.

Figure 2. Live Oaks as monumental architecture. St. Charles Avenue, c. 1915.

more deeply bucolic than its counterparts in New York, Philadelphia, Chicago, or San Francisco (Figure 2). Few of its houses are built to so vast a scale as the sprawling residences on Euclid Avenue in Cleveland, nor was St. Charles ever dominated by a few palaces, as occurred on Summit Avenue in St. Paul. Heavily traveled and a haven for gawkers, it nonetheless was never the parade ground that was Fifth Avenue in its heyday, nor did it even achieve the degree of stiff propriety of Monument Avenue in Richmond. To be sure, St. Charles was, and to some extent is still, a showcase for the affluent. Yet from the start it was wide open to the common person, unlike such pompous conceits as Vandeventer Place in St. Louis.

For all its charm, St. Charles Avenue always fell short of most other American grand avenues according to such measures as the size of its greatest residences, the amount of stone and marble lavished on them, their shoulder-to-shoulder proximity to one another, and the formal grandeur of the streetscape as a whole. Yet it possesses certain characteristics that were common to most American grand avenues and that help define them as a group. Like many American avenues developed before the twentieth century, it is a monument to spontaneous privately initiated growth rather than to planning. No officially imposed standards defined its streetscape; no guidelines shaped its architecture. In spite of this, it conformed to an order as strict as that imposed on Paris by Napoleon III. The size of houses, the sprinkling of church and civic structures in their midst, and the clear relationship of these structures to each other and to the overall streetscape—all contribute to the order of the whole.

Of all these points, only the size of the lots was described by governmental action. All the rest must be attributed to the specific social and economic circumstances of the Crescent City in the late nineteenth century. In their day, these forces exerted a decisive influence on the avenue. Like other grand American avenues and unlike their European counterparts, St. Charles was created not by governmental action from above but through the direct actions of citizens. Yet it is not the product of democracy so much as of the open oligarchy that came into being as the New Orleans economy, and that of the United States generally, expanded in the late nineteenth century.[1]

Which Avenue Should Be Grand?

Haussmann's plan for Paris conceived of a network of intersecting concourses embracing the entire city. These in turn were lined with apartment houses built with inexpensive governmentally subsidized loans for the great bourgeois families. By this means the Second Empire co-opted the business and social elite. In America, by contrast, those who possessed new industrial and commercial wealth sought to organize the cityscape around themselves, co-opting the government as necessary. The difference reflects the fact that France was a statist monarchy while the United States was an increasingly oligarchic democracy.

For an American grand avenue to fulfill its function, it was therefore crucial that the oligarchs of an entire city come together in a single group and reach consensus over where they would make their collective architectural statement. Most cities boasted a single social elite whose members agreed on where they should settle. New Orleans did not. Before St. Charles could be established as the grand avenue, two alternatives were tried and rejected.

New Orleans' uncertainty in siting a grand avenue traces to the old split between the small but proud group of French Creoles and the rapidly expanding ranks of Anglo-Saxon and Jewish newcomers who increasingly dominated local life. The former concentrated in the eastern part of the city, especially on or near Esplanade Avenue, which ran from the Mississippi to the banks of Bayou St. John to the north. The latter were domiciled mainly in the western side of the city and particularly in the Garden District, settled in the 1840s and 1850s. Canal Street demarcated these two broad zones and would appear to have been the obvious compromise solution as a grand avenue acceptable to both groups. It began in the very center of the city, was as wide as any street in America, and ran north through land perfect for estate development.

Canal Street came closest to becoming a grand avenue in the period after 1838, when the waterway from which it derives its name was filled in. In that year an elaborate project for beautifying the street was devised.[2] Appearing as it did only months after the Panic of 1837, this proposal proved stillborn. In 1854, however, Judah Touro, a New Orleans philanthropist, left $150,000 in his will for the adornment of Canal Street. The city fathers accepted the bequest and had the work carried out.

Three serious impediments prevented Canal Street from becoming New Orleans' principal boulevard. First, while there was money to develop the short route as far as Rampart Street, the several miles beyond the urban core remained a marshy path. Second, Canal Street led nowhere except to the city's cemeteries. Because of this, neither the city government nor the public had reason to invest in it as a grand concourse. Third, and most important, Canal Street was probably too close to the Creole enclaves for the Anglo-Saxon immigrants and too close to the Yankee business center for the Creoles. Far from representing a social consensus, Canal Street symbolized the persisting division in New Orleans society (Figure 3).

The Creoles had their own grand thoroughfare in Esplanade Avenue. Following a slight ridge, Esplanade Avenue was physically more stable than marshy Canal Street and had the further advantage of connecting two significant points in the city. Like Canal Street, it had a broad center strip (or "neutral

Figure 3. Canal Street, handsomely developed and renamed, c. 1850s.

Figure 4. Esplanade Avenue in the mid-nineteenth century.

ground," as New Orleanians call it) in its lower reaches and had long been recognized by the populace as a promenade (Figure 4).

The chief reason Esplanade did not evolve into a true grand avenue is that the people most likely to build there—members of the Creole elite—were neither sufficiently wealthy nor numerous in the post–Civil War years when such avenues were the vogue. The *Illustrated Visitors' Guide to New Orleans* of 1879 listed Esplanade Avenue as "one of the most desirable" streets in the city, but it failed to attract many of those who made significant fortunes after that date.[3]

A serious effort to dramatize Esplanade and hence foster its development was made when a noble statue of the Confederate hero P. G. T. Beauregard was placed at its junction with Bayou St. John. But not one major cultural institution or new church was constructed on Esplanade in the late nineteenth century. "New money" did not flock to this locale, and to the extent it did, Esplanade Avenue offered no real competition to St. Charles, which by 1880 was firmly established as the Crescent City's main showcase avenue.

FROM PLAYGROUND OF THE NAYADES TO GRAND THOROUGHFARE

It is ironic that stately St. Charles Avenue was laid out initially as a roadbed for steam trains. Incorporated in 1833, the New Orleans and Carrollton Rail Road Company linked the historic downtown and the suburban village of Carrollton.[4] The entrepreneurs who built the railroad wanted to provide easy access from the city to the resort hotel and gardens they were building on the Mississippi levee at the line's western terminus. One of the earliest to use steam trains in the country, the new railroad eventually met its builders' financial expectations and even attracted some individuals to build along its route (Figure 5). In 1850 a writer for the *Daily Delta* observed that, "One of the greatest pleasures of a trip to Carrollton is the view of the many beautiful little villas which are springing up all along the road. Nothing could be more charming or lovely than the little gardens and groves in this delightful region...."[5]

Figure 5. The eastern end of St. Charles Avenue at Tivoli (later Lee) Circle, c. 1870s.

Americans, with their restless infatuation with motion, are quick to credit positive social changes to the application of new technologies of transportation. While this is justified in the case of so-called "streetcar suburbs" created in the late nineteenth century after the rise of electric interurban lines, it is not a defensible explanation for the proliferation of grand avenues, all of which were comfortably geared to the horse and pedestrian. Indeed, the steam trains on the Carrollton line actually thwarted the avenue's development, even though its engines today look like mere toys (Figure 6). Not only did prospective residents object to the

Figure 6. A noisy engine of the Carrollton line.

smoke and noise of the little engines, but the relatively high cost of their operation meant that only three trains could run per hour—too few to meet the needs of business commuters.

The railroad's managers tried valiantly to address the first problem by encouraging the development of cleaner and quieter engines. Thanks to their efforts, the New Orleanian Emile Lamm became a world pioneer in the development of cleaner and cheaper locomotives in the 1870s. His answer was an engine powered by a boiler of water that was preheated at the station house and piped into the cars at stops along the route (Figure 7). In the end the directors reverted to the sturdy mule. Not only were they cleaner, cheaper, and more reliable than the alternatives, but the low cost of mules meant that cars could be scheduled to run every five minutes.

Richmond, Virginia, had opened the nation's first electric trolley line in 1887–88, and by 1890 fully fifty-one cities had followed suit.[6] Only in 1893 were electric trolleys introduced on St. Charles Avenue, the first street in New Orleans to be served by them. The relatively late date was due to the local Electric Traction and Manufacturing Company's belief that cars driven by battery-operated motors would soon be practical and as cheap to operate as mules. Once the trolleys were installed they were an instant success, however, and by 1895 the new fleet was supplemented with carpeted "palace cars" outfitted with silk tapestry, Honduran mahogany, and plush. These contrasted sharply with the common cars, of which an English visitor wrote that "even when ladies and children are fellow passengers the men smoke and expectorate all over the place…."[7] Obviously, the palace cars were intended to lure onto public transportation those upper-class avenue residents who preferred to commute by carriage. But by the time the palace cars were fully in operation, the private automobile was already looming on the horizon. With the rise of the automobile, palace cars were no longer needed or wanted by the affluent.

Thus, although St. Charles Avenue owes its existence to steam engines and is associated today with the electric trolley, neither of these technologies was significant to its development as a grand avenue. Scarcely a decade separated the introduction of electric streetcars and the rise of private automobiles, which were soon carrying residents downtown. This crucial aspect of timing may well warrant a reconsideration of electric (as opposed to horse-drawn) streetcars in the development of grand avenues and suburbs elsewhere.

Partly because of the presence in its center strip of a rail line, St. Charles remained unpaved down to the 1880s. In the very years when many of the grandest homes were constructed, it alternated between being a dusty track and a pair of muddy ruts, often filled with water. As if recognizing this, the name of the thoroughfare until 1855 was Nayades Street, after the Greek spirits who inhabited rivers and streams. Yet if pavement would have rendered the avenue more passable and attractive, its absence seems not to have prevented large numbers of the city's most wealthy and influential citizens from settling their families on St. Charles. On this point as on others, social and economic considerations took precedence over concerns of planning and architecture.

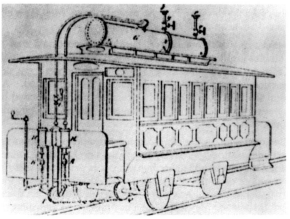

Figure 7. Emile Lamm's experimental "chloride engine."

Grand Avenues on an Empty Treasury

The Parisian grand avenues represented the French state's effort to organize society in conformity with its plan, rather than the society's effort to organize the public realm in its image. This situation was reversed in America thanks both to governmental poverty and to private affluence. Nowhere was this more evident in the late nineteenth century than in New Orleans, and particularly in the development of St. Charles Avenue.

The city's deficit constituted the single most important fact in the civic life of the Crescent City between the Civil War and 1900. This state of chronic indebtedness had begun before the Civil War, but in the antebellum years a rising economy tempered its impact. Indebtedness continued to mount during the postwar boom due to the spendthrift policies of the Carpetbag government. In an abrupt reversal, revenues then plunged after 1873 when the city was hit frontally by a financial panic that was worldwide in scope.

A decade later the city was still reeling under its accumulated debt. When the New Orleans and Carrollton Rail Road prepared to pay $275,000 for the franchise to operate the St. Charles Avenue line, the city fathers quite reasonably wanted to use the money to pave the road. By now many handsome homes had been built along the route, and the lack of paving was becoming a civic embarrassment. But fearing that the city's creditors would garnish the funds if they flowed into the city's treasury, they arranged to have the street railway company contract directly for the paving.[8]

This windfall provided the city's sole investment in St. Charles Avenue, with the exception of sidewalks and a few trees added later (Figure 8). The paving was significant nonetheless. However modest the asphalt

Figure 8. Upper St. Charles Avenue in the 1880s. Photograph shows curbs, trees, and sidewalks, but not yet pavement.

Figure 9. Uptown lane of the avenue, paved, curbed, and planted, c. 1915.

Figure 10. The Robert E. Lee Monument, terminus of the avenue, erected 1884–85.

topping on St. Charles, it set the avenue off from most other streets in the city (Figure 9). Only 94 of the city's 566 streets had any surface but dirt as late as the 1880s, and nearly all of these were covered not with concrete, brick, or macadam but with shell, plank, or cobblestones brought in as ballast in the holds of ships.[9]

The city's financial plight constrained the development of St. Charles Avenue in other ways. In 1880 the total budget of the city government amounted to $8.70 per capita, as compared with $14.70 for Baltimore, $16.30 for Louisville, $27.60 for Philadelphia, and $50.00 for Boston.[10] Sewer pipes were laid in the downtown area only in the mid-1890s, and on the city's grandest avenue only several years after that. Nor was city water available until about the same time, which forced avenue residents to continue the old practice of building silo-like cisterns to store rainwater piped from the roofs.[11]

160

Given the city government's financial plight, it is no wonder that St. Charles Avenue shows virtually no influence of the so-called City Beautiful ideal put forward at the Columbian Exposition in Chicago in 1893. For example, it has no long, straight stretches with monuments at the key intersections that characterized the City Beautiful. However attractive it may have been, this conception of what an American grand avenue should be demanded public funds far in excess of those available in New Orleans.

The grand avenues of Europe were characterized by their great breadth and characteristic streetscape, featuring sculpture, arches, and other monumental elements. These celebrated and were financed by the government, be it Franz Joseph II's Austro-Hungarian state or the Prussia of Wilhelm II. With the exception of Massachusetts Avenue in Washington, none of America's most handsome new avenues were in the capitol and none received subsidies from the central government. In this respect, all were provincial.

The only two civic structures on the entire length of St. Charles Avenue are the Lee monument at the eastern terminus and the classical arches at the gateway of Audubon Park near its western end. Significantly, they both trace their origin to private rather than public initiative. The Robert E. Lee monument was erected in 1884–85 through public subscription (Figure 10), and the entrance portico at Audubon Park is a legacy of the Cotton Centennial Exposition of the same year (Figure 11). Tax money paid for the stone entrance that remains today, but not for most of the pavilions, which were donated by private citizens.

New Orleans' most grand avenue came into being at a time when the city government was underinvesting in most public works, including roads and avenues. Worse, much of the money designated for public works was misspent, due to corruption. The Department of Improvements (after 1882 the Department of Public Works) was renowned for its peculation, as were the city offices most directly involved with the St. Charles Avenue streetcar franchise (Figure 12).[12]

Figure 11. Gateway to Audubon Park.

Figure 12. A political cartoon from 1882.

In spite of this bleak picture, several public works projects undertaken near St. Charles Avenue were successfully completed and had the effect of protecting the avenue from commercial encroachment. As the Civil War was ending, the city government encouraged the development of a commercial district along Magazine Street near Jackson Avenue. It built an outdoor market there and also a spacious covered market on Prytania Street, only a block from St. Charles. Together, these facilities contributed to a functional division of labor, with commercial development concentrated on Magazine Street, mixed commercial and residential development on Prytania Street, and largely residential and cultural development on St. Charles Avenue. In a city with no land use laws for another half-century, this constituted a kind of *de facto* zoning.

Private Wealth, New and Old

Given the city government's depleted coffers, the existence of private wealth in late-nineteenth-century New Orleans was all the more essential to the development of St. Charles as a grand avenue. From the 1820s through the 1860s, New Orleans had generated what in that day were immense fortunes. As the nation's second port, the city was responsible for over a quarter of U.S. exports in the immediate pre–Civil War years and was the chief entrepôt for goods shipped by packet boat throughout the inland waterways.

Most of the fortunes thus created were amassed by self-made Yankee immigrants with commercial ties to New York, Philadelphia, and such foreign centers as Liverpool. These men consigned their families to suburban life in the newly formed Garden District and account for most of the comfortable homes that grace that pioneer American suburb even today.[13] St. Charles Avenue ran through the Garden District for part of its length, but up to the Civil War it was not considered a prime address within the Garden District. True, a number of important homes were built there, among them Lavinia Dabney's fine Greek Revival house at 2265 St. Charles Avenue and the pair of handsome Italianate *palazzos*, also in the Garden District (and since demolished), built by Samuel P. Griffin. But Jackson Avenue, Prytania Street, Washington Avenue, and several other interior streets of the Garden District were all considered preferable locations.

The tempo of new construction on lower St. Charles Avenue up to Louisiana Avenue quickened after the Civil War. Shepherd Brown's elaborate "raised cottage" in the Garden District and, nearby, the imposing Italianate extravaganza designed by architect Lewis Reynolds for coffee importer Lafayette Folger (both since demolished) are but two of many new dwellings of the postbellum era that set the tone for future developments. Many other houses of considerable scale also rose on lower St. Charles Avenue in the half-dozen years following Appomattox. Prime building sites on the more prominent streets within the Garden District were already becoming scarce, causing a miniature boom on St. Charles even before mule-drawn cars reduced the clatter and belching smoke in the 1870s. Suffice it to say that one of the Garden District's greatest bon vivants, Cuthbert Bullitt, built his new Swiss chalet on St. Charles Avenue just a few blocks beyond the Garden District. It now stands at 3627 Carondolet Street.

The existence of "old money" in uptown New Orleans was not in itself sufficient to create a grand avenue there. Families with wealth from the earlier booms had for the most part already built homes for themselves. Also, Confederate sympathizers who had lost their fortunes or departed left behind large homes that were available for purchase by many newly rich families who might otherwise have built on the avenue. Down to the late 1870s, there was not sufficient new wealth to shift decisively the center of prestige from the old Garden District enclave to the ribbon of St. Charles.

In contrast to New York, with its vast commercial fortunes, or Chicago, with its merchandising and railroad wealth, or Cleveland, with its huge industrial fortunes, New Orleans remained something of an economic backwater. Bypassed by the transcontinental railroads and slow to supplement a declining river trade with its own network of rail links, New Orleans lost ground. Other ports on the Gulf and the Atlantic were more aggressive in meeting the country's emerging economic needs. As a result, by the 1890s New Orleans' share of U.S. exports had shrunk by two-thirds to eight percent of the total while it handled a scant two percent of the nation's imports.[14]

Notwithstanding these various negative trends, the economy of New Orleans staged a limited comeback beginning in the 1880s that continued up to the recession that set in after 1893. Few wholly new industries appeared during these years, and the large-scale industrialization that gained ground in the North had no parallel in the Crescent City. Yet this modest renaissance of the 1880s expanded certain older fortunes and created many new ones. This limited boom created a new class of what Samuel Clemens called New Orleans' "long-headed men." These people were responsible for many civic improvements, including the World's Industrial and Cotton Centennial Exposition that opened in 1884.[15] The exposition itself was far from a financial success, but its location on upper St. Charles did much to promote the notion that this was New Orleans' one true grand avenue.

Many of the men who promoted this project themselves settled on St. Charles. They were sympathetic to the so-called New South ideology, which held that the economic renewal of the former Confederate states would come only by their adopting the North's aggressive business practices. In the wake of the devastating Panic of 1873 many of the older and more established local businessmen grew more cautious and felt little sympathy for this frankly entrepreneurial program. The younger and bolder men who succeeded in the face of such doomsayers felt entitled to celebrate and to proclaim publicly their worldly achievements. A residence on St. Charles Avenue was the perfect way to make such a statement.

The New Men

Who were these new entrepreneurs? John S. Wallis, who built the Queen Anne house at 4125 St. Charles, was president of the Louisiana Sugar Refining Company. William Mason Smith, whose massive stone dwelling still stands at 4534 St. Charles Avenue, served as president of the New Orleans Cotton Exchange. Joseph Hernandez turned the New Orleans and Carrollton Rail Road Company into a profitable enterprise by the late 1870s, at which time he built his spacious Italianate home at 4803 St. Charles Avenue. Both

Samuel Zemurray, who lived at 2 Audubon Place at the corner of St. Charles, and Joseph Vaccaro, at 5010 St. Charles Avenue, built their fortunes by importing fruit from Central America. Robert Roberts, whose home formerly stood at St. Charles and Conery Streets, had enriched himself in the lumber business, and Leonard Krower of 4630 was a Canal Street jeweler. Alfred Hiller at 4417 was the Massachusetts-born owner of a cement factory, and Simon Hernsheim, whose home at 3811 St. Charles Avenue is now the Columns Hotel, was one of the country's largest manufacturers of cigars.[16]

Even this brief enumeration indicates the wide range of fields in which those who built on St. Charles Avenue amassed their fortunes. Among avenue residents were to be found Montreal-born Joseph A. Walker, a major investor in Colonel Merriam's fabled Crescent City Billiard Parlor, at 2503, and the New Jersey–born president of the notorious Louisiana Lottery, John Morris, down the street at 2525. It is all but impossible to generalize about these men, except to observe that none of them derived his wealth from industries that were on the cutting edge of American industrial development at the time. Unlike those who had earlier settled in the Garden District, these new men did not initially constitute a group, let alone a close-knit community. The Garden District had been the perfect expression of an earlier phase of New Orleans' economic life, in which leadership was exercised by a self-conscious coalition of leaders in allied fields. St. Charles Avenue mirrored the changed circumstances of the later nineteenth century, in which economic leadership was dominated by entrepreneurs who had spread out in seemingly random directions. Such people had little in common with one another yet were eager to demonstrate that they had achieved affluence and status. St. Charles Avenue was not the only street on which they chose to settle, but its character as a linear showcase met their social needs to a rare degree. St. Charles Avenue enabled a whole class of *arrivistes* to proclaim its arrival.

Those who built the great houses on St. Charles Avenue in the last third of the nineteenth century were diverse in their backgrounds and professions, but there were strong elements of cohesion among them. These were given physical expression in the various cultural institutions that sprang up along the avenue, and which will be considered shortly. Before doing so, a qualification regarding the diversity must be entered, namely, the presence along the avenue of a large number of Jewish families whose heads had enriched themselves in the generation following the outbreak of the Civil War. While precise statistical evidence is lacking, it is clear that Jews constituted one of the largest and most coherent groups within the diverse population along St. Charles Avenue.

The coherence of New Orleans' Jewish elite traces to its background in the German-speaking French province of Alsace and in the German Rhineland generally. For the most part they had received little education in their homeland, nor were they political exiles driven abroad by the collapse of the Revolutions of 1848, as was the case with so many Germans and German Jews in St. Louis, Cincinnati, and Milwaukee. Yet if they did not stand in the direct assimilationist tradition established by Moses Mendelsohn in eighteenth-century Berlin, they were nonetheless quick to adapt to their new land. The early prominence of philanthropist Judah Touro and politician Judah P. Benjamin in the life of New Orleans and the region encouraged other wealthy Jews to participate actively in the community as a whole. Engaging in a range of commercial enterprises, they commanded sufficient wealth to do so effectively. Many of these prosperous Jewish citizens took up residence on St. Charles Avenue, especially in the area beyond the intersection with Napoleon Avenue.

For example, Marks Isaacs, a Canal Street retailer, in 1907 built the spacious home at 5120 St. Charles Avenue that is now the Latter Library, and the commission merchant Abraham Ermann built the home standing at 4217. Cigar maker Simon Hernsheim resided in his lavish home at 3811, and the jeweler Henry Krower built the house at 4630. Several members of the large Newman family took up residence on the avenue, including its elder, Isidore Newman, who had begun as a peddler to plantations before the Civil War and built a fortune extending credit to plantation owners after the war. Among other prominent Jewish leaders who resided on St. Charles Avenue were Simon Hirsch, president of J. C. Morris Ltd. (4631), Henry Fichtenberg (4920), Jacob Abraham (5504), and several members of both the prominent Godchaux and Lehmann families. By the late nineteenth century these Jewish leaders could get together at the Harmony Club, on St. Charles Avenue. They also built Touro Synagogue at 4238 St. Charles and established the Jewish Widows and Orphans Home near Jefferson (Figure 13). This massive Italianate structure by architect Thomas Sully remained the largest building on the entire avenue down to the completion of Loyola University's main building early in the new century. The presence on St. Charles of these institutions and the people who built them attests to their importance to, and acceptance by, the larger economy and society of New Orleans.

Figure 13. The Jewish Widows and Orphans Home, Thomas Sully, architect.

Figure 14. Academy of the Sacred Heart, 1900.

The absence of a single dominant new industry in New Orleans or of a group of related industries meant that few of the Protestants and Catholics on St. Charles Avenue had the kind of daily business contact with one another that an earlier generation of New Orleanians had. Nonetheless, they and their families built strong elements of community through a wide range of clubs and churches. Many of these were headquartered on the avenue. For men there was the Round Table Club at 6330 St. Charles Avenue, while for women there was the Orleans Club, headquartered after 1909 in the old Mrs. George G. Garner mansion at 5005 St. Charles. Churches representing most of the mainline Protestant denominations and, with the addition of Loyola University, the Catholics as well, were also built along the avenue.

This movement of cultural institutions of all faiths to St. Charles confirmed its status as the city's premier avenue. The churches and synagogue especially imparted an aura of dignity and solidity that could not have been achieved by dwelling houses alone, even if they were mansions.

Many institutions besides clubs and places of worship lent stature to St. Charles Avenue by their presence there. Among them were several that had no physical headquarters in the usual sense of the word and were present on the avenue for only a few hours each year. These were the carnival "krewes," private men's associations committed to mounting lavish masqued parades on Mardi Gras and to frivolity and conviviality at other times. Their parades of floats centered on the downtown area, particularly Canal Street and the Vieux Carre. However, nearly all of them approached downtown from the west, proceeding along St. Charles Avenue from either Jackson or Napoleon. This annual ritual involved many of the men living on the avenue. Their masqued procession down the grand concourse in parades lit by sputtering flambeaux was the kind of ritual that transformed a plain streetscape into a legendary zone, not only on Mardi Gras but throughout the year. Such parades confirmed St. Charles's reputation as a center of attention and truly a grand avenue.

Yet another civic function that increasingly focused on St. Charles Avenue was education. The first major educational institution to be established on the avenue was St. Mary's Dominican College. After buying the land in 1864, the group of Irish-born Dominican nuns commissioned architect William Fitzner to build the main building in 1892. This step reflected the growing Catholic presence in what had earlier been the largely Protestant uptown section of New Orleans. At almost the same time, the Sisters of the Sacred Heart undertook to build their academy further down St. Charles near the Garden District. In 1887 their academy moved to the new site and construction of their handsome French Colonial building commenced in 1900 (Figure 14). By this year the Jesuits, too, were close to realizing their hopes for a Catholic men's college uptown. Having purchased a large plot near the former Exposition grounds, now Audubon Park, they began construction of their French Gothic academic buildings and chapel in 1904. By the end of the decade Loyola University was firmly established there.

A year before the Cotton Centennial Exposition opened its doors, Paul Tulane, a New Jersey–born New Orleans businessman, left money in his will to establish a nonsectarian university in New Orleans. In 1888 the trustees named by Tulane's will decided to move the fledgling institution from downtown, where it had briefly existed, to the former sugarcane plantation across St. Charles Avenue from the former exposition grounds. Seven years later the main building on St. Charles Avenue was opened, giving the avenue its most prominent building in the neo-Romanesque style pioneered by the Louisiana-born H. H. Richardson.

The concentration of churches, schools, clubs, and colleges on St. Charles Avenue indicate the readiness of avenue residents to strengthen the civic presence there. In spite of their diverse backgrounds and lack of close business links, they came increasingly to constitute a community, or at least a group of related subcommunities. To some extent, the avenue itself served as a social condenser for these people, placing each in a relationship to the others and to the city that might not have formed so easily had they lived elsewhere.

The strong community orientation of residents of St. Charles Avenue and uptown New Orleans generally is attested by the failure of private streets to make headway there. Modeled on Vandeventer Avenue in St. Louis, private streets excluded the public and denied to passersby even the role of gawker. Such closed thoroughfares looked inward rather than outward and were limited to residences, with no place for churches or

Figure 15. Audubon Place, St. Charles Avenue.

civic buildings. The first such street in New Orleans was Rosa Park, which was built off St. Charles Avenue in the boom year of 1891. Named for the colorful wife of Durant DaPonte, a nearby avenue resident, Rosa Park had fewer than a dozen homes. New Orleans' other private street, Audubon Place, was conceived in 1895, and its twenty-eight residences were built largely in the early twentieth century. Here, finally, was a private street of grandly scaled homes adjoining St. Charles Avenue yet separated from it by a formidable stone gate (Figure 15). This project was the work not of New Orleanians but of a Fort Worth developer. Even though New Orleanians bought all the lots on Audubon Place, they showed little further disposition to flee from St. Charles Avenue to private streets.

ARCHITECTS AND ARCHITECTURE

To achieve their aspirations, those moving to St. Charles Avenue needed not only money but architects capable of translating their dreams into reality. Their choice of architects and the character of the buildings they ordered or accepted from those architects tells much about the patrons and their world. Did they aspire to compete with those wealthy families building grand avenues elsewhere in the United States? Were certain architects considered status symbols? Were houses on the avenue notable for their advanced style, their size, or their comfort? The answers to such questions not only provide keys to understanding St. Charles Avenue but help position it among other such avenues nationally.

Many different architects worked on St. Charles Avenue. Individuals such as Emile Weil, Louis Lambert, Frank P. Gravely, and William Fitzner were active there, as were such partnerships as Favrot and Livaudais, Harrod and Andry, Andry and Bendernagel, and Sully and Toledano. Some, like Fitzner, were familiar figures on the New Orleans architectural scene. Most of the others were young designers who began their careers only in the 1870s or 1880s and matured professionally with the rise of the avenue.

Had St. Charles Avenue developed earlier in the nineteenth century, most of the houses would have been designed by builders rather than architects. But by 1870 nearly all those designing the larger residences identified themselves as architects. While most had received training only as apprentices, they joined the American Institute of Architects and increasingly conducted their professional life according to national standards.

Was this shift from builders to architects complete on St. Charles Avenue? Probably not. A striking feature of the streetscape as a whole is the concentration of commissions in the hands of a few architects and firms. Nearly all those listed above produced three or more residences for the avenue. Emile Weil, who was among the first to promote the Renaissance Revival locally, did at least half a dozen homes there. The New Orleans native Thomas Sully, who lived in a house of his own design at 4010 St. Charles, designed more than two dozen known houses on the avenue, and probably more.[17]

Even a cursory look at St. Charles Avenue indicates that a wide range of architectural styles was employed there and that the neat—too neat—chronological sequence of styles that historians detect elsewhere was not systematically observed here. But there were limits to this diversity. Many patrons shared the same architects and firms, and received from them work in the same general stylistic vein. This suggests that it was not particularly important for avenue residents to build a house that was startlingly original in its architecture. Had it been, we would expect greater diversity from the architects who dominated the local scene. Also, many patrons would surely have gone outside of New Orleans in search of architects, which they did not do. Unlike such showcase thoroughfares as Euclid Avenue in Cleveland, Vandeventer in St. Louis, or Erie Avenue in Cincinnati, St. Charles boasts no major buildings by the best-known national architects of the era. It is not that avenue residents were provincials. They had close commercial ties to the rest of the country and traveled frequently for business and pleasure. One of the best-known national architects was Henry Hobson Richardson, who was raised just off St. Charles Avenue downtown on Julia Row and was known personally to many New Orleanians. Avenue residents did not turn to such national architects as Richardson for their homes because they felt no need to bring in outsiders, no matter how prominent nationally, to perform a task that was considered largely utilitarian in nature.

This is not to say that style was unimportant. The fact that several members of the Newman family commissioned large stone residences in the same ponderous Richardson Romanesque style says much about the sense of permanence they sought to build (Figure 16). Favrot and Livaudais' palatial residence in the same

Figure 16. Isadore Newman residence. Photo etching, 1892.

Figure 17. William Perry Brown residence, 4717 St. Charles Avenue.

Figure 18. Picard house. St. Charles Avenue between Marengo and Milan Streets, Thomas Sully, architect.

style for William Perry Brown, at 4717 St. Charles, reflects that patron's decision in the last decade of the century to break with the styles favored by older members of the Anglo-Saxon elite (Figure 17). At least one "castle" (now demolished) was built at the uptown end of the avenue, and there were several buildings each in the Renaissance Revival and Colonial Revival styles, each of them attesting to their owner's boldness in matters of taste.

For all this variety, one style set the overall tone for the avenue in the period of most intensive building, namely, the Queen Anne in both its "pure" and Italianate variants. Thomas Sully, who was adept at both the Renaissance Revival (4417 St. Charles) and the "Shingle style" (his own home at 4010), was the local master of the Queen Anne (Figure 18). Raised in the Garden District and trained as an architect in Austin, Texas, and New York, Sully built more houses in this style than any other local architect. More comfortable than imposing, the Queen Anne permitted the creation of very large rooms opening onto hallways that were themselves rooms and were therefore perfect for entertaining.

Architectural historians love chronological tidiness, but the blending of styles of different periods was a regular feature of St. Charles Avenue architecture. Several delightfully florid Italianate homes showing strong Queen Anne influences still adorn the avenue, notably 4801 (Figure 19), while other fine ones at 5401 and 3905 (Figure 20) have been demolished.[18] Incongruously, several of these also featured mansard roofs and other traits of the Second Empire style. As often happened in Victorian architecture, "style" was something added at the end of the design process rather than a principle used to define interior spaces.

The fact that all the Queen Anne houses and most of the Italianate and Second Empire residences were built of wood underscored the resemblance among structures built in differing styles.[19] This led to similar sur-

Figure 19. 4801 St. Charles Avenue, Italianate villa.

Figure 20. 3905 St. Charles Avenue, Italianate villa. Demolished.

face treatments, textures, and colors, and to identical treatment of all elements not dictated by the specifics of the given style. Due to large-scale cutting of cypress trees in the Atchafalaya basin in central Louisiana and commercial logging of the pine forests in nearby Mississippi, wood was in ample supply and cheap. By contrast, all stone, exterior brick, and even mortar had to be imported from as far away as Tennessee and Missouri. It is no wonder that nearly all houses built before the boom years of the late 1880s were of plastered over wood or soft "river brick" and that the more expensive materials were employed mainly in the later residences on the avenue's uptown end.

In spite of the exceptionally high cost of materials, a number of avenue residents built monumental homes on a scale rivaling their counterparts on other American grand avenues (Figure 21). Nonetheless, St. Charles Avenue houses are more notable for their comfort than their scale, and for their general compatibility with one another rather than their ostentation or eccentricity. The DaPonte's exuberant seraglio just outside the Garden District, with its onion-shaped cupola and backyard theater, does not invalidate this generalization, nor do the several other similarly extravagant residences (Figure 22).

The Whitney estate, which formerly occupied an entire block along St. Charles Avenue in the Garden District, is a good example of this restraint

Figure 21. 5809 St. Charles Avenue.

171

Figure 22. The DaPonte seraglio.

Figure 23. M. L. Whitney residence.

in architecture. Frequently cited in guidebooks of the day as one of the sights of the city, M. L. Whitney's house featured a separate wing devoted to the paintings and objet d'art collected by this wealthy banker and his wife. Yet the house itself was not large, and may even have been constructed around an earlier raised cottage on the site. Except for its mansard roof, the house was not particularly distinctive in design. It goes without saying that the owner of one of the region's largest banks could have afforded a more imposing residence. That he did not build one suggests that there was neither a social necessity nor a personal desire to do so (Figure 23).

The key variable was in all likelihood the relationship of the avenue resident to the older elite of the Garden District. The Whitneys were part of that world and felt no need to outshine its members. This was not the case with Samuel Zemurray, the immigrant who revolutionized the fruit business nationally by importing bananas through the inexpensive Mississippi Gulf ports rather than through New Orleans, and who built the palatial columned residence at the corner of St. Charles and Audubon Place (Figure 24). Nor was this the situation of Emmanuel P. Benjamin, the Cincinnati-born owner of the Italian Renaissance palace at 5531 St. Charles.

Figure 24. The Zemurray residence.

Most patrons fell between the extremes of Whitney and Benjamin and Zemurray. As a group, however, they tended more toward dignified restraint than vulgar ostentation. It goes without saying that many avenue residents who built less grandly may not have had the money to do more. Whatever the cause, and however many exceptions to the rule, the stylistic norm for private residences on New Orleans' grand avenue was less imposing and pretentious than on most other grand avenues in the Northeast and Midwest.

SUBSEQUENT FATE

From Napolean Avenue uptown St. Charles Avenue remains today much the way it was in the 1920s. This section will doubtless enter the twenty-first century intact. But the area from Lee Circle to Napolean has deteriorated badly over recent decades. In conclusion, it is well to inquire into the reasons for the architectural erosion of the lower sections of the avenue and the preservation of its upper reaches.

The simplest explanation for the decay of lower St. Charles Avenue is economic. Had more new fortunes been formed in the years before the boon unleashed by the OPEC oil embargo in 1973, many houses that fell to the wrecking ball might well have been sold instead to private purchasers. This was not the case, so when some of the larger properties changed hands, developers eyed them for their commercial potential. Zoning laws came late to New Orleans, and were easily altered to accord with the interest of politically well-connected real estate agents and developers.

In some cases the demolition of historic residences occurred without there being a developer in sight. The several barren lots visible behind handsome cast-iron fences along the avenue attest to their "transitional" owners' failed hope of quick profits from demolition and development. Also, willful demolition by arson occurred at the hands of cash-short owners eager to collect insurance money in order to invest it elsewhere.

New Orleans was among the scores of major American cities to witness "white flight" from the historic center and suburbanization during the 1950s and 1960s. This created a vacuum on lower St. Charles that was readily filled by tacky shops, gas stations, and bars. St. Charles Avenue's status as an arterial road exacerbated this process, especially as the intensive development of new neighborhoods uptown placed heavier traffic on the thoroughfare (Figure 25).

Which contributed more to the decay of lower St. Charles Avenue: urban poverty, or prosperity and new construction? While both played a part, a strong case can be made that prosperity has been the worst culprit. During the boom years following the 1973 oil embargo, New Orleans was awash with cash. Large drugstores, franchised restaurants, and gas stations filled lots that were heretofore occupied by single- or multiple-family

Figure 25. St. Charles Avenue, c. 1950.

dwellings. Other owners who had long been content to rent to families now seized the opportunity to develop retail shops in the old houses.

In spite of these powerful destructive pressures, large parts of the avenue remain intact as fashionable residential districts. Several factors have contributed to this happy situation. First, New Orleans lacks a large and readily accessible hinterland in which fancy new suburbs can be built. Old Metairie and the lakefront doubtless drew many high-income residents from the avenue and adjoining areas, but both of them are too small in area to accommodate the number of houses needed to cause the collapse of the older residential areas. Second, the rise of the tourist industry has renewed St. Charles Avenue's status as a prime attraction in the city. This has generated interest in preserving the avenue and its streetcar line when both might have been neglected. Third, New Orleans' very low property taxes have enabled many people to stay in large homes on St. Charles Avenue who would have been financially unable to do so had they been in other major cities.

Finally, the fact that New Orleans' grand avenue had few gargantuan palaces contributed to the preservation of the street as a whole. In other cities, the largest residences rarely have found buyers. Their downward spiral begins with their division into small apartments and ends with their utter decay and demolition. This essay began with the observation that in many respects St. Charles Avenue is less "grand" than many comparable avenues in America. Various economic and social causes for this relative lack of "grandeur" have been noted. It is paradoxical that while the social ambitions and pretensions of the newly wealthy stimulated the development of St. Charles Avenue, they were not so great, and the homes to which they gave rise were not so vast, as to render the avenue unfit for use in our more modest age.

CHAPTER SEVEN

MASSACHUSETTS
Avenue
WASHINGTON, D.C.

IT IS SAID THAT IN WASHINGTON, D.C., momentous decisions are made, not in government offices, but over dinner in private homes. If that is true, then it is probable that more such decisions have been made on Massachusetts Avenue than on any other street in the city. For nearly one hundred years it has been the capital's premier residential thoroughfare, rivaled only by Sixteenth Street at the beginning of this century.[1]

On L'Enfant's plan for Washington, dated 1791, Massachusetts Avenue stands out above all others, running through the entire city in a strong diagonal from southeast to northwest. It runs north of, and parallel to, the official street of power, Pennsylvania Avenue.

L'Enfant's plan, derived primarily from French sources, depended heavily on diagonal avenues and broad vistas, with circles and squares as focal points. Massachusetts Avenue, throughout its length, is punctuated with these "pauses"; they break up vistas, keeping distances within human comprehension (Figure 1). With their open space, green planting, and invariably a monumental statue, the circles offer welcome respite from the rigidity of building-lined streets. An interesting result of their placement, at points where several avenues intersect the orthogonal grid pattern of the streets, is the creation of triangular and other polygonal lots. These odd shapes have encouraged architectural variety. Victorian architecture lent itself particularly well to them; a turret with a high, conical roof was often placed at the apex, and together with various other protuberances, gave the appearance of the prow of a great fanciful ship.

Because of their special qualities, the circles always attracted upper-class resi-

ESSAY BY SUE KOHLER

Figure 1. Massachusetts Avenue in 1900. Map showing U.S. Reservations, drawn by the Army Corps of Engineers.

dential development. During the late nineteenth and early twentieth centuries they were essentially outdoor parlors, cool oases in Washington's tropical summers, where children played and neighbors gathered to talk and promenade. Unfortunately, the residential development that enhanced the circles has all but disappeared, and where it still exists, as around Sheridan Circle, heavy traffic makes it difficult for the pedestrian to reach the circle itself.

Massachusetts Avenue, in spite of its prominence on the map of 1791, sustained very little substantial development until after the Civil War. After leaving the Capitol Hill area, its strong northwesterly direction took it quickly away from the early areas of settlement—around the Capitol, between the Capitol and the White House, and along the western section of Pennsylvania Avenue leading to the established city of Georgetown.

In 1809 the city council passed *An Act to Prevent Swine from Going At Large*; this act named Massachusetts Avenue as the boundary beyond which pigs were allowed to roam. By the 1840s the future grand avenue was still no more than a single wagon track. Even as late as 1862, the English writer Anthony Trollope wrote:

> Massachusetts Avenue runs the whole length of the city, and is inserted on the maps as a full-grown street about four miles in length. Go there, and you will find yourself not only out of town, away among the fields, but you will find yourself beyond the fields, in an uncultivated undrained wilderness. Tucking your trousers up to your knees you will wade through the bogs; you will lose yourself among the rude hillocks; you will be out of the reach of humanity.[2]

To be fair, it should be stated that Mr. Trollope's bogs were probably in the Dupont Circle area, far out at that time, and still crossed by Slash Run, which drained into Rock Creek near P Street. Closer to town there was considerable residential development on the avenue, although it was generally modest.

The development of Massachusetts Avenue as a desirable residential area for the well-to-do began in the 1870s, a decade that ushered in a long period of prosperity and industrial expansion throughout the country. Vast fortunes were made, and although Washington was strictly a government town with no industry to speak of, it felt the effects of the country's confident mood. To make the shabby and backward city look like the nation's capital it was, a massive public improvement program was undertaken.

"Boss" Alexander Shepherd, head of the Department of Public Works under Washington's new territorial government set up by Congress in 1871, pushed through a program that included the regrading and repaving of streets (many were paved for the first time), new sewers, sidewalks, and street lighting; an additional amenity was the planting of 60,000 street trees, which, when grown, gave Washington a unique character among American cities. Unfortunately, the program was carried out almost overnight, before adequate studies had been made, with the result that it bankrupted the city and brought an end to territorial government in the District.[3] The results were not all bad, however; Washington at last received the look of the capital of a great nation, and large areas, particularly in the northwest quadrant, were opened up to development. While a certain number of people were attracted to Lincoln Square on lower Massachusetts Avenue, in the Capitol Hill area, the trend after the Civil War was to the northwest, to generally higher ground and cooler air. Massachusetts Avenue led straight in the right direction, and its circles and vistas gave it a distinction many other streets lacked. When the circles received their impressive statues of Civil War heroes in the 1870s and 1880s, they took on an additional importance and became monumental in character.

Late-nineteenth-century residential development on Massachusetts Avenue occurred primarily between Ninth Street NW and Dupont Circle (Twentieth Street). Washington was gaining steadily in wealth, and well-to-do professionals, businessmen, merchants, and highly placed government officials began to build in this conveniently located area, still sparsely settled but certainly no longer the outer boundary of civilization. In the book *Picturesque Washington*, published in 1884, one finds this assessment of the new Washington and the development in the far northwest section of the city:

> It is on this spacious plain, but a few years ago an almost valueless area of swamps, that those palatial mansions, the pride and boast of the capital, are erected. Here are the residences of the wealthiest citizens, and those of the millionaires from sections of the United States who make Washington their winter home.... Here are the foreign legation buildings, and here the leaders of society have congregated under splendid roof-trees. On every side is a dazzling spectacle of luxury and grandeur, and one can obtain by a stroll through the avenues and streets, a realization of the enormous wealth that is centering in Washington at the present time....
>
> From its early days the national capital has been noted for being a gay and pleasure-loving city, and its social life had been unusually brilliant and delightful. Of late it has developed its social qualities to a very considerable extent, and society now has the claim of cosmopolitan characteristics.... The houses of the wealthy are now constructed with special reference to the giving of grand entertainments, very large drawing-rooms and dining rooms made, and accommodations provided for a host of guests.[4]

At this time there was no one grand avenue in the capital. Massachusetts Avenue, Connecticut and New Hampshire Avenues in the Dupont Circle area, as well as Sixteenth Street and K Street in the vicinity of the White House all had their mansions as well as many handsome rows of fine houses that were a bit below the mansion level. Henry Hobson Richardson, America's finest architect of the period, built four great houses in Washington, all near the White House, on Sixteenth and K Streets.[5]

For the most part, the "palatial mansions" were not built by native or even long-time Washingtonians. It was the peculiarity of Washington, a city built "from scratch" as the seat of government, that its residents were primarily transients. This is, to some extent, still true today. Of course, by the end of the Civil War, there were Washington families who could be called "old," and even older families who had settled in Georgetown as far back as the eighteenth century. But these families were small in number and tended to remain in their old family homes in the White House/Georgetown area or in outlying "country" estates.

Those who were building on upper Massachusetts Avenue and other streets in the West End, as it was called, can be divided roughly into three groups. One group consisted of members of Congress and other high-ranking government officials who expected to be in the capital for some time; many stayed on after their tours of duty had ended, having become accustomed to the excitement of Washington society. The second group included businessmen, professionals, and well-to-do merchants; these men were usually not native Washingtonians but had spent a good part of their lives in the capital. A third group, which increased in number as the turn of the century approached, consisted of self-made men from the Middle and Far West, usually retired from the businesses that had made them wealthy. They were drawn to the capital because of its brilliant social season, the chance to mingle with figures of political and diplomatic prominence, and, very likely, to do a little lobbying for their businesses back home. Washington was used to newcomers, and society was not nearly as rigid as it was in other East Coast cities; the right amount of money plus at least reasonable behavior almost guaranteed acceptance.

THOMAS AND SCOTT CIRCLES — THE GILDED AGE

City directories paint a graphic picture of the enormous growth that took place in Washington beginning in the 1870s: in 1871, the year "Boss" Shepherd began his city improvements, there were three architects and twenty-five real estate agents listed in the business section; by 1883 those numbers had increased, respectively, to twenty-one and eighty-seven.

On Massachusetts Avenue the area between Ninth and Seventeenth Streets filled up rapidly. This stretch includes both Thomas and Scott Circles, which were particularly attractive to the affluent. Following the pattern seen elsewhere in the city, large freestanding residences were built around the circles and on the corner lots, with row house development filling in the blocks. The more impressive examples were usually nearest the circles. These houses were generally the work of local architects, and they were characteristic of the period—picturesque in outline and embellished with a wealth of detail inside and out. They were often not great mansions in the usual sense of the word, and only rarely did they achieve true architectural distinction; the effect came from the ensemble. Washington houses of this period were invariably built of a bright red brick, made from local clay. The red color made an attractive combination with the green of the deep front lawns (the result of generous building setbacks along the avenue) and the luxuriant foliage of the trees in side and back gardens. Contributing significantly to the effect were the thousands of American elms and other trees that lined the city streets, thanks to Shepherd's improvements.

Although the character of Massachusetts Avenue at this time was due largely to these Victorian houses, the spiritual life of the residents was not neglected. In 1874 two imposing churches, still standing, were built: the Episcopal Church of the Ascension, at Massachusetts Avenue and Twelfth Street, designed in the English

Victorian Gothic style, and the Luther Place Memorial Church at Thomas Circle, also a Gothic structure, though of less well-defined origin (Figure 2). Several other large church edifices, now gone, were built in the area in the 1880s. Their tall spires, breaking the tree canopy, made a pleasant contrast to the low residential development. At Scott Circle stood the First Baptist Church, with a fine tower in the manner of H. H. Richardson. Deemed too small to accommodate its congregation, it was demolished in 1950 and replaced by a church without a tower.

Massachusetts Avenue crosses Thomas Circle at Fourteenth Street and Scott Circle at Sixteenth Street. Thomas Circle received its equestrian statue of General George Thomas in 1879; General Winfield Scott's statue had already been erected on Scott Circle in 1874. Each statue was set on a high pedestal so that it would be visible along the main streets coming into the circle. A green carpet of grass surrounded the statue, interspersed with flower beds and specimen trees; ornamental gas street lamps ringed the perimeter.

The earliest grand house on Thomas Circle was built in the 1840s, when the area was still rural. It was a large, three-story brick in a simple Greek Revival style, erected by brick maker Charles Coltman, and it remained a well-known landmark until its demolition in 1947. It was for many years the home of Judge Andrew Wylie and his family. The judge's daughter-in-law, Katherine, kept the Wylie name alive in Washington society with her Christmas night dances in the Thomas Circle house, a tradition until her death in 1941 (Figure 2).[6]

Coming into Thomas Circle from the east, one encountered the eighty-foot length of Mrs. Madeleine Vinton Dahlgren's mansion at 1325 Massachusetts Avenue. Built in 1883 on one of the triangular lots, it had a large Chateauesque tower at the apex and numerous bays and gables; the windows were detailed in the Gothic mode. The house was not noted for its architectural excellence, but it was a center of cultural and social life in the city until Mrs. Dahlgren's death in 1898.

Figure 2. Thomas Circle looking north, c. 1910, showing Luther Place Memorial Church with Wylie residence to the right.

Madeleine Dahlgren was the daughter of a congressman from Ohio and the widow of Admiral John Dahlgren, chief of the Bureau of Ordnance and commandant of the Washington Navy Yard. She had spent the greater part of her life in the capital and was well acquainted with Washington society. To guide others in its mysterious ways, she wrote a popular treatise, *Etiquette of Social Life in Washington* (1873). Although it might seem strange that she would build such a large house after her husband's death, this was a common practice for wealthy Washington widows. In Mrs. Dahlgren's case, it made some sense. She was a founder and vice president of the Washington Literary Society as well as a prolific author, and her house became a sort of literary salon, the site of numerous meetings, conferences, and elegant dinner parties.[7]

Thomas Circle itself was dominated by two large structures: Luther Place Memorial Church on the north side, and to the south, a six-story apartment building called the Portland Flats (Figure 3). The Portland was a

luxury apartment with an elevator—a new residential type for Washington.[8] It was built in two sections, in 1880 and 1883, to the designs of German-born architect Adolph Cluss, one of the more distinguished Washington architects of the period. He was the architect of the Department of Agriculture building (now demolished), the former National Museum (presently the Smithsonian's Arts and Industries building), numerous schools and markets in the city, and an unknown number of fine houses.[9] Like most of Cluss's work, the Portland was eclectic in style, although it recalled British work of

Figure 3. The Portland Flats looking south from Thomas Circle to McPherson Square, c. 1900.

the period; it had an incredibly rich facade. It was built on one of the triangular lots coming into the circle, and a great domed tower, ringed with balconies, took full advantage of its position.

The Portland was particularly well suited to the capital, because it offered members of Congress and other transient officials spacious quarters in a fashionable neighborhood, without the maintenance required of a house. Traditionally such officials lived in hotels and entertained in the public rooms. Around the turn of the century, prominent residents included two secretaries of the navy—Charles J. Bonaparte and John D. Long—and Secretary of Agriculture J. Sterling Morton. Apartments in the building did not come cheaply; historian James Goode notes that the seven-room apartments rented for $150 per month, at a time when $50 would rent an entire house in a comfortable suburban area.[10]

On the west side of the circle, Shepherd's regrading in the early 1870s formed a steep bank on the north side of Massachusetts Avenue. This bank was called Highland Terrace, although the houses all had Massachusetts Avenue addresses. Between the 1870s and the turn of the century, it was home to a number of distinguished men: Senator and later Secretary of State Thomas F. Bayard; Associate Supreme Court Justice Samuel F. Miller; several members of Congress; the Right Reverend Henry Y. Satterlee, first Episcopal Bishop of the Diocese of Washington; and Samuel H. Kauffmann, president of the *Evening Star* newspaper (Figure 4). The German embassy occupied several houses in the block from 1893 until December 1941, when they were seized after the United States entered World War II. Spencer F. Baird, secretary of the Smithsonian Institution, director of the National Museum and the U.S. Commission of Fisheries, lived at 1445 Massschusetts Avenue and used 1443 as his office. The basement of the latter house was the first home of the Bureau of Fisheries, which Baird founded. One cannot help thinking that such a combination of residence and government bureau would not have been acceptable twenty years later in the newly fashionable Sheridan Circle area.[11]

Breaking the pattern of residential development between Thomas and Scott Circles was the Louise Home with its spacious landscaped grounds, taking up the entire south side of Massachusetts Avenue from Fifteenth to Sixteenth Streets (Figure 5). It was built in 1871, early in the development of the area when land was plentiful, by banker/philanthropist William Wilson Corcoran.[12] Corcoran had been a Southern sympathizer during the Civil War, and he built the home (named for his deceased wife and daughter) to support and maintain a number of "gentlewomen reduced by misfortune," which meant at the time primarily Southern women impoverished by the war.[13] One of the residents was Letitia Tyler Semple, daughter of President Tyler, but little is known of the other ladies who benefited from Mr. Corcoran's largesse.

Figure 4. Highland Terrace, 1400 block of Massachusetts Avenue NW, north side. Samuel H. Kauffmann residence in foreground, c. 1900.

Figure 5. Louise home, 1500 Massachusetts Avenue NW, 1871, Edmund G. Lind, architect.

The Louise Home was an elegant structure, inside and out, designed in the French Second Empire style. The plan, based on central and lateral atrium spaces to bring additional light to the rooms, was particularly noteworthy. There was a central octagonal space, rising four stories to a stained-glass skylight, and skylit halls or "palm courts" running east-west, ringed with three floors of open corridors.[14] The architect for the Louise Home was Edmund G. Lind of Baltimore.

On Scott Circle, the second of Massachusetts Avenue's Victorian circles, were the large, square, red brick houses of Senator Cameron of Pennsylvania and Secretary of the Treasury William Windom, and the residence of Stilson Hutchins. All three houses were built in the early 1880s. Hutchins was the founder of the *Washington Post* newspaper and the donor of the statue of Daniel Webster that was placed across from his house, in 1900, in the landscaped triangle at the west side of the circle. In the same year, the memorial to homeopathic physician Dr. Samuel Hahnemann was erected in the triangle on the east side of the circle. The use of these triangles for parks rather than buildings, and the unusual configuration of roads around them, give Scott Circle an especially open, green appearance.

A word should be said about the urban design of these two Victorian circles. There seems to have been no strong feeling on the part of the architects that their houses should acknowledge the circle in siting and placement of dominant architectural features. Those built on the triangular lots could hardly fail to show some respect, but others were conceived with only the grid pattern of the city streets in mind. This was encouraged by the post–Civil War boom, which brought about many subdivisions and the creation of smaller lots, usually laid out in reference to the orthogonal streets, rather than to the circles. The effect was that the unity of the circle was broken, surely not what an eighteenth-century planner like L'Enfant had envisioned. At Scott Circle, particularly, the strength of the circle was diminished by the grounds of the Louise Home, attractive as they were, which allowed the space to leak out in that direction.[15]

Two houses that stood out because of their strong relationship to the circle were the Greek Revival Coltman/Wylie house on Thomas Circle (Figure 2) and Senator Cameron's house on Scott Circle (Figure 6). The Coltman/Wylie house's orientation might be explained by the survival of the classical tradition into the 1840s, or by the fact that it was the first house of any size on the circle and the lots were large. In the case of the

Figure 6. Scott Circle, c. 1890. 1500 Rhode Island Avenue NW, to the right. Senator Cameron's residence, far left behind Scott's statue.

Cameron house, the architect, John Fraser, was a former partner of Frank Furness in Philadelphia and more sophisticated in his approach to urban design than many of the Washington architects.[16] His client purchased five of the narrow rectangular lots facing Sixteenth Street—perhaps at his architect's request—allowing Fraser enough space to turn the house diagonally so that it could face the circle.

One of the most interesting of the large houses at Scott Circle (and still standing) is the Alexander Graham Bell/Levi Morton residence at 1500 Rhode

Figure 7. Levi Morton residence, 1500 Rhode Island Avenue NW; John Fraser, architect. Dining room addition, 1889.

Island Avenue. It started life as a red brick Victorian mansion, became a white limestone palace in the Academic Classical style, and at present, after extensive interior remodeling, is the headquarters of the National Paint and Coatings Association. Although it has a Rhode Island Avenue address, it sits close to the intersection of that avenue with Massachusetts Avenue at the circle and is considered part of the Massachusetts Avenue upper-class residential development.

As built in 1879, it was rather typical for its period, with a corner turret, mansard roof, the usual bays, and an unusually delicate wood-spindled carriage porch. John Fraser was also the architect for this house, less than a block away from Senator Cameron's residence. Soon after completion the owner sold it to Gardiner Hubbard, a developer of public utilities in the Boston area and organizer of the telephone industry; Hubbard bought it for his daughter, Mabel, wife of Alexander Graham Bell. The Bells lived in the house until 1889 when they sold it to the newly elected vice president, Levi P. Morton, a New York banker, who purchased it as a base for his official entertaining; he immediately asked John Fraser to put on a large dining room addition (Figure 7). Morton was not renominated in 1892, and he returned to New York, becoming governor in 1895.

Levi Morton did not sell his Washington house, however, preferring to lease it to a number of tenants; the most colorful was the Russian ambassador, Count Arturo Cassini. From 1903 to 1907 the house functioned as the Russian embassy and was the scene of many balls and dinners arranged by the count's young daughter, Marguerite, who, with her friend Alice Roosevelt caused quite a stir in Washington society. Marguerite loved clothes, jewels, and dogs—it was reported that she kept twenty wolfhounds at the embassy—and she was one of the first Washingtonians to own and drive an automobile. The next tenant, from 1907 to 1909, was decidedly different. He was Secretary of State Elihu Root, one of the most distinguished figures in twentieth-century American history. Secretary of state, secretary of war, senator from New York, winner of the Nobel Peace Prize, he commanded universal respect for his extraordinary ability.

Levi Morton retired from active business life in 1909 and made plans to move back to his Washington home. By this time the section of Massachusetts Avenue east of Scott Circle was not as fashionable as it had been when Morton bought his house in 1889; the Victorian architectural styles and the use of Washington red

Figure 8. Levi Morton residence, 1500 Rhode Island Avenue NW, after "remodeling" by John Russell Pope, architect, 1912. Photograph, 1970.

brick were definitely passé. The Chicago Columbian Exposition of 1893, with its dazzling white classical buildings, changed the architectural scene for the next forty years. Dark brick houses, picturesque in detail and outline, gave way to light stone and marble structures, formal in shape and plan. In Washington, this seemed a natural return to the city's architectural heritage, the classical architecture of the Capitol and the White House. Washington once again became a white city.

Massachusetts Avenue northwest of Scott Circle boasted many grand residences in the Academic Classical style when Levi Morton moved back to Washington. The circle itself was crossed by another street then rivaling Massachusetts Avenue as the capital's most prestigious thoroughfare: Sixteenth Street. Mary Henderson, the doyenne of that street, in her determination to make it Washington's embassy row had already erected several great houses in the Meridian Hill section.

Considering his situation—just a stone's throw from each of the grand avenues—Levi Morton decided to keep his house but bring it up to date architecturally. Perhaps having seen what John Russell Pope had done with an old house owned by *Washington Post* publisher John R. McLean, he hired the prominent New York architect in 1912 to transform his Victorian mansion into an Italian Renaissance *palazzo* (Figure 8).

Levi Morton lived in the Pope house until his death in 1920. His daughter Edith, who was married to William C. Eustis, grandson of W. W. Corcoran, resided there after her husband's death in 1921 until the early 1930s. One of her daughters, Margaret, later married David Finley, who became director of the National Gallery of Art and president of the National Trust for Historic Preservation. Mrs. Eustis sold the house in 1936 to the National Paint and Coatings Association, which uses it as its headquarters.

THE DUPONT CIRCLE AREA: "MILLIONAIRES' ROW"

Levi Morton was a transplanted New Yorker, but the greater number of non-Washingtonians who built houses on upper Massachusetts Avenue at the turn of the century were drawn to the capital from the Midwest. Beriah Wilkins was one of them. He served three terms in the House of Representatives from his Ohio district and then decided to stay on. He acquired an interest in the *Washington Post* and became its editor and publisher in 1899. In 1909, several years after Wilkins's death, his widow built a grand white limestone residence, resembling an Italian Renaissance palace, at the corner of Massachusetts Avenue and Seventeenth Street (Figure 9). A grocery store had occupied the site until 1899. The architect for Mrs. Wilkins's house was Jules Henri de Sibour, one of the best of Washington's architects of the period. De Sibour's family was prominent in

Washington society, and he moved easily among the elite, a number of whom would become his clients.[17]

Mrs. Wilkins died soon after the house was completed and left it to her son, banker and real estate executive John F. Wilkins. Now the chancery for the Peruvian embassy, it stands with its entrance facade set diagonally to the two principal street elevations; it marks the beginning of "Millionaires' Row."

At the turn of the century, many of Washington's political, social, and intellectual elite resided on the 1700 block of Massachusetts Avenue. Thomas Nelson Page, author and ambassador to Italy under Wilson, lived for a while at 1708 (now the embassy of Trinidad and Tobago) until he engaged McKim, Mead & White in 1896 to build him a mansion nearby at 1759 R Street NW. Frances Hodgson Burnett, the author of *Little Lord Fauntleroy*, resided at 1770; William Gibbs McAdoo, secretary of the treasury under Wilson, lived at 1709 (Beriah Wilkins's former home), Senator Henry A. duPont of Delaware at 1711, and Henry Cabot Lodge at 1765. In the midst of these elegant residences, on the south side of Massachusetts Avenue, stood the Peter Force public school. It was attended by the children of Presidents Theodore Roosevelt and William Howard Taft, and those of Beriah Wilkins, General Philip Sheridan, and many other Washington notables; General Douglas MacArthur was a student at one time.[18]

Figure 9. Mrs. Beriah Wilkins residence, 1700 Massachusetts Avenue NW, 1909, J. H. de Sibour, architect. Currently the Peruvian Chancery. Photograph, c. 1915.

Next to Force School was erected one of the finest houses in Washington, 1746 Massachusetts Avenue. For many years the Canadian embassy, it was built for Clarence Moore, a West Virginian who had developed coal, oil, and timber property in his home state. In 1890 he came to Washington, where he engaged in large real estate transactions through his association with a local banking and brokerage firm. In 1906 he and his wife, the former Mabelle Swift, heiress of the Chicago meat-packing firm, built their Massachusetts Avenue residence (Figure 10).

Like Beriah Wilkins's widow, Clarence Moore selected Jules Henri de Sibour as the architect for his house. De Sibour's design is at once exceptional and typical for its time. The exterior is based on eigh-

Figure 10. Clarence Moore residence, 1746 Massachusetts Avenue NW, 1906, J. H. de Sibour, architect. Formerly the embassy of Canada. Photograph, c. 1915.

Figure 11. Apartment house, 1785 Massachusetts Avenue NW, 1915, J. H. de Sibour, architect. Currently the headquarters for the National Trust for Historic Preservation. Photograph, 1970.

teenth-century French antecedents, a popular choice during the twentieth-century period of Academic Classicism, but like most great houses of the period, the interior does not carry out the historical origin of the exterior. The rooms are primarily English in feeling, spanning the sixteenth to the eighteenth centuries. In terms of proportion, detailing, and craftsmanship, the house is truly exceptional.

Clarence Moore had only a few years to enjoy his magnificent new residence. He went alone to England in March 1912 to vacation and to purchase fifty pair of English foxhounds for the Loudon County (Virginia) hunt. Moore liked to travel in style, and the trip was very likely planned so that he could book passage home on the maiden voyage of the highly touted White Star liner R.M.S. *Titanic*; fellow Washingtonians making the trip were Colonel Archibald Butt, aide to Presidents Roosevelt and Taft, and prominent mural painter Frank Millet. All three were among the 1,514 lost at sea; the dogs were left behind, to be delivered by less elegant, but not so ill-fated, transportation.[19]

Mrs. Moore remarried in 1915, becoming the wife of Aksel Wichfield, a Danish diplomat. When they were not living abroad, the Wichfields made 1746 Massachusetts Avenue their home, entertaining the elite of Washington's diplomatic and social circles. By 1927 Mrs. Wichfield had decided she no longer wanted to keep the house, and it was sold to the government of Canada for embassy purposes. It was used as both the ambassador's residence and chancery until 1946, and after that solely as a chancery, until the new Canadian embassy on Pennsylvania Avenue opened in 1988. At this writing it is used as an annex, its future uncertain.

In 1915 de Sibour designed a luxury apartment house in the Beaux-Arts style at the corner of Eighteenth Street and Massachusetts Avenue, replacing a large and handsome Victorian house built in the 1880s by lumberman Belden Noble at 1785 Massachusetts Avenue. The apartment house was built by Stanley F. McCormick of Chicago, son of the inventor of the reaper and founder of what later became International Harvester Company. It represented the ultimate in luxurious and spacious apartment living (Figure 11). There were six apartments: two flanking the vestibule and four principal apartments above, each occupying an entire floor. Accommodations for over forty servants were ingeniously arranged in ten service levels to ensure privacy for the tenants. The apartments featured such niceties as oval reception foyers and twenty-four- by forty-five-foot living rooms, curved at the fireplace end; there were six bedrooms. From 1917 to 1940 the building was home to a number of wealthy individuals who were in Washington on assignments of several years' duration; among them were diplomat Robert Woods Bliss, financier Thomas Fortune Ryan, and the State Department's Sumner Welles. It was in this building that Lord Duveen rented an entire floor to display an art collection so that his client, industrialist Andrew Mellon, then secretary of the treasury, would not have to leave his home to view the art in a residential setting. Duveen's expensive gamble paid off; Mellon bought forty-two items from the collection for $21 million.[20]

In 1940, 1785 Massachusetts Avenue was converted to offices. In 1977 it was purchased by the National Trust for Historic Preservation for use as its headquarters and was then completely renovated and restored.

Just beyond the McCormick apartment house, Dupont Circle opens up the avenue and provides a park-like setting for the buildings around it. In the center of the circle is one of the most beautiful fountains in Washington (Figure 12). It was a gift from the duPont family, designed by the architect of the Lincoln Memorial, Henry Bacon, with sculpture by Daniel Chester French. Dedicated in 1921 to Rear Admiral Samuel Francis duPont, it replaced an unimpressive statue of the admiral that had been erected in 1884, when the name of the circle was changed from Pacific to Dupont (Figure 13).[21]

The name duPont automatically conjures up images of wealth, so it is the perfect name for the focal point of the truly grand part of Massachusetts Avenue. Three major avenues and two streets run through Dupont Circle. Two of these thoroughfares,

Figure 12. Fountain dedicated to Rear Admiral Samuel Francis duPont, 1921, Henry Bacon, architect. Sculpture by Daniel Chester French. Photograph, 1971.

Connecticut and New Hampshire Avenues, rivaled Massachusetts Avenue in the elegance of their residential development during the last quarter of the nineteenth century; the erection of the British embassy on Connecticut Avenue in 1874 had drawn the wealthy like a magnet. But in 1912 one-half of an elegant duplex at the intersection of Massachusetts and Connecticut Avenues was demolished and replaced by a bank (1826 Massachusetts Avenue/1347 Connecticut Avenue). Even though the residents could take some comfort in the fact that de Sibour was the architect, it signaled the end of this part of Connecticut Avenue as a residential street and the beginning of its commercialization, with Dupont Circle as the hub. In fact, to many Washingtonians, Dupont Circle "belongs" to Connecticut Avenue more than it does to Massachusetts; this can be ascribed to the dynamic quality of present-day Connecticut Avenue as an upper-class shopping area, in contrast to the quieter institutional and residential character of Massachusetts Avenue.

Like Thomas and Scott Circles, the Dupont Circle area lay undeveloped (and nearly impassable) until Shepherd's improvements in the 1870s. Writing in the late 1860s, the "Poet of Washington," John A. Joyce, gave a distinctly unglamorous description:

> ...I have seen domestic beasts of all kinds feeding on the grass and garbage clumped about the sites of the British Legation, Blaine, Leiter, Patterson, and Walsh mansions, and I have warmed myself in the midnight hours on my way to Georgetown by the roaring and flashing fires of brick kilns along P Street and Massachusetts Avenue....[22]

The brick kilns had belonged to the Hopkins family for many years and remained on the site until 1870, when the astute George Hopkins took note of the rising land prices, subdivided his land, sold it off at a handsome profit, and moved his business elsewhere.[23]

The big developers of the Dupont Circle area were a group of men known as the "California Syndicate." These were no ordinary real estate brokers; the principals were California Senator William Morris Stewart, who had made his fortune in gold mining; Thomas Sunderland, another gold miner; and Curtis Hillyer, a lawyer with a lucrative practice in mining litigation. All three were closely associated with the state of California. There were frequent complaints from those who lived elsewhere in the city that powerful men such as these received special treatment when it came to money for street improvements. True or not, the *Reports of the District Commissioners* in the 1880s noted the need for improvement and extension of the major avenues and streets in the fast-growing northwest section of the city; Massachusetts Avenue was extended to what is now Wisconsin Avenue (the future site of the National Cathedral) by the end of the century. Those who had bought land earlier at ridiculously low prices and held on to it were ecstatic.[24]

In the early 1870s, both Curtis Hillyer and Senator Stewart built fashionable mansard-roofed Second Empire–style mansions in the Dupont Circle area, hoping to encourage other wealthy Washingtonians to do the same. Hillyer bought all of Square 66 for $25,000 in 1871, subdivided it, and built his house on a large lot on the corner of Massachusetts and Florida Avenues, at 2121 Massachusetts Avenue. Stewart bought all of Square 113 from his friend Hillyer and built visibly on the circle what was always known as "Stewart Castle," at Massachusetts and Connecticut Avenues (Figure 14). When it was built, the house was described as having

Figure 13. Dupont Circle, c. 1880s. Blaine residence at left, Stewart Castle at right.

a picturesque setting in the woods.

Architect Adolph Cluss's design was based, it was said, on Rhenish castles Mrs. Stewart had seen on her travels abroad. Unfortunately, the expenditures for the "castle" left Stewart somewhat embarrassed financially; the lots around it were sold off and the house was leased to the Chinese government for embassy purposes from 1886 to 1893. It was then sold to Senator William A. Clark of Montana, who demolished it in 1900, intending to build a new house on the lot. Apparently there was a disagreement over the plans, and he built a palatial winter residence in New York instead. The land remained vacant until Clark sold it in 1921; by that time the circle had taken on a commercial character, and a bank was erected on the site.

Another early resident of the area was James G.

Figure 14. Stewart Castle, 1913 Massachusetts Avenue NW, c. 1873, Adolph Cluss, architect. Photograph, c. 1893.

Blaine—speaker of the House, twice secretary of state, a powerful orator, and a controversial figure who never achieved his goal of becoming president. His prominent position made it inevitable that he would be stung by the mansion-building bug; early in 1881 he had architect John Fraser prepare plans for a site just north of Scott Circle on Sixteenth Street. The lot had already been graded when Blaine suddenly changed his mind and decided to build on Dupont Circle instead (2000 Massachusetts Avenue). Mrs. Blaine noted in a letter to her son, Emmons, that his father had "conceived a sort of disgust with the Sixteenth Street place, on account

Figure 15. Blaine residence, 2000 Massachusetts Avenue NW, 1881, John Fraser, architect. Photograph, c. 1890.

of the vicinage of stables...."[25]

The very large red brick house that went up at 2000 Massachusetts Avenue was similar to Fraser's Bell/Morton house, but heavier and squared-off; its large and complicated mansard roof is clearly visible from the circle (Figure 15). No photographs of the interior have been found, but descriptions mention a massive oak staircase, a baronial hall and fireplace, and a stained-glass window directly above the carriage porch on Massachusetts Avenue.

Like the Stewarts, the Blaines spent little time in the house after they built it, finding it too large and expensive to maintain. In 1883 Mrs. Blaine wrote to her daughter, Margaret: "How does it happen that the large mansion and the large family came in different portions of my life?"[26] In 1901, several years after Blaine's death, Mrs. Blaine sold the house to George Westinghouse, inventor and founder of the Westinghouse Electric Company. The Westinghouses used it for large-scale entertaining when they were in Washington but never considered it a home.

In 1920 the house was sold, and its life as a single-family dwelling came to an end. The mansion was converted to apartments, the great staircase torn out, and the double stair of the main entrance on Twentieth Street, with its beautifully curved iron railing, removed. Incredibly, four commercial spaces with glass fronts were inserted at ground level on the P Street facade. The house has now been converted to offices, but the stores remain.

The Noble, Stewart, Hillyer, and Blaine houses were part of the Victorian development of Dupont Circle, little of which is left. The area is more closely associated with the early-twentieth-century Academic Classical houses, as part of Massachusetts Avenue's "Millionaires' Row." There was a distinct change in the character of the houses at this time, and to some extent, in the people who built them. The *Evening Star*, December 16, 1902, commented:

> Seventeen years ago there appeared in one of the leading magazines of the country an illustrated article on "Homes in Washington." ...It is interesting to note after this lapse of time that the houses singled out as the largest and most elaborate of those then recently erected were the Anderson house, at the southeast corner of Sixteenth and K streets, and the Noble house, at the northeast corner of Massachusetts Avenue and Eighteenth Street, now the home of the Spanish legation in this city. Both of these houses would be still classed among the more notable private residences of the city, but they would certainly not be selected as typical of the most elaborate and costly homes which now adorn the streets of the residence section.... In this class are the home of Mr. L. Z. Leiter, that of Mr(s). Scott Townsend, and also the very large house which is now being erected by Mr. Thomas F. Walsh....

The people erecting these houses (all of which were on Massachusetts Avenue) were extraordinarily rich; the Smithsonian's Baird and his Bureau of Fisheries near Thomas Circle had been replaced with men like Clarence Moore. In 1905, Bishop Satterlee, at one time Baird's neighbor on Highland Place, expressed concern about the change, noting that the new elite, "while they bring wealth, magnificence and luxury to the capital of the country, are, as a rule, actuated by no sense of civic, moral or religious obligation regarding the welfare of the community...."[27] Although they may have shown these traits in their hometowns, they usually looked on Washington solely as a social and political base and often occupied their houses only during "the season," perhaps three months out of the year.

These grand houses used the most expensive materials—Italian marbles, exotic hardwoods, and custom-made hardware from England and France—but they also exhibited the latest in building technology and labor-saving devices. Both passenger and service elevators were common; there were intercom systems, central vacuuming systems, and even rudimentary air conditioning: as early as 1900 McKim, Mead & White were providing for this amenity in the Patterson house at 15 Dupont Circle.[28] The Everett residence on Sheridan Circle was equipped with a "Webster Air Washer and Humidifier," patented in 1908, and de Sibour's house for Alexander Stewart had an enormous gas-fired clothes dryer, with racks that pulled out from the wall. It was still in use in the 1970s.

The first to build a Dupont Circle mansion in the Academic Classical style was Levi Leiter, one-time partner of retailer Marshall Field. His ponderous mansion at 1500 New Hampshire Avenue, built in 1891 with a four-story classical portico, is only a memory; it was replaced by a hotel in the late 1940s. Across the circle stood whiskey distiller Edson Bradley's great castle, designed in 1907 by New York society architect Howard Greenley (Figure 16). The work was described on the building permit as a remodeling and addition to an existing Victorian house, but what emerged from Greenley's drawing board was a very large, romantic concoction, basically late Medieval/early Renaissance English in derivation; the Victorian house had been blotted out (Figure 17). The sumptuous interiors were filled with Bradley's art collection, which included whole interiors brought from Europe.

Despite such luxury, the Bradleys tired of Washington and decided to move to Newport; per-

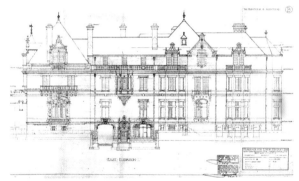

Figure 16. Edson Bradley residence, 1328 Connecticut Avenue NW, 1907, Howard Greenley, architect. Original drawing, 1907.

Figure 17. Edson Bradley residence, 1328 Connecticut Avenue NW. Photograph, c. 1915.

haps de Sibour's new bank across the street helped them make up their minds. Sixteen years after the house was designed, Greenley began the three-year process of dismantling and moving it, piece by piece, to Newport, where it was incorporated into a villa with over one hundred rooms.[29] An office building was erected on the Dupont Circle site in 1926.

Only two of the great mansions remain directly on the circle, both on the northeast side. One was completed in 1903 for Robert W. Patterson, a Chicago newspaperman. Patterson had become editor of the *Chicago Tribune* in 1899 when his wife's father, Joseph Medill, died and left the position vacant. Apparently deciding that his new status required a residence in the nation's capital, Patterson went to McKim, Mead & White, one of the country's most prestigious architectural firms, and asked the flamboyant Stanford White to design his house. The architect had previously designed Patterson's Chicago residence.[30]

Figure 18. Robert W. Patterson residence, 15 Dupont Circle, 1903, Stanford White, architect. Currently the Washington Club. Photograph, 1971.

White decided on a heavily ornamented, white marble and glazed terra cotta Italian palace for the Washington house (Figure 18). Its polygonal plan, with a diagonal entrance loggia, accommodated admirably its position facing two streets and a circle. The main floor was made for entertaining: it contained an ample hall for circulation, a grand ballroom and dining room, and for the family and more intimate groups, a paneled library. On the ground floor were more mundane spaces—one marked "bicycles"—as well as a billiard room and one of the earliest interior automobile garages in Washington. Just owning an automobile at this time was a mark of distinction, but a garage contained within a house was almost unheard of.[31]

The Patterson house is known principally as the home of Eleanor "Cissy" Patterson, Robert's daughter. As a young woman Cissy was a constant party-goer and -giver and a close friend of Alice Roosevelt and Marguerite Cassini. She took up her parents' involvement with the newspaper world and eventually, through inheritance and purchase, accumulated stock in the *Chicago Tribune* and the *New York Post*, as well as buying two Washington papers from William Randolph Hearst and combining them in 1939 to form the *Times-Herald*. She took firm control of the paper and used it to express her often controversial opinions, which were described by critics as "pro-Americanism, pro-Hearst, pro–Marion Davies, and anti-everything else."[32]

Cissy was married twice, first, when she was only twenty, to Count Josef Gizycka of Austria-Hungary, in a ceremony in the Dupont Circle house. It was a brief marriage that ended in a bitter child custody battle. Later in life she married corporate lawyer Elmer Schlesinger.

In 1927 the Patterson house was used by President and Mrs. Coolidge while the White House was being renovated. Charles Lindbergh was their guest after his historic transatlantic flight in June of that year, and cheering crowds besieged the house to get a glimpse of the nation's newest hero.

Eleanor Patterson lived at 15 Dupont Circle until her death in 1948; in her will she left the house and its contents to the Red Cross. Most of the furnishings were auctioned off; what remained, including a number of tapestries and some period furniture, were then sold with the house to the Washington Club in 1951.

The other remaining mansion, across P Street from the Patterson house, is also the home of a women's organization, the Sulgrave Club. It occupies an entire triangular block at 1801 Massachusetts Avenue. The Academic Classical structure was built in 1900 as a winter residence for Herbert Wadsworth, a gentleman farmer from Geneseo, New York, and his wife, Martha. The Wadsworths were the only occupants of the house until it was sold to the Sulgrave Club in 1932.[33]

Until 1970 a handsome white limestone house by John Russell Pope stood just north of the Patterson house (Figure 19). It was designed in 1908 for Sallie Hitt, widow of Representative Robert R. Hitt of Illinois. The house was remarkable for its delicate Adamesque ornamentation, both on the exterior and interior; its demolition for an office building, when the preservation movement was already under way, was a great loss to the city.

Northwest of Dupont Circle the original turn-of-the-century fabric of Massachusetts Avenue remains reasonably intact. Here is the largest collection of the grand mansions; a brief discussion of a few will give some indication of the character of Washington's grand avenue at its zenith.

Just off Dupont Circle and within a few hundred feet of Massachusetts Avenue stands the former home of businessman and inventor Thomas T. Gaff of Cincinnati; it is now the embassy of Colombia (Figure 20). Designed by J. H. de Sibour in 1904, early in his career, it is one of his finest works, reminiscent of seventeenth-century French country houses. It is more intimate and less formal than the Clarence Moore house, and it has a spectacular two-story vaulted and skylit Edwardian-style ballroom

Figure 19. Sallie Hitt Residence, 1511 New Hampshire Avenue NW, 1908, John Russell Pope, architect. Demolished.

Figure 20. T. T. Gaff residence, 1520 20th Street NW, 1904, J. H. de Sibour, architect. Main entrance, c. 1910. Currently the embassy of Colombia.

Figure 21. T. T. Gaff residence, 1520 20th Street NW, 1904, J.H. de Sibour, architect. Ballroom. Photograph, 1991.

Figure 22. Thomas Walsh residence, 2020 Massachusetts Avenue NW, 1901, Henry Andersen, architect. Currently the embassy of Indonesia. Photograph, 1970.

(Figure 21). The room comes as a complete surprise to the visitor, as there is no indication of it from the exterior. Mr. Gaff was apparently an erudite man, with intellectual as well as social leanings; much of his extensive library remains in the house, as do many of the original furnishings. After her husband's death in 1923, Mrs. Gaff leased the house to a succession of tenants, including Senator Peter Goelet Gerry of Rhode Island, Secretary of War Dwight Filley Davis (of Davis Cup fame), and the Grecian legation. It was purchased by the government of Colombia in 1944.

One of Mr. Gaff's Massachusetts Avenue neighbors was Thomas Walsh, perhaps best described as nouveau riche. Walsh was a native of Ireland who emigrated to the United States, went prospecting in Colorado, and discovered one of the richest gold mines in the world; he lived extravagantly ever after. Walsh moved his family to Washington in 1897, and in 1901 he commissioned New York architect Henry Andersen to design his house (Figure 22), a very large "French" creation whose most memorable aspect is seen immediately upon entering: a three-story, galleried, skylit stairhall, recalling strongly the interior of European steamships of the day (Figure 23). No expense was spared, according to the Walsh daughter, Evalyn.[34] The house cost an exceptional $835,000 to build, exclusive of furnishings, which took several years to collect from here and abroad. Entertaining was on a grand scale, with exotic flowers shipped in from tropical climes, and a gold flatware service (made from nuggets from the Walsh mine) that was used when the guest list was not too long. In 1919, when President Wilson was ill, Mrs. Walsh lent the house for a state dinner honoring King Albert and Queen Elizabeth of Belgium.

Evalyn Walsh became the capital's leading socialite. She eloped with *Washington Post* heir Edward McLean in 1908, and theirs was a stormy marriage that ended in divorce and his commitment to a mental institution. The public was fascinated by her private life, her parties, and her fabulous jewels, among them the 44.5-carat Hope diamond. When Mrs. Walsh died, Evalyn leased the mansion to the government and then lent it, rent free, to the Red Cross during World War II. She died in 1947, and the house was purchased in 1951 by the Indonesian government for embassy use.

In the next block is Anderson House, one of the largest and most costly houses in the capital. Diplomat Larz Anderson's father was a general and his great-grandfather was the founder of the Society of the Cincinnati, a hereditary patriotic society composed of descendants of Revolutionary War officers. Larz married Isabel Weld Perkins, heiress to the fortune of her grandfather, East Indian trader Stephen Weld.

The Andersons built their house with the idea that it would be used to accommodate official government entertaining, particularly of foreign guests, and that it would eventually become the headquarters of the Society of the Cincinnati (Figure 24). Designed by architects Little & Browne of Boston in 1902, it is a monumental limestone structure in the

Figure 23. Thomas Walsh residence, 2020 Massachusetts Avenue NW, 1901, Henry Andersen, architect. Entrance hall and stair. Photograph, 1970.

Figure 24. Larz Anderson residence, 2118 Massachusetts Avenue NW, 1902, Little & Browne, architects. Currently the Society of the Cincinnati. Photograph, 1971.

Figure 25. Larz Anderson residence, 2118 Massachusetts Avenue NW, 1902, Little & Browne, architects. Ballroom.

Academic Classical style that is clearly institutional rather than residential in character. Features of the interior are a great two-story ballroom and a magnificent mural by Jose Villegas on the landing of the main stair, depicting the wedding of the Doge of Venice in 1424 (Figure 25).

In spite of the grandeur of their surroundings, the Andersons seem to have managed to bring some informality into their lives. In her memoirs, Isabel Anderson described a party and a surprise visit from President Taft:

The kitchen is near the music room, and its white-tiled walls are hung with shining coppers. When we have a party there we all put on aprons and begin by taking down the pans and walking around in a procession banging them and singing. Once when we were right in the midst of one of these lively frolics a bell rang and a White House aide appeared with the information that the President was outside in a motor and would like to come in. So L. and I went to the door, aprons and all, to receive him; he gave me his arm and walked straight out to the kitchen, where everybody set to work to make special dishes for him while he kept us in gales of laughter with his funny anecdotes. I wonder who ever had a President in her kitchen before?[35]

Figure 26. Richard Townsend residence, 2121 Massachusetts Avenue NW, 1899, Carrère & Hastings, architects. Currently the Cosmos Club. Photograph, 1970.

The last house to be mentioned in this group is the former Townsend residence, across from Anderson House (Figures 26 and 27). It was built by the retired president of the Erie and Pittsburgh Railroad, Richard Townsend, and his wife, the former Mary Scott, who was from a prominent Washington family. Reportedly the couple wanted a house that resembled the Petit Trianon at Versailles. If so, they made the perfect choice when, in 1899, they chose the firm of Carrère & Hastings of New York as their architects. Eighteenth-century France was the most frequent source of inspiration for this firm, known for its grand residences and public buildings in the New York area.

Figure 27. Richard Townsend residence, 2121 Massachusetts Avenue NW, Carrère & Hastings, architects. Salon. Photograph, c. 1915.

The Townsend house was built on the site of Curtis Hillyer's Victorian house, some part of which was incorporated because of Mary Townsend's belief that evil would result from living in a totally new house. But misfortune came anyway; her husband was killed in a fall from a horse in 1902, soon after completion of the house. She remained in her French palace until her death in 1931, and is said to have spent as much as $240,000 a year on entertaining and maintaining the house with a staff of thirty-four servants. Her daughter, Mathilde, was first married to Senator Peter Goelet Gerry; her second husband was Sumner Welles, FDR's under secretary of state. They lived in the residence until Mathilde's death in 1949; Welles sold it in 1950 to the Cosmos Club, a private social organization, which still occupies it. Additions and remodeling over the years have brought many changes, but the house remains one of the glories of Massachusetts Avenue.

SHERIDAN CIRCLE AND BEYOND

Even the *New York Times* noticed the number of very wealthy people who were building residences in Washington. The headlines of an article in the magazine section of the Sunday paper for January 29, 1911, read "Is Washington Cornering Our Multi-Millionaires? Remarkable Growth of a Colony Whose Wealthy Recruits Come from All Parts of the Country to the Nation's Capital." The article described the families, their financial worth, and their lavish entertainments, focusing on the new development around Sheridan Circle:

> The people and all their class are new to Washington…. Among these people a man with four or five millions is poor almost to deserving charity…. Around Sheridan Circle the bonanza kings, as they are called, have pitched their palace tents…. And so they come, piling millions upon millions into the National Capital…. The gauntlet of the acquisition of that sort of wealth that goes hand in hand with social prominence is thrown down by the National Capital. Where is the city that can enter the lists with her?

Figure 28. Barney studio house, 2306 Massachusetts NW, 1902, Waddy B. Wood, architect. Photograph, prior to 1911.

Figure 29. Barney Studio House, 2306 Massachusetts NW, 1902. Third-floor studio, 1904.

While Dupont Circle has lost its residential character, Sheridan has not; it is one of the few Washington circles still intact. The houses around it, all built in the first decade of the twentieth century, make a first-rate ensemble of Academic Classical architecture. Sheridan is the perfect residential circle; it is relatively small, and it is traversed only by Massachusetts Avenue; three other streets enter, but dead-end at the circle. In the center of the landscaped area is a dashing equestrian statue of General Philip Sheridan, sculpted by Gutzon Borglum and unveiled in 1908 by the general's son.

The first of the "millionaire houses" on Sheridan Circle was the small and deceptively modest Barney Studio House. Designed in 1902 in the Spanish Mission style by Washington architect Waddy B. Wood, it is a maverick on the circle in both appearance and use (Figure 28).[36] It was designed for artist and dilettante Alice Pike Barney as a private cultural center, with studio and stage facilities for artistic pursuits and space for informal entertaining.

Alice Pike was a free-spirited woman, born into a wealthy family from Cincinnati who were avid supporters of the arts. She married Albert Barney, who was also rich, although unfortunately not supportive of her serious interest in painting and playwriting. The Barneys maintained a large house in Washington just off Scott Circle, but Alice was attracted to Paris and its avant-garde art colonies. As the years went by, she and her two daughters spent more and more time in the French capital. In 1901, however, she decided to return to Washington and build her studio house; her husband died late in 1902, before it was completed.[37] The *New York Times* article quoted above said of her:

In the building up of Sheridan Circle as the real social centre of Washington much is due to the clever brain of Mrs. Barney.... She was the pioneer social settler, and many of her smart friends expressed surprise that she should go so far from fashionable Dupont Circle. Mrs. Barney merely smiled, built her quaint Italian home and waited. Now the entire circle of Sheridan is marked by an imposing row of magnificent marble mansions.

Figure 30. Joseph Beale residence, 2301 Massachusetts Avenue NW, at Sheridan Circle, 1907, Glenn Brown, architect. Currently the embassy of Egypt. Photograph, 1970.

At Studio House, Alice lived the artistic life and entertained the elite of Washington society and the art world; occasionally, the neighbors found her behavior eccentric.

Old photographs show the wonderful "arty" furnishings of Studio House, many of which remain today (Figure 29). In accordance with Alice Barney's will (she died in 1931), her daughters, both of whom resided in Paris, gave Studio House and its furnishings to the Smithsonian Institution in 1963. It is now maintained as a museum by the National Museum of American Art.

Undoubtedly the finest house on Sheridan Circle is the present Egyptian embassy at 2301 Massachusetts Avenue (Figure 30). It is the residential masterpiece of Washington architect Glenn Brown, one-time secretary of the American Institute of Architects and crusader for the reinstatement of the L'Enfant plan as the guiding principle for the development of Washington.[38] Brown's client was Joseph Beale, about whom little is known; this was the second house Brown had designed for him in nine years. The first, built in 1898 of red Washington brick, still stands at 2012 Massachusetts Avenue, near the Blaine Mansion.

The Sheridan Circle house, built in 1907, is a monumental white stucco and limestone structure in the Academic Classical style, basically trapezoidal in shape. It faces the circle and complements it in an unusual way—with a convex facade; a fine Palladian loggia on the principal floor provides a central focal point. The interior is notable for its vaulted and domed spaces and its abundance of neoclassical plasterwork (Figure 31).

No image of Sheridan Circle is complete without mention of the impressively large Turkish embassy, at 1606 Twenty-third Street. Its grand curved portico, although oriented toward Twenty-third Street, gives the building command of the circle as one proceeds up Massachusetts Avenue from the east. It was built between

1910 and 1915 by a native of Cleveland, Edward H. Everett, a multimillionaire industrialist known as the "bottle-top king" because of his invention of the crimped metal top for glass bottles. The house was made for entertaining—newspapers described one party for 3,000, complete with footmen dressed in livery; there was even a swimming pool in the basement. In 1936, several years after Everett's death, his widow sold it to the government of Turkey for embassy use. The lavish interiors remain unchanged—marble and parquet floors, dark carved woodwork, coffered ceilings, and elaborately carved mantlepieces (Figure 32).

The architect for the Turkish embassy was George Oakley Totten, a Washington man trained at

Figure 31. Joseph Beale residence, 2301 Massachusetts Avenue NW, at Sheridan Circle, 1907, Glenn Brown, architect. Reception room looking into sitting room. Photograph, 1971.

Figure 32. Edward H. Everett residence, 1606 Twenty-third Street NW, 1910–15, George Oakley Totten, architect. Ballroom looking toward conservatory. Photograph, 1970.

the École des Beaux-Arts in Paris, and at one time in his career architect to the Sultan of Turkey. He designed many luxurious residences on both Massachusetts Avenue and Sixteenth Street. Totten was fascinated with ornament, using it almost indiscriminately on his buildings. While he was not in the same class as de Sibour, the richness of his facades contributes much to the character of the avenue in the Sheridan Circle area. His work appealed to those drawn to the more ostentatious of the revival styles, while others preferred a quiet classicism.[39]

This contrast between classicism and turn-of-the-century opulence is evident on the north side of the avenue from the Egyptian embassy on the circle to Twenty-fourth Street. The embassies of Chile and Haiti, both in the classical tradition, were designed by Washington architect Nathan Wyeth. The former was built in 1908 for his cousin, Sara Wyeth of Philadelphia (2305 Massachusetts Avenue), the latter in 1909 for New York financier Gibson Fahnestock (2311 Massachusetts Avenue). Wyeth was socially prominent, edu-

cated at the École des Beaux-Arts, and like de Sibour (whom he rivaled in talent), had many wealthy clients. He was also the architect for the addition to the west wing of the White House that includes the Oval Office.[40]

Two of George Oakley Totten's fanciful creations stand next to Wyeth's classical designs. Where Decatur Street intersects the avenue is the embassy of Pakistan, designed in 1909 as a residence for Mrs. F. B. Moran (Figure 33). It sits on a triangular lot with two street fronts, the apex anchored by a round tower with a bulbous roof. With its ornamented facades and round-arched dormer windows, it recalls turn-of-the-century Paris. The second Totten building stands at Twenty-fourth Street

Figure 33. F. B. Moran residence, 2315 Massachusetts Avenue NW, 1909, George Oakley Totten, architect. Currently the embassy of Pakistan. Photograph, 1970.

(2349 Massachusetts Avenue) in a similar position. Here we are in the Loire Valley chateau country, but this house, in its sophistication, is far removed from Mrs. Dahlgren's red brick, chateauesque abode on Thomas Circle. The house was built in 1906 for Christian Hauge, Norway's first minister to the United States, and is now the chancery of the embassy of Cameroon.

The "grand avenue" continues out to Observatory Circle at Thirty-fourth Street, but it thins out beyond Christian Hauge's chateau. The vacant spaces between the great houses were filled in with post–World War I development, still upper-class, but not of the magnificence of the Dupont–Sheridan Circle area. Several exceptional buildings deserve mention. One is the present Brazilian embassy, designed as a private house by John Russell Pope in 1908 (3000 Massachusetts Avenue). Two were built as embassies, signaling a change in this part of Massachusetts Avenue from residential to institutional. The Japanese embassy was designed in 1931 in the full Academic Classical tradition by Delano & Aldrich of New York (2516 Massachusetts

Avenue). It sits far back from the street, approached by an elegant courtyard, complete with Belgian block paving, a central parterre, and flanking rows of trees. It is obvious that the now-current idea of having embassy buildings reflect the art and culture of their countries did not cross the mind of the architect or his clients. Across Rock Creek is the British embassy, designed in 1927 in a very personal version of the English country house style by Sir Edwin Lutyens, Britain's finest architect of the period; it was his only building in the United States (3100 Massachusetts Avenue).

This section of Massachusetts Avenue, from Sheridan Circle to Observatory Circle, is undoubtedly the most scenic. Rock Creek Park runs close to the avenue, and in some cases along it; the heavy tree canopy behind the buildings and the broad building-line setbacks give a green, park-like setting to what has become a major traffic artery of the city.

The automobile was to a great extent responsible for a change in the kind of development that took place on Massachusetts Avenue after World War I. The avenue was no less a "straight shot" from the center of the city to its far northwest reaches in the 1920s than it had been in the 1870s, but this time it took people rapidly through the city and out to the suburbs of Maryland. Wealthy house builders began to find areas just off Massachusetts Avenue quieter and more attractive—especially the beautiful wooded areas bordering Rock Creek. Even before World War I, the Kalorama area north of Sheridan Circle and the Massachusetts Heights development in Normanstone Valley, just beyond the avenue's crossing of Rock Creek, were attracting the affluent who did not mind a slight remoteness of location. The developers of these areas, however, were quick to point out the nearness of their lots to Massachusetts Avenue: "160 feet in width, the longest and most important residential thoroughfare in the District...adorned almost to The Heights itself by mansions...."[41] These neighborhoods remain today among the most highly valued residential property in the metropolitan area.

EPILOGUE

Many of the houses on Massachusetts Avenue have been spoken of in the past tense. As in other cities, Washington's grand avenue has suffered serious losses. In many cases, the heirs of the builders of the great houses chose not to remain in Washington. Daughters married and moved away; sons chose careers that offered better opportunities outside this "government town." The houses were expensive to maintain, servants hard to find, and very quickly a number of the great mansions became rooming houses, often with stores on the ground floor. The spread of the commercial core north and west of the city center also brought changes to Massachusetts Avenue. An elegant Victorian townhouse did not seem so desirable when others across the street were being razed for apartment blocks and office buildings.

The circles have been especially hard hit. Thomas Circle retains little of its Victorian charm, the entire area now being turned over to commercial and special-purpose uses. Luther Place Church remains; it has become an activist center for aid to the poor and homeless of the area. Architecturally, there has been one bright spot in the twentieth-century history of the circle: the erection of John Russell Pope's National City

Christian Church in 1930. Unfortunately, it required the demolition of several Victorian residences in the Highland Terrace area, and other losses have not been softened by new buildings of the quality of Pope's church. The circle is ringed by nondescript office buildings, motels, and hotels.

Scott Circle has not turned commercial, since the streets that traverse it are zoned special purpose and residential in that area. However, residential on Scott Circle now means large apartment houses, and special purpose means the Australian chancery office building and the headquarters of the National Rifle Association; none of the old residences remains on the circle itself.

Dupont Circle has not fared much better. As early as 1936 some residents on Massachusetts Avenue just northwest of the circle—where some of the finest Academic Classical residences stand—wanted the area rezoned to permit apartment houses. Alice Roosevelt Longworth, who lived across from the Blaine mansion, added her name to the list.[42] In a few years the rezoning was successful, and a huge apartment house filled the site of the Patten sisters' Victorian mansion and grounds at Twenty-second Street, next to the Society of the Cincinnati and across from the Townsend house.

Demolition began in earnest following World War II. Whole blocks disappeared to make way for apartments and hotels; later, as the residential character weakened, the old houses were replaced by office buildings. The north side of the 1700 block—an exceptional row of turn-of-the-century houses—came down in the 1940s and 1950s. Across the street, a section was razed as late as 1974, this time not without outcries from preservationists and the city's Landmarks Committee, which was in the process of granting historic district status to Massachusetts Avenue from Seventeenth Street NW to Observatory Circle at Thirty-fourth Street NW.[43]

Since that time the situation has stabilized; the preservation movement has gained enough strength to slow the wholesale destruction of the amenities that make our crowded cities liveable. But there is another factor that has "saved" many of the palaces of Massachusetts Avenue. Washington's position as national capital brings representatives of foreign governments, and the size and elegance of the old houses makes them especially attractive as embassies. Sheridan Circle, in particular, is almost exclusively devoted to embassy use, and has been for forty to fifty years. Other residents traditionally complain about the parking and the noise, but without the embassy presence the area would very likely have lost much of its glamorous appeal.

And so, in spite of its losses, Massachusetts Avenue remains one of the capital's finest residential streets, remarkable for the architectural quality, unity, and variety of its facades. The history of those who guided the political and cultural growth of the United States and developed its industries can still be read here in the grand mansions, many of them scarcely changed from their original condition. The lavish large-scale entertaining goes on. More public than private nowadays, it continues the function for which the houses are most admirably suited, and, indeed, for which they were built.

CHAPTER EIGHT

BROADWAY

GALVESTON, TEXAS

BROADWAY IS A THREE-AND-ONE-HALF-MILE, fifty-three-block-long boulevard that bisects the island city of Galveston. During the last quarter of the nineteenth century, it was where the wealth, power, and refinement of Galveston's entrepreneurial elite were exhibited in a parade of high-set, architecturally ambitious, towered villa houses. Collectively, these symbolized Galveston's claim to reign as "Queen of the Mexican Gulf." The exceptional breadth of the avenue, its median esplanades, and the scale and richness of the domestic architecture along its length advertised Broadway as paramount among the grand avenues of Texas's leading cities. Two twentieth-century contributions have magnified the perception of Broadway's civic importance. One was the coordinated planting of palm trees and live oak trees that now frame the avenue spatially. The second was a major shift in traffic patterns that made Broadway the principal path of entrance into the city. These impose a degree of unity on Broadway that nineteenth-century visitors would not have experienced and override some of the finer urban distinctions characteristic of the street during its ascendancy as the grand avenue of Galveston (Figure 1).

THE GROWTH OF GALVESTON

Broadway seemed destined for greatness. Laid out as one of the principal thoroughfares of the city of Galveston in 1837–38, it was 150 feet wide. This was an extraordinary dimension for a street in a new Texan city of the late 1830s. By comparison, Congress Avenue, the ceremonial axis that bisected the town of

ESSAY BY STEPHEN FOX

Figure 1. Broadway and Twenty-fifth Street. Texas Heroes Monument, 1900, Louis Amateis, sculptor. At left is The Open Gates, 1891, McKim, Mead & White, architects. Photograph, 1925.

Austin, laid out in 1839 to serve as the permanent seat of government of the Republic of Texas, was only 120 feet wide.

Broadway was the cross-axial of the town plan that John D. Groesbeck (1815–56), a surveyor who had come to Texas from Albany, New York, platted on the east end of Galveston Island for the Galveston City Company (Figure 2). It was intersected by the axial, 120-foot-wide Twenty-fifth Street (which was also designated Bath Avenue). These cross-axes anchored an immense town plan of 4,605 acres, which the city of Galveston would not fill out until the twentieth century.[1]

What occasioned a city plan of this magnitude was the potential that Galveston's founder, Michael B. Ménard, and his fellow investors in the Galveston City Company saw for a town on Galveston Island. A slender, thirty-mile-long sandbar two miles off the coast of the Texas mainland, Galveston was a low-lying barrier island, flat and treeless. Since the eighteenth century it had been known to possess a fine natural harbor that lay on the bay side at the east tip of the island. The Spanish viceregal government never authorized settlement on Galveston Island, and the Mexican government had explicitly outlawed settlement in Texas within thirty miles of the Gulf coast. Therefore, at the time of its independence from Mexico in April 1836, Texas had no port city. Because water provided the most reliable medium of transportation within Texas and because the republic was economically dependent on the United States, the island occupied an economically strategic position at the transportation and trade gateway to Texas. But due to its location on a barrier island, the Galveston town site was extremely vulnerable to the deadly storm surges accompanying periodic hurricanes.

Galveston's development after 1838 was swift by Texas standards, although compared to the explosive population growth of the industrial cities of the Middle West, it remained quite small throughout the nineteenth century. By 1860 Galveston's population of 7,307 made it the second-largest city in Texas. The Civil War set back the town's prospects. Galveston Island was declared indefensible by the Confederate government and a substantial percentage of the town's population evacuated. Yet despite the impact of the war, Galveston rebounded with surprising speed. By 1870 it had a population of 13,818 and had become the largest city in Texas, a position it would maintain until overtaken by Dallas during the late 1880s.

The period of post–Civil War reconstruction was crucial for business reorganization and expansion in Galveston. Most of the businessmen who would build the houses that confirmed Broadway's role as a grand avenue in the 1880s and 1890s came to Galveston at this time, relocating their mercantile businesses from inland Texas towns. Many of these men had come to Texas in their youth in the 1840s and 1850s, immigrating from the northeastern United States or from Europe. They tended to accumulate fortunes based on mercantile trade, which they amplified by investing in cotton trading, banking, and transportation, especially railroads.

The economy of nineteenth-century Texas was largely based on cotton production. Merchants in towns who sold goods to rural cotton planters were often paid in crops. Becoming commission merchants, these traders would not only broker the sale of cotton to buyers in the northeast or Europe, but finance the cotton planters as well. Thus the wholesaling of dry goods, groceries, or agricultural implements led the most aggressive entrepreneurs into the banking and cotton factorage businesses. Expediting the transport of cotton from the fields to the wharves and processing and packing it for export led to the development of railroad lines, cotton compresses, and steamship companies. To rationalize and regularize these endeavors, the commission merchants, cotton factors, and bankers organized such enterprises as the Galveston, Houston & Henderson Railroad (1853), the first railroad to connect Galveston with Houston and, after the war, the rich cotton country of the Brazos River valley; the Galveston Wharf Company (1854), a private corporation enfranchised by the City of Galveston to operate the public wharves; the Mallory Steamship Line (1866), which provided regular steamship service between Galveston and New York; the Galveston Cotton Exchange and Board of Trade (1872), the first cotton exchange in Texas; and the Gulf, Colorado & Santa Fe Railway, begun in 1873 for the purpose of funneling the bounty of the southwestern United States through the port of Galveston.[2] The wharf company, the cotton exchange, and the Santa Fe railway were the undertakings in which the interests of the occupants of the Broadway houses most frequently intersected.

Figure 2. Map of Galveston, 1845, showing the Groesbeck city plan as surveyed in 1838. Broadway runs east-west and is shown near the center of this map.

Figure 3. Osterman-Kopperl house, 1001 Twenty-fourth Street, 1846, and subsequent additions. At right, The Open Gates. Photograph, 1896.

EARLY BROADWAY

Broadway did not begin to emerge, even tentatively, as a grand avenue until the 1850s. The elite among Galveston's earliest settlers had built their houses on ten-acre, suburban "out-lots" along Avenue O, south of Broadway and well west of Twenty-fifth Street in what was open countryside near the beach. Twenty-third Street (also called Tremont Street) ran from the business district, on the bay side of the island, southward to the beach, and was the town's major north-south thoroughfare.[3] By the 1850s it had become a favored location for elite town houses. One such house was the Frosh house at the intersection of Tremont and Broadway, built about 1840. The Frosh house faced Tremont and turned its side elevation toward Broadway, as did other houses in the neighborhood, such as the Osterman-Kopperl house of 1846 at Twenty-fourth and Broadway.[4] The three-bay-wide, side hall plan of the Frosh and Osterman-Kopperl houses was typical of Galveston's wooden Greek Revival town houses, as were their columned galleries. These faced the street, then wrapped around the side of the house, Charleston-style, even if the south side of the house faced an interior property line rather than the street, as at the Osterman-Kopperl house (Figure 3).

ASHTON VILLA

The house that decisively established Broadway as the incipient grand avenue of Galveston was Ashton Villa, built between 1859 and 1860 at Twenty-fourth and Broadway by the wholesale hardware merchant and railroad corporation president James M. Brown (1821–95). In every apparent way, Ashton Villa stood apart from all that preceded it in Galveston (Figure 4). It faced Broadway rather than Twenty-fourth Street. It was built of brick rather than wood. It was three stories high rather than two. It had a center hall plan configuration rather than a side hall plan. Its porches were fabricated of cast iron, as were the lintels above its first-floor and second-floor windows. And it cost approximately $14,000. In his book *A History of Ashton Villa*, Kenneth Hafertepe notes that the Brown house was equipped with the most advanced domestic conveniences: gas lighting and heating, indoor plumbing for the family (although not for the servants), and built-in closets. The house was offset by a row of architecturally coordinated brick service buildings lined up along a back alley that bisected the block parallel to Broadway. These included a two-story kitchen and laundry building (with accommodations for the Brown family's three slaves above) and a two-story stable and coach house.[5]

The Italianate architecture of Ashton Villa was exceptional in Texas for its currency. It was adapted from the design for "A Suburban Residence" published in *The Model Architect*, a pattern book by the Philadelphia architect Samuel Sloan. J. M. Brown's obituary notice in the *Galveston Daily News* in 1895 stated that "some of the parlor furniture is the same that he selected in New York, after completing his new home."[6] In terms of size, design, construction, cost, and interior appointments and amenities, Ashton Villa marked a clear advance in domestic style, luxury, and convenience. The house's intimations of Philadelphia and New York identified Brown as one whose judgments and tastes were formed by firsthand acquaintance with metropolitan standards rather than their dim, provincial reflections.

Photographs of Ashton Villa taken at the time it was new indicate that J. M. Brown and his wife, Rebecca Stoddart Brown, cultivated the grounds of the house, which comprised four town lots. This required the imposition of topsoil on the island's natural sand surface and intensive watering, an item of conspicuous expenditure before the installation of a waterworks system in 1889.[7] Mr. and Mrs. Brown planted large trees at regular intervals along the Broadway frontage of their property, outside the line of their ornamental iron fence. Their concern with beautifying the public right-of-way along Broadway suggests that Brown deliberately chose to take advantage of the street's civic potential when he built Ashton Villa there.

This civic potential grew out of the reciprocal spatial relationship that existed between the street and the house. This relationship was essential to the ritualized display of newly acquired wealth characteristic of the grand avenue. Broadway provided a spatial foreground that could frame the houses along it, imparting to private domestic accommodation a heightened degree of publicity. Architecture contributed to this relationship by extracting the house from the collective realm of domestic typology and elevating it to the role of individual urban actor. Although Ashton Villa was a single-family dwelling, freestanding on privately owned property, it pre-

Figure 4. Ashton Villa, 2328 Broadway, 1860. Photograph, c. 1860.

211

sented itself as part of this new civic realm, one in which the wealth of J. M. Brown symbolically spilled over to enrich the city and attest to his public-spirited largesse. This implicit representation of private wealth as public good was confirmed on ceremonial occasions, as when ex-President and Mrs. Grant called on Mr. and Mrs. Brown at Ashton Villa in March 1880 as they passed through Galveston near the end of their world tour. It was the only call that the former president made at a private residence in Galveston.[8]

That the garden of Ashton Villa was completely visible from Broadway indicates that it was offered as much for public comment and approval as for the private refreshment of the Brown family. It also implies that despite the priority accorded to single-family dwellings and ornamental vegetation, the grand avenue was essentially urban in nature rather than suburban. The garden district alternative to urban row housing that Broadway presented was not a rejection of the city. Rather it was a reformulation of older American patterns of middle-class town dwelling that rationalized, and ritualized, the mixture of domestic comfort, public display, and vicarious enjoyment.

Ashton Villa was the prototype of what Howard Barnstone in his book *The Galveston That Was* characterized as the "Galveston palace."[9] Although the Broadway houses that began to succeed it in the 1870s were palatial only by Texas standards, they confirmed Ashton Villa's exemplary role in preparing Broadway to serve as Galveston's grand avenue.

BIRTH OF A BOULEVARD

Ashton Villa did not immediately exercise its role as prototype, however, for it was not until after the post–Civil War period of business expansion that transformation of the avenue commenced. A bird's-eye view of Galveston by C. Drie, published in 1871, indicates that Broadway was built up in the neighborhood around Ashton Villa, where it was intersected by the city's most heavily traveled north-south streets, Twenty-first, Tremont, and Twenty-fifth. But it was much less developed on the avenue's east and west ends. In Galveston's East End, where Broadway was crossed by teen streets, and in the West End, in the upper twenties and thirties, Broadway exhibited numerous unimproved lots, sometimes entire block fronts. The 1871 bird's-eye view shows that houses were freestanding and of wooden construction. There was no tradition of row housing in Galveston, and brick-built houses were extremely rare. It also shows that Broadway had acquired one of the two cross-town lines of the streetcar company, which had begun service in 1866. Another bird's-eye view, published by Augustus Koch in 1885, records the increased density of the central section of Broadway in the Tremont district near Ashton Villa, as well as considerable growth in the East End and to a lesser extent in the West End (Figure 5).

A report in one of the Galveston newspapers in August 1869 stated that the city council of Galveston had passed an ordinance designating Broadway a "boulevard." The medians—called esplanades in Galveston—were mentioned in the *Galveston Daily News* in 1873 as having been curbed by the city government. A year later, another report indicated that this was an ongoing process and that in some instances own-

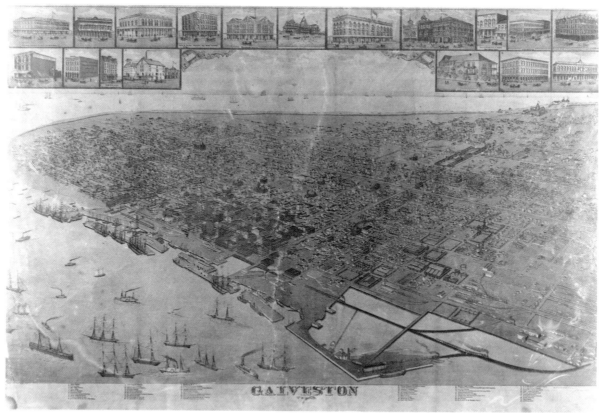

Figure 5. Bird's-eye view of Galveston (north to south), 1885. Published by Augustus Koch.

ers of facing properties had offered to plant and maintain the Broadway esplanades if the city would enforce ordinances against loose animals. The 1885 bird's-eye view depicts the Broadway esplanades as dotted with saplings, as do photographs through the late 1890s. A newspaper article in 1890, reporting the protests that arose when the streetcar company announced that it would double its tracks on the Broadway esplanades and erect wooden poles and cables along them to electrify the system, noted that only a few residents on Broadway maintained the

Figure 6. Broadway looking west from Sixteenth Street, c. 1895. Center left, League house, Castle District. Upper left, tower of St. John's Methodist Church, Tremont District.

esplanades facing their houses.[10] The city apparently had no mechanisms for performing such a task. Hurricanes in 1875 and 1886 sent tidal surges into the East End, which perhaps explains the failure of saplings planted along the streets and in the Broadway esplanades to mature into trees. Sandy soil, salt air, and the lack of piped water during much of the period were probably also contributing factors. One effect of this inability to achieve mature street tree growth was that, by the end of the century, Galveston remained a painfully bare city, except where private gardens had been cultivated (Figure 6).

213

This urbanistic shortcoming notwithstanding, Broadway was the first divided boulevard in a Texas city. Its civic potential, first explored by Ashton Villa, was reinforced after the Civil War by nondomestic building projects that recognized and took advantage of the street's scale. Between 1869 and 1892 three large churches were built on or near Broadway. St. John's Methodist Episcopal Church, South, was completed in 1871 at Twenty-fifth and Broadway for Galveston's oldest Methodist congregation. St. John's was a gawky building, as high as it was long. But its tall tower emphatically marked the crossing of Galveston's axial and cross-axial. St. Patrick's Catholic Church, at Thirty-fourth and Avenue K one block south of Broadway in the West End, was designed by Galveston's outstanding Victorian architect, N. J. Clayton, in a lyrical High Victorian interpretation of Gothic. The body of the church was built between 1874 and 1878. Not until 1898 was Clayton able to construct the church's 225-foot-high Ménard Memorial Tower, completed in 1899. St. Patrick's location off Broadway underscored, however, the lesser status of the West End in comparison to the Tremont district and the East End. Clayton was also the architect of Sacred Heart Catholic Church at Thirteenth and Broadway in the East End. Built between 1889 and 1892 in a spirited High Victorian version of the southern French Romanesque style, Sacred Heart was the largest church in Texas at the time of its dedication. Each of these churches distinctly marked the section of Broadway along which it stood and architecturally monumentalized what were otherwise residential neighborhoods.[11]

THE FASHIONABLE NEIGHBORHOODS

These three neighborhoods were the fashionable enclaves along Broadway. Of them, the Tremont district and the East End were distinctly superior. Broadway's entire extent was never uniformly prestigious. The racial and class composition of adjacent neighborhoods and the character of nonresidential land-use either reinforced or undermined the desirability of Broadway real estate, depending on whether adjacent conditions were accounted high status or low status by elite standards.

The four blocks that separated the Tremont district and the East End, for instance, comprised a social divide, typical of nineteenth-century American cities, that fashion never managed to bridge. Not only were there corner grocery stores and saloons at Twenty-first and Broadway, but at Twenty-second and Broadway lay what I. H. Kempner, in his memoirs, described as the most "exclusive" bordello in Galveston during the 1880s and 1890s.[12] Located on the south side of Broadway between Twentieth and Twenty-first Streets was the oldest Black congregation in Galveston, Reedy Chapel African Methodist Episcopal Church, organized in 1848 as the slave congregation of St. John's Methodist Church. After the Civil War it became the nucleus of a small African-American neighborhood in the 2000 block. In 1888 the Episcopal Diocese of Texas established St. Augustine's Church at Twenty-second and Broadway as a mission to Black West Indians living in Galveston. At the far east end of Broadway, near its terminus at Sixth Street and the beach, was another African-American neighborhood, settled in the late 1860s. East District School in the 900 block of Broadway, a small public elementary school for Black children, was the institutional focus of this neighborhood.[13] There were Black neighborhoods on both sides of Broadway west of Twenty-sixth Street. But so intricate was the social geography of nineteenth-century Galveston that these did not seem to affect the prestige of the Tremont district, which they bracketed. During the last quarter of the nineteenth century, Galveston's railroad, warehouse, and industrial sector lay north of the West End of Broadway. In contrast, the East End, the largest concentrated upper- and middle-income neighborhood in Galveston, developed north of Broadway between Twentieth and Thirteenth Streets in these years.

In the face of competition from the East End of Broadway, the older Tremont district maintained its standing for two reasons. One was its proximity to a zone of prestigious institutions that stood along Twenty-second Street between Broadway and downtown. By the mid-1880s these included Galveston's oldest Episcopal parish, Trinity Church; the synagogue of Congregation B'nai Israel; the offices of the Galveston City Company; Artillery Hall, the home of Galveston's most elite militia unit; and Ball High School. The second, and perhaps more compelling, circumstance was the kinship network that prevailed in this enclave. Three generations of members of four prominent families—Dyer, Brown, Sealy, and Willis—were clustered in this neighborhood by the 1870s. The East End of Broadway did not possess a social network that was this tightly woven. Instead, it made its bid for recognition with architecture.

That the East End proved capable of challenging the Tremont district was due especially to the ability of architect Nicholas Joseph Clayton (1840–1916).[14] Howard Barnstone aptly summarized Clayton's impact on Galveston when he called the last quarter of the nineteenth century there the "Clayton era." In addition to Sacred Heart Church, Clayton designed the LeGierse-Ball, Blum, Trueheart, Gresham, Lasker, and League houses in the East End. What set his work apart from other Texan architects of this period was the coherence with which he organized his extravagant High Victorian displays and the intensely affecting surface animation with which he imbued his buildings.

THE GREAT HOUSES

It was in the East End that the earliest group of houses of exceptional size were built on Broadway, beginning in 1875 with Clayton's $15,000 house for the wholesale grocer Louis LeGierse. Following LeGierse's death in 1877, it was acquired by one of the elder statesmen of Galveston's business community, the commission merchant and banker George Ball (1817–84). The LeGierse-Ball house was the first of the Broadway houses to be raised nearly a full story above grade on an exposed basement, and its verticality was boosted higher still by a tower that rose another story above the roof. The J. N. Sawyer house, built next door about 1879, reproduced this towered villa type. Clayton repeated it again in his H. M. Trueheart house of 1884–86 and again, with modifications, in his Sylvain Blum house of 1884–85.[15] This row of four houses prompted the *Galveston Daily News* to designate East Broadway as Galveston's "Castle District," suggesting the striking contrast that ensued between these dwellings and older Galveston houses.

Despite their commanding heights, the LeGierse-Ball, Sawyer, and Trueheart houses were in some

Figure 7. Blum house, 1424 Broadway, 1885, N. J. Clayton, architect. Demolished 1915. Photograph, c. 1886.

respects conservative. Like Ashton Villa they had center hall plans, although their consistent adherence to the towered villa *parti* disguised the symmetrical implications of this plan configuration. Unlike Ashton Villa, all were built of wood rather than brick. The LeGierse-Ball and Sawyer houses had their kitchens and servants' rooms in detached buildings adjacent to the back alleys. The LeGierse house does seem to have introduced what would become a prestigious appurtenance on Broadway, a conservatory. About 1877, Mr. and Mrs. Brown enclosed the yard between the back of Ashton Villa and its detached kitchen building with a one-and-a-half-story sitting room that incorporated a conservatory. The Trueheart house had a freestanding conservatory in its side garden. The cultivation of exotic plants requiring a protected environment was thus identified architecturally as a high-status leisure pursuit.[16]

The great houses of the Castle District and the Tremont district were, like Ashton Villa, built on the north side of the street. What made real estate on the north side of Broadway so much more desirable was that the houses built there could face the street and be assured that their principal rooms would have unimpeded access to the prevailing southeast Gulf breeze. Houses on the south side were apt to receive the prevailing breeze via the immediate precincts of backyard privies, stables, and the rear alley, whose perennially sordid condition was a staple of late-nineteenth-century Galveston newspaper reports. Although the south side of Broadway in both the East End and the Tremont district was quite respectable, it could not compete with the north side of the street in terms of fashion. Not only were houses on the south side smaller, but there were more houses per block front. Architecturally, the south side of Broadway belonged to the collective realm of domestic typology while the north side was the stage on which urban actors performed. This consistent locational pattern underscored the urbanity of the grand avenue, where elite householders sought to engage the street rather than retreat from it.[17]

It was with the $30,000 house for Sylvain Blum (Figure 7), a partner in the wholesale dry goods, cotton exporting, and real estate investment firm of Leon & H. Blum, that Clayton responded to the architectural precedent—and challenge—posed by Ashton Villa.[18] The brick construction of the Blum house, its giant scale, its projecting polygonal bays and iron porches, its animated stucco wall surfaces, and its fantastic roofscape translated the ebullience of Clayton's public buildings and smaller houses into a large house for the first time in his career.

The house that Clayton designed for the lawyer, politician, and railroad investor Walter Gresham (1841–1920) and his family, built next door to the Blum house, was the apotheosis of Clayton's—and

Galveston's—High Victorian phase (Figure 8). Reportedly costing $125,000 to construct, the Gresham house rose three full stories above an exposed basement. The house was built of Texas granite and was trimmed with limestone, sandstone, and extensive sculptural decoration. Its reception rooms were finished in ornately detailed woods accented by colorful figured marbles. Interior detailing was classical, but it was a baroque, High Victorian classicism, full-bodied and activated (Figure 9). To exhibit Josephine Mann Gresham's collection of ferns, Clayton appended a large, apsidal-ended conservatory to the east wing of the house. The Gresham and Blum houses had only minor outbuildings associated with them. Both incorporated kitchens and servants' rooms in rear wings structurally continuous with the body of the house. Construction of the Gresham house began in February 1887. Colonel and Mrs. Gresham first entertained there on New Year's Day 1893.[19]

A description of the house that Clayton wrote during its construction emphasized its exoticism. "The unusual massive construction, unique appearance, and the majesty of expression conveyed by this building—

the first [stone residence on a large scale erected in architectural design] on the island—and the castellated effects of the picturesque stone walls, recalls to the traveled of our community the stately mansions of England and the chateaux of France." The Gresham house competitively maximized the distance that separated it from other Galveston houses in terms of size, material, and expenditure. Clayton's terminology indicated the basis of such invidious distinctions: durability, rarity, and high status.[20]

Clayton's Sacred Heart Church contributed architecturally to the urbanistic effect produced by the alignment of the Gresham and Blum houses along East Broadway (Figures 10 and 11). Its shaped masses, muscular components, richly detailed exteriors, and striped slate roof echoed the vertical rise and robust surfaces of the adjoining Broadway palaces. Sacred Heart's splendor may have served a compensatory purpose as well. Notwithstanding the urbanistic and architectural prominence of Clayton's two Broadway churches, Galveston's large Roman Catholic population was not well represented in the city's economic elite. None of the builders of major houses in the Tremont district or the East End was Roman Catholic.[21]

Figure 8. Gresham house (the Bishop's Palace), 1402 Broadway, 1892, N. J. Clayton & Co., architects. Photograph, c. early 1900s.

Figure 9. Gresham House, dining room. Photograph, 1981.

Figure 10. Broadway looking west from Fourteenth Street. Right to left: Gresham house, Blum house, LeGierse-Ball house, Sawyer house. Photograph, c. 1894.

Figure 11. Broadway looking east from Fourteenth Street. Sacred Heart Catholic Church, 1302 Broadway, 1892, N. J. Clayton & Co., architects. Destroyed 1900.

Figure 12. The Open Gates, 2424 Broadway, 1891, McKim, Mead & White, architects. Photograph, c. 1894.

Figure 13. The Open Gates, alcove in the Gold Room. Photograph, 1981.

In the competitive building that ensued along Broadway in the 1880s, the Tremont district responded to the challenge issued by the Castle District with The Open Gates, the house of one of George Ball's partners, banker and railroad corporation president George Sealy (1835–1901) and his wife Magnolia Willis Sealy (1854–1933) (Figure 12). Begun after, but completed before, the Gresham house, the Sealy house inverted one crucial term in this architectural competition. It substituted exquisiteness for overstatement. Although nearly as large as the Gresham house, the Sealy house was developed on a different plan. It was two stories high (plus raised basement and attic), not three stories high. And its site was an entire block front on Broadway. Like Ashton Villa and the Gresham house, however, the Sealy house was built almost to the back property line, and its grounds were completely exposed to public view.

The house was designed by McKim, Mead & White. According to family tradition, it was Mrs. Sealy who commissioned the house from Stanford White, although how she became aware of the New York firm is not known. N. J. Clayton was supervising architect. Construction began in late 1887 and was completed at the end of 1890. The house cost $100,000 to build. Mr. and Mrs. Sealy opened their house with a reception on January 24, 1891. Three months later they entertained President Benjamin Harrison and Governor James S. Hogg at a reception given to honor the president's visit to Galveston.[22]

The Sealy house was picturesquely composed but detailed with classical ornament, which was crisp and subtle in treatment rather than florid, highly contrasted, or flamboyant. It was the spirit of Queen Anne that prevailed. Instead of iron porches, a "piazza" was structurally and architecturally integrated into the body of the house. The Sealy house introduced the living hall to Galveston. And in place of double parlors, it had a single drawing room, which the Sealy family called the Gold Room (Figure 13). McKim, Mead & White were responsible for the interior decoration of the house. They detailed the Gold Room with Corinthian pilasters, Corinthian columns, and a delicate frieze of anthemia and palmettes, all finished in enameled white and gold. Upholstered furniture, described as being Louis XVI in style, was also gilded. The effect was perhaps more Texas French than eighteenth century, but it was to strike a very responsive chord in Galveston.[23]

Between 1889 and 1892, a large two-story brick and tile-roofed stable and carriage house, costing $15,842, was built just east of the house, set well back from Broadway. This was designed by Clayton, who carefully coordinated it with the design of the house. A freestanding conservatory was built next to the stable, and Mrs. Sealy retained Herbert Millidge, an English horticulturist, to supervise it.[24] At the four corners of the property McKim, Mead & White designed the pairs of stone gate piers, yoked together by graceful filigrees of wrought iron, from which the house acquired its name. Graveled carriage drives looped around the half-block site and allowed visitors to alight directly at the front steps of the house rather than at curbside on the street. They brought the amenity of the porte-cochère to Broadway and initiated, ever so slightly, the beginning of a retreat from the urban order of the street.

In commissioning McKim, Mead & White, Magnolia Willis and George Sealy obtained, as J. M. Brown had thirty years earlier, a house that was current in style not just by Galveston standards but by metropolitan standards. It introduced a new plan arrangement, a new type of interior decor, the intimation of a new relationship to the public realm, and a significantly modified attitude about the propriety of architectural display in Galveston. The influence of the Sealy house can be measured in the houses that succeeded it on Broadway.

Two houses designed by Clayton in the Castle District attest to his assimilation of the lessons of the Sealy house. The large, pink stucco-surfaced brick house for the real estate investor and banker Morris Lasker (1840–1915) and his family, designed in 1889 and completed in 1892, was more integrated formally and less brittle than the Gresham house (Figure 14). Its Neo-Grec classical decor was not related to the Sealy house, but its plan was. A series of preliminary plan drawings survive to document the Lasker house's evolution from a compressed version of the Gresham house to an arrangement that, while preserving a compartmentally staged central hall, dispensed with double parlors for a single drawing room, entered opposite a large projecting bay, as in the Gold Room of the Sealy house.[25]

Figure 14. Lasker house, 1718 Broadway, 1892, N. J. Clayton & Co., architects. Demolished 1967. Photograph, 1962.

Sharing the block front on Broadway with the Lasker house was an even larger house built to Clayton's design between 1890 and 1893 for the lawyer and real estate investor John Charles League (1849–1916) and his wife Nellie Ball, the daughter of George Ball (Figure 15). This, the last of the palaces that Clayton designed on Broadway, was picturesque in composition and decorated with Colonial Revival detail. Clayton suppressed the L-front arrangement of the towered villa, integrated the piazza into the body of the house, and provided both a drawing room and a living hall finished with white-painted Colonial Revival detail. The League house was built for a reported cost of $80,000. Of brick construction, it was finished with gray stucco and light-colored trim. It was outfitted with a freestanding roofed porte-cochère and occupied one of the few house sites on Broadway that ran the full depth of the block back to Avenue I.[26]

Next door to Ashton Villa, Mrs. Sealy's brother, P. J. Willis, Jr., replaced his existing Greek Revival

Figure 15. League house, 1710 Broadway, 1893, N. J. Clayton & Co., architects. Photograph, 1900.

house between 1889 and 1890 with a house that paraphrased certain elements of The Open Gates, although it abandoned neither the corner tower nor the plain wooden clapboarding customary in Galveston. The Willis house seems to have had the first roofed porte-cochère on Broadway. Like the conservatory and French-style furniture, the porte-cochère acquired an association of high status that made its subsequent replication noteworthy. At Ashton Villa, the Brown family had their house's large parlor redecorated in white and gold, even calling it the Gold Room.[27] It was, however, Mrs. R. S. Willis, the widow of Mrs. Sealy's uncle, who sought to emulate the discriminating patronage of her niece in the last of the Victorian palaces on Broadway.

Narcissa Worsham Willis (1828–99) seems to have begun planning her new house shortly after her husband's death in 1892. Built between 1893 and 1895 on a three-lot, midblock site in the Tremont district, it was reported to cost $80,000 (Figure 16). The three-story house was so big that it was built against the rear alley in place of a wall and against both of the side lot lines. Mrs. Willis's house was designed by William H. Tyndall (1841–1907), an English-born architect who arrived in Galveston in 1879 and advertised himself as having been a pupil of the English architect E. Welby Pugin. The Willis house was built of red pressed brick and white, ashlar-faced Bolton limestone.[28] It was awkwardly composed, with multiple protruding bays and towers. Its one bravura touch was a three-story convex end wall on the west side of the house that rose into a gable. Like the Gresham house, the Willis house incorporated a conservatory. Like the League house, it had a roofed porte-cochère.

What set Mrs. Willis's house apart on Broadway was not just its enormous size but its interior decor. Mrs. Willis retained Pottier, Stymus & Company of New York to detail and decorate the inside of the house. As with

Figure 16. Willis-Moody house, 2618 Broadway, 1895, W. H. Tyndall, architect. Photograph, c. 1913.

the interiors of the Sealy house, the major rooms of Mrs. Willis's house were detailed and furnished in different styles that allowed for a discreetly competitive exhibition of opulence, disciplined by the taste, skill, and implicit prestige that a recognized expert in the field of decorative art such as Pottier, Stymus & Company could be relied upon to provide. In terms of visual richness, Mrs. Willis's very large dining room, with its gilded plaster bas-relief wall friezes and coffered ceiling, outshined the local competition (Figure 17).

Figure 17. Willis-Moody house, 2618 Broadway, 1895. Dining room. Pottier, Stymus & Company, designers. Photograph, 1991.

Mrs. Willis had not completed the decoration of the principal rooms of her house at the time of her death in 1899. In 1900 the house was purchased by Libby Shearn and William L. Moody, Jr. Moody (1865–1954), a cotton exporter and banker, would become the richest man in twentieth-century Galveston. Although Moody corresponded with Pottier, Stymus & Company in 1910 about completing the interior work, he rejected their proposals as too expensive. Instead, he contracted with a Galveston millwork company, whose stock moldings and pine strip floor planks provided a thrifty, if somewhat anticlimactic, conclusion to Mrs. Willis's ambitious decorating project.[29]

A New Civic Identity

Concluding Broadway's evolution at the end of the century was the erection of the Texas Heroes Monument between 1897 and 1900 at Twenty-fifth and Broadway, the symbolic if not operational center of the city (Figure 1). Executed by the Italian-born and -trained Washington, D. C., sculptor Louis Amateis, the Texas Heroes Monument was in the epic style of the American Renaissance. It was the first—and ultimately the grandest— work of public art installed in a Texas city under the auspices of the City Beautiful movement.[30] What made the intersection of Galveston's axial and cross-axial streets the inevitable location for the monument was that it confirmed, with its rhetorical publicity, Broadway's status as Galveston's showplace avenue of power, wealth, and domestic (and therefore refined) luxury, where self-representation acquired a civic and corporate dimension.

By the end of the century, Broadway had gathered together, without rendering indistinguishable, the triumphant expressions of the accumulated wealth of Galveston's self-made men. It coherently organized this exhibition and expanded the subject of representation from the families who built and occupied the Broadway palaces to the city itself. The Strand, the downtown street where the major commission houses and banks were located, also fulfilled this symbolic function, but its tone was different. It was not a place where ladies were encouraged to go.[31] What Broadway offered was a coordination of architectural spectacle that combined respectability, propinquity, and architectural grandeur, advertising not the production of wealth but its refinement into expressions of domestic piety and civic pride. Broadway regularized, rationalized, and ritualized the competitive strivings of Galveston's elite, transforming these expressions of individuality into a civic whole that could in turn advertise Broadway's superiority to the grand avenues of Houston, San Antonio, and the upstart Dallas. When the *Galveston Daily News* asserted in 1888 that "Broadway is to Galveston what Fifth Avenue is to New York, preeminently the aristocratic street of the city," it collectivized these expressions of private wealth into a symbol of civic identity.[32]

The New Century

In the beginning of the new century, public works reinforced Broadway's civic standing but in the context of unanticipated catastrophe. Less than five months after the dedication of the Texas Heroes Monument, Galveston endured the greatest natural disaster to strike an American city, the storm of September 8, 1900. A hurricane with winds as high as 120 miles per hour propelled a tidal surge across the island, burying parts of the city under fifteen feet of pounding surf. Between 5,000 and 6,000 people were killed, out of a population of 37,789. All the large Broadway houses survived and most harbored numerous refugees. Churches, however, proved especially vulnerable because of their large internal volumes and tall towers. Sacred Heart, St. Patrick's, and St. John's Methodist were all destroyed (Figure 18).[33]

To protect Galveston from the recurrence of such a disaster, a seventeen-foot-high reinforced concrete seawall was constructed around the east and south sides of the city between 1902 and 1904. Between 1904

Figure 18. Aftermath of the Storm of 1900, looking southwest from the 1200 block of Avenue I toward the wreckage of Sacred Heart Church. Upper right: Gresham house towers. Photograph, 1900.

and 1910 the entire grade level of Galveston was raised between five and eight feet. The grade raising compromised the mature vegetation that survived the storm. Therefore, even before this engineering feat was completed, an elite women's organization, begun in 1899 and eventually known as the Galveston Civic League, initiated a landscaping program that gave Broadway its present aspect.[34] The league advocated the planting of oleanders and palm trees. Rows of Washingtonia palms, interspersed with live oaks and oleanders, were planted in the esplanades and sidewalk reserves along Broadway. These gave the avenue a tropical appearance that before 1900 had been confined to private gardens in Galveston.[35]

Figure 19. Broadway, looking east from Fifteenth Street past Blum house (left) and Gresham house (center) toward second Sacred Heart Church of 1904. Onion dome, 1910, N. J. Clayton & Co., architects. Photograph, 1914.

Between 1903 and 1904 a new Sacred Heart Church was built. Unlike its predecessor, it faced Fourteenth Street rather than Broadway. The intensely white, stucco-surfaced, reinforced concrete church was designed in a rather naïve Moorish style by Brother Peter Jiménez, S. J., a Jesuit lay brother and carpenter (Figure 19). Clayton prepared plans to reconstruct Sacred Heart in 1902, but these were rejected by the parish pastor. In

Figure 20. Kempner house, 1502 Broadway, 1906, C. W. Bulger, architect. Photograph, c. 1906.

Figure 21. To the left of the Gresham house (on the corner), the Carl C. Biehl and Richard M. Wilkens houses, both 1916 by Anton F. Korn, Jr., architect, replaced the Blum house. Photograph, 1919.

1910 Clayton replaced Jiménez's low dome with the buoyant, firmly profiled onion dome that still rises above the crossing of Sacred Heart. It was his last work on Broadway.[36]

The only major house built in the Castle District in the first decade of the new century was constructed in 1905–1906 for the cotton exporter and sugar refiner I. H. Kempner (1875–1967) and his wife Henrietta Blum, the niece of Sylvain Blum (Figure 20). The Kempner House was designed by Charles W. Bulger, one of a number of younger architects who set up practices in Galveston in the 1890s. Although it retained the big-scale characteristic of the Victorian houses, the Colonial Revival–style Kempner house was symmetrically composed, consistently detailed with classical ornament, and relatively low set, this last an implicit show of faith in the efficacy of the Galveston seawall.[37]

The dearth of new Colonial Revival houses along Broadway reflected Galveston's economic decline in the early twentieth century.[38] Not until the 1910s did architecturally ambitious residential construction resume on Broadway. Anton F. Korn, Jr., a young architect who practiced in Galveston between 1914 and 1917 as a representative of the New York firm of Crow, Lewis & Wickenhoefer, designed four houses on Broadway that were smaller in scale, more academic in their use of historically derived detail, and less assertive than the Victorian and Colonial Revival houses. Yet in their symmetry, planarity, and frontality, these houses continued to engage Broadway, as did the older houses. The shipping agent and cotton exporter Richard M. Wilkens demolished Clayton's Blum house in 1915 and replaced it with two Korn-designed houses, one for his family, the other for the family of his partner, Carl C. Biehl (Figure 21). Korn also designed the house built on the site of St. John's Methodist Church for Eveline Goggan and George N. Copley.[39]

In 1909 property owners along Broadway organized to promote the paving of the street, which was carried out in 1913.[40] This accompanied a development that profoundly affected visitors' perceptions of Broadway and Galveston. Prior to 1911, visitors arriving by train or ship disembarked downtown. But in 1911 the Galveston-Houston Electric Company completed the Galveston Causeway across Galveston Bay and built its rapid-rail interurban line in the Broadway esplanades from Fifty-third Street, at the western edge of the city, to Twenty-first Street, where the Interurban turned to go downtown (Figure 22). Thereafter, most visitors to the city entered Galveston on Broadway. Unified landscaping, paving, and intercity mass transportation transformed Broadway into an urban highway.[41]

This led to Broadway's spatial transformation as a continuous route that traversed various neighborhoods. This perceptual reinterpretation tended to submerge the distinct character of the West End, the Tremont district, and the East End, re-presenting them instead as episodes in a new linear sequence whose most consistent elements were the rows of live oaks and Washingtonia palms that framed the boulevard. This civic landscaping, as it matured, redefined the city's aspect in a more elusive way. The combination of oaks, palms, and oleanders evoked images of southernness and tropicality, impressing Broadway with a romantic allure. The mood, however, was elegiac, as though the plantings were meant to image the city's inability to sustain the entrepreneurial ambitions with which it was begun (Figure 23).

By the late 1920s the publicity that Broadway had offered Victorian entrepreneurs was out of date. The ritualized public display of wealth on which the grand avenue was predicated had given way to less aggressive (and eventually suburban) architectural exhibitions of status. The relative restraint of the Sealy house had been a very early indication of this trend in Texas. Moreover, as a conventional sign of urban progress and civic prosperity, the grand avenue had been eclipsed by the rising skylines of American downtowns. To the extent that Broadway continued to represent Galveston, it portrayed the city as picturesque, eccentric, and economically stagnant, unable to keep pace with its dynamic neighbor, Houston (Figure 24). The novelist Edna Ferber implied this when she described how the "remnant of haunted beauty—gray, shrouded, crumbling" of Galveston in 1939 reminded her of Miss Havisham in Dickens's *Great Expectations*.[42]

The domestic architecture of the grand avenue underwent a similar reversal in estimation. The collective significance of the Broadway palaces became that of picturesque eclectic Victorian architecture everywhere in the United States in the twentieth century: a combination of the ridiculous and the grotesque, defying good taste and sound judgment. John Gunther, in his biography of Morris Lasker's son, Albert D. Lasker, resorted to the castle trope to

Figure 22. Broadway, looking west from Twenty-first Street along the Interurban tracks. Right to left: the Frosh house, 1840; the P. J. Willis, Jr., house, 1890; Ashton Villa, 1860; The Open Gates, 1891. In the distance: the Willis-Moody house, 1895. Photograph, 1911.

Figure 23. Broadway, looking west from Seventeenth Street, Castle District. League house (right), Lasker house (center). Photograph, c. 1920s.

Figure 24. Aerial view of central Galveston showing the east end of Broadway running from the 1400 block (center, left) to the 1900 block (lower left). Background shows downtown Galveston, waterfront and harbor, and railroad yards and wharves. Photograph, 1926.

evoke life on the grand avenue from a mid-twentieth-century perspective:

> The Lasker residence looked like a castle—or prison—out of Grimm…. It had balconies, Corinthian columns, tri-angular porches, and ornate glass bulges set at improbable angles behind clumps of palm—a remarkable hodgepodge indeed, but typical of its time…. Albert's family home became a symbol of everything he wanted to get away from.[43]

Even among those members of the younger generation who did not seek to escape Broadway, discretion as the preferred elite style was evident. The last domestic building projects to occur in the Castle District were comparatively unpretentious. And all entailed the demolition of Victorian houses. In 1924 Mr. and Mrs. I. H. Kempner retained John F. Staub of Houston to add an understated wing to their house. To make room for the addition, Kempner acquired the lot next door and Clayton's LeGierse-Ball house came down. In 1928 Sally Trueheart Williams demolished her parents' Clayton-designed house. She subdivided the site and in 1928–29 built on part of it a compact, pink stucco–surfaced Mediterranean-style house for herself. Mrs. Trueheart Williams sold the corner lots to Dr. and Mrs. Albert O. Singleton, who built a restrained Monterey-style house there in 1931 (Figure 25). Both were designed by the Houston architect Cameron Fairchild.[44]

The Williams and Singleton houses—low set, eclectically styled, suburban "country houses"—were typical of houses being built in Galveston's new restricted residential enclaves, developed after the mid-1920s west of Forty-third Street and well south of Broadway. These subdivisions broke with the street and block pattern of the Groesbeck town plan, within which they were set, to produce internally focused neighborhoods that discouraged through traffic.[45]

During the 1920s gasoline service stations began to be built at key intersections on Broadway west of Twenty-first Street. The Tremont district's location astride the streets where the streetcars, the Interurban, and incoming vehicular traffic along Broadway turned to go downtown led to increasing infiltration by auto-oriented businesses. Between the early 1930s and the late 1940s, most of the large houses in the Tremont district were demolished, leaving only Ashton Villa, The Open Gates, and the Willis-Moody house. The completion of a paved highway between Houston and Galveston in 1928 brought an influx of traffic onto Broadway. This intensified after 1952 when the Gulf Freeway, the first intercity freeway in Texas, opened between Galveston and Houston. The Texas Highway Department accommodated the anticipated increase in

vehicles by adding new traffic lanes to Broadway at the expense of the esplanades, which were reduced from 98 feet in width to 36 feet, reversing the ratio between planting and paving.[46]

What kept Broadway from disintegrating entirely, as Houston's grand avenue, Main Street, had done in the 1920s, was the conservatism of senior members of the Sealy, Moody, and, in the East End, Kempner families. Zoning, adopted by the City of Galveston in 1937, gave the East End a measure of stability by inhibiting the encroachment of busi-

Figure 25. Singleton house, 1602 Broadway, 1931, Cameron Fairchild, architect.

nesses, which had undermined the attractiveness of the Tremont district and the West End of Broadway for residential use. But the "BOI" mentality ("born on the island") of the older generation of Galveston's elite should not be underestimated.[47] Their disinclination to be disturbed by the changes that living on an urban highway entailed—traffic congestion and noise, dirt, and petty crime—meant not only the survival of most of Broadway's greatest houses, but their continued occupation as single-family residences right into the last quarter of the twentieth century.

Preservation and Beautification

During the late 1960s historical preservation emerged as a powerful and compelling focus of civic identity and community activism in Galveston. When the Sawyer house in the Castle District was demolished in 1965, no protest was raised. But when the Lasker house was demolished in 1967, it was only after protracted efforts to save it failed.[48] In between these two demolitions, Howard Barnstone had published *The Galveston That Was*, with photographs by Henri Cartier-Bresson and Ezra Stoller, and the Galveston Historical Foundation initiated a Historic American Buildings Survey inventory of the city's architectural-historical resources under the direction of John C. Garner, Jr. *The Galveston That Was* brought widespread recognition of Galveston's nineteenth-century architectural patrimony, and the HABS inventory provided the data necessary to begin preservation-oriented planning. In 1971 the Galveston City Commission authorized the creation of the East End Historical District, which encompasses the blocks on both sides of Broadway between Eleventh and Nineteenth Streets. The district was listed in the National Register of Historic Places in 1975 and designated a National Historic Landmark in 1976.[49]

History emerged as a new interpretive paradigm for Broadway and for much of the rest of Galveston in the 1970s. Broadway's socioeconomic function between the 1860s and the 1910s had been to legitimize newly made wealth by the symbolic transfer, through architecture and civic improvement, of individual fortunes to a new type of middle-class civic realm that identified successful entrepreneurship with the destiny of the city. After the first decade of the new century, scorn replaced envy as the reflexive response to the superannuated project of the grand avenue. Broadway became a kind of architectural and urbanistic emblem of Galveston's failure to fulfill what became Houston's destiny. By the end of the 1960s, the cautionary morality embodied in this architectural and urbanistic narrative ceased to compel. It was succeeded by historical curiosity that rather than demonizing local artifacts, sought to locate them in a cultural context. Historical curiosity acquired a constituency in Galveston in the 1970s that propelled the city into an urban conservation initiative. Ironically, this gave Galveston a competitive edge over Houston and renewed its sense of civic destiny.[50]

Three of the Broadway mansions have become house museums. Two of these, the Gresham house and Ashton Villa, were sold by the families of their original builders during the 1920s. The Gresham house became the residence of the Roman Catholic Bishop of Galveston, the Most Rev. Christopher E. Byrne, in 1923 (hence the name by which it is now best known, the Bishop's Palace). After Bishop Byrne's death in 1950, the Gresham house was used only intermittently by the diocese, especially after the see was transferred to Houston in 1959. In 1963 the diocese opened the Bishop's Palace as a house museum, the first on Broadway.[51]

Ashton Villa, which was acquired by El Mina Shrine Temple in 1928, was the only Broadway house to be recorded in the original Historic American Buildings Survey in 1934. In 1971 the property was bought by the City of Galveston from El Mina Temple to save the house from demolition and replacement by a service station. Following its restoration, Ashton Villa was opened to the public in 1974 as a house museum operated by the Galveston Historical Foundation.[52] W. L. Moody's eldest daughter and heir, Mary Moody Northen, upon her death in 1986, bequeathed the Willis-Moody house and its contents to a foundation she established. The foundation completed the comprehensive restoration she had begun in 1983 and opened the house as the Moody Mansion and Museum in 1991.[53]

The children of Magnolia and George Sealy presented The Open Gates as an endowed gift to the University of Texas Medical Branch at Galveston in 1969. The university took possession of the property upon the death of the Sealys' youngest son, Robert, in 1979. Commodore Sealy, as he was known in Galveston, had lived at The Open Gates since Mrs. Sealy's death in 1933, maintaining the house and grounds as they had been during his mother's lifetime.[54]

Figure 26. Broadway at Twenty-fifth Street, 1986.

A beautification plan for Broadway, authorized by the City of Galveston in 1985 and prepared by Slaney Santana, landscape architects, William F. Stern & Associates, architects, and other consultants, provides an opportunity to assess the historical evolution of Galveston's grand avenue and its role in the city.[55] The Broadway Beautification Plan emphasizes the continuity of the street through reinforcement of the landscaping installed by the Galveston Civic League after the Storm of 1900. But it used the precedent of the Texas Heroes Monument to propose a series of monuments, staged at intervals, that acknowledge the diversity of Galveston, especially the various neighborhoods abutting Broadway. Broadway's historic ability to display civic symbols of public significance is valued. The plan proposes to make visible a wider range of historic experiences than is alone preserved in what it refers to as the "gallery" of Galveston's best-known Victorian neighborhoods. Galveston at the end of the twentieth century has tried to forge a new identity for itself by confronting the surviving artifacts of its past. Broadway is pressed into service once again to represent this identity, one that encompasses yet is more complex than the images of success and privilege that the grand avenue originally enshrined (Figure 26).

ACKNOWLEDGMENTS

For assistance with the preparation of this essay the author gratefully acknowledges Kenneth Hafertepe, Ph.D.; Drexel Turner; Barrie Scardino; Ellen Beasley; Sadie Gwin Blackburn; Patrick H. Butler, III, museum director, and Bradley C. Brooks, curator of collections, the Moody Mansion and Museum; Lisa Lambert, archivist, Jean Robinson, Casey Greene and Julia Dunn, librarians, Galveston and Texas History Center, Rosenberg Library; Mrs. Albert O. Singleton III; Randy Pace, Galveston Historical Foundation; Bob Nesbitt; Evangeline Loessin Whorton; Houston Metropolitan Research Center, Houston Public Library; College of Architecture, University of Houston; and School of Architecture and the Fondren Library, Rice University.

STEPHEN FOX

VANDEVENTER
Place
St. Louis, Missouri

IN 1895 VANDEVENTER PLACE, only a quarter century old, was proclaimed an ideal representation of the concept of *rus in urbe*, or rural character within an urban context (Figure 1). Drawing upon two earlier private streets, the planners of Vandeventer Place reorganized certain characteristics of those streets on a comprehensive scale, popularizing and perfecting this idea, which continues to some degree to the present day. But this prototype was razed fifty-five years later. Even in the absence of concrete monuments, there is just enough evidence to support a reasonable reconstruction. Perhaps recreating Vandeventer Place here may reveal why this street was considered such an acme of perfection.[1]

THE PRIVATE STREET IN ST. LOUIS AND VANDEVENTER PLACE

Nineteenth-century St. Louis has had a special place in our national development thanks to its strategic location. An inland city situated at the confluence of major natural waterways, its location made it a transportation and commercial center. After midcentury St. Louis made the important transition from river port to overland railway hub (Figure 2). Those few municipal ordinances and regulations that existed both before and after the Civil War continued to favor land speculation. Waves of immigration increased the city's population by more than one hundred thousand persons each decade, putting pressure to subdivide on those who held vacant land on the ever-expanding periphery of the city. Development adhered to the local topography; industry followed the tributary streams—Mill Creek and the Des Peres River—and expanded north and south along the western bank of the

ESSAY BY CHARLES SAVAGE

Figure 1. Vandeventer Place, aerial view west from Grand Avenue, c. 1900.

Mississippi River. The once-scenic bluffs north and south of the city were made intolerable for residential development by the riverside iron furnaces and tanneries below. These years of prosperity saw the rise of a small group who controlled the banks, the major businesses, and a great deal of the real estate. As residential development moved to the central and western portions of the city, the established and affluent members of this oligarchy secured the more desirable highland, much of which had once been the city's common pasture lands. But these higher elevations did not always offer protection from industrial nuisance or foreign strangers. While the introduction of private streets in St. Louis was a reaction to the general absence of zoning, there are examples of private development elsewhere that might have influenced it. More than the development of Bloomsbury and Belgravia, the London squares that presaged similar developments in East Coast cities, it appears that the kernel of St. Louis's private streets may descend from the provincial developments in shire and market towns based on Nash's Regents Park, Calverley Park, Tunbridge Wells, and Peter Frederick Robinson's Nottingham Park Estate. The principles of these park-like residential developments were adapted to the grid pattern prevalent in American cities.

Vandeventer Place was conceived by Charles H. Peck, a builder, successful real estate developer, and early associate of the architect George Ingham Barnett (1815–98), in conjunction with Napoleon Mullikin, Joseph McCune, and the heirs of Peter L. Vandeventer (d. 1859), late of New Brunswick, New Jersey. The parcel that eventually contained Vandeventer Place was situated in the "Grand Prairie" common fields due west of the city on the knob of the ridge along which Grand Avenue now runs.[2] In 1855 the city's western boundary was extended from Eighteenth Street to Grand Avenue; in 1876 the western boundary was extended from Grand to just beyond Forest Park. Vandeventer Place, the third of the nineteen private streets platted in the city, drew upon the characteristics of its two predecessors, Lucas Place and Benton Place.

In 1851, on the advice of Barnett, James H. Lucas (1800–73) donated the block bounded by Olive Street on the south, St. Charles on the north, and Thirteenth and Fourteenth Streets on the east and west, to the city as Missouri Park. (Today the St. Louis Public Library covers the greater part of this block.) Barnett had been apprenticed to the Nottinghamshire builder William Patterson, who had built the private Park Terraces in the Nottingham Park Estate. Barnett arrived in St. Louis in 1839, associating himself with a succession of builder/developers, Charles Peck among them. It is likely that Barnett adapted his early experience in the development of the Nottingham Park Estate to the degree that it was acceptable in St. Louis. Lucas Place was laid out in accord with the city's grid as a continuation of Locust Street but west of the new park. The new street followed the gentle slope up from Fourteenth Street to Eighteenth Street, the city's boundary along the first ridge west of the Mississippi. Lucas and Barnett introduced deed restrictions giving joint ownership and responsibility for maintenance of the street to its residents. The street was a restricted thoroughfare with traffic limited to private pleasure vehicles. No grocers, apothecaries, coffee houses, dram shops, theaters, or circuses could be located or pursue trade in Lucas Place, although schools and churches were not excluded. Lucas Place itself was seventy-two feet wide; lots were twenty-five feet in width with a setback of twenty-five feet. There was a built-in time limit; these restrictions were binding for thirty years.[3]

Buffered from the city by Missouri Park at its foot, Lucas Place needed no physical barriers to identify it as St. Louis's most prestigious address. The city's first capitalists built late Federal and Italianate houses here, houses of common brick fronted with the chalky hued Mississippi River sandstone (occasionally called Joliet stone) or brick painted the color of this stone. Two of the most distinguished, the Thomas Allen house (1858)

Figure 2. Map of the city of St. Louis, c. 1874.

and the George Collier house (c. 1858), both near Lucas and Sixteenth Street, were designed by George I. Barnett. By 1860 Lucas Place had become the most select neighborhood in the city.[4] Business leaders Rufus Lackland, Henry Kayser, Samuel C. Davis, and the Filleys, Oliver and Giles, built there; James Lucas himself bought John How's house, moving from Ninth and Olive in 1867. Athough the restrictions applied only as far as Eighteenth Street, the cachet of Lucas Place stretched west with a group of stone-fronted, mansard-roofed Second Empire houses. Daniel Catlin brought his bride, Justina Kayser, from her father's house in Lucas Place proper to a new red brick Queen Anne house on the corner of Twenty-first Street in 1882.[5]

Benton Place, named for Missouri's provocative legislator Thomas Hart Benton, was established by Montgomery Blair (1813–83). In 1868 he purchased the wooded hillside north of LaFayette Square and employed Julius Pitzman to survey and grade it. Blair, mayor of St. Louis in 1842, made a name for himself nationally as counsel for Dred Scott in 1857. In 1861 Lincoln appointed him postmaster general. LaFayette Square, at the highest point of the old "common pasture" on the city's southwestern edge, had been set aside as a public park by municipal ordinance as early as 1836, despite opposition from speculators who were purchasing sections of the common fields from the city fathers. By 1859 LaFayette Square had become a fashionable neighborhood.[6] Benton Place was Pitzman's first private-street commission, though not his last; after Benton Place, he platted every private street in town except one (Shaw Place, 1878).[7] Julius Pitzman was born in Halberstadt, Prussia, in 1837, but immigrated at the age of seventeen to Wisconsin and then moved to St. Louis to work with his brother-in-law, a surveyor. He served as a topographer to Generals Fremont, Halleck, Sherman, and Grant in the Civil War but was wounded in 1863. Returning to surveying, he compiled a comprehensive corpus of regional surveys and in 1868 published a map of St. Louis.

Benton Place was laid out as forty-nine lots, each twenty-five feet wide. The setback line was the same as that for Lucas Place, but unlike Lucas Place, Benton Place was a cul-de-sac with no through traffic. Except for the six lots fronting the square, the lots within Benton Place run from the back alleys to the middle of the narrow elliptical greensward down its center, a significant innovation. The deed restrictions followed those for Lucas Place. An association to which every property owner had to belong regulated annual assessments for maintenance, and the houses could be for residential use only.[8] The majority of the houses were built in the stone-fronted Second Empire style. The grandest, George I. Barnett's for William L. Huse at 2043 Park Avenue (1878), faced LaFayette Square. Around the corner and unique for Benton Place was the red brick Edward Rowse residence (1892), a composite of the Queen Anne style and the Richardsonian Romanesque, designed by Pierce P. Furber of Peabody & Stearns of Boston.

Pitzman first surveyed Vandeventer Place on June 1, 1869, in a configuration more ambitious than the one he platted a year later.[9] The plat Pitzman filed on June 24, 1870, is the one that was realized (Figure 3).[10] Integrating it into the existing city grid as Barnett had done with Lucas Place, Pitzman laid out Vandeventer Place west of Grand Avenue to Vandeventer Avenue, between and parallel to Enright (subsequently known as Morgan, then Hogan) Avenue to the south and Bell Avenue to the north. But he added a fountain at the entrance and a park-like center strip, an elongation of the Benton Place ellipse. In the deed filed July 1, 1870,

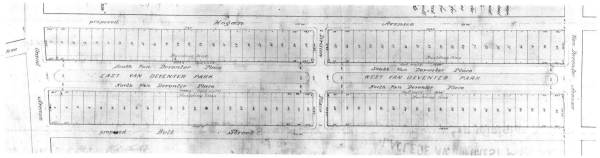

Figure 3. Plat of Vandeventer Place, 1870.

North Vandeventer Place and South Vandeventer Place—the drives and footwalks on either side of the center strip—were dedicated to the use of the persons who purchased and improved the lots and were not for public use. Division Place (later Spring Avenue), the cross street running between Enright and Bell Avenues, separated the landscaped median into East and West Vandeventer Parks and was dedicated to public use in perpetuity. Eighty-six lots were platted; each was fifty feet wide (except for the slightly wider end lots, buffers against the public domain) and one hundred forty-three feet deep. The drives were thirty feet wide, the landscaped medians fifty feet wide. The strip between curb and lawn, including the sidewalk, was twelve feet wide, and the setback line was twenty feet. Most of the people who purchased lots in Vandeventer purchased more than one; sometimes half and occasionally one-quarter of an adjacent lot was added to the one already held. Charles H. Peck and Napoleon Mullikin had four contiguous lots; Edward Mallinckrodt at 22 Vandeventer bought four and Henry C. Pierce at 40 Vandeventer bought five contiguous lots.

Every lot owner was subject to the regulations in the deed restrictions. There was a street association to which every lot owner had to belong and, after an initial payment of $150, an annual assessment for street maintenance, lighting, repairs, and improvements. Enjoyment of the median parks depended on full payment of these dues. Only first-class dwellings could be erected within the first seventy feet of each lot. These could only be single-family dwellings and could not cost less than $10,000. The "principal front" of each house (usually interpreted as the one with the front door) had to face Vandeventer Place. All houses were required to have basement kitchens. Incredible as it may seem today, front steps were to be scrubbed at least twice a week and every window had to be hung with three sets of curtains. (Coal was burned as fuel and its soot, an accepted inconvenience, was dealt with in the most practical manner.) No commercial enterprise of any kind would be tolerated, and service deliveries had to be made through the back alleys. Prohibited were all present and recalled nuisances, from breweries to tanneries.[11] It is interesting that here, unlike Lucas Place, churches, schools, and museums were excluded.

It fell to the three trustees—Charles H. Peck, Napoleon Mullikin, and John S. McCune—to enforce these deed restrictions and to collect the initial payments and the annual assessments. They had the power to appoint additional trustees should their number diminish. The trust was to end only with the death of the last of the original three trustees, although the restrictions were to remain in effect. At that time the owners of each lot would be in control in perpetuity; a two-thirds majority of the lot owners was needed to enact any changes to the restrictions. Unlike Lucas Place, there was no time limit specified; and unlike Lucas Place, Vandeventer was organized by a syndicate, not an individual. The lots on Vandeventer were deeper and twice as wide as those on Lucas and Benton Places. Like Lucas Place, Vandeventer was not a cul-de-sac; like Benton Place, Vandeventer had a green center median (*rus in urbe*). The one characteristic all Vandeventer Place houses shared was an English basement, high enough to light the mandated basement kitchens. Not one of them deviated from this restriction (although one attempted to do so).

One important distinction relevant to the inclusion of a private street within the context of grand residential avenues requires clarification. The characteristics common to America's grand avenues are, in St. Louis, to be found in the succession of private streets that evolved there and nowhere else. Vandeventer Place was not a speculative venture; its residents built in it for themselves. Although St. Louis's private streets were enclaves of the well-to-do, they were not sealed to all others. In 1895 a group of touring journalists, taken to see Vandeventer Place and the new Forest Park Addition west of it, declared that St. Louis was the only city in the United States where the private street had evolved in such a practical and useful manner.[12] Taken together there was little difference between the private streets in St. Louis and the new residential boulevards being platted in other American cities.

ARCHITECTS AND CLIENTS: A SURVEY

Charles H. Peck's mansion at 7 Vandeventer Place (Figure 4) and Napoleon Mullikin's directly opposite were both designed by George I. Barnett in the stone-fronted Second Empire style just before the financial Panic of 1873. Near mirror images, they were the first houses in Vandeventer Place (Figure 5). Barnett and Charles Peck had collaborated as early as 1846; from 1848 until 1854 they were in partnership, Barnett designing and Peck building. Although Peck withdrew to attend to other business interests, he continued to rely on Barnett as an architect.[13] It is likely that Barnett designed two other stone-fronted houses on Vandeventer Place, one for Samuel A. Coale, Jr., at 15 Vandeventer in 1872 (Figure 1, third house on the right),[14] and the other for Hugh Crawford, president of the Sligo Furnace Company, a year later, after the economy had begun to improve (Figure 6).

Pitzman's annotated plats and published building applications corroborate the economic upswing. The Barnett firm began once more to receive commissions in Vandeventer Place, whether from individual patrons such as Crawford or from speculators such as William J. Hegle, Henry Leathe, Thomas Gallagher, and Charles Bland Smith, who each bought parcels of several lots when the market was weak.[15] That these speculative commissions came to Barnett through his erstwhile partner Charles Peck is likely. Pitzman surveyed 45 Vandeventer Place for Barnett in 1885 and the lots at 41 and 62 Vandeventer Place in 1886. The house built at 62 Vandeventer Place, subsequently owned by Jordan W. Lambert, the inventor of Listerine and founder of the Lambert Pharmaceutical Company, was from the Barnett office. Its design may be attributed to Henry G. Isaacs, an Easterner new to the Barnett firm.[16]

Figure 4. Charles H. Peck residence, 7 Vandeventer Place, 1870–71, George I. Barnett, architect.

Barnett's stone-fronted house at 37 Vandeventer was followed by Charles K. Ramsey's houses for John D. Perry and his son-in-law David R. Francis, built in 1880–81 at 12 and 16 Vandeventer, and for Edward Mallinckrodt built just a year later (Figure 7). David Rowland Francis established his own commission company in the wholesale grain trade, becoming president of the Merchants' Exchange in 1884. He was elected mayor of St. Louis

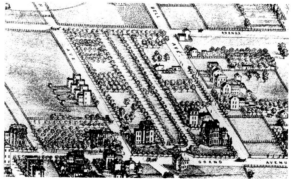

Figure 5. Vandeventer Place, 1873–74.

in 1885, then governor of Missouri in 1889. Francis was appointed secretary of the interior in the second Cleveland administration. He initiated the Louisiana Centennial Exposition in 1902 and during President Wilson's first term served as ambassador to Russia. Edward Mallinckrodt founded the chemical works that still bear his name. Ramsey's High Victorian Gothic Central Presbyterian Church (1874–76) at Lucas Place and Seventeenth Street must have done much to establish his reputation.[17] In these residential commissions he imposed Neo-Grec detail upon the polychromy of the Victorian Gothic.

Figure 6. Hugh A. Crawford residence, 37 Vandeventer Place, 1873, George I. Barnett, architect. Verandah, roof, and dormers, 1892, Alfred F. Rosenheim, architect.

The history of 17 Vandeventer Place, the Queen Anne residence of Watson B. Farr, illustrated in a single commission the earlier phase of the stylistic transition reflected in Vandeventer Place (Figure 8). The foundation had been laid and some work above it done when Farr discovered something other than the conventional stone-fronted dwelling. Halting the work in progress, Farr had the laborers remove all they had completed down to the foundation. Work was resumed according to the designs of his new architects, Burnham & Root of Chicago.[18] The identity of Farr's first architect is not known; that it was Barnett is likely.

Peabody & Stearns of Boston enjoyed a substan-

Figure 7. Edward Mallinckrodt residence, 26 Vandeventer Place, 1881–82, Charles K. Ramsey, architect.

tial presence in St. Louis at least two years prior to the commissions that brought other out-of-town firms, such as Burnham & Root, Fuller & Wheeler, and Henry Hobson Richardson, to Vandeventer Place. Peabody & Stearns won four prestigious commissions in the late 1870s and early 1880s. The Unitarian Church of the Messiah (built 1878–79 and demolished 1988) at Locust and Garrison was commissioned by an affluent congregation whose first pastor, William Greenleaf Eliot, a graduate of Harvard Divinity School, had come to St. Louis in 1843.[19] Several members of his congregation built in Vandeventer Place. The new Museum of Fine Arts (1881) at Locust and Nineteenth Streets was Peabody & Stearns's second important commission. The third was the Turner Real Estate & Building Company building (1881) at Locust and Olive Streets.[20] The commission for the new St. Louis Club (1884–85) at Locust and Ewing Streets was a measure of the firm's success; the club's membership included the commercial and cultural leaders of the city. Peabody & Stearns, through their local representative Pierce P. Furber,[21] also designed at least four residences in the area: Henry Levi Newman's home (1880–81) at 21 Vandeventer;[22] 49 Vandeventer for Isaac Wyman Morton, a principal of Simmons Hardware Company and a member of Washington University's board, in 1885 (Figure 9);[23] 61 Vandeventer for Robert Moore, civil and sanitation expert and Morton's brother-in-law, in 1885–86;[24] and 33 Vandeventer Place for Thomas Howard, a principal in the St. Louis Iron Works (later Thomas Howard & Company), manufacturers of iron water pipe and iron furniture, in 1887 (Figure 10).[25]

Figure 8. Watson B. Farr residence, 17 Vandeventer Place, 1880–81, Burnham & Root, architects.

Figure 10. Thomas Howard residence, 33 Vandeventer Place, 1887, Peabody & Stearns, architects.

Figure 9. Isaac W. Morton residence, 49 Vandeventer Place, 1885, Peabody & Stearns, architects.

Figure 11. John R. Lionberger residence, 27 Vandeventer Place, 1885–87, Henry Hobson Richardson, architect.

Figure 12. John D. Davis residence, 51 Vandeventer Place, 1886–88, Shepley, Rutan & Coolidge, architects.

The Boston firm of Henry Hobson Richardson and its successor, Shepley, Rutan & Coolidge, had several residential commissions from members of the Lionberger family, a father and three of his children. Two of these were located on Vandeventer Place and a third was close by: the John Robert Lionberger house at 27 Vandeventer Place (Figure 11); 51 Vandeventer Place, built for John D. Davis and his wife, Marion Lionberger Davis (Figure 12); and 3630 Bell Avenue (now Grandel Square), constructed for Isaac H. Lionberger.[26] John R. Lionberger established a wholesale shoe business in 1855; it became J. R. Lionberger & Company two years later, the year he organized the Third National Bank of St. Louis. By 1868 his interests included railroads—the Northern Missouri Railroad, the St. Joseph & St. Louis Railroad, and the Eads Bridge Company.[27]

Shepley, Rutan & Coolidge maintained a St. Louis office until 1900. Richardson's son-in-law, George Foster Shepley, was a native St. Louisan, related or connected to many of the people who built in Vandeventer Place.[28] After Washington University, Shepley traveled east to the Massachusetts Institute of Technology, graduating in 1882. With his classmate and future partner Charles A. Coolidge (subsequently also a brother-in-law), he began work in Richardson's Brookline office. Together with their engineer colleague Charles H. Rutan, they formed their partnership upon Richardson's death, becoming a well-organized firm with large offices in both Boston and Chicago. The first of Shepley's commissions in Vandeventer Place was the John D. and Mary Lionberger Davis house mentioned above.[29] Shepley also designed 50 Vandeventer Place for his mother, Mary, widow of the respected attorney John Rutledge Shepley, in 1891.[30] In the following year he designed the house next door for Henry and Mary Collier Hitchcock (Figure 13).[31] Hitchcock, a grandson of the American Revolutionary patriot Ethan Allen, was St. Louis's most eminent attorney and a man of revered integrity. Known for his lofty sense of public duty, he had been a member of the historically decisive Missouri State Convention. Aside from an active law practice, he had organized the law school at Washington University and served as president of the American Bar Association. The Henry Clarkson Scott house, 64 Vandeventer Place, was Shepley's last along the street (Figure 14).[32] Scott, president of both the LaClede Power Company and the Missouri & Illinois Coal Company, was the husband of Bertha

Warburton Drake Scott, whose diary reveals a brief glimpse of life in and around Vandeventer Place in this last decade of the nineteenth century. Mrs. Scott's father, George S. Drake, officer and director of the Boatman's Bank, had purchased the two lots on which the Scotts' house was constructed.

In his weekly newspaper column, William R. Hodges was a steadfast booster of those young local architects whom he knew could provide buildings equal to the ones designed in Chicago or Boston. William Sylvester Eames (1857–1915) was one of these younger men. Born in Michigan, Eames was brought up in St. Louis. He graduated from Washington University, having studied architectural instruction in the School of Fine Arts. Subsequently he worked as a draftsman until 1881, when he went abroad to study, with Hodges as his traveling companion. In 1882 Eames was appointed to a city job, a position for which Hodges supported him. Six months later Hodges wrote, "As soon as people acknowledge his artistic as well as architectural merits, they'll lose a deputy Commissioner of Public Buildings."[33] Thomas Crane Young (1858–1934), born in Wisconsin but raised in Grand Rapids, Michigan, may have been another of the "local" men. He attended the Art School in Cincinnati and Washington University's School of Fine Arts, graduating with Eames. He also went abroad, attending the University of Heidelberg and the École des Beaux-Arts. On his return he worked in Boston, first for Ware & van Brunt and then for E. M. Wheelwright. The partnership of Eames & Young was initiated in 1885 and Hodges published the new firm's first commission.

Eames & Young designed five houses in Vandeventer Place between 1887 and 1892 and

Figure 13. Henry Hitchcock residence, 54 Vandeventer Place, 1892, Shepley, Rutan & Coolidge, architects.

Figure 14. Henry Clarkson Scott residence, 64 Vandeventer Place, 1897–98, Shepley, Rutan & Coolidge, architects.

Figure 15. Asa A. Wallace residence, 67 Vandeventer Place, 1887–88, Eames & Young, architects.

quickly demonstrated their capability in the new residential architectural idiom imported from the East. The first was the Asa A. Wallace house at 67 Vandeventer Place (Figure 15). Asa Wallace was a principal in the Marston, Cupples Dry Goods Company. The second Eames & Young home was designed for Otto L. and Mary Scudder Mersman at 71 Vandeventer Place in 1888–89.[34] Obviously impressed, Mrs. Mersman's brother, Charles White Scudder, had Eames & Young design a house next door for him a year later. Otto Mersman was a real estate developer; his brother-in-law was the city treasurer.

After her husband's death in 1887, Mrs. Silas Bent (the former Miss Tyler) commissioned 48 Vandeventer Place from Eames & Young (Figure 16).[35] Captain Bent had accompanied Commodore Matthew Perry on his historic expedition to Japan. Opposite Mrs. Bent, on the southeast corner of Division Place (Spring Avenue), Eames & Young built 46 Vandeventer Place for John Gilbert Chapman (Figure 17).[36] Chapman owned the Eau Claire Lumber Company, chief distributor of

Figure 16. Mrs. Silas Bent residence, 48 Vandeventer Place, 1889–90, Eames & Young, architects.

Figure 17. John G. Chapman residence, 46 Vandeventer Place, 1891–92, Eames & Young, architects.

Wisconsin lumber in the Mississippi valley. The library extension was designed by Shepley, Rutan & Coolidge's St. Louis representative John Lawrence Mauran, Chapman's son-in-law.

Grable & Weber, the second local firm to attract commissions on Vandeventer Place, completed five residences along the street. Kentucky-born Alfred Grable (c. 1825–97) worked in St. Louis as a carpenter and builder. Auguste Weber (1857–1905), born of Swiss parents in Ohio, worked first in St. Louis for Jerome B. Legg before coming to work for Grable as designer in 1883; they formed their partnership in 1888.[37] The firm's first commission on Vandeventer Place was from David Davis Walker, a principal partner in the dry goods business of Ely, Walker Company, at 53 Vandeventer (Figure 18).[38] The Walker house was followed by Grable & Weber's Smith P. Galt house at 63 Vandeventer Place in the same year. Mr. Galt, a corporate lawyer, was attorney for the St. Louis Railroad Company (trolley lines) and, as executor of the Robert A. Barnes estate, a trustee of Barnes Hospital. Three years later Grable & Weber

Figure 18. David D. Walker residence, 53 Vandeventer Place, 1886–87, Grable & Weber, architects.

Figure 19. Ethan Allen Hitchcock residence, 60 Vandeventer Place, 1891–92, Grable & Weber, architects.

designed 56 Vandeventer Place, the Horatio N. Davis house.[39] Davis, unrelated to John D. Davis across the street, was president of Smith & Davis, manufacturers of iron bedsteads and spring beds. Just down the street, Edmund F. Wickham, president of the Universal Accountant Machine Company, commissioned the house at 28 Vandeventer Place.[40]

A year later Grable & Weber undertook the Ethan Allen Hitchcock house at 60 Vandeventer Place (Figure 19).[41] Brother of Henry Hitchcock, E. A. Hitchcock (1835–1909) owned the Crystal Plate Glass Company, the St. Louis Ore & Steel Company, and the Chicago-Texas Railroad. U.S. ambassador to Russia in the McKinley administration, he served both Presidents McKinley and Theodore Roosevelt as secretary of the interior. His wife, the former Margaret Collier, was the sister of Mary Collier Hitchcock, wife of her husband's older brother Henry. Grable & Weber's last commission in Vandeventer Place was for D. Dexter Tiffany, attorney and husband of a Shepley cousin, Annie Shepley Tiffany, at 72 Vandeventer (Figure 20).[42]

The St. Louis architectural partnership of Stewart, McClure & Mullgardt was a mutation of two predecessor firms, the local builder James Stewart and the firm of Fuller & Wheeler of Albany, New York. Stewart's

Figure 20. D. Dexter Tiffany residence, 72 Vandeventer Place, 1892–93, Grable & Weber, architects.

Figure 21. Henry Clay Pierce residence, 40 Vandeventer Place, 1886–87, Fuller & Wheeler, architects.

first commission was the house at 83 Vandeventer for J. A. McKeighan, the commercial and corporate lawyer, in 1884.[43] There is no evidence that either Thomas Fuller (1825–98) or his partner ever came to St. Louis, but Craig McClure was sent from Albany to open an office and to supervise the construction of two large houses in Vandeventer Place.[44] The Henry Clay Pierce house at 40 Vandeventer (Figure 21) was built on the two easternmost lots of the five Mr. Pierce owned.[45] On the largest single holding in Vandeventer Place, the scale of the Pierce house was just short of monumental. A native of New York State (which may explain his preference for an Albany-based architect), Pierce was involved with the Waters-Pierce Oil Company, a large kerosene distilling and distribution concern. Although much like the Pierce house next door, Fuller & Wheeler's second and concurrent undertaking, the Richard C. Kerens house at 36 Vandeventer Place, was sited on a single lot, its gable end oriented toward the street. Kerens, with mining interests in West Virginia, New Mexico, Colorado, and Arizona, extended his initial stagecoach mail and passenger service to the ownership of several railroads, including the Atchison system, the St. Louis Southern Railroad, and the Los Angeles Terminal Railroad.

Craig McClure remained in St. Louis to work with James Stewart who, at the time that the Pierce and Kerens houses were going up, was constructing a house further west at 70 Vandeventer Place, "Lovenest," for John E. Love, the real estate developer.[46] In 1892 this partnership was expanded to include Louis Christian Mullgardt as designer. Mullgardt (1866–1942), a native of Washington, Missouri, worked first for the German-trained architects Wilhelmi and Janssen in St. Louis, then in 1886 for Shepley, Rutan & Coolidge in Boston. From 1890 until his return to St. Louis he worked in the office of Henry Ives Cobb in Chicago.[47] Their first effort on Vandeventer Place was the Fowler-Drummond house (Figure 22), commissioned by John Fowler, son-in-law of John E. Liggett, founder of the Liggett & Myers Tobacco Company. The Fowlers may have resided there until it was purchased by

Harrison I. Drummond in 1897.[48] Drummond, another tobacco heir, was also a real estate investor.

It is likely that Stewart, McClure & Mullgardt also designed the stable behind 83 Vandeventer for the new owner, Edward C. Dameron, son of L. D. Dameron, steamship owner and commission business founder, in 1894.[49] In the same year Mullgardt designed the identical granite gateways at both the eastern and western extremities of Vandeventer Place (Figures 1 and 23), a commission suggesting John Fowler's concern as an elected trustee for the street's special character. These Ionic screens of smooth-faced ashlar Barre (Vermont) granite

Figure 22. Fowler-Drummond residence, 35 Vandeventer Place, 1892–93, Stewart, McClure & Mullgardt, architects.

Figure 23. Vandeventer Place gateway, Forest Park, 1894, Louis C. Mullgardt, architect.

Figure 24. Thomas K. Niedringhaus residence, 79 Vandeventer Place, 1892–93, Beinke & Wees, architects.

replaced the original cast-iron gates, gateposts, and fencing.

The firm of Beinke & Wees had one house in Vandeventer Place to their credit, at Number 79, sited on two lots (Figure 24). It was built for Thomas K. Niedringhaus, son of the founder of the St. Louis Stamping and Rolling Mills Company.[50] This partnership, like that of Grable & Weber, combined the skills of a carpenter-builder, August M. Beinke, with those of a designer, John Ludwig Wees (1861–1942). Most of their clients were successful second-generation German Americans.

The firm of Tully & Clark was responsible for the designs of two local homes, the Charles Clark house (c. 1886) at 41 Vandeventer and the George D. Barnard house (1887–88) at 47 Vandeventer, both near the northeast corner of Vandeventer and Division Places.[51] Clark had invested in mines, and Barnard was president of his own company of printers and blank book manufacturers.

Several houses along Vandeventer have less definite backgrounds, with only suggested attributions possible. The design of the house for Hiram Shaw Liggett, the tobacco fortune heir and real estate investor, at 32 Vandeventer Place (1888–89) has been attributed to Henry E. Roach.[52] And, on the basis of Jerome B. Legg's design for the chapel that Captain John N. Bofinger gave to Christ Church Cathedral in memory of his wife, Bofinger's house at 76 Vandeventer (1897–98) is attributed to Legg.[53] Bofinger had been a riverboat captain

246

and boat builder before investing in the Texas Pacific Railroad and the telephone.

In 1892 Alfred F. Rosenheim (1856–1943) was commissioned by Mrs. Martha J. Sweringen, widow of J. T. Sweringen, who made a fortune in dry goods, to make major renovations to the exterior of 37 Vandeventer Place (George Barnett's Crawford residence). He removed the mansard roof, replaced it with a dormered hip roof, and added the verandah to the east side of the house.

The last building in this survey, the Thomas E. Tutt house (1894–95) at 11 Vandeventer Place, has defied attribution.[54] A banker, Tutt was president of the Third National Bank and a director of the Mississippi Valley Trust Company. He and John R. Lionberger were pallbearers for their old friend Oliver D. Filley (d. 1881), the father of Mrs. Robert Moore and Mrs. Isaac Morton.

ARCHITECTS AND CLIENTS: A CLOSER LOOK

The architecture of the dwellings in Vandeventer Place reflected the stylistic transition that occurred between 1870 and 1900. The speed at which one superseded another reflected the improvements in communication and transportation of the last quarter of the nineteenth century. The uniform pervasiveness of the stone front, so evident in Lucas and Benton Places, did not prevail in Vandeventer Place. Once past the Peck and Mullikin houses, visitors to Vandeventer Place encountered the glyptic angularity of the Neo-Grec, with its complement of applied and incised conventionalized ornament, and the Queen Anne style, popularized by designers like the Englishman Richard Norman Shaw and illustrated in architectural periodicals along with the related details of the "Aesthetic Movement." They saw a broad representation of the Richardsonian Romanesque style; a few tentative architectural essays in the Italian Renaissance style, introduced to this country by McKim, Mead & White; and one early example of the neo-Elizabethan style, which came to be favored not just for residences but for university buildings as well. And they were introduced to the versatility and beauty of brick. The Peck and Mullikin mansions, flanking the entrance to Vandeventer Place at Grand Boulevard, represented what William R. Hodges had come to dislike most about local architecture:

> A few years ago someone introduced that peculiar phase of French architecture which takes its name from Mansard [*sic*], the architect of Versailles. We all know how like wildfire it swept the country. A style which is admirable in such edifices as the Tuilleries, the Louvre and the Luxembourg Palace, with innumerable statues and infinite ornamentation, becomes bald and hideous when shorn of its proper adornment.[55]

At 7 Vandeventer Place two hallways—broad enough for the appraiser in 1948 to describe them as "reception" hallways—led from the south and west entrances of the Peck house to the main staircase.[56] Disposed on either side of this L-shaped double axis were the public rooms, double parlors, library, music room, and dining room. The ceilings were fourteen feet high. There were polished marble mantels, and every window had louvred interior shutters. In some of the rooms the pier glass frames were polished walnut, in others they were gilded. The plaster work was richly molded and the woodwork was ornately carved; the window pediments were carved and in some instances gilded. There were six bedrooms and five bathrooms on the second floor and on the third, six more bedrooms though only one bathroom.

The Crawford house, the last stone-fronted house in Vandeventer Place, with its high-style Second Empire doorway, window aediculation, and roll-molded corner chamfers, was evidence that the economic depression and consequent building hiatus had left the Barnett office unprepared for the stylistic changes effective by 1881. Built within a five-year period following the brick houses that were built down the street to the designs of Charles Ramsey, the designs of Henry Isaacs and Isaac Taylor for Barnett eschewed the now-unfashionable stone front and were realized in brick with stone trim. Ramsey's houses in Vandeventer Place were brick on basements of rough-cut Mississippi River stone and had high hip roofs, like the Mallinckrodt house.[57] But these polychromatic effects and the Neo-Grec details were superficial; they could not conceal the fact that Ramsey's formal schemes and consequent massing were similiar to those employed by Barnett. The angulated, tall, hipped-roof tower of the Francis house at 16 Vandeventer, as arresting and picturesque a feature as it was, only introduced a novel angle to an otherwise square plan.

Peabody & Stearns were the first prominent eastern architects to build in Vandeventer Place. Hodges described the two-and-a-half-story brick Newman house at 21 Vandeventer as "distinctively Queene [sic] Anne" and "a thoroughly English house transplanted to American soil." Its roof was a special feature; its many gables and "broken lines" gave it a picturesque effect. In lieu of a plan, let Hodges's account of his visit to the Newman house suffice.[58] He reported that the woodwork of the roomy hall was cherry and its upper walls and ceiling "were painted a warm color, in oil, with stenciled ornaments." The dining room woodwork was butternut and had a paneled ceiling. The walls of the library were covered with a paper stamped in imitation of leather. Rather than isolated off corridors, these rooms were juxtaposed round the hall and by opening sliding doors could become extensions of it. Two landings interrupted the stair; the first, with a wide window seat, was lit by a stained-glass window. Five bedrooms and three baths were on the second floor. There were six bedrooms on the third floor and one bath.[59]

Hodges was also pleased to inform his readers that above its original Mississippi stone foundation rose Burnham & Root's house for Watson B. Farr at 17 Vandeventer (Figure 8), of pressed brick, conveniently planned and "embodying taste and refinement," a house that opened the eyes of local architects and builders, as well as those of patrons, to a new approach.[60] One entered not a narrow passageway, but a spacious room with a fireplace and carved mantel, and oak-paneled wainscoting and ceiling. "Some people object to these modern rooms and say they are not high enough. Every inch you add to the height of a room after you have given it proper proportion detracts from its beauty."[61] The windows were filled with stained glass. The floors in this living hall were cherry, as they were throughout the house. Although one room opened to another, heavy portieres and/or sliding doors could close off one from another. The parlor was finished in maple, and the woodwork in the library beyond was oak. Doors with stained-glass transoms opened to the verandah through a quaintly carved sideboard in the dining room. The staircase was not long and straight but turned twice with a broad landing. There were four bedrooms and two bathrooms on the second story and four bedrooms on the third, one with a washstand.

It becomes apparent that the features of a modern house included a compact plan of contiguous, interconnecting rooms (rather than one of high-ceilinged rooms in isolated symmetry on either side of a central stair hall), dog-leg and quarter-turn staircases, built-in furniture, and a variety of wood finishes. These features characterized the new houses going up in Vandeventer Place. But Hodges had little patience for the more extreme manifestations of the "Aesthetic Movement." The architectural components of Grable & Weber's first Vandeventer Place commission, the Walker house (Figure 18)—the moon window and the porch with its broad gable, coupled columns, and pendant lattice—were indicative of the Aesthetic Movement, late for 1886 perhaps, but reminiscent of the work of the Legg firm, with whom Weber had worked and about which Hodges had written, "Much of the recent domestic architecture in St. Louis is like the cat tail and Japanese fan style of interior decoration so fashionable a short time ago, the measles and whooping cough stage."[62]

Hodges explained this invasion of outside architects to St. Louis:

People are fast getting their eyes opened, and they will soon demand of the men who design their homes that comfort, convenience, taste and beauty shall be united in their dwellings; and if these are not furnished by St. Louis architects, they will go to Burnham & Root of Chicago, as did Messrs. Whitaker and Farr, to Peabody & Stearns of Boston, or someone else who will supply their wants.[63]

Henry Hobson Richardson's house for John R. Lionberger at 27 Vandeventer Place (Figure 11) was built entirely of rough-cut "Carolina" granite laid in alternating wide and narrow courses.[64] This containing and stony exterior was pierced by the deep arched entrance and the deep loggia above. Only when the rounded corners were read as turrets and the facade as a granite screen stretched between them was the enigma of this monolithic building clarified. Located on the north side of Vandeventer Place, the house with its fortress-like facade enjoyed the best orientation that Lionberger's single lot afforded.[65]

The Lionberger commission was among Richardson's last, but his expressive use of the French Romanesque and his genius in adapting it to spatial volumes was already admired where it was known. Peabody & Stearns's next commission was the brick Isaac W. Morton house at 49 Vandeventer (Figure 9), which, like the Newman house four years earlier, was two and a half stories and capped with a high hip roof. But the broad arched entrance with its long *voussoirs* and the adjacent buttress of Mississippi stone, the second-story enframement of three windows separated by colonettes, and the diaper pattern in the dormer gable were Richardsonian decorative elements, not Queen Anne.

Like the Newman and Morton houses, the Robert Moore house (61 Vandeventer) possessed a picturesque two-and-a-half-story silhouette, although the massing was simpler and more compact. But where these houses demonstrated Peabody & Stearns's growing awareness of Henry Hobson Richardson's strong personal style, the Thomas Howard house (Figure 10) was the most comprehensive residential study in the Richardsonian canon essayed by Peabody & Stearns in St. Louis. This house (33 Vandeventer), just west of and a year after Richardson's Lionberger house, was a response to the challenge from Richardson, the other big Boston firm. Though not directly imitative of the Lionberger house, the Howard house was built entirely of the chalk-colored rough-cut Mississippi River stone (in emulation of its neighbor), laid in random courses and dressed with tawny Grafton stone. Its simplified silhouette was complemented by familiar Richardsonian ornamental devices: the relatively narrow arched entrance with broad *voussoirs*, the colonette mullion in the second-story window, and the stone diaper work at the top of the gable. The only applied ornaments were the gargoyles projecting from either eave, a Peabody & Stearns signature (Figure 25).[66]

Richardson's influence was visible in the two Fuller & Wheeler commissions of the late 1880s; the designs for the Henry Clay Pierce and the Richard C. Kerens houses, at 40 and 36 Vandeventer Place respectively, came from Albany, New York, with the Richardsonian Romanesque architectural elements intact (Figure 21). The parapet of Pierce's deep, segmentally arched entrance porch, but one of many representative illustrations, was bowed like that of Richardson's house for Grange Sard, Jr., in Albany. Three later examples

Figure 25. Gargoyle fragment, Thomas Howard residence, 33 Vandeventer Place, 1887, Peabody & Stearns, architects.

of the Richardsonian style, generalized to its familiar and distinct components of rough-cut masonry, round towers, and arched entrances and windows, were Tully & Clark's Barnard house at 47 Vandeventer, Harry E. Roach's Hiram Liggett house at 32 Vandeventer, and Legg's Bofinger house at Number 76, and all of them lacking Richardson's characteristic compactness.

The work of Richardson's successors, Shepley, Rutan & Coolidge, as Henry-Russell Hitchcock observed, gradually fell away from the spirit of their mentor to follow the stylistic fashions set by other

firms. But it should come as no surprise that the design of the John D. Davis house at 51 Vandeventer (Figure 12) was believed to have been Richardson's.[67] The uniform wall fabric and the deep reveals of the windows and entrance porch suggest the contained character of his later houses. Indeed, the precedent for the juxtaposed narrow entrance arch and broader porch arch was Richardson's Sard house in Albany. But the Davis house was both more accessible and more homogeneous than its predecessor at 27 Vandeventer. Perhaps the Davises requested a design more open to Vandeventer Place's green median?

Critic William Hodges not only encouraged, he scolded too; the younger, local architects were being neglected. "We have competent architects in our own city, but those who are capable of designing beautiful and artistic buildings have as yet no opportunity of demonstrating their ability. So it is no wonder that progressive men go elsewhere for their designs." And, "It so happens that the best residences we have were designed by architects from other cities. Local men have been given little opportunity."[68] In retrospect it appears that when finally Eames & Young, Grable & Weber, Beinke & Wees, and Stewart, McClure & Mullgardt began to receive commissions in Vandeventer Place, they carefully followed the lead established there by firms from out of town to such a degree that at least three of the houses designed by out-of-town firms became prototypes: Richardson's Lionberger house at 27 Vandeventer, Peabody & Stearns's Howard house next door, and Shepley, Rutan & Coolidge's John D. Davis house just down the street.[69]

The younger designers worked these prototypes into interesting variations. In 1887 Eames & Young gave the Wallace house at 67 Vandeventer Place (Figure 15), their first commission on the street, an asymmetrical facade suggestive of Shepley's John D. Davis house. For the Mersmans just beyond at Number 71, Eames & Young evoked Peabody & Stearns's Howard house in their design of a broad gable-end facing the street and an arched entrance. The house built next door a year later for Mrs. Mersman's brother, Charles Scudder, reflected the same source. Mrs. Bent's house at 48 Vandeventer (Figure 16) was a didactic parody of Richardson's Lionberger house. Eames & Young had taken Richardson's enigmatic screen and rounded corners and articulated them as proper turrets. But in the last three of these four houses, classical ornamental details, vestiges of the Italian Renaissance style, were subtly introduced at the doorways. Grable & Weber's design for the Horatio Davis house at 56 Vandeventer Place is similar to Peabody & Stearns's Morton house almost directly across the street. Architectural elements adapted from models as close to hand as the Morton house, Shepley's John D. Davis house, and Peabody & Stearns's Howard house characterized the Wickham residence (28 Vandeventer Place). But a Renaissance motif distinguished the entrance to the E. A. Hitchcock house at 60 Vandeventer (Figure 19), much as Eames & Young had introduced it in the Mersman, Scudder, and Bent doorway designs. The 1892 house that Beinke & Wees undertook for Thomas K. Niedringhaus on a double lot at 79 Vandeventer (Figure 24), although without the rounded corners, was a broad variation of the Lionberger house facade, reflecting its unity and with its deep arched entrance and sheltering hip roof.

Within the confines of Vandeventer Place, hindsight permits us to see that the novelty of the first Vandeventer prototypes could not endure the pressure of subsequent stylistic innovation. The "local men," no longer as young and without current models nearby, were on their own. A significant departure for Eames & Young, the design of the John Gilbert Chapman house at 46 Vandeventer Place (Figure 17) was not based on local prototypes but tapped a national source, the growing influence of professional publications. The hint of Italian Renaissance motifs in the Mersman, Scudder, and Bent facades and the four-square, classically detailed Chapman house suggest Eames & Young's awareness of the work of McKim, Mead & White; both their Villard houses (New York) and the John F. Andrews house (Boston) received attention in *American Architect and Building News* and *Inland Architect*.[70] Allusions to Renaissance styles were not limited to the Italian only. The central bay in Shepley, Rutan & Coolidge's design for the Henry Hitchcock house (Figure 13) at 54 Vandeventer rose through the broad eaves of the high hip roof to terminate as a dormer in the style of the early French Renaissance.[71]

Grable & Weber, heretofore tactfully derivative, took the familiar Howard prototype and produced a design at once novel and original for the Tiffany house (Figure 20). Rising from the broad sill molding, a narrow arched reveal incorporated the second-story and third-story windows, an attenuated and unconventional Palladian motif. The Tiffany house was entered from the side, in itself an exception.[72] Classical decorative motifs may have replaced earlier ornament, but the "modern" interior, admired by Hodges, had seen little essential change. A broad oak-paneled hall separated the oval living room across the front of the house from the dining room at the rear. When the occasion warranted, the sliding doors could all be opened to create one large space. The dining room was flanked by a small library and the butler's pantry with its dumbwaiter to the basement kitchen. The living room had a mantel of oak and the fireplace a tesselated facing. Built-in and curtained corner niches containing oak seats gave the room its oval appearance. The dining room, paneled in cherry, had upper walls covered with a dark blue and gold embossed Japanese paper. The fireplace overmantel was niched and shelved, and the flue was divided above to frame a stained-glass window depicting pomegranates and butterflies.[73]

Like the Chapman house (itself a prototype for subsequent four-square, three-story, neo-Renaissance residences in St. Louis), the facade of Stewart, McClure & Mullgardt's Fowler-Drummond house (Figure 22) comprised two-story bows flanking a Palladian motif enframing the doorway. Vandeventer Place's new gates, the semicircular Ionic columnar screens at Grand Avenue and Vandeventer Avenue, cut in the center by the roadway, were also designed by Stewart, McClure & Mullgardt. Shepley, Rutan & Coolidge designed the Scott house (Figure 14) at 64 Vandeventer in "the popular English Domestic style," completing the firm's stylistic transition.[74] Eames & Young, Grable & Weber, and Stewart, McClure & Mullgardt—even Shepley's office, although they carried out residential commissions elsewhere in the city—chose Vandeventer Place to introduce their own more independent expressions.

There was a remarkable homogeneity in Vandeventer Place, despite the stylistic transitions, thanks to the adherence to prototypes. But aside from the prototypes, the uniform lot width (some residents had combined several lots), and the setback limits, several other important conceptual factors contributed to this sense of consistency. The deed restrictions were certainly among these factors; they not only required participation in the street association, but they mandated basement kitchens and, furthermore, were interpreted to mean that all principal entrances must face the street. On his visit to the Newman house in 1882, William Hodges noticed that the kitchen, initially planned for the first story adjacent to the dining room, had been replaced by a breakfast room. The kitchen, as directed by the deed restrictions, had to be moved to the basement. Until 1891 every front door of every house faced Vandeventer Place. No doubt Mr. Chapman had to obtain permission from the trustees to relocate his principal entrance from the Vandeventer Place facade of his corner house to the Division Street (Spring Avenue) facade (Figure 17). To appease the trustees, it is likely that Eames & Young placed the Palladian motif framing the central window of the first-story Vandeventer Place facade there to compensate for the missing doorway. Recall the Tiffany house described above; the main entrance was on its western side, indeed far enough behind the building line to have prompted questions relative to the deed restrictions. Apparently the well-proportioned "logetta" [sic] reorienting the entrance toward Vandeventer Place was impressive enough to silence the philistines (Figure 20). Had the trustees been more lenient in 1885, one wonders if Richardson would not have located the principal entrance of the Lionberger house to one side as he was known to have done elsewhere.

Hodges recognized the value of Vandeventer Place as a showcase for the new dwelling, beautiful because it was convenient and comfortable. But convenience and comfort depended on the current advances in residential technology. The introduction of central heating was a major contributor toward the comfortable home that Hodges advocated. A coal furnace made possible the compact plan of contiguous, interconnecting rooms common to most of the houses built in Vandeventer Place after 1880.[75]

The extensive use of brick a third factor contributing to the street's homogeneity. With the exceptions of the few early stone-faced houses and the rough-cut stone Lionberger, Howard, and Bofinger houses, all of the houses in Vandeventer Place were built of brick. Perhaps one reason that the use of brick was seen as a "progressive" reaction to the conventional stone-fronted house was the improved quality and variety of brick in the last quarter of the nineteenth century.[76] In 1882 Hodges wrote from abroad, "Brick is a beautiful material for building purposes and there is no better brick made than in St. Louis, and nothing in Europe compares with it."[77] By the end of the 1880s, brick was available in a variety of shapes and colors: Eames & Young used a fine yellow brick for the Chapman house at 46 Vandeventer Place; the pinkish tone and rough finish of the brick that Mullgardt specified and the frieze-like diaper pattern he designed for the top story of the Fowler-Drummond house were much admired even a decade after the house's completion.[78]

The high basements, front stoops facing the street and green center median, the often asymmetrical fenestration suggestive of a "convenient" interior, and the preponderance of brick all bestow on the architecture that evolved within this enclave a character best described as a Vandeventer Place "idiom," and to this day can be seen in the earliest residences constructed in the Forest Park Addition as well as throughout the city where new houses were being erected, either to the plans of an architect or by builders, at this time.

Social and Cultural Life in Vandeventer Place

To outsiders, life in Vandeventer Place must have seemed punctilious. For example, Monday was the day on which the ladies of Vandeventer Place were at home to callers.[79] So the slightest deviation from the perceived order within this reserve was generally considered news. The threatened strike by the cooks of Vandeventer Place and a simultaneous demand for higher monthly wages must have tickled nonresidents. The two families that initially held out gave in after being "starved," and the strike was over within a day.[80] But the inhabitants of Vandeventer Place did not acquiesce to intimidation from outsiders. Consider the fate of "Russell, the West End Stable Fiend," who attempted to exploit the place's residents. Russell was a subtle blackmailer. He would set up his slipshod livery stable in a prominent neighborhood, forcing the residents to buy him out at double his original investment. In 1882 it was ascertained that Russell was planning to set up near Vandeventer Place. By the spring of 1883, he was established on Grand Avenue. But when it was discovered that he rented out stabled horses when their owners weren't using them, he had gone too far. His new neighbors stabled their horses elsewhere and put him out of business.[81]

In recommending a look into Vandeventer Place in the summer of 1882, Hodges suggested appropriate behavior for the visitor: "...and although a sign hangs conspicuously over the carriageway, warning the public that it is 'No Thoroughfare,' I apprehend that if one be well dressed, and talks in a respectful undertone, he will not be arrested for trespass if he strolls down the beautiful avenue and glances at the exterior of these [the Farr and Newman houses] and other houses."[82]

In early October 1887, President Grover Cleveland and his wife visited St. Louis for three days of near-general adulation and glorious weather. They stayed with Mr. and Mrs. David Francis at 16 Vandeventer Place. Each day a small crowd waited politely on the sidewalk and median for the Clevelands to wave from the Francises' doorstep. In preparation for their distinguished guests, the mayor and his wife had the house redone. Cabinetmakers and upholsterers in and out of St. Louis were taxed to the utmost to finish on schedule. But an unforeseen problem occurred on the morning after the arrival of the presidential couple. Before the cook would return to the kitchen downstairs, breakfast was held up until she had snatched a glimpse of the first lady of the land.

Recollections and diaries suggest that life in Vandeventer Place was a good deal more congenial when not in public view. Families and casual callers gathered on front steps or adjacent verandas on warm summer evenings, sometimes to be regaled by singing quartets of young men and to enjoy cooling refreshments. Isaac H. Lionberger recalled finding Henry Hitchcock on the doorstep of Number 54 one hot July evening; the seasoned jurist and the young attorney talked until dawn. In the morning in good weather those men who had offices downtown preferred to walk the two miles from Vandeventer Place rather than take a trolley. To the young growing up in Vandeventer Place there was the special challenge of "tight-rope walking" the joists and climbing the rafters of the new houses under construction, as Ralph Coale of 15 Vandeventer did. One of the late Ethan Allen Hitchcock Shepley's earliest memories of his visits to the street was of the first motorcar in Vandeventer Place. It was owned by his grandfather's neighbor, Jordan Lambert of 62 Vandeventer.[83]

Bertha Warburton Drake Scott (1866–1945) left a diary in which life in Vandeventer Place can be glimpsed. George F. Shepley and his wife, the former Julia Richardson, were among her wedding guests on St. Valentine's Day 1893 (at "Stancote," in Newtown Center, Massachusetts). Athough she was not to move to Vandeventer Place until 1897, her first home in St. Louis was only a few blocks away. One of the first social events she described in the diary were the round of parties on the occasion of Edward Dameron's stepsister Lucy's marriage to Count Reventlow-Criminil. That winter Mrs. Scott joined a German language club in Vandeventer Place. On May 19 the following year she wrote with deep feeling of Mr. Lionberger's death. On a midsummer visit to New York City from Jamestown, Rhode Island, in 1897 she shopped for her new house going up at 64 Vandeventer Place. She returned to St. Louis in mid-September and went to look at the house the next day. Five days later, Shepley, Rutan & Coolidge's representative in St. Louis, John Lawrence Mauran, who would soon marry the Chapmans' daughter, came to dinner. Apparently there were no major problems either with dinner or construction and the Scotts were moved in time for Thanksgiving.[84]

Vandeventer Place families extended themselves along the street. Mr. Lionberger had three of his children nearby: his son, Isaac H. Lionberger, was just north on Bell Avenue; a daughter, Mrs. John D. Davis, was up the street at 51 Vandeventer; another daughter, Mrs. Henry S. Potter, bought the lot at 85 Vandeventer in 1895; and his youngest daughter lived with him at Number 27. Down the street, Alice Filley Moore (at 61 Vandeventer) and her sister Jeanette Filley Morton (at Number 49), daughters of former mayor Oliver Dwight Filley, late of 2201 Lucas Place, were near neighbors. In 1889 Captain John A. Scudder, owner of the Anchor [steamship] Line, bought the Watson Farr house at 17 Vandeventer Place. Within the year his daughter, Mrs. Mary Scudder Mersman, and his son, Charles W. Scudder, were building houses at Numbers 71 and 75, respectively. John D. Perry (12 Vandeventer) lived next door to his daughter and son-in-law, Mr. and Mrs. David Francis, at Number 16.

George S. Drake bought the lot on which his daughter Bertha Warburton and son-in-law Henry Clarkson Scott built (Number 64), and then himself took a house just a bit west. Nor was intermarriage between Vandeventer Place families uncommon. As mentioned earlier, Henry Hitchcock brought his wife, the former Mary Collier, to their new house at 54 Vandeventer and his brother Ethan Allen Hitchcock brought his wife, the former Margaret Collier, to Number 60; each brother had married a daughter of George and Sarah Collier of Lucas Place. John F. Shepley, the son of Mrs. Mary (John R.) Shepley at 50 Vandeventer and brother of both Louise Shepley (Mrs. Isaac H.) Lionberger and of George F. Shepley, married Margaret, one of E. A. Hitchcock's daughters.

On December 9, 1899, Charles H. Peck, the last charter trustee, died at 7 Vandeventer Place, and the trust that had governed the street was terminated. The deed restrictions remained in effect, but now the owners were in control.[85] But even as the residents prepared for self-governance in a new century, the concept of a residential park, protected from incompatible incursions, was being challenged by the city's growth.

Deterioration and Demolition

The value of Vandeventer Place property had steadily risen in the 1880s. When Henry Newman suffered business reverses in 1887 he exchanged residences with Daniel Catlin, a principal in the American Tobacco Company. Vandeventer Place property was not a commodity to be traded on the open market. The Newman house was valued at $65,000, the Catlin house on nearby Lucas Place at $25,000. Catlin assumed a $40,000 encumbrance. But in 1895 a piece in the *Saint Louis Republic* signaled a trend in the opposite direction. It pointed out that the single-family residential character of the streets adjacent to Vandeventer Place was being replaced by retail establishments and tenements.[86] While the erection of Mullgardt's new granite screen gates marked the zenith of Vandeventer Place, row houses were going up on Vandeventer Street, between Morgan and Delmar Streets, just southwest of Vandeventer Place's western gate.[87]

Between 1905 and 1916 many of the earliest residents, aggravated by the smoky pall from the ever more numerous manufactories to the southeast and the clatter of the streetcars and garish glare of electric signs, moved west to the Forest Park Addition—a private street complex modeled after Vandeventer Place.[88] Vandeventer Place's distinguished antecedents attracted other residents. The Very Reverend Dr. Daniel Tuttle, Episcopal Bishop of the Diocese of Missouri, the street's sole cleric, resided at 74 Vandeventer after 1905. In 1910 upon the death of his wife, H. C. Pierce (of 40 Vandeventer) moved to New York, leaving the largest house on the street inhabited only by a few servants until his death in 1927. An indication that the decay of the surrounding residential neighborhoods might spread to Vandeventer Place came in 1922 when it was discovered that the new owners of Number 12 were running a boardinghouse. The street's residents filed suit, and they won.[89] An effort in the late 1920s to rename the street "Verbeck Place" for a local World War I hero caused a small controversy. Some thought the street snobbish and ripe for a comeuppance; others treasured its dignified, though frayed, respectability. The residents defeated this challenge as well.

In 1932 the Public Service Company took the southeast corner off the backyard of 6 Vandeventer to lay streetcar track.[90] Three years later the city, already an owner through tax delinquency of several parcels whose builders had long since sold them to others, proposed that Vandeventer Place be transformed into a public health park and community health center; a majority of the residents voted against this. The house at 40 Vandeventer, which had been empty the nine years since Pierce's death, was ordered razed by his executors. In these Depression years, eight more houses were demolished and several others sold at a fraction of their original value.

A campaign to preserve Vandeventer Place was mounted in 1941 by Emily Eaton (80 Vandeventer), a third-generation resident, in collaboration with Ralph D'Oench, a local realtor.[91] But any interest in her efforts to make of Vandeventer a Sutton Place (New York) or Beacon Street (Boston) was suddenly diverted by the nation's entrance into World War II. After the war the spirit necessary to resist the challenges from without was seemingly exhausted. Early in 1948 the federal government initiated condemnation proceedings in order to construct the multimillion-dollar John J. Cochran Hospital for the Veterans Administration on the eastern eleven acres.

In August 1948 U.S. Attorney Drake Watson announced a deadline for vacating property of the first of November. However, the deadline was extended to January 1949, and demolition did not begin until mid-1950. Throughout the summer and early autumn of 1950, local newspapers announced the days on which each house was to be destroyed; Charles Peck's house, the first to be built, was razed on August 26, 1950. An anonymous citizen arranged to purchase Richardson's Lionberger house and have it dismantled and moved to a site in St. Louis County, but this person abandoned the project when apprised of the significant reconstruction costs.[92] Eight years later the Board of Aldermen approved a bill to acquire what was left of Vandeventer Place—thirty houses at the western end—for the purpose of constructing a new detention home for the juvenile division of the Circuit Court.

Perhaps the best way to measure Vandeventer Place's now posthumous claim as an ideal representation of the concept of *rus in urbe* is to see it as a model for the matrix of seventeen private streets (plus two relatively recent newcomers) that were subsequently platted. Even as Vandeventer Place saw its busiest decade of building in the late 1880s and early 1890s, plans were underway to repeat Charles Peck's successful venture farther west. The private street concept in St. Louis saw its fullest and most impressive manifestation in the Forest Park Addition of 1888, which is Vandeventer Place "doubled"; the lots there are twice as wide, and there are twice as many streets.[93] It is located just north of the northeast corner of Forest Park, St. Louis's largest park, bearing out the theory that those private streets remaining now are the ones that were platted adjacent to park land and, as a consquence, were insulated against inhospitable urban spread.[94] Ironically, the only remaining intact vestige of Vandeventer Place, one of Mullgardt's granite gateways, now stands alone in the southeast portion of Forest Park (Figure 23).[95]

ACKNOWLEDGMENTS

The author wishes to acknowledge the following for their assistance: the late Martha Helligoss; Lois Duggins; Roy Leimberg of the Pitzman Company; Shannon Paul, Art and Architecture Librarian, St. Louis Public Library; Sister M. Dionysia Brockland, SSND; William D. Merwin; Arbie Rolband; Rick Rosen; Eric Sandweiss; Ethan Allen Hitchcock Shepley, Jr.; Michael Shepley; Duane Sneddeker, Stephanie Klein, Emily Miller, Carol Verble, Barbara Stole, Dennis Northcott, Edna Smith, Jean Streeter, Martha Clevenger, John Furlong, and Dorothy Woods, all of the Missouri Historical Society; David Mesker and Jan Broderick of A. G. Edwards & Son, Inc.; Frederick Medlar; Mrs. J. R. Usher, who grew up at 72 Vandeventer Place and described the interior of the house; Carolyn H. Toft who, like the author, came to St. Louis, but remained to fight the good fight; and Carl Forster.

This essay is dedicated to Norris H. Allen.

CHARLES SAVAGE

CHAPTER TEN

MONUMENT
Avenue

MONUMENT AVENUE MARCHES OUT in a long cadence of homes, a progression of trees lining a boulevard interspersed with a rhythm of statues (Figure 1). In common with many of the other grand residential streets developed during the nineteenth and early twentieth centuries, Monument Avenue in Richmond, Virginia, was the preferred address for the local wealthy and those who aspired to that status. Monument Avenue is lined with a mixture of dwellings, some large and impressive, others more modest, that represent the various fads and styles of American architecture from the 1890s to the 1920s. The avenue also contains spacious apartment blocks and six churches. The total number of buildings is approximately 260.

In many ways Monument Avenue fits the generic character of great American residential avenues of these years: few of the buildings are architecturally distinguished by themselves—the impact comes from the overall harmony of scale, form, materials, and details of buildings and street that stretches for a mile and a half. This is a pattern repeated many times across the United States. What gives Monument Avenue a unique character and distinguishes it from other American avenues can be perceived in its name and its defining feature, the monuments. Many other grand avenues have statues, but none contains a consistent iconographic program as does Monument Avenue. The program or narrative of Monument Avenue's statues is unique in that it is an homage to the leaders of the side that lost the Civil War. On Monument Avenue stand Robert E. Lee, J. E. B. Stuart, Jefferson Davis, Thomas "Stonewall" Jackson, and Matthew Fontaine Maury, each a hero of the "lost cause." These statues are intimately linked with the development of the avenue.

ESSAY BY RICHARD GUY WILSON

Figure 1. Monument Avenue, view west from Stuart Circle, c. 1925. Stuart Circle Apartments (right), 1924, William Lawrence Bottomley, architect. First German (now English) Evangelical Lutheran Church (left), 1912, Charles S. Robinson, architect.

Figure 2. Map of the City of Richmond by Bolton, Clarke and Pratt, Inc., 1914.

Monument Avenue was laid out and built between the 1890s and the 1920s. It is 140 feet wide, a divided boulevard planted with parallel rows of maples and other trees along its center and in a single row in front of the houses. The houses are set back an almost uniform fifteen feet from the street, and although they vary in size, style, and materials, there is an overall consistency. The section containing the five monuments is a mile-and-a-half length of fourteen blocks stretching westward from Stuart Circle to Roseneath Road, which for years constituted the city limits (Figure 2). This is the core of the avenue, and it contains its most distinguished architecture. During the post–World War II years the avenue was extended out into Henrico County for a total length of a little over five miles. This area is of a different character and is not integral to this study.

RICHMOND AND THE NEW SOUTH

The origins of Monument Avenue can be found in the diverse elements of Richmond's growing urban population, the need to express wealth in the form of residences, the desire of many Southerners to erect monuments to the recently vanquished, and the concept of a "New South." The Richmond that built Monument Avenue thought of itself as the "first" city of the "New South."[1] Beginning in the late 1880s and extending well into the early twentieth century, many Southern leaders argued that the South could no longer be tied to its agrarian, and hence poverty-stricken, past. Instead the South had the possibility, with its resources both natural and physical, to establish a great industrial, commercial, and financial empire, along with the requisite cultural emblems, that would rival that of the North. According to these progressive leaders, the South should become modern. Urban rivalry with other Southern cities and especially with Northern cities was paramount. Nowhere was this attitude more prominent than in Richmond.[2]

Prior to the Civil War, Richmond had been the industrial, financial, political, and cultural center of the South. That Richmond had been the capital of the Confederacy merely confirmed this fact. Since the end of Reconstruction, Richmond's business leaders had prospered. The city was the terminus of six railroads; a center of iron, steel, and flour mills; and the tobacco capital of the nation, with more than fifty factories. It was the only Southern city that came close to the national mean of males employed in manufacturing in 1890.[3] But Richmond was slipping, and over the next several decades it would lose some of its economic leadership. New Orleans would become the largest Southern city, and soon other Southern cities would eclipse Richmond as well. But still it was growing, more than doubling in size between 1860 (population 37,910) and 1890 (population 81,338). Richmond's growth stagnated in the 1890s because of the national depression of that decade, but then in the next twenty years the city more than doubled again, reaching a population of 171,667 in 1920. Both the established wealthy and the newly affluent who benefited from this growth needed the appropriate setting to illustrate their accomplishments, and Monument Avenue became one of the prime vehicles for this aspiration.

Richmond's natural growth, topographically and culturally, has always been toward the west. The James River to the south, uneven topography, and the expansion of the manufacturing and transportation belt in the other directions has directed the growth of elite residential neighborhoods largely to the west of the commercial and governmental core.[4] Streetcar lines began to snake out to the west from the downtown in the 1870s, linking outlying parks and suburban developments. Monument Avenue is locally seen as an extension of the "Fan," a group of streets that radiate out from the city at the western end beginning at Monroe Park. Although Monument Avenue formally begins at Lombardy Street with the Stuart statue and circle at its eastern end, it is actually an extension of Franklin Street, whose eastern termination is Capitol Square, the site of the commonwealth's state house, designed by Thomas Jefferson in the 1780s. Franklin Street, which runs west from the capitol, had become since the 1830s the city's most prestigious residential address. In the 1890s the New York architectural firm of Carrère and Hastings designed on Franklin Street Richmond's great hotel, the Jefferson, and remodeled Richmond's elite club for men, the Commonwealth Club.

The area in which Monument Avenue developed encompassed three large tracts of undeveloped land located just beyond the city line at the western end of Franklin Street.[5] This area was bisected by one road, Reservoir Avenue, which was renamed the Boulevard. On the Boulevard was located the R. E. Lee Camp Soldiers' Home for Confederate veterans, which in the twentieth century would become the city's cultural

Figure 3. Davis Monument, Monument Avenue, looking west, c. 1907.

acropolis. On the streets—Broad and Grace to the north, and Grove Avenue to the south—suburban sprawl was already taking place. The owners of the tracts were William C. Allen's family, on whose land the initial development occurred and the Lee and Stuart statues were located; John P. Branch and his heirs, whose property would be the site of the Davis and Jackson monuments; and the Sheppard family, whose land would host the Maury memorial. This last tract, the farthest out from the city center, terminated near present-day Roseneath Road, which also marks a boundary of Confederate earthworks from the Civil War. Monument Avenue was laid out and graded, and the surrounding land was subdivided, between 1889 and 1909. This was not done continuously but took place with starts and stops over the years as the city annexed the area and land was sold. Construction of houses, apartments, and churches followed the progression of the statues (Figure 3).

THE MONUMENTS

Monument Avenue really began in 1870 with the death of Robert E. Lee. Immediately two competing Lee monument groups began campaigning (unsuccessfully) to select a site and erect a monument to the former commander of the Army of Northern Virginia. In March 1886, under the leadership of the newly elected governor, Fitzhugh Lee, a Confederate general and a nephew of Robert E. Lee, the rivalrous groups were unified. On June 18, 1887, the Lee Monument Commission selected a site just outside the western boundary, or "West End," of Richmond. In October 1887 a sculptor was selected: the resultant statue was unveiled on May 29, 1890.[6]

The site of the Lee Monument lay within a tract of fifty-eight acres just beyond the western edge of the city. The tract was owned by the heirs of William C. Allen, who had died in 1874. Allen was a very successful builder who had accumulated property. His son, Colonel Otway S. Allen, was a socially prominent Richmond businessman, a friend of Governor Lee, and later a member of Richmond's Board of Aldermen. He also had served in the war as commanding officer of Virginia's First Battalion. Allen offered to donate a site to the Lee Monument Commission and to build two broad intersecting boulevards around the monument and give them to the city of Richmond.

Although this west-end site was flat and bare, it had several possible advantages. A Richmond newspaper described it as a broad open space on one of the "greatest elevations of the city... several feet above the

Capitol site" that had been proposed earlier. Other, higher sites had been suggested as well but had not been chosen. The newspaper went on to explain, "A too-close proximity of buildings has ruined some of the finest monuments in Europe." Located at the end of prestigious Franklin Street, the site of the Lee Monument lay in a direct line with Capitol Square. Also important were land economics: Richmond was expanding to the west and Governor Lee noted the tax advantages accruing to the city as the land was "almost at the end of the great west-end boom."[7] In 1892 the state legislature passed a law allowing the Allen tract, the Lee Monument, and another 292 acres in the area to be annexed by the city of Richmond.[8]

Although it took many years for Monument Avenue to be built, the concept of a grand boulevard stretching to the west had been intended from the very beginning. A newspaper account of the debate surrounding the Lee Monument site stated that the Allen tract supporters proposed to widen Franklin Street and "to make a grand boulevard, with room for trees down the middle…and to intersect Reservoir Avenue [the Boulevard]."[9] For the planning of his tract Otway S. Allen hired Colonel Collinson Pierrepoint Edwards Burgwyn, a Harvard-trained civil engineer who practiced architecture in Richmond. Burgwyn's scheme (Figure 4) indicated knowledge of American and European boulevards, such as Commonwealth Avenue in Boston, Monument Square in Baltimore, and Baron Haussmann's transformations of Paris. He laid out cross-axial boulevards with a fifty-foot-wide median and a round point of 200 feet in diameter, at the center of which would be placed the Lee Monument. The property was subdivided into standard Richmond-sized lots, with a thirty-foot frontage and a depth of 150 feet. Lots fronting on the circle had more eccentric shapes.

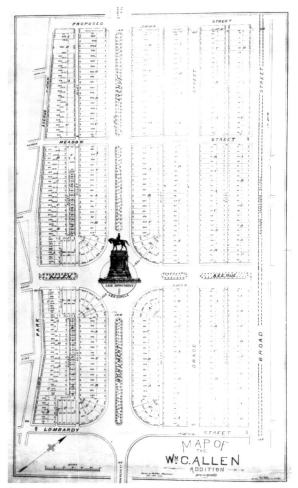

Figure 4. Monument Avenue, "Map of the Wm. C. Allen Addition, Richmond, VA." Surveyed by Bates and Bolton, engineers, December 18, 1888.

While several competitions had been held in the past for the honor of designing the Lee statue, the new Lee Monument Commission chose French sculptor Marius-Jean-Antonin Mercié. A writer noted, "It is alleged that Mercié owes his good fortunes in no small degree to the odd offices of those of the members of the jury."[10] One of the members was Augustus Saint-Gaudens, an eminent American sculptor who had been a member of an earlier jury and praised the entry by Mercié. Of no small coincidence, Saint-Gaudens and Mercié had been fellow students at the École des Beaux-Arts in Paris and in

Figure 5. Lee Monument, Monument Avenue, looking west, c. 1920.

the atelier of Jouffroy. Saint-Gaudens apparently convinced the new Lee Monument Board to select Mercié.[11] Predictably, an outcry ensued over the ignoring of local talent. Still, the selection of Mercié and the success of his work, along with the pedestal by the French architect Paul Pujol, gave the monument an international flavor and elevated it far above parochial sentimentalism. This was no local favorite-son sculptor but one of the leading artists in the world who agreed to provide Richmond with a masterpiece. Lee mounted on his horse Traveler is presented as larger than life-size, monumental and impassive (Figure 5).[12]

The Lee Monument came at a critical juncture, for the war was now several decades in the past and memories of the grim carnage began to fade and be replaced with a romantic nostalgia. In the North the announcements and unveilings of major monuments and memorials gained momentum: Saint-Gauden's Admiral Farragut Memorial, with the base by Stanford White, was unveiled on Madison Square in New York in 1881; the arch at the Grand Army of the Republic Plaza in Brooklyn was proposed in 1885 and completed in 1892; and the Grant Tomb in New York was announced in 1885, though not completed until 1897. All of this activity was part of a wider tendency by Americans to immortalize the American past, to create what was termed an "American Renaissance."[13] In this context the monument to General Lee became part of the monumentalization of the War Between the States. In addition, Lee's reputation underwent a substantial shift in meaning: no longer a rebel but an American hero, he became a tragic personage of noble dimensions caught in an unsolvable conflict between his state (Virginia) and his nation.[14]

The Lee Monument was dedicated in May 1890 at a huge celebration whose audience was estimated at between 100,000 and 150,000—more than the population of Richmond (Figure 6). A grand parade wound through the city and past Lee's former home. At its head as chief marshal was former governor and general Fitzhugh Lee, and more than forty other generals either marched or rode along with governors from the former Confederate states and 15,000 veterans. Especially honored were the widows of "Stonewall" Jackson and George Pickett. As the canvas slid off, there stood the man and horse in bronze monument on an elaborate marble pedestal, with the inscription "LEE" in capital letters. Not every Richmonder hailed the occasion; John Mitchell, Jr., a Black councilman and owner of the newspaper *Planet*, argued vehemently against spending any city money on the occasion. His paper wrote that the entire proceeding handed down to future generations a "legacy of treason and blood." The Lee Monument came at precisely the time when Southern lynchings of Blacks were increasing and "Jim Crow" laws were instated.[15]

From the North came a few expressions of outrage that a statue to Lee could be erected: a Philadelphia newspaper compared him to Benedict Arnold, while the New York *Mail and Express* proposed a congressional law that would ban monuments of Confederate heroes and displays of the Confederate flag. But other Northerners saw it differently. For them the monument was not a rebellious statement. As the *New York Times* editorialized, Lee was brave and honorable and, "His memory is, therefore, a possession of the American people."[16]

The other monuments lining the avenue have similar stories of complicated and conflicted origins and elaborate dedications. Ideas for a monument to Confederate calvary leader J. E. B. Stuart had been announced as early as 1875, but not until 1903 was a competition held. Former Governor Lee chaired the competition committee, and on it was Edward V. Valentine, a Richmond sculptor. Frederick Moynihan, a sculptor from New York who had worked on the monument for years, won the competition; previously he had worked for Valentine as a studio assistant. The selection of the

Figure 6. Dedication of Lee Monument, view north, May 29, 1890.

Figure 7. Monument Avenue, looking east from Lee Monument. Parade for dedication of Stuart Monument, May 30, 1907. The covered Stuart monument is in background.

Figure 8. Dedication of Stuart Monument, view northwest, May 30, 1907.

site on Monument Avenue came in September 1904, and the statue was unveiled on May 30, 1907, as the opening ceremony of the annual Confederate reunion (Figures 7 and 8).[17] In addition to the proximity to Lee, the site further recommended itself because it was close to the site of Stuart's death in 1864 and to the old church from which he was buried. Stuart is portrayed as a calvary leader, twisting in his saddle.

A few days later, on June 3, the monument to Jefferson Davis was unveiled on the ninety-ninth anniversary of his birth, to a crowd variously estimated between 80,000 and 200,000 (Figure 9). The United Daughters of the Confederacy had sponsored the Davis Memorial, and in July 1903 they had selected Edward V. Valentine as the sculptor and William C. Noland, also of Richmond, as the architect of the setting. After much controversy, a site on Monument Avenue was selected because it was the location of the Star Fort, a piece of the Confederate defense line in the siege of Richmond. A cannon is located just east of the Davis Monument to further commemorate the site. Davis stands in front of a sixty-foot-high Doric column capped by Vindicatrix, a representation of the spirit of the South. Behind this is an exedra of thirteen Doric columns symbolizing the states that made up the Confederacy or sent troops in support (Figure 3).[18]

The cornerstone for the "Stonewall" Jackson Monument was laid during the twenty-fifth

Figure 9. Dedication of Davis Monument, view northwest, June 3, 1907.

Figure 10. Jackson Monument, Monument Avenue, looking east, c. 1919.

Confederate reunion of 1915, but a "penetrating misty rain" preempted the large parade of the by-now aging veterans.[19] The unveiling took place four years later on October 11, 1919, on the fifty-sixth anniversary of Jackson's death at Chancellorsville (Figure 10). A parade of Virginia Military Institute and other veterans marked the occasion, and Colonel Robert E. Lee, the great general's grandson, gave the oration.[20] The sculptor was F. William Sievers, who had studied sculpture in Italy and France. In 1910 Sievers won a competition for the Virginia Monument at Gettysburg and moved to Richmond, where he remained for the rest of this life.[21]

Sievers also was the sculptor for the fifth and last monument, honoring Matthew Fontaine Maury (Figure 11). Interest in a monument to Maury began in 1912, when it was pointed out that while he was scarcely recognized at home, he had an international reputation in navigation, meteorology, and oceanography, as well as for his invention of the electric torpedo and service as a Confederate special envoy. A

Figure 11. Maury Monument, Monument Avenue, view east.

Maury Committee formed by the Richmond Woman's Club and the United Daughters of the Confederacy began to raise funds in 1916. The cornerstone was laid in June 1922 during the Confederate reunion. The occasion was marked by a crowd of 100,000, who witnessed the "slowing steps" of veterans marching down the avenue.[22] At the unveiling ceremony held on Armistice Day in 1929, the Confederate connection was noted by Governor Harry Flood Byrd, along with the assertion that until Woodrow Wilson and the founding of the League of Nations, "no other American had been so recognized by the great nations of the world."[23] Although Maury is portrayed as a man of peace who sits in an armchair, a book open in his hand and a Holy Bible at his feet, there are also symbols of his Confederate contributions: on the lower corners of the pedestal are carved electric ray or torpedo fish, symbolic of both deep-water investigation and the invention of the electric torpedo in 1861–62. The giant globe behind him recalls his accomplishments as an oceanographer and explorer.[24]

These statues give Monument Avenue much of its character and indeed its meaning. The district of the monuments is the heart of the avenue and its real public space. No longer the site of Confederate veterans' marches, it remains the ceremonial boulevard of the city, and along it have traveled world leaders and personalities, such as Marshall Foch, Charles Lindbergh, Winston Churchill, Dwight D. Eisenhower, and Queen Elizabeth II.

Figure 12. Monument Avenue, view west from base of Lee Monument, with decorations for Confederate reunion of May-June 1907.

BUILDING ON THE AVENUE

While the Lee Monument and layout by Colonel Burgwyn were intended by Otway S. Allen to be the site of a prestigious neighborhood, in actuality nothing much happened between 1890 and 1901. The Allen family lots sold well to various speculators, but no building occurred. The reasons are not far to seek. The great depression that gripped the United States in the 1890s hit Richmond hard; not until 1898 did the local economy recover to the levels of 1892. Similarly, the city provided little in the way of urban amenities to people seeking to locate on the avenue. In spite of Burgwyn's (and Allen's) projection of lavishly planted central medians, the planting did not get under way until after 1900. In 1901 utilities were extended to the avenue and the first house was built. Henry James visited the Lee Monument in 1905 as part of his "pilgrim's return," and he described the statue as isolated: "The place is the mere vague centre of two or three crossways, without form and void, with a circle half sketched by three or four groups of small, new, mean houses."[25]

James was too critical. In actuality the Lee Monument was laid out and defined, the roads were graded and graveled, curbs and sidewalks were installed, and at least twenty buildings were up with probably a score more under construction (Figure 12).[26] By 1904 over two hundred scarlet and sugar maple trees had been planted from what would be Stuart Circle along three blocks to the west.[27] In late 1905 the city of Richmond begin to lay out the remainder of the avenue westward from the Allen property to the Boulevard, and in August 1906 the name formally became Monument Avenue.[28] Slightly earlier, in 1904, the city had begun permitting property owners to pave the sidewalks in front of their houses. Paving of the avenue with asphalt Belgian blocks did not commence until 1908, and it continued into 1910. These

Figure 13. Monument Avenue, view east, c. 1908.

improvements occurred at the same time as the placement of the Stuart and Davis statues and the begin-ning of substantial home construction. Home construction, as both land records and photographs show, fol-lowed rather than led the westward progression of the monuments that gave the avenue its distinctive character (Figure 13).

The Allen property lots, and later the lots of the Branch and Sheppard tracts, were sold in two ways: about half were sold directly by the family to individuals who erected their own houses, and the others were sold to speculators. The speculators included developers who erected houses for sale, such as William J. Payne, who built four townhouses in the 1600 block in 1903, as well as those who simply purchased property and resold it at a profit. Of the latter, Henry S. Wallerstein is an example. His primary business was wholesale gro-cery, but he was also involved in the Richmond Building Corporation and actively purchased and sold prop-erty throughout the city. He frequently bought land from one of the original families that owned the Monument Avenue area, held it for a year or two, and then sold it at a modest profit.[29] Wallerstein's various enterprises allowed him to build in 1915 one of the most ostentatious houses on the street, a richly orna-mented Jacobean mansion at 2312 Monument Avenue modeled after the designs of the Richmond architec-tural firm of Carnel & Johnson.

The Allen property had been subdivided into lots with a frontage of 30 feet and a depth of 150 feet (except for those on circles). This had been the standard lot size along Franklin Street, and to some degree it was followed by the Branch and Sheppard families, and the developers who purchased from them. However, there were exceptions. In some cases, double lots were used for building, and both the Branches and the Sheppards did sell off irregular-sized plots. Hence there is a breakdown in building rhythm beginning in the 2300 block and a shift from narrower houses to wider detached buildings.

House construction began on the avenue in 1901. The deeds granting the property mandated "brick stone dwellings" set back twenty feet from the street (this changed to fifteen feet when sidewalks were introduced in 1904).[30] By 1905 fourteen houses had been built near the Lee Monument. By 1910 there were fifty-three houses on the avenue, with most clustered at the eastern end. In the next decade home building doubled to 109 houses between the Stuart and Jackson statues. Most of these were owner occupied, with only a very few

Figure 14. Monument Avenue, view of south side of 2300–2500 blocks, with Davis Monument at right. From left: J. P. Taylor house, 2325 Monument Avenue, 1914, Duncan Lee, architect; L. H. Blair house, 2327 Monument Avenue, 1914, Walter D. Blair, architect. At extreme right: John K. Branch house, 2501 Monument Avenue, 1919, John Russell Pope, architect. Photograph, c. 1921.

owned by absentee landlords. Developers did build houses, but they were immediately sold.

Monument Avenue from its beginning was a solid middle- to upper-income neighborhood known for its prestigious residents and elegant houses. Among the earliest residents were Isaac Thalhimer, owner of a large city department store; O. H. Funsten, a leading realtor; Oliver J. Sands, president of the American National Bank; and D. C. Richardson, the mayor of Richmond in 1908. Just prior to his death, Otway Allen commissioned a house in the block east of the Lee statue (at 1631). However, he did not live to see it completed. Several other members of the Allen family also built on the avenue over the years.

John P. Branch, who owned one of Monument Avenue's original tracts, never lived on the street, but a number of his children and other family members built extensively. The Branches' money came from financial investments, especially their ownership of the Merchants National Bank, one of the largest banks in the South. John P.'s son, John Kerr Branch, was given a house site on the south side of Monument Avenue in 1903. He and his wife Beulah did not build there until 1917, when they began construction of the largest house on the avenue after designs of John Russell Pope. The house is stylistically derivative of Compton Wynates in Warwickshire, England, and it became one of Richmond's showpieces.[31] The Branch house's siting was important because it was in one of the most prominent locations on the avenue, a backdrop for the Davis statue (Figure 14). The house was intended as a showpiece for John Kerr Branch's extensive collection of furniture and tapestries. While partaking of twisted chimneys of molded brick, diamond-shaped windowpanes, and other Tudor and early English Renaissance details, it was in plan and in its balanced facades reflective of Beaux-Arts classical composition.

One of John P. Branch's daughters married a cousin, Robert Gamble Cabell (the Cabells are an old Virginia family), who was a member of the various Branch business interests—in this case, a stockbroker. The Cabells were also given a site and commissioned a house from William Lawrence Bottomley (Figure 20).

Figure 15. Monument Avenue, view east from middle of 2000 block (to left, 2023 Monument Avenue; to right, 2026 Monument Avenue) looking toward Lee Monument and spire of St. James Episcopal Church. Photograph, c. 1925.

ARCHITECTURE

The residences erected along Monument Avenue reflected the different architectural forms and styles favored in the years 1900 to 1930. On one level they present a confusing picture in their variation: individual facades, entrances located at the center and the sides, eccentric fenestration patterns, multiple roof heights, turrets and towers, columns and finials, and an assortment of different-colored brick, stone, and trim (Figure 15). Some dwellings are built close to their lot lines and reflect a row house orientation, but the majority are freestanding entities. Far out on the avenue a few houses were erected that were really large suburban or country houses in character, notably the W. S. Forbes mansion, a giant-columned Southern Colonial revival located west of Roseneath (Figure 16). Mixed in with this assortment of individual dwellings were a few apartment houses, normally containing six units and standing three stories in height but with a greater bulk.[32]

Out of this disparate babel of architecture, two types of generic Monument Avenue houses can be defined: the three-bayed house and the five-bayed house. The three-bayed house typically had an entrance located in either of the outer bays. This side entrance was commonly used for the narrow-lot row house. At a slightly larger size, forty feet or wider, the three-bayed house could have the entrance in the center, such as can be seen at the Wickham-Valentine house (1812, by Alexander Parris). The three-bayed design had been widely used in Richmond since the 1780s and can be found repeated constantly throughout town, especially on West Franklin Street and in the Fan.[33] No matter the style of the architecture and the amount of ornament, this three-bayed type was the basic urban house of Richmond. It

Figure 16. W. S. Forbes residence, 3401 Monument Avenue, 1915. Destroyed.

Figure 17. Monument Avenue, view of north side of 1600 block (shown are 1616, 1620, 1626, and 1634, all built 1903 by W. J. Payne, architect unknown), looking toward Lee Monument from near Stuart Circle, c. 1904.

appears on Monument Avenue in the older sections, in the 1600 block (the Stuart Statue) to the 2300 block, and then interspersed farther out (Figure 17).

The second type, the five-bayed house, was usually symmetrical, with a central entrance hall. The historical basis for this house type can be seen in the governor's mansion (1813), also by Alexander Parris. Although the five-bayed type can appear as a row house, in Richmond it almost always signified a freestanding house, and it appeared as such on Monument Avenue. Though a few five-bayed houses do appear in the older sections of the avenue, most were built after 1910 and in the area past the Davis Monument.

Common to both house types was a height of three stories with prominent dormers projecting from the third-floor attic. Front elevations received the majority of detail and ornament. Columned porticoes or porches appeared with great regularity on Monument Avenue and were of two types, either one story or two stories in height with giant columns. The use of columns diminished with houses built in the 1920s, though they still appeared on apartment blocks. Floor plans indicate the impact of Richmond's humid summer climate in the days before air conditioning: openings are placed for cross-ventilation and the porches serve as rooms.

Spatial organization was almost always planned around some type of large entrance hall, and without fail all the major public rooms—living, parlor, dining, and music rooms—were on the ground floor. The placement of these rooms varied depending on entrance; some arrangements shifted the interior orientation away from the street to side or rear gardens. Second floors were always the bedroom floor, though in larger houses a family sitting room may have been included. Spaces for servants, which were common in all the houses, were located at the rear of the second floor or in the large attic. Rear staircases provided vertical communication for the servants. Gardens and their placement varied. In the older row houses they were placed to the rear, but some of the larger individual residences had side gardens that were walled off from the street. The relation of the interior spaces to the garden also varied, with some of the gardens treated as extensions and outdoor rooms.

Finally, there was a third type of Monument Avenue house, which had no generic features. This is the very large house, such as the Branch house by John Russell Pope, which was really a country dwelling squeezed onto a large city lot (Figure 14). Another example is the Forbes house, a giant-columned Southern Colonial (Figure 16).

Stylistically, the houses of Monument Avenue were quite varied, ranging from the restless pyrotechnics of the earliest houses clustered between the Stuart and Lee monuments—the Richardson Romanesque and the Queen Anne—to a much calmer classicism that began to dominate after 1905. The early houses stood out with their towers and rounded bays. After 1905 the various classical idioms dominated, but a few stylistic heretics did appear, including the Jacobean house for Henry S. Wallerstein and several half-timbered designs. Other alternatives included the Mediterranean or the Italio-Spanish idiom, as illustrated by the house designed by William Lawrence Bottomley in 1922 for J. Scott Parrish (president of a local concrete company and a vice president of the Richmond Chamber of Commerce) (Figure 18). Although the light-colored stucco facade made the house stand out against the ubiquitous darker brick of much of the avenue, stylistically it was essentially classical. Bottomley also employed the Mediterranean idiom for the nine-story Stuart Court Apartments (1924–26) located at the eastern end of the avenue at Stuart Circle. Another stylistic variation was the Italian Renaissance idiom, as in the John Wilson house (1911) at 2037 Monument Avenue (Figure 19). Wilson was a successful building contractor and may have used his own designers to create an Americanized—and indeed southernized—version of an Italian Renaissance *palazzo* in red brick with limestone trim.[34]

Figure 18. J. Scott Parrish residence, 2315 Monument Avenue, 1922, William Lawrence Bottomley, architect. Photograph, c. 1924.

Although many styles are present today, most of the houses on Monument Avenue share a common classical basis. The most prominent stylistic expression is a variation on the American Colonial, Georgian, and English revivals. Linked together by their common bonds in that American Colonial is a derivative of English Georgian, and also of late-seventeenth- and early-eighteenth-century Queen Anne style, these choices reflect American Renaissance origins for the avenue. Additionally, there is a Virginia basis to some of the stylistic choices, since the commonwealth was the origin for a number of the red brick and white-trimmed colonial styles in use. Even more localized was the view

Figure 19. John T. Wilson residence, 2037 Monument Avenue, 1911.

that Southern Colonial meant columns and large porticoes. Although in retrospect it is recognized that the large-columned portico is really a Federal and Greek Revival feature, still at the time it was widely believed to be genuinely Southern Colonial and specifically Virginian.[35]

This Colonial-Georgian revival had national and cosmopolitan connotations in that it was the style of the founders of the United States while at the same time it had links both to England and to the great classical heritage of Rome and Greece. As with the monuments, the architecture on Monument Avenue was intended to demonstrate a connection to the great heritage of Western civilization. At the same time, the Colonial-Georgian style had particularized Virginia connections in that stylistic variants were generic to the state, and Virginians liked to claim their—real or imagined—English aristocratic connections. Here was an idiom both national and international, both democratic and aristocratic, and capable of infinite variation.

Figure 20. Robert Cabell III residence, 2601 Monument Avenue, 1924, William Lawrence Bottomley, architect. Photograph, 1985.

While some of the Colonial-Georgian designs were inspired by specific prototypes, none was a total duplication. They were modern houses of their period in plan, materials, and technology. William Lawrence Bottomley, the New York City architect who became such a favorite of the Virginia elite in the 1910s through the 1930s, used the eighteenth-century Mompesson house in Salisbury Cathedral Close as precedent for his design for Robert Cabell's dwelling (Figure 20).[36] Bottomley did not attempt to recreate the English house; rather, he changed the seven bays of the English example to five for the Cabells, and constructed it of brick with stone trim rather than entirely of stone, as with the English example. He freely adopted the English details. Exterior shutters never used in England appeared on the American model.

Henry Baskervill, the founder of one of Richmond's most prominent architectural firms, and his new partner, Gary Lambert, also used the Salisbury Close model for the home of Dr. Stuart McGuire (1925) (Figure 21). McGuire was president of St. Luke's Hospital and of the Medical College of Virginia. Baskervill used only five bays but constructed the house of limestone to imitate much more directly the English prototype. Details such as the pediment of the McGuire house came not from English sources but from American design of the eighteenth century. Baskervill and Lambert employed essentially the same form further down, at 2609 Monument Avenue, in a house for Sallie Perkins (1925). In this case, brick was used, which recalled eighteenth-century Virginia brickwork such as that at Wilton or Williamsburg.

In addition to the previously mentioned Mediterranean designs and the Cabell house, Bottomley designed five other houses on Monument Avenue. All of these reflect a Colonial-English Georgian preference. His house for Coleman and Mary Wortham (designed in 1917 but not built until 1925) had special

Williamsburg-made and -burned bricks laid up in Flemish bond on all four facades. The cut limestone detailing was Adamsesque, and the portico, with its large Corinthian columns, dominated the composition. On the interior, Bottomley designed an oval dining room, which, according to local lore, was adapted from the governor's mansion. In actuality the oval dining room at the governor's mansion was designed in 1906–1907 by Duncan Lee. The Worthams were an old Richmond family; Coleman was a stockbroker with one of Richmond's oldest investment companies. Mary Gilliam Wortham came from a family long known in Presbyterian Church circles.

Bottomley's other houses, such as the Goslan house of 1916, with its all-header brickwork, are equally fine in detail. H. Logan Goslan was in real estate and investments. His wife was from New York and may have recommended Bottomley to her husband. The Goslan house, a four-bay composition with a side entry, was unusual for the avenue. Bottomley composed a different four-bay design with the house for Mrs. T. Archibald Cary (1926), in which the entrance was in one of the inner bays, creating a striking asymmetrical composition within an overall balanced block. Bottomley returned to the more orthodox side entrance in his next Monument Avenue house, the 1927 four-bayed residence for Anna B. and Ellen T. Boykin, members of a family long prominent in railroad and tobacco businesses. Bottomley's final house on Monument Avenue, one for Robert Miller and Elizabeth Talbott Gwathmey Jeffress, was located

Figure 21. Stuart McGuire residence, 2304 Monument Avenue, 1925, Baskervill and Lambert, architects.

near the beginning of the avenue at Lee Circle. This house, designed in 1929 and completed in 1931, illustrates that although there was a westward movement in the building of houses, still many lots remained unbuilt and were later filled in. In this case, the lot was one of the awkward pie-shaped sites, which accounts for its late building date. Here Bottomley used a five-bay format, with the general form being eighteenth-century Georgian but the details more Federal in origin. Robert Jeffress came from a wealthy family involved in real estate, tobacco, and paper, and he was president of a large paper company. His wife came from an equally prominent family.

The presence of so many houses by Bottomley and also of the Branch house by Pope indicates a feature of Virginia architecture observable on Monument Avenue. One of Virginia's great contributions to American culture has been its architecture, but by the mid-nineteenth century many of the important commissions had begun to go to out-of-state architects. There appears to have been a loss of confidence in the local talent, which has continued well into the twentieth century. Although many Richmond and Virginia architects designed for Monument Avenue, the social elite tended to go out of state.

There are reasons for the appearance of Bottomley in Richmond. He was promoted by one of the leading local builder-contractors, Claiborne and Taylor, Incorporated, and many of his commissions came through clients' wives or other female members of the family. Nearly all of the women belonged to the Garden Club of Virginia. The Garden Club was an all-female organization, very social and status oriented; its leading lady, who wrote many of the guidebooks, was married to Herbert A. Claiborne, the builder-contractor.[37]

The significance of Monument Avenue's architecture is to be found not in the individual unit but in the overall totality. Other local architects, such as Duncan Lee, Bascom J. Rowlett, Scarborough and Howell, and D. Wiley Anderson, designed buildings in the various styles. All of these had substantial local reputations but were scarcely known beyond the commonwealth. Duncan Lee showed an ability to move back and forth between the Colonial, as seen in the T. A. Smyth house (Figure 22), and other idioms, such as the Italio-Spanish style of the dwelling at 2325 Monument for Jaquelin P. Taylor, a tobacco broker and banker. Lee

Figure 22. T. A. Smyth residence, 2336 Monument Avenue, 1913, Duncan Lee, architect.

designed at least thirteen houses for the avenue.

Also of importance to Monument Avenue as a neighborhood, and adding an air of architectural counterpoint to the residences, was the ecclesiastical landscape. At the far eastern end, actually on Franklin Street and just beyond the avenue, stands St. James Episcopal Church (1912), designed by Richmond architect William Noland (Figure 23). St. James's tall spire, inspired by Wren and Gibbs's London churches and early American derivatives, provided a visual terminus to the avenue. At Stuart Circle, Charles Robinson designed the German

Figure 23. Monument Avenue, view east of Stuart Circle. St. James Episcopal Church (background), 1912, William Noland, architect. Stuart Circle Hospital (right), 1912–14, Charles S. Robinson, architect. Photograph, c. 1921.

Figure 24. Monument Avenue, Stuart Monument, looking west, c. 1940. To left, First German (now English) Evangelical Lutheran Church, 1912, Charles S. Robinson, architect.

Lutheran (now the First English) Evangelical Church in 1912, and Carl Lindner provided plans for St. John's United Church of Christ of 1932 (Figure 24). Located in the middle of the next block is John Kevan Peebles's Grace Covenant Presbyterian Church (1920–22). Peebles came from Norfolk and was one of the few turn-of-the-century Virginia architects to gain a reputation beyond the state.[38] These churches, with their stumpy towers and finials, break the three-story residential skyline and add a picturesque and medieval note to Monument Avenue.

Other churches were added over the years, such as the very large and imposing Greco-Colonial First Baptist, located adjacent to the Boulevard. This giant 130-room complex was designed in the late 1920s by Richmond architect H. L. Cain, with University of Virginia professor (and later dean at Harvard) Joseph Hudnut as consulting architect. There is no Jewish synagogue on Monument. However, Temple Beth Ahabah was located two blocks east of the Stuart Monument at Ryland and Franklin. Richmond always had a strong Jewish community, and a number of prosperous Jewish families settled on Monument Avenue over the years. All of the churches on the avenue actually had been located closer in to the city core but moved out as the population shifted to the west. In some cases, the land they occupied came through gifts. For example, Whitmell S. Forbes, who built a giant house out beyond Roseneath, donated the land for the First Baptist Church.[39]

Beyond the Maury Monument near Roseneath—which was then the city limit—there tended to be larger, country-styled mansions, such as the Forbes house.[40] Beyond Roseneath the character of the buildings, the landscaping, and the avenue began to change significantly. Greater space appeared between the houses, the scale became more suburban (for instance, the Forbes house), and while a generic Colonial Revival style prevailed, ranch houses and governmental and business buildings appeared. One moves into a very different period, but the avenue's early pattern continues to provide definition.

THE MODERN AVENUE

The Depression of the 1930s brought an end to virtually all building on Monument Avenue, and in the post–World War II years many of the original families sold their homes and departed to the suburbs. Some residences in the area closest to downtown were converted to rooming houses, apartments, or businesses. John Russell Pope's Branch house, for example, became an insurance office. Only a few postwar buildings were constructed on the avenue, the most prominent of which was the Lee Medical Building (1950–51) on Lee Circle. Still Monument Avenue remained an address of distinction, and beginning in the mid-1970s a reverse trend was perceived as some houses were converted back to single-family dwellings and either renovated or restored. Assisting in this development was the designation in 1971 of Monument Avenue as a national, state, and local historical district. More problematical have been the monuments because to many, and especially to African Americans, they symbolize an ignoble past. Consequently there have been proposals to remove them or to also construct monuments to the heroes of the civil rights movement, but to date nothing has been done. Small celebrations are still held on the birthdays of Lee and his accompanying cohorts, and every Easter a giant Easter egg hunt is held for the children of the neighborhood.

Created during the great wave of city rebuilding and civic art at the turn of the century, Monument Avenue remains one of the finest illustrations of the American Renaissance and the City Beautiful movement. With the revived economy that followed the depression of the 1890s, as well as the powerful influence of turn-of-the-century city beautification schemes in Washington, D.C., San Francisco, Denver, and other places, and with the many "White Cities" or expositions that were built across the country, Richmonders turned their attention to the avenue and installed more monuments and built houses.[41] Streets began to display harmonizing landscaping and architecture, a favorite feature of the emerging profession of city planning in the early twentieth century. Although Monument Avenue is part of the City Beautiful movement, it has a unique character that results from its completeness and overall level of thematic design, not to mention its mission as a memorial.

It may be a place of residences and churches, a street of movement and communication, but ultimately Monument Avenue is the site of memorials to the Confederacy. And it is back to these statues one must come, for their message cannot be ignored. The three equestrian statues of Lee, Stuart, and Jackson are all military memorials and give ample indication of a persistent strain in American culture—and especially strong in Southern culture—of a martial spirit. America proclaims its peace-loving nature, yet it fought on its soil one of the bloodiest wars of any nation. But the gore is gone from Monument Avenue. All that remains are ennobling portraits. Maury is essentially depicted as a man of peace, even though a few subtle symbols indicate his Confederate involvement. The Davis statue at the middle of the row is symbolically the center, protected by Lee, Stuart, and Jackson. Davis gestures toward the State House from which he ruled the Confederacy, and on the monument appears the inscription *"Deo Vindice"* or *"God Be Our Vindicator."* The meaning is clear—that right was on the side of the Confederacy; its battle for states' rights and to preserve slavery was a noble and just cause. Certainly there were noble individuals on both sides of the war, Union and Confederate, but there can be no question now of what was right and that the "lost cause" was a wrong cause. Henry James felt this when he viewed Lee's statue in 1905: "I looked back, before leaving it, at Lee's stranded, bereft image, which time and fortune have so cheated of half the significance, and so, I think, of half the dignity, of great memorials, I recognized something more than the melancholy of a lost cause. The whole infelicity speaks of a cause that could never have been gained."[42] If symbolically Monument Avenue recedes into a mixed past of both glory and deprivation of rights, still there is another and possibly a greater message.

As a grand plan, as a public space, as form, and as a unified streetscape, Monument Avenue is an important example of American city building. It represents a particularly American type of urban space, for it has evolved a certain unity in spite of the diversity of its parts. Seldom are great public urban spaces in America created as finite units; instead, they come into being over time. Essential is a good initial plan, but on the scale on which Americans have built, few people can foresee the conclusion. The monuments added to the avenue over the years provide focal points, vertical thrusts against the march of the street and the buildings. On Monument Avenue the buildings are not identical units. Rather, they are closely spaced individual designs. Taken separately they represent a potpourri, an anarchy of styles and forms. They do not present a solid wall: some buildings project oriels and porches, others present facades nearly flush to the street. And there is variation in the size and height of the buildings, ranging from the tall medical center and apartment buildings at Stuart Circle to the different churches, and many houses. But within this mixture of architecture, these counterpoints of rhythm, enough of a repetition occurs to provide order. These structures represent a concurrence of belief on the part of the architects and their patrons as to what makes appropriate architecture.

The greatest unity is provided by Monument Avenue itself. Spatially, it is long and linear; at times, as in the circles around the Stuart and Lee monuments, it pushes out, but ultimately it is a longitudinal space. It is the stretch of the street, its constant width, its paving, curbstones, and sidewalks that help provide unity.[43] The landscaping, the horizontal sweep of the green grass of the median, and the trees soften the conflicting architecture and provide a measured rhythm to the contrasting forms of buildings. The trees provide a necessary sequencing, a stepped pattern of space. And then there are the monuments: different and yet unified in their iconography, they are the focus. It is this interaction between the monuments, the buildings, the landscaping, and the street that makes Monument Avenue a unique American place.

ACKNOWLEDGMENTS

I am greatly indebted to my former student Carden C. McGehee, Jr., and his thesis, "The Planning, Sculpture, and Architecture of Monument Avenue, Richmond, Virginia" (master's thesis, University of Virginia, 1980). He was unable to participate in the preparation of this article, but I do want to acknowledge his assistance. Since his work was completed, more information has come to light and more research has been carried out. Naturally I accept all responsibility for conclusions that are my own. Research materials are located at the Valentine Museum, the Virginia Historical Society, and the Virginia State Library and Archives, all in Richmond, Virginia. Additionally, I want to acknowledge the assistance of Sarah Shields Driggs, an architectural historian in Richmond, who has assisted with research, and Robert Winthrop, AIA, who over many years has conducted extensive research on Richmond and Monument Avenue and has shared with me his catalogue and other information. Additional information, especially on original residents, has come from Richmond city directories. As this chapter was undergoing revision in early 1993, a Historic American Buildings Survey report, *Monument Avenue: History and Architecture* (Washington, D.C.: U.S. Department of the Interior, National Park Service Cultural Resources, HABS/HAER, 1992), written by Kathy Edwards, Esme Howard, and Toni Prawl, was published and provided additional information.

RICHARD GUY WILSON

CHAPTER ELEVEN

WARD
Parkway
KANSAS CITY, MISSOURI

LANDSCAPE ARCHITECT GEORGE KESSLER saw the problem clearly in 1907. The young landowner and attorney Hugh Ward and his even younger land developer, J. C. Nichols, wanted Kessler to create a boulevard that would surpass in value all other residential streets in Kansas City. The reason Kessler could envision what they wanted so easily was that he had planned almost all of the high-value residential boulevards and parkways throughout the city some fifteen years earlier. Indeed, he planned to connect the new boulevard directly with the southern terminus of Kansas City's widely recognized landscape system.

In 1890 Kansas City had been a small city that had grown too fast. It had experienced a tremendous burst of physical expansion in the middle of the preceding decade, thanks to wet weather in its agricultural hinterland and the city-boosting efforts of many real estate entrepreneurs. Like Minneapolis, Milwaukee, Chicago, and even that sleepy little town of Los Angeles on the west coast of California, Kansas City expanded every way it could from 1884 through 1888.[1]

No landowner was more persistent in his boosting during the boom times than the publisher of one of the daily newspapers, William Rockhill Nelson. The newspaperman obviously possessed a myriad of publicity opportunities with his evening publication, the *Kansas City Star*. But Nelson wanted to do more than simply boost the value of his own large landholdings, which lay south of the city limits near a small, meandering stream known appropriately as Brush Creek. Nelson pushed editorially for the city to purchase and finance the construction of what he called "a park and boulevard system." The idea revolved around the notion that a system of parks needed to be created (the city possessed only one small park covering all of

---

ESSAY BY WILLIAM S. WORLEY

one city block at the time) and connected by means of an elaborate design of wider-than-normal streets that he dubbed "boulevards."[2]

Nelson and others convinced the political powers of the city, including a young alderman named Jim Pendergast, that such a plan would benefit the city in the lean times of the early 1890s by providing public works jobs. At Nelson's insistence, the city hired George Kessler in 1891 to lay out the plan. Thus, when in 1907 attorney and landowner Hugh C. Ward approached Kessler about designing a large subdivision for him that would include a new high-value boulevard, Kessler knew instinctively what was needed. Further, Kessler appears to have recognized in J. C. Nichols, then a twenty-seven-year-old land developer, someone who could help perpetuate the land values the landscape architect created.

Frankly, there was little in Nichols's background in 1907 that would have obviously led Kessler to that con-

Figure 1. J. C. Nichols at his offices at 310 Ward Parkway in the Country Club Plaza shopping center, c. 1940.

clusion. J. C. Nichols grew up in the Johnson County, Kansas, county seat town of Olathe, on the main line of the Frisco Railroad, Kessler's initial employer in the Kansas City area. Nichols graduated from the University of Kansas in 1902 with a reputation as a campus organizer who made good grades. The latter capability won him a Phi Beta Kappa key and a scholarship for a postgraduate year at Harvard University.[3]

Completing the requirements for a second Bachelor of Arts degree from Harvard in one year, Nichols returned to the Kansas City area in 1903 just after a devastating flood had forced many to flee the river bottom's residential neighborhoods near the packing houses in Kansas City, Kansas. Over the next two years, he and a young assistant, John C. Taylor, bought land and built quite modest houses with money borrowed from Nichols's father and Johnson County farmers associated with the senior Nichols through his work at the Grange supply store in Olathe. Nichols also gained support in this venture from two fraternity brothers who practiced law in Kansas City, Missouri.

In 1905 Nichols, using the same money sources as before, bought ten acres of Missouri land almost directly south of William Rockhill Nelson's growing upper-income neighborhood, which the publisher had dubbed "Rockhill," his mother's maiden name. Nichols's ten acres comprised the major portion of an old subdivision laid out during the 1880s land boom across Brush Creek from Nelson's prestigious holdings. The young real estate entrepreneur followed his Kansas City, Kansas, plan by building houses on some of the lots in the new subdivision to encourage interest on the part of potential buyers. He constructed the Missouri houses on a somewhat more elaborate scale than the simple $1,000 houses he sold across the river in Kansas. Still, they amounted to only $3,000 to $4,000 houses, designed to appeal primarily to strictly middle-class buyers.

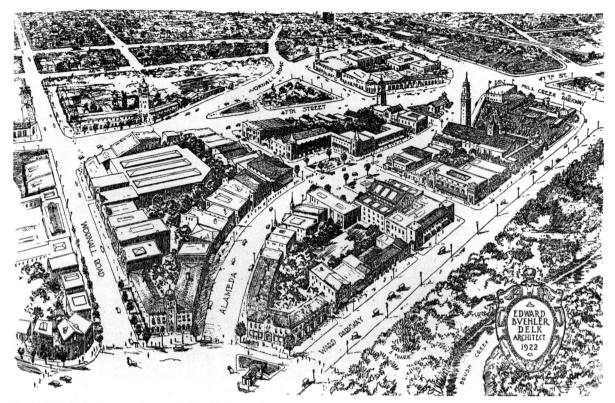

Figure 2. Nichols's land served as the origin for Ward Parkway at the intersection of Mill Creek (now J. C. Nichols Parkway) and Brush Creek. Plan as originally envisioned, c. 1922.

Nichols and his new financial backers from the Kansas City Board of Trade continued to buy land during the next two years in plots adjacent to his initial investment. He opened new subdivisions, trading on the name "Rockhill" as used by Nelson to create a sense of greater prestige and value. All of these early Nichols subdivisions were located along or near the route high-status people from Kansas City had to travel to get to the exclusive pleasure grounds of the Kansas City Country Club, which included a golf course and polo grounds. In the process, Nichols created a distinct community unlike any other residential section of Kansas City (Figure 1).

Hugh Ward had leased the country club its site in 1896 and built his own residence across the roadway from the grounds. He owned over five hundred acres, by virtue of inheritance from his almost legendary father, sometime mountain man and later, improbably, Kansas City banker Seth Ward. Indeed, his father's pre–Civil War house still stood on land west of the polo grounds area of the country club site. Eventually, the boulevard laid out by Kessler at the request of Ward and Nichols undulated to within one building lot of the Seth Ward house, leading later Kansas Citians often to suppose, incorrectly, that Ward Parkway was named for the old pioneer. When Kessler, Ward, and Nichols walked over the acreage Ward wanted transformed into salable house-building sites, they did not apply a name to the potential roadway they discussed. The fact that Hugh Ward died in 1909 before his fiftieth birthday—while the project was still in the planning stages—led Nichols and the grieving widow, Vassie James Ward, to name the planned grand avenue after him (Figure 2).

At the time Kessler commenced his planning in cooperation with Ward and Nichols, the entire area that would become known as the "Country Club District" and would be served by Ward Parkway was south of the city limits. Consisting of mostly unimproved land aside from the Kansas City Country Club itself, the area appeared to have little potential value to most of the Kansas City real estate profession. It was Nichols's imagination, supported by Ward's financial backing and Kessler's design expertise, that transformed farmlands and hillsides into the most desirable residential section in the city.

A Successful Parkway Plan

The route Kessler determined for the parkway began with a connection to his overall boulevard plan just south of what would become Forty-seventh and Main Streets (Kansas City officially annexed the lands controlled by Nichols and the Ward family in 1911). Kessler decided that Ward Parkway should follow the bed of Brush Creek as it led southwest from the boulevard intersection almost to the point where the streambed crossed the Kansas-Missouri state line. The landscape architect noted that a ravine cut into the bluffs overlooking the Brush Creek Valley just east of the state line. He quickly saw that this natural incline provided a more accessible grade for an approach to the more southerly reaches of the Ward lands, which stretched south to what became Fifty-ninth Street. Once the ravine was scaled (between Fifty-third and Fifty-fifth Streets), it

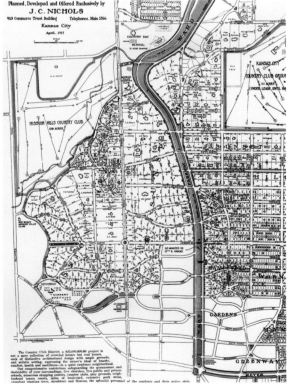

was possible to provide a gentle curve slightly back to the east, creating a slowly widening strip of land for residential building lots between the Parkway and the Kansas state line, which also served as the western boundary of the Ward holdings (Figure 3).[4]

One of Kessler's design techniques resulted in a significant impact on the future grand avenue. Throughout almost all of Kansas City, Missouri, including the areas served by Kessler's previous boulevards, the blocks were oriented with their length running from north to south while the shorter width (usually two building lots deep) ran from east to west. Kessler changed all that in the earliest plats of Sunset Hill, the subdivision name applied to the Ward properties enclosed by Ward Parkway. In these sections, Kessler made the east-west direction dominant, with short north-south blocks. Because the house numbering and street naming were thought to need to conform to previous

Figure 3. This 1917 map illustrates the plan for the section of Ward Parkway discussed in this chapter. The upper portion to Fifty-ninth Street was laid out by George Kessler. The Meyer Circle area, not yet contemplated, was designed by the firm of Hare & Hare.

Figure 4. Park at intersection of two roadways with Ward Parkway. The park allowed residences to face Ward Parkway yet remain distanced from the noise of the thoroughfare.

Figure 5. English cottage–style residence with Tudor half-timbering, 1043 West Fifty-seventh Terrace. This street intersects Ward Parkway diagonally so that the rear elevation of the residence is facing Ward Parkway.

city patterns, blocks lying west of Main Street in land controlled by Nichols and the Ward estate (and affected by Kessler's plan) skipped a digit as they moved west from the Main Street demarcation. Hence, the first block west of Main was the "0" block—houses were numbered in double digits such as "34" rather than "134"; the second block west of Main was the "200" block, with numbers like "234"; the third block west was the "400" block, and so on to State Line Road, which had the "1200" block between it and Ward Parkway to the east from a point south of roughly Fifty-third Street (Figure 4).

The change in orientation also meant that there were two blocks between the normal numbered street intersection distances as they existed in the rest of the city. Because Nichols was insistent that the new additions be made to seem as much a part of the city as possible, making the lots more salable, he hoped, a pattern of naming the intervening streets as "terraces" developed. This meant, for example, that the street running east and west between Fifty-fifth and Fifty-sixth was called Fifty-fifth Street Terrace, with the pattern repeated throughout Nichols's subdivisions as far south as Seventy-first Street (or Gregory Boulevard) (Figure 5).

The direct impact of this pattern on the future of Ward Parkway as a grand avenue is clear because south of Fifty-third Street, Ward Parkway is a north-south thoroughfare. This means that only a relatively small number of lots were designed to face the boulevard directly. On top of that, Nichols specified in his deed restrictions, which were tied directly to the published plat maps and were legally binding on present and future purchasers, the direction each house on street corners was to face. In many instances he specified that houses would face the side streets intersecting with Ward Parkway rather than the roadway itself (Figure 6).[5]

Figure 6. Nichols Company Office, Meyer Boulevard, Meyer Circle. With the design of this elaborate real estate office with fireplace, Nichols wished to encourage formal residential design for Ward Parkway.

Nonetheless, Kessler and Nichols planned from the beginning for the fully developed Ward Parkway to be what it became—"one of the great parades of America." An early advertisement noted that "the plaza treatment of Ward Parkway south of…Fifty-fifth Street lends an air of distinction to the individual homes which front the streets radiating from it." Nichols intended that the building sites on Ward Parkway would be dominated by houses "of the villa type," meaning large mansions, that "…will present a picture to see which travelers will come great distances and from which the people of our own city will receive great inspiration."[6] The advertisement makes it clear that Nichols viewed Ward Parkway primarily as an attraction to raise values along the intersecting streets even more than he expected the roadway to have large numbers of high-value residences lining its path (Figure 7).

That Ward Parkway achieved that goal can be documented from a number of sources. In 1959 a former Kansas Citian published his first novel, set in the neighborhoods in which he had grown up. Evan Connell's *Mrs. Bridge* became a significant success, prompting a sequel from a male's point of view, *Mr. Bridge* (1969). (The two books became the inspiration for the 1990 movie *Mr. and Mrs. Bridge*, starring Paul Newman and Joanne Woodward in the title roles.) Connell suggests the importance of proximity to (but not actual frontage on) Ward Parkway in *Mrs. Bridge*:

> [Mr. Bridge] was as astute as he was energetic, and because he wanted so much for his family he went to his office quite early in the morning while most men were still asleep and he often stayed there working until late at night. He worked all day Saturday and part of Sunday, and holidays were nothing but a nuisance. Before very long the word had gone around that Walter Bridge was the man to handle the case.…Consequently they were able to move to a large home just off Ward Parkway several years sooner than they had expected.…[7]

The fact that Mr. and Mrs. Bridge always "expected" to move nearer to Ward Parkway is taken as a truism. It was just a matter of time and effort.

Further documentation of the desirability of a Ward Parkway location comes from work done in the 1950s concerning Kansas City. A sociological research team from the University of Chicago came to document the class structure of a medium-sized United States city. They discovered through a series of interviews with a cross-section of the population that the most recognizably desirable residential section in the metropolitan area was what they called "the Ward Parkway and Mission Hills Gold Coast." The term "Gold Coast" is taken from earlier sociological studies of residential patterns in Chicago to describe the most wanted residential addresses in that city.[8]

The study concluded that many interviewees of various levels of social standing believed that "the streets leading off Ward Parkway were 'lined with mansions'...."

> The "blue bloods," "the uppercrust," "the Society Crowd," and "the topnotchers" were said to live in this area. A man
> who could afford one of these mansions was assumed to be "one of the big industrialists," "a leading man of commerce,"
> "a well-to-do executive," "a top-ranking lawyer or doctor" or "one of the big shots among the real estate boys and
> stocks and bonds brokers." This was the area thought to supply most of the members of the elite country clubs, leaders
> in the Chamber of Commerce, and board members of various cultural institutions. The Gold Coast precincts were said
> to vote Republican by a nine-to-one majority in election after election.[9]

It is important to note that such descriptions reflect the perceptions of persons interviewed for the study and are not based on actual historical research. The fact that the researchers encountered so many from such a variety of backgrounds who held similar views about the significance of an address near Ward Parkway demonstrates the continuing importance of the street as a symbol.

As recently as 1981, the *Kansas City Star* considered Ward Parkway a synonym for "money, power, and permanence." A reporter noted that "at first sight, it's apparent that Ward Parkway is something special. It's a road like no other in Kansas City. Living there is synonymous with prestige."[10]

That Nichols intended for his centerpiece boulevard to be the prestige address of the city is clear from previous evidence. Throughout the decade of the World War, his advertising emphasized the value of buying land and building a house near the prestigious people of the city. On several occasions in 1911 and 1912 he published large display advertisements in the Sunday *Kansas City Star*, listing the names and featuring drawings of residential structures either completed or under construction for prominent men of the city.[11]

Figure 7. 1980 census tracts for Ward Parkway region. Meyer Circle can be seen at upper left corner of tract 85. Mission Hills, a separate Kansas municipality (tracts 508 and 509), ranks highest in that state in the median value of housing.

287

THE FIRST HOUSES: CORRIGAN AND NELSON

The first two houses on Ward Parkway, which in fact set the tone socially and architecturally for the street, were built by men who had worked their way up in local business firms. Bernard Corrigan had been the operating manager as well as a shareholder in the Metropolitan Street Railway system at a time when the intracity transit company made money. He led in the transformation from horse cars to cable cars and finally to electric trolley lines and was wise enough to get out of the business before it bankrupted itself into receivership in 1913. Similarly, Mack B. Nelson, although not a Kansas City native, had worked his way up to a vice president's position at the Long-Bell Lumber Company, which operated a regional chain of lumberyards as well as a wholesale lumber business out of Kansas City. Both men were quite wealthy, but neither had inherited his wealth and neither was ever fully accepted in the highest reaches of Kansas City society.

While Corrigan's house at Fifty-fifth and Ward Parkway is the first house on the thoroughfare in terms of chronological construction, it does not, in fact, have a Ward Parkway address. Its distinctive style and architectural designs are visible to motorists (and were visible to earlier streetcar riders) as they reach the top of the ravine that climbs the Sunset Hill bluffs from the Brush Creek valley (Figure 8). The 1912 house is something of a composite architecturally, with basic Prairie School lines but featuring Arts and Crafts ornamentation. Local architect Louis Curtiss directed the use of what were then novel construction methods in domestic architecture: long-span girders and reinforced concrete. Much of the thematic unity of the house is provided by repetition of stained-glass wisteria leaves in a delicate purple hue in many of the main floor exterior windows (Figure 9).[12]

The residence was constructed on its three-acre site by the Bernard Corrigan Construction Company for the owner and his family. Corrigan did not live to occupy the house, which his survivors sold to an incoming Oklahoma oil man and banker named P. J. White in 1914. A short while afterward, White sold the house and site to Dwight L. Sutherland, who operated a large lumber business. The Sutherlands occupied the structure from 1920 to the 1970s. Their lumberyard evolved into a regional chain that serves several states.[13]

Under the Sutherlands' ownership, the location attained its greatest prestige. Members of the Sutherland family have been influential in several local and area charities, with one child of the homeowner serving a stint as trustee of the Nelson Art Gallery for a period. Support for the Nelson Gallery is among the most popular of upper-class philanthropies, and membership on its board is among the most prestigious positions in the city.[14]

Figure 8. Southbound lane and trolley car line of Ward Parkway at Brush Creek valley, north of Fifty-fifth Street, c. 1912.

Figure 9. Bernard Corrigan residence, 1200 Santa Fe Road (now Fifty-fifth Street), 1912, Louis Curtiss, architect.

Immediately south of the Corrigan residence, Mack B. Nelson constructed the second Ward Parkway residence. By the time Sutherland bought 1200 Fifty-fifth Street, Nelson was president of Long-Bell, which meant that the CEOs of two large lumber companies were neighbors across the street in the 1920s.

Nelson apparently had three main criteria for his local architect, Henry Hoit. The first was a certain appearance of prestige. Nelson's board chairman, Robert A. Long, had employed Hoit to design a palatial mansion, completed in 1911, in Kansas City's northeast section. The Nelson design bears certain superficial resemblances to the Long mansion, including Greek Revival columns, which indicates that Nelson wanted to emulate the prestige he thought that style imparted.

Second, Nelson had married into what turned out to be an extended family, including his mother-in-law and two sisters-in-law (one of whom was married), and he needed to provide space for its various members. Thus the second floor is divided into three bedroom–living room suites plus a large guest suite, which was generally occupied by the mother-in-law. Such specifications required a house of large dimensions, with the result that the Nelson house is the largest house (with approximately 30,000 square feet) on all of Ward Parkway. This also makes it the only true mansion on the thoroughfare (Figure 10).

Nelson's third criterion was that the house have a Ward Parkway address even though the main entrance clearly faces the Corrigan-Sutherland house across Fifty-fifth. A second, false front made up of French doors alternating with Greek columns provided the formal facade required by Nichols in his restrictions. Later in life he expressed regret that no more mansions were built on Ward Parkway, a fact that he attributed to the introduction of the graduated income tax as his own mansion neared completion in 1914.[15]

Nelson liked to describe the house as being of "the Italian Renaissance style," which satisfied his need for what he considered to be a classically styled residence. The focal point of the interior supports this description. It consists of a center courtyard that extended upward through all three stories to a retractable skylight.

289

Figure 10. Mack B. Nelson residence, directly across the street from the Bernard Corrigan residence on Santa Fe Road (now Fifty-fifth Street), 1914, Henry Hoit, architect. Photograph, 1992.

All major interior rooms opened onto balustrades that encircled the courtyard or patio on all four sides. The center patio floor consisted of Tennessee marble, surrounded by carved wood columns finished with a false marble paint. A working fountain dominated the center of the patio on the first floor.[16]

At the time of its construction, the house created something of a sensation by making the bathtubs work as combination bath-shower facilities:

> The bath equipment is to be exceptional. The tubs are to be built-in and enclosed in glass fitted in nickel plated metal
>
> bars. The other three sides of this bath compartment will be tiled, to permit shower baths. Entrance to the bathtub
>
> through the glass front will be through a glass door. The fixtures will be electric welded to prevent leaking.[17]

One room of the house was featured in the national theatrical release of *Mr. and Mrs. Bridge*. The film producers were unable to find a suitable kitchen on location until the immediate past owner of the Nelson residence, himself a movie and theater producer, volunteered use of the mansion's kitchen. It proved to be the one authentic 1930s-style food preparation area available for the several scenes slated for that portion of the fictional Bridge residence.[18]

Mack Nelson was essentially a self-made man. Born in Arkansas, he had started his working life at age thirteen in the silver mines of Mexico and worked his way to Kansas City by age twenty-two as sales manager for an east Texas lumber company. After a stint in Louisiana, during which he suffered from "chills and fever," Nelson returned to Kansas City in 1898 to work for Long-Bell as its wholesale manager. Nelson reported no hobbies in a 1922 interview, but was reputed to be a formidable golfer at Mission Hills Country Club, whose clubhouse was accessible off of Ward Parkway two blocks north of his dwelling. Nelson occupied his home until his death in 1950, after which his sister-in-law continued to live there until she sold the property in 1956 to Mary Hudson Vandegrift.[19]

Mrs. Vandegrift's money came from the ownership of her father's Hudson Oil Company, a firm that went bankrupt in the 1980s but was considered to be quite solid from the 1950s through the 1970s. In 1966 Mrs. Vandegrift donated the somewhat deteriorated Nelson residence to the University of Missouri at Kansas City for endowment purposes. Mrs. Vandegrift went on to purchase one of the larger houses in Mission Hills, just a few blocks west of the Nelson property.[20]

Local movie producer Wade Williams purchased the Nelson residence in 1968 from the university endowment agency. He lived in it on and off during the next two decades while renting out some of the second-floor suites. In the spring of 1991 Williams sold the Nelson mansion for a reputed $2 million.[21]

The 1991 purchaser authorized a sizeable renovation of the interior, as well as of the exterior grounds. The purchaser allegedly had accumulated the money needed for the acquisition by taking over the operation of a client's questionable puzzle business. Thus, the tradition of "new money" or "first-generation money" finding its way into Ward Parkway real estate has been continued in each of the transfers of this property.[22]

SUBSEQUENT CONSTRUCTION

By the time the Nelson mansion was completed in 1914, fighting had broken out in Europe that would develop into World War I. While President Wilson argued forcefully throughout 1915 and 1916 that Americans should be neutral "in thought, deed, and action," no major home builders were willing to ante up the dollars to build new houses considering the uncertainty of world events.

During the same period, however, a good deal of home building was going on in the adjacent side-street areas within two blocks of Ward Parkway, east and west. The architectural firm of Shepherd, Farrar and Wiser competed strongly with Hoit, Price and Barnes for commissions on these relatively large residential structures. The *Kansas City Star* featured drawings of many of them on the newspaper's Sunday real estate page. It is worth noting that the next large residence announced for Ward Parkway itself was not publicized until September 1917. While it is impossible to trace the prices for lots in the various locations listed, it is likely that there was not a great deal of variation in price from lots fronting Ward Parkway to those quite nearby.[23]

One of the largest houses in the neighborhood was announced almost contemporaneously with the Nelson mansion. Located just west of the Corrigan-Sutherland residence and north of the west end of Nelson's acreage, the C. S. Keith house received publicity in November 1913. Like its neighbors, this house was located on a large (three acres) lot. The owner, president of Kansas City's largest coal company, employed Shepherd, Farrar and Wiser to design a modified Georgian residence that omitted the large columns so often placed on the fronts of such residences. Indeed, the cream-colored stone and dull green tile roof combined to give the structure, even just after completion, the appearance of having been situated

Figure 11. C. S. Keith residence, Santa Fe Road (now Fifty-fifth Street), 1913, Shepherd, Farrar and Wiser, architects. Residence of J. C. Nichols from 1920 to 1950.

there for decades.[24] In 1920 J. C. Nichols purchased this property, and he lived in it until his death in 1950 (Figure 11).

Between the World War I period and the onset of the Great Depression in 1930, fifteen additional houses and one church appeared along the route of Ward Parkway south of Fifty-third Street to Meyer Circle—the portion of Ward Parkway that has always dominated the public perception of the roadway.

The church constructed on Ward Parkway in the 1920s served to create a sense of Gothic majesty. The main portion of the Country Club Christian Church, including the sanctuary, was dedicated in January 1926. Featuring ribbed vaults in its interiors, pointed arches in its divided windows, and tall spires about the main bell tower, the church reproduced the English Gothic style more faithfully than any other structure in Kansas City (Figure 12).[25]

Architecturally distinctive, and destined to become one of the socially prestigious churches of Kansas City, Country Club Christian did much to support the developing tone of Ward Parkway during the 1920s. Many influential residents may have lived just off its roadway on intersecting side streets, but they often went to church right in the middle of the premier section of the thoroughfare. The church dominates the entire 6100 block of the east side of Ward Parkway (Figure 13).

A later study of social patterns and perceptions in the city singled out the image Country Club Christian (referred to as Ward Parkway Christian in the study) carried in the minds of many Kansas Citians:

The Ward Parkway Christian Church was founded by twelve millionaires, and they have more millionaires in that congregation than in any other in Kansas City. It's right in the heart of the wealthy neighborhood, and when anybody moves into town who is high up in the executive ladder he joins that church—that is, if he isn't strongly committed to some other denomination. That's the church to be with for business advantage.[26]

The study concluded that, along with three Episcopal congregations and a Presbyterian church, Country Club Christian was among the five "society churches" in the city.

Of the houses constructed during the same period as Country Club Christian, most were distinguished more by the notoriety of their occupants than by the size of the edifice or the distinctiveness of the architecture. Nothing on the scale of the Corrigan and Nelson houses went up, but two houses owned by well-known political figures did appear during the 1920s.

Figure 12. Country Club Christian Church, 6100 Ward Parkway, 1926.

Figure 13. Block-long reflecting pool in the median opposite Country Club Church. Installed by the J. C. Nichols Company, late 1920s. Sailboat regattas and ice skating were regular seasonal events.

Figure 14. Miles Bulger residence, 5850 Ward Parkway, 1926. Photograph, 1992.

The first political home builder was Miles Bulger, who owned a major interest in a cement business and a good deal of real estate in the Kansas City area. He was also a former city alderman, county judge (a county judge in Missouri was the same thing as a county commissioner in most other states), and state representative in the Missouri Legislature.

A Democrat and an Irishman, Bulger had risen partially under the sponsorship of political boss Jim Pendergast and then under that of Jim's younger brother, Tom. Ultimately, Bulger had attempted to take control of at least part of Pendergast's areas of influence but was defeated in a 1924 political primary.[27]

Possibly as a result of his forced retirement from politics, Bulger decided to build a residence on Ward Parkway. Trained as a plumber, he supervised much of the actual construction work on the structure at 5850 Ward Parkway. Given his background, Bulger might have been expected to put up a showy structure in an attempt to impress either his neighbors or fellow Kansas Citians as they drove to work. Instead, the Bulger residence (completed in 1926) has been described by the former architecture critic of the *Kansas City Star* as "one of the few recessive houses" in this most prestigious section of Ward Parkway. Composed in a modified English Tudor Cottage style, the house sits back somewhat further from the street than some of its neighbors. Additionally, in the 1980s it was carefully screened by overhanging trees in the front (Figure 14).[28]

The best-known political address is that of Tom Pendergast at 5650 Ward Parkway, just two blocks north

Figure 15. Thomas J. Pendergast residence, 5650 Ward Parkway, 1928, Edward Tanner, architect.

of that of Miles Bulger. Born in St. Joseph, Missouri, Pendergast was a product of an Irish immigrant family. Building on his older brother Jim's saloon-and-hotel-based political machine, Pendergast soon learned that there were more ways to make money than just by doing favors for saloon patrons who had little more than their votes to trade. Moving into the wholesale liquor business (and apparently into organized crime subsidiaries, such as gambling, prostitution, and protection), the younger Pendergast cut a wider economic swath than his older brother had ever dreamed.

Pendergast took over his brother's alderman seat in 1910 and kept it for three terms, but the act of holding office kept him tied to a particular part of town. By 1916 he was negotiating with J. C. Nichols to buy a sizeable house at the corner of Fifty-second and Wyandotte, only two blocks from the country club grounds. After 1916 Pendergast never held public office again, and he always lived in the Country Club District (Figure 15).[29]

It can be supposed, but not proven, that Pendergast decided to have the J. C. Nichols Company build him a large mansion on Ward Parkway at least partially as a comeback at Bulger. Nichols's in-house architect, Edward Tanner, designed the rather severe brick house, which features a slate mansard roof, in early 1928. Actual construction proceeded apace during the months before the Wall Street crash. Whether Pendergast's new house was designed to overshadow the residence of his political enemy or not, there was never any love lost between Bulger and Pendergast while the two were ostensibly neighbors. On at least one occasion Pendergast was driving on Ward Parkway when he spied Bulger on foot. The smaller Bulger "gave an impudent gesture" in the direction of the powerfully built Pendergast, who slammed on his brakes and chased the "Little Czar" (Bulger's political nickname) up to the latter's front door. Shenanigans like this brought notoriety to the Ward Parkway neighborhood, but hardly prestige.[30]

One of the most architecturally interesting structures of the decade went up in 1927 a block south of the Bulger location on land not controlled by J. C. Nichols. A competing real estate operator named Harry Clark obtained control of land facing the west side of Ward Parkway between Fifty-ninth Street and Sixty-third Street. The Clark land did not extend all the way to the state line but stopped about halfway between Ward Parkway and State Line Road. Some of the houses built in this stretch are truly outstanding, but only two blocks south are some of the most ordinary and physically "jammed up" houses in the entire area. It proved to make quite a difference whether the Nichols Company continued to control the undeveloped portions of the Parkway area.

In 1927 a wealthy investor named George W. Wright purchased a large lot from Clark at what would be numbered 5940 Ward Parkway. Wright is reputed to have closely supervised the construction of what has been called "the finest Spanish Renaissance palace in the city." Indeed, according to relatives after the investor's death, he personally selected every stone for shape and color. The house is built entirely of stone and features a porch colonnaded with stone columns under Romanesque arches. Hearsay evidence cited in the newspaper indicates that Wright spent upward of $150,000 in 1920s dollars on the construction of the residence. He died before the completion of the interior decoration. In 1931 the real estate was sold to the local manager of the General Electric sales office, who had been born and raised in Kansas City. Today the property is owned by a member of the family that owns the primary Cadillac dealership. The same critic who admired the Bulger house observed that the Wright structure is unique—"In America, one cannot often expect to come across architecture of this quality" (Figure 16).[31]

Immediately next door to the north of the Wright house is what the *Kansas City Star* considered in 1981 as "perhaps the most handsome and picturesque 'medieval' house in the city." Built a year or two later than the Wright house, there are a few features that appear to make it something of an odd, beautiful "bookend" to the mellow excellence of its Spanish Renaissance neighbor—particularly the presence of a north porch (with a second story above), which clearly balances the south porch/cloister of the Wright residence. This fine residence, vaguely reminiscent of Norman architecture, with its octagonal turret next to a "gabled and deeply arched entrance" and featuring a huge triangular gable that reaches the ground just south of the entrance, nonetheless utilizes the Romanesque arch style in entrances and in the north porch/cloister, again echoing choices made in its earlier neighbor. The overall result, architecturally, is that this single block with only two houses involved, both facing the west-side southbound lane of Ward Parkway, may just be the most significant block in Kansas City (Figure 17).[32]

Figure 16. George W. Wright residence, 5940 Ward Parkway, c. 1927. The Romanesque arcade is barely visible today. Photograph, 1992.

The irony of this fact is that the houses are not on land controlled at any time by J. C. Nichols. A section of this most prestigious part of Ward Parkway was bought up by Harry Clark during the period when Nichols and Kessler were attempting to lay out Ward's land in the Sunset Hill subdivision. Clark obtained only the east portion of blocks leading west toward State Line Road along Ward Parkway from Fifty-ninth to Sixty-third Streets. Nichols later obtained control of the land west of Clark's, including frontage on State Line, as well as the land south of Sixty-third Street on both sides of the Parkway.

Michael Katz paid for the construction of his "medieval" structure out of earnings from a drugstore chain he co-owned and managed with his brother, Isaac. "Ike and Mike" Katz, as they were popularly known, established Katz drugstores throughout the Midwest during the 1920s. Brother Isaac built a house in the immediate neighborhood (but not on Ward Parkway) at approximately the same time. Michael was the more publicity conscious of the pair, and that fact may have been one cause of his kidnapping on Ward Parkway in 1930. Kidnappings for ransom were on the upswing as the national economy worsened in late 1929 and early 1930.

Michael Katz was driving north on Ward Parkway in his Packard sports roadster from his new house toward his downtown office on the morning of March 18, 1930. A second car forced Katz's vehicle to the curb near the intersection of Ward Parkway and Fifty-fifth Street; one of the two men in the second car climbed on Katz's running board, knocked the surprised retailer unconscious, and climbed in to drive the

Packard off, following his accomplice in the attack vehicle. An eyewitness turned in the information to police officers who were stationed nearby (Nichols and his residents always insisted on good police protection; they usually got it). The officers jumped to the conclusion that because Tom Pendergast, Jr., lived with his parents just three blocks north of the Katz residence and because he drove a Packard like the one described (although the Pendergast vehicle was a different color from the one stolen), the target must have been the political boss's son. This bit of confusion brought on by the proximity of several well-known Kansas Citians living on Ward Parkway gave even more urgency to the effort of finding the kidnappers than would have otherwise been the case.[33]

Within two hours young Tom Pendergast was discovered by police to be safely in class at Rockhurst College, a fine Jesuit school located on the east edge of Nichols's developments. Later in the day the kidnappers relayed their cash demands to Michael's brother Isaac. After a two-day series of negotiations, a $100,000 payoff was agreed to and Michael Katz was freed. The kidnappers left him hooded but otherwise unbound and unharmed in a small park in the northeast residential section of Kansas City. Michael Katz came home to his medieval retreat on Ward Parkway as probably the second-best-known resident on the famed thoroughfare.[34] Katz continued to live in the dwelling until his death in 1961. Today the house is owned by a retired bank vice president and his wife, who live ever so much more quietly than did the first owner.

Figure 17. Michael Katz residence, Ward Parkway, 1930. Photograph, 1992.

Directly across the street from the Wright and Katz houses, and built before either of them, is the residence at 5921 Ward Parkway originally constructed by trade school and early radio pioneer Emory J. Sweeney. Although this residence is less architecturally distinctive than others in the neighborhood, the site has had a series of quite interesting owners. Sweeney built the structure just after World War I to house his family of six daughters and four sons. The site originally comprised five acres, but one lot to the south facing Ward Parkway has since been sold off, while several others were carved out of the eastern section of the plot facing Fifty-ninth Street Terrace. Sweeney used the extra acres as a playground for his brood of youngsters.

In the pre–World War I era Sweeney conceived a plan to establish a training school for young men to instruct them in automobile mechanics. He correctly guessed that the automobile age was on its way and that there would be a shortage of trained mechanics. The school was quite successful and generated significant revenues for several years. The house went up during this period. After the war, Sweeney's school suffered a setback when several of his students died in the influenza epidemic that swept the country. While Sweeney had no direct responsibility for the deaths, rumors circulated that the dormitory arrangements for the young mechanics-to-be might have encouraged the flu virus to pass more freely. At any rate, Sweeney fought back from this debacle to establish Kansas City's second radio station, WHB, in 1922, both as a training station for

Figure 18. Emory J. Sweeney residence, 5921 Ward Parkway, c. 1920s.

Figure 19. Emory J. Sweeney residence, 5921 Ward Parkway, c. 1920s. Pool and grounds.

his students and as an advertising medium for his expanded trade school offerings. Ultimately nothing worked: the school closed, the station sold, and Sweeney reluctantly had to give up his spacious abode (Figures 18 to 20).[35]

The exterior of the Sweeney house is faced with warm orange and yellow brick. A somewhat pretentious porch with four Corinthian columns projects from above the second-floor level in the center of the front. The regularity of window openings on the third floor indicates something of the utility they represent—most of the ten children's bedrooms were located there. Not visible from the front is a third-floor combined ballroom and theater, which the Sweeney children used to present evening entertainments for their parents and visitors. The house includes a total of thirty-three rooms.[36] Sweeney sold the site to lumberman Harry L. Dierks, whose son-in-law, Dwight Sutherland, already owned the Corrigan house. For many years the Dierks Lumber Company was one of the leading wholesale and retail lumber dealers in Kansas City. After Harry Dierks died in 1940, his wife, Katherine, lived in the residence until her death in 1951. At that time she willed the somewhat decrepit mansion to the Kansas City Archdiocese of the Roman Catholic Church. Both the Sweeney and the Dierks fami-

Figure 20. Emory J. Sweeney residence, 5921 Ward Parkway, c. 1920s, Playground for the Sweeney children, now subdivided into building lots.

lies were of that faith. For fifteen years the site served as the official residence of the resident archbishop.[37]

The property returned to private ownership in 1967 and passed through a number of owners until 1985, when its then-owner consented to have the house become the Designer Showcase House for the Kansas City Symphony League. The resulting publicity resulted in the sale of the property to a Kansas City resident named Farhad Azima.

Azima is an interesting individual who adds much to the current flavor of the Ward Parkway neighborhood, although there is little evidence that he has much contact with his neighbors. When he purchased 5921 Ward Parkway in 1985, Azima was president of RACE Airways, headquartered in Madrid, Spain. Prior to its bankruptcy in 1983, Azima had also operated Global Airways as a charter airline out of Kansas City International Airport. In 1986 a RACE plane reportedly carried twenty-three tons of unspecified armaments to Teheran, Iran, via Spain and Yugoslavia, as a part of what has become known as the Iran-Contra Affair. In 1991 Azima operated a company called Aviation Leasing Group with offices in Kansas City and London. The Kansas City office is located in a small two-story building across the street from the original J. C. Nichols shopping area at Fifty-second and Brookside Boulevard. What kind of business is conducted by Aviation Leasing Corporation is not entirely clear either to investigators or to the general public.[38] One meets, or at least sees, some of the most interesting people in Kansas City on Ward Parkway.

Although it may seem safe to conclude that Ward Parkway between Fifty-third Street and Meyer Circle is the residential address of the rich and famous (Figure 21), if not necessarily the respected and well-born, a balanced presentation of this grand avenue must include the information that there are some very ordinary houses in a three-block section of the west side of the roadway between Sixtieth and Sixty-third Streets. This segment, which is just south of the block that includes the Sweeney, Katz, and Wright residences, with all their size and architectural variety, is a continuation of the real estate controlled during the 1920s and 1930s by Harry Clark rather than by J. C. Nichols.

The original plats filed for this Suncrest subdivision indicate that Clark planned to have large houses built on large lots, just as Nichols had required. The problem is that Clark lost control of the property in the

Figure 21. Ornamental stone piers with commemorative World War I plaques, Meyer Circle, Ward Parkway, 1924. Henry J. Haskell residence (background).

Figure 22. View of Ward Parkway, west side between Sixtieth and Sixty-third streets. Photograph, 1992.

mid-1930s. Beginning in 1936 a number of houses were built that hardly conform to the size and scope one would expect from a Ward Parkway location anywhere else in this prestigious section. Contractors built all the houses in the 6100 block during the late 1930s, but on lots that generally are no more than 60 feet wide and 125 feet deep. The 6200 block of the west side of Ward Parkway lay vacant until 1951–52, when four houses went up on less street frontage than that occupied by the Sweeney house alone. Needless to say, there are no architecturally distinctive structures in this section. Apparently even Ward Parkway had to pay the price of the Depression in certain segments. The fact that later land purchasers were able to carve up the larger lots designed by developer Clark because he had lost control of the area speaks to the importance of the continuity of influence and control by the Nichols Company in the remaining segments of Ward Parkway down to Meyer Boulevard (Figure 22).

The Nichols Company's subdivisions south of Meyer Circle were developed after the Depression as well. While the distinctiveness of architectural style and indeed the very size of the post-Depression houses on Nichols-developed land is certainly inferior to the earlier sections, the lot sizes remained large, which gives the passerby a sense of some continuation of the grandeur of the more northerly portion of the parkway. Only in the unfortunate three-block segment of Suncrest are the houses both small and cramped on insufficient lot space.

While there are other residences of interest on the street, none carries the individuality of the ones on which the focus has been most closely applied. Certainly current residents continue much of the tradition of wealth and influence that owning a residence in this premier segment of Ward Parkway has historically implied. One of the two brothers who founded the nation's largest tax preparation company is a resident, as is the third-generation president of one of the leading truck-freight companies in the region. Older money is represented by the continued presence of widows of some of the city's wealthier grain-brokerage elite and bankers.

Nichols was convinced that a variety of outdoor decorative pieces would lend greater value to the parkway in the minds of potential buyers. As a result, he sprinkled the median with an assortment of items he alleged were Renaissance works of art imported secretively from Italy. In fact, he and landscape architect Herbert S. Hare contracted with manufacturing firms in Italy that turned out this type of work in mass quantities (Figures 23 to 27).

Figure 23. Decorative iron gates, looking south toward Meyer Circle. Installed by J. C. Nichols Company.

Regardless of the size of their houses or their bank accounts, Ward Parkway residents and their neighbors on the intersecting side streets retain into the 1990s a desire that the premier residential avenue of the city should maintain something of its historical character even as it carries tens of thousands of commuters to and from work (43,040 cars per average weekday as of September 1990). A 1991 incident brought this fact home quite clearly.[39]

Figure 24. General view of gates, stone fences, and urns in the Meyer Circle area.

Figure 25. Marble and iron fence with seating area, south side of Meyer Circle.

Figure 26. Dove vase, located near Meyer Circle.

Figure 27. Low stone fences and decorative urns, one of six at Meyer Circle. Photograph, 1924.

MEYER CIRCLE

For more than a decade Kansas City, Missouri, officials, usually in the person of the Board of Commissioners of Parks and Boulevards, which has direct responsibility for maintenance of Ward Parkway, had floated plans for altering Meyer Circle. Repeatedly the proposals were rejected by residents. Meanwhile, several serious traffic accidents, some of which caused fatalities, occurred at the intersection, which is almost the only traffic circle in the entire city.[40]

Essentially without warning in the early spring of 1991, Park and Boulevard personnel descended on Meyer Circle and proceeded to remove the decorative fountain in preparation for changes designed, according to a spokesman for the Park Board, to give cars "a little wiggle room." The stated purpose of the changes as they began was to "repair curbs and fix drainage and electrical problems with the Sea Horse Fountain." The total job was expected to cost $100,000 (Figures 28 and 29).[41]

In less than three weeks it became clear that the project was much greater in scope than was first announced, according to published reports. The Park Board employees were constructing an entirely new, higher wall to go around the fountain. After removing and examining the statuary in the fountain, the city employees learned that the existing statuary would have to be replaced because of deterioration. It was also announced that the traffic patterns were going to be adjusted after all.

The primary objection of residents was the height of the new wall that would enclose the fountain. Park officials estimated that a four- to five-foot wall would be needed to fix drainage problems that were beyond repair within the limits of the two-foot wall that had enclosed the fountain since its placement in 1925 by the Nichols Company. One resident stated that the new wall, more than twice as high as the previous one, "looks like the Berlin Wall has moved to Meyer Circle." It is significant that the *Kansas City Star* considered this to be front-page news.[42]

Shortly after this, a meeting of representatives of fifteen homes associations (all in J. C. Nichols Company–developed areas) met "to voice opposition to the Meyer Circle reconstruction project." The associations represented more than 10,000 Kansas City, Missouri, residents living in the general area. The basic opposition formed around the issue of the height of the retaining wall of the fountain. Residents objected that

Figure 28. Fountain, Meyer Circle, donated by the J. C. Nichols Company to the Ward Parkway region. Photograph, c.1940.

the higher wall would obstruct the view of the fountain as a decorative piece, disrupt "the vista across the circle in every direction," and obstruct the view of automobile drivers near the intersection.[43]

At a public meeting attended by seventy-five residents representing the various homes associations, the president of the Armour Hills association, Brad Max, stated that "What has been destroyed is the element of openness." Park Board representatives explained that they would use landscaping to scale ground up to the fountain so that only two feet of the wall would actually show, and that the fountain itself would be raised to make it just as visible as before.[44]

Within three days of the meeting, the Park Board suspended work on the fountain temporarily. Beatrice Davis, the president of another homes association and wife of a former mayor of the city, commented that she had fielded complaints about the wall from people living miles from the circle. "The importance of Meyer Circle transcends the particular neighborhood," she said. The newspaper writer commented that "Some of Kansas City's finest homes stand along Ward Parkway just north of Meyer Circle." It should be noted that by the time work was halted a little over a month after it began, the Park Board's estimate of the cost of improving and repairing the fountain had tripled to $300,000.[45]

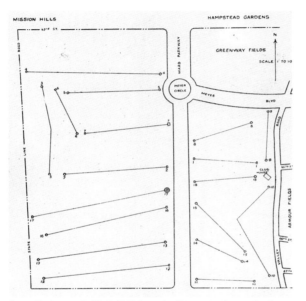

Figure 29. Armour Fields Golf Club, south of Meyer Circle. Membership by ownership of lot or residence from the J. C. Nichols Company.

Finally, almost two months after the first work had begun on the traffic circle and the fountain it encloses, a compromise was reached. The Park Board voted to cut off thirty-two inches of already-completed fountain wall and install an underground drainage system (costing an estimated $8,000) to handle the drainage problem park engineers had cited as the reason for the higher wall in the first place. Lowering the wall would cost approximately $25,000. Area residents, led by Mrs. Davis, had already raised over $20,000 privately to pay for the alterations. After the vote was taken, the outgoing chairperson of the Park Board observed that the clamor to lower the wall around the fountain had come from throughout the metropolitan area. She likened the circle to the Middle East, saying that it was "a small area with a lot of controversy."[46]

As if to underscore the sentimental ties of residents to this location on Ward Parkway, a man from Overland Park, Kansas, who had grown up in the neighborhood reminisced to the reporter about his senior prom. He recalled that on the morning after the senior dance, he went to Meyer Circle "and watched the sun come up. That was in 1927."[47]

The importance of this controversy really has nothing to do with the wisdom or lack thereof exhibited by the city officials involved. What was demonstrated was that area residents, supported by many who by then lived in other parts of the metropolitan area, had rallied to obtain a change in plans that they believed would better retain the sense of openness and order that Ward Parkway and its centerpiece, Meyer Circle, held in their collective memory. Thus, in spite of the fact that the planned parade boulevard had turned into a major traffic artery of the city, residents fought loudly and with their pocketbooks to keep that part of Ward Parkway looking something like they remembered it. With that kind of determination, this grand avenue of America may not soon suffer the change and deterioration that has beset so many of the others as the neighborhoods change and the cities decay. In that respect Ward Parkway can truly continue to serve as a symbol of Kansas City's determination to retain some aspects of its more opulent past.

Chapter Twelve

WILSHIRE
Boulevard

Los Angeles, California

In art as in life, Wilshire Boulevard has loomed large in the Los Angeles psyche. In literature, painting, and film, the 15.6-mile-long avenue has played a dominant role in the world's image of Los Angeles and in the city's image of itself. In Mark Lee Luther's popular novel, *The Boosters* (1923), two Angelenos discuss the westward development of the city, particularly the pastoral Hampton Gardens. "Do you happen to have seen that tract?" one of them asks. "'Out Wilshire way?' he said. 'I walked through there last Sunday. They have a chance to do something rather fine on those rolling hills with their sweeping mountain view.... I wish they'd stick to Spanish or Italian styles. Nothing suits this part of the country so well.'"[1]

Sixty-five years later in Bret Easton Ellis's acclaimed novel, *Less Than Zero* (1986), the tone had become more urban and considerably more violent: "When we got to Rip's apartment on Wilshire, he leads us into the bedroom. There's a naked girl, really young and pretty, lying on the mattress. Her legs are spread and tied to the bedposts and her arms are tied above her head.... Spin digs the syringe into her arm. I just stare. Trent says 'wow.'"[2]

Yet the quintessential treatment of the street and the city occurred in the 1940s in the *noir* novels of Raymond Chandler. In *The Lady in the Lake,* "He drove down to Wilshire and we turned east again. Twenty-five minutes brought us to the Bryson Tower, a white stucco palace with fretted lanterns in the forecourt and tall date palms...up marble steps through a Moorish archway, and over a lobby that was too big and a carpet that was too blue.... There was a desk and a night clerk with one of those mustaches that get stuck under your fingernail."[3]

---

essay by Thomas S. Hines

In *The Little Sister*, Chandler's protagonist admits, "'I used to like this town…. A long time ago. There were trees along Wilshire Boulevard. Beverly Hills was a country town. Westwood was bare hills…. Hollywood was a bunch of frame houses on the inter-urban line. Los Angeles was just a big dry sunny place with ugly homes and no style, but good hearted and peaceful. It had the climate they just yap about now. People used to sleep out on porches. Little groups who thought they were intellectual used to call it the Athens of America. It wasn't that, but it wasn't a neon-lighted slum either."[4]

Chandler's biographer, Philip Durham, confirmed the novelist's power as an image maker. "A few years ago," he recounted in 1963, "a story was told of an English girl arriving in Los Angeles for the first time. She was picked up at the railroad station by her host, who drove her through downtown Los Angeles on the way to his home in Westwood Village. The English girl made no comment as she observed the civic buildings and the streets filled

Figure 1. *Wilshire Boulevard, Los Angeles*, 1964. Painting by David Hockney.

with more automobiles than the sidewalks were with pedestrians. But suddenly she shouted, 'Wilshire Boulevard.' The host, unable to account for so much enthusiasm over Wilshire, looked to the girl for an explanation. Wilshire, the visitor said, was one of the most frequently traveled streets in Raymond Chandler's stories and now that she was on it she was oriented and was at home in the city…."[5]

If Wilshire figured prominently in the Los Angeles novel, it was inevitable that it would also appear in the city's "own" medium, the movies. Local tour guides ballyhooed Wilshire's Westlake Park as "Charlie Chaplin's Bath Tub" since many of his early comedies were filmed around the basin there.[6] In the late 1940s, ironically, the palatial home of the silent film star Norma Desmond in Billy Wilder's *Sunset Boulevard* was actually the Getty mansion on Wilshire near Hancock Park. In 1988, Steve De Jarnett shot his visually brilliant nuclear fantasy *Miracle Mile* almost entirely within a five-block stretch of the avenue, with much of the action centering at "Johnnie's," the legendary pop architecture fast-food restaurant at Wilshire and Fairfax.

The painter Edward Ruscha interpreted another Wilshire landmark from the same area in his *Los Angeles County Museum on Fire* (1965–68). He also gave the title *Wilshire Boulevard* to a painting of a late-modern, 1950-ish apartment house (1965). His contemporary David Hockney used the same blunt nomenclature for a typical painting of 1964, with figures, palm trees, and most prominently, a street sign reading "Wilshire Blvd. 2800" (Figure 1).[7]

ORIGINS

The modern street that inspired such tributes followed roughly the imprint of ancient animal and Indian paths and of Spanish explorers' trails westward from the pueblo on the Los Angeles River to the Pacific Ocean. A polymathic developer, Gaylord Wilshire, had in 1895 honored himself by giving his name to the principal street in his new subdivision west of Westlake Park on the outer fringes of the original pueblo boundaries. Before that in the late 1880s, Orange, a street on the same axis, had developed from the eastward edge of Westlake Park to the center of downtown—later in the twentieth century to become the eastern terminus of Wilshire. Even earlier, in 1875, appeared Nevada Avenue in Santa Monica, one of the two major streets in the gridiron plan of its founder, John Jones, a United States senator from Nevada. Nevada Avenue was later

extended from the ocean to the Sawtelle Veterans Center by the legendary Abbott Kinney, later the founder of the fantastic seaside town of Venice. As such, Nevada would become the western end of Wilshire, linking up with a section of the same phantom thoroughfare in the paper town of "Sunset" from the 1880s, whose curving main street was logically dubbed "Sunset Boulevard." Though the town never materialized and the name Sunset Boulevard was later given to Wilshire's great rival avenue to the north, the first Sunset Boulevard in the proposed

Figure 2. Map of Los Angeles and suburbs, 1906.

town of Sunset became the winding stretch of Wilshire that would run through Westwood Village, the latter a partial reification of the doomed town of Sunset.[8]

Halfway between downtown and Santa Monica, east of the dormant "Sunset," Beverly Hills was born in 1906 with its main east-west avenue joining the incipient Wilshire corridor (Figure 2). A connecting strip between Santa Monica and Beverly Hills through the old forgotten "Sunset" and the vast veterans complex at Sawtelle formed another important linkage, as did the so-called Miracle Mile and Wilshire Center sections east of Beverly Hills in the 1920s. Only in 1934 was the ultimate Wilshire Boulevard finally completed with a causeway cut through Westlake Park. From the north-south line of Grand Avenue downtown to the ocean front in Santa Monica, a completed Wilshire Boulevard surged unbroken for 15.6 miles (Figure 3).[9]

By the mid-twentieth century, Wilshire was acknowledged not only as LA's greatest street, but as one of the great thoroughfares of the planet, largely because it harbored such important businesses and institutions for such a very long and variegated distance. "Wilshire Boulevard," wrote journalist David Lantis in 1960, "stretching westward from the downtown district to the Pacific strand, had become the city's contribution to the famous streets of the world, along with the Champs-Élysées, Broadway, Michigan Boulevard...." One impressed visitor invoking Alexander Woolcott exclaimed that it was "just what God would have done if he had the money."[10]

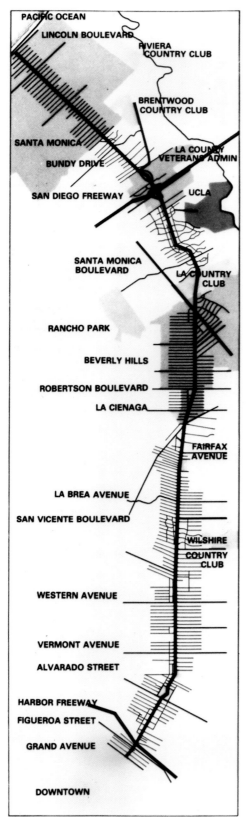

Figure 3. Map of Wilshire Boulevard, from downtown to the ocean, 1981.

Wilshire seemed to most observers to be relatively "contained," with a definite beginning at Grand Avenue downtown and a definite ending at the ocean cliffs in Santa Monica. Each end had, in various ways, a fittingly grand setting—the skyscrapers around Pershing Square at the eastern terminus and the Pacific Ocean at the western end. And there was considerable grandeur in between. Though sections of Wilshire would rise and fall in degrees of urban vitality over the years, the street neither dribbled out at either end nor sagged in the middle. In these ways it has usually seemed an exception to Los Angeles's reputation as a city of endless suburban sprawl or of countless "suburbs in search of a city." Once seen as an extension of the original downtown and then as a stretched-out "rival downtown" itself, Wilshire achieved a relatively self-contained mix of residential, commercial, cultural, and governmental elements, similar in certain ways to West Berlin's postwar Kurfurstendamm.

Still, as a linear spine of a high demographic and architectural density, Wilshire evoked a kindred identity with another Los Angeles image—the false-front stage set of the Hollywood back lot. Columnist Matt Weinstock challenged the argument that by midcentury Wilshire had achieved any sense of grandeur or unity. "A motion picture prop man, in his wildest nightmare," he averred, "could not have dreamed up the fantastic hodge-podge that is Wilshire Boulevard. In its sixteen miles…Wilshire resembles nothing so much as a succession of movie sets strung out incongruously with no beginning, no ending, no pattern."[11]

Journalist Ralph Hancock also resisted the idea of Wilshire as a single self-contained line, arguing that, in fact, it shaped and reflected a much broader corridor of influence. "In the regional classification of scandal," he observed, "Wilshire is to Los Angeles as Park Avenue is to New York. A murder anywhere within five blocks of Park Avenue is automatically a 'Park Avenue murder.' A recent headline in a Los Angeles paper, 'Wilshire Raid Nets Dope,' didn't mean necessarily that the raid actually occurred on Wilshire Boulevard. The locale of this particular case was in the ten hundred block on South Irolo Street, three blocks from Wilshire."[12]

Hancock also noted that by 1950 there were over 200 businesses and institutions from hotels to mortuaries to beauty shops to churches all sporting the fancy name of "Wilshire." What an "irony of fate," Gaylord Wilshire wrote his friend George Bernard Shaw in 1922, that so many Los Angeles churches should have the name of a man who advocated socialism "and incidentally, of course, atheism."[13]

Writing a Los Angeles cover story for *National Geographic* in 1962, Robert De Roos, a native Angeleno, averred that upon "traveling the 15½-mile length of Wilshire Boulevard, I realized that this street is the unifying element in the diversity of Los Angeles. It ties together the city of today with the city's past; virtually everything that has happened to Los Angeles has happened or is represented on Wilshire."[14]

The Linear City

Other Los Angeles boulevards that crossed or ran parallel to Wilshire, such as Sepulveda, Vermont, La Brea, Santa Monica, Olympic, Pico, and Sunset, became, in the twentieth century, significant urban arteries and landmarks, but none came close to the relative "self-containment" that Wilshire had achieved. Wilshire reified perhaps more than any boulevard in the world the avant-garde nineteenth-century concept of the "linear city."

Historian George Collins has argued that the idea of the dense linear strip linking, but not subsidiary to, older nodes at either end can be found in varied forms as far back as Tell-El-Amarna, Egypt (fourteenth century B.C.), in Fatehpur Sikri, India (sixteenth century A.D.), and in Edinburgh, Scotland's, eighteenth-century New Town, but never was it so clearly enunciated as in the visionary planning of the nineteenth-century Spanish urbanist Arturo Soria y Mata (1844–1920).[15]

Soria was an administrative official who had served in the colonial diplomatic corps in Cuba and Puerto Rico. In the 1870s he founded one of Madrid's first tramways, which he administered for about ten years. Indeed rapid urban rail transit was the basis of his idea for *la ciudad lineal*, which he announced in a series of newspaper articles in the early 1880s. As if anticipating the seemingly infinite spaces of another Hispanically created city, Los Angeles, Soria's lineal city was to be a "single street of 500 meters width and of the length that may be necessary—such will be the city of the future, whose extremities could be Cadiz and St. Petersburg, or Peking and Brussels."[16]

Down the center of this "immense belt" would run "trains and trams, conduits for water, gas, and electricity, reservoirs, gardens, and at intervals, buildings for different municipal services—fire, sanitation, health, police, etc.,—and there would be resolved at once almost all the complex problems that are produced by the massive populations of our urban life." Because its density would expand along a single line in only two directions, the "city unites the hygienic conditions of country life to the great capital cities." On either side of the spinal column, two parallel strips would include intermingled units designed for work, recreation, and hous-

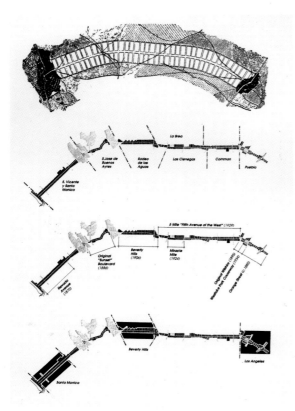

Figure 4. From top: Diagram of Soria y Mata's 1886 proposal for the Linear City, shown connecting two existing principalities; Wilshire Boulevard and its relationship to the pueblo, its common lands to the west, and five ranchos; chronology and names of the segments of development along Wilshire; and Wilshire as a vertebral connector of three independent municipalities. Diagram by Douglas Suisman.

ing, the latter of which would occupy approximately one-fifth of the allotted lands. Soria was certain of "the superiority of the Linear City—in the form of a vertebrate animal—over modern 'point cities,' 'organic cities,' and especially invertebrate cities." His scheme might function in three primary ways: first, as an urban link between already existing towns or cities; second, as a suburban green belt around a traditional, centrifugally oriented city; and third, as an instrument for developing and "colonizing" the underpopulated countryside.[17]

Architect Douglas Suisman, in his excellent short history of the Los Angeles street system, has observed that at one time or another, Wilshire Boulevard would exemplify all three aspects of Soria's model: as a park-like suburban district on the edge of downtown; as a connecting roadway between Los Angeles, Beverly Hills, and Santa Monica; and as a magnet for development along the open fields of the rancho lands that lay in between. Like many vital urban arteries, Wilshire's development resulted from a series of serendipitous convergencies over a long period of time, not from any conscious adherence to Soria's sophisticated vision. But, "that such a singular and powerful urban structure [as Wilshire] could emerge," Suisman argued, "without the benefit of an overall plan or public leadership is a remarkable emblem of Los Angeles urbanism, both in its achievement and in its unfulfilled promise" (Figure 4).[18] Though Wilshire property owners would long resist Soria's rapid transit lines on or under Wilshire Boulevard, and though, as in all Southern California, the automobile would rule the road, indeed Wilshire bore in many other ways remarkable similarities to Soria's Linear City.

THE BOULEVARD SYSTEM

Wilshire became in the late nineteenth and early twentieth centuries one of several major offshoots of the original nuclear village christened in 1781 by its Spanish founders *El Pueblo de la Reina de Los Angeles*—the Town of the Queen of the Angels. Its physical form followed roughly the 1573 Laws of the Indies, the long-established pattern of Spanish colonial settlement. This included a central rectangular plaza with a church and government house on its perimeter. From the plaza a rectilinear grid of streets spread outward two leagues, or 5.25 miles, on all four sides to the pueblo's boundaries, enclosing a 28-square-mile tract. In 1848, following the Mexican War, as United States forces arrived to take control of Los Angeles, a young lieutenant, Edward Ord, surveyed the new holdings and redirected the pattern for future development with two separate grids north and south of the plaza, sufficiently skewed to accommodate existing Hispanic street patterns in what would come to be downtown Los Angeles. Six years later in 1854, another surveyor, Major Henry Hancock, extended Ord's grid all the way to the pueblo's boundaries.[19]

The Hancock Survey, Suisman has noted, "realigned and extended Ord's grid just as Ord had done with the Spanish grid. But while Ord's blocks and lots had closely matched the fine grain of the existing town, Hancock's grid was on the super scale of the U.S. Land Survey which had been in effect since 1783." This would require a later subdivision of tracts into streets and blocks and saleable lots. In this way, Hancock "planted the first real seeds of the boulevard system, whose large scale intervals would prove perfectly suited to a city with so much territory to cover...." The course of the boulevards westward to the sea was affected, of course, by the less regular boundaries of the ranchos and common lands.[20]

HENRY GAYLORD WILSHIRE

Into these emerging patterns of late-nineteenth-century Los Angeles strode Henry Gaylord Wilshire, a figure so colorfully contradictory that he would come to seem over the years a quintessential Los Angeles character. Born in 1861 in Cincinnati, Ohio, into a wealthy family with substantial gas and railroad holdings, Wilshire grew up across the street from the future president, William Howard Taft. He attended Harvard for a year, taking a philosophy course from William James, connections he later exploited to prove that "a wealthy and intelligent man could also be a socialist." Indeed, wrote Howard Quint, a leading historian of American socialism, Wilshire was "something of a poseur, which was unfortunate because he possessed a keen mind, personal warmth, and generosity of spirit."[21]

After Harvard, Wilshire returned briefly to Cincinnati for unprofitable business ventures before moving to California in the mid-1880s to search for success in citrus farming and land development. His course as a capitalist entrepreneur was only slightly deflected in 1887 with his discovery of socialism through Edward Bellamy's utopian novel *Looking Backward*, which led to his founding of the local socialist journal, *The Weekly Nationalist,* and to his running unsuccessfully in 1890 as the Nationalist Party's candidate for the House of Representatives. He was the first American socialist actively to seek a seat in Congress. Despite a vigorous campaign that featured a debate with Henry George, Wilshire lost the race but not the enthusiasm for combat. "I classify all men into two great classes—fools and Socialists," he wrote.[22]

In 1891, after coming into an inheritance, Wilshire temporarily left Los Angeles for the greener socialist—and social—pastures of New York. Despite his lack of legal training, he ran there unsuccessfully as the Socialist Labor candidate for attorney general of New York. The inveterate traveler, he spent four years in England between 1891 and 1895 involving himself in Socialist circles and cultivating friendships with notable

Britons, including particularly George Bernard Shaw, with whom he shared a close physical resemblance. He also apparently shared Shaw's lady friend, Mrs. Stella Patrick Campbell, who later revealed love letters from Wilshire as well as Shaw. In England, incredibly, he stood as a Socialist candidate for Parliament, again unsuccessfully, and returned to Los Angeles in 1895 for another incongruously mixed period of commercial, socialist, and social activities. In the latter category he was one of the founding members of the elite Los Angeles Country Club at Pico and Alvarado, which after its move westward in 1910 straddled the rural lane that would later become Wilshire Boulevard between Westwood and Beverly Hills.[23]

In December 1900, Wilshire's journalistic ambitions resurfaced with a second publishing venture, *The Challenge*, the name of which he intended as a reminder of the standing challenge he had earlier made to debate William Jennings Bryan on the relative merits of capitalism and socialism. At various times during the 1890s Wilshire had offered Bryan as much as $10,000 to meet him on this issue. Bryan ignored him and Wilshire claimed that the Nebraskan feared to confront him. Failing to engage Bryan personally, Wilshire carried his flamboyant style to the pages of *The Challenge*. Still, Howard Quint observed, the journal "had both literary and editorial talent and, contrary to most Socialist magazines of the time…was a well edited and handsomely produced periodical, comparing favorably with many of the better non-Socialist journals of opinion."[24]

Yet to Wilshire, Los Angeles seemed too small and provincial to support his journal and, in 1901, he moved it to Manhattan. It was an ill-advised move since the hysteria over the recent assassination of President McKinley in Buffalo had led to an effort to quell all radical publications. The tactic used was a denial by postal authorities of second-class mailing privileges, but the resourceful Wilshire eluded this gambit by removing the journal to Toronto, Canada, where he mailed copies under the new name of *Wilshire's* unimpeded back across the border. The cost of publication was high, but Wilshire borrowed money from his mother and other wealthy radicals and kept it afloat. He also offered subscription prizes, including player pianos, billiard tables, silk shirts, oil painted tapestries, collie dogs, and a ten-acre fruit ranch in Ontario, California.[25]

Other socialists criticized *Wilshire's* for its having a literary and intellectual, rather than political, focus, to which Wilshire replied that his magazine had "never pursued the narrow petty policy of ignoring good merely because the good does not come from an accredited Socialist source." And indeed Wilshire was able to publish an impressive number of the best thinkers and writers of the early twentieth century, including George Bernard Shaw, Charlotte Perkins Gilman, Jack London, Leo Tolstoy, Eugene Debs, George Herron, and Gustavus Myers. Wilshire interviewed John D. Rockefeller on the trust problem and Wilshire's wife, Mary, an early Jungian psychoanalyst, contributed a column with feminist calls for a greater degree of female participation in political and economic spheres. Upton Sinclair avowed that he was converted to socialism by reading *Wilshire's*. Meanwhile, the editor stayed in the public eye, promoting and hosting the 1906 visit to America of the Russian writer Maxim Gorky.[26]

While his staff ran the magazine, Wilshire spent another four years in England from 1910 to 1914 promoting socialism and selling stock in his Bishop, California, gold mine—chiefly to his socialist friends. Yet, with the outbreak of World War I, he returned to California, financially broken. The last issue of the maga-

Figure 5. Left: Gaylord Wilshire. Right: Advertisement for Gaylord Wilshire's quack health remedy "Ionaco."

zine was published from Bishop in February 1915. Soon even the mine gave out, and Wilshire resorted for sustenance and entertainment to the promotion of an electrically charged belt, the "Ionaco," which he claimed would cure a variety of diseases, including cancer (Figure 5). It was a sad last hurrah for the socialist entrepreneur. Heavily in debt, he died on September 6, 1927, in New York City. The *New York Times* and *Los Angeles Times* each carried respectful three-paragraph obituaries.[27]

Even though something of an itinerant, Wilshire had continued to identify with Los Angeles during the last decades of his life, proclaiming in the brochure advertising his quack cure-all "Ionaco" that he was the "originator of Wilshire Boulevard…another achievement of a Californian whose activities have uniquely embraced many fields in art, literature, and science." He urged his readers to "go where you will around the world from Shanghai to Leningrad, from Capetown to Calcutta, from London to Cairo, and you will hear of the Wilshire District and Wilshire Boulevard of Los Angeles. It will be a monument to his foresight and vision for a thousand years." Indeed, next to Socialist journalism, real estate development was clearly Wilshire's forte.[28]

Wilshire had arrived in Los Angeles in 1886 at the height of the land boom with several thousand dollars that his father had given him to invest. With his brother and a friend, the future Army general Leonard Wood, he bought land in Long Beach, which he developed into what became that city's grand Ocean

Figure 6. Westlake Park, Wilshire Boulevard. Postcard, early twentieth century.

Avenue. In Orange County he did the same with land that became Commonwealth Avenue in Fullerton. In fact, when the boom collapsed, Wilshire retired to his walnut and citrus ranches in Fullerton, where he became one of the first farmers in Southern California to develop the grapefruit as a staple crop.[29]

In Los Angeles, he purchased a triangular wedge between Sixth and Seventh Streets and between the western edge of Westlake Park and the old pueblo boundary at Hoover Street. On December 21, 1895, Wilshire filed a subdivision plot in the Los Angeles County Recorder's office, offering to donate the central 12,000-foot-long "Benton Boulevard" to run west from Westlake Park to another north-south boulevard to be given by the city (Figure 6). This would form a T-square, thus defining his subdivision. The north-south street was originally to have been called Wilshire Boulevard, but Wilshire must have realized the westward potential of Benton, and he presciently switched the names of the streets so that his surname would grace the east-west corridor. Initially Wilshire envisioned his namesake to be a grand avenue of stately homes, buffered against the commercial downtown by Westlake Park. To ensure that identity, he persuaded the city council to pass an ordinance guaranteeing that Wilshire would remain "an open boulevard, along which no railroad franchise shall ever be granted or laid thereon...nor that wagons carrying merchandise or any heavy trucking be permitted." But there was no such provision against a ubiquitous Los Angeles art form, the billboard, a medium boosted by Wilshire himself. He filled the empty lots on Wilshire Boulevard with such signs, most of them initially advertising his own real estate offerings.[30]

AT HOME ON WILSHIRE BOULEVARD

Wilshire's dream of a grand boulevard of impressive homes was quickly confirmed when Harrison Gray Otis, the powerful editor of the decidedly non-Socialist *Los Angeles Times*, became his first customer by buying the corner lot at Wilshire and Park View and building a large villa, "The Bivouac," in the fashionable Mission Revival style (Figure 7). Shortly thereafter, the neighboring lot to the west on Wilshire sold to Otis's friendly business rival, the editor of the Los Angeles *Express*, Edwin T. Earl, who was even more famous for inventing the refrigerated railcar, an event of great significance for the California citrus industry. Earl built a handsome brick mansion designed by the noted architect Ernest Coxhead (Figure 8). Like other Wilshire Boulevard mansions through the years, the Earl house was later featured on a color postcard entitled "A California Home, Wilshire Boulevard, Los Angeles." Otis and Earl, observed the journalist, Ralph Hancock, "though fre-

Figure 7. Harrison Gray Otis residence, c. 1895, architect unknown. Wilshire Boulevard at left, Edwin T. Earl house in center background.

quently attacking each other in their editorial columns, were as chummy as any good neighbors with a mutual back fence."[31]

Figure 8. Edwin T. Earl residence, 1895–97, Ernest Coxhead, architect.

More distinguished than Otis's "Bivouac" next door, the Earl House was one of Coxhead's, and Wilshire Boulevard's, greatest early architectural achievements. Coxhead had moved as a young man in his twenties from his native England to Los Angeles during the boom of the 1880s, presumably due to personal and architectural connections he had cultivated with officials of the Southern California diocese of the Episcopal Church. In the late 1880s, he consequently designed churches in Santa Ana, Pasadena, Sierra Madre, and Los Angeles, all inventive reinterpretations of the English Gothic tradition, in both its ecclesiologically purist forms and its High Victorian variations. In 1890 Coxhead moved his office to San Francisco, where his practice and reputation flourished. Whether or not Edwin Earl had known him in Los Angeles, it was logical that he should choose Coxhead as the architect of what he hoped would be a fashionable new mansion on LA's most fashionable new street. Coxhead originally designed a picturesquely rambling wooden shingle house evoking English and American East Coast precedents, but a fire caused extensive damage just before its completion and, while using the original plan and configuration, Coxhead redesigned the facade into a tauter, brick fortress-like composition.[32]

Historian Richard Longstreth, Coxhead's major interpreter, argues that while a reductive simplicity gave added strength to this more stripped exterior, the effect was "also made somewhat disquieting by the use of small, isolated pieces of ornament, the most conspicuous of which is a single Ionic column surrealistically supporting a tiny slice of entablature and pediment at the corner of the entrance porch." This mischievous element, moreover, suggested the mannered interior extravagances for which the generally plain and abstract exterior served as a foil. "Each room is a remote world," Longstreth observed, with "striking polarities of large and small scale, and ornate and simple embellishment…. In the living room, a great scrolled pediment looms above the fireplace, suspended as if it were a trophy from Baalbek hung on the wall of an art academy. Its size is made even more outrageous by the low ceiling and the flanking tiers of miniature orders. Across the room, Corinthian columns are isolated, again like fragments, punctuating curved bookshelves. The components are separated from their conventional context, and interact in an irregular space that is charged with contrasts between light and dark zones, plain and decorated surfaces." Even more fantastic motifs occurred in the decoration of the hallway, particularly in the overscaled fireplace, which reflected Coxhead's fascination with pre-Columbian Mayan architecture.[33]

Though no evidence survives to document Earl's participation and intentions as a client in such an important commission, Longstreth's speculations on the motifs of "this self-made millionaire, who was an ardent promoter of the region's special character" take the form of provocative questions that extend to other builders and promoters of Los Angeles and Wilshire Boulevard: "Did Earl share Coxhead's love of the unconventional, desiring a house so markedly different from the norm? Or was Coxhead simply reflecting the fantasy world that Angelenos were boosting, pulling out all the stops with a nouveau riche client who believed the design to be 'authentic'?" The answer seems to be that it was paradoxically something of both.[34]

As Wilshire developed westward, the leading citizens moved with it, sometimes bringing their houses with them. One family, at the turn of the century, moved their substantial mansion from downtown Figueroa to the corner of Lucerne and Wilshire, not only staying in the house while it was in transit, but holding a continuous party while the house was being moved. And sometimes houses were moved from Wilshire to the farther west side. The Pasadena architects Charles and Henry Greene, for example, designed an elegant Craftsman villa for Earle C. Anthony, the affluent Packard dealer, at the corner of Wilshire and Berendo in 1909. In 1923, however, because the area was changing from residential to commercial, the film actor Norman Kerry purchased the house and moved it to Beverly Hills (Figure 9). Henry Greene was engaged to handle the re-siting and the design of the garden.[35]

The Anthony House was one of the half-dozen acknowledged masterworks, or "ultimate bungalows," of the Greenes and, as such, one of the greatest houses ever built on Wilshire Boulevard. It was the only example in Los Angeles proper on a select list of the architects' creations that included the contemporary Gamble and Blacker houses in Pasadena, the Pratt house in Ojai, and the Thorsen house in Berkeley. It followed the architects' preferred L-shaped configuration that opened the house via porches and pergolas to the rear and side gardens. Its faithful allegiance, however, to the ethic and aesthetic of the Arts and Crafts Movement led to a conflict between the designers and the client.[36]

Shortly after the house was completed, Mrs. Anthony, according to historian Randell Mackinson, became "disenchanted with the dim interiors, the abundance of wooden expression, and the bungalow character of the house" and summoned her architects to make various alterations. These included a painting of parts of the woodwork to lighten the interior. Her reaction to the natural quality of the design, Mackinson argues, "was an early indication that public taste was turning from the principles of the Arts and Crafts Movement to traditional designs which had previously been identified with affluence."[37]

Because the new century's pressing commercial imperatives made its street frontage too valuable for sustained residential use, Wilshire passed through its residential phase more quickly than its other American nineteenth-century counterparts. Throughout its history, however, elitist neighborhoods continued to thrive directly north and occasionally south of the avenue. These included the posh Hancock Park district between Normandy and Highland, developed in the first decades of the century, and similar areas in Beverly Hills and Westwood that rose in the 1920s and 1930s.

Throughout the late 1890s and early 1900s, however, the *Los Angeles Times* reported frequently on the elegant new homes going up in the Wilshire corridor. On March 28, 1909, a columnist noted the recent opening and improvement of Wilshire Boulevard from Vermont west to Arlington, "which in scope, character and rapidity of home building growth today far surpasses the expectations of the most sanguine. Many fine homes of our best citizens now adorn Wilshire Boulevard, while many sales of the choice corners promise greater things for the future." The paper also recommended the nearby parallel rail lines to the north and the south and on the north-south axis of West Sixteenth Street, "a splendid service...forming the connecting link of the city with Hollywood."[38]

Figure 9. Earle C. Anthony residence, 1909, Greene and Greene, architects. Residence relocated from Wilshire Boulevard to Beverly Hills in 1923. Photograph, after 1923.

In the teens and twenties, not only business and professional people, but early movie celebrities lived in the posh Wilshire district. Joseph Schenck, president of United Artists, built for his wife Norma Talmadge the elegant Talmadge Apartments on Wilshire and Berendo across from the Anthony house. Actor Jackie Coogan lived behind a protective brick wall at the southwest corner of Oxford and Wilshire. Producer Thomas Ince built a house at Wilshire and Hobart. Mary Pickford lived on Wilshire at Fremont Place before she married Douglas Fairbanks and moved to Beverly Hills. More movie stars, however, lived north of Wilshire in the Hollywood Hills, commuting south to the shops, restaurants, and nightclubs that would rise on Wilshire in the 1920s.[39]

The urge to use the cachet of the boulevard's name in residential designations was exemplified in a *Los Angeles Times* headline in 1914 announcing the new "French Renaissance" mansion of C. M. Spitzer at Third and St. Andrews four blocks north of Wilshire. "Ohio banker to build superb Wilshire home," it announced.

Figure 10. Houses, hotels, and Model Ts. Wilshire Boulevard near Westlake Park, 1914.

The "new Wilshire show place" was designed by Spitzer and Burns and would cost approximately $100,000. On the same page, another article boasted of "the notable activity in the magnificent Wilshire district, where highly improved subdivisions are being opened and scores of expensive residences are being built on roomy lots." In the many phases of the city's growth, the *Times* reporter remarked, "none has been more remarkable than the transition from low priced barley fields to residential property valued at $10,000 per acre…in the district west of Westlake Park."[40]

Yet in the same article this journalist noted a new trend that would in time change the character of the boulevard—the growing prominence of the fashionable hotel district just west of Westlake Park and on the eastern edge of the Wilshire district (Figure 10). There, he noted, "The hotel men are claiming site after site…and are gradually but surely replacing the beautiful homes of the 'original Wilshire district' with splendid hostelries and apartments that compare in elegance with those of the metropolis itself." As a result, he observed, real estate prices had soared and had pushed residential development north, south, and especially west.[41]

THE CITY BEAUTIFUL

As private development in the early twentieth century was pushing the boulevard west and, in the process, producing the fashionable "Wilshire district," urban planning officials took note of the need to integrate public and private visions of the Wilshire that was to be. Exactly contemporary with the first decades of Wilshire's existence was the potent force in American urban planning—the City Beautiful movement. Largely influenced by Daniel Burnham's 1893 World's Columbian Exposition in Chicago, and recognizing Burnham as its father and major figure, the City Beautiful movement also included such other important figures as the peripatetic journalist-turned-planner Charles Mulford Robinson. Robinson shared Burnham's commitments to both historicist Beaux-Arts architecture and, at the same time, practical, forward-looking planning for transportation, circulation, commerce, and the public realm.[42]

Robinson's 1907 plan for "Los Angeles, the City Beautiful" included the customary proposals for "civic center" groupings of public and cultural institutions. It also spoke to the needs of outlying areas and neighborhoods and to the improvement of particular streets and of cross-town arteries. The juncture, for example, of Vermont and Wilshire Boulevards, Robinson believed, was of "a civic significance that should be marked." Wilshire, he believed, was more boulevard-like than anything else Los Angeles has. It should be further developed, its great width inviting a strip of middle parking for the whole length. As to the junction with Vermont, Robinson continued, failing to foresee the intersection's role as a traffic nexus, "Here is a place having no real traffic but demanding dignity of treatment, where a Rond Point, such as those which are so striking a feature of Paris, should be arranged." Wilshire never became a Champs Élysées with palm trees, but it steadily took on its own type of grandeur.[43]

Other planners with different visions and priorities offered other kinds of proposals. Seventeen years later, in 1924, a board consisting of Frederick Law Olmsted, Jr., Harlan Bartholomew, and Charles Henry Cheney argued in *A Major Traffic Street Plan for Los Angeles* that, in contrast to Robinson's plans, it would be "extravagant to attempt…a wide central park space" as in the Champs Élysées. Such a result, they argued, would be impractical. Rather, they proposed a "type of design in which a single wide roadway is the dominant feature." They also recommended the seemingly visionary course of extending Wilshire eastward across Westlake Park, absorbing and enlarging Orange Street, and extending the elongated Wilshire Boulevard through the old downtown as far east as Central Avenue and thence across a new bridge over the Los Angeles River to Boyle Heights. This ambitious recommendation was only partially carried out, as the Figueroa Street terminus of the old Orange/Wilshire axis was pushed through only to its ultimate eastern edge at Grand Avenue.[44]

In the same period, moreover, the city rezoned eastern Wilshire, from Westlake to Western Avenues, from class "B" residential to class "C" commercial. The city planning commission in the early 1920s had, in the spirit of Robinson's City Beautiful plan, deferred to downtown business interests that feared Wilshire as a political competitor. The commission then zoned Wilshire residential with the intention of making it a noncommercial parkway from downtown to the ocean. The east Wilshire property owners, however, claimed that the land was too valuable for anything less than commercial zoning and successfully persuaded the city council to overrule the planning commission. The rebuffed commission, then, in league with downtown merchants, petitioned for an election on the matter. After a heated campaign from both sides, the voters defeated the downtown merchants and confirmed the commercial designation of Wilshire by a three to two majority.[45]

DEVELOPMENT

In precisely the same years, developer A. W. Ross was setting in motion a transformation of what was then called Western Wilshire. His work would also illustrate the Olmsted team's sense of a future commercial street rather than a residential parkway. Yet the section west of La Brea that would become a bustling trade nexus by 1929 was in the early 1920s "a meandering dirt road flanked by barbed wire and barley fields" (Figure 11). La Brea Avenue, journalist Ralph Hancock observed, was "little more than a service road for the oil wells in the neighborhood.... The vast, barren acreage of the Hancock ranch, the last of the old Rancho La Brea, spread north of Wilshire to the hills.... There was not a residence or a building except for the occasional ramshackle farm house...." The most visible structure for miles around was a billboard proclaiming "Wilshire Boulevard Center—A. W. Ross, development."[46]

Figure 11. Wilshire Boulevard near Fairfax and La Cienega, c. 1908–10.

A quiet, soft-spoken man, Ross had been a moderately successful realtor in downtown Los Angeles since the 1890s. But in the early 1920s, he realized that the market was clearly moving westward. He later recalled his thinking for Ralph Hancock. First, he reasoned, "the business of this town is becoming more and more predicated on automobile transportation. Someday it will become a completely motorized town and nearly everyone will own a car. Now the question is, how far will they drive to do their shopping? Ten miles? Nope. Eight? Not unless they get better roads than they have now. Five? Maybe. Four? That's it. Four miles is no distance, a man could drive it in a horse and buggy in thirty minutes. In an automobile, he'd consider it his neighborhood."[47]

On a map of Los Angeles, then, Ross redlined a circle with a four-mile radius with the center on Wilshire roughly halfway between the dirt roads of La Brea and Fairfax as his new commercial nexus. This circle included the established residential districts of Westlake, Hancock Park, Hollywood, and West Adams Heights as well as such burgeoning areas as Beverly Hills to the west. As a beginning, Ross purchased from the owners of the old ranchos, La Cienegas and Rodeo de las Aguas, a tract of eighteen acres on the south side of Wilshire for $3,000 an acre, a fabulous sum at the time. Both friendly supporters and suspicious rivals believed that Ross had simply gone "crazy" and referred to the desolate tract as "Ross's bean patch" and "Ross's folly." But the speculative developer ignored them and continued purchasing land on either side of his property as well as across the street on the old Rancho La Brea. He subdivided his holdings and sold business lots on

Wilshire at $100 a front foot, a pittance compared to the hundreds of thousands such lots would ultimately fetch. Soon doubts subsided and other realtors joined the fray, often using bizarre and aggressive tactics to attract buyers. In 1923, at the height of the boom, one observer noted that Wilshire realtors "would literally run out of their offices and intercept automobiles which were driving slowly past; apparently they created many fresh prospects for subdivision lots from the running boards of automobiles."[48]

In 1925 Ross's previously unincorporated development became part of Los Angeles and fell heir to the city's classification of western Wilshire Boulevard as a "B" zone restricted to residential usage. In view of the recent election supporting a "C" classification for eastern Wilshire, Ross and other property owners challenged the planning commission and the downtown businessmen against their insistent opposition to giving over more of Wilshire to a commercial classification. The referendum that followed in 1926 was an even hotter contest than the earlier fight between the same two opposing sides. One tabloid cartoon, opposed to rezoning, featured a huge octopus with tentacles crushing beautiful homes on Wilshire but leaving untouched a line of large billboards with such "advertisements" as "Good location for cat and dog hospital" and "This home to be wrecked—splendid locations for filling stations, garages, hot dog stands, laundries, etc.—Greed and Grab, Agents." An accompanying article argued that "because Wilshire Boulevard is the principal street leading to the new University of California [in Westwood], the real estate speculators have seen an opportunity for enriching themselves...and they are asking *you* to use *your* vote to help them realize their financial ambitions." Though indeed the issues were much the same as in the earlier east Wilshire referendum, this time the electorate returned western Wilshire to residential classification.[49]

Undaunted, Ross and his cohorts resorted to what in Los Angeles was curiously called "spot zoning." Even though voters could dictate the overall classification of a district, the city council retained the right to rezone individual parcels. Property owners pressed for variances on the grounds that they were being denied the rights and price values enjoyed by east Wilshire developers. The popular movie actress Ruth Roland, for example, made headlines and was photographed with impressed and grinning councilmen when she petitioned for a variance to erect a commercial building and a filling station on her property at Wilshire and Fairfax. Such exceptions became the justification for granting each subsequent one until ultimately Ross's Wilshire was effectively rezoned commercial.[50]

In this instance, the piecemeal approach worked to the district's benefit since the quality of buildings along the street was more carefully scrutinized than under a system of free enterprise development. The city board reviewed and thus to a great degree controlled the final design and contemplated use of each planned building. Ross himself was also consulted on the plans before the presentations were made. His informal "quality codes" frowned upon too vivid red or green neon or neon with a nervous tic. Billboards were now discouraged. Attractively designed and, in the early years, relatively low-rise buildings frequently styled in the Spanish Colonial mode multiplied on the acres of "Ross's folly." Though he probably would have denied having a conscious and explicit "vision" for the area, Ross became the street's godfather, interested not only in selling property but in promoting the quality of the street's character and

Figure 12. Miracle Mile. Postcard.

Figure 13. Wilshire Boulevard near Western Avenue, looking east, 1940. Wilshire Boulevard Temple in left background, Pellisier Building in right background.

Figure 14. Wilshire Boulevard near Western Avenue, looking west, 1940. Pellisier Building at left, Spanish Colonial commercial buildings at right.

welfare. Under his guidance, for example, Wilshire became probably the first street in the world with coordinated Christmas decorations.[51]

Through 1928, Ross was still calling his original redlined area the Wilshire Boulevard Center when a friendly investor, Foster Stewart, noticing the bustling activity of the district, suggested that he name it the Miracle Mile. "I liked Stewart's idea," Ross later recalled. I talked to advertising men and also to merchants of the area. They all liked it. So I changed Wilshire Boulevard Center to Miracle Mile" (Figures 12, 13, and 14).[52]

NEW TOWNS

By 1929 the *Los Angeles Times* was marveling at the miracle: "Long retarded from the spectacular development that now is sweeping its way, Wilshire Boulevard is rapidly shaking its shackles, namely residential and income zoning restrictions. And, as various districts are opened for business, principal merchandising houses of Los Angeles are seizing the opportunity to place branches where, they assert, is the highest class purchasing power of Los Angeles."[53]

Beverly Hills, just west of Ross's Miracle Mile, developed more slowly even though it ultimately attracted an even higher class of "purchasing power," particularly along its central spine of Wilshire Boulevard. The young city lay on portions of the old 4,500-acre Rancho Rodeo de las Aguas, owned by Señora Rita Villa. She was the granddaughter of one of the first settlers of Los Angeles and the widow of another, who sold her holdings in 1854 to two Americans, Benjamin (Don Benito) Wilson and the ubiquitous Major Henry Hancock, who subdivided them and sold them to others. Attempts were made there in the 1870s to found a town called Santa Maria and in the boom of the 1880s to establish another one called Morocco, but these were not to last.[54] In 1906, however, a developer, Burton Green, of Beverly Farms, Massachusetts, organized the Rodeo Land and Water Company, which laid out subdivisions flanking Wilshire and Santa Monica Boulevards and named them Beverly and Beverly Hills, the latter becoming the name of the city when it was incorporated in 1914. Beverly Hills flourished during the boom of the 1920s thanks to the stimulus of the actor and pundit Will Rogers, who served as "honorary mayor" until his death in 1935. "Lots are sold so quickly and often here," he wrote in August 1923, "that they are put through escrow made out to the twelfth owner." As an extension of the Miracle Mile, Wilshire in Beverly Hills followed the same architectural patterns, with low-rise stores and office buildings of largely historicist styling. These gave way in the late 1920s and 1930s to various modernist modes and to taller and taller buildings (Figure 15).[55]

Beyond Beverly Hills and the sprawling acres of the Los Angeles Country Club rose Westwood Village, developed in the 1920s by Arthur Letts and the Janss Corporation on the lands of the Wolfskill Ranch and the older Rancho San Jose de Buenos Aires. The stretch of Wilshire that linked it with the city was roughly the same as the undulating street that had once been "Sunset Boulevard" of the phantom town of "Sunset" (Figure 16). Like the new University of California campus that would rise a mile to the north, the original buildings of this college town between Wilshire and UCLA would favor "Mediterranean" architecture, a romantic blending of various Spanish and Italian modes. Indeed, if Beverly

Figure 15. Wilshire Boulevard in Beverly Hills, looking west, 1931. Warner Theater in left foreground, Beverly Wilshire Hotel in left background, Van de Kamp's Bakery with windmill in right foreground.

325

Hills seemed a posh residential suburb of Ross's Miracle Mile district, Westwood in the late 1920s and 1930s conveyed the ambience of a stylish Hollywood version of a Mediterranean village amidst the bean fields.[56]

Between Westwood and Santa Monica lay one of the oldest establishments on what came to be Wilshire Boulevard—the Veterans home, hospital, and cemetery at Sawtelle, developed on land donated by the Wolfskill interests and Santa Monica's Senator Jones (Figure 17). Opened in 1888, seven years before Gaylord Wilshire pioneered his subdivision, the center was established to care for disabled soldiers of the Civil War as well as veterans of recent Indian campaigns. When the home reached its peak capacity around the turn of the century, Los Angeles families paid homage to the Cause by taking a picnic lunch and spend-

Figure 16. Wilshire Boulevard at Westwood Boulevard, 1937. Westwood Village and UCLA, upper right.

ing Sundays with the "dear old boys in blue." The dear old Confederate boys in gray were not permitted entry. Later the center would house veterans of the Spanish-American War and of America's twentieth-century wars. The Victorian "Stick" and Shingle-style barracks, demolished in the mid-twentieth century, were designed with exuberant panache by the firm of Peters and Burns. Only a few houses and the handsome chapel by J. Lee Burton (1900) would survive. By the 1990s the gingerbread chapel would be the oldest extant structure on all of Wilshire Boulevard.[57]

Figure 17. Sawtelle Veterans Center, Wilshire at Sawtelle, c. 1880. Dormitories at left, demolished. Chapel at right, extant.

In 1901, at Wilshire and Sawtelle, when the chapel was new and the center was flourishing, the Old Boys were paid a visit by none other than President McKinley. "A fine carriage had been procured," remembered Josephine Potter, who had come from Santa Monica for the occasion, "and four white horses were in harness, the two leaders being on loan from the Santa Monica Fire Department. For some reason the Los Angeles train had been delayed and by the time the presidential party arrived, the crowd was fit to explode with excitement. A great 'Hurrah!' went up as McKinley entered the carriage. Whistles blew! Horns sounded! And, unfortunately for the President, someone clanged a fire bell." Then, Miss Potter continued, "the next thing I remember is that the President's feet shot out from under him as he catatapulted into his seat, and the four-horse team was off in a cloud of dust." As the least commercial part of the boulevard, this spot remained dusty until 1928, when the government cooperated with the city to pave this last stretch of the boulevard as it traversed the grounds of the center on its way to Santa Monica.[58]

Traffic

In recognition of the street's growing prominence, various steps were taken in the late 1920s and early 1930s to confirm its status as a grand commercial avenue. In 1929 a cluster of Wilshire neighborhood groups "from Westlake Park to the sea" formed a parent organization to advertise and promote Wilshire as the "Fifth Avenue of the West." $100,000 was budgeted to boost the avenue as "a street of fine shops and office buildings, catering to the motorizing public." That motorizing public was increasing in geometric proportions. In February 1928, according to an official traffic check, the *Los Angeles Times* reported that Wilshire and Western was the busiest corner in the nation. About 74,755 vehicles passed through it on one particular Saturday and 64,405 traversed it the following Sunday. Traffic on weekdays was presumably even denser. By comparison, Chicago's Michigan Avenue at Wacker Drive clocked 62,459 vehicles on a day surveyed five months before. A similar survey counted 42,377 automobiles on New York's Park Avenue at Fifty-Seventh Street. The *Times* concluded, however, that the city should have mixed feelings about the numbers, which suggested prosperity but also problems. "Her street cars are jammed," it noted, "and her telephones are nests of bumble bees. Traffic is tramping upon the heels of her fondest dreams and her plans for keeping ahead of the procession have gone awry. A Boulder Dam would almost seem necessary to save us from traffic inundation.... Boston may have been laid out by cows, but Los Angeles was laid out by real estate men. No two appear to have cooperated."[59]

Several months later, in April 1929, the traffic records of the Wilshire-Western intersection were introduced in a lawsuit to remove the restrictions against commercial development of the Pellisier residential tract. Clarence Snetten, head of the Los Angeles Traffic Commission, testified that statistics obtained from New York, Chicago, Paris, Berlin, and London showed that none of those cities had a traffic nexus as busy as Western and Wilshire, indicating forcibly that the area should be rezoned.[60]

The commercial development of the boulevard led inevitably to a greater concern with both necessi-

Figure 18. New street lights, late 1920s. Brown Derby, right foreground. Wilshire Boulevard Christian Church, 1923, right background, Robert Orr, architect.

Figure 19. Traffic jam, 1940s. Wilshire Boulevard, near downtown.

ties and amenities, in particular to paving and widening, not only in and to the east of the Miracle Mile, but west of Beverly Hills as Wilshire passed through the Los Angeles Country Club and through the Veterans Hospital grounds at Sawtelle. Then, on the evening of February 8, 1928, 393 new street lights "of copyrighted design" were switched on between Westlake Park and Fairfax Avenue, turning Wilshire into a "great white way," with a radiance of one million amps greater, the paper noted, than that of Broadway in the old city center (Figure 18). Thousands of spectators lined the streets as Mayor Cryer turned the switch. The occasion was celebrated with bands stationed at six points along the boulevard, which continued their concerts into the night.[61]

Such amenities naturally increased the traffic juggernaut, which called for the then-novel device of white lines painted on the street to indicate traffic lanes. The 27 million cars that crossed the Wilshire-Western intersection in 1929, as opposed to the mere 15 million that passed through New York's Holland Tunnel in the same period, were cited as the basis for the new lined corridors. "As Wilshire has been established as the busiest street in the world," the *Times* exclaimed, "this improvement is felt to be of the utmost importance for the traffic conditions of the city." The same conditions also led in 1930 to the installation of synchronized traffic lights. Each light, the *Times* explained to its uninitiated readership, "is cast in heavy bronze and is provided with a green 'go' light, an amber 'caution' and a red 'stop,' and has a soft-toned gong to indicate a change in the signal." Robert Breyer, president of the Los Angeles Traffic Association, characterized the signals as the "most pronounced improvement made in Los Angeles traffic regulations in many years" (Figure 19). Subsequently, such devices were introduced throughout the city.[62]

THE DECO CITY

The development of Wilshire Boulevard in the early 1920s fostered low-rise buildings of two to four stories in Hispanic and other historicist styles, the same sort of buildings that were going up all over Los Angeles. The later twenties, by contrast, witnessed a rapid increase in the building of larger-scale, high-rise retail and office buildings in various modernist modes, distinguishing Wilshire as the city's chief showcase for advanced commercial architectural design. Three structures, Bullocks-Wilshire, the Pellisier Building, and the Wilshire Tower, stood out as landmarks on this commercial landscape. All represented variations on the Art Deco style, so named after its prominent display in the 1925 Paris "L'Exposition Internationale des Arts Decoratifs et Industrials Modernes." Art Deco was the most eclectic and the most popular of modernist styles in the twenties and thirties. It drew from a number of historic sources, from Egyptian to pre-Columbian to the more recent Jugendstil—the soberer, more rectilinear German manifestation of Art Nouveau. It also imbibed some of the high modern movement's fascination with the Machine and especially with the imagery of transportation and motion. It favored polychrome and the oblique angle of the chevron. While its cousin the Streamline Moderne usually embraced a horizontal orientation, Art Deco, whatever its actual height, generally tended toward a vertical thrust. For that reason it seemed to many to be the ideal "skyscraper style." More concerned with

Figure 20. Bullocks-Wilshire, 1928–29, Parkinson and Parkinson, architects. Note large Craftsman house in left foreground.

packaging and less with the modulation of interior space than such modernist modes as the International Style, Art Deco epitomized "modernity" for most ordinary people, who preferred its obvious sensuousness to the International Style's more intellectually demanding abstractions.

Bullocks-Wilshire, completed in 1929, was the first major downtown business to build a branch store "way out west" on Wilshire Boulevard (Figure 20). At the time it seemed a daring, if not risky, commercial venture. But soon Bullocks proved to be an eminently sound and progressive move, and other businesses followed. Designed by John and Donald Parkinson, the five-story structure with its soaring ten-story tower was sheathed in light tan terra cotta and trimmed with brown copper, soon to weather to a mellow green. Along with its contemporary, the Wilshire Tower on Miracle Mile, Bullocks was truly designed for the age of the automobile. Its handsome front facade featured display windows large enough to engage the passing Wilshire motorists, but the real and more impressive entrance was at the rear of the building facing the ubiquitous Los Angeles parking lot. There the porte-cochère ceiling mural by Herman Sachs paid homage to the age of transportation with images of trains, planes, and zeppelins reflecting the era's fascination with speed, flight, and "getting away." Interiors by

Jock Peters and other artists spread the spirit of modernity throughout the various departments.[63]

The Los Angeles journal *Saturday Night* praised this new "cathedral of commerce" for its "inculcation of beauty as an unselfish element in modern commercial enterprise…." As importantly, however, "the building is a concrete expression of faith in the boulevard's rich destiny. One part of it has become known all over America as the 'Miracle Mile'…but there is no need to confine this appellation to any single mile of the thoroughfare…. It is a 'miracle highway' for it is doubtful if any other artery in any large city can show comparative increases in so brief a space of time." Later, Raymond Chandler typically placed Bullocks-Wilshire in a darker, less buoyant context. In his novel *The Big Sleep*, "The motor of the gray Plymouth throbbed under her voice and the rain pounded above it. The violet light at the top of Bullocks green-tinged tower was far above us, serene and withdrawn from the dark, dripping city. Her black-gloved hand reached out and I put the bills in it. She bent over to count them under the dim light of the dash."[64]

In the same years, 1929 to 1930, Gilbert Stanley Underwood designed the similar, if less opulent, Wilshire Tower, a store and office building farther west in the heart of the Miracle Mile. The block-long two-story store space featured rounded corners, marquees over the entrances, a fourteen-carat gold ceiling mural in the lobby, and display windows trimmed in black and red granite and maroon synthetic rhyolite.

Figure 21. Carpenter's Drive-In, Wilshire Boulevard at Western Avenue, 1938. Note surviving Craftsman house at left.

The "Wilshire Tower" that soared above it rose in a series of Art Deco setbacks. Like Bullocks-Wilshire, the building's major entrance and parking spaces were at the rear of the building.[65]

The third great flagship of the Deco towers on Wilshire was the Pellisier Building (1930–31), which stood between Bullocks and the Wilshire Tower at the corner of Western Avenue (Figures 13 and 14). Designed by the leading Los Angeles commercial firm of Morgan, Walls, and Clements, the blue-green and gold terra cotta tower with its vertically attenuated fenestration seemed to soar much higher than its mere twelve stories. Its most distinctive element, however, was the ground-floor corner Wiltern Theater, designed by G. A. Lansburgh and

Figure 22. May Company, 1940, A. C. Martin and S. A. Marx, architects. Wilshire Boulevard at Fairfax.

Anthony Heinsbergen "with enough razzle-dazzle zigzag Moderne ornament and steaming jungle colors on the walls," architect Charles Moore observed, "to make the movie as incidental as the popcorn."[66]

Kindred Deco cousins filled the spaces in between these towers. Meyer and Holler's Wilson Building at La Brea (1930) sported a dirigible mast on its top. Morgan, Walls, and Clements's Dominguez-Wilshire Building of the same year, between Cochran and Cloverdale, featured a spectacular recessed boulevard entrance opening through to the rear parking lot. Smaller nearby structures that helped to place Los Angeles, along with Miami and New York, at the top of the list of major Deco cities included Cliff Balch's El Rey Theater (1928); Morgan, Walls, and Clements's Kohram Building (1929); Marcus Miller's Chandler Shoe Store (1938); and Marcus Priteca's Warner (later Beverly) Theatre in Beverly Hills (1931). Varieties of Deco and Streamline Moderne were also the styles of choice for another ubiquitous Los Angeles genre of the 1930s, the drive-in restaurant. Carpenter's Drive-In on Wilshire near Western was typical (Figure 21). In 1949 Ralph Hancock proclaimed that on Wilshire there were "forty-three drive-in businesses ranging from the Altos Drive-In market to Zinke's Drive-In Shoe Repair." Before giving way to huge apartment blocks in the 1960s, Deco and Moderne also vied with historicist styles in the new apartment buildings on Wilshire between Westwood and Beverly Hills. Indeed one of the area's most handsome Deco structures was the small building at Wilshire and Comstock of the Los Angeles Department of Water and Power.[67]

A. C. Martin and Albert Marx's 1940 May Company branch store at Wilshire and Fairfax was a fitting finale to LA's Deco decades (Figure 22). Its dominant feature, a bold and gold cylindrical corner tower, contrasted with its street facades of almost International Style severity. The powerful critic Henry Russell Hitchcock, during his 1940 visit to the city, cited the May store on Wilshire as a masterpiece of modern commercial architecture.[68]

Figure 23. "A Dream That Is Coming True," by Charles Owens. Drawing for *Los Angeles Times*, February 25, 1928.

Wilshire's Deco profile indeed reified a visionary drawing by *Times* staff artist Charles Owens, first published in the heat of Ross's rezoning fight. The drawing depicted a dense line of soaring towers and was captioned "A Dream That Is Coming True" (Figure 23). It represented the artist's conception of what Wilshire and Western "may look like in a few years."[69]

GRAND HOTELS

It was natural that the city's grandest commercial avenue should also call for great hotels, the earliest of which was the Hershey Arms near Westlake Park, which opened in 1902. This luxury hotel proudly proclaimed Wilshire Boulevard "the finest residential thoroughfare of Los Angeles, where there is an entire absence of the disturbing noises and traffic of the business streets." But this was soon to change. The nearby Bryson Hotel was built in 1913 because its owner prophesied that Wilshire "was never destined to be a street of single family homes." The slightly later Gaylord Hotel, at Wilshire and Catalina, was purportedly named for Gaylord Wilshire himself.[70]

Yet the most famous hotel in Wilshire's history was undoubtedly the Ambassador. Designed by Myron Hunt, the grand Ambassador opened near Wilshire and Berendo in 1921 (Figure 24). Along with the Beverly Hills Hotel on Sunset Boulevard and the Bel Air Hotel north of Sunset in Westwood, the Ambassador was among the city's first great resort hotels. It boasted a landscaped cluster of large and small structures of salmon-tinted stucco and red-tiled roofs, designed in a mode that realtors called Mediterranean.

The Ambassador's legendary grounds spread across vast lawns, exotic gardens with shady pergolas, fountains, tennis courts, a putting green, jogging track, a health club, and a pool with its own sandy beach. Yet its most famous attraction was the Coconut Grove nightclub, renowned for its exotic floor shows and movie star clientele. The Ambassador, observed Charles Moore, was "one of the prime reasons Wilshire Boulevard became the extended main street of Los Angeles. When construction of the hotel began in 1919, Wilshire was a dirt road running between bean and barley fields on the fringes of rather tentative residential subdivisions.... Its activities moved the city's center of gravity westward and spurred the commercial development of Wilshire Boulevard."[71]

At the far western end of the boulevard on the coast in Santa Monica "where Wilshire meets the sea," the smaller Miramar Hotel featured similar if more modest accoutrements. Its detached cottages were particularly favored by movie celebrities in search of a getaway or hideaway. The happiest images, for example, of novelist and screenwriter William Faulkner were snapshots taken of him at the Miramar with his Hollywood lover, Meta Carpenter. The Miramar was in fact a modern reincarnation of Santa Monica's grand old Victorian hotel, the Arcadia, demolished before Nevada Avenue became Wilshire Boulevard.[72] In Beverly Hills, halfway between the Ambassador and the Miramar, rose the urban and urbane Beverly Wilshire Hotel, which prided itself on its East Coast ambience. Following the war, the nearby Beverly Hills Hilton would take its place at the commanding intersection of Wilshire and Santa Monica. Like the great Wilshire restaurants, Perino's and Romanov's, these grand hotels served as popular Hollywood watering holes.

Figure 24. Ambassador Hotel, 1921, Myron Hunt, architect.

MIMETIC ARCHITECTURE

As counterpoint to such establishments as hotels, stores, and office buildings designed in both modernist and traditionalist styles, Wilshire also harbored the famous or infamous Los Angeles phenomenon of mimetic architecture, buildings constituting a semiotic parody of the product or service the tenant offered for sale. This bizarre architecture of coffeeshops shaped like coffee pots and camera shops shaped like cameras was reflected in other aspects of Los Angeles life. For all its grandeur, Wilshire was still a part and product of the city's fantastic, free-spirited popular culture. The variety of such outrageous behavior was pungently evoked in Mark Lee Luther's novel, *The Boosters*. There, in Wilshire's Westlake Park, he observed "a vast amount of therapeutic lore was to be had for nothing…." The daily denizens of the park "seemed to have experienced all ailments, tried all cures. Allopathy, homeopathy, osteopathy, chiropractic, faith healing and Christian Science, vegetarianism and unfired food, the bacillus bulgaricus and the internal bath had each its disciples

Figure 25. The Brown Derby restaurant, 1926.

and propagandists. They also had the diversion of alfresco theatricals. Not content with their broad acres on the outskirts, the moving picture cohorts continually invaded the city's parks and streets…. Bibulous youths in evening dress propelled one another in wheelbarrows, or eluded grotesque policemen or flirted with beauteous nursemaids…. Even the ducks and swans were impressed as extras and for the low wage of a few grains of corn willingly held the mirror up to nature."[73]

Such zany predilections of the City of the Angels were indeed manifested in gloriously absurd mimetic buildings—surrealist images on the already

Figure 26. Bob's Air Mail Service, Wilshire and Cochran, c. 1940.

334

surreal landscape. The good food and goofy shape of the Brown Derby restaurant (1926) across from the Ambassador Hotel attracted stars and celebrities, as would its later branches in Hollywood and Beverly Hills (Figure 25). Alice Faye's Club Car at Wilshire and San Vicente, built in 1938 in the shape of a train, drew on the cachet of its popular movie star namesake. The incongruously christened Sander's System Ben Hur Coffee Pot bore no trace of the Roman warrior but was fashioned in the shape of a mammoth coffee pot. The Darkroom on the Miracle Mile (1938), which sold photographic supplies, was shaped like a giant camera. Bob's Air Mail Service at Wilshire and Cochran featured gas pumps surrounding an actual renovated airplane (Figure 26).[74] Such structures evoked both the comic and the tragic sides of the Los Angeles character, the manic hilarity and the garish nightmare of southern California in the 1920s and 1930s.

Public Places

By contrast, Wilshire also harbored public and private institutions of the most conservative sobriety. These were primarily religious structures, designed to serve the residential neighborhoods clustered north and south of the boulevard. Albert C. Martin designed the handsome Craftsman-style Catholic Church of St. Basil's, which first opened on Catalina south of Wilshire in 1920. Diocesan redistricting led in 1923 to the church's being moved to Wilshire at Harvard, where it sheltered its influential parish membership until it burned in 1969. To replace it, a later generation of the Martin firm designed the strikingly handsome new church with its alternating vertical slabs of concrete and stained glass.[75]

In the 1920s David Allison, who designed UCLA's Royce Hall, teamed up with Abraham Adelman to create the Wilshire Boulevard Temple at Wilshire and Harvard, next to St. Basil's, for the city's oldest and most prominent Jewish congregation. The Byzantine-inspired edifice, with its black marble, inlaid gold, mosaics, rare woods, and rich murals, observed historians David Gebhard and Robert Winter, suggested "the mystery and opulence of the eastern Mediterranean." Robert Orr echoed various Romanesque sources in his handsome nearby Wilshire Boulevard Christian Church of 1923. St. James Episcopal Church near Wilshire and Western (1926) continued the tradition along central Wilshire of imposing historicist religious structures ensuring an element of grace and texture in an increasingly dense commercial fabric.[76]

Similarly inspired churches and temples of the 1930s and 1940s enriched the Wilshire landscape in Westwood, in the spirit of their older neighbor of 1900, the Veterans Chapel at Wilshire and Sawtelle. At the western end of Wilshire in Santa Monica, John Byers and Edla Muer designed one of the boulevard's most significant public structures, the Miles Memorial Playhouse of 1926, a gracefully sober rendering of the Spanish Colonial Revival.

Richard Neutra, the Los Angeles modernist architect with the greatest international reputation, considered it one of his life's darkest disappointments that he never received a Wilshire Boulevard commission. The closest he came in the 1930s and 1940s were four stunning apartment houses just north of Wilshire in Westwood. Sited amidst the semitropical foliage, the Strathmore and Landfair (1937), the Kelton (1941), and the Elkay (1948) epitomized the best of the Los Angeles–based International Style.[77] Following World War II, near the eastern end of the boulevard, Neutra designed an imposing late International Style commercial building for the Northwestern Mutual Fire Association Building, a block north of Wilshire on Westmoreland. Neutra's great modernist colleague Rudolph Schindler was likewise neglected by Wilshire Boulevard builders, but in 1934, one block to the south at Eighth and Genesse near Fairfax, he built the elegant Buck House, one of his most memorable essays in the International Style.

In addition to the public spaces of Wilshire in MacArthur Park at the eastern end, in Palisades Park on the cliffs at Santa Monica, and on such precious private real estate as the Los Angeles Country Club in Westwood, the most significant open spaces on Wilshire in the 1920s and 1930s were its several small but significant airfields. Two private fields belonging to Charlie Chaplin and Cecil B. deMille flanked Wilshire near Fairfax until commercial development gobbled them up in the early 1920s. Another airfield lay in Santa Monica next to the factory, a remodeled film studio, where Donald Douglas manufactured his first airplanes. The last pilot to land on and the last to take off from the old Douglas field on Wilshire before it was superseded by the nearby Clover Field was Charles A. Lindbergh, en route to San Diego to discuss the building of his new plane, "The Spirit of St. Louis."[78]

Figure 27. Roadway through Westlake Park looking east, 1934. The completion of Wilshire Boulevard. Los Angeles City Hall, left background.

THOROUGHFARE

Nothing could better serve as a symbolic bridge between pre- and postwar Los Angeles than Donald Douglas and the aircraft industry that he pioneered. The Los Angeles aerospace industry was crucial to America's winning World War II. It was equally crucial to California's postwar economic and population boom. Yet, if the war years formed the decisive era of transition in the city's twentieth-century history, the corresponding benchmark in Wilshire's history was 1934, when the boulevard was extended through Westlake Park (Figure 27). At the dedication of the "causeway" on December 7, the *Los Angeles Times* recorded that a "garland of roses dropped to the pavement midway over the long span as Mayor Shaw cut the last obstruction to Los Angeles's main artery to the sea." Completion of this final link, Shaw declared, symbolized "the spirit of Los Angeles progress. It is a fitting end to a chapter of our history that began when California's only roads were wagon trails." It would assure Wilshire's prominence, he predicted, as "California's most famous thoroughfare" (Figure 28).[79]

Figure 28. View east from Bullocks at Wilshire and Westmoreland.

In 1945, as World War II ended, Wilshire Boulevard marked its fiftieth birthday. Its continuous redevelopment in the next half century would not seriously alter its basic configuration as the ultimate "linear city." As it approached its centennial in 1995, it was still Los Angeles's grandest avenue and showed every sign of retaining that distinction as the City of the Angels entered the twenty-first century.

ACKNOWLEDGMENTS

For help and support on this essay, I am indebted to Alan Onoye, Richard Longstreth, Douglas Suisman, Donald Shoup, David Gebhard, Ann Bergren, Claire Rogger, Thomas Zimmerman, Thomas Jimmerson, and Jon Mochizuki.

THOMAS S. HINES

NOTES

Introduction

1. Virginia Robie, "The City of Homes," *House Beautiful* 10 (July 1904): 6.

2. Across Europe, state-appointed architects and gardeners laid out royal avenues and radiating vistas in Versailles, Richelieu, Karlsruhe, Bath, Brussells, Prague, Madrid, Barcelona, St. Petersburg, and the new town of Edinburgh. See Werner Hegemann and Elbert Peets, *The American Vitruvius: An Architect's Handbook of Civic Art* (1922, reprint, New York: Princeton Architectural Press, 1988); I. Kotelnikova, comp., *Panorama of Nevsky Prospekt* (Leningrad: Aurora Art Publishers, 1974).

3. John W. Reps, *Monumental Washington: The Planning and Development of the Capital Center* (Princeton, N.J.: Princeton University Press, 1967), 15, 42.

4. Hunt's photographic "journal" of his European travels is in the Prints and Drawings Collection, Octagon Museum, American Architectural Foundation, Washington, D.C.; Charles Beveridge and David Schuyler, *Frederick Law Olmsted Papers, v. 3, Creating Central Park, 1857 to 1861* (Baltimore: John Hopkins University Press, 1983).

5. Charles Mulford Robinson, *Modern Civic Art or The City Made Beautiful* (New York: G. P. Putnam's Sons, 1904, 2d ed.), 216.

6. Christopher Tunnard and Henry Hope Reed, *American Skyline: The Growth and Form of Our Cities and Towns* (Boston: Houghton Mifflin, 1955), 137.

7. Kenneth T. Jackson, *Crabgrass Frontier: The Suburbanization of the United States* (New York: Oxford University Press, 1985), 14–19, 45–46; Karl Baedeker, ed., *The United States, With an Excursion into Mexico: A Handbook for Travellers* (Leipzig and New York, 1893; reprint, New York: Da Capo Press, 1971), 348, 351.

8. Eric H. Monkkonen, *America Becomes Urban: The Development of U.S. Cities and Towns, 1780–1980* (Berkeley and Los Angeles: University of California Press, 1988), 158–62; Tunnard and Reed, 95–128; Jackson, 34–41.

9. Andrew Jackson Downing, *A Treatise on the Theory and Practice of Landscape Gardening* (New York: O. Judd, 1841). Downing began publication of *The Horticulturalist* periodical in 1846.

10. Doris B. Townshend, *The Streets of New Haven: The Origin of Their Names* (New Haven, Conn.: New Haven Colony Historical Society, 1984), 76.

11. Robert Campbell and Peter Vanderwarker, *Cityscapes of Boston: An American City Through Time* (Boston: Houghton Mifflin, 1992), 78, 207; Tunnard and Reed, 61, 134. Also, William Dean Howells, *The Rise of Silas Lapham*, reprint of 1885 novel, edited by George Arms (New York: Holt, Rinehart and Winston, 1949), 57.

12. Daniel M. Bluestone, "Detroit's City Beautiful and the Problem of Commerce," *Journal of the Society of Architectural Historians* 47 (September 1988), 245–62; Michigan State Administrative Board and U.S. Work Projects Administration, *Michigan: A Guide to the Wolverine State* (New York: Oxford University Press, 1941), 277.

13. Even when Fifth Avenue patrons built summer "cottages" on Newport's Bellevue Avenue, some retained favored society architects, notably Mr. Hunt and McKim, Mead & White.

14. See George W. Sheldon, *Artistic Houses–Interior Views of Homes in the United States*, 2 vols. (1883, reprint, New York: Benjamin Blom, 1971); Metropolitan Museum of Art, *In Pursuit of Beauty: Americans and the Aesthetic Movement* (New York: Rizzoli, 1986).

15. Montgomery Schuyler, "The Art of City-Making," *Architectural Record* 12 (May 1902): 5.

16. Fairmount Parkway was renamed Benjamin Franklin Parkway, in David B. Brownlee, *Building the City Beautiful: The Benjamin Franklin Parkway and the Philadelphia Museum of Art* (Philadelphia: Philadelphia Museum of Art, 1989).

17. Cited in Peter Hall, *Cities of Tomorrow: An Intellectual History of Urban Planning and Design in the Twentieth Century* (London: Basil Blackwell, 1988), 183.

18. The residents of St. Paul, Minnesota, stood out as the exception in early zoning history: they established a restricted residence district along Summit Avenue in 1916, creating the best insurance policy for their grand avenue; in Ernest R. Sandeen, *St. Paul's Historic Summit Avenue* (St. Paul, Minn.: Macalester College, 1978), 32.

1. Fifth Avenue

1. Unless noted otherwise, all houses on Fifth Avenue discussed here are demolished. For an illustration and discussion of this phase of Washington Square's development, see Sarah Bradford Landau's article in Mindy Cantor (ed.), *Around the Square 1830–90*, New York University, 1982, p. 19. We look forward to the future book on A. J. Davis currrently being completed by Jane B. Davies.

2. For an illustration of the house, see *Harper's Weekly*, 3, April 23, 1859, pp. 264–65.

3. For an illustration of Col. Thompson's Inn, see Henry Collins Brown, *Fifth Avenue Old and New*, New York, 1924, p. 53.

4. M. G. van Rensselaer, "Fifth Avenue," *Century Magazine*, vol. 47, March, 1894, p. 12. The Davis houses were demolished in the 1870s for George B. Post's Chickering Hall.

5. My thanks to Jane B. Davies for telling me about the bay windows and iron railings and for confirming that they were demolished for Chickering Hall. The commission to the Town & Davis office is quite logical as was the rural appearance of the house, because Henry H. Elliott's brother, Charles Wyllys Elliott, studied horticulture with A. J. Downing before joining his brother in the iron business in New York.

6. For Griffith Thomas, see the obituary in *American Architect and Building News*, vol. 5, March 1, 1879, p. 7, and "Career of a Successful Architect," *Carpentry and Building*, Feb. 18, 1879, pp. 28–29.

7. For example, Kissam built for W. B. Astor extensively on the side streets in the blocks around Thirty-fourth Street in 1868–69 and again in 1870–71. These houses were rental units.

8. For an illustration of the Marshall O. Roberts house, see Brown, *Fifth Avenue Old and New*, p. 46.

9. See Gore Vidal's novel, *1876*, for a fictional account of life at the Fifth Avenue Hotel; see also Henry Collins Brown, *Fifth Avenue Old and New*, pp. 55–65.

10. Bayrd Still quotes from Mrs. Trollope in her 1832 book on America in his *Mirror for Gotham*, New York, 1956, p. 118. Still also notes that women's fashion was decidedly French: "If it were not for the peculiar manner of walking which distinguishes all American women, Broadway might be taken for a French street...the dress is entirely French," in Still, *Mirror*, quoting again from Mrs. Trollope.

11. The quote from Trollope here is from Ellen Kramer, *The Domestic Architecture of Detlef Lienau, A Conservative Victorian*, Ph.D. dissertation, Institute of Fine Arts, NYU, 1958, p. 88.

12. Kramer quotes the diarist Philip Hone on the "palaces" being built on Fifth Avenue in 1850 on page 96. Kramer discusses the French background of the house on page 98, including the reaction to the house in *Putnam's Magazine* of 1854. Robin Middleton of Columbia University has brought to my attention several French publications on nineteenth-century chateaux which do look much like the Shiff house.

13. Kramer, *Lienau*, p. 99.

14. Kramer certainly noticed the doodles, *Lienau*, p. 108.

15. William Allen Butler, *Harper's Weekly*, vol. 1, Feb.7, 1857, p. 84.

16. Sarsaparilla Townsend had made a fortune in the soda business. In 1854–55 he spent an excess of $100,000 on a crude, freestanding house that defies architectural description. Townsend then lost his money and sold the property to Stewart who originally intended to remodel the place but demolished the ten-year-old house. See Jay E. Cantor, "A Monument to Trade," *Winterthur Portfolio*, vol. 10, 1975, p. 178 for an image of the Townsend house.

17. *The Diary of George Templeton Strong 1835–75*, as quoted in Cantor, *Trade*, p. 178.

18. Cantor, *Trade*, p. 181.

19. Although Kellum used a commercial technique of iron rods reinforcing the floor beams, see Cantor, p. 184.

20. See Alfred J. Bloor, *AIA Proceedings*, 1873, p. 19.

21. Elizabeth Drexel Lehr in *King Lehr*, New York, 1935, p. 18, recalls that visitors from the provinces used to stand before the Stewart house in openmouthed admiration.

22. See *Valentine's Manual 1916–17* for "Old Fifth Avenue," p. 87.

23. Henry-Russell Hitchcock believed that the High Second Empire style in America in the mid-nineteenth century came equally from the London of the period as from Paris. The developers of the Grosvenor Estate in the mid-1860s, particularly Grosvenor Gardens, may have contributed to the American acceptance of the Second Empire in equal proportion to contemporary work in Paris. My research of the last decade seems to confirm this. Andrew Saint and Sarah Bradford Landau are also convinced of the "British" factor.

24. Catherine Howland Hunt, *Diary*, unpublished manuscript in the Avery Architectural Library as edited by Alan Burnham, pp. 123–24.

25. Tales about the Vanderbilt party abound in all social histories of the period. My account comes from the daily newspapers of March 24, 1883, particularly *The World*. Pictures of the Vanderbilt house just before demolition can be found in John V. Van Pelt, *A Monograph of the William K. Vanderbilt House*, New York, 1925.

26. Elizabeth Drexel Lehr, *op. cit*, p. 18.

27. Edith Wharton, *A Backward Glance*, New York, 1934, pp. 54–55. Mrs. Wharton's aunts were the Jones sisters who built the white rows on upper Fifth Avenue. Mrs. Wharton herself would abandon the palatial character of early twentieth-century Newport for the more intellectual and rustic charms of Lenox, Massachusetts, where she built her new home, The Mount. Mrs. Wharton would eventually move to Europe.

28. John Kennion, *The Architect's Guide*, New York, 1867, part I, p. 33.

29. Speculative houses by landowning and socially well-connected developers enjoyed a boom again in the early twentieth century on Fifth Avenue.

30. Wayne Andrews, *Architecture, Ambition and Americans*, New York, 1964, p. 179. When celebrations were called for (such as Washington's

1889 Centennial and the 1893 Columbian parade in honor of the discovery of America), Fifth Avenue was the location of the festivities. When the City mourned the death of Lincoln, Grant, and General Sherman, Fifth Avenue was the focus of the public procession.

31. Alva Forbes Smith helped to run a boardinghouse with her mother before she married William Kissam Vanderbilt.

32. Three Fifth Avenue was the first house on the avenue to be altered into a boardinghouse since the City of New York began to keep building records in 1866–67; it was altered in 1869. Other houses were clearly boardinghouses but their owners did not file for building permits.

33. For a discussion of the apartment hotel, see Sarah Bradford Landau's article in Susan R. Stein (ed.), *The Architecture of Richard Morris Hunt*, Chicago, 1986, and Ellen Kramer, *Lienau*, pp. 211–14.

34. Lots on Fifth Avenue were going for $100,000 a plot in the early 1870s; see *A History of Real Estate, Building, and Architecture in New York City*, New York, reprint, 1967, p. 71.

35. The Stevens House failed in 1879 and was renovated to become the Victoria Hotel; see Landau, *Hunt*, p. 66.

36. On May 11, 1875, Peter Townsend turned 129 Fifth Avenue into a boardinghouse and William H. Barmor converted 388 Fifth Avenue into the same type of residence.

37. On June 16, 1876, at 72 Fifth Avenue, John C. Babcock spent $20,000 remodeling the interior and exterior as an apartment hotel and at 170 Fifth Avenue, Russell Sturgis raised the roof on a new commercial building for John Hoey, June 20, 1876.

38. In 1879, the former private house of Levi P. Morton at 503 Fifth Avenue across the street from the Bristol was transformed by William Field into French flats at a cost of $85,000. The flats must not have been a success so Morton had J. E. Terhune remove the mansard roof, add a fifth floor, and transform the building into a family hotel. The Morton house was frequently altered and survived, miraculously, until 1991 when it was razed without going before New York City's Landmarks Preservation Commission. As of the summer of 1992, the empty site may be used as a billboard.

39. See Mardges Bacon, *Ernest Flagg, Beaux-Arts Architect and Urban Reformer*, Architectural History Foundation Press, New York and Cambridge, Mass., 1886, p. 14.

40. For the Plaza Apartment house, see Sarah Bradford Landau, *Edward T. and William A. Potter*, New York and London, 1979, pp. 428–29 and Bacon, *Flagg*, pp. 14–15. The prospectus for *The Fifth Avenue Plaza Apartments*, 1883, is in the New York Public Library.

41. *Record & Guide*, Oct. 27, 1883, p. 830.

42. *American Architect and Building News*, July 5, 1884, p. 6 for the text; the illustration is plate 445.

43. *Record & Guide*, Feb. 27, 1886.

44. The old Halstead house of 1835 was converted into Brewster Hall.

45. Such as the building on the west side of Fifth Avenue just north of Twenty-sixth Street of 1872 designed by A. H. Thorp and already discussed.

46. The tall buildings were the Empire State building and the Fred French building.

47. The information on Altman comes primarily from the *New York Times*, especially the obituary notices of October 8, 1913, p. 1, and October 10, 1913, p. 11. The Thirty-fourth Street store is a New York City Landmark. See also the *Designation Report* of March 12, 1985. Very useful was a pamphlet in the New-York Historical Society of 1914, *B. Altman's & Co.'s Enlarged Store*.

48. *New York Times*, Jan. 7, 1990, section II, p. 31.

2. Delaware Avenue

1. For a discussion of Ellicott's plan, see William Wyckoff, *The Developers's Frontier, The Making of the Western New York Landscape*, New Haven, 1986, pp. 144–47.

2. Timothy Dwight, *Travels in New England and New York*, edited by Barbara M. Solomon, Cambridge, Mass., 1969, vol. 4, p. 43.

3. Henry-Russell Hitchcock, Jr., "Buffalo Architecture, 1816–1940," unpublished exhibition catalogue, Buffalo, 1940, p. 10. Hitchcock identified this dwelling as the Ganson house in reference to Congressman John Ganson. a subsequent owner. Later, the house became the first home of the Buffalo Club. Frank Severance stated that the residence was built by S. Buck and cost $30,000 (see F. Severance, *Picture Book of Earlier Buffalo*, vol. 16 of the *Buffalo Historical Society Publications*, Buffalo, 1912, p. 160).

4. "I recall a number of its buildings vaguely now," wrote Julian Streit of his visit to Buffalo in 1914, "but there is one which I admired every time I saw it, and which still clings to my memory as a building and as a good sermon on the enduring beauty of simplicity and good, old-fashioned lines—the offices of Spencer Kellogg & Sons." Julian Streit, *Abroad at Home, American Ramblings*, New York, 1914, p. 37.

5. Potter's letter, dated April 13, 1835, to Town and Davis is preserved in the A. J. Davis Papers in the Rare Books and Manuscripts Division of the New York Public Library. In the letter, Potter asks a number of specific questions, the answers to which are noted in the margin in Davis's hand. In Davis's *Day Book*, vol. 1, p. 171 (New York Public Library), the architect recorded having spent three days on six sheets of drawings for Potter, who was billed $30. In the opinion of Davis scholar Jane B. Davies, this fee was not enough for the design of a large house; she suggests that the firm sent Potter working drawings for details, as well as other advice, for a dwelling being erected by a local builder. I am indebted to Jane B. Davies for calling my attention to the material mentioned above.

6. "The Post Office," [Buffalo] *Daily Commercial Advertiser*, April 19, 1836, p. 3.

7. Ellen Bigelow, "Letters Written by a Peoria Woman in 1835," *Journal of the Illinois State Historical Society*, 22 (1930), pp. 339–40. The interiors of the house were apparently elaborately furnished, for Ellen Bigelow wrote: "The walls were splendidly finished with stucco work and the room furnished magnificently with a fine pianoforte, marble center and pier tables, elegant books scattered about, damask couches and ottomans, mirrors, busts and statues in niches about the walls, in short nothing was wanting to make the room perfectly splendid. We went into many others furnished in the same expensive manner…. I never saw a house which so entirely corresponded with my ideas of perfection as this of Dr. Johnson's." The Johnson house resembled Hornby Lodge, the rural retreat of Dr. Johnson's brother, Elisha, located south of Rochester, New York. It is possible that Elisha, who was an engineer, provided his brother with plans for his Buffalo house. See John Conlin, "The Johnson Cottage," *Landmarks* (Newsletter of the Landmark Society of the Niagara Frontier), Summer 1992, pp. 4–6. Further information about the house can be found in Chase Viele, "The First of the Delaware Avenue Mansions," *Niagara Frontier*, 28 (1980), pp. 17–23.

8. Samuel M. Welch, *Home History: Recollections of Buffalo During the Decade from 1830 to 1840 of Fifty Years Since*. Buffalo, 1891, p. 59.

9. The Wilcox house is now maintained by the Department of the Interior as the Theodore Roosevelt National Historic Site.

10. A history of the attempt to establish the University of Western New York is found in Walter McClausland and Julian Park, "Higher Education in Early Buffalo," *Niagara Frontier Miscellany*, edited by R. W. Bingham, vol. 34 of the *Buffalo Historical Society Publications*, Buffalo, 1947, pp. 59–78.

11. *Ibid*, p. 51.

12. Dwight, vol. 4, p. 45.

13. Entries for the Buffalo project appear on September 14, 1836, in Davis's *Day Book*, vol. 1, p. 181 (New York Public Library) and his *Journal*, p. 55 (Metropolitan Museum of Art). I am indebted to Jane B. Davies for calling these items to my attention. For other collegiate works by Davis, see Amelia Peck (ed.), *Alexander Jackson Davis, American Architect, 1803–1892*, New York, 1992.

14. See the author's "Richard Upjohn and the Gothic Revival in Buffalo," in *Preservation Report of the Preservation Coalition of Erie County*, 8 (1986), pp. 8–10.

15. "Seeing Buffalo of the Olden Times, Old Richmond Homestead," *Buffalo Evening Times*, January 23, 1909, p. 5.

16. Kate Burr, "Ghosts of Old Mansions," *Buffalo Courier*, May 30, 1826. (In *Buffalo Streets Scrapbook*, vol. 1, Buffalo and Erie County Public Library, p. 30.)

17. See Welch, p. 93.

18. The Reverend Lord had earlier in his career showed his willingness to transgress authority when he persuaded the daughter of Ebenezer Johnson to elope with him. Quoting scripture, the headstrong bride left behind a note gently mocked her pious father who had opposed the wedding. "The Lord giveth and the Lord taketh away," she wrote.

19. The Buffalo Iron Works' 1859 catalogue is reprinted in Diane S. Waite, *Architectural Elements: The Technical Revolution*, Princeton: Pyne Press, undated. See "Style No. 33," p. 9, and "Style No. 32," p. 11, both of which match elements visible on the Howard house.

20. In 1871, James Metcalfe, one of Buffalo's early park commissioners, acquired the house. His widow commissioned McKim, Mead & White to design a smaller dwelling for her on the western edge of the Rumsey property. A rare survivor on the avenue of an Italianate villa stands at the corner of Barker Street. Dating from mid-century, the brick house, which later received a mansard roof and columned portico, is commonly identified with William B. Hoyt, a prominent lawyer who later lived there.

21. Frank Severance, *Picture Book*, pp. 430–31. Towle also designed a huge Second Empire mansion on the west side of town for William G. Fargo, co-founder of the Wells Fargo Company.

22. Severance, *Picture Book*, p. 411.

23. Hitchcock, p. 18.

24. "Homes of Wealth," *Buffalo Morning Express*, August 25, 1869.

25. "Homes of Wealth," *Buffalo Morning Express*, August 16, 1869, p. 4. "In this house social history was made," wrote a later society editor, "for it was within these walls that the first debut known as a 'rosebud party' was given for…Cornelia Altman, one of the most beautiful girls Buffalo ever had to her credit." ("Ghosts of Old Mansions That Once Lined Delaware Avenue," *Buffalo Courier*, May 30, 1926, p. 33.) Unfortunately, both father and daughter lived to see hard times; he lost his fortune and had to sell the house, and Cornelia ended her days in a sanitarium. But Altman's three-storied, red brick and Ohio stone house with its central tower marking the entrance was a presence on the avenue until it was demolished in the 1950s.

26. "Ghosts of Old Mansions," p. 31.

27. *Ibid*.

28. *Ibid*.

29. For Olmsted and Vaux's work in Buffalo, see F. R. Kowsky (ed.), *The Best Planned City: The Olmsted Legacy in Buffalo*, Buffalo, 1992.

30. Speaking of the area of the Terrace, Samuel Welch wrote that "it had been the intention of Mr. Ellicott to lay out, grade and beautify it in a picturesque manner, making of it a sort of 'Champs Élysées,' terminating in Niagara Square, where should be a Triumphal Arch as at the Champs Élysées in Paris at the Arc de Triomphe, which it would be not unlike, for the resort of the people in their leisure hours, having a beautiful overlook to the lake and river beyond, fanned in summer by our lake breezes" (Welch, p. 13).

31. Richardson's unbuilt arch found a legacy in the work of Stanford White, who at the time was an assistant in Richardson's office. White's Washington Square arch stands in relationship to Fifth Avenue and Washington Square as Richardson's arch would have stood relative to Delaware Avenue and Niagara Square.

32. See the author's "The William Dorsheimer House: A Reflection of French Suburban Architecture in the Early Work of H. H. Richardson," *Art Bulletin*, 62 (1980), pp. 134–47.

33. Although he seldom mentioned the avenue in the articles he wrote, Clemens is believed to have based the "Discontented Graveyard" on the cemetery that at the time stood at the southwest corner of Delaware and North Street.

34. Allan Nevins, *Grover Cleveland, A Study in Courage*, New York, 1934, p. 31.

35. Jacob Wrey Mould, whose decorative genius was responsible for the embellishment of the Terrace in Central Park, planned a house erected on Main Street for Charles G. Williams, part owner of a steam forge mill.

36. Oakey and Bloor's imaginative design was published in *American Architect and Building News*, Vol. 2, September 8, 1877.

37. These latter two windows were donated to the church by Stephen Van Rensselaer Watson, who lived across the street in a large Second Empire house (now the Buffalo Club). He agreed to have the La Farge windows displayed at the Paris Exposition of 1889 before they were set in place in Trinity Church. Two other buildings of note share the site of Trinity Church: Christ Chapel (c. 1867) by Arthur Gilman (remodeled in 1913 by Cram, Goodhue and Ferguson) and the parish house (1904) by Cram, Goodhue and Ferguson.

38. *L'Architecture Americaine* was reprinted in Arnold Lewis and Keith Morgan (eds.), *American Victorian Architecture, A Survey of the 70s and 80s in Contemporary Photographs*, New York, 1975. The Folwell house is illustrated on pages 123 and 124.

39. See the (Buffalo) *Real Estate and Building Monthly*, 2 (December 1885), p. 6 and frontispiece.

40. Other neighbors on Delaware who built notable examples of the Queen Anne style were John Satterfield, the general manager of the Union Oil Company, whose large red brick house by Milton E. Beebe and Son stood at Number 1022, and H. M. Gerrans, the proprietor of Buffalo's fashionable Iroquois Hotel, whose nearly symmetrical shingle dwelling proudly faced the avenue at Number 513. Both buildings have been demolished.

41. Inside, the Gratwick house was a succession of monumental spaces focusing on the living hall with its floor-to-ceiling mantelpiece. Richardson made several sketches for the house before his death and worked out the plan on paper in a series of drawings that are preserved at Harvard's Houghton Library.

42. See the author's "The Metcalfe House: A Building in the 'Early Colonial' Style by McKim, Mead and White," in the *Little Journal of the Western New York Chapter of the Society of Architectural Historians*, 4 (1980), pp. 2–11.

43. The Root house was published in *American Architect and Building News*, 91 (January 12, 1907), p. 31.

44. Virginia Robie, "The City of Homes," *House Beautiful*, 10 (July 1904), p. 6.

45. The Midway stands on land that formerly housed the Cornell Lead Works, which until 1889 was the one industrial wart on the physiognomy of the avenue. Taking advantage of the stream that flowed beneath Delaware Avenue in this area, S. Douglas Cornell had erected his lead works there in 1865. Thirty years later, Cornell built a house across the street, facing the site of his former factory. The architect for this large stone French Renaissance dwelling was Buffalonian Edward Austin Kent (died 1912) who placed in the attic a small theater to accommodate the amateur plays that the Cornell family liked to perform. It was here that Cornell's granddaughter, Katherine, got her first taste of stage life.

46. The charming garden behind the club was laid out by Harold Olmsted, a talented local architect and artist.

47. The members of the Society believed that "the principles found good in Delaware Avenue will be found good everywhere else. Street by street and avenue by avenue the whole city may be made clean, easy to traverse, pleasing to the sight and notable for its genuine civilization. This means a thousand little things, but only five or six greater things. Buffalo stands in the front rank of cities to be proud of in the country, but it is the curse of vanity that it stops content with a fine achievement and so loses position while bragging of what it has done." (See "Beautifying the City of Buffalo," *Buffalo News*, December 22, 1901. The *Minutes* of the Society are in the Rare Book Room of the Buffalo and Erie County Public Library.) In November 1901, the Delaware Avenue Improvement Association met at the club. "The association is being organized for the purpose of preserving the beauty of Delaware Avenue," reported the *Buffalo Commercial*. (See "Delaware Avenue," *Buffalo Courier*, November 30, 1901 [in *Buffalo Streets Scrapbook*, vol. 1, p. 101, Buffalo and Erie County Public Library]). Among its members were Edward H. Butler, George L. Williams, George V. Forman, Robert K. Root, John Milburn, and industrialist Charles W. Goodyear. The latter had recently moved into a large French Renaissance mansion that Green and Wicks had designed at 888 Delaware and which was touted as the largest residence on the avenue. Perhaps more remarkable than its elaborate stone carving and distinctive brickwork was its fireproof construction, which took full advantage of modern engineering advances. The floors were of cement supported by steel I-beams and the spaces between all partitions were filled with hollow brick. (See "A Handsome Home," *Buffalo Express*, December 12, 1901 [in *Buffalo Streets Scrapbook*, vol. 1, p. 101, Buffalo and Erie County Public Library]).

48. Samuel Gompers, *History of the United Trades and Labor Council of Erie County*, Buffalo, 1897, p. 39.

49. Mabel Dodge Luhan, *Intimate Memoirs: Background*, New York, 1933, in Elwin H. Powell, *The Design of Discord, Studies of Anomie*, New York, 1970, pp. 67–68.

50. Mary B. Swan, "Work of Author Depicts City's Early Social Life," *Buffalo Courier Express*, March 16, 1933, p. 8.

51. Powell, *op. cit.* For more on Mabel Dodge Luhan and Buffalo, see Lois Palken Rudnick, *Mabel Dodge Luhan, New Woman, New Worlds*, Albuquerque, 1984, and Christopher Lasch, *The New Radicalism in America, 1889–1963*, New York, 1965, chapter 4, "Mabel Dodge Luhan: Sex as Politics."

52. "Mrs S. H. Knox Buys Howard Property," *Buffalo Commercial Advertiser*, November 22, 1915, p. 5.

53. Hitchcock, p. 32.

54. Here the avenue's collection of stately buildings was added to by the construction of such now-demolished dwellings as those for attorney Harlow C. Curtiss at 864 Delaware by the local firm of August Carl Esenwein and James J. Johnson, for lumberman and industrialist F. H. Goodyear (1907) by Carrère and Hastings, and for lawyer Porter Norton (before 1907) at 33 Gates Circle by Grosvenor Atterbury.

55. A drawing of this proposal is in the Buffalo and Erie County Historical Society.

56. Richard W. Goode, "Delaware Avenue as a High-Grade Business Street," (Buffalo) *Truth*, October 31, 1925 (in *Buffalo Streets Scrapbook*, vol. 2, p. 20, Buffalo and Erie County Public Library).

57. "Despite the modest changes which had occurred prior to the fall of 1919, when the Statler was begun," wrote Smith, "Delaware Avenue property was still at the time of the Statler announcement in the transition stage in which it reflected only the loss of caste as high-grade residential property, with no premium set upon it for business use. From the Square to Allen Street, the old homes, for the most part on broad lots, were for sale at from $300 to $600 a front foot, corner values being only slightly higher, according to the quality of the structures. After the Statler announcement, prices advanced generally, and sales of old homes were made at from $750 to $2000 a foot south of Chippewa Street, and from $500 to $1000 a foot above Chippewa Street. Recently [1925], sales from Tupper Street down have been recorded at from $2500 to $3000 a foot...." Louis Graham Smith, "From a Country Lane to a Metropolitan Thoroughfare," (Buffalo) *Truth*, October 31, 1925 (in *Buffalo Streets Scrapbook*, vol. 2, p. 25, Buffalo and Erie County Public Library).

58. "The Duchess Strolls Pomander Walk," *Buffalo Express*, July 14, 1934, p. 6.

59. Goode, p. 20.

60. "Mechanical Process in Making the Avenue," (Buffalo) *Truth*, October 24, 1925 (in *Buffalo Streets Scrapbook*, vol. 2, p. 28, Buffalo and Erie County Public Library).

61. "City Begins Demolishing Delaware Avenue Trees," *Buffalo Commercial*, February 2, 1930, p. 5.

62. Welch, p. 8.

3. Woodward Avenue

1. W. Hawkins Ferry, *The Buildings of Detroit: A History* (Detroit: Wayne State University Press, 1968), xix.

2. Silas Farmer, *History of Detroit and Wayne County and Early Michigan*, 3rd ed. (Detroit: Silas Farmer & Co., 1890; reprint, Detroit: Gale Research Company, 1969), 957–58 (page references are to reprint edition).

3. Surveying of the new town began in 1805 and in 1806 Governor Hull, Judge Woodward, and Associate Justice Frederick Bates were authorized to lay out the new town. Although conceived in 1806, the plan that accompanied the report to Congress was drawn by Abijah Hull and dated February 1, 1807. Clarence M. Burton, ed., *The City of Detroit, Michigan 1701–1922* (Detroit-Chicago, The S. J. Clarke Publishing Co., 1922), 1: 312.

4. Farmer, *History of Detroit*, 927.

5. Campus Martius (military field), at the present-day intersection of Woodward Avenue, Michigan Avenue, and Monroe Street, was named after the principal square in the first capital of the Northwest Territory at Marietta. The most celebrated Campus Martius was that of ancient Rome. *Ibid.*, 74.

6. Detroit's population:

1810	1,650
1820	1,442
1830	2,222
1840	9,124
1850	21,019
1860	45,619
1870	79,603
1880	116,340
1890	205,876
1900	285,784
1910	465,766
1920	993,739
1930	1,568,662

George W. Stark, *In Old Detroit* (Detroit: Arnold-Powers, Inc., 1939), 183–88, and Burton, *City of Detroit*, 2: 1503.

7. Originally the court house was to be at the center of the Grand Circus and Woodward was to be called Court House Avenue. In the final 1806 plan, it was named Woodward Avenue. In 1818, an act of the Governor and Judges officially changed the name of that portion between Campus Martius and Adams Avenue to Congress Avenue. However, the common name of Woodward Avenue prevailed. North from Adams Avenue, it was opened only half of the Avenue's width and was called Witherell. Witherell was changed to Woodward Avenue on July 9, 1867. Present-day Witherell Street was named after Judge James Witherell in 1868. Farmer, *Detroit*, 947–51.

8. "Palaces of the City of the Straits." *Detroit News*, 10 April 1892, section 1A: 1.

9. After 1836 all available Jefferson Avenue fronts were occupied by retail trade. Burton, *City of Detroit*, 1: 509.

10. An initial effort to develop Campus Martius was undertaken in 1835 which resulted only in grading the area. Farmer, *Detroit*, 74.

11. *Detroit Free Press*, 2 August 1851.

12. Burton, *City of Detroit*, 360.

13. *Detroit Free Press*, 19 May, 20 May, and 31 August 1852.

14. Territorial Judge James Witherell (1759–1838) lived at the northeast corner of Woodward and Campus Martius and north of his property the narrow dirt road was called Witherell's Lane. The Detroit Opera House later stood on this site. The name was officially changed by city ordinance on July 9, 1867, Farmer, *Detroit*, 951.

15. The Detroit-Pontiac plank-road opened in November 1849 and was eighteen miles long with three toll gates. The first of these gates was located near the intersection of Woodward and Canfield. Farmer, *Detroit*, 926.

16. The Jefferson and Woodward lines opened on August 3, 1863, the Gratiot line on September 12, and the Michigan line in November 1863. The Woodward line was three and a quarter miles long. *Ibid.*, 931–33.

17. *Detroit Free Press*, 24 December 1851; Farmer, *Detroit*, 773–79; Ferry, *Buildings of Detroit*, 74; and Burton, *The City of Detroit*, 509–10.

18. Farmer, *Detroit*, 376.

19. *Detroit Journal*, 29 April 1891. Winder (1804–97) lived on the northeast corner of Woodward Avenue and High Street. Winder served as clerk of the Supreme Court of Michigan (1836–43), clerk of Court of Common Pleas (1836–43), clerk of Wayne County Circuit Court (1837–41), was appointed lifetime commissioner for U.S. courts in 1838, and served as clerk in U.S. District Court (1837–48). Winder Street which abuts Woodward Avenue was named after him in 1852. His house was still standing in 1902.

20. Duffield (1794–1868) was born in Pennsylvania and graduated from the University of Pennsylvania at age 16. He attended the Theological Seminary of the Reformed Presbyterian Church in New York City and was licensed in 1815. Duffield served as pastor in Carlisle, Pennsylvania, for 19 years, in Philadelphia for 2 years and at Broadway Tabernacle in New York City for a year before accepting his position at the First Presbyterian Church, Detroit in 1837. He was editor of the weekly *Evangelical Observer* (1844–46), president of the Detroit City Tract Association (1846) and first president of the Detroit City Temperance Society in 1860. In 1852 he traveled to Europe and Palestine for a year to restore his health. Duffield and Jacob S. Farrand were among the first trustees of Harper Hospital, and Duffield served as president from 1859–68. Duffield Street was named after him in 1853.

21. *Detroit News*, 5 June 1905.

22. Detroit Historical Museum photograph 61.223.3. This information is found in a handwritten notation on the reverse by Colin E. Campbell.

23. Clarence M. Burton, *History of Wayne County and the City of Detroit, Michigan*, 3: 697–700.

24. "Home Matters," *Detroit Daily Advertiser*, 25 February 1859, 1. Mandlebaum (1818–76) made his money in tobacco and real estate. A native of Bohemia, he came first to St. Louis and settled in Detroit in 1843. En route to Cleveland on the steamer *Northwest*, he fell overboard and drowned on May 4, 1876. His body washed ashore at Vermillion, Ohio, the following August 23. Antoinette Avenue, which intersects Woodward, was named after his wife in 1870, and Bohemian Avenue was so named in honor of Mandlebaum's birthplace.

25. In 1862, Martin and Magnus Butzel, Heineman's brothers-in-law, were admitted as partners. Both Butzels lived on Woodward Avenue—Martin on the west side at 397, between Henry and Sibley Streets, and Magnus at the northeast corner of Winder Street, at 406. Samuel Heavenrich, a prominent men's clothing manufacturer, built his home at 468 Woodward, northeast corner of Alfred Street, in 1872.

26. She was president in 1865–69 and 1883, and was secretary in 1872–76. Their son, David E. Heineman, later designed the Detroit city flag.

27. He was a grandson of Michigan Territorial Justice James Witherell.

28. Leander L. Farnsworth purchased ten acres on Woodward in 1850 for $1,000, now the site of the Detroit Institute of Arts. Palmer purchased part of this land and the existing farmhouse from Farnsworth for $8,000.

29. Palmer Scrapbook, 18a: 183; Burton Historical Collection, Detroit Public Library. Palmer, a Detroit native, studied briefly at the University of Michigan and in 1848, at age 18, traveled to Spain and South America for several months. He worked as a lake transportation agent and merchant in Wisconsin until 1853 when he returned to Detroit.

30. Palmer was a vocal supporter of suffrage for women throughout his public career.

31. "Dismantled—the Elegant Home of Thomas W. Palmer." *Detroit News*, 31 May 1896.

32. The Detroit Museum of Art trustees secured options on the land in 1908 and successfully lobbied the Library Commission to acquire the facing block on the west side of Woodward for the new public library.

33. Wallace built midblock between Warren and Farnsworth, just south of Palmer's estate. He was a partner in James Powell & Company, a scythe and grindstone works. The company became the Lake Huron Stone Company about 1870.

34. James Wallace is first listed in Detroit directories as living on Woodward Avenue near Farnsworth in 1864 and remains at 990 Woodward until 1883. Henry Stephens is listed at 990 Woodward from 1883 to 1885.

35. The firm was established in 1866 with Charles H. Smith. Baldwin was an early resident on Woodward at High Street and Smith hired architect William Scott to design a brick mansion for the southwest corner of Canfield and Woodward Avenue in 1884. Frank C. Pingree, Hazen's brother, lived for a time at 665 Woodward, southwest corner of Parsons.

36. Burton, *City of Detroit*, 3: 836, and *Wayne County*, 5: 506–13.

37. "Passing of Pingree Home Recalls Days of a Colorful Era." *Detroit Saturday Night*, 6 December 1919, 2. The Horace H. Rackham Educational Memorial Building (Harley, Ellington & Day, 1941) now occupies the Pingree site.

38. Charles Endicott, his business partner, built a house on the west side of Woodward between Holden Road (now West Palmer) and Antoinette about 1870. Christopher R. Mabley, another prominent Detroit dry goods merchant, built a house in 1873 at the southwest corner of Holden Road.

39. Burton, *City of Detroit*, 3: 82–6.

40. Originally published by André, Daly fils Cie, Paris, it was reprinted by Dover Publications, Inc. Arnold Lewis and Keith Morgan, eds., *American Victorian Architecture* (New York: Dover Publications, Inc., 1975).

41. This appeared as Plate III: 23.

42. *Detroit Journal*, 9 September 1885, 1: 1–2.

43. Farlin's house occupied the site from 1872 to 1883. Farlin lived on East Jefferson Avenue before moving to this upper Woodward Avenue address. William Scott created an elaborate design to reflect Murphy's wealth and social standing. The residence represents a transition from Second Empire to Queen Anne in its high mansard roof and unorthodox incorporation of classical elements. This was featured as plate II: 21 in *L'Architecture Américaine* and published in *Inland Architect and News Record*, November 1887. Two original drawings from Scott's office are preserved in the Burton Historical Collection of the Detroit Public Library. A full-page plate of the residence is in *The Inland Architect and News Record*, November 1887.

44. The building was designed by Donaldson & Meier and was located on Fort Street. The current forty-seven-story Penobscot Building was designed by Wirt Roland of Smith, Hinchman & Grylls in 1927.

45. Farmer, *Detroit*, 352.

46. Gearing (1862–1932) was associated with his father and brother in the Gearing Brothers Company, Ltd., building contractors. He was also a charter member of the DAC. Gearing Brothers Company was the contractor for the Woodward Avenue First Unitarian Church, southeast corner of Edmund Place, in 1889–90. *Detroit News*, 30 October 1887, and Burton, *City of Detroit*, 5: 859–60.

47. "The D. A. C. Heritage." *D.A.C. News*, 50th Anniversary Issue, 50 (April 1965), 53–60.

48. Baldwin built an Italian style pressed-brick mansion with brown freestone trimming. Jordan & Anderson were the architects. *Detroit Daily Advertiser*, 25 February 1859.

49. Baldwin subsequently donated another $18,000 toward the construction. Farmer, *Detroit*, 585–86. He served as Michigan governor (1869–73) and U.S. senator (1879–81).

50. Kellys Island is located in Lake Erie.

51. Woolfenden, William E., "A Study of Nineteenth-century Church Architecture in Detroit, Michigan." (M.A. Thesis, Wayne State University, Detroit, 1941), 35–36.

52. *Detroit Free Press*, 16 January 1877, and *Detroit News*, 29 December 1880.

53. The First Unitarian Church originally had four large stained-glass windows executed by John La Farge in 1899. Three of the windows were removed in 1934 and are now in the Detroit Institute of Arts, and the fourth window was removed in 1993.

54. Woodward Avenue resident Mrs. Lucetta R. Medbury donated land and erected the stone St. Joseph's Protestant Episcopal Chapel on the northeast corner of Woodward Avenue and Medbury Street in 1884. After this merger, the small chapel was greatly enlarged by architect Malcomson & Higginbotham for the Church of the Holy Rosary.

55. Cram was connected to Detroit through his involvement in the Arts and Crafts Movement. He was a friend of Mary Chase Perry, founder of Detroit's Pewabic Pottery, and frequently incorporated her handcrafted tile in his architectural work.

56. The Marine Hospital and Russell House Hotel (1857), residences for Z. Chandler and H. P. Baldwin (1858–59), St. John's Episcopal Church (1860), and the U.S. Post Office and Custom House (1860).

57. Jordan appears in city directories from 1852 to 1861. Anderson completed plans for the Italianate City Hall on Campus Martius in 1861, but it was not erected until 1870–71 because of the Civil War. The building was razed in September 1961 with much public outcry.

58. Christian was a noted church architect who later became president of the Royal Institute of Architects.

59. Smith's brother Oliver P. Smith began practicing and teaching architecture in Jamestown, New York, in the late 1840s and published a book *The Domestic Architect* in 1854.

60. Thomas J. Holleman and James P. Gallagher, *Smith, Hinchman & Grylls—125 Years of Architecture and Engineering, 1853–1978* (Detroit: Wayne State University Press, 1978), 27.

61. *Detroit Advertiser & Tribune*, 13 March 1869.

62. William Scott maintained an office in Detroit, but resided across the Detroit River in Windsor, Ontario.

63. Their partnership began on September 1, 1878, and ended by agreement on January 15, 1899. Rice (1855–1929) was a family friend from Oswego, New York, who came to Detroit with his parents in 1861. Following graduation from Detroit High School in 1871, Rice entered the office of Brush & Smith as a draftsman.

64. Mortimer L. Smith, George D. Mason, Zach Rice, John Donaldson, Henry Meier, and John Scott were involved in the 1884 organization. A constitution and bylaws were adopted by twelve charter members on October 26, 1887. The charter members were John Donaldson, George D. Mason, Zach Rice, E. W. Arnold, Arthur B. Cram, Richard E. Raseman, Joseph V. Gearing, Henry J. Meier, Joseph S. Rogers, Jr., Walter Mac Farlane, John Scott, and Edward C. Van Leyen. Officers were Donaldson, president; Smith, senior vice president; Mason, junior vice president; Rogers, secretary; and Raseman, treasurer.

65. "History, Michigan's First Architectural Society," *Michigan Architect and Engineer*, 2 (February 1920), 27–31. There was an earlier architects' union called the Detroit Association of Architects.

66. The Chicago residence of Dr. J. A. McGill, designed by Henry Ives Cobb about 1890, is similar to Hecker's home. Ferry, *Buildings of Detroit*, 227.

67. Hecker purchased two lots facing Woodward for $27,859 and Freer acquired two lots facing East Ferry Avenue for $11,487.46 on March 16, 1887. Hecker's property had a 172-foot frontage on Woodward and was 250 feet deep on East Ferry.

68. McKim, Mead & White, to Louis Kamper, September 28, 1888, in possession of Kamper's granddaughter, Mrs. Ann E. Lesesne, Grosse Pointe, Michigan. "While we wish you every success in your new venture, you can be sure you will find a home with us at any time you feel like returning." Kamper was born in Bavaria and graduated from Koenigliche Bayriche Acadame in Reinpfalz in 1879. He came to America the following year and began work in the architectural office of McKim, Mead & White in New York. His partnership with John and Arthur Scott lasted two years.

69. Freer sought advice of artist friends in New York on Hecker's behalf. Michigan-born artist Frederick Stuart Church recommended Garnsey for the Hecker decorative work, inasmuch as Garnsey had just finished a commission for the Rockefellers at Tarrytown, New York. Letter, Church to Freer, 30 August 1890, Freer Gallery of Art Archives. Garnsey (1862–1946) is known for his decorative work at the World's Columbian Exposition, the Andrew Carnegie residence, now the Cooper-Hewitt Museum, the color decoration of the Library of Congress, and the Boston Public Library.

70. *Detroit Free Press*, 1 February 1891, 4.

71. *The Critic*, 30 August 1890.

72. Major alterations and additions were made in 1897, 1905, 1910, and 1913. "The House That Freer Built," *Dichotomy*, Spring 1984 (entire issue).

73. Karl Baedeker, ed., *The United States with Excursions to Mexico, Cuba, Porto Rico, and Alaska*, (Leipzig, Karl Baedeker, 1909), 359. "The finest private art gallery in Detroit is that of Mr. Charles L. Freer, 33 Ferry Ave. East (Pl. A, B, 1), for which free cards of admittance may be obtained at 915 Union Trust Building. This gallery contains the largest group of works by Whistler in existence and good examples of Tryon, Dewing, and Abbott Thayer, as well as many Oriental paintings and potteries."

74. Plans are not known to exist, but the building permit was granted May 10, 1890, with a valuation of $70,000, and Whitney moved into the house in December 1893. Contemporary accounts report that the residence cost $400,000 and took four years to build. Its decoration cost $250,000, and Whitney's art collection cost $300,000. Whitney first lived on Woodward Avenue and High Street from 1866 to 1872 in a mansion built for Henry P. Baldwin (Jordan & Anderson, 1859). He then moved four blocks north along the avenue to the corner of Sproat in a home that he commissioned of Mortimer L. Smith in 1872.

75. *Detroit News*, 10 April 1892, 1.

76. *Detroit Free Press*, 4 February 1894, part 3, 19.

77. Surprisingly, the Whitneys did not publish interior views of their residence nor have any come to light.

78. Whitney died in 1900. Heirs had the Grand Circus Building razed in 1914 and erected the David Whitney Building designed by Daniel H. Burnham on this site in 1915.

79. "Will Begin At Once." *Detroit Free Press*, 3 July 1890.

80. *Ibid.* The Association was incorporated by 1894, and its offices are listed in Detroit city directories until 1905. Little else is known about the group or its activities. Mention is found in the *Detroit News*, October 7, 1929, regarding the group's support of a political issue, but it is unclear if the 1929 organization and the 1890 association are the same.

81. For example, Col. Hecker's two lots, residence, and furnishings cost him $144,936.54 in 1892, but at his death in 1927, his residence and lots excluding furnishings were valued for tax purposes at $900,000.

82. Frank B. Woodford, *Parnassus on Main Street* (Detroit: Wayne State University Press, 1965), 208–27.

83. *Little Stick*, 19 December 1914.

84. Letter, Freer to Jerome, 1 December 1911, Freer Gallery of Art Archives.

85. Frank J. Hecker residence (1889) at 5510, Samuel L. Smith residence (1889) at 5035, the David Whitney, Jr., residence (1890) at 4421, the George L. Beecher residence (1893) at 5475, and the Lemuel W. Bowen residence (1911) at 5435 Woodward Avenue. The Charles L. Freer mansion and art gallery (1890) on East Ferry Avenue is the property of Wayne State University.

4. Euclid Avenue

1. Karl Baedeker, ed., *The United States, With an Excursion into Mexico: A Handbook for Travellers* (Leipzig and New York, 1893; reprint, New York: Da Capo Press, 1971), 268.

2. John Fiske, *American Political Ideas Viewed from the Standpoint of Universal History* (Boston and New York: Houghton Mifflin Co., 1911), 14.

3. Mark Twain [Samuel Clemens], letter to *Alta California*, reprint, *Leader*, Dec. 19, 1868.

4. Robert A. Wheeler, *"Pleasantly Situated on the West Side"* (Cleveland: Western Reserve Historical Society, 1980).

5. Harlan Hatcher, *The Western Reserve: The Story of New Connecticut in Ohio* (Kent, Ohio: Kent State University Press, 1991), 21–26, 202–203.

6. U.S. Department of Commerce, *Bureau of the Census, 1890 Report on Manufacturing Industries in the U.S.* (Washington, D.C.: U.S. Government Printing Office, 1895), 154–62.

7. William G. Rose, *Cleveland: The Making of a City* (Cleveland, 1950; reprint, Kent, Ohio: Kent State University Press, 1990), 38; *Herald*, Feb. 3, 1827, Feb. 4, 1828.

8. The eastern edge of the developed village was at Ninth Street, and corporation limits at Fourteenth Street; Gertrude Van Rensselaer Wickham, *The Pioneer Families of Cleveland, 1796–1840*, II (Cleveland: Evangelical Publishing House, 1914), 530; S. J. Kelly, *Cleveland Plain Dealer*, Mar. 18, 1937, Aug. 9, 28, 1938; Maurice Joblin, pub., *Cleveland, Past and Present: Its Representative Men* (Cleveland: Fairbanks, Benedict & Co., 1869), 220; *Leader*, Oct. 4, 1854.

9. Artemus Ward, 1860, reprint, W. R. Rose, *Plain Dealer*, Nov. 27, 1914.

10. *Leader*, June 25, 1857, and May 5, 1858.

11. *Leader*, June 26, 1857, and July 20, 1866; *New York World*, May 25, 1863; reprint, *Plain Dealer*, June 13, 1946.

12. Mark Twain [Samuel Clemens], letter to *Alta California*, reprint, *Leader*, Dec. 19, 1868.

13. *Leader*, Aug. 16, 1855, and Apr. 28 and 30, 1874; and see Mark Girouard, *Cities & People* (New Haven: Yale University Press, 1985), 170–89, 286–91.

14. The intent of Euclid Avenue residents to create assets that would be inherited by their children and grandchildren is noted in letters and diaries of these families, as well as spoken about frequently by descendants in interviews with the author; Diary, John Henry Devereux, 1873, Devereux Family Papers, Western Reserve Historical Society, Cleveland; Diary, Antoinette Devereux, 1873, Devereux Family Papers; Letterbook, Charles F. Brush, 1887, Brush Papers, Special Collections, Freiburger Library, Case Western Reserve University, Cleveland; Letters, Jeptha H. Wade to Randall P. Wade (and vice versa), March-Oct. 1866, Wade Family Papers, Western Reserve Historical Society.

15. Everard M. Upjohn, *Richard Upjohn* (New York: Columbia University Press, 1939), 128, 200–201.

16. Account Books, Joseph Perkins, Simon Perkins Papers, Western Reserve Historical Society; Letter, Joseph Perkins to Richard Upjohn, Feb. 24, 1853, Richard Upjohn Papers, New York Public Library, New York City, cited in Judith S. Hull, "Richard Upjohn: Domestic Architecture and Professional Practice," Ph.D. dissertation, Columbia University, 1987, A17.

17. Letter, Perkins to Upjohn, May 5, 1853, in Hull, A17.

18. Joblin, 123.

19. Rose, 250; Mrs. W. A. Ingham, *Women of Cleveland and Their Work* (Cleveland: W. A. Ingham, 1891), 183, 189.

20. Ohio was the leading U.S. manufacturer and shipper of clay brick and pottery products in the late nineteenth century, accounting for 90 to 95 percent of the U.S. industry as measured by the value of products. Cited in *Ohio Architect, Engineer & Builder*, IV, no. 2 (Aug. 1904), 24.

21. Jeptha H. Wade to R. P. Wade, Apr. 2, 1856, Cleveland; Randall P. Wade to Anna Wade, Dec. 18, 1866, Cleveland, Wade Family Papers; and see John R. Stilgoe, *Borderland: Origins of the American Suburb, 1820–1939* (New Haven: Yale University Press, 1988), 105–10.

22. R. P. Wade to J. H. Wade, May 10, Sept. 20 and 23, Oct. 5 and 9, 1866, Cleveland; William M. Milliken, *A Time Remembered* (Cleveland: Western Reserve Historical Society, 1975), 22; *Cleveland Press*, Oct. 16, 1934; *Plain Dealer*, July 15, 1878.

23. Jeptha H. Wade, "Sketch of the Life of Jeptha Homer Wade, from 1811–1867," July 1, 1889, written for J. Homer Wade II, original in former Guardian Trust Company vault, courtesy E. E. Worthington Private Collection, Kirtland, Ohio; Wade Family Papers; Rose, 374.

24. *Plain Dealer*, Mar. 21, 1866; W. R. Rose, *Plain Dealer*, Nov. 5, 1923; Lease, J. D. Rockefeller to Miss Augusta Mittleburger, Sept. 1, 1880, Worcester R. Warner Papers, Special Collections, Freiburger Library, Case Western Reserve University, Cleveland, Ohio.

25. Allan Nevins, *A Study in Power: John D. Rockefeller* (New York: Scribner's Sons, 1953), 267.

26. *New York Times*, Mar. 13, 1915; Nevins, 36–37; *Plain Dealer*, Mar. 21, 1866.

27. Edward Merritt to Myron T. Herrick, U.S. Ambassador to Paris, June 21, 1912, Cleveland, Myron Timothy Herrick Papers, Western Reserve Historical Society.

28. *Cleveland Press*, Jan. 29, 1938.

29. John Hay to Whitelaw Reid, June 3, 1875, in William Roscoe Thayer, *The Life and Letters of John Hay* (New York: Houghton Mifflin, 1908), v. I, 390.

30. Approximately two-thirds of the builders and carpenters working in Cleveland, and on Euclid Avenue, in the 1870s and 1880s were foreign immigrants from Scotland, Germany, England, and Bavaria; *Cleveland City Directory*, 1870, 1880; *U.S. Census of Population*, *1870, 1880, Cleveland, Cuyahoga County, Ohio*.

31. John Hay to Flora Stone, Feb. 26, Aug. 14, 1876, July 10, 1877, Cleveland, Mather Family Papers. Hay also enjoyed a friendly correspondence with Richard Morris Hunt, architect of the Tribune Building in Manhattan (1873), while that building was under construction; Richard Morris Hunt to John Hay, Apr. 7, 1873, New York, in Richard Morris Hunt Collection, Prints and Drawings Collection, Octagon Museum, American Architectural Foundation, Washington, D.C. In much the same way, he would later write frequently to Henry Hobson Richardson while his Lafayette Square house in Washington, D.C., was under construction (1884–86). See Patricia O'Toole, *The Five of Hearts* (New York: Clarkson Potter, 1990), pp. 141–45; Frank Barnum, "Architecture," *A History of Cleveland, Ohio*, I, Samuel P. Orth, ed. (Chicago and Cleveland: S. J. Clarke, 1910), 473.

32. Nevins, 22–23; Tom Barensfeld, *Cleveland Press*, Dec. 17, 1977.

33. Reportedly, Andrews's wife wished to return to her native New York City, but this is undocumented hearsay.

34. The movies included "House Without Children," "Women Men Love," and "Dangerous Toys." *Cleveland Town Topics*, June 23, 1923; Winsor French, *Cleveland Press*, May 13, 1950.

35. *Ohio Architect, Engineer & Builder*, III, no. 2 (Sept. 1903).

36. Charles W. Bingham House, Peabody & Stearns Collection, original drawings and office records, Boston Public Library; Charles W. Bingham to Messrs. Peabody & Stearns, May 1, 1883, Cleveland; Bingham Papers, Bolton Family Private Collection, Cleveland.

37. Julius A. Schweinfurth (1859–1931), Charles's brother, joined Peabody & Stearns in 1879 and was the firm's chief designer by the mid-1880s, probably the most influential of the partners' designers until he left in 1892. If there was a connection between the Bingham commission of 1882–83 and the Everett commission of 1883–87, I have been unable to pinpoint it. For an excellent discussion of the Peabody & Stearns office, see Wheaton A. Holden, "The Peabody Touch: Peabody and Stearns of Boston, 1870–1917," *Journal of the Society of Architectural Historians*, 32 no. 2 (May 1973), pp. 114–31; Wheaton A. Holden, interview with author, Millis, Mass., Mar. 29, 1991.

38. Jeptha H. Wade to mother, Apr. 12, 1883, Cleveland; J. H. Wade to Anna Wade, Apr. 8, 1883, Cleveland, Wade Family Papers.

39. Charles E. Jenkins, "Charles F. Schweinfurth," *Architectural Reviewer*, I, no. 3 (Sept. 30, 1897), 107.

40. J. H. Wade to mother, Apr. 2, 1883, Cleveland; Clay Herrick, *Plain Dealer*, Nov. 6, 1938; Milliken, 18; Ruth Everett Worthington, "History of Our Family," undated, E. E. Worthing Private Collection, Kirtland, Ohio.

41. Mrs. G. C. Cleveland, "Charles F. Brush House," Historic Ohio Homes Series (Cleveland: Western Reserve Historical Society, Feb. 1930). Brush and Euclid Avenue neighbor John Severance commissioned Smith in 1889 to design their commercial office and retail arcade on Euclid Avenue, known as the Arcade. The Brush house was built during 1887–88 by local contractors William B. McAllister and Andrew Dall, both Irish immigrants.

42. Warren C. Wick, *My Recollections of Old Cleveland* (Cleveland, 1979), 37; unidentified newspaper article, Nov. 18, 1888, in Brush Papers.

43. In one instance, Brush returned Herter's dining room drawing and told the furniture designer to "please note carefully." He admonished Herter for the design of the table, which was too small: "Now this top must be not less than 10' in diameter…. This was carefully considered when the drawings for the sideboard were made by [Mr. Smith and me]." Brush, never known

to be reticent with his opinions, went on at length to spell out for Herter's benefit what he expected in every detail of the rosewood furniture for the library and reception room. C. F. Brush to Herter Brothers, Apr. 6, 1887, Cleveland, Brush Papers.

44. C. F. Brush, "The Arc-Light," *Century Magazine*, 70 (1905): 110–18; Rose, 423, 440, 526, 539; *Scientific American*, Sept. 1929, 141; *National Cyclopedia of American Biography*, 21 (New York: White & Co., 1931): 1–3.

45. Charles F. Brush to Charles F. Brush, Jr., Dec. 18, 1911, Nov. 26 and Dec. 29, 1917; Sept. 27 and Dec. 6, 1918, Cleveland, Brush Papers.

46. Regina A. Perry, "The Life and Works of Charles Frederick Schweinfurth: Cleveland Architect—1856–1919," Ph.D. dissertation, Western Reserve University, 1967, 156–57.

47. *Cleveland News*, Oct. 19, 1950; *National Cyclopedia of American Biography*, 21 (1931): 375–76.

48. *Plain Dealer*, Jan. 3, 1928; Ella Grant Wilson, *Famous Old Euclid Avenue of Cleveland*, vol. 2 (Cleveland, 1932, 1937), 220.

49. None of the architects that began practicing in Cleveland and on Euclid Avenue in the 1890s and early 1900s was trained at the prestigious École des Beaux-Arts in Paris, where many prominent Eastern architects of the period studied.

50. "The Work of Mr. J. Milton Dyer," *The Architectural Record*, 20, no. 5 (Nov. 1906): 391–92.

51. Hunt and Warner first met in 1886 when each had been retained by the federal government to collaborate on the design of the U.S. Naval Observatory in Washington, D.C.—Hunt for the observatory buildings and Warner for the telescope mountings. The architect was then commissioned in 1889 by Adelbert College of Western Reserve University, of which Warner was a trustee, to design Clark Hall and the president's house. Paul R. Baker, *Richard Morris Hunt* (Cambridge: MIT Press, 1980), 374–76, 380–81; Catharine Howland Hunt, "The Biography of Richard Morris Hunt," undated (post-1895), Prints & Drawings Collection, Octagon Museum, American Architectural Foundation, Washington, D.C.

52. W. R. Warner to A. Swasey, Apr. 28, 1948, Cleveland, Warner & Swasey Papers, Special Collections, Freiburger Library, Case Western Reserve University, Cleveland; *Cleveland City Directory*, 1918, 11.

53. Warner & Swasey Papers; John G. Rae, "Ambrose Swasey," *Dictionary of American Biography*, vol. 22, 642–43.

54. Samuel Mather, a major donor to many Cleveland institutions, was influential in bringing Schweinfurth a number of major design commissions, notably for University School, Trinity Cathedral, Kenyon College, and Western Reserve University. Perry, 199.

55. Perry, 199.

56. C. F. Schweinfurth to Alfred Stone, Oct. 12, 1896, AIA Archives, Washington, D.C.; interview with C. F. Schweinfurth by S. J. Kelly, in *Massillon News Leader*, Oct. 10, 1892.

57. S. J. Kelly, *Plain Dealer*, May 14, 1945; Perry, 72; Molly Mather Anderson (daughter of Philip Mather), interview with author, Oberlin, Ohio, Feb. 15, 1988.

58. Philip Mather to Constance Mather, Nov. 3, 1912, Mather Family Papers.

59. Flora Stone Mather to Clara Stone Hay, Aug. 8, 1908, Cleveland, Mather Family Papers.

60. Restoration of the dining room, drawing room, library, reception hall, and master bedroom completed by the Cleveland architecture firm Dalton, van Dyke, Johnson & Partners; cited in *Plain Dealer*, Feb. 23, 1978.

61. McKim, Mead & White also designed the Farmington, Conn., summer home of Euclid Avenue resident Alfred A. Paper in 1898–1901. See Leland M. Roth, *McKim, Mead & White, Architects* (New York: Harper & Row, 1983); *Cleveland Press*, June 24, 1958, and May 17, 1975.

62. *Cleveland Press*, Mar. 15, 1950.

63. Hotels and restaurants would come into vogue as places of rest and entertainment for affluent Clevelanders after Euclid Avenue's heyday.

64. This profile of servants is based on demographic analysis of 20 percent of Euclid Avenue households in 1850, 5 percent in 1880, and 10 percent in

1900. *U.S. Census of Population, Cleveland, Cuyahoga Country, Ohio, 1850, 1880, 1900*; Mrs. Henry Melcher, granddaughter of Edwin B. Hale, interview with author, June 15, 1988, Cleveland.

65. Ingham, *Women of Cleveland*, 188–89; Flora S. Mather to Samuel Mather, Jan. 11, 1889, Cleveland, Mather Family Papers; other tales are told in letters, such as Cornelia Brown to Fayette Brown, Oct. 25, 1857, Cleveland, Fayette Brown Papers, Western Reserve Historical Society; and in diaries, such as Antoinette K. Devereux, Feb. 13, 1873, Cleveland, Devereux Family Papers, Western Reserve Historical Society.

66. The description of Euclid Avenue servants' living quarters is based on a review of available house plans and descriptions by family members. Separate servants' houses were built by only a few residents, including Edwin B. Hale, Andrew Squire, and Charles W. Bingham.

67. John Hay to Flora Stone, Mar. 2, 1876, Cleveland, Mather Family Papers.

68. *Cleveland Town Topics*, n.d., 8; *Plain Dealer*, Feb. 9, 1889; Charles A. Otis, *Here I Am: A Rambling Account of the Exciting Times of Yesteryear* (Cleveland: Buehler Printcraft Corp., 1951), 68.

69. Grace Goulder, *John D. Rockefeller: The Cleveland Years* (Cleveland: Western Reserve Historical Society, 1972), 35. See Robert H. Bremner, *American Philanthropy* (Chicago: University of Chicago Press, 1960, 1988), 85–133, for a history of charitable giving and philanthropic organizations in the United States, 1865–1930.

70. Rose, 540, 742; Milliken, *Born Under the Sign of Libra* (Cleveland: Western Reserve Historical Society, 1977), 64–66; and see Albert Fein, "The American City: The Ideal and the Real," *The Rise of an American Architecture*, Edgar Kaufman, ed. (New York: Praeger Publishers, 1970), 93.

71. I. T. Frary, "The Passing of a Famous Avenue," *Architectural Record*, 43, no. 4 (Apr. 1918): 301–302.

72. *Cleveland Press*, Apr. 2, 1952.

73. *City Council Proceedings*, Cleveland, Dec. 28, 1896, 370–71.

74. *City Council Proceedings*, Cleveland, Apr. 19, 1897, 499–500.

75. Samuel E. Williamson to Charles W. Bingham, Dec. 29, 1897, Cleveland, Bingham Papers; *City Council Proceedings*, Cleveland, May 21, 1900, 48.

76. See Thomas S. Hines, *Burnham of Chicago* (Chicago: University of Chicago Press, 1974), 158–73; "The Grouping of Public Buildings at Cleveland," *The Inland Architect*, 42 (Sept. 1903): 13–15.

77. Rose, 49, 618.

78. Committee of Euclid Avenue Property Owners to Worcester R. Warner, Sept. 18, 1908, Cleveland, Warner & Swasey Papers.

79. *The City Record*, Cleveland, Oct. 13, 1915, 13.

80. Kenneth L. Kusmer, *A Ghetto Takes Shape: Black Cleveland, 1870–1930* (Urbana, Illinois: University of Illinois Press, 1976), 41–47, 157–65. And see *Cleveland Gazette*, May 5 and 12, Aug. 18, 1917, May 11, Aug. 17, 1918; *Plain Dealer*, Aug. 4, 1917. Langston Hughes, an eminent Cleveland Black, claimed that "the white neighborhoods resented Negroes moving closer and closer—but when the whites did give way, they gave way at very profitable rentals"; cited in Langston Hughes, *The Big Sea* (New York, 1940), 27.

81. Cuyahoga County tax duplicates for 22 Euclid Avenue residential properties, 1890–1950, Cuyahoga County Archives, Cleveland. Based on these assessments, the city was apparently valuing the property's commercial potential: land value constituted at least 90 percent of total property assessments. Property values for the area between Fourteenth and 107th Streets increased from $88.8 million in 1920 to $118.1 million in 1924, a 33 percent increase; the area west of Fifty-fifth Street accounted for a disproportionate amount of the escalation. *Plain Dealer*, Nov. 11, 1927.

82. *Cleveland Press*, Jan. 15 and 26, Aug. 13, 1937; S. E. Williamson to C. W. Bingham, Dec. 29, 1897, Cleveland.

83. *Plain Dealer*, Nov. 11, 1927.

84. See Christopher Alexander, *A Pattern Language* (New York: Oxford University Press, 1977).

85. Richard J. Miller, "The Glittering Slum on Main Street," *Architectural Forum* (Apr. 1959).

86. *The City Record*, Cleveland City Council Archives, July 6, 1949, 33–35.

87. James M. Lister, "A Little Story About a Great Street That Is Dying," *The Clevelander*, Apr. 1952, 8, 31; Stone, cited in *Plain Dealer*, Sept. 17, 1965.

5. Prairie Avenue

1. Ascribed to "one who seems to have been of Prairie Avenue" by Robert Shakleton in *The Book of Chicago* (Philadelphia: Penn Publishing Co., 1920), 116.

2. Emanations of Second City Syndrome should probably be protected by anonymity; those recounted here, however, were perpetrated in print. The guilty are, respectively: Rand McNally & Co., *Bird's Eye Views and Guide to Chicago* (Chicago: Rand McNally & Co., 1898), 229. Wayne Andrews, *Battle for Chicago*, (New York: Harcourt, Brace, 1946), 80. "Silver Wedding: Mr. and Mrs. J. W. Doane Take Possession of Their New Mansion—A Brilliant Social Event," *Chicago Tribune*, November 11, 1882. Emmett Dedmon, *Fabulous Chicago* (New York: Random House, 1953), 116. C. Dean, *The World's Fair City and Her Enterprising Sons* (United Publishing, 1892), 390. Rand McNally, *Views*, 235.

3. John E. Goold, Interview, Vivien M. Palmer, *Documents: History of the Near South Side Community, Chicago*, Document #1, interviewed July 1927. Arthur Meeker, *Chicago, With Love* (New York: Knopf, 1955), 31. (Although Meeker ascribes this, the street's most frequent sobriquet, to his mother, it was really coined by Oliver Wendell Holmes with reference to Beacon Street, Boston. See George F. Weston, Jr., *Boston Ways* (Boston, Beacon Press, 1955), 47.) Shackleton, *Book of Chicago*, 114. "Prairie Avenue Stirs Again," *Chicago Tribune*, December 12, 1937. Arthur Bissell, "The Original Gold Coast: A Mature Consideration of Old Prairie Avenue Days, Part I," *The Chicagoan*, August 11, 1928, 9. "Chicago's Nest of Millionaires" and "New Things in Town," newspapers and dates unknown, "Glessner Scrapbook," Chicago Historical Society, Architectural Collection, 20, 21; internal evidence suggests December 1887 dates.

4. Union Park, the focus of West Side society, was the "Bois de Boulogne of the West Side," according to Carter H. Harrison, "A Kentucky Colony," *Chicago Yesterdays: A Sheaf of Reminiscences* garnered by Caroline Kirkland (Chicago: Daughaday, 1919), 177.

5. The Olmsted and Vaux firm was hired in October 1869 to lay out a boulevard linkage of carriage roads between the Loop and the as yet undeveloped South Side Park, which was completed as Washington and Jackson Parks after the World's Columbian Exposition was held there in 1893.

6. Everett Chamberlin, *Chicago and Its Suburbs* (Chicago: T. A. Hungerford & Co., 1874), 242, 200; "Palace Avenue," *Chicago Daily Inter Ocean*, January 2, 1887. At $500 per frontage foot, the Pullman figure may be deceptive since the property, with its 100-foot frontage, was 300 feet deep, twice the usual Chicago depth.

7. Unless otherwise noted, this "tour" cites Rand McNally, *Views*, 232–36. "Palace Avenue" and *The Elite News*, February 6, 1886, mention the Pullman doors. The P. D. Armour house was built at 2115 Prairie Avenue in 1871 for lumberman David Kelley; its architect is unknown.

8. The "splendid pavements" of white macadam had been installed to provide carriage drives in "the luxurious part of Chicago" in the mid-1880s at a cost of $100,000 a mile, according to Mrs. John Sherwood, "Chicago. No. 10," publication and date unknown (found in the Glessner Scrapbook, 54). Elsewhere, according to Mrs. Sherwood, lay "Pandemonium. The pavements are dreadful and in strong contrast with those of the pleasure drives."

9. Thomas Wakefield Goodspeed, *The University of Chicago Biographical Sketches* (University of Chicago Press, 1922), II, 31.

10. John J. Flinn, *The Marvelous City of the West* (Chicago: National Book and Picture Co., 1893), 604. C. B. Blackall, "Notes of Travel. Chicago—IV," *The American Architect and Building News*, XXIII, 639 (March 24, 1888), 140–42; he avers, "The West is too busy for the elaboration and quiet thought involved in good domestic architecture." Montgomery Schuyler, "Glimpses of Western Architecture: Chicago," *Harper's Magazine*, 83 (September 1891), 563–604; he answers himself by noting that anarchism, "being distinctly an exotic," did not spring up in Chicago. No one outside socialist circles admitted that conditions in Chicago fostered its growth.

11. Fort Dearborn imported provisions to survive, Prairie Avenue built conservatories. For presettlement conditions, see William H. Keating, *Narrative of an Exploration to the Source of St. Peter's River*, 2 vols. (London: George B. Whittaker, 1825), I, 162–75, as quoted in Bessie Louise Pierce, ed., *As Others See Chicago: Impressions of Visitors, 1673–1933* (Chicago: University of Chicago Press, 1933), 33; Philip C. Hanson, "The Presettlement Vegetation of the Plain of Glacial Lake Chicago in Cook County, Illinois," *Ohio Biol. Surv. Biol. Notes* No. 15 (Stuckey & Reese, 1981); and "Map of Chicago in 1830" in A. T. Andreas, *History of Chicago*, 3 vols. (Chicago: A. T. Andreas Publishing, 1884), I, insert between 112–13. Of the three most photographed properties on Prairie Avenue, the Field, Pullman, and Glessner plots, only the Pullman site shows persistent attempts at landscaping while conservatories are conspicuous on all three homes. Shoreline conditions were very different north of the Chicago River and south of Thirty-first Street, which were both heavily forested.

12. The 1893 sculptural group by Carl Rohl-Smith was removed to the Chicago Historical Society in 1931 and returned to the Prairie Avenue Historic District in 1987.

13. Adelaide Hibbard Gregory, *Reminiscences of Lydia Beckman Hibbard* (Chicago: Privately printed, 1929), 34, describes in these terms a house at Michigan Avenue and Eleventh Street that her father rented from 1865 to 1867. The Staples house address would eventually be 1702 Prairie Avenue. It was sold in 1880 to lumberman Turlington W. Harvey, who had architect C. A. Alexander add a stone-fronted mansard facade that demonstrated a better than average understanding of Neo-Grec ideas. In 1901 John J. Glessner had the Staples/Harvey house demolished to make room for townhouses, for his two children, designed by Shepley Rutan and Coolidge.

14. *London Times* reporter William H. Russell as quoted in Lois Wille, *Forever Open, Clear and Free* (Chicago: Regnery, 1972), 31. Wille documents the price Chicago continues to pay for the breakwater. Property records indicate that at least two large parcels came into the hands of developers in 1853–54 but were not sold off as individual lots until 1863–65.

15. John Wellborn Root, "The City House in the West," *Scribner's Magazine*, vol. 8, no. 42 (October 1890), 419–21. Root states that he is describing the situation twenty years earlier. Carl Keith, a son of Elbridge Keith, whose home stands at 1900 Prairie Avenue, used very similar terms to recall his family's house before a remodeling of about 1880 in "The Home" (Unpublished, 1920), 11.

16. Rand McNally, *Views*, 235. The author of "Palace Avenue" found the Thompson/Allerton house to be a "rare and costly jewel" of "no one pronounced style." Rather it had French and Gothic characteristics "harmoniously blended." The stable was the best feature on the property, an essay in Renaissance details worked out in brick.

17. *The Land Owner*, May 1974, 74, where the illustration is on page 68; and Chamberlin, *Chicago*, 241, 242. The addresses for these houses were: Thompson, 1936; Pullman, 1729; Field, 1905; Wahl, 2026; Edson Keith, 1906; Dewey, 1730; Henderson, 1816; Law, 1620 Prairie Avenue. All have been demolished.

18. "New Things in Town," date and newspaper unknown, Glessner Scrapbook, 21.

19. Readers familiar with the Prairie Avenue literature will observe that most of the dates I have used thus far are several years earlier than those in general circulation. The case of the John G. Shortall house, a Hudson River Gothic frame that stood at 1638 Prairie Avenue, will suffice to document the extent of the typical discrepancy. Adelaide Hibbard Gregory, in *A Great-Grandmother Remembers* (Chicago: Kroch, 1940), 105, gives the Shortall house an 1870 date and says the building of two marble fronts to its north in 1875 caused it to be remodeled; John Drury, *Old Chicago Houses* (Chicago: University of Chicago Press, 1941), 27, even has a very young Gregory watching the Shortalls moving in. Other sources contradict this: The *Chicago Tribune* reported that architect J. W. Roberts was constructing the Shortall house on August 18, 1868, and occupancy information from Chicago city directories indicates that Josiah W. Preston, a grain trader, was living in one of the troublesome marble fronts in 1870 while Amos Tuttle Hall, treasurer of the Chicago, Burlington and Quincy railroad, occupied the other by 1873. Shortall, by building immediately north of his father-in-law, Staples, launched a Prairie Avenue habit of keeping the second generation near the patriarch. William Gold Hibbard continued it in 1881 by buying Shortall's house for Gregory upon her marriage and, eventually, building three other houses nearby for other daughters; the area became known as Hibbardville. A building permit dated May 11, 1881, establishes that it was Hibbard and not Shortall who remodeled 1634 Prairie Avenue.

20. The Neo-Grec aesthetic refined to a minimum the Baroque eclecticism of the historic Louis XII architecture. It was confusing to many, especially to John Trebble, author of *The Marshall Fields: A Study in Wealth* (New York: E. P. Dutton, 1947). On page 48 he found the Marshall Field house to be "in some respects, a masterpiece"; by page 94 it had become "an architectural failure in most respects."

21. Sanford E. Loring and W. L. B. Jenney, *Principles and Practice of Architecture* (Chicago: Cobb, Pritchard & Co., 1869), 54. Jenney published elevations, plans, and detail drawings of the Hibbard house as Example D in this, his only book. As Louis H. Sullivan noted in *The Autobiography of an Idea* (American Institute of Architects, 1924), 203, Jenney was "intelligently conscientious in the interests of [his] clients." Most of the reminiscences of life on Prairie Avenue note that residents chose to sit on their front stoops in summer, however splendid the rear view might be.

22. Gregory, *Great-Grandmother*, 29. Gregory adds that the interiors were only the second ones in Chicago finished throughout with hardwood trimmings, specifically black walnut and butternut. They were probably also Jenney's work. Hibbard altered the house so often that others on Prairie Avenue used him as a construction consultant (*Ibid.*, 105).

23. Letter, F. L. Olmsted to James B. Angell, president of the University of Michigan, August 8, 1776, as quoted by Theodore Turak, "Jenney's Lesser Works: Prelude to the Prairie Style?," *Prairie School Review*, III, 3 (Third Quarter 1970), 12.

24. Peter Bonnett Wight, "Correspondence" (unsigned), *American Architect and Building News*, April 1, 1876, 110; as quoted in Sarah Bradford Landau, *P. B. White: Architect, Contractor, and Critic, 1838–1925* (Chicago: Art Insititue of Chicago, 1981), 33. The house was the first Chicago commission and first urban residence for Hunt, the first American educated at the École des Beaux-Arts, Paris. Edwards' *Annual [Chicago] Directory for 1869–70* lists eighteen "Architects and Superintendents." Anyone wanting more than could be seen from these men's hands had to seek elsewhere. Field had supervised the buying in the five years since he and Levi Leiter had bought into Potter Palmer's dry goods business in 1865, the year he also married Nanny Scott, daughter of an Ironton, Ohio, foundry owner. He worked primarily in New York, soon controlling the output of several mills and also increasing his personal fortune, half of which he kept in real estate, primarily in downtown New York and Chicago. This placed him in the commercial and financial circles from which Hunt received his commissions. Both men would have been pleased with their association.

25. Francis R. Kowsky details these in "The William Dorsheimer House: A Reflection of French Suburban Architecture in the Early Work of H. H. Richardson," *The Art Bulletin*, 62 (March 1980), 134–47. In addition to the imposing garden elevation, they included brick construction, which appealed to middle-class notions of economy; a roof with a height nearly one-third that of the total building, which catered to French sensibilities about proportion; and overall articulation of the walls with horizontal and vertical bands forming panels, which carried romantic references to French architecture of the first half of the seventeenth century. According to Field's statement of affairs dated January 1, 1874, his lots, house, furniture, stables, horses, and carriages cost about $175,000, of which the lots accounted for $71,000. This is reported in Bessie Louise Pierce, *A History of Chicago*, 3 vols. (New York: Alfred A. Knopf, 1957), III (1871–93), 59, n. 110; subsequent writers have invented figures as high as $2 million. I am indebted to Kevin Harrington for pointing out similarities in the Field and Dorsheimer houses, which led me to Kowsky's work.

26. Montgomery Schuyler, "The Works of the Late Richard M. Hunt," *Architectural Record*, 5 (October-December 1895), 110.

27. Hunt had developed the plan after trying "dozens of alternate schemes" for the J. N. A. Griswold house on Belleview Avenue, Newport, R.I., in 1862–63, according to David Chase, "J. N. A. Griswold House and Stable," in William H. Jordy and Christopher P. Monkhouse with contributors, *Buildings on Paper: Rhode Island Architectural Drawings, 1825–1945* (Providence, 1982), 88. He continued to use it with modifications through-

out the decade. The manipulation of the two octagons in the Field house so that their short ends, rather than angled sides, abutted the hexagonal hall allowed the conservatory to be tucked neatly into the south elevation, rather than being thrust well beyond it, as in the plan's earlier manifestations. This plan would soon disappear from Hunt's repertoire, swept away by the impact of the publication in 1875 of drawings of Richardson's Watts Sherman house, in which a hall became a living and not merely a circulating space.

28. The relationship between French department stores and Chicago ones is explored by Russell Lewis, "Everything Under One Roof: World's Fairs and Department Stores in Paris and Chicago," *Chicago History*, vol. 12, no. 3 (Fall 1983), 28–47. It is unfortunate that the only two known views of the interior of the Field home do not show the sun-drenched southern rooms. Instead they show the central hall and the library. They were first published, printed reversed, in George William Sheldon[?], *Artistic Houses*, 2 vols. (New York, D. Appleton and Co., 1883–84), II, 43. They are printed correctly in Arnold Lewis et al., *The Opulent Interiors of the Gilded Age* (New York: Dover, 1987), 72 and 73.

29. Andreas, *Chicago*, III, 69. Victor Dyer, in his "Lecture on the Homes of Mr. and Mrs. George Pullman given at the Chicago Historical Society November 12 and 14, 1978" (Unpublished), 9, established Jaffray as the Pullman house architect. A number of sources misquote Andreas (III, 71) and credit John M. Dunfrey, who was the builder. Jaffray, a native of St. Louis, had established himself in Chicago in 1868. He was listed as an architect with an office in the Hyde Park area until the start of World War I, but he is known today solely for his 1882–84 partnership with Isaac E. Scott, a major figure in the Modern Gothic furniture movement in Chicago (see, for example, Sharon Darling, *Chicago Furniture: Art, Craft & Industry, 1833–1983* [Chicago Historical Society, 1984], 166–69.

30. For example, the Thomas P. Rossiter house of 1855, which is illustrated in Susan R. Stein, ed., *The Architecture of Richard Morris Hunt* (Chicago: University of Chicago, 1986), plate 3; and elsewhere.

31. Construction is outlined in a letter to Victor Dyer from Pullman biographer Liston E. Leyendecker dated September 29, 1978, which includes extracts from Mrs. Pullman's diary for March 26, 1871–May 2, 1879. Under March 18, 1872, Mrs. Pullman wrote, "Mr. Jaffry [sic] [was here] to see about altering house." Jaffray, in a letter dated May 15, 1872, in Pullman Folder No. 2, Manuscript Collection, Chicago Historical Society, mentions "the design with the bay window," which does not appear to have been executed. Dyer generously shared with me his entire Pullman file.

32. Tebbel, *Fields*, 47, and Wayne Andrews, *Battle for Chicago* (New York: Harcourt, Brace, 1946), 167–68, deal with Pullman's response to challenges. Pullman protected his lake view to the southeast by acquiring the land south of Eighteenth Street, selling the western portion to William W. Kimball, and developing the eastern part with a greenhouse for over 6,000 plants in a park setting. The architect for this and an 1891 remodeling of the house that added a palm court was not Jaffray. Rather it was S. S. Beman, whom Pullman had brought to Chicago in 1880 to develop his model town. The one surviving monument to the Pullmans' domestic taste is the home built at 1125 Sixteenth Street NW, Washington, D.C., by Mrs. Pullman for her son-in-law, Frank O. Lowden, when he was in the House of Representatives. Designed by Nathan Wyeth in 1909, it is now the Russian Embassy.

33. Harriet Monroe, *John Wellborn Root* (Boston and New York: Riverside Press, 1896), 154. Monroe adds that Root felt that strong, slanting roofs were necessary in the Chicago climate, and therefore he made them an important element of his residential designs. Root himself concluded ("City House," 432), "nothing so much adds to the interest of street vistas as outlines of high-pitched and well-modeled roofs."

34. Sullivan, *Autobiography*, 285. This remark and the conclusion that the Sherman house was the "best-designed residence he had seen in Chicago" reflect as much the merits of the house as the fact that Sullivan, age 18, was fresh from his stint in the Philadelphia office of Frank Furness and accustomed to his powerful expressions of Ruskinian polychromy.

35. The elevation and plan were published in *American Architect and Building News*, vol. 1 (September 30, 1876). The Burnham and Root partnership had been struggling to keep alive when Sherman responded to the challenge to give a very young firm a chance. Before the house was finished Burnham had married Sherman's daughter, Margaret, and the firm had the commission for

the first of several buildings it would construct on or near the Union Stock Yards. Similarly Root's brief marriage to Mary Louise Walker, who died of tuberculosis six weeks after their 1879 wedding, provided association with the various interests of her father, James M. Walker, who lived at 1720 Prairie Avenue. It led particularly to commissions for stations in Illinois and Iowa for the Chicago, Burlington and Quincy railroad, for which Walker was general solicitor and eventually president. In all, Burnham and Root were associated with the design or remodeling of ten houses on upper Prairie Avenue and at least eleven on lower Prairie Avenue and numerous commissions elsewhere that these connections generated.

36. These houses are pictured in *American Victorian Architecture* (New York: Dover, 1975), 73, where "W. L. B. Jenney" is given as architect, probably erroneously. George O. Garnsey, editor of *The National Builder*, used a plate made from this photograph to sell plans for one of his designs and was reported in the press as having designed houses for Hutchinson at an unspecified address. Hutchinson's home received a new facade in an extensive remodeling by Burling and Whitehouse in 1888. Margaretta E. Otis, in *Documents*, 3a, 2, claims that Hutchinson's father had been unable to buy land on upper Prairie Avenue and "so went south and started Lower Prairie Avenue."

37. Burnham and Root designed the Kinsley home, at 2638 Prairie Avenue, in 1882, the A. A. Sprague home, at 2710 Prairie Avenue, in 1883 and the Hughitt home, 2828 Prairie Avenue, in 1881. For the Bartlett house, 2720 Prairie Avenue, Cobb and Frost almost rivaled their work on the Potter Palmer mansion. Otho Sprague's home, at 2700 Prairie Avenue, was designed in 1888 by Burling and Whitehouse. John J. Glessner recorded the snowballing growth of lower Prairie Avenue in his wife's journal on July 2, 1883: "Thursday morning A. A. Sprague called to tell me he and his brother were about buying property on west side of Prairie Avenue near 27th Street and asked if I wished to buy in same vicinity. I invited him and Mrs. Sprague and Miss Amelia to drive with me that evening to see the property." The Glessners opted for an upper Prairie Avenue site.

38. Blackall, "Notes," 141: "The basement is built of a buff or brown sandstone; the first story is of a chocolate brick, with stone trimmings; above this is a panel of terra-cotta; the second story is of a light-buff Milwaukee brick; a wide frieze of blue enamel brick with brown enamel patterns runs around the building above the second story; the trimmings of the second story and of the dormers are of terra-cotta; the roof is of purple slate, and the ridges and side bay-window are of copper left its natural color. The combination of tones looks as strange as it sounds." Blackall also reports that Pardridge had been in Europe while the house was being thus dressed and "was very much disgusted with it when he returned." Nonetheless the Pardridge family remained in the house for over 30 years.

39. The addresses were O. R. Keith, 1901 Prairie Avenue (L. B. Dixon was the architect); Doane, 1827 Prairie Avenue; Dent (a lawyer), 1823 Prairie Avenue; and Sears, 1815 Prairie Avenue. The peripatetic O. R. Keith, who would build four houses on Prairie Avenue, sold this one in 1887 to Norman B. Ream, a livestock speculator, who had Burnham and Root remodel it.

40. "Homes of the Rich. Prairie Avenue Gems." *The Daily Inter Ocean* (Chicago), August 5, 1882. Field's estate was estimated conservatively at $120 million, compared to Armour's $30 million and Pullman's $17 million. From the early 1880s onward, newspaper accounts of social events usually placed "Mr. and Mrs. Marshall Field" at the head of all guest lists. Similarly, Frances Macbeth Glessner, in her diary account of the first receiving day in her new home, January 10, 1888, recorded that callers came from 1:30 to 10:00 P.M., but she mentioned by name only Marshall Field, who "called in the evening," and Mrs. Field, who "was ill" and did not come.

41. *Artistic Houses*, II, 59, where the photographs are printed reversed; *Opulent Interiors*, 162, corrects this. The Doane residence was a particularly apt demonstration of Root's contention that western houses were "better finished within than their exterior would seem to indicate" ("City House," 432). According to the *Illinois Society of Architects Monthly Bulletin*, February-March 1934, 7, Wadskier was born in the Danish West Indies, educated in Denmark, and since 1857 had been designing residences, churches, and business blocks in Chicago, including one for Doane right after the fire (1872). The Prairie Avenue house is described frequently as Chicago's first palace, which is an especially dreadful case of misquoting

the Rand McNally 1898 guide (*Views*, 234), which states that during construction the Doane residence "was perhaps the first 'Chicago palace' to arrest the attention of city editors."

42. The hall is regarded as "an odd combination of open contemporary space and old-fashioned tactile overstatement" in Lewis, *Opulent Interiors*, 163. A rumor persists that the Field house was the first in Chicago to have electric lighting, but there is sufficient documentation in the archives of the Commonwealth Edison Company to prove that this distinction should be reserved for the Doane house. Power was supplied by a high-speed Armington and Sims engine and a belted shunt-wound generator installed by the Western Edison Light Company in the basement of the Doane barn. Soon the homes of Edson Keith, Dent, Sears, and Field, in that order, were wired and connected to the Doane generator. Jethro Meriwether Hurt III has graciously shared with me this, from his "Why Prairie Avenue?" (Unpublished, 1984), 4 and n. 6, and many other pieces of Prairie Avenue lore.

43. Bissell, "Original, I," 10 and "Original, II" (August 25, 1928), 13. To discuss life on Prairie Avenue one must use recollections such as Bissell's. These were invariably childhood viewpoints recorded late in life. There are no firsthand accounts written by adult participants. Therefore, I can neither confirm nor deny the accuracy of most of this section.

44. Gregory, *Reminiscences*, 42.

45. Otis in Palmer, *Documents*, #3a. The skating rink was on the property north of Field's house; O. R. Keith acquired the land and built there in 1882–83.

46. "Silver Wedding." *Artistic Houses* (II, 55) comments with reference to the Doane house (emphasis Sheldon's): "Whether rich or poor, a man may *die* anywhere, but to own a residence in which to *live* on Prairie Avenue, he is obliged to be a member, in good standing, of the aristocracy of wealth."

47. The Mikado Ball was a rare event at the Field house, where most entertainments were bachelor affairs because Mrs. Field lived apart from her husband most of the year. The ball is described by Dedmon, *Fabulous*, 119–20, and by Hurt, "Why," 4–5, who observes that Prairie Avenue's preferred photographer, "Commodore" M. J. Steffens, took the first flash light picture in Chicago at this event. Steffens was not allowed to take another picture because the unusual smoke and noise had been frightening. Field's daughter, Ethel, was joined in portraying the operetta's three little maids by two Prairie Avenue friends, Alice Keith, daughter of the O. R. Keiths of 1901 Prairie Avenue, and Florence Otis, whose parents were the Joseph E. Otises of 1730 Prairie Avenue.

48. The Pullmans' entertaining habits are outlined in Dyer, "Lecture," 20.

49. Dedmon, *Fabulous*, 120.

50. Sherwood, "Chicago No. II." "They are thinking of music, of art, of internal decoration, of 'first editions,' of which they are great collectors. They think of pleasure last."

51. Carrol H. Quenzel, "'Society' in New York and Chicago, 1888–1900," Ph.D. dissertation. (University of Wisconsin, 1938), 17. The women were on a list of ten outstanding hostesses supplied by "a social leader of the Nineties." The list also included Delia Spencer (Mrs. Arthur) Caton, whose home, at 1910 Calumet Avenue, was immediately east of the Fields. "Nobody," declared Arthur Meeker's mother, "ever gave such wonderful parties as Delia Caton" (*Chicago*, 57). Delia Caton became the second Mrs. Field in 1905, a scandalously short time after her first husband's demise.

52. Meeker (*Chicago*, 55) describes Mrs. Dexter's walk, adding that she "shed a peculiar grace as she moved serenely on her way under the rustling elms of the Eighties." Herma Clark, *The Elegant Eighties* (Chicago: A. C. McClurg, 1941), 175, dwells on her wit, which "always makes her the center of a lively group." The Dexters' entertaining is described in Wirt Dexter's obituaries (Chicago Historical Society clipping files, dates and sources not given). Josephine Dexter's antecedents appear to have been curious; an anonymous gossip columnist described her as the "pretty, fascinating gray-eyed Mrs. Wirt Dexter, who once upon a time sold cigars in the Palmer House. Her face was her fortune and she married a rich man." ("A Woman's Walks in Chicago. No. II," Glessner Scrapbook, 64.)

53. Meeker, *Chicago*, 55. Bissell ("Original, II," 14) explained, "A handsome, vivacious woman, she once told my mother that 'trouble didn't agree with her, so she never had any.'" Some of the troubles Mrs. Stone avoided were the childhood deaths of two children, the early demise of her hus-

band, and the run-away marriage of her only daughter. "In Chicago Palaces. Glimpses Into the Tasteful Drawing-Rooms of Well-Known Residences," *The Chicago Times*, April 15, 1888, 1, describes her salon and maintains, "In the morning, after breakfast, Mrs. Stone sits at the organ in a flowing gown of black silk that opens on a mass of soft creamy lace, and with the radiant sunlight streaming through the jeweled panes and falling upon her upturned face and about her beautiful figure one sees a living copy of the 'Lost Chord' or the 'Day Dream.'"

54. The Calumet's first building, a Queen Anne design by Burnham and Root, was destroyed by fire and replaced in 1893 by a Renaissance Revival design of Frost and Granger. The Standard Club, by Adler and Sullivan, opened in 1888 and was expanded in 1892. For the race course, see "The Story of the Famous Washington Park Club," *South Shore Country Club Magazine*, March 1930, 16–18. It was "one of the largest race tracks in the country," according to "The Washington Park Club," *The Graphic News*, June 26, 1886, 267, with stables "said to be the most complete in the world." The architect was S. S. Beman.

55. For the history of the Commercial Club, see John J. Glessner, *The Commercial Club of Chicago* (Privately printed, 1910). A frequent observation that forty members lived within five blocks of each other on Prairie Avenue appears to have had its origins in "Chicago's Alarm," *New York Herald*, January 17, 1887 (Glessner Scrapbook, 19).

56. "The Art Institute of Chicago: An Informal History," typescript (origin and date unknown), 2. Confusion exists because the meeting was called to reorganize a failing art school. Armour, a grain elevator owner and no relation of the meat packer, was the first president of the new Chicago Academy of Fine Arts, which changed its name to Art Institute of Chicago in December 1882.

57. Quoted by Frederic Cople Jaher in *The Urban Establishment: Upper Strata in Boston, New York, Charleston, Chicago and Los Angeles* (University of Illinois Press, 1982), 542. In 1910–11 visitorship at the Art Institute far outstripped both New York's Metropolitan Museum of Art and Boston's Museum of Fine Arts, but endowment lagged well behind either institution.

58. Armour's remark, made in an interview with Elbert Hubbard, is quoted in numerous places. The New York press mocked the Demidoff coup, claiming Hutchinson had probably bought the Rembrandts, Van Dykes, and Rubenses by the foot and that their arrival in Chicago would call for a triumphal procession led by Berkshire hogs. The Commercial Club's role in Chicago cultural affairs is documented by Thomas J. Schlereth in "Big Money and High Culture: The Commercial Club of Chicago and Charles L. Hutchinson," *Great Lakes Review*, vol. 3, no. 1 (April 1976), 15–27.

59. Meeker, *Prairie Avenue* (New York: Alfred A. Knopf, 1949), 60. Meeker is vitriolic and condenses impressions from all over Chicago to belittle the real Prairie Avenue.

60. Florence Lowden Miller, "The Pullmans of Prairie Avenue" *Chicago History*, Spring 1971, 154. The gulf between the Pullman and Glessner tastes is apparent in their responses to the art of Guillaume-Adolphe Bougeureau. Far from prizing it, John Glessner, "went to see Bougeureau's picture of Mother Earth but did not find it pleasing. A large female figure— a sort of cross between Mrs. Langtry and the Statue of Liberty, with a slight suggestion of a state seal with innumerable naked babies gathered about her." Jethro Hurt supplied this quote, which he ascribes to the Glessner journals about 1883.

61. Bissell, "Original, III," 13. A photograph of the room appeared in *Inland Architect and News Record*, 28 (August 1896–January 1897); the architect is not identified. Mrs. Gorton, an accomplished pianist, was also a founding member in 1873 of the Amateur Music Club, which continues today as the Musicians Club of Women. Her home was a very early Burnham and Root design from 1877 for O. W. Clapp.

62. One version of the story is in "Four Blocks on Prairie Avenue Peopled by Widows and Widowers Whom Fortune Has Favored," *Chicago Tribune*, January 9, 1898, 38.

63. Bissell, "Original, I," 9–10; Flinn, *Marvelous City*, 529.

64. Charles Dudley Warner, "Studies of the Great West, III. Chicago," *Harper's New Monthly Magazine*, 76 (May 1888), 875. Sufferers' reports, such as Gregory's of 500 trains a day (*Great-Grandmother*, 225), which translates into a train every two minutes, are understandable exaggerations.

65. Carl Keith, "Home," 13, recalled that "the lawn in front [of 1900 Prairie Avenue] was always the same, with two trees that lived only so long and were then replaced." Photos of Glessner House over the years show at least five different trees in the same location in the parkway to the north of the porte cochère drive; the most recent tree was planted in spring 1989. The spread of the vice district, which always engulfed Black neighborhoods, permeates the pages of Allan H. Spear, *Black Chicago* (University of Chicago Press, 1967).

66. "Hunger's Black Flag," *Chicago Tribune*, November 28, 1884, 1. Newspapers variously estimated the crowd at a morning rally as numbering one thousand, fifteen hundred, or two thousand, with five hundred participating in the actual march. Prominent among the numbers were three of the men charged with the Haymarket bomb throwing in 1886, Albert Parsons, August Spies, and Michael Schwab.

67. Lyman J. Gage, president of the First National Bank of Chicago, quoted in "Chicago's Armed Camp," *New York Herald*, January 18, 1887; and an unidentified clipping, Glessner Scrapbook, 20. Accounts such as these affirm that plans were underway long before the Haymarket Riot.

68. John J. Glessner, "Let me explain…," March 1923, printed in various works including Henry-Russell Hitchcock, *The Architecture of H. H. Richardson and His Times*, revised edition (Cambridge, Mass.: MIT Press, 1966) 328–30. On the site was the brick house built in 1858 for Andrew Jackson Galloway. It had been abandoned since about 1882 and the subject of estate wrangling that prevented J. W. Doane from acquiring it. Glessner purchased his lot for $50,500 in March 1885. He would pay $108,712.71 including architects' fees to build and outfit the house, a figure similar to the one Marshall Field had paid fifteen years before, when construction costs had been particularly high. Compared to the paucity of information about the rest of Prairie Avenue, there is a veritable cornucopia to delight students of Glessner House, including first-person accounts and correspondence, drawings, and specifications and other primary materials and both historic and contemporary critical studies, of which the most recent is Elaine Harrington's *H. H. Richardson: J. J. Glessner House, Chicago* (Tubingen: Wasmuth, 1993). Most importantly, the house itself, a national landmark, stands at 1800 South Prairie Avenue and is open regularly for tours.

69. Frances Macbeth Glessner and John J. Glessner, "Journals (1879–1921) of Frances Glessner, with Occasional Entries by Her Husband, John J. Glessner," Chicago Historical Society. "Remarks about the House" are at the end of the volume covering May to September 1887. Josephine Dexter's letter, dated March 30, 1886, is inserted in the diary entry for April 4 and is a classic of its day. Richardson's efforts to ensure the Glessners would keep faith were the subject of my paper, "Richardson's Web: A Client's Reassessment," read at the Society of Architectural Historians' meeting, April 16, 1988.

70. Frances Glessner, "Journals," February 11, 1888.

71. The Kimball house library measures 27.6 x 20.4 feet without including the generous bay, and the drawing room is about 18 x 15 feet.

72. The Reid house claim is made in Carl Condit, *The Chicago School of Architecture* (Chicago: University of Chicago Press, 1964), 111, n. 3. The domed space is documented in photographs dated August 21, 1962, in the Chicago Historical Society collection. Monroe, *Root*, 155–57, selected the Meyer house as one of eight Burnham and Root homes to which to devote a paragraph; she found it a "perfect little composition" that was "beyond criticism" and included illustrations of its facade and hall. Meyer was an officer of the Selz Schwab & Co. boot and shoe firm. The "house-like" facade encompassed Burnham and Root Chicago buildings as varied as the Art Institute and St. Gabriel's Church (before the obscuring porch), both of 1886–87; the six-story, three-bay Herald newspaper building and the 20-story Masonic Temple, of 1890–92; and the completely ignored, ultra-simple Immanuel Presbyterian Church, 1892, now a bingo parlor in Bridgeport. Whitehouse did several houses in about 1890 modeled on the roughly contemporary London work of J. J. Stevenson and Richard Norman Shaw on Pont Street, Cadogan Square, Harrington Gardens, and elsewhere throughout Chelsea and Kensington. Root, therefore, called Whitehouse's designs Pont Street Dutch ("City House," 417, where he used the image of one of these, the C. B. McGenniss residence on lower Prairie Avenue, to open his article).

73. Meeker, *Chicago*, 35; the house stands unused. Meeker himself grew up in the yellow limestone house at 1815 Prairie Avenue, which was designed by Burnham and Root in 1882 for Joseph Sears, and remodeled by Arthur Heun so that it had acquired "a faintly French air" (*Ibid.*, 19).

74. "He died in his chair," *Chicago Herald*, May 19, 1890, and Walter Knight Sturges, "Arthur Little and the Colonial Revival," *Journal of the Society of Architectural Historians*, May 1973, 162–63. The Dexter addition was illustrated in *Inland Architect*, 17 (June 1891), 5. Sturges infers from the placement of the entrance at its northern end that, as was characteristic of Little's work, the Dexter house plan would have been unusual; Dexter's obituaries indicate only that the principal room in the addition was devoted to music. Sturges maintains this style did not travel well, even when executed outside of New England by Boston firms. Shepley, Rutan and Coolidge employed it in 1895 on their home for Elizabeth Sprague and Dr. Frederick Coolidge at 2636 Prairie Avenue, published in *Inland Architect*, 26 (January 1896), 6, and for the children of John J. Glessner in 1901 in townhouses at 1700 and 1706 Prairie. Confirmation of Sturges's claim is impossible; all these structures have been demolished. The house Little and Brown built for Josephine Dexter in 1899 survives at 393 Commonwealth Avenue, Boston.

75. "Four Blocks," *Tribune*, January 9, 1898, 38, reports the deaths to that date; Flinn, *Marvelous City*, 582, notices the ages of the houses. Second Presbyterian Church purchased its Michigan Avenue site just before the Chicago Fire; James Renwick was the architect. After a fire in 1900, the church received an Arts and Crafts interior designed by Howard Van Doren Shaw and enhanced by murals of Frederick Clay Bartlett. The building also features an outstanding collection of Tiffany and other period windows. In 1908 the church established an endowment to provide for the building once the neighborhood changed. The most thorough discussion of the factors of Prairie Avenue's decline is Robert Pruter, "The Prairie Avenue Section of Chicago: The History and Examination of Its Decline" (Master's Thesis, Roosevelt University, 1976).

76. The licensed vice district was abolished in 1915. Photographs before and after the demolition of lower Prairie Avenue are in Harold M. Mayer and Richard C. Wade, *Chicago: Growth of a Metropolis* (University of Chicago Press, 1969), 383. The later photograph is incorrectly dated 1963; St. Paul's church is visible, and its demolition permit was issued in 1953. The replacement housing, called Prairie Courts, is regarded as architecturally the best of the developments of the period. Keck and Keck were the architects. See Devereux Bowly, Jr., *The Poorhouse: Subsidized Housing in Chicago, 1895–1976*, 73–75.

77. In 1905 Hill and Woltersdorf's design for the Eastman Kodak Company building was executed at 1727 Indiana Avenue, and Christian A. Eckstorm's Western Bank Note Company building went up at 1916–1934 Indiana. The rapidity of Michigan Avenue's transformation is covered in Peter B. Wight, "The Transmutation of a Residence Street. Resulting in Another Solution of a Utilitarian Problem by Architects," *Architectural Record*, vol. 27, no. 4 (April 1910), 285–93. Donnelley's photographic documentation of the construction of their facility, designed by Howard Van Doren Shaw, also records the demolition of an entire block of homes.

78. Alfred S. Alschuler, a specialist in factory design, was the architect. Alschuler's work as a designer of printing plants has been documented by Connie Casey, "Alfred S. Alschuler's Buildings for the Printing Industry" (Unpublished, 1991). Casey established that the Columbia Colortype Company building of 1920, standing at Twenty-first Street and Calumet Avenue, was seminal in Alschuler's perception of a printing plant as "one large operating machine." The Atwell Printing Company (1922), at 2000–2016 Prairie Avenue, repeats its features.

79. A long-time neighbor commented in 1927, "Only poor whites will live here now, and they must take in roomers to pay their rent." Goold in Palmer, *Documents*, 1.

80. The Field house generated the following, from the *Chicago Tribune*, November 19, 1954: "Chicago has plowed under many of the big old homes which embellished its early years. But among those still struggling to justify their existence—successfully, we hope—are the two Chicago homes designed by that fabulous architect, Richard Morris Hunt.
"One of them is the 1020 Art center, the old Borden home on Lake Shore dr., which is seeking to expand its club activities. The other is the home at 1905 Prairie av. built for Marshall Field in 1877 [sic] and now used

as an aeronautical engineering laboratory. Hunt, who died in 1895, is the man who livened up American architecture by importing the 16th century French chateau. He found his most extravagant customers in the east, where he built palaces in Newport and New York.... They are the sort of homes that make you choke on your coffee....

"Hunt also designed the administration building for the Columbian exposition, from which we are well spared. But we hope his two houses stick around a while. Chicago would not seem like home without a few relics of that age of architectural flamboyance.

"And think how much better off we are than Newport."

81. Robert Campbell, "Irony in Chicago," *Boston Globe*, November 5, 1978. The same overblown language found that the final resting place of many Prairie Avenue residents, Graceland Cemetery on Chicago's North Side, was "by a lavish expenditure of money and the exercise of good taste and engineering skill...worthy to rank with the famous cemeteries of America" (*Chicago Illustrated* [Chicago: N. F. Hodson, 1883], 48–49, as quoted by Walter L. Creese in *The Crowning of the American Landscape: Eight Great Spaces and Their Buildings* [Princeton, 1985], 208).

6. St. Charles Avenue

1. See Robert Fishman's discussion of France and the U.S. in *Bourgeois Utopia; the Rise and Fall of Suburbia*, New York, 1987, chapter 4.

2. The *Bulletin*, January 12, 1838; see John Smith Kendall, *History of New Orleans*, 2 vols., Chicago and New York, 1922, II, pp. 676–77.

3. J. Curtis Waldo, *Illustrated Visitors' Guide to New Orleans*, New Orleans, 1879, p. 56.

4. J. L. Guilbeau, *St. Charles Street Car or the New Orleans and Carrollton Rail Road*, New Orleans, 1975, pp. 2 ff.; see also *A Streetcar Named St. Charles*, N. A., New Orleans, 1972; see Louis C. Hennick, E. Harper Charlton, *The Streetcars of New Orleans*, Gretna, 1975.

5. *Transit Writers' Digest*, 1968, May 27, n.p.

6. Arthur M. Schlesinger, *The Rise of the City, 1878–1898*, New York, 1933, p. 92.

7. *London Daily Telegraph*, 2 February 1885; cited by Joy J. Jackson, *New Orleans in the Gilded Age: Politics and Urban Progress 1880–96*, Baton Rouge, 1969, p. 162.

8. *Daily Picayune*, 1882, August 2, 8; cited by Jackson, *New Orleans in the Gilded Age*, p. 159, footnote 38.

9. George E. Waring and George W. Cable, Tenth Census, *Report on the Social Statistics of Cities*, XIX, pt. 2, Washington, D.C., 1887, p. 272.

10. George W. Waring, Jr., "A Tale of Six Cities," *Daily Picayune*, 11 January 1881.

11. Kendall, *History of New Orleans*, II, pp. 577 ff.

12. Jackson, *New Orleans in the Gilded Age*, pp. 156–63.

13. See S. Frederick Starr, *Southern Comfort: The Garden District of New Orleans: 1800–1900*, Cambridge, MIT Press, 1989, chapter 2.

14. Jackson, *New Orleans and the Gilded Age*, pp. 212–13.

15. Mark Twain [Samuel Clemens], *Life on the Mississippi*, New York, 1977, p. 249; on the exposition of 1884–85 see the fine M.A. thesis by D. Clive Hardy, "World's Industrial and Cotton Centennial Exposition and the New South, 1884–85," Tulane University, 1964.

16. For several of the identifications in the following pages the author is indebted to the excellent and detailed "Architectural Inventory" by the compilers of *Jefferson City, New Orleans Architecture*, vol. 7, Gretna, 1989, especially pp. 156–71.

17. For this and other aspects of the career of Thomas Sully, the reader should consult the excellent unpublished monograph by John Ferguson of New Orleans.

18. Jefferson City, pp. 66, 72.

19. Starr, *Southern Comfort*, pp. 129 ff.

7. Massachusetts Avenue

1. This essay is based on a publication of the U.S. Commission of Fine Arts, *Massachusetts Avenue Architecture* (2 vols.; Washington, D.C.: U.S. Government Printing Office, 1973, 1975). The writer was a coauthor of Volume II, and of a companion publication documenting the architecture of Washington's other grand avenue, *Sixteenth Street Architecture* (2 vols.; Washington, D.C.: U.S. Government Printing Office, 1978, 1988). Dates of construction and names of owners and architects are from the District of Columbia Building Permits file at the National Archives, Washington, D.C., Record Group 351. Dates for sculpture are from H. P. Caemmerer's *Washington, the National Capital* (Washington, D.C.: U.S. Government Printing Office, 1932), an excellent source of information on the capital's public architecture and sculpture.

2. John Clagett Proctor and Edwin Melvin Williams, eds., *Washington Past and Present, A History*, 5 vols. (New York: Lewis Historical Publishing Company, 1930, 1932), 1:123–24. Trollope's comments appear in his *North America*, 2 vols. (1869 edition: reprint, London: Dawson's of Pall Mall, 1968), 1:2–3.

3. Constance McLaughlin Green, *Washington, Village and Capital* (Princeton: Princeton University Press, 1962), chapter 14. This and a second volume, *Washington, Capital City* (Princeton: Princeton University Press, 1963), are an invaluable source for the student of Washington history through the 1950s. Another excellent history, of the earlier period, is Wilhelmus Bogart Bryan, *A History of the National Capital*, 2 vols. (New York: MacMillan Company, 1914, 1916).

4. Joseph West Moore, *Picturesque Washington* (Providence, R. I.: J. A. and R. A. Reid, 1884), p. 240.

5. U.S. Commission of Fine Arts, *Sixteenth Street Architecture*, 1, 1603 H St.-800 Sixteenth St., pp. 57–87; 1515 K St., pp. 121–43; 1530 K St., pp. 144–57.

6. U.S. Commission of Fine Arts, *Massachusetts Avenue Architecture*, 2, 1205 Vermont Avenue NW, pp. 31–36. Judge Wylie had issued the writ of *habeas corpus* in the Lincoln assassination conspiracy case of Mary Surratt; when President Johnson ignored the writ, she was hanged with the other conspirators.

7. The Dahlgren house is illustrated in Stilson Hutchins and Joseph West Moore, *The National Capital, Past and Present* (Washington: Post Publishing Company, 1885), p. 307. Biographical information is from Allen Johnson and Dumas Malone, eds., *Dictionary of American Biography* (New York: Charles Scribner's Sons, 1930).

8. James M. Goode, *Best Addresses* (Washington, London: Smithsonian Institution Press, 1988), pp. 8–10.

9. For more information on Cluss, see Tanya Edwards Beauchamp, "Adolph Cluss: An Architect in Washington during Civil War and Reconstruction," *Records of the Columbia Historical Society, 1971–72* (Washington: Columbia Historical Society, 1973), pp. 338–58.

10. Washington city directories; Fremont Rider, *Rider's Washington, A Guidebook for Travelers* (New York: MacMillan Company, 1924), p. 220; James M. Goode, *Capital Losses* (Washington: Smithsonian Institution Press, 1979), pp. 180–82.

11. Washington city directories, 1870s-1890s; *Washington, City and Capital*, Federal Writers' Project, Works Progress Administration, American Guide Series (Washington: U.S. Government Printing Office, 1937), pp. 682–83; *Evening Star* (Washington), 24 Nov. 1959 (German embassy). Senators Edmund and Bayard sued over the effect of Shepherd's regrading on the value of their property. The amount started out at $2500 and $3000, respectively, but they settled for $400 each. See Bryan, *National Capital*, 2:618.

12. W. W. Corcoran (1798–1888), a founder of the parent bank of Riggs National Bank, was one of the capital's greatest benefactors. In addition to the Louise Home, he gave the land for Oak Hill Cemetery in Georgetown and its chapel designed by James Renwick. He also gave the city his art collection, housed in another Renwick building (now called the Renwick Gallery); the present Corcoran Gallery of Art occupies a building designed by Ernest Flagg. For a biography, see *Sixteenth Street Archictecture*, 1, pp. 33–36.

13. *House of Rep., 49th Cong., 1st sess., Report No. 3050.* Quotes from the deed of 21 Nov. 1869, Corcoran to James M. Carlisle and others, trustees.

14. The best description of the Louise Home is found in Goode, *Capital Losses*, pp. 226–29. See also *Washington Post*, "Sale of Louise Home to Slash Expenses Would Wipe Out Ties," 7 Jan. 1946.

15. An exception is Logan Circle, a few blocks northeast of Thomas Circle. Built up during the 1870s and 1880s, it has a unity that Thomas and Scott Circles lack, due, most likely, to the lots being laid out in reference to the circle, rather than to any design consciousness of the architects.

16. The firm of Fraser, Furness & Hewitt was dissolved in 1871, the year Fraser came to Washington. He designed a significant number of residences in the city, as well as commercial buildings. His most notable work was the British embassy on Connecticut Avenue, the first building erected in Washington specifically for that purpose. For a biography of Fraser, see *Massachusetts Avenue Architecture, 2*, pp. 119–21. Information on the British embassy comes from Beckles Wilson, *Friendly Relations, A Narrative of Britain's Ministers and Ambassadors to America (1791–1930)* (Boston: Little, Brown & Company, 1934), chapter 15.

17. De Sibour was born in Paris, the son of a French diplomat directly descended from Louis XI. He married Margaret Clagett, who was from a prominent Washington family. Although he did not attend the École des Beaux-Arts, de Sibour entered one of the Paris ateliers associated with the school; he was forced to leave after a year because of financial difficulties. He went to work for Bruce Price in New York, later becoming his partner. Several years after Price's death in 1903, de Sibour confined his practice to the Washington area. For a biography, see *Sixteenth Street Architecture, 2*, pp. 166–69.

18. Washington city directories; *WPA Guide*, p. 684; John Clagett Proctor, *Washington and Environs*, articles written for the *Washington Sunday Star*, 1928–49 (Washington: privately printed, 1949), pp. 303–304; *Rider's Washington*, p. 224.

19. Walter Lord, *A Night to Remember* (New York: H. Holt & Company, 1955), p. 13.

20. Like Corcoran, Mellon turned over his collection to the public and built a gallery in which to display it; in Mellon's case it was John Russell Pope's National Gallery of Art.

21. Although the name of the circle is Dupont, the correct spelling for the family name is duPont.

22. John A. Joyce, *Beautiful Washington* (Washington: Gibson Brothers, 1903), p. 123.

23. For examples of Hopkins's subdivisions, see Subdivisions Book JHK, Office of the Surveyor of the District of Columbia, folios 371 and 373, sub-divisions in Square 94, 17 June 1878, and folio 213, subdivision in Square 96, 20 Oct. 1877; the latter subdivided the square into 58 lots.

24. Green, *Village and Capital*, pp. 347–48; *Capital City*, pp. 47–48; *Annual Report of the Commissioners of the District of Columbia for the year ended June 30, 1887* (Washington: U.S. Government Printing Office, 1887), pp. 21, 39–54; Proctor, et al., *Washington Past and Present*, 1:154–57.

25. Harriet S. Blaine Beale, *The Letters of Mrs. James G. Blaine*, 2 vols. (New York: Duffield & Company, 1908), 1, p. 201.

26. Beale, *Letters*, 2. p. 95.

27. Green, *Capital City*, p. 193. Quoted from an article in the *Evening Star*, 26 March 1905.

28. New-York Historical Society, McKim, Mead & White collection, Patterson House drawings; two pieces of correspondence regarding air conditioning.

29. The villa, "Seaview Terrace," is now used as a dormitory by Salve Regina University.

30. Leland Roth, *McKim, Mead & White* (New York: Harper & Row, 1983), p. 139.

31. At the same time, plans for the Herbert Wadsworth house at 1801 Massachusetts Ave. (Jan. 1900) showed an interior garage, and up the street at 2201, Captain Frederick Miller's house, also built in 1900, had a miniature chateau-type garage, placed prominently in front and to the side of the house (*Massachusetts Avenue Architecture, 1*).

32. Quoted in Green, *City and Capital*, p. 418.

33. The name of the architect for the Wadsworth house, George Cary of Buffalo, was unknown until recently because the building permit is missing. It was discovered by architectural historians Judith H. Lanius and Sharon C. Park while doing research on the house for the Sulgrave Club.

34. Evalyn Walsh McLean, *Father Struck It Rich* (Boston: Little, Brown, and Company, 1936), p. 92.

35. Isabel Anderson, *Presidents and Pies* (Boston & New York: Houghton Mifflin Company, 1920), pp. 115–16.

36. Waddy Wood was another of the local architects who designed houses for well-to-do clients in the Sheridan Circle–Kalorama area. He practiced alone early in his career, then as a partner in the firm of Wood, Donn & Deming. The firm's work included many commercial and public structures, among them the Department of the Interior Building.

37. See Jean Kling, "Alice Pike Barney, Bringing Culture to the Capital," in *Washington History*, vol. 2, no. 1, Spring 1990 (Washington: Historical Society of Washington, 1990), pp. 68–89. This is an excellent and well-illustrated account of Alice Barney's life in Washington.

38. For a brief biography of Brown, see *Massachusetts Avenue Architecture, 2*, pp. 80–81. For a detailed assessment of Brown's career, see William B. Bushong, "Glenn Brown, The American Institute of Architects, and the Development of the Monumental Core of Washington, D.C." (Ph.D. Dissertation, George Washington University, 1988).

39. For a biography of Totten, see *Sixteenth Street Architecture, 2*, pp. 435–36.

40. Like many other architects of the time, Wyeth was hard-hit by the Depression. He gave up his practice in 1934 and became municipal architect, designing numerous public buildings and a major Potomac River crossing, the Key Bridge in Georgetown. For a biography of Wyeth, see *Sixteenth Street Architecture, 1*, pp. 182–86.

41. *Massachusetts Avenue Heights*, a promotional brochure published in 1911 by the developers of the property, pp. 5, 12. A copy is in the Washingtoniana Division of the Martin Luther King Public Library, Washington, D.C.

42. *Washington Daily News*, "Zoning Row Stirs Residents Along Massachusetts Avenue," 10 Oct. 1936; *Evening Star*, "Dupont Circle Zoning Plan Is Argued," 4 Dec. 1940. Mrs. Longworth lived at 2009 Massachusetts Avenue in a house designed by de Sibour.

43. *Evening Star*, "Dupont Mansion Razing Starts for $2,500,000 Apartment," 4 Nov. 1949; *Washington Post*, "Preservation Frustration," 23 May 1974, A22.

8. BROADWAY

1. David G. McComb, *Galveston, A History*, Austin: University of Texas Press, 1986, pp. 42–44; Charles W. Hayes, *Galveston, A History of the Island and the City*, Austin: Jenkins Garrett Press, 1974, 2 vols., vol. 1, p. 260; vol. 2, pp. 898–900; John W. Reps, *Cities of the American West: A History of Frontier Urban Planning*, Princeton: Princeton University Press, 1979, pp. 129–34. Reps reproduces a preliminary version of the town plan that was even more complex and monumental than the executed plan. The original plan of Houston, located 50 miles northwest of Galveston and laid out in 1836, encompassed a site of only 62 blocks. See Reps, pp. 127–30.

2. Margaret Swett Henson, "Proud and Determined: Galveston's History in Review," in Kirsten Mullen, editor, *Texana III: The Victorian Era—Texas Comes Of Age*, Austin: Texas Historical Commission, 1987, pp. 15–19; McComb, pp. 47–48; Hayes, vol. 2, pp. 956–61.

3. The "out-lots," equal in size to four city blocks including the intervening streets, occupied the southern and western margins of the town plan. Eventually, streets were cut through many of these superblocks, which accounts for the use of the "½" designation for the alphabetical east-west avenues (example: Avenue M ½). Broadway is also designated Avenue J. The Galvestonian custom of designating city streets by more than one name seems to date from the city's inception.

4. On the Frosh and Osterman-Kopperl houses, see Anne Brindley, editor, *Historic Galveston Homes*, Galveston: Galveston Historical Society, 1951, pp. 46–47. Both houses were demolished in the 1940s.

5. The authoritative source on the Brown house is Kenneth Hafertepe, *A History of Ashton Villa: A Family and Its House in Victorian Galveston, Texas*, Austin: Texas State Historical Association, 1991. See also John C. Garner, Jr., James Moreau Brown House, Historic American Buildings Survey Photographic-Data Book Report, Galveston, Texas 333–3, 24 March 1967; Texas Anderson, "The Urban Residence: Archaeology Explores Victorian Domestic Life," in Mullen, editor, *Texana III*, pp. 47–51; and Susan and Michael Southworth, *Ornamental Ironwork, An Illustrated Guide to Its Design, History, and Use in American Architecture*, Boston: David R. Godine, Publisher, Inc., 1978, pp. 68, 70–71.

6. "A Leading Man Gone," *Galveston Daily News*, 26 December 1895.

7. Sadie Gwin Blackburn emphasizes the differences that introduction of a waterworks system had for ornamental gardening in Houston in her essay "The Evolution of the Houston Landscape" in Dorothy Knox Howe Houghton, Barrie M. Scardino, Sadie Gwin Blackburn, and Katherine S. Howe, *Houston's Forgotten Heritage: Landscape, Houses, Interiors, 1824–1914*, Houston: Rice University Press, 1991, pp. 32–33. Mrs. Blackburn observes that gardening as an elite pastime came to be pursued more seriously in Houston than in Galveston because Galveston's poor soil and salt air made plant cultivation so difficult. The garden at Ashton Villa is noted in Mac Griswold and Eleanor Weller, *The Golden Age of American Gardens: Proud Owners, Private Estates, 1890–1940*, New York: H. N. Abrams, 1991, p. 238.

8. "Parting Guests," *Galveston Daily News*, 26 March 1880.

9. Howard Barnstone, *The Galveston That Was*, New York: Macmillan Company, 1966, p. 55.

10. "City Council Passes Ordinance for Making Broadway a Boulevard," *Flake's Semi-Weekly Bulletin*, 19 August 1869; "The Boulevard," *Galveston Daily News*, 17 April 1872; "The Esplanades," *Galveston Daily News*, 13 May 1873; "The Esplanades," *Galveston Daily News*, 16 January 1874; "Broadway Esplanades," *Galveston Daily News*, 12 November 1890; "Where Put the Track?" *Galveston Daily News*, 14 November 1890; "A Public Walk on Broadway," *Galveston Daily News*, 10 August 1888; "Beautify Broadway," *Galveston Daily News*, 26 November 1891.

11. "Methodist Church," *Galveston Daily News*, 12 February 1871; "St. Patrick's Church," *Galveston Daily News*, 23 October 1877; "Michael B. Ménard Memorial Tower, St. Patrick's Church, Galveston," *Southern Messenger*, 24 March 1898; "Dedication Ceremonies," *Galveston Daily News*, 18 January 1892.

12. I. H. Kempner, *Recalled Recollections*, Dallas: Egan Company, 1961, pp. 25–26. The 1899 Sanborn's insurance map of Galveston labeled this building "female boarding."

13. "Local Improvements," *Galveston Daily News*, 1 January 1888; William Manning Morgan, *Trinity Protestant Episcopal Church, Galveston, Texas, 1841–1953*, Houston: Anson Jones Press, 1954, p. 50; Bob Nesbitt, *Bob's Galveston Island Reader*, Galveston: Privately published, 1983, p. 96. Reedy Chapel still occupies its 1887 church building at 2013 Broadway, designed by B. G. Chisolm. African American neighborhoods in Galveston were small in size and scattered throughout the city rather than concentrated in one or two locations. Even so, Black neighborhoods were less likely to be interspersed among high-income housing. In the late nineteenth century some of the most prominent members of Galveston's African American community lived on or near the far east end of Broadway. This neighborhood was decimated in the Storm of 1900 because of its proximity to the beach.

14. Drexel Turner has amassed considerable data on Clayton's career in preparation for a book on his architecture, to which Turner has generously given the author access. Major collections of Clayton's drawings and office records are at the Galveston and Texas History Center of the Rosenberg Library, Galveston, and at the Architectural Drawings Collection and the Eugene C. Barker Texas History Research Center, both at the University of Texas at Austin.

15. The practice of raising houses on piers is common along the Gulf coast. Although Galveston's oldest house, the Samuel May Williams house of 1838 in the out-lot district, is raised on high piers, the practice of raising houses a full story above grade does not seem to have become common

until after 1875. According to Sally B. Woodbridge, high-raised houses in Sacramento are known as "Galveston" houses. "Improvements," *Galveston Daily News*, 30 May 1875; "Building Improvements," *Galveston Daily News*, 3 October 1875; "Rapidly Gaining Ground," *Galveston Daily News*, 4 April 1886; "The Building Boom," *Galveston Daily News*, 4 August 1884; "Stray Notes," *Galveston Daily News*, 12 June 1885.

16. The Sanborn Map Publishing Company's map of Galveston of 1889 notes kitchens and servants' quarters as well as conservatories. Haferetepe, pp. 25–26.

17. The north side of the street was the preferred side of the street on all east-west avenues in Galveston. There were, however, Clayton-designed houses on the south side of Broadway in the East End. A typical alley report is contained in the article "Dirty Alleys," *Galveston Daily News*, 6 August 1869. Ellen Beasley will deal with alley life and culture in her forthcoming book on the back buildings of Galveston, to be published by Rice University Press.

18. "The Building Boom," *Galveston Daily News*, 4 August 1884; "Stray Notes," *Galveston Daily News*, 12 June 1885; *Inland Architect and Builder*, 5 (June 1885), p. 81.

19. "Local Improvements," *Galveston Daily News*, 1 January 1888; "Recent Improvements," *Galveston Daily News*, 1 January 1889; "A New Year's Reception," *Galveston Daily News*, 3 January 1893.

20. "A New Departure in Building," *Galveston Daily News*, 17 April 1887.

21. In her illuminating essay "Women, Religion, and Reform in Galveston, 1880–1920," published in Char Miller and Heywood T. Sanders, editors, *Urban Texas: Politics and Development*, College Station: Texas A&M University Press, 1990, pp. 80, 188–89, Elizabeth Hayes Turner noted the absence of Roman Catholics in Galveston's elite women's civic organizations, although she does not ascribe this to purposeful exclusion. In contrast to the ambivalent position of Roman Catholics in relation to Galveston society, Galveston's elite Jewish families do not seem to have encountered obstacles to social acceptance (although John Gunther, in his biography of Morris Lasker's son, Albert Lasker, implies that the Lasker family's status in Galveston society was tenuous. See John Gunther, *Taken at the Flood, the Story of Albert D. Lasker*, New York: Harper & Brothers, 1960, p. 27). Male members of the Dyer, Osterman, and Kopperl families in the Tremont district and the Blum, Lasker, and Kempner families in the East End belonged to the Galveston Artillery Company. By the time of its dissolution as a militia unit in 1893, the Artillery Company had become Galveston's most prestigious social club. After its members reorganized themselves as the Galveston Artillery Club, they took quarters in one of the former Willis family houses at Tremont and Broadway in 1899, where the club remained until the 1930s. It was under the auspices of the Artillery Club that Galveston debutantes were—and are—presented.

22. "Local Improvements," *Galveston Daily News*, 1 January 1888; "Recent Improvements," *Galveston Daily News*, 1 January 1889; "The Sealy Reception," *Galveston Daily News*, 1 February 1891; "A Quiet Sabbath," *Galveston Daily News*, 20 April 1891; Elizabeth Gustafson, "'The Open Gates,' the George Sealy House in Galveston," *The Magazine Antiques*, 108 (September 1975), pp. 508–14; Leland M. Roth, *The Architecture of McKim, Mead & White, 1870–1920: A Building List*, New York: Garland Publishing, Inc., 1978, p. 139; Richard Guy Wilson, *McKim, Mead & White, Architects*, New York: Rizzoli International Publications, Inc., 1983, pp. 124–27; Jane Burton Pinckard and Rebecca Pinckard, *Lest We Forget, The Open Gates*, privately printed, 1988.

23. The article "The Sealy Reception" describes the drawing room as "white and gold of the Louis XVI design." Mrs. Burton Pinckard, a Sealy granddaughter, and her daughter, Rebecca Pinckard, also describe the furniture as being "Louis XVI" (Pinckard and Pinckard, pp. 50–51). This gilt, French-style furniture became extremely popular among rich Texans in the first decade of the twentieth century. The McFaddin-Ward House Historical Museum in Beaumont preserves such decor in its Pink Room, as does the Moody Mansion and Museum in Galveston. Katherine S. Howe in *Houston's Forgotten Heritage* illustrates several Houston examples (pp. 209, 211, 213) as does Cynthia A. Brandimarte in *Inside Texas: Culture, Identity, and Houses, 1878–1920*, Fort Worth: Texas Christian University Press, 1991.

24. N. J. Clayton & Co., Statement of Expenditures, 9 March 1892, Galveston and Texas History Center, Rosenberg Library, Galveston; Julius

Trousdale Sadler, Jr., and Jacqueline D. J. Sadler, *American Stables, An Architectural Tour*, Boston: New York Graphic Society, 1981, p. 97; Pinckard and Pinckard, pp. 52–53; Griswold and Weller, p. 238. That the Sealy stable cost more than the reported construction cost of Clayton's LeGierse-Ball house of 1875 suggests its exceptional status.

25. "Recent Improvements," *Galveston Daily News*, 1 January 1889; "Little Locals," *Galveston Daily News*, 19 February 1890.

26. "Little Locals," *Galveston Daily News*, 10 March 1893; "Buildings Erected," *Galveston Daily News*, 22 July 1894. Despite its unusually deep site, the League house was set no farther back from Broadway than the Lasker house and its principal rooms resolutely faced south, toward Broadway. Perhaps J. C. League intended the rear portion of the property to be a future house site for his daughter. It was never built upon and the property has remained intact.

27. "The Fifth Avenue of Galveston," *Galveston Daily News*, 7 April 1889. Clayton's drawings survive for the addition of a porte-cochère to the Lasker house, which had been built without one. William Seale, *The Tasteful Interlude: American Interiors Through the Camera's Eye, 1860–1917*, New York: Praeger Publishers, 1975, p. 201; and Hafertepe, pp. 33–35. Hafertepe dates the redecoration at Ashton Villa to about 1890. The arrangement of chimney stacks on the house's west side, the blocking-up of west side windows on the first floor, and the Sloan plan in *The Model Architect* imply that Ashton Villa might originally have had double parlors, which at this time were consolidated into a single drawing room. However, Hafertepe's research did not uncover any evidence to suggest that the single drawing room was not original to the Brown house.

28. "Little Locals," *Galveston Daily News*, 10 March 1893; "A Fatal Fall," *Galveston Daily News*, 2 September 1893; "Buildings Erected," *Galveston Daily News*, 22 July 1894; "Galveston's Building Progress," *Galveston Daily News*, 1 September 1895; "W. H. Tyndall, A Pupil of the Late E. W. Pugin of England…" (advertisement), *Galveston Daily News*, 20 December 1885; David Woodcock, "Restored Island Anchor," *Texas Architect*, 41 (July-August 1991), pp. 38–41.

29. "Mrs. Willis' Funeral," *Galveston Daily News*, 12 September 1899; "The Willis Will Contest," *Galveston Daily News*, 26 November 1899; Henry Wiencek, *The Moody Mansion & Museum*, Galveston: Mary Moody Northen, Inc., 1991; Arthur M. Louis, "It's Moody versus Moody in the Struggle for American General," *Fortune*, 83 (March 1971), pp. 108–12. Patrick H. Butler III, director of the Moody Mansion and Museum, and Bradley C. Brooks, curator of collections, believe that when Mr. and Mrs. Moody bought the Willis house, they acquired much of Mrs. Willis's Pottier, Stymus & Company–installed furniture as well. Dr. Butler states that Mrs. Willis never had Pottier & Stymus finish and furnish her drawing room. This was the room that Mr. and Mrs. Moody declined to have designed by Pottier & Stymus in 1910. Butler to author, 12 August 1992.

30. "Monument Exercises," *Galveston Daily News*, 22 April 1900; *Henry Rosenberg, 1824–1893*, Galveston: Rosenberg Library, 1918, pp. 125–38.

31. Virginia Eisenhour, *The Strand of Galveston*, 1973, p. 1. According to N. J. Clayton's office book for 1887, a copy of which is now in the Galveston and Texas History Center of the Rosenberg Library, when Mrs. Sealy called at Clayton's office on the Strand on some matter relating to the design of her house, she did not go "up" to Clayton's office. Rather, he went down to her carriage.

32. "Building Improvements on Broadway," *Galveston Daily News*, 16 February 1888. A year later, on 7 April 1889, the *News* ran an article on Tremont Street titled "The Fifth Avenue of Galveston." The houses on Tremont, with two early exceptions, were not as grand as those on Broadway. But the street continued to be a fashionable address into the twentieth century.

33. Clarence Ousley, editor, *Galveston in 1900*, Atlanta: William C. Chase, 1900.

34. Lillian E. Herz, "Galveston's Civic League to Honor Pioneers of Organization," *Galveston Daily News*, 22 May 1949; Pinckard and Pinckard, pp. 21, 24, 28–29; Turner, pp. 86, 192. According to Lillian Herz's article, this organization was begun in 1899 for the purpose of landscaping Broadway. The Storm of 1900 caused it to become involved with a much broader range of public welfare issues, but civic landscaping retained a high priority.

35. It was reported in the *Galveston Daily News* on 18 January 1872, when a shipment of palmettos arrived from Florida to be planted in Magnolia Cemetery, there there was only one palm tree in Galveston. The popularity of palm trees as street trees in Texas in the 1900s testifies to the importance of Pasadena as an arbiter of subtropical urban landscaping. Because of Pasadena, the palm tree was associated not only with tropical allure but high status.

36. "To Build a Church," *Galveston Daily News*, 9 January 1903; "Church Dedicated," *Galveston Daily News*, 18 January 1904; "Galveston's New Church," *Southern Messenger*, 25 June 1903; "New Church Dedicated," *Southern Messenger*, 21 January 1904; "Bids Wanted," *Commercial Recorder*, 6 June 1910; "Construction and Building," *Commercial Recorder*, 22 August 1910.

37. "Galveston's Improvements," *Galveston Daily News*, 1 September 1906; On the Kempner family, see Harold M. Hyman, *Oleander Odyssey, The Kempners of Galveston, 1856–1980s*, College Station: Texas A&M University Press, 1990.

38. San Antonio and Houston contained large numbers of pretentious, columned, Colonial Revival–style houses, and they were very visible in such smaller coastal towns as Beaumont, Victoria, Corpus Christi, and Brownsville. Tim Matthewson, "The Colonial Revival and the McFaddin-Ward House," lecture presented at the McFaddin-Ward House Museum Conference, 30 October 1987.

The Storm of 1900 dramatically punctuated, but did not cause, Galveston's economic decline. During the 1890s Galveston began to lose ground to Houston. In the late 1880s Dallas demonstrated that rail connections to Kansas City, St. Louis, and Chicago were of more consequence to the economy of Texas than shipping connections to the eastern seaboard and Europe. Between 1880 and 1890 Dallas grew in population from 10,358 to 39,067 to become the largest city in the state. Houston's superior rail connections enabled it to outgrow Galveston between 1890 and 1900. Between 1900 and 1910 Houston, Dallas, and San Antonio nearly doubled their populations. Galveston, as a result of the storm, lost population. The discovery of oil on the Texas Gulf coast in 1901 rebounded to Houston's benefit. And after the U.S. Army Corps of Engineers dredged a 50-mile ship channel from the Gulf of Mexico through Galveston Bay and up Buffalo Bayou to Houston between 1902 and 1914, Galveston's one natural advantage, its harbor, was no longer a unique asset.

The organization of certain types of cultural institutions provides an index of civic development among Texas cities: first, a public library, then a symphony orchestra, then an art museum. Galveston acquired a public library, but never a symphony orchestra nor an art museum.

39. "Demolishing Old Blum House," *Galveston Daily News*, 12 December 1915, and Ellis A. Davis and Edwin H. Grobe, *The New Encyclopedia of Texas*, Dallas: Texas Development Bureau, undated (c. 1921), vol. 2, pp. 544–45. Crow, Lewis & Wickenhoefer specialized in hospital design and sent Korn to Galveston to supervise their alterations and additions to Clayton's John Sealy Hospital. Korn left Galveston in 1917 to establish an independent and highly successful practice in Dallas.

40. "Campaign for Paving Beautiful Broadway," *Galveston Daily News*, 25 May 1909, and "Twenty-Thousand View Broadway Lighting and Cheer Monster Parade," *Galveston Daily News*, 14 March 1914.

41. Robert H. McGhee, "History of the Townplan of Galveston," unpublished manuscript, 1976, pp. 42–43; Herb Woods, *Galveston-Houston Electric Railway*, Interurbans Special Number 22, vol. 16, Glendale, 1976. The Interurban ran until 1936. Between 1947 and 1952 the Gulf Freeway was built following the Interurban's right-of-way.

42. Another early indication of the trend toward subtlety appeared in an article by the journalist Julian Ralph, "Joyous Galveston," in *Harper's Weekly*, 39 (9 November 1895), p. 1064, in which he observed that "the fine seats of the old aristocracy and the showy homes of the new generation of successful men in trade exhibit strong contrasts. Only a few of the old-style, galleried, and colonnaded planters' mansions are left, and they accentuate with some pathos the loss of taste that occasioned their extinction. They are today the finest houses in Galveston."

Ralph went on to assert that "Galveston will remain peculiar and Southern in spite of the new bird cage palaces" (i.e., the "showy homes"). That the "seats of the old aristocracy," the "planters' mansions" (such as the Frosh house), were built by an earlier generation of those "successful men in trade" would no doubt have pained Ralph had he known it. Edna Ferber, *A Kind of Magic*, Garden City: Doubleday, 1963, p. 102.

43. John Gunther, *Taken At the Flood, the Story of Albert D. Lasker*, New York: Harper & Brothers, 1960, p. 18.

44. Howard Barnstone, *The Architecture of John F. Staub, Houston and the South*, Austin: University of Texas Press, 1979, p. 317; *Texas General Contractors Association Monthly Bulletin*, 9 (November 1928), p. 30, and 12 (May 1931), p. 23. During the 1920s new houses of modest proportions were also built on the south side of Broadway in the Castle District and on the West End of Broadway.

45. These include the subdivisions of Cedar Lawn, developed by W. L. Moody's son-in-law, Clark W. Thompson, and settled by relatives and business associates of the Moody family; Westmoor; the one-block-long private street of Caduceus Place; and Denver Court, where members of the Kempner family lived.

46. Bob Wood, "Man Who Cut Isle Esplanades Called 'Butcher of Broadway,'" *Houston Chronicle*, 9 April 1967.

47. In her novel *The Shadow Line*, Laura Furman has a Galvestonian explain to a visitor the significance of being a native-born Galvestonian: "This BOI business. It's really important to people around here.... Did you notice those huge red stone mansions as you drive down Broadway? The esplanade with the giant palms? Well, one of those belongs to the richest lady in town. It's the family mansion and this is their town. But the Dairy Queen's right next door. Now what can anyone say about that?" *The Shadow Line*, New York: Viking Press, 1982, p. 194.

48. Barnstone, *The Galveston That Was*, p. 95. "Landmark Demolition," *Galveston Daily News*, 8 October 1967; Martin Dreyer, "Farewell to a Galveston Landmark," *Texas Magazine*, 22 October 1967; Constance M. Greiff, *Lost America: From the Mississippi to the Pacific*, Princeton: The Pyne Press, 1974, p. 105.

49. Paul Goeldner, compiler, *Texas Catalog: Historic American Buildings Survey*, San Antonio: Trinity University Press, 1974, pp. 21–28; Gianni Longo, Jean Tatge, and Lois Fishman, *What Makes Cities Livable? Learning from Galveston*, New Brunswick: Institute for Environmental Action, 1983, pp. 55, 93–97; James Wright Steely, compiler, *A Catalog of Texas Properties in the National Register of Historic Places*, Austin: Texas Historical Commission, 1984, p. 64.

50. James P. Sterba, "Galveston, Texas, Is Reawakening After a Long Slumber," *New York Times*, 18 May 1975; Ellen Beasley, "History in Towns: Galveston, Texas," *The Magazine Antiques*, 108 (September 1975), pp. 478–89; John Cornforth, "The Venice of Texas: Galveston-1," *Country Life* (27 April 1978), pp. 1160–62 and "The Resilience of a Texas Town: Galveston-2," *Country Life* (1 June 1978), pp. 1574–78; David Woodcock, "Texas Contexts: Keeping the Past in Texas," *The Architectural Review*, 164 (November 1978), pp. 322–23; Lawrence W. Cheek, "Galveston Defies the Odds," *Historic Preservation*, 41 (September-October 1989), pp. 28–35.

51. John Raines, "Old Bishop's Castle to Open to Public," *Galveston Daily News*, 24 October 1963.

52. Hafertepe, pp. 40–47; Longo, Tatge, and Fishman, pp. 51–55.

53. Woodcock, "Restored Island Anchor," pp. 40–41.

54. Pinckard and Pinckard, p. 55. The University of Texas has never used the Sealy house for any purpose. It is cared for but not occupied and is not open to the public.

55. Jeffrey Karl Ochsner, "Broadway Beautification Plan," *Cite*, Fall 1986, p. 6; William F. Stern, "Galveston: A Master Plan for Broadway," *Houston Chapter/American Institute of Architects Newsletter*, July-August 1988, p. 4.

9. VANDEVENTER AVENUE

1. There remain three prime sources to facilitate an approximate reconstruction: the architectural criticism of William R. Hodges, critic of the weekly *The Spectator*; the photo archive of the late Dr. William Swekosky, dentist and indefatigable amateur photographer of houses, now housed at

Convent of the School Sisters of Notre Dame in Carondelet, Missouri; and the original plat books, so carefully maintained at the Pitzman Company that each of the eighty-six neatly annotated lots in Vandeventer Place remains a key to the street's early development. These three are supplemented by Enno Kraehe's "Appraisal of City Block 2289, Vandeventer Place," (May 21, 1948), at the Landmarks Association of St. Louis, Inc.; Bertha Warburton Drake Scott's "Diary," Isaac H. Lionberger's "Memoir," and Emily Eaton's "Scrapbook—Vandeventer Place" of 1941, all at the Missouri Historical Society. Some of this essay has been extracted, with the permission of University of Missouri Press, from *The Architecture of the Private Streets of St. Louis* (Columbia, Mo.: University of Missouri Press, 1987) by this author. Additional research was carried out in St. Louis in 1989, 1991, and 1992.

2. Vandeventer's heirs were his two sons William and Henry Vandeventer of New York and his daughter Emily V. Vallean of Ohio. William was his father's executor. The earliest purchases within Vandeventer Place were made from Vandeventer's heirs. For example, the indenture from the "Executors" to Samuel A. Coale, Jr., for lot 14 (15 Vandeventer), dated April 19, 1872, for $3750, can be seen in Pitzman Plat Book 8, pp. 122–23. In the first distribution of public land early in the century, this parcel stretching all the way to Kingshighway was assigned to a farmer named Marechal. (An arpent is a unit of measurement still employed in Quebec and Louisiana. It is a strip of land 192 feet, six inches wide but its length is determined by the needs of a family directly proportional to the number of progeny.) Emily Eaton records in "Scrapbook—Vandeventer Place" that Marechal exchanged a portion of his arpents for medical treatment and subsequently the doctor, strapped, sold it to Peter Vandeventer. A note in the Bates Papers at the Missouri Historical Society indicates that in 1854 Vandeventer and the city schools reached a compromise over an apparent claim and counterclaim; Vandeventer would take ground on the west side of Grand Avenue, approximately four-and-a-half acres, and the schools would take ground on the east side.

3. E. A. Behymer described the Lucas Place time limit as an immanent death warrant in "Rise and Fall of Lucas Place," *Post-Dispatch* ("Everyday Magazine"), March 3, 1941. Whether or not the framers of the deed restrictions foresaw the commercial and industrial growth that engulfed the neighborhood in any pragmatic way continues to be discussed.

4. Richard Edwards and M. Hopewell, M.D., *Great West, History of St. Louis* (St. Louis, 1860).

5. Now only the Campbell house (1851) at 1508 Locust Street remains, the last of the initial Lucas Place houses and a historic house museum.

6. *Missouri-Republican*, May 20, 1859; Lucas Place was mentioned also.

7. Subsequently Pitzman was retained by several of the private street associations as the only nonresident trustee.

8. There was no restriction against rooming houses, which may have been a contributing factor in Benton Place's survival.

9. Pitzman plat-exhibit, June 1, 1869, p. 1549, to Book 478, p. 204, City Records Office. There is a double entrance to Vandeventer Place at Grand Avenue, two drives separated by a center median, but each of these splits on either side of a subordinate median strip.

10. Pitzman plat-exhibit, June 24, 1870, p. 1917, to Book 478, p. 204, City Records Office. The plat for Vandeventer Place is in Pitzman Office Records, Grand Prairie Book 10-A, p. 4, June 24, 1870. Vandeventer Place was integrated into city blocks 2289 north and 3748, 2289 south and 3749.

11. Here is the full list of prohibited nuisances: breweries, distilleries, public museums, theaters, circuses, exhibitions, businesses, dangerous and noxious undertakings, tenement houses, taverns, hotels, public schools, warehouses, places of trade, livery stables, slaughter houses, smithies, forges, furnaces, steam engines, brass foundaries, rail factories, gun powder, glue/varnish, vitriol, ink, turpentine, tanning, dressing and preparing furs.

12. "Private Residential Places," *Saint Louis Republic* (May 5, 1895).

13. Barnett had designed a double house at Locust between Sixth and Seventh Streets for Peck—the facade was articulated with a major order of Corinthian pilasters. Barnett's stylistic preference stayed close to the classical canon. He is best known for his surviving work, country houses in the Tuscan idiom in the 1840s and 1850s and the Second Empire residences following the Civil War. Several other architects worked with Barnett,

among them Henry G. Isaacs (1835–95) who had come to St. Louis from New York where he had worked for Richard Michell Upjohn. Isaac S. Taylor (1856–1917), best known as supervising architect of the Louisiana Purchase Exposition which opened in 1904, started in Barnett's office and was his partner from 1874 to 1880. All three of his sons trained in his office. The oldest, Absalom, moved to San Francisco. Subsequently George Dennis Barnett, Thomas P. Barnett, and their brother-in-law, John Ignatius Haynes, carried the firm into this century. In 1885 the firm became George I. Barnett & Son; in 1890 Barnett & Haynes; and Barnett, Haynes & Barnett five years later. In 1912 Thomas P. Barnett started his own practice.

14. The Coale house was noticed in "Building Intelligence," *American Architect & Building News*, v. 9, no. 281, (May 14, 1881), p. 240. The two-story, fourteen-room house was to cost $16,500.

15. Pitzman's Record, pp. 2289, 3748–49. In the late 1870s and early 1880s Henry Leathe, owner of lots 48–60 (49–55 Vandeventer Place) and William J. Hegel, owner of lots on both sides of Vandeventer's westernmost reach, may have employed the Barnett firm to improve their investments. Particularly provocative is Francis D. Lee's commissioning a survey of lots 53 and 55 for a Mr. Stewart in 1882. Although each of these lots was built on in 1891 and 1889 respectively, neither commission could have been carried out by Lee. Indeed, it is doubtful that Lee, a prominent antebellum Charleston architect, undertook a commission in Vandeventer Place.

16. Numbers 55, 68, 74, 85, even 87, are similar to Number 62 and it is likely that Isaacs designed them as well. Carolyn Toft prefers Isaac Taylor as the member of the Barnett firm to design these brick houses. In 1899 Jordan Lambert commissioned Eames & Young to design an addition to 62 Vandeventer.

17. The church, built of rough-cut ashlar limestone dressed with smooth-faced gray sandstone, was illustrated in *American Architect and Building News*, 2 (Dec. 9, 1876), p. 397. Ramsey is best known today as the local architect Adler & Sullivan chose to supervise their St. Louis work for the Wainwrights. Ramsey had worked for the Wainwright family in 1886.

18. Burnham & Root carried out two other residential commissions in St. Louis, though neither was in Vandeventer Place.

19. There he had met Ephraim Peabody, later pastor of Kings Chapel in Boston and father of Robert Swain Peabody, the architect. Eliot's leadership and humane spirit were responsible to a great degree for St. Louis's cultural growth. In establishing Washington University, Eliot received substantial assistance from Bostonians as well, among them Nathaniel Thayer whose house on Commonwealth Avenue had been designed by Peabody & Stearns. To prepare students for Washington University, Eliot founded both Smith Academy for young men and Mary Institute, the first nonsectarian secondary school for young women in St. Louis.

20. Hodges used the Turner Building as an example in one of his six "Lessons in Architecture," serialized in *The Spectator*, 233 (Dec. 20, 1884), pp. 234–35.

21. See a discussion of Furber's responsibilities in *The Architecture of the Private Streets of St. Louis*, pp. 133–34. In 1882–83 he was in Colorado Springs supervising the construction of the Antlers Hotel. There is reason to believe that he supervised the construction of the James H. Hill mansion on Summit Avenue in St. Paul, 1887–88. All evidence suggests that Furber was responsible for drumming up local trade as well as supervising the work of the firm in the West. It appears that the bulk of the designing was done in Boston, but Furber may have been able to modify the work somewhat. In 1877 Furber was one of a group of several young draftsmen who met in the rooms of Howard Walker and Willson Bates to sketch twice a week; Cass Gilbert, Clarence Johnston, Francis Bacon, and Thomas Hastings were some of the other members. David Gray, *Thomas Hastings, Architect* (Boston: Houghton Mifflin Co., 1933), p. 21. It would appear that a portion of Furber's background was in design.

22. Mr. Newman's three-story, fourteen-room house was projected to cost $20,000, "Building Intelligence," *American Architect & Building News*, v. 8, no. 239 (July 24, 1880), p. 48. Newman had purchased his two-and-a-half lots from one P. P. Runyon of New Brunswick, New Jersey—perhaps a speculator acquaintance of the Vandeventers.

23. Mr. Morton's building permit was published in "Building Intelligence," *American Architect & Building News*, v. 17, no. 473 (Jan. 17, 1885), p. 36. The house was projected to cost $22,000, and the contractor was Samuel Morrison.

24. Mr. Moore's new building permit was published in "Building Intelligence," *American Architect & Building News*, v. 18, no. 514 (Oct. 31, 1885), p. 216. Projected cost of the house was $12,000, and the contractor was J. Strimple & Son.

25. The Howard house was noticed in "Building Intelligence," *American Architect & Building News*, v. 21, no. 579 (Jan. 29, 1887), p. xii. The house was to cost $30,000, and the builder was E. C. Clark.

26. Only the J. R. Lionberger house was cited in Marianna Griswold van Rensselaer's biography, *Henry Hobson Richardson and His Work*, 1967, pp. 108, 140. The fourth house, the shingled Henry S. Potter house for Margaret Lionberger Potter and her husband at 5814 Cabanne, may have been the first of the four commissions. William R. Hodges visited the house and described it in early 1883. Bequeathed to the city as a park, the house was demolished in 1958. The Isaac Lionberger house alone remains but has been subjected to controversial alterations and additions. Hitchcock gave this design to Shepley, Rutan & Coolidge on chronological grounds, *The Architecture of H. H. Richardson and His Times*, 1966, p. 281. Ochsner has determined that it was designed before Richardson's death, *H. H. Richardson, Complete Architectural Works*, 1984, p. 425.

27. In 1888 Shepley designed a $315,000 wholesale building of brownstone for John R. Lionberger at the corner of Washington Avenue and Eighth Street to be occupied by the Ely, Walker Dry Goods Co. and Gauss, Shelton & Co. Norcross of Boston were the builders. "Building Intelligence," *American Architect & Building News*, v. 23, no. 633 (Feb. 11, 1888), p. xvi.

28. Both his father, John R. Shepley, and his brother, John F. Shepley, were distinguished attorneys. His brother practiced law in partnership with Isaac H. Lionberger and his sister Louise became Lionberger's wife. His brother married Sarah Collier Hitchcock, the daughter of Ethan Allen Hitchcock and his wife, Margaret Dwight Collier, daughter of George and Sarah Collier of Lucas Place. Henry Hitchcock, at 54 Vandeventer Place, the uncle of Shepley's sister-in-law, had also married a daughter of George and Sarah Collier, Mary Collier Hitchcock. And Annie Shepley, his niece, married Dexter Tiffany; they built 72 Vandeventer Place.

29. New building permits were published for the Davis house, "Building Intelligence," *American Architect and Building News*, v. 21, no. 588 (April 2, 1887), p. xiii, and the stable, no. 589 (April 9, 1887), p. xiii. The house was to cost $22,000 and the stable $2,800. The builder was S. Maraten.

30. Unfortunately, Dr. Swekowsky did not photograph in Vandeventer Place until after Number 50 was demolished; no reproduction of it exists in the Missouri Historical Society or the Swekowsky Collection housed at the Cardinal Ritter Library, Convent of the School Sisters of Notre Dame. When queried, descendents could not locate an image of the house. Mrs. Shepley had lot 49 surveyed on Nov. 16, 1889, and the adjoining half of lot 51 surveyed in March 18, 1891. The new building permit was noted twice in *American Architect & Building News*, v. 27, no. 73 (Jan. 18, 1890), p. xvii, and v. 28, no. 750 (May, 10, 1890), p. viii.

Two years earlier Shepley had designed a $45,000 retail store building at the corner of Locust and Seventh Streets for his father's estate, "Building Intelligence," *American Architect & Building News*, v. 23, no. 633 (Feb. 11, 1888), p. xvi.

31. Although lot 53, 54 Vandeventer Place, was surveyed on Sept. 7, 1891, the new building application for the Henry Hitchcock house was twice noted in the "Building Intelligence" section of the *American Architect and Building News*: v. 35, no. 837 (Jan. 9, 1892), p. xviii; and v. 37, #872, (Sept. 10, 1892), p. xix. The house was to cost $20,000, and Givens & Steinhoff were the contractors.

32. The Scott's intention to build was published in "Building Intelligence," *American Architect & Building News*, v. 56, no. 1122 (June 26, 1897), p. xii; the house was to cost $20,000.

Shepley, Rutan & Coolidge undertook alterations and additions to two other houses: at 21 Vandeventer Place (the former Newman house—Peabody & Stearns), a new front entrance for Daniel Catlin, 1888, and at Number 47 (the George D. Barnard house—Tully & Clark), a renovated eastern elevation for John Fowler in 1899. Both Catlin and Fowler commissioned Mauran, Russell & Garden, the firm that evolved from Shepley, Rutan & Coolidge's local office, to carry out further additions in 1903.

33. *The Spectator*, v. 85 (April 8, 1882), p. 359; v. 100 (Oct. 21, 1882), p. 125.

34. The Mersmens had their lots (Numbers 70 and 72) surveyed Sept. 8, 1888. A building permit was published in "Building Intelligence," *American Architect & Building News*, v. 24, no. 676 (Dec. 8, 1888). The house was to cost $16,000, and the contractors were Kerr & Allen.

35. Mrs. Bent's building permit was published in "Building Intelligence," *American Architect & Building News*, v. 27, no. 733 (Jan. 11, 1890), p. xvii. It was projected to cost $20,000. The contractors were Kerr & Allen.

36. Eames & Young had one final commission in Vandeventer Place, for Jordan W. Lambert at Number 62 in 1899, an addition to the existing house.

37. See Carolyn Hewes Toft & Jane Molloy Porter, *Compton Heights* (St. Louis: Landmarks Association of St. Louis, Inc., 1984), p. 43.

38. David D. Walker was the great-grandfather of the forty-second president of the United States, George Walker Bush.

39. The building permit for the H. N. Davis house was published in "Building Intelligence," *American Architect & Building News*, v. 25, no. 686 (Feb. 16, 1889), p. xix. The house was to cost $10,000, and the contractors were Goesse & Remmers.

40. The Wickham house was noticed in "Building Intelligence," *American Architect & Building News*, v.26, no. 712 (Aug. 17, 1889), p. xvii; the house was to cost $15,000, and the contractors were Goesse & Remmers.

41. The permit for the E. A. Hitchcock house was published in "Building Intelligence," *American Architect & Building News*, v. 35, no. 836 (Jan. 2, 1892), p. xvii. The house was to cost $20,000, and the contractors were Goesse & Remmers.

42. The Tiffany house was noticed in "Building Intelligence," *American Architect & Building News*, v. 36, no. 861 (June 25, 1892), p. xxii. The cost of the house was projected at $20,000, and S. L. Jones was the contractor.

These last Grable & Weber commissions raise a question. Was it the firm's new inventiveness that drew to them commissions that might just as well have gone to Shepley, Rutan & Coolidge? Ethan Allen Hitchcock was the father-in-law of Shepley's brother. It was he who commissioned Richardson to design the Crystal City, Missouri, church project (1885–86) and Mrs. Dexter Tiffany was a Shepley cousin and her husband the son of John R. Shepley's law partner. The Crystal City church project is discussed in James F. O'Gorman, *Henry Hobson Richardson and His Office* (Cambridge, Mass.: 1974), pp. 62–65, and J. K. Ochsner, *H. H. Richardson, Complete Architectural Works* (Cambridge, Mass.: 1984), pp. 408–409. Why would these people, likely Shepley clients, take their business to Grable & Weber? It is known that a William T. Brainerd became chief of the Shepley, Rutan & Coolidge office in St. Louis in 1890 but that he was replaced by John Lawrence Mauran two years later, Ernest J. Russell, "Impressions," Russell file, Missouri Historical Society. Were these likely clients dissatisfied with Brainerd?

43. The intention to build the McKeighan house was published in "Building Intelligence," *American Architect & Building News*, v. 15, no. 423 (Feb. 2, 1884), p. 59. To cost $10,000, the house's architect and contractor was Stewart.

44. Fuller may be best known for his many partnerships: with Chilion Jones he designed the Parliament Buildings, Ottawa, Canada; again with Jones he won the first competition for the New York State Capitol. But to retain this commission through the subsequent political battles surrounding the design of the new Capitol, he modified partnerships: Fuller, Nichols & Brown, then Fuller & Laver. See Henry-Russell Hitchcock and William Seale, *Temples of Democracy* (New York: Harcourt Brace Jovanovich, 1976). It is possible that it was Lorenzo B. Wheeler (d. 1899) who was Fuller's partner in the 1880s and 1890s. Dennis Steadman Francis tracked Wheeler in New York: Wheeler began his practice in New York with Hugh Lamb from 1878 to 1882, then worked alone until 1884, *Architects in Practice in New York City, 1840–1900* (New York: Committee for the Preservation of Architectural Records, 1980). In his obituary, and after his partnership with Lamb in New York, Wheeler is recorded as sequentially maintaining offices in Atlanta, Memphis, and St. Louis, returning to Connecticut, his place of birth, only when forced to by ill health, *American Architect & Building News*, v. 63, no. 1212 (March, 1899), p. 82. Francis cites Wheeler back in New

York in 1898–99. For Craig McClure being sent from Albany to represent Fuller & Wheeler in St. Louis, see "Personal," *Northwest Architect*, v. 10, no. 2 (Feb., 1892), p. 15. Fuller & Wheeler designed the Ellis house in Schenectady, N.Y.; *American Architect & Building News*, v. 17, no. 474 (Jan. 1885). Though more in the Queen Anne style than the Romanesque, the Ellis house is similar to the Pierce house. Fuller & Wheeler designed the Montreal YMCA, which gained notoriety when the floors collapsed, *American Architect & Building News*, v. 32, no. 799 (April 18, 1891), p. 44, and the Baths at Saratoga, *Moniteur des Architectes*, v. 41, no. 6 (1892), pp. 67–68. Fuller & Wheeler's plans for the Masonic Temple in Albany were noticed in "Building Intelligence—Advanced Rumors," *American Architect & Building News*, v. 47, no. 1003 (March 16, 1895), p. xiii.

45. Pierce's intention to build was announced in "Building Intelligence," *American Architect & Building News*, v. 20, no. 563 (Oct. 9, 1886), p. xi, immediately below his neighbor, Richard Kerens, same page, same architect. Both contracted with the same builder, C. E. Clark.

46. Mr. Love's house was noticed in "Building Intelligence," *American Architect & Building News*, v. 20, no. 567 (Nov. 6, 1886), p. xii. It cost but $5000. J. B. Asper was the contractor.

47. Mullgardt's work is best known in the San Francisco Bay Area. See Robert Judson Clark, *Louis Christian Mullgardt* (Santa Barbara: University of California Art Gallery, 1966). L. C. Mullgardt is not to be confused with his brother Oscar, who after a career with Mauran & Russell in St. Louis was made a partner in 1939.

48. Mr. Fowler's intent to build was published in "Building Intelligence," *American Architect & Building News*, v. 38, no. 879 (Oct. 29, 1892), p. xviii; the house was to cost $21,000 and the contractors were Kelly & Lawton.

49. Mr. Dameron had had Pitzman survey this site (lot 80 and half of 82) on Jan. 22, 1894. Kelly & Lawton, frequent contractors for Stewart, McClure & Mullgardt, were noticed for this job in "Building Intelligence," *American Architect & Building News*, v. 43, no. 947 (Feb. 17, 1894), p. xii. Mr. Dameron's stable was to cost $15,000.

50. The Niedringhaus building permit was published in "Building Intelligence," *American Architect & Building News*, v. 36, no. 857 (May 28, 1892), p. xxii; the house was to cost $18,000.

51. Not enough is known about the firm of Kivas K. Tully and Charles P. Clark to do more than record their partnership. See *The Architecture of the Private Streets*, p. 66. Pitzman had surveyed this lot for George I. Barnett in 1886, but Barnett was not the architect of this house. Clark, the architect of the much maligned Fagin Building, "Architectural Aberrations—No. 7, Fagin Building, St. Louis," *Architectural Record*, v. 2, no. 4 (April-June, 1893), pp. 470–72—repeated that building's overscaled and eccentric ornament here, integrating it into the design of this unique brick house. Apparently Clark was inspired by the individualism of the Philadelphia architect Frank Furness. See also Lawrence Lowic, *The Architectural Heritage of St. Louis* (St. Louis: Washington University Art Gallery, 1982), p. 141.

The Barnard house was carried in "Building Intelligence," *American Architect & Building News*, v. 22, no. 611 (Sept. 10, 1887), p. xiii; the cost of the house was projected at $15,000, and R. P. McClure was to be the contractor.

52. Mr. Liggett's new building permit was published in "Building Intelligence," *American Architect & Building News*, v. 28, no. 747 (April 19, 1890), p. xvii; it was to cost $20,000, and H. E. Roach was the contractor. Because Roach was responsible for the Liggett & Myers Tobacco Building at 1900 Pine Street, built in 1889, it is not unlikely that Roach designed this house also.

53. Mr. Bofinger's intention to build was published in "Building Intelligence," *American Architect & Building News*, v. 56, no. 1122 (June 26, 1897), p. xii; it was to cost $13,000.

54. Might it have been the design of Grable & Weber? The Italian Renaissance style was in vogue and the principal entrance was on the side and accessible from the street through a columned veranda, as in Grable & Weber's Tiffany house at 72 Vandeventer Place.

55. Hodges, "Architectural Renaissance," *The Spectator*, v. 98 (July 29, 1882), p. 824.

56. Enno Kraehe, *Appraisal of City Block 2289—Vandeventer Place*, unpublished report, May 28, 1948.

57. The coincidence of the Mallinckrodt commission and Ramsey's let-ter—"Roofing Tile," *American Architect and Building News*, v. 9, no. 282 (May 21, 1881), p. 250—in which he asks for sources for red tile suggests the tile is to cover the Mallinckrodt house. He was directed to Merrill, Ewart & Co. of Akron, Ohio.

58. Hodges, "Architectural Renaissance," *The Spectator*, v. 98 (July 29, 1882), p. 824.

59. The ratio of second-story bedrooms to those on the third story is an indication that servants were needed to make things work.

60. Hodges, "Residence of Watson B. Farr, Vandeventer Place," *op.cit.* Burnham & Root carried out two other residential commissions in St. Louis, though neither was in Vandeventer Place.

61. Hodges, "Residence of Mr. Watson B. Farr in Vandeventer Place," *The Spectator*, v. 97 (July 22, 1882), p. 812.

62. *Ibid.*

63. *Ibid.* Burnham & Root's house for John Whitaker was noticed in "Building Intelligence," *American Architect & Building News*, v. 8, no. 243 (Aug. 21, 1880), p. 96. This eighteen-room, $25,000 house was not built in Vandeventer Place. Nor was Burnham & Root's house for Halstead Burnett, "Building Intelligence," *American Architect & Building News*, v. 13, no. 383 (April 28, 1883), p. xi; the Halstead house was illustrated the year before, *American Architect and Building News*, v. 12, no. 350 (Sept., 1882).

64. "Carolina" granite: the material was identified in "Too Costly," *Webb Spinner*, v. 4, no. 10 (Sept., 1950), p. 11.

65. Henry-Russell Hitchcock found fault with the scale of the J. R. Lionberger house, *The Architecture of H. H. Richardson*, p. 280. Hitchcock compared this house to the McVeigh house, c. 1885–87, in Chicago. Both possess rounded corners and loggias in the upper stories. But the Lionberger facade is also the Glessner house Prairie Avenue facade rounded into a nar-rower lot. Where the McVeigh house entrance is around the corner, free-ing the more desirable Lake Michigan orientation for rooms and loggias, the entrance to the Lionberger house was prescribed by the street's deed restrictions. It is unlikely that Hitchcock knew this in 1965.

66. These griffins will be recognizable to those familiar with the gargoyles that animated the decorative scheme of the Turner Building. The earliest of Peabody & Stearns's signature gargoyles were those on the Gardner Brew Building, 1874, in Boston, *American Architect and Building News*, v. 2 (April 4, 1877).

67. It was believed locally for many years that Richardson designed the J. D. Davis house, Mary Powell, "Public Art in St. Louis," *Saint Louis Public Library Monthly Bulletin* (July-August, 1925), p. 218. Miss Powell states that there were two houses in Vandeventer Place designed by H. H. Richardson and finished by Shepley, Rutan & Coolidge. Miss Powell was art and archi-tecture librarian and subsequently head of the Art Museum's Education Department. Recent scholarship does not place designs for the Davis com-mission before Richardson's death, April 27, 1886. While drawings existed for the J. R. Lionberger house in late 1885, the lot at Number 27 wasn't sur-veyed until January 29, 1886. Pitzman did not survey the Davis lot until July 6, 1886.

68. "The Whitaker Residence," *The Spectator*, v. 93 (June 24, 1882), p. 726; "Residence of Mr. Watson B. Farr in Vandeventer Place," *Ibid.*, v. 97 (July 22, 1882), p. 812.

69. Shepley enjoyed a double reputation. On one hand he could be thought of as Bostonian and the inheritor of a nationally respected prac-tice; on the other he was St. Louis–bred, understanding the requirements of the private street residents. He could assimilate his adaptations of current styles into the evolving texture of Vandeventer Place.

70. Eames & Young had one final commission in Vandeventer Place for Jordan W. Lambert at No. 62 in 1899, an addition to the existing residence designed by George I. Barnett & Co in 1886.

71. Perhaps the Mrs. Mary Shepley house was a link in the stylistic transi-tion between the John D. Davis house across the street and the Hitchcock house next door.

72. The plan of the Tiffany house resurrected and made the old "flounder house" plan respectable. "Flounder house" is not used here in its original sense, which indicated a house built on a very narrow lot and so close to

one side of the lot that the house lacked windows on that side. The Tiffany house had fenestration on all sides, but its principal entrance was on the side, a characteristic it shared with earlier "flounder houses."

73. This description was taken from a letter to the author from Mrs. J. R. Usher, December 26, 1987, in which she described with gratifying clarity the interior of her childhood home.

74. The quotation is from Samuel L. Scherer, "Interesting Brickwork and Terra Cotta Architecture in Saint Louis," *Brickbuilder*, v. 12 (Feb. 1903), pp. 32–36.

75. In 1889 Eames & Young specifed a furnace manufactured by Vrot Iron Range Co. for Charles W. Scudder's new house at 75 Vandeventer Place. Scudder Family Papers, 58–0127, Missouri Historical Society.

76. By 1890 there were thirty-two structural brickyards in the metropolitan area of St. Louis, and Missouri ranked fifth nationally in brick production, *Eleventh Census*, 1890, v. 6, No. 3.

77. Hodges, "Art," *The Spectator*, v. 97 (July 22, 1882), p. 812.

78. Samuel L. Scherer, "Interesting Brickwork," *The Brickbuilder*, v. 12 (Feb. 1903), p. 32.

79. The customs of Lucas Place informed those of the next generation in Vandeventer Place. The ladies of Lucas Place had not all agreed to a single day, but the day that each was "at home" followed her listing in *Gould's Blue Book*. Many of their married daughters moved to Vandeventer Place: Mrs. Orrick (nee Allen) at Number 25; Mrs. Chapman (nee Bridge) at 46; Mrs. Daniel Catlin (nee Kayser) at 49; Mrs. Morton at 49 and her sister Mrs. Moore at 61 (nee Filley); and the two Mrs. Hitchcocks (the sisters Mary L. and Margaret D., daughters of Sarah and George Collier) at 54 and 60 Vandeventer Place respectively.

80. *The Spectator*, v. 368 (Oct. 1, 1887), p. 74.

81. *The Spectator*, v. 106 (Sept. 23, 1882), p. 25; v. 114 (Nov. 18, 1882), p. 216; v. 138 (May 3, 1883), p. 721; v. 141 (May 26, 1883), p. 791; v. 149 (July 21, 1883), p. 927.

82. Hodges, "Architectural Renaissance," *The Spectator*, v. 98 (July 29, 1882), p. 824.

83. Ralph Coale: "Old Vandeventer," *Reedy's Mirror* (Aug. 18, 1916), pp. 523–33. E. A. H. Shepley's recollection, *Post-Dispatch* (March 17, 1958).

84. Bertha Warburton Drake Scott, "Journals and Diaries," Missouri Historical Society.

85. Arthur B. Shepley, another of Mary Shepley's offspring, was elected treasurer. The residents voted (one vote per lot) to assess themselves $6540 per annum ($75 per lot) for street maintenance. They selected officers and agreed to meet annually.

86. "Private Residential Places," *Saint Louis Republic*, May 5, 1895.

87. "Building Intelligence," *American Architect & Building News*, v. 40, no. 909 (May 27, 1892), p. viii. In retrospect, replacing the simple iron gates and fencing suggests that the residents felt not only forced to compete with the new private streets going up to the west—the Forest Park Addition, et al., but to isolate themselves from a changing quarter.

88. Instead of rebuilding in Vandeventer Place, the Newmans built anew in Westmoreland Place in 1889. Isaac Lionberger moved to Westmoreland Place in 1905. Arthur Shepley moved there three years later. Miss Marion Lionberger followed her brother in 1910. George Barnard moved to Portland Place in 1911 and Mrs. Morton the year after. John and Cora Liggett Fowler moved to Westmoreland Place in 1912, Mrs. Scott in 1913, the Mallinckrodts in 1914, and Daniel Catlin in 1916.

89. *Globe-Democrat*, Jan. 1, 1928.

90. Lot #1—a taking duly recorded in Pitzman's plat book.

91. Simultaneous to Miss Eaton's labors were the successful negotiations to save the Campbell House, the last residence on what had been Lucas Place.

92. "Too Costly," *Webb Spinner*, v. 4, no. 10 (Sept., 1950), p. 11. This issue of the Del E. Webb Construction Co. newsletter carried the particulars and illustrations of the demolition of Vandeventer Place.

93. Savage, *The Architecture of the Private Streets of St. Louis* (1987), pp. 42–67; Julius K. Hunter, *Westmoreland and Portland Places* (Columbia, Mo.: University of Missouri Press, 1988).

94. Indeed, about a quarter of Missouri Park—now called Lucas Park—remains, and only the Campbell House, a historic house museum, stands as a reminder of Lucas Place itself.

95. Fragments of the wrought iron veranda from Number 27 were reconstituted in a wall and as a garden loggia at 9 Westmoreland by the late Norris Allen, to whom this essay is dedicated.

10. Monument

1. The term "New South" comes from Henry Grady, the editor of the *Atlanta Constitution* in the 1880s. See Henry Grady, *The New South, Writings and Speeches of Henry Grady* (Savannah: The Beehive Press, 1971). The classic study is C. Vann Woodward, *Origins of the New South, 1877–1913* (Baton Rouge: Louisiana State University, 1951).

2. For Richmond I have relied on Virginius Dabney, *Richmond, The Story of a City* (Garden City: Doubleday & Co, 1976). On southern cities, see David R. Goldfield, *Cotton Fields and Skyscrapers, Southern City and Region, 1607–1980* (Baton Rouge: Louisiana State University Press, 1982), and Blaine A. Brownell and David R. Goldfield, eds., *The City in Southern History* (Port Washington, N. Y.: Kennikat Press, 1977).

3. Howard N. Rabinowitz, "Southern Development, 1860–1900," in Brownell and Goldfield, *The City in Southern History*, p. 109.

4. Ginter Park, laid out in 1892, is to the north and is an exception to this observation.

5. The western part of Richmond onto which Monument Avenue was attached is known as the Fan because of the radiating pattern of streets; it also is known as the West End.

6. *Richmond Dispatch*, May 25, 29, 30, 31, and June 3, 1890, all cover the unveiling. Jay Killian Bowman Williams, *Changed Views and Unforeseen Prosperity: Richmond of 1890 Gets a Monument to Lee* (Richmond: Privately Printed, 1969) is an excellent study of the Lee Monument and the beginnings of Monument Avenue. Also of importance for chronology is "The Lee Monument at Richmond," *Southern Historical Society Papers*, 17 (1890), pp. 187–355.

7. "Statue and Sculptor," *Richmond Dispatch*, May 29, 1890; and June 19, 1886. Additional accounts of debate for the site can be found in the *Richmond Dispatch*, October 12, 1886. See also Williams, *Changed Views*, chapter III.

8. City of Richmond, *Common Council Journal*, 1890–1894, p. 262; and Williams, *Changed Views*, p. 41.

9. *Richmond Dispatch*, June 19, 1886.

10. "Equestrian Monuments, XLIV," *American Architect and Building News*, 34 (November 1891), pp. 104–105. See also Ulrich Troubetzkoy, "The Lee Monument," *Virginia Cavalcade Magazine*, 12 (Spring 1962), pp. 5–10.

11. Homer Saint-Gaudens, ed., *The Reminiscences of Augustus Saint-Gaudens* (New York: The Century Company, 1913), Vol. II, p. 47; see also Vol. I, pp. 74–77.

12. Joseph T. Knox, "Le général Lee," *Virginia Cavalcade* 38 (Autumn 1988), pp. 76–85.

13. Richard Guy Wilson, Dianne Pilgrim, and Richard N. Murray, *The American Renaissance, 1876–1917* (Brooklyn: The Brooklyn Museum, 1979).

14. Thomas L. Connelly, *The Marble Man: Robert E. Lee and His Image in American Society* (New York: Alfred A. Knopf, 1977) covers the transformation of the Lee myth. Gaines M. Foster, *Ghosts of the Confederacy: Defeat, The Lost Cause, and The Emergence of the New South, 1865 to 1913* (New York: Oxford University Press, 1987) covers the various memorials and activities of the organizations.

15. *Richmond Planet*, May 31, 1890, quoted in Williams, *Changed Views*, p. 60; and Dabney, *Richmond*, p. 242. See also Foster, *Ghosts*, pp. 101–103.

16. *New York Times*, May 30, 1890; others quoted in Williams, *Changed Views*, p. 63.

17. Ulrich Troubetzkoy, "The Best Picture of General Stuart," *Virginia Cavalcade Magazine*, 12 (Winter 1962–63), pp. 40–47.

18. John H. Moore, "The Jefferson Davis Monument," *Virginia Cavalcade Magazine*, 10 (Spring 1961), pp. 29–34; Foster, *Ghosts*, pp. 158–59.

19. *Richmond Times-Dispatch*, June 3–4, 1915.

20. *Richmond Times-Dispatch*, October 11–12, 1919.

21. Ulrich Troubetzkoy, "F. William Sievers, Sculptor," *Virginia Cavalcade Magazine*, 12 (Autumn, 1962), pp. 5–12.

22. Richmond *Times-Dispatch*, June 22–23, 1922; *Richmond Newsleader*, June 22–23, 1922.

23. Troubetzkoy, "F. William Sievers," p. 11; and *Richmond Dispatch*, November 12, 1929.

24. *Richmond News-Leader*, March 9, 1929.

25. Henry James, *The American Scene* (New York: Horizon Press, 1967 [1907]), p. 393. James originally published the Richmond section in *Fortnightly Review*, 86 (1906).

26. Information derived from contemporary photographs and from Robert Winthrop's survey.

27. City Engineer, *Trees of the City* (Richmond: O. E. Flanhart Printing Co, 1904), p. 4. Maple trees are still used east of The Boulevard to Stuart Circle. From The Boulevard west to Roseneath penoaks and willow oaks are used. West of Roseneath the landscaping is more varied, with various trees, and none near the end.

28. Richmond Virginia, *Board of Alderman Journal 1901–1906*, entry for August 14, 1906; October 11, 1906; and, *Common Council Journal 1902–1906*, entry for January 2, 1906, August 16, 1906.

29. Winthrop survey.

30. Williams, *Changed Views*, p. 47.

31. William B. O'Neal, "The Multiple Life of Space," *Arts In Virginia Magazine*, 5 (no. 3, 1965), pp. 1–11, gives a basic history of the Branch house. According to Stephen Bedford, who is writing a book on John Russell Pope, the design is probably the work of Pope's partner, Otto R. Eggers, with Pope as critic.

32. Only a few apartment houses occur between the Stuart Monument and the Boulevard; the majority are beyond The Boulevard.

33. Robert Winthrop has defined this type of house. See his *Architecture in Downtown Richmond* (Richmond: Junior Board of Historic Richmond Foundation, 1892).

34. Wilson did some projects with William L. Carneal, and Robert Winthrop has suggested to me that Carneal may have lent a hand to the design. However, the Wilson house also has some similarities to Noland and Baskervill's YWCA in Richmond, at 6 North Fifth Street, of 1913.

35. For a fuller development of this topic, see my "Building on the Foundations, The Historical Present in Virginia Architecture, 1870–1990" in Charles Brownell, Calder Loth, William Rasmussen, and Richard Guy Wilson, *The Making of Virginia Architecture* (Richmond: Virginia Museum of Fine Arts, 1992), pp. 108–27.

36. William B. O'Neal and Christopher Weeks, *The Work of William Lawrence Bottomley in Richmond* (Charlottesville: University Press of Virginia, 1985), pp. 69–73. This book covers the work of Bottomley, but see also Davyd Foard Hood, "William Lawrence Bottomley in Virginia: The 'Neo-Georgian' House in Richmond," (M. A. Thesis, University of Virginia, 1975).

37. This issue is covered in Wilson, "Building on the Foundations." I owe a debt to Davyd Foard Hood, who pointed out the Bottomley Garden Club connection to me.

38. Peeble's biography is frequently misstated; see Brownell, et al., *The Making of Virginia Architecture*, pp. 115–16, 382.

39. Ulrich Troubetzkoy, *Richmond City of Churches* (Richmond: Whittet and Shepperson, 1957) p. 18.

40. Richard Morse, Richmond City Planning Department, in personal communication, September 22, 1989, has explained that in 1915 the City of Richmond acquired all the land along what would be the continuation

of Monument Avenue between Roseneath and the intersection of what is now Glenside Drive and Three Chopt Road, even though this was in Henrico County. In 1924 the City continued constructing the avenue out to the 1914 city line at Commonwealth. Beyond that a two-lane road existed. At various times in the next decades work and widening took place; fianally in 1963 the County of Henrico widened and completed a boulevard extending Monument Avenue all the way out to its termination at Glenside and Three Chopt.

41. For background on the City Beautiful, see Wilson, Pilgrim, and Murray, *The American Renaissance*; and William H. Wilson, *The City Beautiful Movement* (Baltimore: Johns Hopkins University Press, 1989).

42. James, *The American Scene*, p. 394.

43. The paving of Monument Avenue in recent years has been a subject of controversy. After repeated protests against asphalt surfaces, some Belgian blocks remain between Stuart Circle and The Boulevard. The remainder out to the end is a continuous asphalt surface.

11. WARD PARKWAY

1. An assessment of the 1880s land boom is included in my book-length study of the young land developer mentioned in the first paragraph. See William S. Worley, *J. C. Nichols and the Shaping of Kansas City: Innovation in Planned Residential Communities* (Columbia: University of Missouri Press), 1990, pp. 44–55.

2. The best overall study of the origin and development of the Kansas City park and boulevard system is William H. Wilson, *The City Beautiful Movement in Kansas City*, (Columbia: University of Missouri Press), 1964, [now available in a paperback reprint from the same publisher]. A quick summary of the impact of the movement and J. C. Nichols's relation to it and to W. R. Nelson is in Worley, *J. C. Nichols and the Shaping of Kansas City*, pp. 55–62.

3. Details of Nichols's early life and work are summarized in *Ibid.*, pp. 63–68.

4. The initial plan for Ward Parkway is best seen in the plat filed for the land subdivision named "Sunset Hill," available in the Office of the Register of Deeds, Jackson County Court House, Kansas City, Missouri. The plat map is reproduced in the J. C. Nichols *Scrapbook #3*, p. 245.

5. One of the earliest plats of the Sunset Hill subdivision is reproduced with deed restrictions in the J. C. Nichols Company *Scrapbook #2*, p. 48.

6. Taken from an undated (presumably World War I era from content) advertisement reproduced in the J. C. Nichols Company *Scrapbook #2*, pp. 49–50. Other relevant portions of the advertisement point out:

"Sunset Hill in reality is a high ridge, one of the loftiest elevations in Kansas City, its highest point being Westover Road and Belleview. The valley of Brush Creek is its northern boundary and a view of its abrupt hills and wooded slopes is available from many parts of the residence.

"The home plots in Sunset Hill purposely were made large; the smallest being 100 feet [in frontage], in order that proper free space might be secured. Many tracts are from 300 to 400 feet deep, greatly exceeding the depth of homesites in any other section of Kansas City.

"Home life in Sunset Hill is made excellent and comfortable by literally a hundred influences. It has excellent fire protection, any part of it being from three to five minutes from the Sixty-third and Baltimore and the Westport stations. Its excellent police protection is an outstanding advantage, the entire section being under private patrol in addition to the city's patrol and the city also maintains a motorcycle patrol on Ward Parkway.

"Splendid educational facilities are enjoyed by Sunset Hill residents. The Country Day School for Boys is the only school of its kind in the city. It has a large campus and ideal surroundings for work and play. Sunset Hill School for girls is one of the foremost schools for girls in the city, and St. Theresa's, a finishing school for girls, is most conveniently located. The William Cullen Bryant School for girls and boys ranks among Kansas City's best grade schools. The Parkview Riding Academy affords Sunset Hill residents an opportunity for instruction and practice in horsemanship, within a few minutes ride or walk from their homes. Within the boundaries of Sunset Hill is the Kansas City Country Club, comprising 111 acres of improved ground. Its vast and private character make it extremely desirable to the surrounding residences.

"Sunset Hill is but twenty minutes by motor from the downtown shopping centers. The entire section is conveniently served by the Sunset Hill car line, which traverses the length of Ward Parkway.

"All public improvements, street construction, sewers, gas mains, winding drives, parks and boulevards, are built with a view to meeting every requirement that might be imposed on them.

"All these advantages, and many others, make Sunset Hill essentially a home-owning neighborhood, where one may build a home with assurance of future protection—knowing it will be free from undermining influences which invariably prey upon residential sections less carefully safeguarded."

7. Evan S. Connell, *Mrs. Bridge*, paperback edition (San Francisco: North Point Press), 1981.

8. Richard P. Coleman and Bernice L. Neugarten, *Social Status in the City* (San Francisco: Jossey-Bass), 1971, pp. 31–33.

9. *Ibid.*, p. 34.

10. James C. Fitzpatrick, "Ward Parkway means money, power, and permanence," *Kansas City Times*, June 15, 1981, pp. C1–2.

11. See *Kansas City Star*, September 10, 1911, p. 10A; October 15, 1911, p. 9A; and September 22, 1912, p. 7A, for examples.

12. This house, carrying an address of 1200 55th Street (originally Santa Fe Road), is the only Ward Parkway house cited in the two major guidebooks to Kansas City area architectural originality and significance: *Kansas City: A Place in Time* (Kansas City: Landmarks Commission), 1977, p. 254; and *Kansas City* (Kansas City: Kansas City Chapter of the American Institute of Architects), 1979, p. 161.

13. See Corrigan, P. J. White, and Dwight Sutherland clipping files at the Missouri Valley Room, Kansas City Public Library, Kansas City, Missouri. Also see "Innovations in a $142,000 Home," *Kansas City Star*, May 24, 1914, p. 7C.

14. Richard P. Coleman alludes to the popularity and influence of the Nelson Gallery in *Social Status in the City*.

15. Mack B. Nelson Home file, Western Historical Manuscripts Collection, University of Missouri, Kansas City, Missouri. See particularly the souvenir program, 1991 Designer Showcase House. See also "Home With Glass Encased Bathtubs," *Kansas City Star*, December 21, 1913, p. 16A.

16. All information concerning interior room arrangements and furnishings is from the 1991 Designer Showcase Home souvenir program in Western Historical Manuscripts Collection, UMKC, except as otherwise noted.

17. "Home With Glass Incased Bathtubs," p. 16A.

18. *Ibid.*

19. "Who's Who in Kansas City," *Kansas City Star*, May 21, 1922, p. 3D. Land List Records, Sunset Hill Subdivision, Register of Deeds, Jackson County Courthouse, Kansas City, Missouri.

20. Robert T. Nelson,"Money is Not Enough to Enter the Circle Called Society," *Star Magazine*, *Kansas City Star*, August 27, 1978, pp. 20–21.

21. "Movie Maniac," *Ingrams*, May 1990, p. 30.

22. "The House That Puzzling Bought," *Pitch Magazine*, #164, June 19, 1991, p. 12.

23. See, for example, "Lyman Reid's New Home at 5252 Sunset Drive Just Started," August 6, 1916, p. 5A; "A. P. Osborne's New Home a Western Type," October 22, 1916, p. 13A; "The New Home of L. H. Fox in Sunset Hill," December 12, 1916, p. 3B; "A Residence of the Italian Type—H. L. Root's New Home," December 24, 1916, p. 6A; "New Home of W. S. McLucas One of Many Distinctions," January 14, 1917, p. 10A; "An Observatory an Unusual Feature in William Pitt's New Home in Sunset Hill," February 4, 1917, p. 15A; "An English Country House Being Built by Frank McDermid in Sunset Hill," March 25, 1917, p. 13A; and "The F. J. Dean Home to be Built at Fifty-Fourth and Sunset Drive," May 6, 1917, p. 8A, all in the *Kansas City Star*.

24. The front elevation and landscaping plan can be found in "C. S. Keith's New Home," *Kansas City Star*, November 2, 1913, p. 7C.

25. J. C. Nichols Company *Scrapbook #8*, p. 119.

26. Richard P. Coleman, *Social Status in the City*, p. 50.

27. "Miles Bulger is Dead," *Kansas City Star*, January 3, 1939, pp. 1, 14.

28. Donald Hoffmann, "Kansas City, step by step: The lavish homes on Ward Parkway tour speak of old money," *Kansas City Star*, October 16, 1981, p. 1B.

29. The best source for Tom Pendergast information is William Reddig, *Tom's Town: Kansas City and the Pendergast Legend* (Philadelphia: J. B. Lippincott Company), 1947. It is also available in a paperback reprint version from University of Missouri Press.

30. "Miles Bulger is Dead."

31. George W. Wright Clipping File, Missouri Valley Room, Kansas City Public Library. Donald Hoffmann, "Kansas City, step by step," p. 1B.

32. Donald Hoffmann, "Kansas City, step by step," p. 1B.

33. The Katz kidnapping is well-reported in Reddig, *Tom's Town*, pp. 147–50.

34. Without question, Tom Pendergast, Sr., was the best-known resident as witnessed by the fact that Kansas City publications routinely refer to the house at 5650 Ward Parkway as "the Pendergast house" while Katz's home and even the Emory J. Sweeney home across the street elicit little attention in the early 1990s.

35. Information on E. J. Sweeney and on 5921 Ward Parkway is available on pp. 252–53 of Volume 5 of the J. C. Nichols Company *Scrapbooks*. Additional information is available in the Sweeney clipping file at the Missouri Valley Room of the Kansas City Public Library.

36. Additional material about Emory J. Sweeney is available in his obituary (1953), reprinted in the J. C. Nichols Company *Scrapbook #6*, pp. 54–57.

37. The dates of the transitions are derived from Kansas City directories published by the J. L. Polk Company for the years indicated.

38. An investigative report is done on Azima as his activities tie in with those of a failed bank in Kansas City, Kansas—the Indian Springs State Bank—where he had some contact with the Kansas City organized crime family, the Civellas. Stephen Pizzo, Mary Fricker, and Paul Muolo, *Inside Job: The Looting of America's Savings and Loans* (New York: McGraw-Hill Publishing Company), 1989, pp. 89–91, 304, 341–42.

39. Amy Snider, "Meyer Circle gets more 'wiggle room'," *Kansas City Star*, March 23, 1991, p. C-3.

40. A sense of the concern, agitation, and reaction to suggested changes is gained simply by reviewing the titles of newspaper articles and dates over the last fourteen years: "Plan Debated: Meyer Circle Called a Speed Problem," *Kansas City Times*, November 23, 1977; "City in Quandary Over Circle," *Times*, October 14, 1978; "Death renews debate over Meyer Circle," *Times*, June 12, 1985; "Stop signs are an option: Meyer Circle safety changes suggested," *Times*, June 26, 1985; "Traffic death renews Meyer Circle debate," *Kansas City Star*, June 29, 1986; "Fatal crashes raise pressure for safety measures," *Times*, June 27, 1987; "New plan would widen Meyer Circle approach," *Times*, December 5, 1987; "Some oppose plan for circle: Park board sets hearing," *Times*, April 13, 1988; "Warnings urged for Meyer Circle: Residents oppose realignment," *Times*, May 4, 1988; "Wreck at Meyer Circle paralyzes legs," *Times*, January 24, 1990.

41. Snider, "Meyer Circle gets more 'wiggle room'."

42. James C. Fitzpatrick, "Wall puts neighbors on edge," *Kansas City Star*, April 11, 1991, pp. 1, 5.

43. "Homes groups to meet to speak against Meyer Circle project," *Kansas City Star*, April 29, 1991, p. 2.

44. Calvin Wilson, "Meyer Circle wall riles residents," *Kansas City Star*, April 30, 1991, p. B2.

45. James C. Fitzpatrick, "As wall rises, so does anger; work halted," *Kansas City Star*, May 2, 1991, p. C1.

46. James J. Fitzpatrick, "The Meyer Circle wall will fall (a little)," *Kansas City Star*, May 15, 1991, pp. 1, 7.

47. *Ibid.*

12. WILSHIRE BOULEVARD

1. Mark Lee Luther, *The Boosters* (New York: Grossett and Dunlap, 1923), p. 181.

2. Brett Easton Ellis, *Less Than Zero* (New York: Penguin Books, 1986), p. 188.

3. Raymond Chandler, *The Lady in the Lake*, in Elizabeth Word and Alain Silver, editors, *Raymond Chandler's Los Angeles* (Woodstock, New York: Overlook Press, 1987), p. 62.

4. Raymond Chandler, *The Little Sister*, in *Ibid.*, p. 6.

5. Philip Durham, "Raymond Chandler's Los Angeles," in John and Laree Caughey, *Los Angeles: Biography of a City* (Berkeley and Los Angeles: University of California Press, 1977), p. 333.

6. Ralph Hancock, *Fabulous Boulevard* (New York: Funk and Wagnalls, 1949), pp. 130–31. Hancock's is a popular rather than a scholarly essay, written in a breezy journalistic style, yet containing much valuable information, particularly interviews with now deceased figures.

7. *The Works of Edward Ruscha* (New York: Hudson Hills Press, 1982), pp. 65, 95–96; Nikos Stangos, editor, *Pictures by David Hockney* (New York: Harry N. Abrams, Inc., 1979), p. 44.

8. See Hancock, *Fabulous Boulevard*, passim; Douglas R. Suisman, *Los Angeles Boulevard, Eight X-Rays of the Body Public* (Los Angeles: Forum for Architecture and Urban Design, 1989), passim; and Esther McCoy and Marvin Rand, "Wilshire Boulevard," *Western Architect and Engineer* (September, 1961).

9. *Ibid.*

10. David W. Lantis, *Los Angeles* (Garden City, New York: Doubleday, 1960), p. 44; Stanley Haggert and Darwin Porter, *TWA Getaway to Los Angeles* (New York: Frommer/Pasmantier Publishing Corporation, 1971), p. 99; Robert Bobrow, "Wilshire Boulevard, A Profile: Part I," *Westways* (April, 1964), p. 5; see also Arthur James Krim, *Imagery in Search of a City, The Geosophy of Los Angeles, 1921–1971*," unpublished dissertation, Clark University, 1980.

11. Matt Weinstock, quoted in Hancock, *Fabulous Boulevard*, p. 3.

12. Hancock, *Fabulous Boulevard*, pp. 64–65.

13. Howard Quint, "Introduction," to Greenwood reprint of *Wilshire's* (Westport, Conn.: Greenwood Reprint Corporation, 1970), p. 1.

14. Robert De Roos, "Los Angeles," *National Geographic* (October, 1962), p. 484.

15. George R. Collins, "Linear Planning and Its Bibliography," *Urban History Group Newsletter*, no. 29 (April, 1980), pp. 2–12.

16. *Ibid.*; George R. Collins, "Arturo Soria y Mata," *Macmillan Encyclopedia of Architects*, vol. 4 (New York: The Free Press, 1982), pp. 107–108; Françoise Choay, *The Modern City: Planning in the 19th Century* (New York: George Braziller, 1969), pp. 99–102.

17. *Ibid.*

18. Suisman, *Los Angeles Boulevard*, pp. 23–24.

19. *Ibid.*, pp. 11–15.

20. *Ibid.*

21. Quint, "Introduction," pp. 1-2; Jack Smith, "Gaylord Wilshire, the Father of the Boulevard and the Belt," *Los Angeles Times* (April 1, 1984).

22. *Ibid.*; Hancock, *Fabulous Boulevard*, pp. 85–111.

23. *Ibid.*

24. Quint, "Introduction," pp. 1–3; Hancock, *Fabulous Boulevard*, pp. 85–111.

25. *Ibid.*

26. *Ibid.*

27. *Ibid.*; Arthur J. Cramp, "I-on-A-Co—The Magic Horse Collar," *Hygeia* (February, 1927), pp. 69–72; "Gaylord Wilshire Dead," *New York Times* (September 8, 1927); "Wilshire Passes in New York," *Los Angeles Times* (September 8, 1927).

28. George J. Duraind, "The Remarkable Invention of Gaylord Wilshire," pamphlet, reprinted from *San Francisco Chronicle* (July 18, 1926).

29. Hancock, *Fabulous Boulevard*, pp. 85–111; Quint, "Introduction," pp. 1–3; Suisman, *Los Angeles Boulevard*, pp. 24–27.

30. *Ibid.*

31. Hancock, *Fabulous Boulevard*, pp. 113–23.

32. Richard Longstreth, *On the Edge of the World: Four Architects in San Francisco at the Turn of the Century* (New York: Architectural History Foundation, 1983), pp. 47–51, 206–11.

33. *Ibid.*

34. *Ibid.*

35. *Ibid.*; "Reaching Ever to the West," *Los Angeles Times* (March 28, 1909); "From Barley Fields to Palatial Homes," *Los Angeles Times* (March 29, 1914); Randell Mackinson, *Greene and Greene, Architecture as a Fine Art* (Salt Lake City and Santa Barbara: Peregrine Smith, Inc., 1977), pp. 184–86.

36. Mackinson, *Greene and Greene*, pp. 206–11.

37. *Ibid.*

38. "Reaching Ever to the West," *Los Angeles Times* (March 28, 1909).

39. Hancock, *Fabulous Boulevard*, pp. 124–35.

40. "Ohio Banker to Build Superb Wilshire Home," and "From Barley Fields to Palatial Homes," *Los Angeles Times* (March 29, 1914).

41. *Ibid.*

42. See Thomas S. Hines, *Burnham of Chicago: Architect and Planner* (New York: Oxford University Press, 1974).

43. Charles Mulford Robinson, *Los Angeles, The City Beautiful* (Los Angeles, 1907), n.p.

44. Frederick Law Olmsted [Jr.], Harlan Bartholomew, and Charles Henry Cheney, *A Major Traffic Street Plan for Los Angeles* (Los Angeles: 1924), pp. 38–39, 47–48.

45. Robert M. Fogelson, *The Fragmented Metropolis, Los Angeles, 1850–1930* (Cambridge: Harvard University Press, 1967), pp. 261–62.

46. Hancock, *Fabulous Boulevard*, pp. 150–63.

47. *Ibid.*

48. *Ibid.*

49. *Ibid.*; Fogelson, *The Fragmented Metropolis*, pp. 262–63; Mark Stewart Foster, "The Decentralization of Los Angeles During the 1920s," unpublished dissertation, University of Southern California, 1971.

50. "Ruth Roland's Plea Wins Audience," *Los Angeles Times* (February 10, 1933).

51. Wesley Marx, "The 'City' of Wilshire," *Los Angeles Magazine* (August, 1963), pp. 26–31; Hancock, *Fabulous Boulevard*, pp. 150–63.

52. W. W. Robinson, *History of the Miracle Mile* (Los Angeles: Columbia Savings and Loan, 1965), pp. 1–2.

53. "Wilshire Paces Growth of City," *Los Angeles Times* (January 20, 1929); "Wilshire Boulevard Business Growth in Five Year Period Declared Phenomenal," *Los Angeles Times* (November 24, 1929).

54. Hancock, *Fabulous Boulevard*, pp. 165–75; Fred E. Baston, *Beverly Hills, Portrait of a Fabled City* (Los Angeles: Douglas West Publishers, 1975).

55. *Ibid.*

56. Hancock, *Fabulous Boulevard*, pp. 176–86.

57. "Wilshire Boulevard," *Westways*, v. 56 (May, 1964), pp. 2–6.

58. *Ibid.*; "New Wilshire Link Widened," *Los Angeles Times* (February 26, 1928).

59. "Wilshire Will Advertise," *Los Angeles Times* (November 28, 1928); "The Busiest Corner," *Los Angeles Times* (February 26, 1928).

60. "Record in Traffic Set Right Here," *Los Angeles Times* (April 3, 1928); "Pellisier Restriction Rule Voided," *Los Angeles Times* (April 11, 1928).

61. "Projects Aid Major Street," *Los Angeles Times* (January 29, 1928); "New Lights on Wilshire Turned On," *Los Angeles Times* (February 9, 1928).

62. "Step Taken to Make Wilshire Greatest Artery," and "White Lines Divide Wide Boulevard Into Efficient Lanes," in *Los Angeles Times* (September 7, 1930). "Progressive Timing Ready Next Month," and "Stops Removed By New Wilshire Signals," *Los Angeles Times* (June 14, 1931), and "Wilshire Signals Work," *Los Angeles Times* (October 4, 1931).

63. "Expansion of Bullock Store," *Los Angeles Times* (April 28, 1928).

64. "Beauties and Future of Wilshire Boulevard," *Saturday Night* (January 11, 1930); Raymond Chandler, *The Big Sleep* [1939] (New York: Vintage Books, 1976), p. 168.

65. Joyce Zaitlin, *Gilbert Stanley Underwood, His Rustic, Art Deco, and Federal Architecture* (Malibu, California: Pangloss Press, 1989), pp. 120–23.

66. Charles Moore, Peter Becker, and Regula Campbell, *The City Observed: Los Angeles* (New York: Vintage Books, 1984), pp. 151–54.

67. Moore, Becker, and Campbell, *The City Observed*, pp. 151–54. David Gebhard and Robert Winter, *A Guide to Architecture in Los Angeles and Southern California* (Santa Barbara and Salt Lake City: Peregrine Smith, Inc., 1977), passim; David Gebhard and Harriette von Breton, *LA in the Thirties, 1931–1941* (Santa Barbara and Salt Lake City: Peregrine-Smith, Inc., 1975), passim; Hancock, *Fabulous Boulevard*, p. 4.

68. Gebhard and von Breton, *LA in the Thirties*, p. 46.

69. "A Dream That is Coming True," *Los Angeles Times* (February 25, 1928).

70. Hancock, *Fabulous Boulevard*, pp. 285–305.

71. *Ibid.*; Moore, Becker, and Campbell, *The City Observed*, pp. 148–49.

72. Hancock, *Fabulous Boulevard*, pp. 285–89; Meta Carpenter Wilde and Orin Borsten, *A Loving Gentleman, The Love Story of William Faulkner and Meta Carpenter* (New York: Simon and Schuster, 1976).

73. Luther, *The Boosters*, pp. 48–49.

74. Jim Heimann, Rip Georges, and David Gebhard, *California Crazy, Roadside Vernacular Architecture* (San Francisco: Chronicle Books, 1980), passim.

75. Rev. Francis J. Weber, *Christ On Wilshire Boulevard, St. Basil's Catholic Church* (Los Angeles: Westernlore Press, 1969), passim.

76. Marco R. Newmark, "Wilshire Boulevard Temple," *Historical Society of Southern California Quarterly*, vol. 38 (June, 1956), pp. 167–84; Gebhard and Winter, *A Guide to Architecture in Los Angeles*, p. 194.

77. Thomas S. Hines, *Richard Neutra and the Search for Modern Architecture: A Biography and History* (New York: Oxford University Press, 1982), passim.

78. Hancock, *Fabulous Boulevard*, pp. 199–205.

79. "Throngs See Dedication of New Artery to Ocean," *Los Angeles Times* (December 8, 1934).

ILLUSTRATION CREDITS

Introduction

Figure 1. Original by Johannes Covens, reprinted by *Historic Urban Plans*, 1966.

Figure 2. Illustration by Matthew Seutter. Courtesy Library of Congress.

Figure 3. Illustration by E. Dufrenoy. Courtesy Library of Congress.

Figure 4. Photograph by George M. Edmondson, 1910. Courtesy Cleveland Public Library.

Figure 5. Photograph by Charles L. Frank, c. 1925. Courtesty Historic New Orleans Collection.

1. Fifth Avenue

Figure 1. Prepared by M. Dripps for *Valentine's Manual*. Private collection.

Figure 2. Courtesy New-York Historical Society.

Figure 3. Courtesy Museum of the City of New York.

Figure 4. Courtesy Avery Architectural and Fine Arts Library, Columbia University.

Figure 5. Courtesy New-York Historical Society.

Figure 6. Courtesy New-York Historical Society.

Figure 7. From *Fifth Avenue Old and New 1824-1924*, by Henry Collins Brown, The Fifth Avenue Association. New York: Wyndoop Hallenbeck Crawford Co., 1924.

Figure 8. Courtesy New-York Historical Society.

Figure 9. Courtesy New-York Historical Society.

Figure 10. Photograph by George P. Hall. Courtesy New-York Historical Society.

Figure 11. Courtesy New-York Historical Society.

Figure 12. Illustration by Richardson Cox in *Putnam's Monthly*, March 1854. Courtesy New-York Historical Society.

Figure 13. Courtesy New-York Historical Society.

Figure 14. Photograph by Bernice Abbott. Courtesy Museum of the City of New York.

Figure 15. From *Valentine's Manual*. Courtesy New-York Historical Society.

Figure 16. Courtesy Museum of the City of New York.

Figure 17. Courtesy Avery Architectural and Fine Arts Library, Columbia University.

Figure 18. Courtesy Prints and Drawings Collection, The Octagon, The Museum of the American Architectural Foundation.

Figure 19. From *Harper's Weekly*, January 21, 1882. Courtesy New-York Historical Society.

Figure 20. Painting by J. F. Raffaelli, date unknown. Oil on canvas. Courtesy Metropolitan Museum of Art.

Figure 21. Courtesy New-York Historical Society.

Figure 22. Photograph by Byron. Courtesy Museum of the City of New York.

Figure 23. Photograph by Richard Hoe Lawrence. Courtesy New-York Historical Society.

Figure 24. Courtesy Museum of the City of New York.

Figure 25. Courtesy Avery Architectural and Fine Arts Library, Columbia University.

Figure 26. From *Puck Magazine*, 1882. Courtesy Museum of the City of New York.

Figure 27. Courtesy New-York Historical Society.

Figure 28. Courtesy New-York Historical Society.

Figure 29. Courtesy New-York Historical Society.

Figure 30. Courtesy Museum of the City of New York.

Figure 31. Courtesy the Wurts Collection, Museum of the City of New York.

Figure 32. Courtesy Avery Architectural and Fine Arts Library, Columbia University.

Figure 33. Photograph by Browning. Courtesy New-York Historical Society.

2. Delaware Avenue

Figure 1. From *Picture Book of Earlier Buffalo*, by F. Severance, 1912.

Figure 2. From *Picture Book of Earlier Buffalo*, by F. Severance, 1912.

Figure 3. From *Picture Book of Earlier Buffalo*, by F. Severance, 1912.

Figure 4. Courtesy Buffalo and Erie County Historical Society.

Figure 5. Courtesy Buffalo and Erie County Public Library, Rare Book Room.

Figure 6. Courtesy Buffalo and Erie County Public Library, Rare Book Room.

Figure 7. From *Picture Book of Earlier Buffalo*, by F. Severance, 1912.

Figure 8. Courtesy Buffalo and Erie County Historical Society.

Figure 9. Courtesy Buffalo and Erie County Historical Society.

Figure 10. Courtesy Buffalo and Erie County Public Library, Rare Book Room.

Figure 11. From *Picture Book of Earlier Buffalo*, by F. Severance, 1912.

Figure 12. Courtesy Buffalo and Erie County Public Library, Rare Book Room.

Figure 13. From *Beautiful Homes of Buffalo*, by Mark Hubbell, 1915. Courtesy Buffalo and Erie County Public Library, Rare Book Room.

Figure 14. Courtesy Houghton Library, Harvard University.

Figure 15. Courtesy Buffalo and Erie County Historical Society.

Figure 16. From *American Architect and Building News*, Sept. 8, 1877.

Figure 17. From *L'Architecture Americaine*, 1886.

Figure 18. Courtesy Ohio State University.

Figure 19. From *Beautiful Homes of Buffalo*, by Mark Hubbell, 1915. Courtesy Buffalo and Erie County Public Library, Rare Book Room.

Figure 20. Courtesy Ohio State University.

Figure 21. Courtesy Buffalo and Erie County Historical Society.

Figure 22. From *Beautiful Homes of Buffalo*, by Mark Hubbell, 1915. Courtesy Buffalo and Erie County Public Library, Rare Book Room.

Figure 23. Courtesy Buffalo and Erie County Historical Society.

Figure 24. Courtesy Buffalo and Erie County Historical Society.

Figure 25. Courtesy Buffalo and Erie County Historical Society.

Figure 26. Courtesy Buffalo and Erie County Historical Society.

Figure 27. Courtesy Buffalo and Erie County Historical Society.

Figure 28. Courtesy Buffalo and Erie County Historical Society.

Figure 29. Courtesy Buffalo Friends of Olmsted Parks.

Figure 30. Courtesy Buffalo and Erie County Historical Society.

3. WOODWARD AVENUE

Figure 1. Lithograph by J. R. Chapin. Courtesy Detroit News Archive.

Figure 2. Photograph by James V. Pierse. Courtesy Detroit News Archive.

Figure 3. Courtesy Burton Historical Collection, Detroit Public Library.

Figure 4. National Lithograph Company. Courtesy Thomas W. Brunk Collection.

Figure 5. Courtesy Burton Historical Collection, Detroit Public Library.

Figure 6. Photograph by Godfrey & Company, in *Detroit: Its Points of Interest and Representative Business Men*, 1896.

Figure 7. Courtesy Burton Historical Collection, Detroit Public Library.

Figure 8. Courtesy Burton Historical Collection, Detroit Public Library.

Figure 9. Courtesy Burton Historical Collection, Detroit Public Library.

Figure 10. Courtesy Burton Historical Collection, Detroit Public Library.

Figure 11. Courtesy Burton Historical Collection, Detroit Public Library.

Figure 12. Courtesy Burton Historical Collection, Detroit Public Library.

Figure 13. Photograph by Godfrey & Company, in *Detroit: Its Points of Interest and Representative Business Men*, 1896.

Figure 14. Courtesy Henry Ford Museum, Greenfield Village.

Figure 15. Courtesy Burton Historical Collection, Detroit Public Library.

Figure 16. Courtesy Henry Ford Museum, Greenfield Village.

Figure 17. Courtesy Burton Historical Collection, Detroit Public Library.

Figure 18. Courtesy Burton Historical Collection, Detroit Public Library.

Figure 19. Courtesy Burton Historical Collection, Detroit Public Library.

Figure 20. Courtesy Burton Historical Collection, Detroit Public Library.

Figure 21. Courtesy Burton Historical Collection, Detroit Public Library.

Figure 22. Courtesy Burton Historical Collection, Detroit Public Library.

Figure 23. Courtesy Detroit Institute of Arts, Research Library.

Figure 24. Courtesy Freer Gallery of Art, Smithsonian Institution.

Figure 25. Courtesy Thomas W. Brunk Collection.

Figure 26. Photograph by Jessica Trevino, 1989.

Figure 27. Courtesy Marti Edwards.

Figure 28. Courtesy Henry Ford Museum, Greenfield Village.

Figure 29. Courtesy Detroit News Archive.

Figure 30. Photograph by Marilyn Zimmerman and David Doubley.

4. EUCLID AVENUE

Figure 1. Courtesy Western Reserve Historical Society.

Figure 2. Cram, Beers & Bennett, *Surveyors, Atlas of Cuyhoga County*.

Figure 3. Facsimile by Carlos A. Smith, 1908. Courtesy Western Reserve Historical Society.

Figure 4. Photograph by George M. Edmondson, 1930s. Courtesy Western Reserve Historical Society.

Figure 5. Courtesy Avery Architectural and Fine Arts Library, Columbia University.

Figure 6. From *Lake Atlas*, 1874.

Figure 7. Photograph by G. M. Edmondson. Courtesy Cleveland Public Library.

Figure 8. Courtesy Western Reserve Historical Society.

Figure 9. Courtesy Western Reserve Historical Society.

Figure 10. Photograph by G. M. Edmondson, 1889. Courtesy Western Reserve Historical Society.

Figure 11. Courtesy Boston Public Library.

Figure 12. Courtesy Boston Public Library.

Figure 13. Courtesy Western Reserve Historical Society.

Figure 14. From *Beautiful Homes of Cleveland*, 1917.

Figure 15. Photograph by G. M. Edmondson, 1937. Courtesy E. E. Worthington.

Figure 16. Photograph by G. M. Edmondson. Courtesy Western Reserve Historical Society.

Figure 17. Courtesy Western Reserve Historical Society.

Figure 18. Photograph by G. M. Edmondson, 1939. Courtesy Western Reserve Historical Society.

Figure 19. Photograph by G. M. Edmondson, 1939. Courtesy Western Reserve Historical Society.

Figure 20. Courtesy Western Reserve Historical Society.

Figure 21. Photograph by G. M. Edmondson. Courtesy Case Western Reserve University.

Figure 22. Courtesy Cleveland Public Library.

Figure 23. Courtesy Western Reserve Historical Society.

Figure 24. Courtesy New-York Historical Society.

Figure 25. Courtesy Western Reserve Historical Society.

Figure 26. Courtesy Western Reserve Historical Society.

Figure 27. Courtesy Western Reserve Historical Society.

Figure 28. Courtesy Western Reserve Historical Society.

Figure 29. Group Plan Commission. Courtesy Western Reserve Historical Society.

Figure 30. Courtesy Western Reserve Historical Society.

Figure 31. From *Cleveland Plain Dealer*, August 31, 1958.

5. PRAIRIE AVENUE

Figure 1. Courtesy Chicago Historical Society.

Figure 2. Courtesy Chicago Historical Society.

Figure 3. Courtesy Chicago Historical Society.

Figure 4. Courtesy Chicago Historical Society.

Figure 5. Courtesy Chicago Historical Society.

Figure 6. Courtesy Chicago Historical Society.

Figure 7. Courtesy Chicago Historical Society.

Figure 8. Courtesy Chicago Historical Society.

Figure 9. From *Principles and Practice of Architecture*, 1869, by Sanford E. Loring and William L. B. Jenney. Courtesy Art Institute of Chicago.

Figure 10. From *Principles and Practice of Architecture*, 1869, by Sanford E. Loring and William L. B. Jenney. Courtesy Art Institute of Chicago.

Figure 11. Photograph by George Glessner, c. 1889. Courtesy Chicago Architecture Foundation.

Figure 12. Courtesy Prints and Drawings Collection, The Octagon, The Museum of the American Architectural Foundation.

Figure 13. Courtesy Art Institute of Chicago.

Figure 14. Courtesy Chicago Historical Society.

Figure 15. In *American Architect and Building News*, September 30, 1876. Courtesy Art Institute of Chicago.

Figure 16. Courtesy Chicago Historical Society.

Figure 17. Courtesy Art Institute of Chicago.

Figure 18. Courtesy Chicago Historical Society.

Figure 19. Courtesy Chicago Historical Society.

Figure 20. Courtesy Chicago Historical Society.

Figure 21. Courtesy Art Institute of Chicago.

Figure 22. Photograph by J. W. Taylor. Courtesy Chicago Historical Society.

Figure 23. Courtesy Chicago Historical Society.

Figure 24. In *Inland Architect and News Record*, October 1896. Courtesy Art Institute of Chicago.

Figure 25. Courtesy Society for Preservation of New England Antiquities.

Figure 26. Photograph by Kaufmann and Fabry, 1923. Courtesy Chicago Architecture Foundation.

Figure 27. Courtesy Architectural Collection, Chicago Historical Society.

Figure 28. Courtesy Chicago Historical Society.

Figure 29. Burnham and Root, Perspective Rendering of the Max A. Meyer house, 2009 Prairie Avenue, Chicago (demolished), 1888. Watercolor on paper, 63.5 x 40.6 cm. Lent by Mr. and Mrs. Dale Crowel, RX16763. ©1989 The Art Institute of Chicago. All Rights Reserved.

Figure 30. Courtesy Chicago Historical Society.

Figure 31. In *Inland Architect and News Record*, July 1891. Courtesy Art Institute of Chicago.

Figure 32. Courtesy Chicago Historical Society.

Figure 33. Walker Evans (American, 1903–1975), *2033 Prairie Avenue*, 1936. Gelatin silver print, 26.3 x 21.7 cm. Gift of David C. and Sarajean Ruttenberg. Photograph courtesy The Art Institute of Chicago. © Estate of Walker Evans.

6. St. Charles Avenue

Figure 1. Photograph by Jan White Brantley, 1990. Courtesy New Orleans Public Library.

Figure 2. Courtesy Historic New Orleans Collection.

Figure 3. Courtesy Historic New Orleans Collection.

Figure 4. Courtesy Historic New Orleans Collection.

Figure 5. Courtesy Historic New Orleans Collection.

Figure 6. Courtesy Historic New Orleans Collection.

Figure 7. In *The St. Charles Streetcar*, by J. L. Guilbeau. Photograph by Jan White Brantley, 1990.

Figure 8. Courtesy Historic New Orleans Collection.

Figure 9. Courtesy Historic New Orleans Collection.

Figure 10. Courtesy Historic New Orleans Collection.

Figure 11. Photograph by Robert S. Brantley, 1990.

Figure 12. Photograph by Jan White Brantley, 1990. Courtesy Louisiana State Museum.

Figure 13. Courtesy Louisiana Collection, Tulane University Library.

Figure 14. Photograph by Robert S. Brantley, 1990.

Figure 15. Photograph by Robert S. Brantley, 1990.

Figure 16. From *New Orleans Illustrated in Photo Etching*, 1892.

Figure 17. Courtesy Louisiana Collection, Tulane University Library.

Figure 18. Courtesy Southeastern Architectural Archive, Tulane University.

Figure 19. Collection of Samuel Wilson, Jr.

Figure 20. Courtesy Friends of the Cabildo. Photograph by Jan White Brantley, 1990.

Figure 21. Photograph by Robert S. Brantley, 1990.

Figure 22. Courtesy Historic New Orleans Collection.

Figure 23. Courtesy Historic New Orleans Collection.

Figure 24. Photograph by Robert S. Brantley, 1990.

Figure 25. Photograph by Robert S. Brantley, 1990.

7. Massachusetts Avenue

Figure 1. Courtesy Library of Congress.

Figure 2. Courtesy Martin Luther King Library.

Figure 3. Courtesy Kiplinger Collection.

Figure 4. Courtesy Martin Luther King Library.

Figure 5. Courtesy Historical Society of Washington.

Figure 6. Courtesy Historical Society of Washington.

Figure 7. Courtesy Library of Congress.

Figure 8. Photograph by Jack Boucher, 1970. Courtesy U.S. Commission of Fine Arts.

Figure 9. Courtesy Library of Congress.

Figure 10. Courtesy Library of Congress.

Figure 11. Photograph by Jack Boucher, 1970. Courtesy U.S. Commission of Fine Arts.

Figure 12. Photograph by J. Alexander, 1971. Courtesy U.S. Commission of Fine Arts.

Figure 13. Courtesy Historical Society of Washington.

Figure 14. Photograph by F. B. Johnston, c. 1893. Courtesy Library of Congress.

Figure 15. Courtesy Historical Society of Washington.

Figure 16. Courtesy National Archives.

Figure 17. Courtesy George Washington University.

Figure 18. Photograph by J. Alexander, 1971. Courtesy Library of Congress.

Figure 19. Courtesy Wurts Collection, National Building Museum.

Figure 20. Courtesy Library of Congress.

Figure 21. Photograph by Maxwell McKenzie, 1991.

Figure 22. Photograph by Jack Boucher, 1970. Courtesy Library of Congress.

Figure 23. Photograph by Jack Boucher, 1970. Courtesy Library of Congress.

Figure 24. Photograph by J. Alexander, 1971. Courtesy Library of Congress.

Figure 25. Photograph by F. B. Johnston. Courtesy Library of Congress.

Figure 26. Photograph by Jack Boucher, 1970. Courtesy Library of Congress.

Figure 27. Photograph by F. B. Johnston, c. 1915. Courtesy Library of Congress.

Figure 28. Courtesy National Museum of American Art, Smithsonian Institution.

Figure 29. Courtesy National Museum of American Art, Smithsonian Institution.

Figure 30. Photograph by Jack Boucher, 1970. Courtesy U.S. Commission of Fine Arts.

Figure 31. Photograph by J. Alexander, 1971. Courtesy Library of Congress.

Figure 32. Photograph by Jack Boucher, 1970. Courtesy Library of Congress.

Figure 33. Photograph by Jack Boucher, 1970. Courtesy Library of Congress.

8. BROADWAY

Figure 1. Photograph by Cecil Thomson, c. 1925. Courtesy San Jacinto Museum of History Collection, Houston Metropolitan Research Center, Houston Public Library.

Figure 2. Courtesy Galveston and Texas History Center, Rosenberg Library.

Figure 3. Courtesy Galveston and Texas History Center, Rosenberg Library.

Figure 4. Courtesy Galveston and Texas History Center, Rosenberg Library.

Figure 5. Published by Augustus Koch. Courtesy Galveston and Texas History Center, Rosenberg Library.

Figure 6. Courtesy Galveston and Texas History Center, Rosenberg Library.

Figure 7. Courtesy Drexel Turner.

Figure 8. Courtesy Galveston and Texas History Center, Rosenberg Library.

Figure 9. Photograph by Paul Hester, 1981.

Figure 10. Photograph from *The Art Work of Galveston*, c. 1894. Courtesy Galveston and Texas History Center, Rosenberg Library.

Figure 11. Photograph from *University of St. Mary's, Galveston, Texas, Souvenir Volume of the Silver Jubilee of the College Under Jesuit Administration.* Courtesy Galveston and Texas History Center, Rosenberg Library.

Figure 12. Photograph from *The Art Work of Galveston*, c. 1894. Courtesy Galveston and Texas History Center, Rosenberg Library.

Figure 13. Photograph by Paul Hester, 1981.

Figure 14. Photograph by Ezra Stoller, ESTO, 1962.

Figure 15. Photograph from *Picturesque Galveston*, 1900. Courtesy Galveston and Texas History Center, Rosenberg Library.

Figure 16. Photograph by Verkin Photo Co., c. 1913. Courtesy Galveston and Texas History Center, Rosenberg Library.

Figure 17. Photograph by Katherine Wetzel, 1991. Courtesy Moody Mansion & Museum.

Figure 18. Photograph from *Galveston in 1900*. Courtesy Galveston and Texas History Center, Rosenberg Library.

Figure 19. Courtesy Galveston and Texas History Center, Rosenberg Library.

Figure 20. Photograph by Trube, c. 1906. Courtesy Galveston and Texas History Center, Rosenberg Library.

Figure 21. Photograph from *Texas Port and Playground*, 1919. Courtesy Galveston and Texas History Center, Rosenberg Library.

Figure 22. Photograph from *The Tangent*, 1911. Courtesy Houston Metropolitan Research Center, Houston Public Library.

Figure 23. Courtesy Galveston and Texas History Center, Rosenberg Library.

Figure 24. Photograph by Verkin Photo Co., 1926. Courtesy Galveston and Texas History Center, Rosenberg Library.

Figure 25. Courtesy Galveston and Texas History Center, Rosenberg Library.

Figure 26. Photograph by Paul Hester, 1986.

9. VANDEVENTER PLACE

Figure 1. Courtesy Missouri Historical Society.

Figure 2. By Parsons & Atwater, published by Currier & Ives. Courtesy Mariners Museum.

Figure 3. Courtesy Pitzman Company.

Figure 4. Courtesy Swekosky Photo Collection, School Sisters of Notre Dame.

Figure 5. Compton & Dry, *Pictorial Saint Louis*, 1875.

Figure 6. Courtesy Missouri Historical Society.

Figure 7. Courtesy Missouri Historical Society.

Figure 8. Courtesy Missouri Historical Society.

Figure 9. Courtesy Swekosky Photo Collection, School Sisters of Notre Dame.

Figure 10. Courtesy Missouri Historical Society.

Figure 11. Courtesy Swekosky Photo Collection, School Sisters of Notre Dame.

Figure 12. Courtesy Missouri Historical Society.

Figure 13. Courtesy Missouri Historical Society.

Figure 14. Courtesy Missouri Historical Society.

Figure 15. Courtesy Swekosky Photo Collection, School Sisters of Notre Dame.

Figure 16. Courtesy Missouri Historical Society.

Figure 17. Courtesy Swekosky Photo Collection, School Sisters of Notre Dame.

Figure 18. Courtesy Swekosky Photo Collection, School Sisters of Notre Dame.

Figure 19. Courtesy Missouri Historical Society.

Figure 20. Courtesy Missouri Historical Society.

Figure 21. Courtesy Missouri Historical Society.

Figure 22. In *The Builder*, October 1905.

Figure 23. Photograph by Charles Savage.

Figure 24. Courtesy Missouri Historical Society.

Figure 25. A. D. Edwards & Son, 1991. Photograph by Charles Savage.

10. MONUMENT AVENUE

Figure 1. Courtesy Valentine Museum.

Figure 2. Courtesy Library of Congress.

Figure 3. Courtesy Valentine Museum, Cook Collection.

Figure 4. Published by Wm. Baist Map Ub., 806 Walnut Street, Philadelphia, Pennsylvania. Courtesy Valentine Museum.

Figure 5. Courtesy Valentine Museum, Cook Collection.

Figure 6. Courtesy Valentine Museum, Cook Collection.

Figure 7. Courtesy Valentine Museum.

Figure 8. Courtesy Valentine Museum.

Figure 9. Courtesy Valentine Museum, Cook Collection.

Figure 10. Courtesy Valentine Museum, Cook Collection.

Figure 11. Courtesy Valentine Museum.

Figure 12. Courtesy Valentine Museum, Cook Collection.

Figure 13. Courtesy Valentine Museum, Cook Collection.

Figure 14. Courtesy Valentine Museum, Cook Collection.

Figure 15. Courtesy Valentine Museum, Cook Collection.

Figure 16. Courtesy Valentine Museum, Cook Collection.

Figure 17. Courtesy Valentine Museum, Cook Collection.

Figure 18. Courtesy Valentine Museum, Cook Collection.

Figure 19. Courtesy Valentine Museum, Cook Collection.

Figure 20. Photograph by Richard Cheek, 1985.

Figure 21. Courtesy Valentine Museum, Cook Collection.

Figure 22. Courtesy Valentine Museum, Cook Collection.

Figure 23. Courtesy Valentine Museum, Cook Collection.

Figure 24. Courtesy Valentine Museum, Cook Collection.

11. Ward Parkway

Western Historical Manuscript Collection-Kansas City, J. C. Nichols Company Records= WHMC-KC106

Western Historical Manuscript Collection-Kansas City, J. C. Nichols Company Scrapbooks= WHMC-KC54

Figure 1. WHMC-KC54N2.

Figure 2. WHMC-KC54N42.

Figure 3. WHMC-KC54N83.

Figure 4. WHMC-KC54N80.

Figure 5. WHMC-KC54N67.

Figure 6. WHMC-KC54N72.

Figure 7. WHMC-KC54N84.

Figure 8. WHMC-KC54N22 .

Figure 9. WHMC-KC54N65.

Figure 10. Photograph by William S. Worley, 1992.

Figure 11. WHMC-KC54N37.

Figure 12. WHMC-KC54N38.

Figure 13. WHMC-KC54N79.

Figure 14. Photograph by William S. Worley, 1992.

Figure 15. WHMC-KC54N59.

Figure 16. Photograph by William S. Worley, 1992.

Figure 17. Photograph by William S. Worley, 1992.

Figure 18. WHMC-KC54N70.

Figure 19. WHMC-KC-54N68.

Figure 20. WHMC-KC54N69.

Figure 21. WHMC-KC54N78.

Figure 22. Photograph by William S. Worley, 1992.

Figure 23. WHMC-KC54N75.

Figure 24. WHMC-KC54N77.

Figure 25. WHMC-KC54N71.

Figure 26. WHMC-KC54N74.

Figure 27. WHMC-KC54N73.

Figure 28. WHMC-KC54N82.

Figure 29. WHMC-KC54N81.

12. Wilshire Boulevard

Figure 1. *Wilshire Boulevard, Los Angeles,* 1964. Acrylic on canvas, 36 x 24 in. Courtesy David Hockney.

Figure 2. A. Humitsch. Courtesy UCLA, Special Collections, University Research Library.

Figure 3. Map from *Los Angeles: An Architectural Design Profile,* edited by Derek Walker. London: Architectural Design, 1981.

Figure 4. From David Suisman, "Wilshire Boulevard," in *Los Angeles Boulevard,* Los Angeles Forum for Architecture and Urban Design, 1989.

Figure 5. Photograph of Gaylord Wilshire courtesy UCLA, Special Collections, University Research Library. Photograph of advertisement for Gaylord Wilshire's quack health remedy "Ionaco" courtesy UCLA, Special Collections, University Research Library.

Figure 6. Collection of Thomas S. Hines.

Figure 7. Courtesy Seaver Center for Western History Research, Natural History Museum of Los Angeles County.

Figure 8. Courtesy Seaver Center for Western History Research, Natural History Museum of Los Angeles County.

Figure 9. Photograph by Marvin Rand.

Figure 10. Courtesy Los Angeles Public Library.

Figure 11. Courtesy Seaver Center for Western History Research, Natural History Museum of Los Angeles County.

Figure 12. Collection of Thomas S. Hines.

Figure 13. Courtesy Seaver Center for Western History Research, Natural History Museum of Los Angeles County.

Figure 14. Courtesy Seaver Center for Western History Research, Natural History Museum of Los Angeles County.

Figure 15. Courtesy Marc Wanamaker, Bison Archives, Raleigh Studios.

Figure 16. Courtesy Seaver Center for Western History Research, Natural History Museum of Los Angeles County.

Figure 17. Courtesy UCLA Special Collections, University Research Library.

Figure 18. Collection of Tom Zimmerman.

Figure 19. Courtesy Los Angeles Public Library.

Figure 20. Collection of Tom Zimmerman.

Figure 21. Courtesy Seaver Center for Western History Research, Natural History Museum of Los Angeles County.

Figure 22. Courtesy Marc Wanamaker, Bison Archives, Raleigh Studios.

Figure 23. Drawing for *Los Angeles Times,* February 25, 1928.

Figure 24. Courtesy Seaver Center for Western History Research, Natural History Museum of Los Angeles County.

Figure 25. Courtesy Marc Wanamaker, Bison Archives, Raleigh Studios.

Figure 26. Collection of Tom Zimmerman.

Figure 27. Courtesy Seaver Center for Western History Research, Natural History Museum of Los Angeles County.

Figure 28. Courtesy UCLA Department of Geography Aerial Photo Archives, Spence Collection.

AUTHORS

JAN CIGLIANO, coeditor of *The Grand American Avenue: 1850–1920*, is a Washington, D.C., architectural historian and real estate economist. She is the author of *Showplaces of America: Cleveland's Euclid Avenue* and coauthor of *Southport: The Architectural Legacy of a Connecticut Village*.

SARAH BRADFORD LANDAU, coeditor of *The Grand American Avenue: 1850–1920*, is associate professor of fine arts at New York University and vice chair of the New York City Landmarks Preservation Commission. The author of two books and many articles, she has recently contributed to *Greenwich Village: Culture and Counterculture* (1993), and her book (with coauthor Carl W. Condit) on the early New York skyscraper is scheduled for publication by Yale University Press.

MOSETTE BRODERICK teaches architectural history at New York University. She is working on books on McKim, Mead & White, and on an expanded study of the houses of Fifth Avenue.

THOMAS W. BRUNK is an architectural historian noted for his scholarship on Leonard B. Willeke, Charles Lang Freer, and Pewabic Pottery.

STEPHEN FOX is a Fellow of the Anchorage Foundation of Texas.

THOMAS S. HINES is professor of history and architecture at UCLA. His books include *Burnham of Chicago: Architect* and *Richard Neutra and the Search for Modern Architecture*.

SUE KOHLER is historian of the U.S. Commission of Fine Arts in Washington, D.C. An architectural historian, she is coauthor of *Massachusetts Avenue* (Volume II) and *Sixteenth Street* (Volumes I and II), and author of *A Brief History of the Commission of Fine Arts: 1910–1990*.

FRANCIS R. KOWSKY is professor of art history in the Fine Arts Department at SUNY College, Buffalo, New York.

MARY ALICE MOLLOY is an independent architectural historian specializing in Chicago subjects. She is the author of *Chicago Since the Sears Tower* and editor of the *AIA Guide to Chicago Architecture*.

CHARLES SAVAGE is an architectural historian of the New York City Landmarks Preservation Commission. His book *The Architecture of the Private Streets of St. Louis* was published in 1987.

S. FREDERICK STARR, president of Oberlin College, is an architectural historian and leading authority on Russian affairs. A prolific author, he has written or edited sixteen books, including *Melnikov: Solo Architect in a Mass Society* and *Southern Comfort: The Garden District of New Orleans, 1800–1900*.

RICHARD GUY WILSON is professor of architectural history at the University of Virginia and author of numerous books and articles. His most recent publication is *Thomas Jefferson's Academical Village: The Creation of an Architectural Masterpiece.*

WILLIAM S. WORLEY is assistant professor of history and government at Sterling College. He is the author of *J. C. Nichols and the Shaping of Kansas City.*

ACKNOWLEDGMENTS

THIS PROJECT REPRESENTS THE WORK of many individuals, without whose assistance the museum exhibition, panel reproduction exhibition, two video productions, and *Educational Resource Guide* would not have been completed. Their collective talent, dedication, and energy are immeasurable, and to them all I owe my appreciation.

In 1988 Jan Cigliano, who has worked extensively on the history of Euclid Avenue, suggested that the Octagon Museum host an exhibition on that street. Because the exhibition program at the Octagon strives to present architectural subject matter on a broad national or international basis, focusing on one avenue seemed inappropriate for a national constituency. As curator of the Prints and Drawings Collection, I recognized that our collection held drawings for several significant American avenues and that other repositories across the country had similar holdings. With an idea toward providing a national focus and adhering to the mission of the museum, I suggested we expand the theme from one to many avenues...hence, *The Grand American Avenue: 1850-1920.*

In 1989 an advisory committee was brought together to work with the museum staff to determine the scope and purpose of the project, to identify the avenues and select their authors, to develop the themes and topics of the exhibition, and to discuss methodology for presenting these ideas in a realistic and stimulating manner. John Zukowsky and Sarah Bradford Landau, with assistance from Morrison Hecksher, worked with the staff to develop the framework for the project. Ms. Landau has served as coeditor of this book and has been a steadfast and able advisor for all aspects of the project.

The twelve scholars and historians whose essays form the content of this publication have been actively involved throughout, provoiding invaluable assistance with selecting illustrations for the book, locating objects for the exhibition, and suggesting potential funding sources. Their patience, endurance, enthusiasm, and support have been limitless. To these individuals—Mosette Broderick, Thomas W. Brunk, Jan Cigliano, Stephen Fox, Thomas S. Hines, Sue Kohler, Francis R. Kowsky, Mary Alice Molloy, Charles Savage, S. Frederick Starr, Richard Guy Wilson, and William Worley—I owe my sincerest thanks and appreciation.

The advisory committee to the Octagon Museum gave freely of their ideas, criticism, and support. In particular, former chairperson Damie Stillman willingly shared his expertise. Always accessible, he brought an encouraging and enthusiastic attitude that was much appreciated.

I would also like to thank Selwyn Garraway, program associate of the Lila Wallace-Reader's Digest Fund, and Wendy Clark, program officer of the National Endowment for the Arts, for their encouragement.

The teamwork that has developed throughout the project has been its greatest strength. The cooperation, assistance, and dedication of all the authors, museum staffs, collectors, and private individuals involved has been extraordinary. To these colleagues and associates, I extend special thanks: David Anderson, Ann Anninger, Patrick Ashley, Ada Bartolucci, Deena Bedigian, Mary Bell, Kathleen Betts, Mary Beth Betts, David Boutros, Leslie Greene Bowman, Tim Brant, Sister Dionysia Brockland, Christine Brown, Elizabeth Brown, Louise Brownell, Anne Caiger, Joan Caldwell, Carol Callahan, Cristina Carbone, Janice Chadbourne, Richard Cheek, Karen Chittenden, Joan Clark, Kimberly Cody, Brenda Corbin, Dale Cowell, Mary Cropley, William Cullison III, Arthur Curley, Sam Daniels, Barbara Debs, William Delvac, Linda Dishman, Simon Elliott, John Engman, George Eslinger, Janet Evander, Wayne Everard, William Scott Field, Jim Francis, Wayne Furman, David Gebhard, Jack Germain, Doris Germenian, Luke Gilliland-Swetland, Angela Giral, Susan Godlewski, Abbye Gorin, John Grabowski, Hank Griffith, Chuck Hamilton, Sue Hanson, J. B. Harter, Paul Hester, John Hill, David Hockney, Lou Cinda Holt, Tambra Johnson, Dorothy Kellet, Susan King, Carolyn Kozo, Karen Kuhlman, John Kukla, Marguerite Lavin, Priscilla Lawrence, Penny Leveritt, Daniel Lincove, William Loos, Maxwell MacKenzie, John Magill, Louis Marchiafava, Barbara Martin, Marilyn Gell Mason, Ann Masson, Edward C. Mathes, William Menearay, Cheryl Miller, Sister Shirley Miller, Lois Oglesby, Octavio Olvera, Stephen Ostrow, Minora Pacheco, Janet Parks, David Philips, Kermit Pike, Lieschen Potuznik, Anne Powell, Sandra Powers, Marvin Rand, Stan Richey, Teresa Roane, Lisa Royce, Sandra Rushing, Rise Rutter, Theodore Sande, Cheryl Saunders, Margaret Schlankey, Karen Shackelford, Ann Sindelar, Margaret Smith, Megan Smith, Duane Sneddeker, Errol Stevens, Ezra Stoller, John Taormina, Daisy Tarver, Abigail Terrones, Suzanne Thorin, Frances Turgeon, Drexel Turner, Noel Van Gorden, William Walker, Marc Wanamaker, Gloria Werner, Robert Wilburn, Kevin Williams, Don Wilson, Samuel Wilson, Shirley Wilson, Wim de Witt, Andrea Wittstock, Mary Alice Wollam, Barbara Woytowicz, Tony Wrenn, Richard Wurts, Valle Zale, Jim Zeender, David Zeidberg, Marilyn Zimmerman, Tom Zimmerman, and Betty Zweirankin.

In particular, Jan and Robert Brantley of New Orleans gave generously of their time, expertise, and humor. They assisted in the research and location of objects for the exhibition, and, as professional photographers, produced and copied photographs for the book, exhibitions, and video production. In Los Angeles, the research assistance of Tom Zimmerman was extraordinary during a time when various repositories closed temporarily or permanently due to the recession. He worked patiently and diligently to secure images of Wilshire Boulevard and is also a lender to the exhibition. Simon Elliott, archival assistant at UCLA, Special Collections, University Research Library, ably and cheerfully assisted with the location of objects under difficult circumstances. His knowledge of the collections and willingness to help with the project made it a pleasure to work with him.

A publication of this type must rely heavily on primary material from the late nineteenth and early twentieth centuries, particularly photographic images. The photography departments in dozens of museums and repositories across the country have extended their staffs and resources to provide the best photographs possible. Although some images may appear blurry, foxed, or torn, the decision was made to provide the reader with as much information as possible. This meant using images that, in many cases, were the only ones in existence. Lee Stalsworth of Art Through Photography has been unfailing in his photography efforts towards this end.

Melissa Houghton, former assistant curator/registrar, initially coordinated the massive job of securing all the images and permissions for the publication. Her system made it easy to continue the process. Susan Ciccotti has managed the coordination of images and permissions for the reproduction panel exhibition, maintained the status of loan agreements with over sixty lenders to the museum exhibition, and assisted us all in performing a variety of difficult tasks. Her organizational skills and willingness to tackle any assignment with determination and humor have been an asset to the project.

Every member of the Octagon Museum and American Architectural Foundation staff has participated in this project. President Norman L. Koonce, FAIA, supported the project from the beginning and has worked to give it a truly national focus. Nancy E. Davis, director of The Octagon, supported the project from its infancy and provided a willing ear as well as expertise. Judith S. Nyquist, former curator of exhibitions, helped to shape the project and assisted with the initial fundraising. Marilyn Montgomery, former director of development, worked creatively with the staff to secure funding. Julia Becker, director of development, ably continued this effort.

Suzanne Rosenblum, curator of education, worked tirelessly with Annie V. F. Storr, educational consultant on the *Educational Resource Guide*. She assisted the curators with the exhibition scripts and coordinated all educational activities associated with the project. Her fresh approach and desire to bring the project to the public in a challenging manner made her an asset to the team.

Linnea Hamer, associate curator, served as co-curator of the exhibition with Jan Cigliano and worked with every aspect of the project. In addition to assisting with the selection of objects, she spearheaded the loan process and directed the design and production of the panel reproduction exhibition. Her skill, sense of design, and dedication have contributed immeasurably.

Jan Cigliano, guest curator of the exhibition and coeditor of this publication, worked patiently, tirelessly, and diligently. She has given generously of her time and expertise, attended countless meetings, and greatly assisted the staff. Her dedication and enthusiasm have been unwavering.

Larry Klein, Production Group, Inc., assisted by Rebecca Goldfield, associate producer, developed the scope and content of the two video productions. Working closely with the project director and staff, they brought a new and fresh perspective that added an additional dimension to all areas of the entire project.

Thomas F. Burke, publisher, Pomegranate Artbooks, underwrote the production of this publication. I am deeply indebted to him and to his hardworking staff, especially Allen Eddington and Jill L. Anderson, as well as to Peter Howells of Bonnie Smetts Design.

Alan Sandler, director of environmental education, AAF, provided expertise in the initial development of the *Educational Resource Guide*; Ray Rhinehart, vice president of AAF, lent his editorial expertise; Melissa Downey, AIA Component Affairs, presented ideas regarding the panel exhibition; Pete McCall, editor of

MEMO, kept the AIA membership informed about project activities; Kevin Frye and Jan Johnson, AIA Public Affairs, shared information regarding video production; Lynne Lewicki, director, AIA Public Affairs, guided the public relations and press efforts; Meredith Senold, contract specialist, AIA General Counsel, provided great assistance with contracts; and B. J. Musselman and Brigitte Johnson of the AAF staff gave encouragement in times of crisis.

The scope of *The Grand American Avenue: 1850-1920* generated an unprecedented level of interest, to the delight of those who worked most closely on this multifaceted endeavor. It has been my privilege to participate with such talented colleagues.

SHERRY C. BIRK
Curator, Prints and Drawings Collection
The Octagon Museum, The American Architectural Foundation
Project Director

LENDERS TO THE EXHIBITION

ACADEMY OF THE SACRED HEART, *New Orleans, Louisiana*

THE AIA LIBRARY AND ARCHIVES, *Washington, D.C.*

THE AMERICAN INSTITUTE OF ARCHITECTS, *Washington, D.C.*

ANDERSON HOUSE—*Headquarters, Library, and Museum of the Society of the Cincinnati, Washington, D.C.*

AVERY ARCHITECTURAL AND FINE ARTS LIBRARY, *Columbia University, New York, New York*

CHARLES P. BOLTON COLLECTION

BOSTON PUBLIC LIBRARY, PEABODY & STEARNS COLLECTION, *Boston, Massachusetts*

THE CARNEGIE MUSEUM OF ART, *Pittsburgh, Pennsylvania*

CHICAGO ARCHITECTURE FOUNDATION, *Chicago, Illinois*

CHICAGO HISTORICAL SOCIETY, *Chicago, Illinois*

CITY OF LOS ANGELES, DEPARTMENT OF PUBLIC WORKS, BUREAU OF STREET LIGHTING, *Los Angeles, California*

CLEVELAND PUBLIC LIBRARY, *Cleveland, Ohio*

MR. AND MRS. DALE A. COWEL

FOGG ART MUSEUM, HARVARD UNIVERSITY ART MUSEUMS, *Cambridge, Massachusetts*

GALLIER HOUSE, *New Orleans, Louisiana*

J. B. HARTER

JOY HEBERT

THOMAS S. HINES

THE HISTORIC NEW ORLEANS COLLECTION, *New Orleans, Louisiana*

THE HISTORICAL SOCIETY OF WASHINGTON, *Washington, D.C.*

THE HOUGHTON COLLECTION

THE LIBRARY OF CONGRESS, *Washington, D.C.*

THE LOS ANGELES CONSERVANCY, *Los Angeles, California*

LOUISIANA STATE MUSEUM, *New Orleans, Louisiana*

THE MARINERS' MUSEUM, *Newport News, Virginia*

THE MATHES GROUP, *New Orleans, Louisiana*

THE METROPOLITAN MUSEUM OF ART, *New York, New York*

THE METROPOLITAN MUSEUM OF ART, THOMAS J. WATSON LIBRARY, *New York, New York*

MUSEUM OF THE CITY OF NEW YORK, *New York, New York*

NATIONAL ARCHIVES, *Washington, D.C.*

NATIONAL GALLERY OF ART, *Washington, D.C.*

NATIONAL MUSEUM OF AMERICAN ART, SMITHSONIAN INSTITUTION, *Washington, D.C.*

THE NEW-YORK HISTORICAL SOCIETY, *New York, New York*

THE NEW YORK PUBLIC LIBRARY, *New York, New York*

NOTARIAL ARCHIVES, *New Orleans, Louisiana*

PARKINSON ARCHIVES, PARKINSON FIELD ASSOCIATES, *Los Angeles, California*

THE PLAIN DEALER ARCHIVES, *Cleveland, Ohio*

THE PRINTS AND DRAWINGS COLLECTION, THE AMERICAN ARCHITECTURAL FOUNDATION, *Washington, D.C.*

RATKOVITCH ASSOCIATES

JOHN J. SIMMERLING

DOUGLAS R. SUISMAN, AIA

TOURO SYNAGOGUE, *New Orleans, Louisiana*

TIMOTHY TRAPOLIN

TULANE UNIVERSITY LIBRARY, LOUISIANA COLLECTION, *New Orleans, Louisiana*

TULANE UNIVERSITY LIBRARY, SOUTHEASTERN ARCHITECTURE ARCHIVES, *New Orleans, Louisiana*

UNIVERSITY OF CALIFORNIA, LOS ANGELES, SPECIAL COLLECTIONS, UNIVERSITY RESEARCH LIBRARY, *Los Angeles, California*

UNIVERSITY OF CALIFORNIA, SANTA BARBARA, *Santa Barbara, California*

U.S. NAVAL OBSERVATORY LIBRARY, *Washington, D.C.*

THE WESTERN RESERVE HISTORICAL SOCIETY, *Cleveland, Ohio*

TOM ZIMMERMAN

INDEX